Regulative Verses of the Qur'an

Al-Mahdi Institute

VOLUME 1

The titles published in this series are listed at *brill.com/ami*

Regulative Verses of the Qur'an

From Historical Trends to Contemporary Trajectories

Edited by

Karen Bauer
Seyed Mohammad Ghari S. Fatemi
Robert Gleave
Devin J. Stewart

AL-MAHDI INSTITUTE

BRILL

Published in partnership with Al-Mahdi Institute, 60 Weoley Park Road, Birmingham B29 6RB, UK, www.almahdi.edu.

ISSN 3117-910X
ISBN 978-90-04-75555-0
ISBN 978-90-04-75556-7 (PDF)
DOI https://doi.org/10.1163/9789004755567

Library of Congress Control Number: 2026936938

Brill and Koninklijke Brill BV are part of De Gruyter Brill.
www.degruyterbrill.com

Questions about General Product Safety Regulation: productsafety@degruyterbrill.com

Al-Mahdi Institute

The Al-Mahdi Institute (AMI) was established in Birmingham, United Kingdom, in 1993 with the aim of advancing research, teaching, and scholarship in Islamic Studies. Its work is grounded in the conviction that the classical heritage of Islamic scholarship in theology, Islamic law and jurisprudence, Qur'ānic studies, philosophy and the mystical sciences remains a living resource for rigorous academic inquiry rather than merely a historical artefact. AMI is an institute of higher learning that not only transmits this tradition through its teaching programmes but subjects it to sustained scholarly inquiry, encouraging an approach that is both traditionally grounded and intellectually open. Within the broader field of Islamic Studies, AMI gives particular attention to areas that have historically received insufficient scholarly scrutiny: the theological and juridical thought of the Imāmī Shīʿī tradition, the development of Shīʿī legal theory and its relationship to questions of religious authority, the intersection of Islamic philosophy and theology, and the transmission and reception of classical texts across different periods and regions.

Published in collaboration with Brill, the Institute's peer-reviewed book series is devoted to original scholarship in its intellectual, textual, and historical dimensions, with particular commitment to rigorous engagement with primary sources and languages, careful philological analysis, and historically grounded interpretation.

The Institute's academic publications fall into several interrelated categories:

- Monographs presenting original research in Islamic theology, jurisprudence, philosophy, Qur'ānic studies, and related disciplines.
- Edited volumes and collected studies addressing major themes in Islamic scholarship and the history of Islamic thought.
- Critical editions and annotated translations of significant primary texts in the Islamic intellectual tradition.
- Works on Shīʿī intellectual history and the place of the Shīʿī tradition within the broader landscape of Islamic thought.
- Proceedings of conferences and symposia convened or supported by the Institute.

While every effort is made to ensure the highest academic standards through editorial oversight and peer review, the opinions expressed in individual volumes are those of their respective authors alone and do not represent the institutional position of Al-Mahdi Institute. (*www.almahdi.edu*)

Contents

PART 5
Contemporary Legal and Ethical Trajectories

Figures and Tables

Figures

Tables

Introduction: Regulative Verses of the Qur'an – from Historical Trends to Contemporary Trajectories

Karen Bauer, Seyed Mohammad Ghari S. Fatemi, Robert Gleave and Devin J. Stewart

The present volume is devoted to the investigation of the regulative verses of the Qur'an, a topic that sits at the intersection of law and scripture. Law has been a crucial aspect of the Islamic religion throughout its history, and for this reason it is widely assumed that the Qur'an is the fundamental source of Islamic law. Indeed, for the jurists themselves, this was the case. Their claim is not simply the result of ideas prevalent in the Muslim community, a sign of reverence for and belief in the centrality of Islam's sacred text. Nor is it the result of the hegemony of legal discourse in many Islamic historical and geographical contexts. Rather, their claim relates to the Qur'an's own claim about itself as the source of law for its community.

In many contexts, such as the various centres of Islamic legal education, whether in Cairo, Fez, Najaf, or Qom, it hardly seems necessary to argue that the Qur'an is in some sense a legal document. But the nature of 'law' in the Qur'an has been long contested, as has the relationship between law in the Qur'an and law in Muslim tradition (*fiqh*). Modern scholars have shown that many different factors influenced the making of Islamic law and its practice, and that *fiqh* was not an inevitable result of the norms, laws, or wording of the Qur'an itself.[1] Even the term 'law' can be misleading: we use this term with the caveat that modern, secular law is not equivalent to law in the Qur'an or in *fiqh*. Moreover, various theological, mystical, and philosophical approaches to Islam have downplayed the legal aspects of the sacred text, arguing against the views of Muslim jurists. It is therefore worth pointing out that the conviction

1 Patricia Crone, *Roman, Provincial and Islamic Law: The Origins of the Islamic Patronate* (Cambridge: Cambridge University Press, 1987); Patricia Crone, 'Two Legal Problems Bearing on the Early History of the Qur'ān', *Jerusalem Studies in Arabic and Islam* 18 (1994): 1–37, esp. 20; Behnam Sadeghi, *The Logic of Law Making in Islam: Women and Prayer in the Legal Tradition* (Cambridge: Cambridge University Press, 2013); Lena Salaymeh, *The Beginnings of Islamic Law: Late Antique Islamicate Legal Traditions* (Cambridge: Cambridge University Press, 2016); Mariam Sheibani, Amir Toft, and Ahmed El Shamsy, 'The Classical Period: Scripture, Origins, and Early Development', in *The Oxford Handbook of Islamic Law*, ed. Anver M. Emon and Rumee Ahmed (Oxford: Oxford University Press, 2017), 403–36.

 | HTTPS://DOI.ORG/10.1163/9789004755567-002

of law's central role in defining faith and of the Qur'an's primacy as a source of the law arguably go back to the sacred text itself.

The Qur'an refers to itself and characterises its contents in many different ways: as guidance, a warning of the apocalypse, a cure for worry and need, a source of prayers and blessings, a repository of beautiful stories, and so on. In a crucial passage in Sūrat al-Mā'ida, the Qur'an presents itself as the primary source of law, parallel to the Torah and the Gospel, which are equally presented as the primary sources of law for their communities:

> 43 But why do [the Jews] come to you for judgement when they have the Torah
> with God's judgement, and even then still turn away? These are not believers.
> 44 We revealed the Torah with guidance and light, and the prophets, who had sub-
> mitted to God, [and] the rabbis and the scholars all judged according to it for the
> Jews in accordance with that part of God's Scripture which they were entrusted
> to preserve, and to which they were witnesses. So [Children of Israel] do not fear
> people, fear Me; do not barter away My messages for a small price; those who do
> not judge according to what God has sent down are rejecting [God's teachings].
> 45 In the Torah We prescribed for them a life for a life, an eye for an eye, a nose
> for a nose, an ear for an ear, a tooth for a tooth, an equal wound for a wound: if
> anyone forgoes this out of charity, it will serve as atonement for his bad deeds.
> Those who do not judge according to what God has revealed are the wrongdoers.
>
> 46 We sent Jesus, son of Mary, in their footsteps, to confirm the Torah that had
> been sent before him: We gave him the Gospel with guidance and light, confirm-
> ing the Torah that had already been revealed – a guide and lesson for those who
> take heed of God. 47 So let the followers of the Gospel judge according to what
> God has sent down in it. Those who do not judge according to what God has
> revealed: it is they who are the unrighteous.
>
> 48 We sent to you [Muhammad] the Scripture with the truth, confirming the
> Scriptures that came before it, and with authority over them: so judge between
> them according to what God has sent down. Do not follow their whims against
> the truth that has come to you. We have assigned a law (*shir'a*) and a way (*min-
> hāj*) to each of you. If God had so willed, He would have made you one commu-
> nity, but He wanted to test you through that which He has given you, so take the
> lead in good works: you will all return to God and He will inform you about the
> matters over which you differed. 49 So [Prophet] judge between them according
> to what God has sent down. Do not follow their whims, and beware of them, lest
> they tempt you away from any of what God has sent down to you. If they turn
> away, remember that God intends to punish them for some of the sins they have
> committed: a great many people are unrighteous. 50 Do they want judgement

> according to the time of pagan ignorance? Who can be a better judge than God for those of firm faith? (Q. 5:43–50)[2]

The overarching principle conveyed by the passage is that law – real, correct law – derives from God's revelation, what He has sent down. It thus stands in opposition to people's 'whims' (*ahwāʾ*) (Q. 5:49) and to 'the judgement according to the time of pagan ignorance' (*ḥukm al-jāhiliyya*; Q. 5:50), which have not been revealed as a source of guidance by God.

According to this passage, God's revealed law is embodied in scriptures conveyed to humankind through prophetic messengers. In the first section of the passage presented above, the Prophet Muḥammad is asked how contemporary Jews could request that he settle their legal disputes when the Torah is available to them (Q. 5:43). This question implies that the Torah is a legal text, containing God's rulings on legal issues, an interpretation confirmed in the next two verses. Q. 5:44 stresses that the prophets of the biblical past gave judgements in accordance with the Torah, and Q. 5:45 refers to lex talionis or the law of retaliation (cf. Deuteronomy 19:16–21). Law is thus a fundamental part of the Jewish religion, and the contemporary Jews are remiss in failing to follow the dictates of the Torah in their legal disputes: 'Those who do not judge by what God has sent down are rejecting [God's teachings]!' (Q. 5:44).

This tripartite passage, referring to Judaism in Q. 5:43–45, Christianity in 5:46–47, and nascent Islam in 5:48–50, thus conveys the idea that in all three Abrahamic religions, law represents a fundamental framework for believers, and that law is a major component of the sacred text. Both Christianity and the community of believers following the Prophet are similar and parallel to Judaism with regard to God's law. Just as the Torah that God sent down provides 'guidance and light' with which to judge legal cases, so too does the Gospel (Q. 5:46–47), and the Scripture revealed to the Prophet Muḥammad confirms this (Q. 5:48–49). The commonalities are emphasised by the parallel statements referring to judging according to the contents of scripture: 'the prophets, who had submitted to God, [and] the rabbis and the scholars all judged according to it [i.e. the Torah] for the Jews in accordance with that part of God's Scripture which they were entrusted to preserve, and to which they were witnesses' (Q. 5:45); 'So let the followers of the Gospel judge according to what God has sent down in it' (Q. 5:47). The Prophet Muḥammad is commanded, 'So [Prophet] judge between them according to what God has sent

2 M.A.S. Abdel Haleem, trans., *The Qurʾan* (Oxford: Oxford University Press, 2010) (translation modified).

down' (Q. 5:49), evidently referring to the statement in the preceding verse, 'We sent to you the Scripture with the truth' (Q. 5:48). Parallel negative statements indicate that there is no other proper basis for judgement other than revelation: 'Those who do not judge according to what God has revealed are wrongdoers' (Q. 5:45) and 'unrighteous' (Q. 5:47) and 'a great many people are unrighteous' (Q. 5:49). According to this passage, then, scripture provides guidance for the nascent community of Muslims and the precedent religions of Judaism and Christianity, and the repeated references to judging suggest that the scriptures contain explicit legal rulings.

This passage in Sūrat al-Mā'ida also makes clear that while the Abrahamic religions share a concept of revealed law, Jewish, Christian, and Islamic law differ in detail and represent distinct legal dispensations.[3] Just as Christianity ushered in a new legal dispensation, confirming the earlier revelations but modifying the law, so did Islam. For this reason, each group must be judged according to its respective scripture, the Jews by the Torah, 'the followers of the Gospel' (*ahl al-injīl*) by the Gospel, and the believers in the Prophet Muḥammad by 'the Scripture' (*al-kitāb*) mentioned Q. 5:48, evidently the Qur'an. Judaism, Christianity, and Islam have distinct but parallel legal regimes; in the statement 'We have assigned a law (*shirʿa*) and a way (*minhāj*) to each of you', the context indicates that the key terms *shirʿa* and *minhāj* both refer to the law. The passage as a whole places tremendous emphasis on law as a central component of scripture, to such an extent that even the statements that the scriptures are 'guidance' and 'light' (Q. 5:44, 5:46) arguably refer to their legal content and not to general spiritual guidance or inspiration.

While this passage in Sūrat al-Mā'ida refers to scriptures as the only correct source of revealed law for their respective believing communities, a perusal of the sacred texts shows that they could not be described as legal manuals.[4] The Hebrew Bible contains many passages that are blatantly legal, such as the Ten Commandments and the detailed instructions regarding ritual law such as the rules for building the Tabernacle or presenting a burnt offering at the Temple. However, many other passages of the Hebrew Bible are devoted to tales of travel, sibling rivalry, battles, conquests, and other matters that are not

3 Holger Zellentin has written extensively on the different legal communities represented in the Qur'an. See especially Holger M. Zellentin, *Law beyond Israel: From the Bible to the Qur'an* (Oxford: Oxford University Press, 2022); Holger M. Zellentin, 'Gentile Purity Law from the Bible to the Qur'an: The Case of Sexual Purity and Illicit Intercourse', in *The Qur'an's Reformation of Judaism and Christianity: Return to the Origins*, ed. Holger M. Zellentin (Abingdon: Routledge, 2019), 115–215.

4 On the Qur'an not being a legal manual, see Joseph E. Lowry, *Reading the Qur'an as a Law Book* (New Haven, CT: Yale Law School Occasional Papers, 2015).

obviously legal in nature, and it would be difficult to argue that the narratives of Jesus' birth and the many descriptions of travels and encounters during his mission in the Gospels present specific legal rulings. Similarly the Qur'an contains passages that are devoted to clear legal issues, such as the list of all the women a Muslim man cannot marry or the shares of inheritance due to various relatives, but, at the same time, it contains other passages which may be construed as general exhortations to do good works or to deal with others fairly, and yet others that may even be more tenuously associated with legal rulings, such as injunctions to 'eat of the good things We have provided for you' (Q. 2:172). This is not to mention many passages that seem to have no legal content, such as descriptions of paradise and hell or the horrors associated with the eschaton. Such scenes portray the ultimate consequences of following, or failing to follow, God's path, and clearly cannot be implemented by any humans. The portrayal in Sūrat al-Māʾida of the Qur'an as a legal manual, to be implemented in the human realm, thus cannot be taken as a strict characterisation of the entire text. It is therefore not a trivial matter to address the legal content of the Qur'an.[5]

In response to this challenge, scholars in the Islamic legal tradition devoted a great deal of energy and ingenuity to the explication and analysis of the relationship between law and the text of the Qur'an. The genre of *aḥkām al-Qurʾān* is based on the recognition that the Qur'an's verses with clear, enforceable legal content – termed *āyāt al-aḥkām*, literally 'verses of legal rulings' – represent only a fraction of the Qur'anic text. These verses have often considered to reach a particular number, whether 200, 500, or 600. Some thinkers insisted that there was not a limited number of such verses and that legal rulings could be extracted from many passages, but this latter view went against the general

5 Publications on this topic, which have been few and far between in the Western tradition of Islamic studies, include Robert Roberts, *Das Familienrecht im Qorān* (Leipzig: A. Pries, 1907); Robert Roberts, *The Social Laws of the Qoran, Considered and Compared with Those of Hebrew and Other Ancient Codes* (London: Williams and Norgate, 1925); Josef J. Rivlin, *Gesetz im Koran: Kultus und Ritus* (Jerusalem: Bamberger & Wahrmann, 1934); Wael B. Hallaq, 'Quranic Magna Carta: On the Origins of the Rule of Law in Islam', in *Magna Carta, Religion and the Rule of Law*, ed. Robin Griffith-Jones and Mark Hill (Cambridge: Cambridge University Press, 2015), 157–76. Joseph E. Lowry is working on a forthcoming, comprehensive study on the topic. In the meantime, see Joseph E. Lowry, 'When Less Is More: Law and Commandment in *Sūrat al-Anʿām*', *Journal of Qurʾanic Studies* 9, no. 2 (2007): 22–42; Lowry, *Law Book*; Joseph E. Lowry, 'Law, Structure, and Meaning in Sūrat al-Baqarah', *Journal of the International Qurʾanic Studies Association* 2, no. 1 (2017): 111–48; Joseph E. Lowry, 'A Guide to the Legal Material in Sūrat al-Nisāʾ (Q 4)', in *Unlocking the Medinan Qurʾan*, ed. Nicolai Sinai (Leiden: Brill, 2022), 422–79; Joseph E. Lowry, 'Quranic Law and Its "Biblical" Intertexts', *Asiatische Studien – Études Asiatiques* 78, no. 3 (2024): 431–67.

constitution of the genre. Works on *aḥkām al-Qurʾān* are legal commentaries on the Qurʾan, arranged either according to the chapters of the law as presented in legal manuals, such as the work of Abū Jaʿfar Aḥmad b. Muḥammad al-Ṭaḥāwī (d. 321/933), or according to the order in which the relevant verses appear in the *muṣḥaf*, the Qurʾan as it has come down to us, as in the case of the work of Abū Bakr al-Jaṣṣāṣ al-Rāzī (d. 370/980).

As legal commentaries on the Qurʾan, *aḥkām al-Qurʾān* works served two important functions. On the one hand, they evinced that Islamic law was based squarely on the Qurʾan, something that one may understand as making an unstated defence against the argument that Islamic law was based mainly on *ḥadīth*, the views of early jurists, or other non-Qurʾanic material. On the other hand, they served as a convenient pedagogical or consultative support for law students and jurists, who could have recourse to the necessary material for legal interpretations without having to skim through much larger commentaries on the entire Qurʾan. They were thus similar to the *ṣaḥīḥ* or *sunan* works of *ḥadīth*, which could function as convenient reference works for jurists because they arranged *ḥadīth* reports according to the well-known chapters of legal manuals.

The origins and early history of the genre of *aḥkām al-Qurʾān* are obscure. Al-Shāfiʿī wrote a work on *aḥkām al-Qurʾān*, but it appears to have been incomplete in its coverage of the Qurʾan and may have been ignored for centuries. Other purportedly early works such as the *Tafsīr khams miʾat āya* of Muqātil b. Sulaymān (d. 150/767) were probably written later and falsely attributed to early authors. The genre was certainly already well established by the fourth/tenth century, and it has continued to be a productive genre up until the present day. It has also exhibited considerable variety. Over the centuries, *aḥkām al-Qurʾān* evolved to adapt to different cultural contexts and historical circumstances while maintaining its foundational connection to Qurʾanic exegesis. This evolution highlights the dynamic nature of Islamic jurisprudence, characterised by ongoing scholarly debate and interpretative diversity. The plurality of methodologies within Islamic legal discourse reflects the intellectual richness of Islamic traditions, illustrating how various schools of thought engage with and apply Qurʾanic principles to address normative challenges.

Many exemplars focused narrowly on legal rulings, while others, such as *al-Jāmiʿ li-aḥkām al-Qurʾān* by al-Qurṭubī (d. 672/1273), were more expansive and included other topics. Because it constituted a genre of Islamic legal literature, it ramified according to the divisions among Islamic legal schools. Works in this genre were authored by adherents of the four well-known Sunnī schools of law: Shāfiʿīs, Ḥanafīs, Mālikīs, and Ḥanbalīs. Examples include the Shāfiʿī work of Abū al-Ḥasan ʿAlī b. Muḥammad al-Kiyā al-Harrāsī al-Baghdādī

(d. 504/1110), the Ḥanafī work of Abū Bakr Aḥmad b. ʿAlī al-Jaṣṣāṣ al-Rāzī (d. 370/980), the Mālikī work of Abū Bakr Muḥammad b. ʿAbd Allāh Ibn al-ʿArabī (d. 534/1148), and the Ḥanbalī work of al-Qāḍī Abū Yaʿlā (d. 458/1066). Dāwūd b. ʿAlī (al-Ẓāhirī, d. 270/884), the founder of the Dāwūdī or Ẓāhirī legal school, is also reported to have written a work in the genre. Works on *aḥkām al-Qurʾān* according to the Twelver Shīʿī legal school were authored by Quṭb al-Dīn Saʿīd b. Hibat Allāh al-Rāwandī (d. 573/1177), who wrote *Fiqh al-Qurʾān*, and Miqdād al-Suyūrī al-Ḥillī (d. 826/1423), who wrote *Kanz al-ʿirfān fī fiqh al-Qurʾān*. Influential works according to the Zaydī Shīʿī school of law include *al-Rawḍa wa-l-ghadīr* (*The Garden and the Pool*), by Sayyid Muḥammad b. al-Hādī b. Tāj al-Dīn (d. 720/1320), and *Taysīr al-bayān li-aḥkām al-Qurʾān*, by Jamāl al-Dīn b. Nūr al-Dīn al-Mawziʿī (d. 825/1422). Ilyās Dandūr recently extracted an *aḥkām al-Qurʾān* work from the well-known, thirty-volume commentary *al-Taḥrīr wa-l-tanwīr*, by Ibn ʿĀshūr (1879–1973), published as *Rawāʾiʿ al-bayān fī tafsīr al-ʿAllāma Muḥammad Ṭāhir Ibn ʿĀshūr li-āyāt al-aḥkām*.[6]

The genre of *aḥkām al-Qurʾān* is one of many in legal literature. Much attention has been paid to compendia on the points of law, which are the principal works studied in the legal curriculum of all schools of Islamic law. These range from short manuals that merely present the accepted opinion within the legal school to multivolume works that provide extensive discussions of the justification of specific legal rulings. Significant attention has been paid to the genre of *uṣūl al-fiqh*, 'the principles of the law', which focuses on legal hermeneutics, the derivation of the law from the sources. *Fatwā*s, responsa to specific, individual legal questions, have also served as the basis for many studies that have focused not only on legal reasoning but also on social history. In contrast, there has been relatively little scholarly attention to the genre of *aḥkām al-Qurʾān*, aside from some studies in Turkish and Arabic on the works of al-Jaṣṣāṣ and Ibn al-ʿArabī. The chapters in Part 2 of the present volume, 'The Historical Genre of *Aḥkām al-Qurʾān*', represent a substantial engagement with the history, conventions, sub-traditions, and content of this genre.

Many questions are raised by the attempt to distinguish the legal content of the Qur'an neatly from the remainder of the sacred text. One issue related to the creation of such a dichotomy is the question of whether the law subsumes ethics or morality. The topics certainly overlap, but the exact relationship between them is not a simple matter to define, and this is the subject of the

---

6 Ilyās Dandūr, *Rawāʾiʿ al-bayān fī tafsīr al-ʿAllāma Muḥammad Ṭāhir Ibn ʿĀshūr li-āyāt al-aḥkām* (Beirut: Dār Ibn Ḥazm, 2021); Geraldine Jenvrin, *Exégèses de la «mécréance» (kufr) et statut légal du non-musulman dans le commentaire coranique d'al Qurtubi (m.671/1273)* (Turnhout: Brepols, 2024).

chapters in Part 1, 'The Qur'an, Ethics, and Law'. In the question of the relationship between law and ethics, one may mount arguments on either side: that Qur'anic law encompasses Qur'anic ethics or that the two fields are essentially distinct despite the overlap and that not all of ethics is covered by the law.[7] This question remains highly contested, and the contributors to this volume express distinct views on the issue.

Part 3, 'Interpretation of Regulative Verses', focuses on Muslim scholars' application, or lack thereof, of Qur'anic verses when formulating law. The questions of what makes a Qur'anic verse a regulative verse and how the believer is supposed to implement the Qur'an's legal content have been addressed in many ways in various genres in the Islamic religious sciences, and not only in legal genres. Various answers to these questions were provided, often implicitly. Scholars such as Najm al-Dīn al-Ṭūfī (d. 316/716) held the view – a minority view among jurists – that it was possible for narrative and other passages of the Qur'an to play a role in determining Islamic legal rulings. It seems obvious that the stories of earlier communities in salvation history are meant to provide moral guidance to the Prophet Muḥammad's immediate audience and to later Muslims. Similarly, instructions to the Prophet, texts of consolation, prayer, or blessing, and other formal text of the Scripture may be interpreted as conveying legal or ethical principles, even though they were regularly ignored by Muslim jurists. Strict lines between edification, warning, moral instruction, and legal rulings are thus difficult to draw.[8] The texts in which such expansive conceptions of the legal content of the Qur'an are to be found have tended to be non-legal and have included literary anthologies, sermons, orations, aphorisms, theological treatises, mystical manuals, and others. Ethical treatises such as Miskawayh's (d. 421/1030) *Tahdhīb al-akhlāq* and Naṣīr al-Dīn al-Ṭūsī's (d. 672/1274) *Akhlāq-i Nāṣirī* drew extensively both on Qur'anic examples and

7 Publications that address the relationship between Islamic law and ethics in the Qur'an include Amira Naim Abou-Taleb, 'The Concept of *Iḥsān* (Beauty/Goodness) in the Qur'ānic Moral Worldview' (PhD diss., University of Helsinki, 2023); Mutaz al-Khatib, '*Āyāt al-akhlāq: su'āl al-akhlāq 'inda al-mufassirīn* (Verses on Ethics: The Question of Ethics among the Qur'ān Exegetes)', *Journal of Islamic Ethics* 1, no. 1–2 (2017): 84–121; A. Kevin Reinhart, 'Islamic Law as Islamic Ethics', *Journal of Religious Ethics* 11, no. 2 (1983): 186–203; A. Kevin Reinhart, 'Origins of Islamic Ethics: Foundations and Constructions', in *Encyclopedia of Religious Ethics*, vol. 2, *Moral Traditions*, ed. William Schweiker (Hoboken, NJ: Wiley Blackwell, 2022), 244–53; Nora K. Schmid, 'From Ethico-Religious Exhortation to Legal Paraenesis: The Function of Qur'anic *Wa'ẓ*', *Islamic Law and Society* 28 (2021): 317–51.

8 For a collection of studies on the ethical implications of Qur'anic narratives, see the recently published work by Samer Rashwani, ed., *Behind the Story: Ethical Readings of Qur'ānic Narratives* (Leiden: Brill, 2024).

on the Greek philosophical tradition, inviting the investigation of the complex relationship between Islamic law and philosophy.[9]

In contemporary contexts, the study of Qurʾanic ethics and law continues to evolve in response to emerging social, political, and environmental challenges. Just as medieval scholars sought to demonstrate that the Qurʾan justified their own ethical perspectives, many modern scholars engage in contextual reinterpretations of Qurʾanic verses to reconcile it with modern ethical values and global perspectives. The extent to which they engage with and accept the legacy of historical and traditional interpretations varies widely. Some scholars, including many reformists, feminists, and others, eschew traditional interpretations and seek answers directly from the Qurʾan itself, often arguing that the tradition has narrowed, obscured, or misinterpreted the sacred text and its implications.

The chapters in Parts 4 and 5, 'Contemporary Philosophical Perspectives' and 'Contemporary Legal and Ethical Trajectories', respectively, reflect a dynamic engagement and an ongoing effort to maintain the relevance of Qurʾanic teachings in a rapidly changing world. Issues such as human rights, gender equality, environmental sustainability, and interfaith dialogue are increasingly addressed within the framework of Qurʾanic principles, demonstrating a commitment to adapting Islamic ethics to contemporary realities while remaining faithful to the Qurʾan as a source. Such contemporary approaches to Qurʾanic interpretation emphasise a holistic perspective that encompasses not only legal and ethical dimensions but also the spiritual and philosophical insights conveyed by the Scripture. Multidimensional modern approaches seek to integrate Qurʾanic teachings into broader discussions on human flourishing and societal well-being, highlighting principles of compassion, justice, and stewardship of the earth. Through comprehensive engagement with the Qurʾan, scholars aim to cultivate a nuanced understanding of Islamic ethics that resonates with current global challenges and aspirations for a more equitable and sustainable world.

The five parts of this volume, presented at the First AMI International Annual Qurʾanic Studies Conference on Regulative Verses of the Qurʾan (*āyāt al-aḥkām*), held on 27–28 April 2023, represent a variety of responses to the trajectories outlined in this Introduction.

---

9 Mohammed Hashas and Mutaz al-Khatib, 'Introduction: Modern Arab-Islamic Scholarship on Ethics: A Reflective Contextualization', in *Islamic Ethics and the Trusteeship Paradigm: Taha Abderrahmane's Philosophy in Comparative Perspectives*, ed. Mohammed Hashas and Mutaz al-Khatib (Leiden: Brill, 2020), 1–31.

1 The Qur'an, Ethics, and Law

Ethical and legal verses form a significant part of the Qur'an, offering a comprehensive framework for moral conduct, social justice, and legal principles that guide the lives of Muslims. These verses emphasise ethical behaviour, such as honesty and fair treatment, while also providing detailed legal instructions on matters like marriage and inheritance. This integration of ethical teachings and legal mandates ensures that Islamic principles are not only believed but actively practised, thereby imposing an ideal of cohesive social norms. Historically, these principles have been applied differently in different Islamic contexts, and continue to influence contemporary discussions on Islamic law. While the Qur'an's normative guidance underscores the central role of normativity within Islam as a faith, questions have been raised around certain ethical issues, such as fairness and justice in gender relations.[10] Some of the chapters in this part address such issues.

In Chapter 1, 'Towards a Prehistory of Islamic Law: the Hebrew Bible, the New Testament, and the Qur'an', Holger Zellentin summarises recent scholarship on the Qur'an's engagement with the heritage of law in the biblical tradition. He focuses on legal practices derived from the Bible that were adapted by Jews and Christians in late antiquity. Special attention is given to the laws concerning non-Israelite residents in the Holy Land, known as *gerim* (literally, 'strangers, foreigners, aliens'), which influenced Jewish and Christian interpretations of biblical law. These laws, particularly the 'Noahide Laws' and the 'Decree of the Apostles', played a significant role in shaping rabbinic and Christian legal thought and served as a foundation for key aspects of Qur'anic law while critiquing rabbinic and Christian legal practices based on gentile laws.

In Chapter 2, 'The Place of Divine Law in the Qur'an's Moral Theology', Nicolai Sinai argues that the Qur'an presents a moral theology centred on the

---

10 There have been many discussions of gender justice in the Qur'an. A few of the English-language works on this subject include Kecia Ali, *Sexual Ethics in Islam: Feminist Reflections on Qur'an, Hadith and Jurisprudence* (London: Oneworld, 2006); Nimat Hafez Barazangi, *Woman's Identity in the Qur'an: A New Reading* (Gainesville: University Press of Florida, 2004); Asma Barlas, *"Believing Women" in Islam: Unreading Patriarchal Interpretations of the Qur'ān* (Austin: University of Texas Press, 2002); Karen Bauer and Feras Hamza, *Women, Households, and the Hereafter in the Qur'an: A Patronage of Piety* (Oxford: Oxford University Press in association with the Institute of Ismaili Studies, 2023); Abla Hasan, *Decoding the Egalitarianism of the Qur'an: Retrieving Lost Voices on Gender* (Lanham, MD: Lexington Books, 2019); Celene Ibrahim, *Women and Gender in the Qur'an* (Oxford: Oxford University Press, 2020); Irene Schneider, *Der Islam und die Frauen* (Munich: C.H. Beck, 2019); Amina Wadud, *Qur'an and Woman: Rereading the Sacred Text from a Woman's Perspective* (New York: Oxford University Press, 1999).

idea that God created the world to test moral agents, ultimately rewarding or punishing them in the hereafter. In early Meccan suras, legislative commands are not central; rather, revelation serves to remind humans of God's moral expectations and to counteract their forgetfulness. While humans possess an inherent grasp of moral behaviour, they are prone to ingratitude and assumptions that they are self-sufficient. Some Meccan passages even criticise humans for creating unnecessary rules that restrict God's generosity. However, Medinan suras mark a shift towards a more legislative focus, while maintaining integration with the Qur'an's overarching moral framework.

In Chapter 3, 'Qur'anic Morality as Qur'anic Law', Karen Bauer and Feras Hamza explore the relationship between Qur'anic law and morality, challenging the assumption that they exist as separate realms. The Qur'an contains various commands, prompting the question whether all these commands – legal or moral – should be considered part of God's law. The authors argue that in the Qur'anic context, 'law', 'morality', and 'piety' are interconnected and cannot be separated into distinct categories. They emphasise that the Qur'an integrates concepts of right and wrong with what is licit, pious, or impious in alignment with the Scripture's broader aim of salvation. Moreover, Qur'anic commands have different aims and purposes: some commands are not ideal but aim to prevent a worse harm and others impose temporary obligations based on the exigencies of the time. In either case, believers are always encouraged to fulfil more than the moral minimum, to do good and pursue a path of higher moral purity.

In Chapter 4, 'The Myth of the Elite Male Addressee and Its Implications for Regulative Verses', Abla Hasan challenges the mainstream view that the Qur'an addresses elite men, proposing new readings of Q. 4:3, on marriage to more than one woman; Q. 4:6, on the bestowal of property to orphans; and Q. 4:34, on the husband's right to discipline his wife. Hasan begins from the premise that these verses of the text should not be abrogated or negated, a position that has been taken by some prominent interpreters of the Qur'an. With regard to Q. 4:34, Hasan proposes that the addressee is made clear in the previous and following verses, that is to say, the addressee is the community itself, rather than husbands, and that this verse which seems to be addressed to husbands instead informs the community about how they should manage female criminals. Hasan shows that in Q. 4:6, marriageable age is equated with holding sound judgement; therefore, the Qur'an cannot be interpreted to endorse child marriage. Hasan re-reads Q. 4:3 not as endorsing polygyny in any kind of unlimited way, but only under very specific circumstances, with the mothers of orphans. Hasan's contribution offers a rich and thoughtful engagement with Qur'anic verses that, for some modern readers, pose ethical issues.

In Chapter 5, 'On the Universality of Divine Commands versus the Casuistic Interpretation of the Regulative Verses', Gholamreza Aavani emphasises defining these verses within the broader context of the Qur'an. He examines the perspectives of four major Muslim philosophers – Fārābī, Avicenna, Ghazālī, and Mullā Ṣadrā – to clarify the role of law in relation to the Qur'an. This analysis illuminates the interplay between divine commands and their legal interpretation through these thinkers' lenses.

2 The Historical Genre of *Aḥkām al-Qur'ān*

Aḥkām al-Qur'ān is a well-established genre within Islamic scholarly disciplines that focuses on the legal rulings derived from the Qur'an. This genre emerged in the early centuries of Islamic history as scholars sought to categorise and interpret Qur'anic verses related to legal and ethical issues systematically. Examining its historical development and reception provides valuable insights into the evolution of Islamic jurisprudence. Early scholars played a crucial role in its formation, and over time, it gained prominence as a key genre within Islamic legal literature. Understanding its origins and evolution is essential for analysing its impact on the broader field of Islamic studies and its continued relevance in contemporary jurisprudential discourse.

In Chapter 6, 'Legal Hermeneutics and Religious Authority in *Kitāb Aḥkām al-Qur'ān* by al-Jaṣṣāṣ al-Rāzī (d. 370/981)', Devin J. Stewart examines the *Kitāb Aḥkām al-Qur'ān* of the Ḥanafī jurist Abū Bakr Aḥmad b. ʿAlī al-Jaṣṣāṣ al-Rāzī. This contribution points out that al-Jaṣṣāṣ's analysis included not only typical legal analysis but also concepts such as consensus, analogy, *ijtihād*, and the role of lay Muslims consulting legal experts. The chapter addresses rival legal theories and anti-Shīʿī arguments, possibly in response to the Shīʿī prominence in tenth-century Iraq under the Buwayhids. This study contributes to existing scholarship by analysing key passages and clarifying misconceptions about al-Jaṣṣāṣ's other influential work, *al-Fuṣūl fī al-uṣūl*.

In Chapter 7, 'The Imāmī Reception of the Qur'an's Regulative Verses (*Āyāt al-Aḥkām*)', Seyed Mohammad G.S. Fatemi and Syed Wajee ul-Hasan Shah explore the reception and challenges surrounding the regulative verses of the Qur'an within the Imāmī tradition. The emergence of Imāmī works on *āyāt al-aḥkām* arguably began with Muḥammad b. al-Sā'ib b. Bishr al-Kalbī's *Kitāb Aḥkām al-Qur'ān* in the second/eighth century, marking the genre's inception and subsequent reception among Imāmī scholars. Prominent texts like *Fiqh al-Qur'ān* by Quṭb al-Dīn al-Rāwandī illustrate its evolution. Unlike most Sunnī counterparts, which are organised by the order of suras in the received text of the Qur'an, Imāmī works in this genre typically adopt the structure of legal manuals, following their standard order, beginning with the book of purification. However, chronological analysis remains underexplored within this genre of scholarship. Certain Imāmī scholars challenge normative Qur'anic authority through methods such as hermeneutics, considerations of trans-historical applicability, concerns about distortion, issues related to recitation, and arguments regarding redundancy, thereby emphasising nuanced interpretations beyond the text's apparent meanings.

3 Interpretation of Regulative Verses

The historical discourse surrounding the interpretation of normative verses in the Qur'an illustrates the dynamic nature of Islamic exegetical thought. This discourse reveals a rich diversity of methodologies employed by scholars, reflecting how different schools of thought and historical contexts contribute to the understanding and application of these verses. The evolution of interpretations highlights the diverse intellectual tradition within Islam, including Sunnī, Shīʿī, and Ibāḍī interpretations, from the perspective of law, theology, philosophy, and other disciplines, demonstrating its adaptability to new challenges over time.

In Chapter 8, '*Āyāt al-Aḥkām* in Early Ibāḍī Thought', Nora K. Schmid examines the role of Qur'anic legal verses in early Ibāḍī thought in the second/eighth and third/ninth centuries. Schmid analyses three key sources: the sermons of Abū Ḥamza al-Mukhtār b. ʿAwf al-Azdī al-Salīmī al-Baṣrī (d. 130/748), the epistle of Sālim b. Dhakwān (fl. second/eighth century), and the *Tafsīr* of Hūd b. Muḥakkam (fl. late third/ninth century). Her study reveals that while Abū Ḥamza and Sālim b. Dhakwān both emphasised strict adherence to Qur'anic regulations, their views diverged on Khārijī militancy. Hūd's *Tafsīr* aligns with earlier ideas but introduces distinctive Ibāḍī interpretations. Schmid thus explores how early Ibāḍīs understood and implemented these verses, arguing that they advocated for the literal application of Qur'anic laws in both personal conduct and the legitimisation of rulers.

In Chapter 9, 'The Irrelevance of "Qur'anic Meaning": Akhbārī Shīʿī Interpretive Techniques and the Legal Verses of the Qur'an', Robert Gleave critiques the conventional view of the Qur'an as Islam's primary legal source. He explores how movements like the Akhbāriyya in Twelver Shīʿism challenged this perspective, asserting that the Qur'an may be irrelevant to Islamic law, even without claiming textual corruption. This view posits that variations in interpretation arise from historical contexts, emphasising interpretive authority over textual reliability in understanding divine law.

M. Ashraf Adeel's Chapter 10, 'Arguments for Conditional Variability of *Ḥudūd* Punishments', presents four significant arguments for flexibility in legal interpretation. First, he argues that the term *ḥudūd Allāh* does not necessarily indicate fixed punishments. Second, he asserts that the concept of *maqāṣid al-sharīʿa* necessitates legal adaptations to meet evolving societal conditions. Third, he discusses an axiological hierarchy within Qurʾanic values that prioritises higher values over lower ones, allowing for varied interpretations. Finally, he emphasises that the Qurʾan's epistemology supports this hierarchical view and the application of *maqāṣid* principles.

Imranali Panjwani's Chapter 11, 'Metaphysical and Legal Implications of the Earliest Instance of *Āyāt al-Aḥkām*', examines the spiritual dimensions of regulative verses in light of the Prophet Muḥammad's obligations, particularly regarding the Night Prayer Vigil (*Ṣalāt al-Layl*) presented in Sūrat al-Muzzammil (Q. 73). He argues that these verses should be viewed not only as legal mandates but also as instructions integral to spiritual growth and metaphysical understanding. His analysis draws on narratives about the Companions' challenges in performing night prayers, which may influence jurisprudential discussions on fulfilling ritual obligations.

4 Contemporary Philosophical Perspectives

The philosophical debate surrounding the nature, normative authority, and existential dimensions of the regulative verses of the Qurʾan remains an underexplored area in scholarly discourse. Investigating these aspects may yield valuable insights into how these verses influence Islamic ethical and legal frameworks. Although considerable attention has been paid to their practical applications, the philosophical foundations and implications of these verses warrant further examination. This exploration may illuminate the Qurʾan's role in shaping both individual lived experience and the collective experience of communities, emphasising the complex interplay between divine commands and human experience.

In Chapter 12, 'Making Sense of Obligatory Faith in the Qurʾan', Hamid Vahid interprets Qurʾanic verses that mandate the acquisition of faith. He employs contemporary philosophical theories regarding belief and justification to secure freedom of belief and epistemic agency. Vahid's analysis presents two solutions to the challenge of obligatory faith: one focuses on a specific analysis of faith, while the other engages with the broader discourse on the status of epistemic norms – whether they are hypothetical or categorical. The first section of his chapter discusses the initial solution through a recognised analysis of faith, while the second section proposes a framework of doxastic freedom that addresses concerns about involuntary belief and epistemic agency. The chapter concludes by examining how the Qur'anic perspective on faith aligns with this conceptual framework.

Mahmoud Morvarid's Chapter 13, 'A Decision-Theoretical Approach to the *Ḥujjiyya* of Regulative Qur'anic Verses', introduces a philosophical methodology aimed at reconciling moral intuitions with seemingly contradictory verses without significantly altering traditional theological views on revelation and divine speech. He critiques the prevalent jurisprudential notion of *ḥujjiyya* (normative authority) concerning the prima facie meaning (*ẓāhir*) of regulative verses, employing analytical tools from modern decision theory and rationality studies. Morvarid argues that the *ḥujjiyya* of a Qur'anic verse in a specific ruling should not be determined solely by its assigned probability or associated risks, since this often leads to an excessive attribution of authority to verses. Instead, he advocates for understanding *ḥujjiyya* within a framework of practical rationality, proposing an alternative approach that incorporates both revelation- and non-revelation-based evidence in legal deductions.

In Chapter 14, 'The Existential Perspective on the Regulative Verses (*Āyāt al-Aḥkām*) of the Qur'an', Arif Abdul Hussain contends that the dynamic nature of existence informs the distinction between 'the actual' and 'actuality'. He argues that Qur'anic principles such as justice, ease, and non-hardship are existential and meta-legal, shaping regulative forms according to their audiences' contexts and aptitudes. Abdul Hussain concludes that (a) Qur'anic regulative forms were tailored to their immediate audience; (b) these forms are not universally applicable beyond their original contexts; (c) they encapsulate essential values for growth; and (d) new regulative forms should be developed considering these values and contemporary contexts to foster rational, moral, and spiritual development.

5 Contemporary Legal and Ethical Trajectories

Contemporary trajectories of the regulative verses of the Qur'an reflect a dynamic engagement with normative issues. Scholars are increasingly re-examining these verses through a contextual lens, seeking to reconcile traditional interpretations with contemporary values. This approach advocates for human flourishing, legal reform, human rights, and sustainable environmental practices, while also promoting interfaith dialogue and understanding. By interpreting regulative verses to address modern challenges, scholars ensure that Qur'anic teachings remain relevant and adaptable, providing meaningful guidance in an evolving world.

Oliver Leaman's Chapter 15, 'Rules and Rituals in the Qur'an: Is There a Role for Reason?', explores whether religious laws in Islam should justify obedience by offering rationales. The discussion contrasts the laws of the Qur'an, understood to have divine origin and inherent perfection, with civil laws, which typically provide explanations, even when controversial. Leaman examines the challenge of reconciling morally contentious issues sanctioned by religious law, such as historical practices like slavery and gender roles. While some argue that these laws reflect moral progress over time, traditional perspectives emphasise their immutable nature. Ultimately, the chapter argues that believers should accept divine laws without explicit rationales, underscoring the profound gap between human comprehension and divine wisdom in religious discourse.

One of the major questions in Islamic legal studies is the extent to which Islamic law is amenable to reinterpretation. In Chapter 16, 'Reconstruction of Sharīʿa through Judicial *Ijtihād*: Inheritance Rights of Childless Widows under the Ithnā ʿAshariyya School in Pakistan', Muhammad Zubair Abbasi examines the inheritance law for childless Shīʿa widows, a case in which judges in Pakistan have updated the law in response to changing times and circumstances. To describe the mechanism by which the jurists have modified the centuries-old law, Abbasi traces the evolution of legal thinking in Pakistan beginning in the British colonial period. Initially in that period, there was a recognition of different legal opinions. Of these, the judges chose a preferred legal opinion, and this opinion established precedent for later legal rulings. In the 1950s, following independence in 1947, judges established the Qur'an as the main source of law, but only for the Sunnī majority. The Shīʿa ruling, depriving the childless widow of her inheritance of land, was based on a saying of Imām ʿAlī, but it was contradicted by the Qur'an. The judges at that stage were unwilling to contradict an established legal opinion; they left the door open to such a change being made by the legislature after consultation with the Shīʿa community, a consultation that never took place. In 2016, this law was again challenged, and now a juridical consultation did take place, with the result that the law was revised in the Muslim Family Laws (Amendment) Act of 2021. Rather than relying on earlier legal precedent, the consultation relied on the opinions of modern jurists who follow the Qur'an in allowing a childless widow a quarter of the estate, and the law has now been reformulated on that basis.

In Chapter 17, '"Do Not Prohibit the Good Things That God Has Made Lawful to You" (Q. 5:87): Ethical Vegetarianism in Islam and Beyond', Sarra Tlili evaluates the arguments of advocates for moral vegetarianism according to Islamic principles. In this systematic study, Tlili rejects the common conception that humans killing animals for food is inherently anthropocentric and argues that killing for food is consistent with the principles of egalitarianism and justice, as long as it is undertaken in accordance with specific rules. She shows that the Qur'an is unambiguous on the point of humans killing animals for food and describes the benefits of animal sacrifice in the Qur'an, which include increasing the believers' gratitude to God and their feeding of the poor. One major point made in this piece is that killing animals is never meant to be unreflective. Rather, animals must be treated with care and dignity in life and in death. Finally, she shows that, although the advocates for Islamic vegetarianism may have valid concerns, their answers are not consistent with Qur'anic principles.

The environment is very much at the forefront of ethical discussions today, and in Chapter 18, '"Clear" Verses of the Qur'an (*Āyāt al-Aḥkām*) and Environmental Ethics', Etin Anwar raises the question of how to use the 'clear' (*muḥkam*) verses to address questions of environmental ethics in Islam. She outlines several theories of the *muḥkam* and *mutashābih* verses mentioned in Sūrat Āl ʿImrān (especially Q. 3:7) and uses these theories, particularly that of Ibn ʿĀshūr, as a starting point for outlining a theory of environmental ethics. Anwar's theory takes into account several principles outlined by Muḥammad Rashīd Riḍā, Muḥammad ʿAbduh, Ibn ʿĀshūr, and other scholars, such as the principle of ease, the principle of God's unity, and the principle of not causing corruption on the earth (*al-fasād fī al-arḍ*). Finally, Anwar focuses on the 'glory motif' to show that both humans and nature glorify God, ultimately arguing that to cause harm to the environment is to create 'corruption on the earth', whereas a glorification of God would involve caring for His creation.

The individual contributions gathered here address a variety of traditions within Islam and without, touching on Judaism and Christianity. They focus on several different fields of inquiry, including law, history, theology, and philosophy, and adopt several distinct interpretive approaches. This collection, while by no means exhaustive, addresses many of the historical and contemporary perspectives on law and ethics in the Qur'an, a subject that is of great importance to contemporary Muslims.

Bibliography

Abdel Haleem, M.A.S., trans. *The Qur'an*. Oxford: Oxford University Press, 2010.

Abou-Taleb, Amira Naim. 'The Concept of *Iḥsān* (Beauty/Goodness) in the Qur'ānic Moral Worldview'. PhD diss., University of Helsinki, 2023.

Ali, Kecia. *Sexual Ethics in Islam: Feminist Reflections on Qur'an, Hadith and Jurisprudence*. London: Oneworld, 2006.

Barazangi, Nimat Hafez. *Woman's Identity in the Qur'an: A New Reading*. Gainesville: University Press of Florida, 2004.

Barlas, Asma. *"Believing Women" in Islam: Unreading Patriarchal Interpretations of the Qurʾān*. Austin: University of Texas Press, 2002.

Bauer, Karen, and Feras Hamza. *Women, Households, and the Hereafter in the Qur'an: A Patronage of Piety*. Oxford: Oxford University Press in association with the Institute of Ismaili Studies, 2023.

Crone, Patricia. *Roman, Provincial and Islamic Law: The Origins of the Islamic Patronate*. Cambridge: Cambridge University Press, 1987.

Crone, Patricia. 'Two Legal Problems Bearing on the Early History of the Qurʾān'. *Jerusalem Studies in Arabic and Islam* 18 (1994): 1–37.

Dandūr, Ilyās. *Rawāʾiʿ al-bayān fī tafsīr al-ʿAllāma Muḥammad Ṭāhir Ibn ʿĀshūr li-āyāt al-aḥkām*. Beirut: Dār Ibn Ḥazm, 2021.

Hallaq, Wael B. 'Quranic Magna Carta: On the Origins of the Rule of Law in Islam'. In *Magna Carta, Religion and the Rule of Law*, edited by Robin Griffith-Jones and Mark Hill, 157–76. Cambridge: Cambridge University Press, 2015.

Hasan, Abla. *Decoding the Egalitarianism of the Qur'an: Retrieving Lost Voices on Gender*. Lanham, MD: Lexington Books, 2019.

Hashas, Mohammed, and Mutaz al-Khatib. 'Introduction: Modern Arab-Islamic Scholarship on Ethics: A Reflective Contextualization'. In *Islamic Ethics and the Trusteeship Paradigm: Taha Abderrahmane's Philosophy in Comparative Perspectives*, edited by Mohammed Hashas and Mutaz al-Khatib, 1–31. Leiden: Brill, 2020.

Ibrahim, Celene. *Women and Gender in the Qur'an*. Oxford: Oxford University Press, 2020.

Jenvrin, Geraldine. *Exégèses de la «mécréance» (kufr) et statut légal du non-musulman dans le commentaire coranique d'al Qurtubi (m.671/1273)*. Turnhout: Brepols, 2024.

al-Khatib, Mutaz. '*Āyāt al-akhlāq: suʾāl al-akhlāq ʿinda al-mufassirīn* (Verses on Ethics: The Question of Ethics among the Qurʾān Exegetes)'. *Journal of Islamic Ethics* 1, no. 1–2 (2017): 84–121.

Lowry, Joseph E. 'A Guide to the Legal Material in Sūrat al-Nisāʾ (Q 4)'. In *Unlocking the Medinan Qur'an*, edited by Nicolai Sinai, 422–79. Leiden: Brill, 2022.

Lowry, Joseph E. 'Law, Structure, and Meaning in Sūrat al-Baqarah'. *Journal of the International Qur'anic Studies Association* 2, no. 1 (2017): 111–48.

Lowry, Joseph E. 'Quranic Law and Its "Biblical" Intertexts'. *Asiatische Studien – Études Asiatiques* 78, no. 3 (2024): 431–67.

Lowry, Joseph E. *Reading the Qur'an as a Law Book*. New Haven, CT: Yale Law School Occasional Papers, 2015.

Lowry, Joseph E. 'When Less Is More: Law and Commandment in *Sūrat al-Anʿām*'. *Journal of Qurʾanic Studies* 9, no. 2 (2007): 22–42.

Rashwani, Samer, ed. *Behind the Story: Ethical Readings of Qurʾānic Narratives*. Leiden: Brill, 2024.

Reinhart, A. Kevin. 'Islamic Law as Islamic Ethics'. *Journal of Religious Ethics* 11, no. 2 (1983): 186–203.

Reinhart, A. Kevin. 'Origins of Islamic Ethics: Foundations and Constructions'. In *Encyclopedia of Religious Ethics*, vol. 2, *Moral Traditions*, edited by William Schweiker, 244–53. Hoboken, NJ: Wiley Blackwell, 2022.

Rivlin, Josef J. *Gesetz im Koran: Kultus und Ritus*. Jerusalem: Bamberger & Wahrmann, 1934.

Roberts, Robert. *Das Familienrecht im Qorān*. Leipzig: A. Pries, 1907.

Roberts, Robert. *The Social Laws of the Qoran, Considered and Compared with Those of Hebrew and Other Ancient Codes*. London: Williams and Norgate, 1925.

Sadeghi, Behnam. *The Logic of Law Making in Islam: Women and Prayer in the Legal Tradition*. Cambridge: Cambridge University Press, 2013.

Salaymeh, Lena. *The Beginnings of Islamic Law: Late Antique Islamicate Legal Traditions*. Cambridge: Cambridge University Press, 2016.

Schmid, Nora K. 'From Ethico-Religious Exhortation to Legal Paraenesis: The Function of Qurʾanic *Waʿẓ*'. *Islamic Law and Society* 28 (2021): 317–51.

Schneider, Irene. *Der Islam und die Frauen*. Munich: C.H. Beck, 2019.

Sheibani, Mariam, Amir Toft, and Ahmed El Shamsy. 'The Classical Period: Scripture, Origins, and Early Development'. In *The Oxford Handbook of Islamic Law*, edited by Anver M. Emon and Rumee Ahmed, 403–36. Oxford: Oxford University Press, 2017.

Wadud, Amina. *Qurʾan and Woman: Rereading the Sacred Text from a Woman's Perspective*. New York: Oxford University Press, 1999.

Zellentin, Holger M. 'Gentile Purity Law from the Bible to the Qurʾan: The Case of Sexual Purity and Illicit Intercourse'. In *The Qurʾan's Reformation of Judaism and Christianity: Return to the Origins*, edited by Holger M. Zellentin, 115–215. Abingdon: Routledge, 2019.

Zellentin, Holger M. *Law beyond Israel: From the Bible to the Qurʾan*. Oxford: Oxford University Press, 2022.

PART 1

The Qur'an, Ethics, and Law

CHAPTER 1

Towards a Prehistory of Islamic Law: the Hebrew Bible, the New Testament, and the Qur'an

Holger Zellentin

The formation of Sharīʿa proper, as defined by the development of the various Sunnī *madhāhib* (legal schools, sing. *madhhab*) and by Shīʿī and Ibāḍī jurisprudence, was moulded both by the legal practice of the earliest jurists and by the legal passages of the Qur'an, to which this volume is dedicated.[1] A comprehensive prehistory of Islamic law would therefore need to focus on the Hejazi basis of the legal actions of the earliest practitioners of Islamic law, namely, the Prophet, his Companions, and those who functioned as *fuqahā'* (jurisconsults, sing. *faqīh*) avant la lettre in the early caliphates.[2] Here, a dual emphasis would need to be placed, on the one hand, on the stability of pagan Arabian legal norms that often endured from antiquity into the early Islamic period and, on the other, on the Prophet's interventions that often tended to abrogate or modify these norms.[3] At the same time, however, such a prehistory needs to

---

1 This study is part of a project that has received funding from the European Research Council (ERC) under the European Union's Horizon 2020 research and innovation programme (grant agreement no. 866043).

2 See esp. Harald Motzki, *The Origins of Islamic Jurisprudence: Meccan Fiqh before the Classical Schools* (Brill: Leiden, 2002); see also Lena Salaymeh, *The Beginnings of Islamic Law: Late Antique Islamicate Legal Traditions* (Cambridge: Cambridge University Press, 2016); and Behnam Sadeghi, *The Logic of Law Making in Islam: Women and Prayer in the Legal Tradition* (Cambridge: Cambridge University Press, 2013).

3 The importance of the Qur'an's Arabian context has been rightfully emphasised in recent publications such as Suleyman Dost, 'Pilgrimage in Pre-Islamic Arabia: Continuity and Rupture from Epigraphic Texts to the Quran', *Millennium: Yearbook on the Culture and History of the First Millennium* C.E. 15 (2023): 15–32; and Fred M. Donner and Rebecca Hasselbach-Andee, eds., *Scripts and Scripture: Writing and Religion in Arabia, 500–700* CE (Chicago: Oriental Institute, 2022). For the ancient Near Eastern context, see e.g. Mehmetcan Akpınar, 'False Accusations of Adultery (*Qaḏf*) in the Quran and in Near Eastern Legal Traditions', in *Normativität des Koran im Zeichen gesellschaftlichen Wandels: Theologische und religionspädagogische Perspektiven*, ed. Fahimah Ulfat, Mouez Khalfaoui, and Mohammed Nekroumi (Frankfurt: Nomos, 2022), 249–76; David Powers, 'The Qur'ān and Its Legal Environment', in *Deconstructing Islamic Studies*, ed. Majid Daneshgar and Aaron W. Hughes (Boston: Harvard University Press/Mizan, 2020), 9–32; and Lena Salaymeh, 'Legal Traditions of the "Near East": The Pre-Islamic Context', in *Routledge Handbook of Islamic Law*, ed. Khaled Abou El Fadl,

 | HTTPS://DOI.ORG/10.1163/9789004755567-003

consider what I would describe as the 'biblical impulse' that marks most of the Prophet's interventions into established pagan Arabian legal practices. Only a full understanding of both the pagan Arabian continuities and of the biblical innovations will, eventually, give due credit to the nuanced position vis-à-vis both traditions taken in the Qur'an and, *mutatis mutandis*, in Islamic law.[4]

Since the lofty goal of combining the study of biblical Jewish and Christian, pagan Hejazi, and Islamic jurisprudence has not yet been established in scholarship, the present chapter will offer a more modest, preliminary contribution. It retraces the continuous legal developments that connect the laws first formulated in the Hebrew Bible to the Prophet's biblically oriented amendments to pagan Arabian law, as evidenced by the Qur'an. Perhaps surprisingly to many, these developments pass through the New Testament and Christian legal culture much more so than through the Jewish tradition as formulated in the Talmudic literatures of Palestine and Babylonia, and attention to this point is important for a proper understanding of Qur'anic law.[5]

This chapter will restate in detail and slightly update the case I have made in a recent monograph, *Law beyond Israel: From the Bible to the Qur'an*.[6] The

---

Ahmad Atif Ahmad, and Said Fares Hassan (Abingdon: Routledge, 2021), 275–85. Note, however, that Wael Hallaq has equally emphasised the Meccan basis of many of the later Qur'anic principles. See Wael Hallaq, 'Groundwork of the Moral Law: A New Look at the Qur'ān and the Genesis of Sharīʿa', *Islamic Law and Society* 16 (2009): 239–79.

4 For my views on the Qur'an's 'biblical impulse' and its incremental implementation when it comes to narrative (here 'the biblicisation of the Qur'an and the qur'anicisation of the Bible'), see Holger Zellentin, 'The Synchronic and the Diachronic Qur'ān: Sūrat Yā Sīn, Lot's People, and the Rabbis', in *The Making of Religious Texts in Islam: The Fragment and the Whole*, ed. Asma Hilali and S.R. Burge (Berlin: Gerlach Press, 2019), 111–72. Note that the 'biblical impulse' is neither ubiquitous in the Qur'an (which leaves many pagan Arabian rites, laws, and customs intact, see the previous note and note 44 below), nor absent from later Islamic law. For example, in the case of the Islamic punishment of stoning for adultery, which eventually superseded the Qur'anic one prescribing flogging, one could even argue that the introduction of the punishment of stoning effectively constitutes a reversion to perceived biblical, i.e. Israelite law for Muslims despite the Qur'an's diverging instructions on stoning and its non-Israelite ethno-legal perception of its community; on the matter, see Pavel Pavlovitch, 'The Islamic Penalty for Adultery in the Third Century AH and Al-Shāfiʿī's *Risāla*', *Bulletin of the School of Oriental and African Studies* 75 (2012): 473–97.

5 On the Qur'an's reactions to rabbinic legal thought, see Holger Zellentin, 'What Is "within Judaism" according to the Quran?', in *Within Judaism? Interpretive Trajectories in Judaism, Christianity, and Islam from the First to the Twenty-First Century*, ed. Karin Hedner Zetterholm and Anders Runesson (Lanham: Lexington Books/Fortress Academic, 2023), 282–308.

6 See Holger Zellentin, *Law beyond Israel: From the Bible to the Qur'an* (Oxford: Oxford University Press, 2022), open access at https://doi.org/10.1093/oso/9780199675579.001.0001, which develops the groundwork laid in Holger Zellentin, *The Qur'ān's Legal Culture: The Didascalia Apostolorum as a Point of Departure* (Tübingen: Mohr Siebeck, 2013; repr., 2023), open access

volume sought to rectify a lack of nuance that has marred most previous comparative approaches to biblical and Qur'anic law, which often placed both Scriptures next to each other, without due consideration of one or more of the following three key issues:

1. *The dual nature of biblical law* that formulates laws not only for the Israelites but also for those non-Israelites who are commonly termed 'gentiles' both in Western scholarship and in the Jewish and Christian traditions. The notion of 'gentile law' thus proves fundamental for situating the Qur'an's legal discourse, yet the Muslim Scripture, conversely, resists the classification of its community as 'gentile'. Rather, it seeks to surpass the ethnic binary that divides 'Jews' from 'gentiles' in late antique legal discourse, offering first, in Mecca, a multipolar legal worldview and eventually, in Medina, a more universalist approach that gently, and sometimes not so gently, hints at a (never fully realised) supersessionist and universalist perspective.
2. *The multifaceted development of biblical law* in the roughly fourteen centuries that lie between the Hebrew Bible and the Qur'an. Very often, the Qur'an stands in closer relationship to late antique Jewish or especially Christian practice than to these practices' biblical foundations. Conversely, the Qur'an seeks to convince Jews and Christians to re-establish what it perceives, often with good cause, to be the original and unadulterated form of biblical commandments.
3. *The vibrancy of Christian legal culture* that, far from conforming to the neo-Pauline idea of the full abrogation of biblical law, reformulated the laws of the Hebrew Bible for Christian communities that understood many – though not all – of these laws as positive divine law, i.e. as both eternal and as binding for themselves. The Qur'an often stands closest to Christian groups endorsing Biblical law for gentiles, which likely constituted the mainstream of many forms of Greek-, Syriac-, and Ethiopic-speaking churches, despite occasional patristic resistance to

at https://doi.org/10.1628/978-3-16-162701-9. The present chapter expands the summary given in *Law beyond Israel*, 15–29. Note that I had published a number of preparatory studies whose findings I largely corroborated in the monograph, such as 'Judaeo-Christian Legal Culture and the Qur'ān: The Case of Ritual Slaughter and the Consumption of Animal Blood', in *Jewish Christianity and the Origins of Islam*, ed. Francisco del Río Sánchez (Turnhout: Brepols, 2018), 117–59; 'Gentile Purity Law from the Bible to the Qur'an: The Case of Sexual Purity and Illicit Intercourse', in *The Qur'an's Reformation of Judaism and Christianity: Return to the Origins*, ed. Holger Zellentin (New York: Routledge, 2019), 115–215; and 'Law in the Medinan Qur'an: The Case of Biblical Incest Law and Its Qur'anic Re-iteration', in *Unlocking the Medinan Qur'an*, ed. Nicolai Sinai (Leiden: Brill, 2022), 315–89.

specific aspects of positive divine law. Conversely, the Qur'an also positions itself in clear contradistinction to the type of legal overreach with which it associates the rabbinic leaders of the Jewish community.

In order to rectify these problems, *Law beyond Israel* argued that the Hebrew Bible in effect formulates two sets of law: one for the Israelites and one for the gentile 'residents' living in the Holy Land. It illustrated how these biblical laws for non-Israelites form the historical basis of Qur'anic law, corroborating its central claim by assessing laws for gentiles in late antique Jewish and especially in Christian legal discourse. As a result, the study established a previously under-appreciated legal continuity from the Hebrew Bible to the New Testament and from late antique Christianity to nascent Islam.

In what follows, I will summarise the key findings of my volume first by outlining the legal obligations that the Hebrew Bible imposes on gentiles, on humanity more broadly, and, more specifically, on the non-Israelite residents of the Holy Land. I will then very briefly note how these laws developed through Second Temple Judaism to the early Jesus movement, illustrating how the biblical laws for residents inform those formulated in Acts of the Apostles. Building on this legal continuity, I make three propositions that seek to provide a more nuanced view of the developments that connect the laws of the Hebrew Bible to those of the Qur'an: first, the rabbinic laws for gentiles, the so-called Noahide Laws, while offering a more lenient interpretation than what one finds in Acts, are equally based on the biblical laws for gentiles. Secondly, Christians generally appreciated and even expanded the gentile laws of Acts. Thirdly, the Qur'an reinvents Arabian religious practice by formulating its own distinctive approach to the biblical laws for gentiles, in close continuity with – and at times in critical distance from – late antique Jewish and especially Christian gentile law.

With this background situation, the way in which the Qur'an deals with biblical law is best told in a linear, diachronic fashion as a story of four successive iterations of God's law for gentiles, beginning with the Hebrew Bible and tracing the ways in which Jews and Christians deal with their legal heritage over the fourteen centuries leading up to the time of the Qur'anic community. The following narrative is represented visually in the Appendix at the end of this chapter, with Table 1.1 offering a simplified view of major conceptual continuities in law and ethnicity from the Hebrew Bible through late antique Judaism and Christianity up to the Qur'an, and Table 1.2 providing a simplified view of the very same developments based on central prohibitions and commandments given to gentiles and, eventually, to the nascent Islamic community, thereby laying the foundation for the Qur'an's legal verses and, eventually, for Islamic law.

1 Laws for Israelites and for Gentiles in the Hebrew Bible

The composition and canonisation of the Hebrew Bible broadly straddle the history of the Israelites leading up to and following the destruction of the First and the Second Temples in the seventh century BCE and the first century CE, respectively.[7] As a Scripture, the Bible addresses the people of Israel: its primary focus lies squarely within the bounds of its implied audience. Non-Israelites, however, appear throughout the Bible. To begin with the patriarchal history: the Bible relates the long prehistory of the election of Jacob as Israel (in Genesis 32:22–32) by telling the story of a pre-Israelite past. The Hebrew Bible, it is true, inseparably connects Abraham to the fate of the Israelites.[8] Late antique Jews, Christians, and early Muslims, however, fully laid claim to Jacob's grandfather Abraham, portraying him, respectively, as a Jewish, a Christian, and eventually a Muslim figure. Some of the Bible's late antique readers, accordingly, pointed out that it equally casts every patriarch and matriarch from Adam and up to Abraham's father, and even up to Sarah's and Abraham's initial lives as Sarai and Abram, as not yet belonging to Israel, and therefore, in the view of these readers, as gentile.[9]

In addition to the figures that flourished before the advent of Israel, the Bible uses gentiles repeatedly in its later narratives as well. The Egyptians, for example, host and then suppress the Israelites, God uses the Assyrians as His rod to punish Israel, and gentiles feature centrally in Daniel's eschatological visions. In addition, books such as Ruth, Esther, Ezra, and Nehemiah divergently approach the appropriateness of intermarriage. While it is obvious that gentiles can be punished for certain actions – such as the Egyptians who refuse to release the Israelites, other nations who hinder their progress during the Exodus, or the Canaanites who are expelled from the Holy Land – the Bible

7 See e.g. Konrad Schmid, *The Scribes of the Torah: The Formation of the Pentateuch in Its Literacy and Historical Contexts* (Atlanta: The Society of Biblical Literature, 2023); and Cana Werman, ed., *From Author to Copyist: Composition, Redaction, and Transmission of the Hebrew Bible: Studies in Honor of Zipi Talshir* (Winona Lake: Eisenbrauns, 2015).

8 See e.g. Jakob Wöhrle, 'Abraham amidst the Nations: The Priestly Concept of Covenant and the Persian Imperial Ideology', in *Covenant in the Persian Period: From Genesis to Chronicles*, ed. Richard J. Bautch and Gary Knoppers (Winona Lake: Eisenbrauns, 2015), 23–39; and Ronald Hendel, *Remembering Abraham: Culture, Memory, and History in the Hebrew Bible* (Oxford: Oxford University Press, 2005).

9 On the interpretation of Abraham in later traditions, see e.g. Carol Bakhos, *The Family of Abraham: Jewish, Christian, and Muslim Interpretations* (Cambridge, MA: Harvard University Press, 2014); and Jon Levenson, *Inheriting Abraham: The Legacy of the Patriarch in Judaism, Christianity, and Islam* (Princeton: Princeton University Press, 2012).

does not normally describe God as giving any specific laws to them.[10] There are two main exceptions to this rule. First, when Noah and his offspring reach dry land after the flood, in Genesis 9, God imposes on them the double prohibition of blood – concerning the prohibition of shedding of human blood and the injunction to shed animal blood – that many late antique readers of the Bible understood as applicable to Israelites and gentiles alike. Secondly, especially in Leviticus 17–26, texts emanating from the Holiness School,[11] the Hebrew Bible specifies that certain laws given to Israel equally apply to a specific subset of non-Israelites, the so-called *gerim*, the permanent 'residents of the Holy Land', who are, as Noah's offspring, already prohibited from 'blood'.[12]

These biblical laws given to the non-Israelites residing in the Holy Land can be briefly summarised; taken together, they can be identified as the first iteration of God's law for gentiles. Idol worship, to begin with, is prohibited to Israelite and *ger* alike in Deuteronomy (Deut 29:10–29), and the prohibition of idol worship also provides the frame narrative in which the laws for the *gerim* are presented in Leviticus 17. After a short approval of consuming properly slaughtered animals, this passage likewise denounces the alleged Israelite practice to 'offer their sacrifices for goat-demons, to whom they prostitute themselves' (Lev 17:7), and then extends *some* purity regulations not only to Israelites but also to the *gerim* that I will presently define as governing either 'prohibited' or 'regulated' types of impurity. The further laws applicable

10 On the view of the nations in the Hebrew Bible, see e.g. Jacob L. Wright, *War, Memory, and National Identity in the Hebrew Bible* (Cambridge: Cambridge University Press, 2020); and Reinhard Achenbach, Rainer Albertz, and Jakob Wöhrle, eds., *The Foreigner and the Law: Perspectives from the Hebrew Bible and the Ancient Near East* (Wiesbaden: Harrassowitz, 2011).

11 The concept of the 'Holiness School' as responsible for the edition of Leviticus 17–26 and other biblical passages is a contemporary construct subject to constant revision; see most recently Julia Rhyder, *Centralizing the Cult: The Holiness Legislation in Leviticus 17–26* (Tübingen: Mohr Siebeck, 2019); and the foundational work by Jacob Milgrom, *Leviticus 17–22: A New Translation with Introduction and Commentary* (New Haven: Yale University Press, 2007).

12 The meaning of the biblical term *ger* (pl. *gerim*) constitutes the basis for but differs from its later usage as designating 'a convert to Judaism'. Most of the rulings for these *gerim* can be found in the so-called Holiness School of the Hebrew Bible, encompassing Leviticus 17–26, yet related rulings equally appear elsewhere in the Pentateuch, especially in Exodus and Deuteronomy. On the term *ger* in its biblical context, see especially Joram Mayshar, 'Who Was the *Toshav*?', *Journal of Biblical Literature* 133, no. 2 (2014): 225–46; and Reinhard Achenbach, '*gêr – nakhrî – tôshav – zâr*: Legal and Sacral Distinctions regarding Foreigners in the Pentateuch', in *The Foreigner and the Law*, 29–51; for a lucid summary, see also Adi Ophir and Ishay Rosen-Zvi, *Goy: Israel's Multiple Others and the Birth of the Gentile* (Oxford: Oxford University Press, 2018), 23–56.

to *gerim* set out especially in Leviticus 17–26 include the prohibition of murder, the injunction to drain animal blood during slaughter and the prohibition from consuming it, a detailed list of illicit forms of sexual intercourse in Leviticus 18, and a variety of other prohibitions and ritual obligations. Whereas all *gerim* were required to follow certain ritual laws and enjoyed certain privileges, the Hebrew Bible allows for the circumcision of those male *gerim* who wish to partake of the paschal feast (see Exod 12:48–49 and Num 9:14), but it does not demand that all *gerim* be circumcised. In other words, *gerim* likely form part of the *people* of Israel, yet within the people they remain distinguishable from *Israelites* proper, even if they undergo circumcision.[13]

In the Bible, moreover, it is apparent that both Israelites and *gerim* are susceptible to two types of impurity whose distinction from each other marks most Jewish and Christian legal cultures up to the Qur'an: *regulated* and *prohibited* impurity. In the Hebrew Bible, contracting the former, regulated type of impurity is permitted and sometimes even necessary when fulfilling commandments; it results from mundane actions such as licit sexual intercourse or contact with corpses during burial. Prohibited impurity, by contrast, is contracted through acts such as idolatry, the shedding of human blood, or the consumption of animal blood and by committing sexual transgressions. The distinction between the two types of impurity is not categorical: the failure to implement the safeguards for regulated impurity turns what is merely regulated into prohibited impurity.[14] Significantly, the Hebrew Bible applies the rules for the most severe cases of prohibited impurity – caused by idolatry, blood-consumption, bloodshed, and a catalogue of sexual transgressions – both to Israelites and to the *gerim*, the non-Israelite residents of the Holy Land, and, arguably, even to all human beings. In the Hebrew Bible, *gerim* are required to undergo forms of ritual purification if they contract the regulated impurity and are cut off from the people if they contract the prohibited type.[15]

13 See Zellentin, *Law beyond Israel*, 36–50, 129–43, 236–49.

14 A woman, for example, contracts regulated impurity during the time of her menses, yet engaging in otherwise licit intercourse in this period would impart prohibited impurity both on her and her sexual partner. On the matter of prohibited and regulated impurity, alternatively classified as 'moral' vs 'ritual' impurity, see ibid., esp. 36–41, 282–319; Andrew Brower Latz and Arseny Ermakov, eds., *Purity: Essays in Bible and Theology* (Eugene: Wipf and Stock, 2014); and Jonathan Klawans, *Impurity and Sin in Ancient Judaism* (Oxford: Oxford University Press, 2000).

15 The precise status of the biblical as well as of the rabbinic *ger* vis-à-vis a natural born Israelite remains a matter of dispute. I am fully convinced by the general argument that Israel as such remains an ethnically distinct category in all forms of ancient thought: one can become an Israelite only by birth. See esp. Matthew Thiessen, *Contesting Conversion: Genealogy, Circumcision, and Identity in Ancient Judaism and Christianity* (Oxford: Oxford

One seemingly innocuous detail of biblical law, governing the issue of carrion, may have prepared a decisive dichotomy between late antique conceptions of gentile law. While Deuteronomy (Deut 14:21) prohibits Israelites from eating carrion at all and instead enjoins them to sell carrion to the *gerim* for the expressed purpose of consumption, a passage in Leviticus (Lev 17:15–16) states that Israelites and *gerim* must purify themselves if they consume carrion, implying that doing so is licit yet conveys regulated impurity. The ensuing tension between these two biblical attitudes towards carrion, and their underlying assumptions about gentile purity, prepared the main fault-line between the more *lenient* rabbinic laws for gentiles, on the one hand, and the *stricter* Christian and Qur'anic law, on the other. The historical record on the precise legal development on this question is wanting, yet Christian along with Qur'anic law unanimously prohibits such consumption to gentiles as causing *prohibited* impurity, likely based on developments in Second Temple Judaism and in contradistinction to its classification as causing *regulated* impurity in Leviticus 17, whereas the rabbis seem to have permitted most forms of carrion to gentiles, in line with Deuteronomy 14.[16] Accordingly, Christian and Qur'anic law largely adopted the biblical notions of both prohibited and regulated impurity for non-Israelites, whereas the rabbis, along with some tendencies in Christian legal thought, reject the applicability at least of the latter type of impurity for gentiles, as we will see below.

2 Law for Gentiles in the New Testament

Post-biblical Jewish sources of the Second Temple period offer limited reflections on gentile law. It is obvious that many of the Dead Sea Scrolls, sectarian Jewish texts mainly composed in the two centuries leading up to the Common Era, understand the biblical term *ger* in the sense of 'a convert to Judaism' rather than in terms of 'a gentile resident of the Holy Land', anticipating the later rabbinic understanding of the term that is also partially reflected in the Bible's most influential Greek translation, the Septuagint. By the first century of the Common Era, therefore, a general disjunction between the reception of the biblical term *ger*, on the one hand, and the individual laws extended to

University Press, 2011). The rabbis equally seem to consider only people who are the offspring of an Israelite woman to be Israelites (and, for example, permitted to marry a priest; see Mishna *Yevamot* 6:5 and *Bikkurim* 1:5); converts under rabbinic law may thus well be 'Jewish', but remain in an ethnically distinct category. See also note 17 below.

16 See Zellentin, *Law beyond Israel*, 36–56.

(uncircumcised) non-Israelites, on the other, seems to have occurred, as can be seen in the New Testament and in the early rabbinic corpus.[17]

The issue of gentile law again rose to discernible prominence among Jesus-oriented Jews straddling the period of the destruction of the Second Temple, as reflected in their texts that were later collected in the New Testament. Some of the genuine epistles of Paul, written in the first half of the first century CE, address gentile law, and so does the so-called Decree of the Apostles in the Acts of the Apostles, a text that was composed in the late first or more likely in the early second century CE, as part of a twofold composition along with the Gospel of Luke. The Decree of the Apostles is presented as the product of the apostles of Christ under the guidance of the Holy Spirit. The decree is directed to those among 'the nations' – i.e. non-Israelites – who believe in Christ; the decree to the gentiles is here carefully distinguished from the more complex set of commandments that continue to apply to Jews. The Acts of the Apostles is thus evidently a 'Jewish' text in as far as it fully endorse the Law's validity for Jews, yet Acts equally offers one of the first attestations of the designation of gentile believers in Jesus as 'Christian', a term which is used to refer to the Church in Antioch (Acts 11:26). 'Jews', for Acts, are simply Jews no matter what their messianic orientation; 'Christians', at the same time, are Jesus-oriented gentiles who must obey the Decree of the Apostles as a precondition for their salvation. It is to them alone that the short decree in Acts 15 is addressed; it encompasses only the pithy prohibition of meat sacrificed to an idol, blood, 'strangled things', and improper sexual relations, four classes of prohibitions which summarise a sizeable body of biblical law. A considerable volume of critical scholarship, however, has established the notion, already surfacing across patristic literature, that the decree is based on the laws governing prohibited impurity given to the *gerim* in Leviticus 17 and 18, in conjunction with the laws given to Noah in Genesis 9, as discussed above. After Leviticus, the Decree of the Apostles therefore forms the second scriptural iteration of God's law for the gentiles.[18]

---

17 On the notion of the *ger* in Qumran, see Carmen Palmer, *Converts in the Dead Sea Scrolls: The gēr and Mutable Ethnicity* (Leiden: Brill, 2018); and Kengo Akiyama, 'The גר and Interpretive Integration in the Damascus Document 6:20–21 and 14:3–6', *Journal of Jewish Studies* 67 (2016): 249–66. On rabbinic Judaism, see Moshe Lavee, *The Rabbinic Conversion of Judaism: The Unique Perspective of the Bavli on Conversion and the Construction of Jewish Identity* (Leiden: Brill, 2017); and notes 12 and 15 above.

18 See Zellentin, *Law beyond Israel*, 56–77; Pieter B. Hartog, 'Noah and Moses in Acts 15: Group Models and the Novelty of the Way', *New Testament Studies* 67, no. 4 (2021): 496–513; Isaac Oliver, *Torah Praxis after 70 CE: Reading Matthew and Luke-Acts as Jewish Texts* (Tübingen: Mohr Siebeck, 2013); and esp. Jürgen Wehnert, *Die Reinheit des 'christlichen Gottesvolkes'*

3 Law for Gentiles in Late Antique Judaism and Christianity

Late antiquity, roughly speaking, stretches from the third to the seventh century of the Common Era, the period that saw the rise of the Sassanian Empire, its repeated clashes with the Roman Empire, the latter's Christianisation since the fourth century, and finally the establishment of the Rāshidūn caliphate and the Umayyad dynasty in the seventh century.[19] This period saw the emergence of rabbinic Judaism, the emergence of a variety of Christianities, many of which eventually or even initially rejected Judaism and Jewishness, and finally the emergence of the Qur'anic community, which in turn understood itself as spiritually and legally superior in many ways at least to the majority of the Jews and the Christians of its time.[20] Each of these three streams of late antique thought – rabbinic Judaism, Christianity in its many forms, and nascent Islam – in its own way endorsed the content if not the form of the main body of the *gerim* laws first promulgated in Leviticus. While among the three traditions, only the Christian one makes this connection explicit (and only marginally so, in a few patristic references), the very continuity of gentile law and of the legal narratives sanctifying them (on which more below) illustrates this central affinity between the three otherwise often divergent Abrahamic traditions. A few words on the rabbinic laws for gentiles and their biblical basis will lead us to the respective Christian traditions, which I hold to be a more direct antecedent to Qur'anic law.

There is ample discussion about when the rabbinic movement took shape; my own view is that it only gained traction in the second half of the second century at the earliest, after the failure of the Bar Kokhba revolt. We can, however, date the movement's earliest records. The so-called Tannaitic texts, among them the Tosephta, were edited in Roman Palestine in the third and

---

aus Juden und Heiden: Studien zum historischen und theologischen Hintergrund des sogenannten Aposteldekrets (Göttingen: Vandenhoeck & Ruprecht, 1997).

19 A broad introduction into the religious movements of this period is Josef Lössl and Nicholas J. Baker-Brian, eds., *A Companion to Religion in Late Antiquity* (Chichester: Wiley-Blackwell, 2018); a more general overview is provided by Gillian Clark, *Late Antiquity: A Very Short Introduction* (Oxford: Oxford University Press, 2011).

20 On the relationship of the Qur'anic community to Jews and Christians, see Nicolai Sinai, *Key Terms of the Qur'an: A Critical Dictionary* (Princeton: Princeton University Press, 2022), s.v. '*isrā'īl*' (45–53), '*ahl al-kitāb*' (108–18), '*alladhīna hādū, al-yahūd*' (728–35), '*naṣārā*' (666–77); see also Holger Zellentin, '*banū isrā'īl, ahl al-kitāb, al-yahūd wa-l-naṣārā*: The Qur'anic Community's Encounters with Jews and Christians', *Entangled Religions* 13, no. 2 (2023): https://doi.org/10.46586/er.13.2023.10991; as well as Mohsen Goudarzi, 'The Ascent of Ishmael: Genealogy, Covenant, and Identity in Early Islam', *Arabica: Journal of Arabic and Islamic Studies / Revue d'études arabes et islamiques* 66 (2019): 415–84.

perhaps up to the early fourth centuries CE. It is the Tosephta that presents the rabbinic version of laws for gentiles, the so-called Noahide Laws. These laws are based on the rabbis' joint reading of Genesis 9 and of the *gerim* laws in Leviticus 17–26. In the rabbinic reading, these laws become applicable beyond the borders of the Holy Land, as universal law for those gentiles who want to draw near to the God of Israel. The rabbis' Noahide Laws – whose historical, let alone systematic implementation in any way, shape, or form is unlikely – constitute a third iteration of God's laws for gentiles after that of Leviticus and the Decree of the Apostles; the close exegetical relationship between the Noahide Laws and the Decree of the Apostles, along with their patent differences when it comes to the status of carrion, has already been mentioned. Later rabbinic texts of the Amoraic period, such as the Palestinian and the Babylonian Talmud that were redacted after the late fourth century, preserve the memory of the concept of the Noahide Laws, yet do not develop their content much further. The Noahide Laws apparently played only a minor role in Amoraic and perhaps even already in Tannaitic late antique Judaism: since the emergence of the rabbinic movement at the turn of the third century CE, then, the rabbis seem to have favoured conversion to Judaism – rather than the observation of Noahide, gentile Law – as the preferred method for gentiles to join the fold.[21]

Roughly contemporarily to the rabbinic movement, or plausibly a bit earlier, various forms of Christianity began to arise throughout the late ancient world from the early second century CE onwards. The linguistic denominations 'Greek', 'Latin', and 'Syriac' are useful shorthand for culturally distinguishable forms of Christianity; there are of course broad theological overlaps especially between the Greek and Syriac churches. Overall, it appears that very few church fathers maintained the distinction between Jewish and gentile ethnicity and therefore between Jewish and gentile law that marked the Acts of the Apostles and other New Testament texts. Instead, Latin and Greek Christians seem to have increasingly dismissed the importance of Jewish ethnicity as legally prescriptive for a person's mode of salvation – many Christians effectively subsumed 'the nation' of Israel as one of the many 'nations', the gentiles. The Latin and Greek tendency to subsume Israel under the nations was shared by strands within the Syriac churches, whereas other strands among Syriac Christians, inversely, subsumed 'the nations' under the one 'nation' of Israel, the church: here, we find an essential model explaining why the Qur'an

21 See Zellentin, *Law beyond Israel*, 66–77; and Christine Hayes, 'Were the Noahide Commandments Formulated at Yavne? Tosephta Avoda Zara 8:4–9 in Cultural and Historical Context', in *Jews and Christians in the First and Second Centuries: The Interbellum 70–132 CE*, ed. Joshua Schwartz and Peter J. Tomson (Leiden: Brill, 2017), 225–64.

would understand both Jews and Christians as two parties among the Children of Israel.[22] The Decree of the Apostles, at the same time, was endorsed by all recorded late antique church councils, and by the vast majority of church fathers.[23] A few Christian individuals, along with a few relevant Christian and plausibly Jewish texts, however, prove particularly momentous for understanding how divergently Christians dealt with the legal aspect of their apostolic heritage, displaying, respectively, a dismissive, an appreciative, or an expansive attitude towards the Decree of the Apostles.[24]

A *dismissive* attitude towards the Decree of the Apostles was displayed mainly by Augustine and, to a much lesser degree, by Chrysostom, two central fathers of the fourth and early fifth century CE, who, perhaps in their push against perceived aspects of Jewish practice among Christians, tended to reject any form of gentile law that derives from positive biblical rather than from natural law. These fathers alone went as far as explicating their dismissal of key provisions of the Decree of the Apostles (Augustine) or at least questioning its centrality (Chrysostom). Despite the general importance of these fathers for Christian discourse, however, it is unclear if and when their legal attitude towards the Decree became dominant.[25]

By contrast, significant strands of the entire Christian tradition at least up to the seventh century CE, and in some traditions to this day, stand much closer to the *appreciative* attitude towards the Decree, as a plethora of Greek and Latin alongside East and West Syrian patristic sources, church councils, and canons, as well as later apostolic writings, illustrate. These appreciative writings endorse the Decree in its entirety, and, just like the Decree itself, see

22 See Zellentin, '*banū isrāʾīl*'; and esp. Sebastian P. Brock, *Synagogue and Church in Dialogue: Four Syriac Poems from Late Antiquity* (Oxford: Journal of Jewish Studies, 2019), 9. Note that according to Simcha Gross, the Syriac notion of the church's ethnic continuity with Judaism has no basis in actual history; see Simcha Gross, 'A Long Overdue Farewell: The Purported Jewish Origins of Syriac Christianity', in *Jews and Syriac Christians*, ed. Simcha Gross and Aaron Michael Butts (Tübingen: Mohr Siebeck, 2020), 121–44.

23 The most fundamental study remains Karl Böckenhoff, *Das apostolische Speisegesetz in den ersten fünf Jahrhunderten: Ein Beitrag zum Verständnis der quasi-levitischen Satzungen in älteren kirchlichen Rechtsquellen* (Paderborn: Schöning, 1903); Böckenhoff's derisive attitude towards purity laws is typical of much of the scholarship. A more helpful approach is displayed by Moshe Blidstein, *Purity, Community, and Ritual in Early Christian Literature* (Oxford: Oxford University Press, 2017), esp. 61–92; and David M. Freidenreich, *Foreigners and Their Food: Constructing Otherness in Jewish, Christian, and Islamic Law* (Berkeley: University of California Press, 2011).

24 See Zellentin, *Law beyond Israel*, 77–105.

25 See Zellentin, *The Qurʾān's Legal Culture*, 80–86.

gentiles as susceptible mainly to prohibited impurity, diverging on the issue of regulated impurity.[26]

The historical record for the relevance of the *expansive* attitude towards the Decree of the Apostles, finally, is solid, yet far less robust than that of the dismissive and the appreciative attitude. Yet this expansive attitude is especially important in order to understand the Qur'an's respective formulation of laws for its own, non-Israelite community. The evidentiary basis for the expansive attitude is substantially broadened by the example of the nascent Islamic community itself, if one allows for a triangulation between three key texts over a broad expanse of time and space.[27]

The two key sources attesting to an expansive attitude towards the Decree of the Apostles in late antiquity – which form the other two legs of the triangle of which the Qur'an, in my view, forms the third one – incorporate older material yet seem to have been redacted largely in the fourth or fifth century CE: first, the Didascalia Apostolorum, which appreciates the Decree but strongly rejects a specific list of additions to it, and, secondly, a text called the Clementine Homilies, which endorses both the decree and the very additions rejected in the Didascalia. Each of the two texts is unique, at least in its own time, in the way in which it constructs Israelite and gentile ethnicity and in the way in which it constructs gentile law based on the Decree of the Apostles. The legal and hermeneutical correspondence between these two texts as well as between them and the Qur'an points not so much to a textual relationship but to a continuity of legal hermeneutics and especially of legal practice between theses sources' chronologically and geographically widely dispersed audiences.

The Didascalia Apostolorum, to begin with, is an apostolic text likely based on a third-century Greek source, of which only a few snippets have survived. Its earliest full attestation is a Latin palimpsest from the fifth century and a Syriac manuscript from the early eighth century CE, pointing, along with the text's archaic Syriac, to its circulation at the time of the Qur'anic community. The Didascalia became a foundational document for the West Syrian (sometimes referred to as the 'Jacobite') church, the Syriac-speaking church prevalent in parts of the Eastern Roman and of the Western Sassanian Empire.[28]

26 Ibid., 86–90, 154–58.

27 Ibid., 90–105, 158–81.

28 A proper introduction to the Didascalia remains a desideratum. For an overview of the relevant literature, see ibid., esp. 1–54; and Maria E. Doerfler, 'Didascalia Apostolorum', in *Gorgias Encyclopedic Dictionary of the Syriac Heritage*, ed. Sebastian P. Brock, Aaron M. Butts, George A. Kiraz, and Lucas Van Rompay (Piscataway: Gorgias Press, 2011), 124–25.

The Didascalia will prove valuable for this chapter in three respects, furnishing Christian views both on gentile law and on legal narratives connected with it:

1. The Didascalia, along with earlier Syriac fathers such as Aphrahat, conceives of Christianity in a distinctly 'Israelite' way. The church, in this view, is neither Jewish nor gentile, but constitutes an amalgamation of 'the nation' – i.e. Israel – with 'the (gentile) nations', i.e. the gentiles who joined the nation of Israel under Christ. For the Didascalia, to put it simply, Israel *is* the church – there is no distinction between spiritual and carnal Israel.
2. The Didascalia takes on a very distinct attitude towards the Decree of the Apostles, which it cites and fervently appreciates. It declares the content of this decree, along with its own version of the Decalogue and a number of observances and laws – pertaining, for example, to prayer, fasting, charity, chastity, veiling of women, and financial honesty, along with the strict prohibition of murdering infants, giving false witness, or committing slander – to be the original, *primary* divine law given to Moses. This primary law is clearly delineated from the *secondary* 'punitive' laws given after the incident of the Golden Calf. In this account, only this secondary law was abrogated by Jesus, who left the primary law intact and extended its validity by welcoming all nations to join Israel as Christians. The Didascalia can therefore be said to consider the primary Israelite law as potentially universal, as applying to all gentiles joining the church.
3. The Didascalia offers an emphatic endorsement of the appreciative Christian attitude towards the Decree of the Apostles, which it cites and discusses in detail. It rejects the concept of *regulated* impurity as applicable to its community. In line with other heresiological writings, the Didascalia thereby becomes a significant witness that negatively testifies to the *expansive* attitude towards gentile law that seems to have been held by some or even many of its community members, with whom it thoroughly disagrees. In its view, certain aspects of both prohibited and regulated impurity, such as 'distinctions of meat', or engaging in ritual ablutions before prayer or after sexual intercourse, were part of the punitive law given after the Golden Calf that Jesus had abrogated. Those who continue to observe these laws seen as punitive effectively deny God's abolishment of them, which marked His forgiveness of the worship of the Golden Calf – and since they deny the forgiveness, they are accused of continuing to commit the very same sin.[29]

29 See Zellentin, *Law beyond Israel*, 55–76, 101–2; Michael Pregill, *The Golden Calf between Bible and Qur'an: Scripture, Polemic, and Exegesis from Late Antiquity to Islam* (Oxford: Oxford University Press, 2020), 175–264; and Zellentin, *The Qur'ān's Legal Culture*, 55–202.

The expansive attitude towards the Decree of the Apostles decried by the Didascalia (which also includes the prohibition of pork and wine) is equally condemned – and thereby negatively attested – by a number of other Latin, Greek, and Syriac patristic sources. Many of these sources, such as Epiphanius (d. 403 CE), follow their heresiological instincts to such a degree that they nearly become unsuitable to reconstruct actual practices among Christians of the time.[30] There is, however, one source prior to the Qur'an that fully endorses the expansive attitude towards the Decree of the Apostles explicitly condemned by many fourth and fifth-century sources: the so-called Clementine Homilies make not only the Decree but also several significant additions incumbent on gentiles, positively substantiating the very same list of additional observances the Didascalia had decried. The Clementine Homilies are another apostolic text composed in Greek in the fourth or early fifth century, again likely based on earlier sources. They were subsequently translated into, or at least epitomized in, several languages, including Syriac, Ge'ez, and eventually (plausibly after the Qur'anic period) also Arabic. The formative role of the Clementine Homilies for the Christian tradition and their reception history in the Greek tradition are negligible.[31] The Homilies, however, prove invaluable for the prehistory of Islamic law since they, just like the Didascalia, testify to three important late antique views on gentile law and on legal narratives connected with it:

1. The Clementine Homilies are unique in as far as they maintain and even sharpen the formulation of the strict differentiation between Jewish and gentile law evident in the Acts of the Apostles. The text fully endorses the validity of Jewish law for Jews (who do not need Jesus) and the validity of the Decree of the Apostles for gentiles (who do not need Moses). By declaring Judaism to be a valid tradition based on the teachings of Moses alone, the Homilies certainly constitute a Jewish text, yet within this

30 See e.g. Annette Yoshiko Reed, 'Retelling Biblical Retellings: Epiphanius, the Pseudo-Clementines, and the Reception History of *Jubilees*', in *Tradition, Transmission, and Transformation from Second Temple Literature through Judaism and Christianity in Late Antiquity: Proceedings of the Thirteenth International Symposium of the Orion Center for the Study of the Dead Sea Scrolls and Associated Literature, Jointly Sponsored by the Hebrew University Center for the Study of Christianity, 22–4 February, 2011*, ed. Menahem Kister, Hillel I. Newman, Michael Segal, and Ruth A. Clements (Leiden: Brill, 2015), 304–21.

31 On the Clementine Homilies, see e.g. Karin Hedner Zetterholm, 'Christ Assemblies within a Jewish Context: Reconstructing a Social Setting for the Pseudo-Clementine "Homilies"', in *Negotiating Identities: Conflict, Conversion, and Consolidation in Early Judaism and Christianity (200 BCE–600 CE)*, ed. Karin Hedner Zetterholm, Anders Runesson, Cecilia Wassén, and Magnus Zetterholm (Lanham: Lexington Books/Fortress Academic, 2022), 329–49; and Holger Zellentin, 'Scriptural Hermeneutics and Purity Laws in the Clementine Homilies: Mainstream or Marginal, Progressive or Conservative, Jewish or Christian?', in *Negotiating Identities*, 423–54.

framework, their endorsement of the Decree of the Apostles for gentiles and especially their focus on the salvation of gentiles place them into the specific tradition of a 'Christian' understanding of Judaism as pioneered by the Acts of the Apostles.

2. The Clementine Homilies also attest to a second legal narrative about gentile law, in addition to the one about punitive law found in the Didascalia, that proves relevant for the Qur'an. Along with earlier patristic sources, in particular from the Alexandrian tradition, the Homilies present their version of gentile law as underlying God's command to the demons not to attack any humans unless they first make themselves liable by breaking any of the divine and universal commandments. These laws are based on the Decree of the Apostles, yet in this reading include aspects pertaining not only to prohibited but also to regulated impurity. The Clementine Homilies, unlike the Didascalia, do not distinguish between an eternal primary and a temporary secondary law. They do, however, offer a related concept of a bipartite law in which Jesus confirms 'the Law' while abrogating *part of it*. The Homilies endorse a salvation history in which the Law is given orally to Moses and subsequently corrupted and falsely expanded by human error and satanic intervention. Jesus here serves as the prophet who restores the law to its original state, abrogating the erroneous additions to the Bible and seeking to save the gentiles. This constitutes a partial structural parallel to Jesus' role as the abrogator of the punitive law in the Didascalia within a different narrative framework.
3. The Homilies, finally, formulate their version of gentile law by expanding the Decree of the Apostles in a way that closely resembles the observances specifically condemned in the Didascalia. The key aspect of regulated impurity law which it imposes on gentiles, beyond the stipulations of the Decree of the Apostles, is the requirement to wash after sexual intercourse and, arguably, before prayer; the Clementine Homilies also associate pigs and wine with demons.[32]

In addition to the aforementioned texts, a vast number of Jewish and Christian sources corroborate the central legal developments from the Bible to the Qur'an by providing additional unique perspectives on aspects of law. For example, several further Palestinian and Mesopotamian rabbinic texts offer

32 See Zellentin, *Law beyond Israel*, 90–101; and Zellentin, *The Qur'ān's Legal Culture*, 77–126. On the problem of satanic verses in late antiquity, see Holger Zellentin, '"One Letter *Yud* Shall Not Pass Away from the Law": Matthew 5:17 to *Shabbat* 116a–b', in *Religious Identities in Antiquity and the Early Middle Ages: Walking Together & Parting Ways*, ed. Ilkka Lindstedt, Nina Nikki, and Riikka Tuori (Leiden: Brill, 2021), 204–58.

glimpses of Jewish practices that have affinity to those of Christians and of the nascent Islamic community.[33] Furthermore, the Apostolic Constitutions, a Greek apostolic text from the fourth century that was based on a version of the Didascalia Apostolorum, are important in that they view the laws given to Noah as natural law, a tendency also found, *mutatis mutandis*, in the Qur'an.[34] Various early church fathers, such as Tertullian, Cyprian, and Origen in the second and third centuries CE, Eusebius in the third and fourth, as well as Jerome in the fourth and fifth, allow for tracing the development of gentile laws in Latinate and Greek Christianity.[35] Aphrahat and Ephraem, the two foundational fathers of both the East and the West Syrian traditions that flourished in the fourth century, in the Eastern Roman Empire and in the north of the Sassanian Empire respectively, offer crucial information on the development both of Christian law and of Christian legal narrative. Both Syriac fathers display close affinities with, yet also evident differences from the legal concepts offered by the Didascalia Apostolorum.[36] Likewise, Mar Aba, the sixth-century father of the East Syrian church, sometimes referred to as the 'Nestorian' church prevalent in Mesopotamia and in the Gulf region, proves especially significant for the Qur'an's view of incest laws,[37] as does the Justinian Code, the collection of laws promulgated by the eponymous sixth-century CE Christian emperor whose rulings further help to contextualise some of the Qur'an's rules for dealing with same-sex intercourse along with punishments for a variety of acts deemed criminal.[38]

---

33 See e.g. Holger Zellentin, 'Between Bible and Byzantium: "Corruption on Earth" (fasād fī l-arḍ) and the Qur'an's Penal Code (Q 5:33-34.38-39)', *Journal of the International Qur'anic Studies Association* 10 (2025): 11–56; and Shari L. Lowin, '*The Jews Say the Hand of God Is Chained*: Q. 5:64 as a Response to a Midrash in a *Piyyut* by R. El'azar ha-Kallir', *Journal of Qur'anic Studies* 21, no. 2 (2019): 108–39.

34 On the importance of natural law, or 'natural morality', for the development of late antique and Qur'anic law and morality, see Saqib Hussain, *Wisdom in the Qur'an: Law and Morality from the Bible to Late Antiquity* (Oxford: Oxford University Press, 2026); Julien Decharneux, *Creation and Contemplation: The Cosmology of the Qur'ān and Its Late Antique Background* (Berlin: De Gruyter, 2023); Zellentin, *Law beyond Israel*, 153–57; and Zellentin, *The Qur'ān's Legal Culture*, 41–50.

35 See Zellentin, *Law beyond Israel*, 77–90.

36 See Zellentin, '"One Letter *Yud* Shall Not Pass Away from the Law"'; Zellentin, *Law beyond Israel*, 79–80, 102–3, 157; and Brock, *Synagogue and Church in Dialogue*.

37 See Zellentin, *Law beyond Israel*, 157, 232–37.

38 See Juan Cole, 'Late Roman Law and the Quranic Punishments for Adultery', *The Muslim World* 112, no. 2 (2022): 207–24; and Zellentin, 'Between Bible and Byzantium', 36–48.

4 Law in the Qur'an, in Arabian Epigraphy, and in the Islamic Tradition

As indicated above, when seeking to balance the Qur'an's broader 'biblical' context against its continuity with specifically Arabian cultural paradigms, the modern scholar must strictly avoid two fallacies:

1. One must not construct a false dichotomy between Judaism and Christianity, on the one hand, and Arabian culture, on the other, since by the turn of the seventh century CE, Jews and Christians had long developed distinctly Arabian forms of their traditions. A growing archaeological record firmly locates Jewish and Christian communities in South-West Arabia, e.g. in and around Najrān, Qaryat al-Fa'w, and Ḥimā', in North-West Arabia, e.g. in al-ʿUlā, Taymā', and Madā'in Ṣāliḥ, and finally in historical Bahrain and several Gulf islands, including Ṣīr Banī Yās. The Qur'an, furthermore, engages many aspects of Jewish and Christian forms of culture. Judaism and Christianity had therefore long become fully naturalised Arabian religions.[39]
2. However, it is apparent that pagan Arabian culture as such continued to thrive in the Hejaz at the time of the Prophet. Meccan paganism had likely become broadly henotheistic. Meccans may not have shunned idols, and they did not deny the power of adjacent divine and angelic or *daimonic* forces (such as the 'daughters of God', or the jinn), yet they evidently surmised the primacy of the one God, whom they seem to have referred to largely in terms similar to those employed by the Qur'an itself. The Meccans also seem to have been somewhat acquainted with certain aspects of the Israelite tradition, as becomes clear, for example, when the Meccans, confronted with the Qur'an, dismiss it as irrelevant and categorise it among the 'tales of the ancients' (*asāṭīr al-awwalīn*, see e.g. Q. 6:25, 8:31, 83:13). Arabian paganism thus remains the central touchstone for an understanding of the Qur'an's biblicisation of Arabian culture, and ignoring it would distract from recognising its revolutionary message.[40]

---

39 See e.g. Iwona Gajda, 'Remarks on Monotheism in Ancient South Arabia', in *Islam and Its Past: Jāhiliyya and Late Antiquity in Early Muslim Sources*, ed. Carol Bakhos and Michael Cook (Oxford: Oxford University Press, 2017), 247–56; and Christian Julien Robin, ed., *Le Judaïsme de L'Arabie Antique: Actes du Colloque de Jérusalem (février 2006)* (Turnhout: Brepols, 2015); as well as note 3 above.

40 I agree with Gerald Hawting and others that the Meccans were likely henotheists. At the same time, it should be noted that loose ends remain, such as apparently accurate and precise references to idols in pre-Islamic Arabic poetry and historiography; see G.R. Hawting, *The Idea of Idolatry and the Emergence of Islam: From Polemic to History* (Cambridge:

In order to avoid both pitfalls – the image of Arabian culture untouched by the Israelite tradition, on the one hand, and the dismissal of Arabian paganism as long defunct, on the other – three approaches, albeit with decreasing centrality, are helpful when trying to balance the Qur'an's own emphasis on the richly documented biblical tradition with the much more scarcely attested pagan Arabian records:

1. The primary source for pagan Arabian culture in the Hejaz remains the Qur'an itself, whose commensurate continuity and break with Meccan discourse and practice resonates in most of its verses. While the perspective of the Qur'an does not allow for a 'thick' description of Meccan culture, the body of text is in my view sufficiently rich and detailed to allow for a historical approach to the Qur'an's context through the Qur'an.[41]
2. A large number of pagan inscriptions in various forms of Arabic offer occasional help in locating the Qur'an's vocabulary in its historical environment. Among these, a growing corpus of epigraphy in forms of Safaitic and ancient South Arabian, i.e. Sabean – southern, central, and northern – offers surprising affinity with biblical, late antique, and Qur'anic vocabulary. The study of these inscriptions, and their relationship to the Qur'an, is the subject of rapid ongoing scholarly developments, to which the present study cannot contribute in any systematic way. The corpus of inscriptions, however, is sufficiently well studied to use extant lexicography to guide our attempt to situate the Qur'an at the confluence of biblical and pagan Arabian traditions in a broad sense. Even though a more differentiated approach would palpably sharpen the focus of the findings, ancient Safaitic and South Arabian epigraphy already offers comparanda for the Qur'an's unmistakably Western Arabian vernacular.[42]

Cambridge University Press, 1999); see now also Ahmad Al-Jallad and Hythem Sidky, 'Late Antique Allāh: Ancestral Arabian Religion and the Monotheistic Zeitgeist', *Arabian Archaeology and Epigraphy* 2026: 1–10, https://doi.org/10.1111/aae.70019; as well as Patricia Crone, *The Qur'ānic Pagans and Related Matters*, ed. Hanna Siurua (Leiden: Brill, 2016).

41 See e.g. Walid Saleh, 'Meccan Gods, Jesus' Divinity: An Analysis of Q 43 Sūrat al-Zukhruf', in *The Qur'an's Reformation of Judaism and Christianity: Return to the Origins*, ed. Holger Zellentin (New York: Routledge, 2019), 92–111; and note 3 above.

42 See e.g. Ahmad al-Jallad, *An Outline of the Grammar of the Safaitic Inscriptions* (Leiden: Brill, 2015); Christian Julien Robin, 'Marib et Makka: deux pelerinages de l'Arabie préislamique qui se tenaient a la veille de l'équinoxe de printemps', *Graeco-Arabica* 12 (2017): 661–73; and Suleyman Dost, 'Language of Ritual Purity in the Qur'ān and in Old South Arabian', in *Scripts and Scripture*, 157–74, partially based on Jacques Ryckmans, 'Rites du paganism de l'Arabie méridionale avant l'islam', *Bulletin de la Classe des lettres et des sciences morales et politiques* 4 (1993): 125–42. See also note 3 above.

3. Another obvious corpus to engage would be that of the 'Islamic tradition', which includes a wealth of historiographical, bibliographical, lexical, and exegetical information. Any full appreciation of the Qur'an must of course pay very close attention to the tradition which preserved the text of its Scripture, a tradition whose historical contextualisation of its Scripture in Mecca and Medina at the turn of the seventh century CE has recently gained ever growing support from all but the most sceptical of Western scholars.[43] Yet the contextualisation of Qur'anic law and literature in its pre-Islamic biblical, Jewish, Christian, and pagan context, as here proposed, must take procedural primacy, and this effort remains far behind schedule, as the present chapter itself amply illustrates.

In other words, it is high time that scholars re-evaluate the present findings and take the entirety of the Islamic tradition into account when situating Qur'anic law at the confluence of the increasingly well-known pagan Arabian and late antique biblical traditions.[44] Yet fulfilling this task, I hold, will only be possible once we more fully establish the ways in which the Qur'an deals with the Hebrew Bible and its late antique interpreters in both legal and literary ways.

The Qur'an endorses the individual laws given in the Decree of the Apostles as binding for its community. It does not mention the Decree itself, yet it stands in demonstrable continuity with all its stipulations – despite measured modifications – as they were formulated and practised throughout late antiquity. It also shows select lexical continuity with the Decree's Syriac versions. In addition, among those rules governing regulated and prohibited impurity in the Hebrew Bible and especially those extended to the *gerim*, the Qur'an

43 Note that two ongoing research projects funded by the European Research Council are dedicated, in diverging ways, to close the gap between late antiquity and early Islam: Qur'anic Commentary: An Integrative Paradigm (QuCIP; see https://cordis.europa.eu/project/id/771047 as well as https://qucip.web.ox.ac.uk/home), led by Nicolai Sinai, and The Qur'an as a Source for Late Antiquity (QaSLA; see https://cordis.europa.eu/project/id/866043 as well as www.qasla.eu/), led by myself.

44 Important precursors to this attempt are Hallaq, 'Groundwork of the Moral Law'; David Powers, *Muḥammad Is Not the Father of Any of Your Men: The Making of the Last Prophet* (Philadelphia: University of Pennsylvania Press, 2009); Joseph E. Lowry, 'Early Islamic Exegesis as Legal Theory: How Qur'ānic Wisdom (*Ḥikma*) Became the Sunna of the Prophet', in *Jewish Biblical Interpretation and Cultural Exchange*, ed. Natalie B. Dohrmann and David Stern (Philadelphia: University of Pennsylvania Press, 2008), 139–60; and Patricia Crone, 'Two Legal Problems Bearing on the Early History of the Qur'an', *Jerusalem Studies in Arabic and Islam* 18 (1994): 1–37; despite their broad scope, the studies of Powers and Crone severely limit their potential by exposing an overly critical attitude towards the traditional Islamic historiography.

precisely promulgates those that had been previously imposed upon gentile believers by the late antique Christians who endorsed an expansive attitude towards the Decree of the Apostles.[45]

Initially, however, the Qur'an had dismissed another set of food laws, namely, those practised by its Meccan contemporaries. This initial reluctance soon transitions into an appreciative and even expansive attitude towards the very food laws found in the Decree of the Apostles, maintaining the prohibition of wine and swine – two prohibitions attested in the expansive tradition of interpreting the Decree.[46] When it comes to *prohibited* sexual impurity, the Qur'an censures pagan Arabian practices – some of them also known through the pre-Islamic Arabic poetry – and in their stead endorses biblical rulings. The case of *regulated* sexual impurity, however, stands out, since it enables us to situate the Qur'an at the confluence of biblical, Christian, and pagan Arabian practices. In addition, the Qur'an also expands and modifies the laws of the Decree of the Apostles by specifying some of the stipulations, arguably with recourse to pagan Arabian customs, such as those governing the hunt, and to the biblical formulations, for example, of incest prohibitions and tort law.[47] Finally, the Qur'an offers a series of punishments for a variety of transgressions, mechanisms for atonement, and dispensations for specific circumstances, some of which are previously attested in Arabian epigraphy, whereas others closely correspond to aspects of West and East Syrian as well as Byzantine legal practice. Conversely, many Qur'anic laws, such as those governing the sacred months, the *ḥajj*, or inheritance, fully or largely endorse what appears an unbroken Arabian tradition that is untouched by the Prophet's 'biblical impulse'.[48]

In addition to its continuity with late antique law, the Qur'an includes a prominent legal narrative portraying God as stipulating law to the nascent Islamic community, much as He is portrayed as giving law to the Israelites in the Hebrew Bible. In its Medinan phase, the Qur'anic law itself constitutes or reinforces legal aspects both of the Israelite past and of the nascent

---

45 See Zellentin, *Law beyond Israel*, 105–28, 181–218, 249–66; and Zellentin, *The Qur'ān's Legal Culture*, 77–126, 155–74.

46 See Zellentin, *Law beyond Israel*, 105–28; and Nicolai Sinai, 'The Qur'ān's Dietary Tetralogue: A Diachronic Reconstruction', *Jerusalem Studies in Arabic and Islam* 46 (2019): 113–46.

47 See Zellentin, *Law beyond Israel*, 181–218, 249–81.

48 On the *ḥajj*, see e.g. Sinai, *Key Terms of the Qur'an*, s.v. '*ḥajja*' (208–11); and Zellentin, *Law beyond Israel*, 282–333.

Islamic present.[49] Yet the Qurʾan also integrates a number of other biblical and post-biblical legal narratives, albeit always by reflecting its own prophetological paradigms. Just like the rabbis, Tertullian, Ephrem, and the Apostolic Constitutions, for example, the Qurʾan eventually implies that Noah was given law, and it retains a sense of the protection of 'the land' from prohibited impurity. Yet for the Qurʾan, Noah mainly functions as warner to his generation, and it conceives of both 'the land' and its susceptibility to impurity somewhat differently from either the Jewish or the Christian tradition.[50]

The Islamic Scripture's apostolic nature places it in continuity with the narrative surrounding the Decree of the Apostles. The Qurʾan combines two central legal narratives regarding Israelite law. It operates, on the one hand, with the notion of a primary and enduring law that was first expanded by a temporary punitive law and subsequently abrogated, very much in the tradition of the Didascalia Apostolorum and related texts. On the other hand, it accuses the Israelites – both Jews and Christians – of having partially corrupted the law that was entrusted to them by textual alteration, addition, or misinterpretation, in the mould of the Clementine Homilies and other traditions that put their focus on the danger of satanic verses. The Qurʾan thus presents itself as restoring the primary divine message, 'in which there is no doubt' (Q. 2:2), and it presents Jesus as abrogating *some* of the previous laws given to the Israelites as a punishment for the sins they had committed (Q. 3:50), prominently including the veneration of the Golden Calf. In all this, the Qurʾan continues late antique legal discourse at the same time as constituting a 'Scripture which confirms [the Scripture of Moses] in the Arabic language' (*wa-hādhā kitābun muṣaddiqun lisānan ʿarabiyyan*, Q. 46:12) in a far more precise sense than hitherto acknowledged. It is indeed a confirmation of biblical law for gentiles and of some of the legal narratives connected to these laws both in the Bible and throughout late antiquity.[51]

The investigation of the development of gentile law throughout late antiquity, therefore, must include the Qurʾan as another one of its focal points. In my view, the Qurʾan's laws, just like the rabbinic Noahide Laws and the Decree of the Apostles, stand in *indirect yet broad* and *practical* continuity with the Bible's *gerim* laws, especially in the way in which these laws were understood

49 See Mohsen Goudarzi, 'Unearthing Abraham's Altar: The Cultic Dimensions of *Dīn*, *Islām*, and *Ḥanīf* in the Qurʾan', *Journal of Near Eastern Studies* 82, no. 1 (2023): 77–102; and Zellentin, '*banū isrāʾīl*', 11–25.

50 See Zellentin, 'Between Bible and Byzantium', 30–36; and Zellentin, *Law beyond Israel*, 282–333. On the Qurʾanic Noah, see also Carlos Segovia, *The Quranic Noah and the Making of the Islamic Prophet* (Berlin: De Gruyter, 2017), any reference to which is lacking in Zellentin, *Law beyond Israel*.

51 See Pregill, *The Golden Calf*, 265–379; and Zellentin, *The Qurʾān's Legal Culture*, 127–54.

and practised throughout late antique Christianity. The Qur'an, after the Hebrew Bible, the New Testament, and the Tosephta, therefore may be considered as formulating the fourth version of God's law for gentiles. Based on the cumulative evidence of closely aligned legal pathways, the Qur'an stands in dialogue with the appreciative and with the expansive Christian attitude towards the Decree of the Apostles, which it endorses and modifies when formulating its own laws given to its community. The Qur'an portrays Hejazi Arabians as non-Israelites, and thereby, arguably, as 'gentiles' if one were to follow the definition here employed very narrowly. However, while the Qur'an obviously displays an increasing sense of its community's distinctness from Israel, it effectively surpasses the Jews vs gentile dichotomy that marked late antiquity and continues to define aspects of Western discourse and scholarship to this day, in its stead creating a distinct Abrahamite self-identity that would eventually form the basis of the Muslim *umma*. At the same time, the Qur'an subsumes 'the Christians', with which its community stands in contact, under the broader category not only of the (mainly Medinan) 'Scripture People', but also under the category's (mainly Meccan) predecessor, 'the Sons of Israel' – even if the Qur'anic Christians remain differentiated from 'the Jews' by disputes over Jesus and his partial abrogation of the Law. The Qur'an's view of the Israelite identity of Christians, along with the legal positions it attributes to the Christians, roughly correspond to the ethnic self-identity and legal observances prevalent in the West Syrian and possibly also in the Aksumite church, and to some strands of Byzantine political theology.[52]

To conclude, then, scholars of the Qur'an should keep in mind that the extant Jewish and Christian writings are but a faint written echo of the rich oral discourse that permeated Arabia at the turn of the seventh century CE. Yet an echo they are, and using what we have may reduce our margins of error compared with not attempting to contextualise the Qur'an's legal tendencies at all. The greatest strength of my approach as outlined here and spelled out in detail in *Law beyond Israel*, then, may be the way in which it presents the laws of the Arabian Qur'an and its legal narratives in light of their continuity with, and their departure from, specific strands of late antique law and literature known from outside of Arabia. This strength equally points to this approaches greatest weakness, since its focus on extant late antique sources

52 See note 20 above. By defining the Islamic community as distinct from "Israel," i.e. from the Jews and Christians, the Qur'an laid the groundwork for later Muslim self-identity. This development parallels a shift in late antique Christian discourse, where Christians began to view themselves as a "new people" rather than as part of Israel. On this Christian context, see Denise Kimber Buell, *Why This New Race? Ethnic Reasoning in Early Christianity* (New York: Columbia University Press, 2008).

leaves us with very few witnesses from within the Arabic peninsula. Beyond a growing number of published inscriptions, plausibly aspects of the Christian martyrological record, and some texts of pre-Islamic Arabic poetry, hardly any Arabian witnesses have yet been verified to stem from this period. Yet if my argument will stand, then my study is precisely an attempt to establish pre-Islamic Arabian law by using those *shared* Jewish and Christian practices which the Qur'an endorses alongside those which it rejects as evidence of its affinity with the established legal and literary record, helping us reconstruct pre-Islamic Arabian legal culture while also allowing us to contextualise major strands of Qur'anic legal thought.

Appendix

TABLE 1.1 A simplified overview of concepts regarding law and ethnicity, from the Bible to the Qur'an, excluding 'direct'continuities between the Bible and the Qur'an and rabbinic, East Syrian, and Byzantine law

I Hebrew Bible		
ethnic identity	'Israel'	Non-Israelites
applicable law	Torah	*gerim* laws (within the Holy Land)

(broad arrow denotes broad legal continuity, maintaining divide between Jews/Israelites and gentiles)

II	Acts of the Apostles		Tosephta (Tannaitic early rabbis)	
ethnic identity	'Jews' / 'Israelites'	'the nations'	'Israel'	'the Children of Noah'
applicable law	The Torah	Decree of the Apostles	Written and Oral Torah	Noahide Laws

(narrow arrow denotes continuity with a new ethnic self-identity)

III Late antiquity	Clementine Homilies (partially paralleled by the Amoriac later rabbis)		parts of West Syrian and Aksumite church	Latin, Greek, and parts of West Syrian church
ethnic identity	'Jews' / 'Israel'	'the nations'	Israelite: 'the nations' subsumed under Israel	gentile: Israel subsumed under 'the nations'
applicable law	Torah (for rabbis along with Oral Torah)	Expansion of Decree of the Apostles (for rabbis of Noahide Laws)	The Primary Law, Secondary Law is abrogated by Jesus	Decree of the Apostles, often alongside Imperial or Natural Law

IV The Qur'an			
ethnic identity	'Children of Israel' (two parties among whom God will judge)		non-Israelite Arabians → Abrahamites
applicable law	'Jews': Torah, historically including 'punitive' laws	'Christians': Torah, partially abrogated by Jesus	Qur'an (in continuity with the expanded Decree of the Apostles)

TABLE 1.2 A simplified overview of major legal continuities, from the Bible through late antique Christianity to the Qur'an, based on central prohibitions and positive commandments (in italics), excluding pagan Arabian and rabbinic law

Hebrew Bible	Late antique Christianity	Qur'an
***gerim* laws**[a]	**Decree of the Apostles**[b]	**laws for the believers**[c]
Blood (also Gen. 9)	Blood	Blood
Draining animal blood	*Draining animal blood*	*Draining animal blood*
Idol meat (also Dtn 29)	Idol meat	Idol meat
Carrion	Carrion	Carrion
Incest	Incest	Incest
Sex during menstruation	Sex during menstruation	Sex during menstruation
Adultery	Adultery	Adultery
'Sacrificing offspring to Molech'	Intermarriage with pagans or heretics	Intermarriage with pagans and, for women, with Jews and Christians
Sex between males	Sex between males	Sex between males
***gerim* not mentioned**[d]	**appreciative attitude**[e]	
Ez 18	Robbery	Robbery
Ez 18	Oppression of the poor	Oppression of the poor
Ez 18	Usury	Usury
(Lev 19:35–36, Ez 45:10)	Altering weights or measuring deceitfully	Altering weights or measuring deceitfully
(Ex 20:19 and Dtn 5:20)	False witness and slander	False witness and slander
–	Murder of infants	Murder of infants
(Is 58)	*Fasting*	*Fasting*
(Dtn 26)	*Prayer*	*Prayer*
(Jer 7:6)	*Care for orphans*	*Care for orphans*
(Is 58:7)	*Charity for the needy*	*Charity for the needy*
–	*Veiling of women (head)*	*Veiling of women (bosom)*
	expansive attitude[f]	
Lev 15	*Washing after intercourse*	*Washing after intercourse*
(Ex 30, *for priests*)	*Washing before prayer*	*Washing before prayer*
Lev 11:7, Dtn 14:8	Pork as demonic	Pork as satanic impurity (*rijs*)
(Lev 10)	Wine as demonic	Wine as 'from the works of Satan'
	criminal law[g]	
2 Sam 4:12, Targum (*as ad hoc punishment*)	*(Crucifixion,) execution, exile, or amputation of limbs for violent crimes*	*Crucifixion, execution, exile, or amputation of limbs for violent crimes*
(Dtn 25:11–12, *for women touching a man's genitals*)	*Amputation of hand for theft*	*Amputation of hand for theft*

a Zellentin, *Law beyond Israel*, 36–50, 130–43, 236–49.

b Ibid., 86–90, 154–58; Zellentin, *The Qur'ān's Legal Culture*, 77–81.

c Zellentin, *Law beyond Israel*, 105–28, 181–218, 249–66; Zellentin, *The Qur'ān's Legal Culture*, 77–126, 155–75.

d Zellentin, *Law beyond Israel*, 94, 137–39; Zellentin, *The Qur'ān's Legal Culture*, 68.

e Zellentin, *The Qur'ān's Legal Culture*, 55–76; with special attention to the concept of the Decalogue, see now also Hussain, 'Wisdom in the Qur'an', 176–229.

f Zellentin, *Law beyond Israel*, 90–105, 158–81; Zellentin, *The Qur'ān's Legal Culture*, 81–126, 175–202.

g Cole, 'Late Roman Law'; Zellentin, *Law beyond Israel*, 327–33; Zellentin, 'Between Bible and Byzantium', 36–48.

Bibliography

Achenbach, Reinhard. '*gêr – nakhrî – tôshav – zâr*: Legal and Sacral Distinctions regarding Foreigners in the Pentateuch'. In *The Foreigner and the Law: Perspectives from the Hebrew Bible and the Ancient Near East*, edited by Reinhard Achenbach, Rainer Albertz, and Jakob Wöhrle, 29–51. Wiesbaden: Harrassowitz, 2011.

Achenbach, Reinhard, Rainer Albertz, and Jakob Wöhrle, eds. *The Foreigner and the Law: Perspectives from the Hebrew Bible and the Ancient Near East*. Wiesbaden: Harrassowitz, 2011.

Akiyama, Kengo. 'The גר and Interpretive Integration in the Damascus Document 6: 20–21 and 14:3–6'. *Journal of Jewish Studies* 67 (2016): 249–66.

Akpınar, Mehmetcan. 'False Accusations of Adultery (*Qaḏf*) in the Quran and in Near Eastern Legal Traditions'. In *Normativität des Koran im Zeichen gesellschaftlichen Wandels: Theologische und religionspädagogische Perspektiven*, edited by Fahimah Ulfat, Mouez Khalfaoui, and Mohammed Nekroumi, 249–76. Frankfurt: Nomos, 2022.

Bakhos, Carol. *The Family of Abraham: Jewish, Christian, and Muslim Interpretations*. Cambridge, MA: Harvard University Press, 2014.

Blidstein, Moshe. *Purity, Community, and Ritual in Early Christian Literature*. Oxford: Oxford University Press, 2017.

Böckenhoff, Karl. *Das apostolische Speisegesetz in den ersten fünf Jahrhunderten: Ein Beitrag zum Verständnis der quasi-levitischen Satzungen in älteren kirchlichen Rechtsquellen*. Paderborn: Schöning, 1903.

Brock, Sebastian P. *Synagogue and Church in Dialogue: Four Syriac Poems from Late Antiquity*. Oxford: Journal of Jewish Studies, 2019.

Buell, Denise Kimber. *Why This New Race? Ethnic Reasoning in Early Christianity*. New York: Columbia University Press, 2008.

Clark, Gillian. *Late Antiquity: A Very Short Introduction*. Oxford: Oxford University Press, 2011.

Cole, Juan. 'Late Roman Law and the Quranic Punishments for Adultery'. *The Muslim World* 112, no. 2 (2022): 207–24.

Crone, Patricia. *The Qur'ānic Pagans and Related Matters*. Edited by Hanna Siurua. Leiden: Brill, 2016.

Crone, Patricia. 'Two Legal Problems Bearing on the Early History of the Qur'an'. *Jerusalem Studies in Arabic and Islam* 18 (1994): 1–37.

Decharneux, Julien. *Creation and Contemplation: The Cosmology of the Qur'ān and Its Late Antique Background*. Berlin: De Gruyter, 2023.

Doerfler, Maria E. 'Didascalia Apostolorum'. In *Gorgias Encyclopedic Dictionary of the Syriac Heritage*, edited by Sebastian P. Brock, Aaron M. Butts, George A. Kiraz, and Lucas Van Rompay, 124–25. Piscataway: Gorgias Press, 2011.

Donner, Fred M., and Rebecca Hasselbach-Andee, eds. *Scripts and Scripture: Writing and Religion in Arabia, 500–700 CE*. Chicago: Oriental Institute, 2022.

Dost, Suleyman. 'Pilgrimage in Pre-Islamic Arabia: Continuity and Rupture from Epigraphic Texts to the Quran'. *Millennium: Yearbook on the Culture and History of the First Millennium C.E.* 15 (2023): 15–32.

Dost, Suleyman. 'Language of Ritual Purity in the Qur'ān and in Old South Arabian'. In *Scripts and Scripture: Writing and Religion in Arabia, 500–700 CE*, edited by Fred M. Donner and Rebecca Hasselbach-Andee, 157–74. Chicago: Oriental Institute, 2022.

Freidenreich, David M. *Foreigners and Their Food: Constructing Otherness in Jewish, Christian, and Islamic Law*. Berkeley: University of California Press, 2011.

Gajda, Iwona. 'Remarks on Monotheism in Ancient South Arabia'. In *Islam and Its Past: Jāhiliyya and Late Antiquity in Early Muslim Sources*, edited by Carol Bakhos and Michael Cook, 247–56. Oxford: Oxford University Press, 2017.

Goudarzi, Mohsen. 'Unearthing Abraham's Altar: The Cultic Dimensions of *Dīn*, *Islām*, and *Ḥanīf* in the Qur'an'. *Journal of Near Eastern Studies* 82, no. 1 (2023): 77–102.

Goudarzi, Mohsen. 'The Ascent of Ishmael: Genealogy, Covenant, and Identity in Early Islam'. *Arabica: Journal of Arabic and Islamic Studies / Revue d'études arabes et islamiques* 66 (2019): 415–84.

Grasso, Valentina. 'The Gods of the Qur'ān: The Rise of Ḥijāzī Henotheism during Late Antiquity'. In *The Study of Islamic Origins: New Perspectives and Contexts*, edited by Mette Bjerregaard Mortensen, Guillaume Dye, Isaac W. Oliver, and Tommaso Tesei, 297–324. Berlin: De Gruyter, 2021.

Gross, Simcha. 'A Long Overdue Farewell: The Purported Jewish Origins of Syriac Christianity'. In *Jews and Syriac Christians*, edited by Simcha Gross and Aaron Michael Butts, 121–44. Tübingen: Mohr Siebeck, 2020.

Hallaq, Wael. 'Groundwork of the Moral Law: A New Look at the Qur'ān and the Genesis of Sharī'a'. *Islamic Law and Society* 16 (2009): 239–79.

Hartog, Pieter B. 'Noah and Moses in Acts 15: Group Models and the Novelty of the Way'. *New Testament Studies* 67, no. 4 (2021): 496–513.

Hawting, G.R. *The Idea of Idolatry and the Emergence of Islam: From Polemic to History*. Cambridge: Cambridge University Press, 1999.

Hayes, Christine. 'Were the Noahide Commandments Formulated at Yavne? Tosephta Avoda Zara 8:4–9 in Cultural and Historical Context'. In *Jews and Christians in the First and Second Centuries: The Interbellum 70–132 CE*, edited by Joshua Schwartz and Peter J. Tomson, 225–64. Leiden: Brill, 2017.

Hedner Zetterholm, Karin. 'Christ Assemblies within a Jewish Context: Reconstructing a Social Setting for the Pseudo-Clementine "Homilies"'. In *Negotiating Identities: Conflict, Conversion, and Consolidation in Early Judaism and Christianity (200 BCE–600 CE)*, edited by Karin Hedner Zetterholm, Anders Runesson, Cecilia Wassén, and Magnus Zetterholm, 329–49. Lanham: Lexington Books/Fortress Academic, 2022.

Hendel, Ronald. *Remembering Abraham: Culture, Memory, and History in the Hebrew Bible*. Oxford: Oxford University Press, 2005.

Hussain, Saqib. *Wisdom in the Qur'an: Law and Morality from the Bible to Late Antiquity*. Oxford: Oxford University Press, 2026.

Klawans, Jonathan. *Impurity and Sin in Ancient Judaism*. Oxford: Oxford University Press, 2000.

Latz, Andrew Brower, and Arseny Ermakov, eds. *Purity: Essays in Bible and Theology*. Eugene: Wipf and Stock, 2014.

Lavee, Moshe. *The Rabbinic Conversion of Judaism: The Unique Perspective of the Bavli on Conversion and the Construction of Jewish Identity*. Leiden: Brill, 2017.

Levenson, Jon. *Inheriting Abraham: The Legacy of the Patriarch in Judaism, Christianity, and Islam*. Princeton: Princeton University Press, 2012.

Lössl, Josef, and Nicholas J. Baker-Brian, eds. *A Companion to Religion in Late Antiquity*. Chichester: Wiley-Blackwell, 2018.

Lowin, Shari L. '*The Jews Say the Hand of God Is Chained*: Q. 5:64 as a Response to a Midrash in a *Piyyut* by R. El'azar ha-Kallir'. *Journal of Qur'anic Studies* 21, no. 2 (2019): 108–39.

Lowry, Joseph E. 'Early Islamic Exegesis as Legal Theory: How Qur'ānic Wisdom (*Ḥikma*) Became the Sunna of the Prophet'. In *Jewish Biblical Interpretation and Cultural Exchange*, edited by Natalie B. Dohrmann and David Stern, 139–60. Philadelphia: University of Pennsylvania Press, 2008.

Mayshar, Joram. 'Who Was the *Toshav*?'. *Journal of Biblical Literature* 133, no. 2 (2014): 225–46.

Milgrom, Jacob. *Leviticus 17–22: A New Translation with Introduction and Commentary*. New Haven: Yale University Press, 2007.

Motzki, Harald. *The Origins of Islamic Jurisprudence: Meccan Fiqh before the Classical Schools*. Brill: Leiden, 2002.

Oliver, Isaac. *Torah Praxis after 70 CE: Reading Matthew and Luke-Acts as Jewish Texts*. Tübingen: Mohr Siebeck, 2013.

Ophir, Adi, and Ishay Rosen-Zvi. *Goy: Israel's Multiple Others and the Birth of the Gentile*. Oxford: Oxford University Press, 2018.

Palmer, Carmen. *Converts in the Dead Sea Scrolls: The gēr and Mutable Ethnicity*. Leiden: Brill, 2018.

Pavlovitch, Pavel. 'The Islamic Penalty for Adultery in the Third Century AH and Al-Shāfi'ī's *Risāla*'. *Bulletin of the School of Oriental and African Studies* 75 (2012): 473–97.

Powers, David. 'The Qur'ān and Its Legal Environment'. In *Deconstructing Islamic Studies*, edited by Majid Daneshgar and Aaron W. Hughes, 9–32. Boston: Harvard University Press/Mizan, 2020.

Powers, David. *Muḥammad Is Not the Father of Any of Your Men: The Making of the Last Prophet*. Philadelphia: University of Pennsylvania Press, 2009.

Pregill, Michael. *The Golden Calf between Bible and Qur'an: Scripture, Polemic, and Exegesis from Late Antiquity to Islam*. Oxford: Oxford University Press, 2020.

Reed, Annette Yoshiko. 'Retelling Biblical Retellings: Epiphanius, the Pseudo-Clementines, and the Reception History of *Jubilees*'. In *Tradition, Transmission, and Transformation from Second Temple Literature through Judaism and Christianity in Late Antiquity: Proceedings of the Thirteenth International Symposium of the Orion Center for the Study of the Dead Sea Scrolls and Associated Literature, Jointly Sponsored by the Hebrew University Center for the Study of Christianity, 22–4 February, 2011*, edited by Menahem Kister, Hillel I. Newman, Michael Segal, and Ruth A. Clements, 304–21. Leiden: Brill, 2015.

Rhyder, Julia. *Centralizing the Cult: The Holiness Legislation in Leviticus 17–26*. Tübingen: Mohr Siebeck, 2019.

Robin, Christian Julien, ed. *Le Judaïsme de L'Arabie Antique: Actes du Colloque de Jérusalem (février 2006)*. Turnhout: Brepols, 2015.

Robin, Christian Julien. 'Marib et Makka: deux pelerinages de l'Arabie préislamique qui se tenaient a la veille de l'équinoxe de printemps'. *Graeco-Arabica* 12 (2017): 661–73.

Ryckmans, Jacques. 'Rites du paganism de l'Arabie méridionale avant l'islam'. *Bulletin de la Classe des lettres et des sciences morales et politiques* 4 (1993): 125–42.

Sadeghi, Behnam. *The Logic of Law Making in Islam: Women and Prayer in the Legal Tradition*. Cambridge: Cambridge University Press, 2013.

Salaymeh, Lena. 'Legal Traditions of the "Near East": The Pre-Islamic Context'. In *Routledge Handbook of Islamic Law*, edited by Khaled Abou El Fadl, Ahmad Atif Ahmad, and Said Fares Hassan, 275–85. Abingdon: Routledge, 2021.

Salaymeh, Lena. *The Beginnings of Islamic Law: Late Antique Islamicate Legal Traditions*. Cambridge: Cambridge University Press, 2016.

Saleh, Walid. 'Meccan Gods, Jesus' Divinity: An Analysis of Q 43 Sūrat al-Zukhruf'. In *The Qur'an's Reformation of Judaism and Christianity: Return to the Origins*, edited by Holger Zellentin, 92–111. New York: Routledge, 2019.

Schmid, Konrad. *The Scribes of the Torah: The Formation of the Pentateuch in Its Literacy and Historical Contexts*. Atlanta: The Society of Biblical Literature, 2023.

Segovia, Carlos. *The Quranic Noah and the Making of the Islamic Prophet*. Berlin: De Gruyter, 2017.

Sinai, Nicolai. *Key Terms of the Qur'an: A Critical Dictionary*. Princeton: Princeton University Press, 2022.

Sinai, Nicolai. 'The Qur'ān's Dietary Tetralogue: A Diachronic Reconstruction'. *Jerusalem Studies in Arabic and Islam* 46 (2019): 113–46.

Thiessen, Matthew. *Contesting Conversion: Genealogy, Circumcision, and Identity in Ancient Judaism and Christianity*. Oxford: Oxford University Press, 2011.

Wehnert, Jürgen. *Die Reinheit des 'christlichen Gottesvolkes' aus Juden und Heiden: Studien zum historischen und theologischen Hintergrund des sogenannten Aposteldekrets*. Göttingen: Vandenhoeck & Ruprecht, 1997.

Werman, Cana, ed. *From Author to Copyist: Composition, Redaction, and Transmission of the Hebrew Bible: Studies in Honor of Zipi Talshir*. Winona Lake: Eisenbrauns, 2015.

Wöhrle, Jakob. 'Abraham amidst the Nations: The Priestly Concept of Covenant and the Persian Imperial Ideology'. In *Covenant in the Persian Period: From Genesis to Chronicles*, edited by Richard J. Bautch and Gary Knoppers, 23–39. Winona Lake: Eisenbrauns, 2015.

Wright, Jacob L. *War, Memory, and National Identity in the Hebrew Bible*. Cambridge: Cambridge University Press, 2020.

Zellentin, Holger. 'Between Bible and Byzantium: "Corruption on Earth" (fasād fī l-arḍ) and the Qur'an's Penal Code (Q 5:33-34.38-39)', Journal of the International Qur'anic Studies Association 10 (2025): 11–56.

Zellentin, Holger. '*banū isrāʾīl, ahl al-kitāb, al-yahūd wa-l-naṣārā*: The Qur'anic Community's Encounters with Jews and Christians'. *Entangled Religions* 13, no. 2 (2023): https://doi.org/10.46586/er.13.2023.10991.

Zellentin, Holger. 'What Is "within Judaism" according to the Quran?'. In *Within Judaism? Interpretive Trajectories in Judaism, Christianity, and Islam from the First to the Twenty-First Century*, edited by Karin Hedner Zetterholm and Anders Runesson, 282–308. Lanham: Lexington Books/Fortress Academic, 2023.

Zellentin, Holger. *Law beyond Israel: From the Bible to the Qur'an*. Oxford: Oxford University Press, 2022. https://doi.org/10.1093/oso/9780199675579.001.0001.

Zellentin, Holger. 'Law in the Medinan Qur'an: The Case of Biblical Incest Law and Its Qurʾanic Re-iteration'. In *Unlocking the Medinan Qur'an*, edited by Nicolai Sinai, 315–89. Leiden: Brill, 2022.

Zellentin, Holger. 'Scriptural Hermeneutics and Purity Laws in the Clementine Homilies: Mainstream or Marginal, Progressive or Conservative, Jewish or Christian?'. In *Negotiating Identities: Conflict, Conversion, and Consolidation in Early Judaism and Christianity* (200 BCE–600 CE), edited by Karin Hedner Zetterholm, Anders Runesson, Cecilia Wassén, and Magnus Zetterholm, 423–54. Lanham: Lexington Books/Fortress Academic, 2022.

Zellentin, Holger. '"One Letter *Yud* Shall Not Pass Away from the Law": Matthew 5:17 to *Shabbat* 116a–b'. In *Religious Identities in Antiquity and the Early Middle Ages: Walking Together & Parting Ways*, edited by Ilkka Lindstedt, Nina Nikki, and Riikka Tuori, 204–58. Leiden: Brill, 2021.

Zellentin, Holger. 'Gentile Purity Law from the Bible to the Qur'an: The Case of Sexual Purity and Illicit Intercourse'. In *The Qur'an's Reformation of Judaism and Christianity: Return to the Origins*, edited by Holger Zellentin, 115–215. New York: Routledge, 2019.

Zellentin, Holger. 'The Synchronic and the Diachronic Qur'ān: Sūrat Yā Sīn, Lot's People, and the Rabbis'. In *The Making of Religious Texts in Islam: The Fragment and the Whole*, edited by Asma Hilali and S.R. Burge, 111–72. Berlin: Gerlach Press, 2019.

Zellentin, Holger. 'Judaeo-Christian Legal Culture and the Qur'ān: The Case of Ritual Slaughter and the Consumption of Animal Blood'. In *Jewish Christianity and the Origins of Islam*, edited by Francisco del Río Sánchez, 117–59. Turnhout: Brepols, 2018.

Zellentin, Holger. *The Qur'ān's Legal Culture: The Didascalia Apostolorum as a Point of Departure*. Tübingen: Mohr Siebeck, 2023. Originally published in 2013. https://doi.org/10.1628/978-3-16-162701-9.

CHAPTER 2

The Place of Divine Law in the Qur'an's Moral Theology

Nicolai Sinai

1 Introduction[1]

The present chapter is an attempt to explore how Qur'anic legislation fits into the Qur'an's wider ideas about moral norms and about the relationship between humans and God. To get one important clarification out of the way immediately, I owe my working definition of Qur'anic 'legislation' or 'law' to Joseph E. Lowry. Lowry proposes to demarcate legislative passages in the Qur'an as those that 'impose obligations on the qur'ānic audience to engage in specific, repeatable physical (i.e., not purely mental) conduct'.[2] Lowry thus insists on three criteria in order for a Qur'anic statement to count as 'legal' or 'legislative': 'it (1) enjoins specific, repeatable behaviour that (2) could plausibly be undertaken by the Qur'anic audience and that (3) is not purely mental.'[3] In accordance with this proposal, I would be reluctant to class as legislative Qur'anic verses that, say, warn against oppressing orphans (e.g. Q. 93:9) or utter generic demands to pray to God (e.g. Q. 108:2). Nor would I class as legislative a passage like Q. 2:10–13, where a group accused of being 'sick of heart' are prohibited from 'wreaking corruption on earth' and are commanded to 'believe like the people believe'. By contrast, verses that I would consider to fall under the category of Qur'anic law are the commandment, in Q. 2:144, that the Qur'anic recipients are to orient themselves towards the Meccan sanctuary when praying (on which see further below), or the prohibition of consuming

1 This chapter was produced in the framework of the research project "Qur'anic Commentary: An Integrative Paradigm" (*QuCIP*), funded by the European Research Council under the European Union's Horizon 2020 research and innovation programme (grant agreement no. 771047). I am grateful to Joe Lowry for miscellaneous comments and corrections on a draft version.

2 Joseph E. Lowry, 'Law, Structure, and Meaning in Sūrat al-Baqarah', *Journal of the International Qur'anic Studies Association* 2, no. 1 (2017): 118.

3 Joseph E. Lowry, 'A Guide to the Legal Material in Sūrat al-Nisā'', in *Unlocking the Medinan Qur'an*, ed. Nicolai Sinai (Leiden: Brill, 2022), 424–25n5.

carrion, blood, or pork in Q. 2:173 and elsewhere.[4] In these latter two cases, all of Lowry's criteria are sufficiently met: the Qur'an's contemporary audience is given specific, repeatable, and not purely mental behavioural instructions. It merits noting that Lowry's proposal has the distinct advantage of not defining the classifiers 'legal' or 'legislative' in terms of a stipulation of 'practical sanctions enforceable by human agencies', to employ a formulation by Noel Coulson.[5] As Coulson rightly observes, the Qur'an frequently omits to specify this-worldly sanctions for infringing upon a given Qur'anic commandment or prohibition.[6]

My preceding endorsement of Lowry's working definition of Qur'anic law prompts an important caveat. Evidently, if the distinction between legislative and non-legislative is drawn in accordance with Lowry, it will not be a sharp line. Rather, it will span an inevitably ill-defined transitional spectrum. This is so because Lowry appeals to the contrast between general and specific, which plainly admits of gradation. For instance, are calls to invoke God *in the morning and the evening* (Q. 3:41, 33:42, 76:25) sufficiently specific in order to count as legislative? Yet this is just what philosophers call a 'sorites paradox': how many grains of sand does it take to constitute a heap? How many residual hairs are still compatible with being bald?[7] There are no hard and fast answers to these questions; yet the inherent vagueness of concepts like baldness or constituting a heap, or indeed of the general contrast between generality and specificity, does not entail that they are vacuous and should (or indeed could) be avoided. Still, the inevitable vagueness of discriminating between what is legal in the Qur'an and what is not, in addition to the frequent lack of this-worldly sanctions noted above, are perhaps important enough in order

4 On the Qur'anic dietary taboos, see Nicolai Sinai, 'The Qur'ān's Dietary Tetralogue: A Diachronic Reconstruction', *Jerusalem Studies in Arabic and Islam* 46 (2019): 113–46.

5 Noel J. Coulson, *A History of Islamic Law* (Edinburgh: Edinburgh University Press, 1964), 12.

6 Of course, the Qur'anic wording can sometimes offer sufficient grounds for some basic inferences about the this-worldly consequences of certain actions or omissions. But in general, the vanishing point of normative demands imposed by the Qur'an is an eschatological one, which tends to overshadow the need for a detailed stipulation of penalties in the present world. See, for example, Q. 2:278–81, which prohibits 'usury' (*ribā*) and exhorts the addressees to be lenient with debtors who experience hardship. While the passage is not concerned to define in any detail the financial practices deemed to constitute usury or to specify what a reasonable extension to a repayment deadline might look like, the concluding verse is entirely dedicated to reminding the hearers of the need to 'fear a day on which you shall be returned to God'.

7 See Dominic Hyde and Diana Raffman, 'Sorites Paradox', *The Stanford Encyclopedia of Philosophy* (Summer 2018 edition), ed. Edward N. Zalta, https://plato.stanford.edu/archives/sum2018/entries/sorites-paradox/.

for a Qur'anic interpreter to make occasional use of the more hesitant adjective 'quasi-legal', rather than 'legal' or 'legislative' *simpliciter*, when seeking to capture the particular register of Qur'anic discourse under consideration.[8] The category of Qur'anic law is certainly not an unproblematic one, and there is no reason to assume that the Qur'an itself is drawing an impermeable boundary between two normative domains, that of the merely moral and that of the properly legal.[9]

As has been noted before, the ultimate reason for the fact that there is no cleanly demarcatable legal sphere in the Qur'an is the fact that the Qur'an's overriding concern is to instruct its addressees how to evade eschatological damnation and merit paradise.[10] I shall return to this general issue below, but it will be useful to confront the impact that this eschatological horizon has on Qur'anic (quasi-)legislation right away. Consider Q. 2:280, which demands that debtors who are in difficulty are to be given 'respite until a time of ease' (*wa-in kāna dhū ʿusratin fa-naẓiratun ilā maysaratin*). This might look like a legally enforceable claim similar to a tenant's protection against a no-fault eviction, and a legally trained mind would no doubt have all sorts of follow-on questions about the degree of difficulty that triggers a debtor's right to an extension of the term of payment and the minimum delays that must be granted

---

8 Thus e.g. Nicolai Sinai, 'The Unknown Known: Some Groundwork for Interpreting the Medinan Qur'an', *Mélanges de l'Université Saint-Joseph* 66 (2015–16): 66, 71.

9 Cf. Karen Bauer and Feras Hamza, *Women, Households, and the Hereafter in the Qur'an: A Patronage of Piety* (Oxford: Oxford University Press in association with the Institute of Ismaili Studies, 2023), 24, who note that 'there is no separation of law from ethics in the Qur'an'. See also Nora K. Schmid, 'From Ethico-religious Exhortation to Legal Paraenesis: Functions of Qur'anic *Waʿẓ*', *Islamic Law and Society* 28 (2021): 342: 'Legal discourse framed as *waʿẓ* in the Medinan period is an outgrowth and articulation of Qur'anic ethics.' For further remarks on the importance of Schmid's article, see the final section of this chapter. The fact that the Qur'an does not deploy a terminologically well-established distinction between the legal and the moral could give rise to another objection against talk of 'legal' or 'quasi-legal' material in the Qur'an: if the text that we are interpreting does not make the distinction, who are we to impose it? However, it would be methodologically dubious to insist that an interpreter of the Qur'an is not entitled to introduce analytic descriptors that are not present in the Islamic scripture itself. In fact, in studying documents from other historical periods or other cultural contexts we routinely invoke distinctions that are not explicitly made in the documents we endeavour to interpret, and this can be perfectly legitimate and illuminating. For example, the Qur'an itself does not have an explicit terminological equivalent for, say, 'inclusio' (meaning a literary bracket structure), yet this is nonetheless an eminently useful concept to apply to the Qur'an. Finally, it is also not entirely correct to say that something like our distinction between the legal and the moral is entirely untranslatable into Qur'anic Arabic; see what follows in the main text.

10 The common eschatological horizon that ties together Qur'anic law and Qur'anic ethics is stressed, for instance, in Bauer and Hamza, *Women*, 23–24.

in response to different levels of hardship. Yet the verse simply continues by saying that 'being charitable is better for you (*wa-an taṣaddaqū*), if you have knowledge'. This probably means that creditors are told to do more than just giving a struggling debtor extra time to repay and instead ought to charitably write off the debt itself, or at least part of it. Thus, rather than providing crucial legal detail the verse morphs into a moral appeal to its addressees to do as much as they can, in the hope that their divine judge will eventually take this into due account when determining their fate in the afterlife. Quite obviously, the relatively firm distinction that secular legal systems make between minimum standards of acceptable behaviour that are codified in law and are penally enforced, on the one hand, and more ambitious ethical ideals, such as generosity and fair-mindedness, on the other, which citizens are free to espouse or not, is not present here to the same degree. What the Qur'an has to offer in the way of behavioural regulations therefore doubly transcends a preoccupation with spelling out precise legal circumstances and consequences in the here and now: human actions are placed against the transcendent horizon of an eschatological reckoning followed by an eternity of consequences; and human agents are frequently enjoined to transcend a minimum threshold of well-defined lawfulness. This is why passages like Q. 2:178, 2:237, 2:280, 4:92, or 5:45 all exhibit a palpable concern with encouraging the Qur'anic addressees to charitably forego certain entitlements, such as the right to proportionate retaliation or timely repayment of a debt. Nonetheless, despite everything just said it is not the case that the general contrast between the legal and the ethical is completely unilluminating when it comes to the Qur'an: after all, the present paragraph could not have been written without invoking it. Moreover, it would seem that the Qur'an itself has an expression for what I have just called 'minimum standards of acceptable behaviour', namely: 'God's boundaries' (*ḥudūd allāh*).[11]

11 References to 'God's boundaries' conclude certain behavioural rules in Q. 2:187 (permission to have intercourse with a spouse during 'the night of the fast' but not during the day and a rule for determining the time when the day is considered to commence), Q. 2:229–30 (on the maximum number of revocable divorce pronouncements), Q. 4:13–14 (following an allocation of minimum shares of inheritance in vv. 11 and 12), Q. 58:4 (atonement for breaking an oath of *ẓihār*), Q. 65:1 (on divorce and a divorced wife's residence during her waiting period or *ʿidda*). There are further general references to God's 'boundaries' in Q. 9:97 and 9:112. For recent comments on the term, see Bauer and Hamza, *Women*, 230 (where the authors similarly understand the *ḥudūd* as a 'minimum for proper action'), 258, 284 ('an outer limit of bad behaviour' that implies 'that there is a moral space in which good people behave in ways that go nowhere near these limits').

Having duly problematised, but hopefully also to some degree defended, talk of 'Qur'anic law', I can now go on to explain my primary interest in thinking about Qur'anic legislation in this chapter, namely, to arrive at a better understanding of the relationship between the Medinan suras of the Qur'an and the earlier Meccan ones. For the purposes of the present discussion, I am assuming,

- first, that scholars have at least some reliable sense of the relative date of Qur'anic suras and are able to draw a reasonably sound dividing line between the Meccan and Medinan parts of the Qur'an;
- and secondly, that virtually all legislative material in the Qur'an is Medinan, i.e. belongs to a chronologically secondary layer of the Islamic scripture.[12]

Therefore, like many other readers of the Qur'an, I discern a palpable shift towards legislation in the Medinan suras. It is ultimately my interest in capturing this difference in tonality between different parts and, diachronically speaking, stages of the Qur'an that makes it seem expedient to me to use descriptors like 'legal' or 'quasi-legal', in spite of the reservations just noted.

What the present chapter aims to elucidate, then, is the Medinan shift towards what is, minimally, a tangibly greater quantity of legal or quasi-legal statements. In particular, I am interested in the question whether this shift amounts to a rupture, to a doctrinal discontinuity. In order to appreciate the pertinence of the problem just posed, it may help to recapitulate here an earlier attempt of mine to describe the change under discussion: the Meccan suras, I wrote,

> do not seem particularly concerned to provide detailed instruction about how to behave; rather, they seem concerned to enjoin and motivate their hearers to abide by a set of previously familiar moral norms, such as solidarity with the poor and the marginalised. The problem seems to be less that the audience does not know how to behave but that they are not properly motivated to behave as they know they ought to. Medinan texts, on the other hand, are keen to provide detailed behavioural instructions pertaining to a wide range of human activities that stretches far beyond the sphere of religious ritual.[13]

12 For my general views on Qur'anic chronology, see Nicolai Sinai, *The Qur'an: A Historical-Critical Introduction* (Edinburgh: Edinburgh University Press, 2017). On the Medinan Qur'an in particular, see the contributions to Nicolai Sinai, ed., *Unlocking the Medinan Qur'an* (Leiden: Brill, 2022), with numerous references to earlier scholarship.

13 Sinai, 'The Unknown Known', 67.

This statement at least hints that the transition from the Meccan to the Medinan suras involves a fundamental transformation of the Qur'anic understanding of the reach of human practical reason: in the Medinan Qur'an, it might seem, the crucial moral task confronting human agents shifts from the domain of *doing* – i.e. from the challenge of implementing what deep down most humans know, or could easily know, they ought to do – to the domain of *knowing* – i.e. to the challenge of attaining an adequately specific understanding of how God expects humans to behave, such knowledge not being available via ordinary moral intuitions and deliberations and therefore needing to derive from revelation. It is, in other words, tempting to view the transition from the Meccan to Medinan suras in terms of a shift from a Muʿtazilī-type insistence that human agents have substantial extra-revelatory access to valid norms of behaviour to an Ashʿarī-adjacent insistence that humans need to be informed about such norms by divine revelation.

Indeed, one might be tempted to go even further and to view the Medinan suras as organically paving the way towards the seminal claim of al-Shāfiʿī (d. 820 CE) that 'nothing befalls any adherent of God's religion (*fa-laysat tanzilu bi-aḥadin min ahli dīn illāhi nāzilatun*) without there being in God's scripture an indication (*al-dalīl*) of the path of guidance concerning it'.[14] What al-Shāfiʿī posits is that scripture – at least when supplemented by the Prophet's *sunna* – points to a legal system that is comprehensive and exhaustive, containing a normative assessment of all conceivable courses of action that might present themselves in response to particular circumstances in the world.[15] So when the Medinan suras offer guidance on how to conduct a divorce (e.g. Q. 65:1–7), how to divide up inheritances (e.g. Q. 4:7–12, 4:176), or how to record loans (Q. 2:282), this may well appear not only as the emergence of a novel, revelation-centred moral epistemology but also as the momentous beginning of a trend towards the idea of a comprehensive divine law as eventually explicated by al-Shāfiʿī.

14 See al-Shāfiʿī, *The Epistle on Legal Theory*, ed. and trans. Joseph E. Lowry (New York: New York University Press, 2013), 12–13 (§16; translation modified).

15 See David R. Vishanoff, *The Formation of Islamic Hermeneutics: How Sunni Legal Theorists Imagined a Revealed Law* (New Haven: American Oriental Society, 2011), 34 (al-Shāfiʿī 'imagined law as a comprehensive and coherent set of rules ... dictated entirely by God and accessible to humans through the textual record of Prophetic revelation') and 38–39 (on the passage cited in the main text). For other scholars who have remarked on the crucial premise of legal comprehensiveness, see A. Kevin Reinhart, *Before Revelation: The Boundaries of Muslim Moral Thought* (Albany: State University of New York Press, 1995), 16–17, commenting on Ibn Surayj's view that 'Revelation spoke to all human activity', and Sohaira Z.M. Siddiqui, *Law and Politics under the Abbasids: An Intellectual Portrait of al-Juwaynī* (Cambridge: Cambridge University Press, 2019), 106, 187n3, employing the notion of 'scriptural universalism'.

Now, I do think that the plausibility of al-Shāfiʿī's epoch-making claim does to an important degree rest on the form and content of the Medinan suras; if one were to counterfactually imagine a Qur'anic canon consisting only in the Meccan suras, al-Shāfiʿī's claim would have had significantly less prima facie credibility.[16] Yet I will nonetheless argue that there is no reason to consider the Medinan suras' legislative shift to entail a fundamental theological or epistemological rupture with earlier parts of the Qur'an. Rather, Medinan law remains tightly and coherently embedded in the Qur'an's basic worldview.

2 The Qur'an's Moral Theology

I commence with a summary outline of what I take to be the Qur'an's fundamental moral framework, shared by Meccan and Medinan texts alike. In explicating this framework, I would accord axiomatic significance to the notion that God's creation of the world serves the basic purpose of 'testing' moral agents, as explicitly stated in several verses (e.g. Q. 11:7, 67:2).[17] The idea that God's creation aids His supreme objective of moral testing is in fact operative throughout the entire Qur'an, resonating well into the Medinan period (Q. 3:191, 5:48). The cosmos is therefore an environment in which God has placed moral agents in order to subject them to a discriminating assessment of their individual moral performance. It is in accordance with their individual moral track record that these agents will eventually be punished and rewarded in the hereafter,[18] culminating in an eternal state of festive communion with God or, alternatively, one of agonising torture and separation from Him.[19] Thus, one may think of the Qur'anic cosmos as being a sort of examination hall that presents moral subjects with various problems and challenges to which they can respond correctly or incorrectly.[20] For instance, humans might find themselves blessed with wealth yet fail to be duly grateful to God or fail to make charitable use of

16 Of course, it is also entirely feasible for exegetes of a scriptural canon to go against what is prima facie plausible and persuade a substantial audience that they are right.

17 See in more detail Nicolai Sinai, *Key Terms of the Qur'an: A Critical Dictionary* (Princeton: Princeton University Press, 2023), 138–41. For other recent publications that underline the importance of the Qur'anic notion of testing, see Bauer and Hamza, *Women*, 3–4, 21–23, 59, and elsewhere; and Julien Decharneux, *Creation and Contemplation: The Cosmology of the Qur'ān and Its Late Antique Background* (Berlin: Walter de Gruyter, 2023), 18, 40–43.

18 While the Qur'an insists on God's justice, there is a complementary theme of divine mercy: righteous believers will receive their reward several times over, and God will compassionately pass over or efface their moral slips. See Sinai, *Key Terms*, 23–24, 610–11.

19 Ibid., 194–95, and also 341 (on Q. 57:13).

20 This idea is further developed in my forthcoming 'Social Hierarchy and Inequality in the Qur'an'.

their wealth; or they might find themselves subject to dire straits but nonetheless respond to these in the manner of Job, who despite his suffering did not doubt God's supreme mercy (Q. 21:83).[21]

By way of a philosophico-theological addendum to the preceding, it may be helpful to make two further remarks. First, despite the Qur'an's recurrent emphasis on divine omnipotence, the Islamic scripture can in my view generally be read as accepting what philosophers call the 'liberty of indifference', meaning that the Qur'an credits humans (and also the jinn) with a real ability to select between different courses of action: sinners could in principle have acted righteously (though perhaps at some point inveterate sinners will forfeit the possibility of repenting) and the righteous could in principle have sinned.[22] Secondly, I hold that the Qur'anic notion of moral testing implies the epistemological indeterminacy of future human actions. As Daud Rahbar has shown in detail, Qur'anic assertions of divine omnipotence should therefore not be deemed to entail that God has advance knowledge of everything that human agents will go on to do.[23]

---

21 When I speak of 'moral agents', my primary intent are humans, though the Qur'an views the jinn, too, as moral agents who may either do right or wrong and who will accordingly be subject to eschatological recompense. See Sinai, *Key Terms*, 180–90.

22 See e.g. Daud Rahbar, *God of Justice: A Study in the Ethical Doctrine of the Qur'ān* (Leiden: E.J. Brill, 1960), 67–90; Sinai, *Key Terms*, 445–50; Bauer and Hazma, *Women*, 21–23. On the distinction between liberty of spontaneity (being able to do what one wants to do) and liberty of indifference (being able to do something different than what one actually does), see Roy C. Weatherford, 'Spontaneity and Indifference', in *The Oxford Companion to Philosophy*, 2nd ed., ed. Tod Honderich (Oxford: Oxford University Press, 2005), www.oxfordreference.com.

23 See Rahbar, *God of Justice*, 51–66. As Rahbar notes, some Qur'anic verses state rather clearly that the trials and challenges with which God confronts humans will enable Him to 'know who are the believers' (Q. 3:140: *wa-li-yaʿlama llāhu lladhīna āmanū*) or that God 'does not yet know … who will prove to be steadfast' (Q. 3:142: *wa-lammā yaʿlami llāhu lladhīna jāhadū minkum wa-yaʿlama l-ṣābirīn*). It follows that at least normally God only comes to know the ethical qualities of human agents in real time, as it were: as these humans make decisions and act on them. In other words, God does not harbour such knowledge from all eternity. There is admittedly a tension here with Q. 17:4, according to which God did have advance knowledge that the ancient Israelites would 'twice wreak corruption on the earth'; cf. Rahbar, *God of Justice*, 99–101, who among other things highlights the exceptional character of this statement. Discounting Q. 17:4, therefore, it would seem that when the Qur'an says that God 'has knowledge of all things' (*huwa bi-kulli shay'in ʿalīm*), this should be taken to mean that He has full awareness of all of the states of entities existing at a given moment in time, including 'what is in people's chests' (Q. 3:154), and also that God has an unfailingly accurate memory of all past events. I do not think it would be correct to say that in denying God foreknowledge of morally relevant human actions the Qur'an is placing a *limitation* on God's knowledge. Clearly, from

In thinking about the world as akin to a divine examination hall, it must be borne in mind that the Qur'an unmistakably maintains that the cosmic habitat in which humans have been placed provides them not only with moral tests but also with significant resources for tackling the moral challenges with which they are confronted. This is foregrounded by the Qur'an's extensive discourse on the many 'signs' or *āyāt* that it claims riddle the natural world. In highlighting various natural phenomena like rain and vegetation or even the existence of rivers and mountains, the Qur'an is concerned to demonstrate that the world is designed to enable human flourishing, thus evidencing God's wisdom, generosity, and power.[24] The point is not just that the cosmos is factually set up in such a way as to ensure that vital human needs are met; the cosmos is also set up in such a way as to enable humans to *take cognisance* of this fact and to invite some fundamental theological inferences, namely: that the world has a creator who is supremely wise and powerful, who has certain moral claims on humans, and who is therefore both motivated to reward and punish them according to their moral performance and capable of posthumously resurrecting them in order to face precisely such a reckoning. As for the role of revelation within this veritable 'natural theology',[25] it is very frequently presented as aiming to 'remind' (*dh-k-r*) humans of, and draw their attention to, theological insights that are writ large across the cosmos.[26] Overall, the Qur'an does not give grounds for assuming that the expectation, however rarely fulfilled, that humans understand (*ʿaqala*) God's signs (e.g. Q. 2:164, 16:12, 16:67) and that they be grateful (*shakara*) to their creator (e.g. Q. 45:12, 67:23) becomes incumbent upon them only from the moment when they have been accosted by a divinely sent messenger or prophet.

---

the Qur'anic vantage point God could have created a world in which every occurrence is fully predictable to a divine mind. Instead, I am suggesting, the Qur'an takes God to have created a world marked by a quantum of indeterminacy, due to the existence in this world of moral agents. In other words, it is something of a tautology that once God has created moral agents, defined by their ability to choose between alternative courses of action, it is not fully predictable even to God what an individual will or will not do in a given situation. To say that this is an infringement upon divine omniscience would be rather like saying that it is an infringement upon divine omniscience that God is unable to compute the greatest positive number or that He is unable to create a square circle.

24 See Sinai, *Key Terms*, 38–42, with further references.

25 See Julien Decharneux, 'The Natural Theology of the Qur'ān and Its Late Antique Christian Background: A Preliminary Outline', in *The Study of Islamic Origins: New Perspectives and Contexts*, ed. Mette Bjerregaard Mortensen, Guillaume Dye, Isaac W. Oliver, and Tommaso Tesei (Berlin: Walter de Gruyter, 2021), 177–99.

26 On the Qur'anic root *dh-k-r* and its various derivatives, see Sinai, *Key Terms*, 306–18.

From the Qur'anic vantage point, therefore, an unbiased contemplation of the cosmos not only ought to lead humans to conclude that a creator exists but also to realise that they have certain obligations towards Him. To unpack this further, on my reading the Qur'an is committed to two basic assumptions about normative propositions, that is, about statements involving the word 'ought' (e.g. 'humans ought to be grateful to God'). One of these assumptions concerns the ontology of such norms, that is, their nature and basis in reality, while the other one concerns their epistemology, that is, the manner in which human subjects can come to have knowledge of them.[27] Specifically, I would take the Qur'an to be implicitly committed to the following two propositions:

(1) At least the normative principle that one ought to be grateful to a benefactor (traditionally expressed as the duty of *shukr al-munʿim*)[28] is valid objectively, that is, regardless of whether it is declared to be so by textual revelation. Hence, in the Qur'anic worldview there is at least one fundamental norm whose validity is not contingent upon a positive divine decree.

(2) Humans are in principle capable of appreciating the validity of this principle, in addition to their assumed ability to understand that they are inhabiting a cosmos whose design is such that its creator is in fact a benefactor. That is to say, even without being accosted by revelation, the Qur'an takes humans to be capable of realising the truth of at least one fundamental normative proposition (regardless of whether more than a minority of humans are actually likely to do so).

It is true that the Qur'an is under no illusion that many humans will be prone to overlook and forget what the cosmos ought to tell them. This is why they require revelatory reminders – *dhikr* – of God's existence and of His claims upon humans. But it is not, I think, the case that textual revelation is considered to be that which *grounds* God's claims upon humans to begin with, or that textual revelation is understood to *inform* humans of something of which they had absolutely no prior inkling.[29]

---

27 For the same distinction between the ontology and epistemology of values, see George F. Hourani, *Reason and Tradition in Islamic Ethics* (Cambridge: Cambridge University Press, 1985), 23.

28 See Reinhart, *Before Revelation*, 107–23 and *passim*. The term *shukr al-munʿim* as such is of course not Qur'anic, but there are some Qur'anic verses that combine the roots *sh-k-r* and *n-ʿ-m* in such a manner as to betray the assumption that the bestowal of grace engenders an obligation of gratitude; see Q. 5:6, 16:114, 16:121, 27:19, 31:31, and 46:15.

29 Or perhaps one should say: that which grounds God's normative claims upon humans and informs them of these claims is indeed revelation – but it is God's cosmic revelation-through-creation rather than textual revelation. See Daniel Madigan, 'Themes

What I have just said aligns with the argument of an article first published in 1980 by George Fadlo Hourani. Based on a survey of Qur'anic ethical language, Hourani finds that the Qur'an 'frequently refers to objective values, which cannot be analysed completely in terms of commands and obedience. This conclusion coincides with that of the classical Muʿtazilites.' Hourani also concludes that 'the Muʿtazilites were right in their interpretation of the Qur'ān as allowing some scope for rational ethical judgements by believers and unbelievers' (although Hourani simultaneously stresses his view that revelation is nonetheless considered to be the 'chief source of ethical knowledge').[30] Hourani's carefully argued conclusion that the Qur'an's ontology of values and its moral epistemology have a fundamental affinity with Muʿtazilī theology should not be dismissed as theological partisanship. It certainly does not entail that the Ashʿarī preoccupation with divine omnipotence and majesty is an alien projection onto the Qur'an, only that there are good reasons for a historical interpreter of the Qur'an to hold the themes of divine power and of the pervasive presence of divine agency in the world in balance with other ideas. Nor is Hourani's judgement problematically anachronistic. As Kevin Reinhart has remarked, 'Muʿtazilism represents an archaic form of Muslim thought carrying forward earlier ideas formed in a missionary, that is to say a minoritarian context.' This readily explains some fundamental continuities with the Qur'an, 'itself at its beginning a product of a minoritarian missionary environment'.[31]

3 Religious Law in the Meccan and Medinan Suras

I shall now attempt to take a closer look at the place of what one might call religious law in the general picture just sketched, with the category of 'law' being used with all the caveats set out earlier. By speaking of 'religious law' in the Qur'an, I mean in the first instance legislatively specific norms that are based on divine revelation, such as those that are imposed by the Qur'anic

---

and Topics', in *The Cambridge Companion to the Qur'ān*, ed. Jane Dammen McAuliffe (Cambridge: Cambridge University Press, 2006), 83: 'God's first revelation, then, is in creation. Just as the creative activity of God is continuous and not merely confined to an initial moment, the Qur'ān insists that God is constantly providing "signs" ... that manifest all we need to know about God and about our rightful place in relationship to God.'

30 George F. Hourani, *Reason and Tradition in Islamic Ethics* (Cambridge: Cambridge University Press, 1985), 37, 45. I am inclined to be somewhat less cautious with regard to the Qur'an's acceptance of rational ethical knowledge than Hourani, in part based on the use of the phrase *bi-l-maʿrūf* in Qur'anic legislation (see below).

31 Reinhart, *Before Revelation*, 178.

proclamations themselves or those that the Qur'an takes to have been contained in previous scriptural revelations (e.g. Q. 5:45, attributing to the Torah a version of the law of talion). In a secondary and broader sense, I would expand the category of 'religious law' to mean any legislatively specific norms that are anchored in a worldview, a comprehensive vision of how human individuals and societies fit into the cosmos. In this broader sense, various taboos around crops and livestock that appear to have been observed by the Qur'an's pagan opponents (Q. 6:136, 6:138–39) will also qualify as 'religious law', though not of course as religious law observed by the Qur'anic believers but rather as the religious law of their 'associating' antagonists. I should note here that I consider the Qur'an to be deploying at least two approximate equivalents of the modern category of 'religion', consisting in the Arabic terms *dīn* and *milla*, which in the Qur'an function as umbrella categories encompassing diverse beliefs about deities and practices of worshipping them, both monotheistic and non-monotheistic.[32]

The most salient feature of the Meccan view of religious law seems to be an assumption that humans have an innate tendency to tie themselves up in unnecessary ritual rules and prohibitions: humans, it appears, have a penchant to subordinate themselves to gratuitous and needlessly onerous taboos, rather than – as one might have expected the Qur'an to insist – displaying the opposite tendency of wanting to evade inconvenient prohibitions. It is true, of course, that the Meccan Qur'an does amply criticise human selfishness and humans' flouting of basic moral principles. But specifically with regard to what one may call ritual matters, what the Qur'an criticises is a contrary predisposition to 'proscribe' (*ḥarrama*) many of the 'good things' (*al-ṭayyibāt*) that God has generously conferred on humans.[33] A case in hand would be the above-mentioned pagan taboos to do with crops or livestock that are criticised in some detail in Q. 6 (vv. 136ff.).[34] While it is difficult to reconstruct these taboos in detail, the Qur'anic assessment of them is very clear: according to Q. 10:59, to divide up God's 'provision' (*rizq*) into permitted (*ḥalāl*) and forbidden (*ḥarām*) is to 'fabricate' (*iftarā*) egregious lies about God.[35] The idea seems to be that inventing unwarranted and onerous prohibitions that allegedly restrict the human consumption of the world's resources is tantamount to a denial of God's generosity.

32 See Sinai, *Key Terms*, 293–300 (on *dīn*) and 645–50 (on *milla*). For example, Q. 40:26 implies that the term *dīn* applies to the religion of the Egyptians, and in Q. 38:7 the expression 'the contemporary *milla*' (*al-milla al-ākhira*) appears to refer to Meccan polytheism.

33 See Sinai, *Key Terms*, 218–23.

34 In addition to the previous note, see also Joseph E. Lowry, 'When Less Is More: Law and Commandment in *Sūrat al-An'ām*', *Journal of Qur'anic Studies* 9, no. 2 (2011): 22–42.

35 Sinai, 'Dietary Tetralogue', 124–25.

Clearly, a matter of ritual practice is here treated as having significant (and flatly objectionable) theological purport.[36]

From verses like Q. 10:59, it would appear that the Meccan attitude to dietary prohibitions is basically antinomian: humans ought to gratefully and unreservedly accept the manifold blessings that the creator liberally bestows upon them; there is nothing inherently illicit or impure in what nature has to offer.[37] Of course, this position is substantially qualified in the Medinan suras, which do lay down a number of unequivocal dietary taboos, such as the prohibition to consume blood or carrion (Q. 2:172–73, 5:3, 6:145, 16:114–15).[38] The Qur'anic position on dietary taboos thus constitutes a particularly conspicuous illustration of the Medinan suras' legislative shift. Yet Medinan passages containing dietary taboos also exhibit a noticeable attempt to display theological continuity with the permissivist attitude of the Meccan suras. This is achieved, for example, by reiterating that God munificently provides humans with 'good things'.[39] All four passages, moreover, supplement their dietary taboos with a hardship clause that permits exceptions in cases of emergency and, in one instance, with the concession that animals killed by hunting beasts may be consumed, meaning that they do not count as carrion (Q. 5:4).[40] The conspicuous exceptions and concessions at hand can be understood as concrete exemplifications of the explicit insistence in one Medinan verse that God 'desires ease for you, not difficulty' (Q. 2:185: *yurīdu llāhu bikumu l-yusra wa-lā yurīdu bikumu l-ʿusra*) and related statements elsewhere.[41] This stress on legislative ease also expresses itself in the frequency with which Qur'anic legislation

36 For a potential Medinan echo of this theme of gratuitous human self-denial, see Q. 3:93 (cited in n. 44 below).

37 The qualifier 'antinomian' is introduced in Sinai, 'Dietary Tetralogue', 124–27. Lowry speaks of 'legal minimalism'; see Lowry, 'When Less Is More', 22 (including n. 1).

38 See in more detail Sinai, 'Dietary Tetralogue' (defending the claim that all four relevant passages are Medinan).

39 E.g. Q. 2:172: 'O believers, eat of the good things with which We have provided you and be grateful to God, if it is Him whom you worship.'

40 Sinai, 'Dietary Tetralogue', 136. Q. 5:5, too, may well have an alleviating thrust; see Sinai, 'Dietary Tetralogue', 137; as well as Sinai, *Key Terms*, 112 (including n. 8).

41 See Joseph E. Lowry, 'Exculpatory Language in the Qur'an: A Survey of Terms, Themes, and Theologies', *Mélanges de l'Université Saint-Joseph* 66 (2015–16): 107–8. For an excellent monograph-length study of the nexus between exceptions and special dispensations in Qur'anic legislation, on the one hand, and the Qur'an's general insistence on the feasibility of God's normative demands, on the other, see now Johanne L. Christiansen, *The Exceptional Qur'ān: Flexible and Exceptive Rhetoric in Islam's Holy Book* (Piscataway: Gorgias Press, 2021), which I only managed to peruse after the present chapter had been written.

resorts to what Lowry has aptly termed 'exculpatory' phrases.[42] Finally, the motif of the Qur'an's legislative ease in comparison with earlier, in particular Jewish, law is probably also reflected in the closing verse of the second sura, Q. 2:286, which caps off a composition containing a significant proportion of legislative material with a prayer by the community not to be 'burdened by what we cannot bear', like 'those before us' (*wa-lā taḥmil ʿalaynā iṣran ka-mā ḥamaltahū ʿalā lladhīna min qablinā*).[43]

As intimated by the verse just quoted, the counterfoil to the Qur'an's presentation of its own legislation as easy is Jewish law, which is portrayed as punitively harsh: it is due to Jewish wrongdoing, one Medinan passage (Q. 4:160–61) says, that God 'forbade' to the Jews certain 'good things that had [previously] been permitted to them' (Q. 4:160: *ḥarramnā ʿalayhim ṭayyibātin uḥillat lahum*; cf. also Q. 6:146 and 16:118, which, by using the first-person verb *ḥarramnā*, likewise identify God as the originator of Jewish prohibitions).[44] Such cursory Medinan comments on Jewish law could be animated by a concern to forestall the impression that the Medinan suras' incorporation of legislative material amounts to a sort of reversal to Jewish law, assumed to be notoriously burdensome. I would venture the conjecture that the Qur'an is here seeking to anticipate potential objections by Christians, who might have been minded to view the Medinan suras as an anachronistic throwback to the caricature of Old Testament legalism that Christian polemicists liked to think their own religion had decisively overcome.

Against a deep-seated Christian reflex to think of law as onerous and punitive, Medinan law is thus presented as compatible with, and indeed as a major

42 Lowry, 'Exculpatory Language.'

43 Lowry, 'Law, Structure, and Meaning', 140. Note that the word *iṣr* also occurs in Q. 7:157, a verse that is very likely Medinan (Sinai, *Key Terms*, 97). This verse invokes the legislative activities of Muhammad (here styled as the 'prophet of the scriptureless', *al-nabī al-ummī*, on which see Sinai, *Key Terms*, 94–99) with verbs like 'to prohibit' (*ḥarrama*) or 'to permit' (*aḥalla*) and then says that Muhammad relieves people – or perhaps the recipients of the Torah and the *injīl* in particular – of 'the burden and the fetters that used to be upon them' (*wa-yaḍaʿu ʿanhum iṣrahum wa-l-aghlāla llatī kānat ʿalayhim*). Q. 7:157 thus provides support for the hypothesis that the word *iṣr* in Q. 2:286 connotes burdensome legal norms in particular. This is, of course, also made likely by the reference to 'those before us' (*alladhīna min qablinā*).

44 On Q. 4:160, see Holger M. Zellentin, *The Qurʾān's Legal Culture: The Didascalia Apostolorum as a Point of Departure* (Tübingen: Mohr Siebeck, 2013), 144–54. By contrast with the Qur'anic verses just cited in the main text, Q. 3:93 speaks of Jewish self-prohibition: 'All food was permitted to the Israelites, except what Israel prohibited to himself (*illā mā ḥarrama isrāʾīlu ʿalā nafsihi*), before the Torah was sent down.' Here, the name *isrāʾīl* refers to the ancestor of the Israelites (in biblical terms, Jacob; cf. Q. 19:58).

vehicle of, divine mercy and lenience.[45] In this way, Medinan legislation is retrospectively tied to prominent aspects of established Meccan theology, mitigating the prima facie impression of significant doctrinal discontinuity. In what remains, I would like to supplement this basic insight of previous scholarship (most notably Lowry's) by some additional observations about the function and character of Medinan law, hoping to illuminate in further detail why and how the Medinan suras are casting Qur'anic law as expressive of God's mercy and leniency.

4 Religious Law as Community-Relative

My key propositions with regard to the wider question just posed are three: (i) the Qur'an is explicit that legislative prescriptions have the function of governing the life and defining the identity of a community; (ii) the Qur'an accepts an irreducible diversity of religious communities, and of the legal frameworks governing them, as divinely intended; and (iii) the Qur'an does not limit the prospect of salvation to members of the Qur'anic *umma* alone.

One important Qur'anic passage in which all of the three claims just set out can be glimpsed is the Medinan verse Q. 5:48. Its second half runs as follows:

> For each of you [plural] we have instituted a normative practice and a custom (*li-kullin ja'alnā minkum shir'atan wa-minhājan*). Had God willed, He would have made you a single community (*umma*); but [He did not do so] in order to test you with regard to that which He gave you. So race with one another towards good works (*fa-stabiqū l-khayrāti*). To God you will all return, and He will inform you about that with regard to which you were in disagreement.[46]

---

45 I am entirely sympathetic to the view that this polemical Christian cliché ought to be questioned with regard to rabbinic law as well; but this chapter is exclusively concerned with the Qur'an, and the small number of Qur'anic allusions to rabbinic law just referenced are indeed continuous with Christian presuppositions about the onerousness and harshness of Jewish law.

46 That *istabaqa* can mean 'to race one another' is clear from Q. 12:25 (Joseph and the wife of his Egyptian owner *istabaqā l-bāba*). The latter verse also illustrates that the accusative object of *istabaqa* is that towards which the parties are racing. As for the noun *khayr* (literally, 'something good'), this can of course refer to wealth, but in the context of Q. 5:48 'good deeds' is clearly the more suitable rendering. This meaning is, for example, clearly in evidence at Q. 21:73, where *fi'l al-khayrāt* is 'doing good deeds'. See also A. Kevin Reinhart, 'What We Know about Ma'rūf', *Journal of Islamic Ethics* 1 (2017): 58. Finally, to those familiar with Lessing's *Nathan the Wise*, Q. 5:48 is bound to be reminiscent of the parable of the three rings. There is in fact a historical link between the two texts; see Jan Loop, 'Islam and

The statement comes towards the end of a passage (Q. 5:41ff.) discussing God's revelation of the Torah, the *injīl* (conventionally rendered as 'the Gospel'),[47] and the Qur'an. All three of these scriptures are said to have been revealed in order to govern a particular religious community: Jews, Christians (here called the 'people of the *injīl*'), and Qur'anic believers are all expected to 'adjudicate according to' (*ḥakama bi-*) the scriptural revelations they have received (Q. 5:44, 5:47, 5:48). Interestingly, it is implied that even the Christian scripture, the *injīl*, has legislative content to which Christians can be expected to adhere (Q. 5:47): however much Christians are wont to insist that they are not under the yoke of the law anymore, the Qur'an is here applying to Christianity, too, the general assumption that *any* human community requires legislatively specific prescriptions, and that a community defined in *religious* terms ought to have legal prescriptions that are *religiously* based.[48]

Given the context, the expression 'for each of you' (*li-kullin ... minkum*) in Q. 5:48 may be supposed to range not just over a certain set of human individuals but rather over human communities – or, specifically, over human communities defined in terms of their allegiance to a scriptural revelation: Jews, Christians, and Qur'anic believers. This is supported by Q. 22:67, where a similar statement is unequivocally formulated as referring to *communities* (sing. *umma*).[49] The Qur'an accordingly recognises the diversity of existing legislative behavioural norms – or, in the language of Q. 5:48, of 'normative practices and customs' (*shirʿatan wa-minhājan*) – among Jews, Christians, and Qur'anic believers as divinely willed.[50] By virtue of such an appeal to God's will, Q. 5:48

the European Enlightenment', in *Christian–Muslim Relations: A Bibliographical History*, vol. 13, *Western Europe* (1700–1800), ed. David Thomas and John A. Chesworth (Leiden: Brill, 2019), 17.

47 For more detail, see Sinai, *Key Terms*, 103–7.

48 If one equates the *injīl* with the Gospels or with the New Testament as a whole, Q. 5:47 will of course seem curious. However, I have suggested elsewhere that perhaps the *injīl* is to be identified with the Christian Bible as a whole (Sinai, *Key Terms*, 105–7). But quite apart from the question of how the Qur'an and/or its recipients imagined the Christian canon and its contents, the charitable way of reading the Qur'an here would be to construe it as saying that Christian communities evidently do require legal norms in their daily existence and that therefore these norms ought to be in some sense informed by the Christian canon, whatever form the latter might take concretely.

49 The relevant segment of Q. 22:67 runs, 'For every community We have instituted a rite to which they adhere' (*li-kulli ummatin jaʿalnā mansakan hum nāsikūhu*). It is possible that *mansak* refers specifically to rituals to do with a sanctuary and/or sacrifice here, in view of the other Qur'anic occurrences of the word in Q. 2:128, 2:200, and 22:34.

50 On the terms *shirʿa* and *minhāj*, see Sinai, *Key Terms*, 406 (including n. 34). It is conceivable, of course, that the Qur'an assumes considerable legal overlap between the Torah, the *injīl*, and the Qur'an. However, the context of Q. 5:48 undoubtedly requires that the

goes beyond the observation that one of the principal effects of Medinan law was a demarcation of the Qur'anic *umma* from the pagan 'associators' and from the Medinan Jews.[51] In fact, an accurate understanding of Q. 5:48 requires an awareness that each of the three legal frameworks that figure in Q. 5:41ff. allows for a genuine prospect of attaining eschatological salvation, for a number of Qur'anic verses make it clear that it is by no means only members of the Qur'anic *umma* who will qualify for paradise if they 'believe in God and the final day and do righteous deeds' (Q. 2:62, 5:69; see also 3:199).[52] The Qur'an does of course insist that there are certain factually held Jewish or Christian beliefs – such as belief in the divinity of Jesus (e.g. Q. 5:17, 5:72) – that violate Qur'anic theology. Yet this is undoubtedly not taken to preclude that there can be a theologically valid type of Christianity that conforms to the requirements of Qur'anic monotheism.

The preceding interpretation is confirmed by the parallel of Q. 5:48 in Q. 2:148 (also Medinan). This latter verse comes towards the end of a passage extending from Q. 2:142 to 2:152, whose thematic focus is a change of the Qur'anic community's direction of prayer (*qibla*) towards the Meccan sanctuary. Q. 2:142–52 therefore deal with one particular example of the 'normative practices and customs' from Q. 5:48, namely, with a case belonging to the general domain of ritual. In Q. 2:148, the parallel just noted, the divine voice offers a meta-commentary of sorts, explaining that 'everyone has a direction towards which he turns (*wa-li-kullin wijhatun huwa muwallīhā*); so race with one another towards good works (*fa-stabiqū l-khayrāti*)'. The phraseological overlap with Q. 5:48 (*li-kullin*, *fa-stabiqū l-khayrāti*) is obvious, making it certain that the assertion that 'everyone has (*li-kullin*) a direction towards which he turns' is again to be understood in a communal rather than an individualistic sense: every *community* has a direction towards which they turn. Also implicit is the disavowal of any claim to absolute validity for the Qur'anic community's direction of prayer (in Q. 2:148), just as for its 'normative practices and customs' in general (Q. 5:48): other communities may have different practices

divinely intended diversity of different religious communities goes hand in hand with a real diversity of divinely mandated 'practices and customs'.

51 See on this function of Medinan law Sinai, *The Qur'an*, 202–5.

52 See Mun'im Sirry, *Scriptural Polemics: The Qur'ān and Other Religions* (Oxford: Oxford University Press, 2014), as well as Sinai, *Key Terms*, 340–41, 404–5. Although it is by no means the case that the Qur'an deems one particular communal affiliation to be soteriologically necessary, one specific Qur'anic community – i.e. the Qur'anic 'associators' or *mushrikūn* – is indeed treated as irredeemably beholden to doctrines and customs that violate fundamental Qur'anic teachings. Associators who would qualify for paradise will therefore need to convert.

or observe a different direction of prayer, but these are not therefore necessarily invalid – provided, one may surely add, that these practices have not just arisen from the lamentable human penchant for gratuitous self-prohibition that is castigated in verses like Q. 10:59, discussed above. The performance of good works (*khayrāt*) is clearly assumed to be possible within more than one legislative framework.[53] The upshot, in any case, is that the *qibla* comes across as 'community-relative', to borrow an expression by Lowry.[54]

This disavowal of the *qibla*'s absolute validity is further reinforced later in Q. 2, in v. 177. It seems clear that this verse refers back to, and is meant to put in context, the *qibla* passage in Q. 2:142–52, with which it shares the collocation of *wallā* and *wajh* (Q. 2:144, 2:149, 2:150; cf. 2:142). Q. 2:177 unequivocally relativises the importance of turning one way or another in prayer by expressly distinguishing such details of ritual praxis from a more fundamental tier of moral and religious norms:

> Righteousness (*al-birr*) does not consist in turning your faces (*an tuwallū wujūhakum*) to the east or to the west. Rather, righteousness is [exhibited by] someone who believes in God, the final day, the angels, the scripture, and the prophets; who gives away property, however beloved (*ʿalā ḥubbihi*), to relatives, orphans, the indigent, wayfarers (*ibn al-sabīl*), beggars, and with regard to slaves; who performs prayer and gives alms; and [righteousness is exhibited by] those who fulfil their covenant when they concluded one; and those who are steadfast (*al-ṣābirīn*) in hardship and adversity and in times of violent fighting. Those are the ones who are truthful (*alladhīna ṣadaqū*) and those are the ones who are God-fearing (*al-muttaqūn*).

The verse is bookended by references to righteousness (*birr*) and fear of God, two comprehensive virtue terms that are clearly credited with paramount importance.[55] Whether or not somebody exhibits them is said to be

53 Conversely, it is manifestly also the case that adherence to a particular legislative framework does not *guarantee* the performance of good works. For example, the Qur'an condemns charitable spending or prayer that is undertaken 'in order to be seen by people' (see Q. 2:264 and 4:38 on charity, and 4:142 and 107:6 on prayer).

54 Lowry, 'Law, Structure, and Meaning', 124. Note that Lowry employs this expression in connection with Q. 2:177 (treated immediately below in the main text) and that his phrasing is much more circumspect than mine ('leaves open the possibility that the prayer direction is community-relative').

55 On *birr*, see Reinhart, 'What We Know about Maʿrūf', 56–58 (including a discussion of Q. 2:177 that makes similar points to my comments in the main text). On fear of God (*taqwā*), see Sinai, *Key Terms*, 719–14.

determined by his commitment to fundamental beliefs having to do with God, the eschatological reckoning, and God's revelatory communication with humans as well as by his performance of certain basic forms of moral action such as the charitable sharing of one's possessions, prayer (which must here be intended in a general sense that transcends the execution of a precise set of ritual movements and utterances that would, for instance, involve a particular direction of prayer), honest compliance with prior agreements, and steadfast patience (*ṣabr*).[56] It is surely these fundamental beliefs, virtues, and types of moral comportment – which jointly define the high-level virtue terms 'righteousness' (*birr*), 'truthfulness', and 'fear of God' – that furnish the criteria by which the divine judge will eventually assess humans at the final judgement, as a host of Qur'anic parallels make clear (see e.g. Q. 2:62 and 5:69, discussed below). By contrast, the precise modalities of where to face in prayer are relegated to secondary importance. Structurally, Q. 2:177's distinction between *birr* and 'turning one's faces' in a particular direction resembles Q. 5:48's contrast between 'good works' (*al-khayrāt*), on the one hand, and 'normative practices and customs', on the other.

The secondary importance of the Meccan direction of prayer (which is clearly not taken to contradict the basic stipulation, in Q. 2:144, that the believers are to face Mecca in prayer) is sufficiently important for the sura to anticipate it even prior to the *qibla* passage, in Q. 2:115:

> To God belongs the east and the west (*li-llāhi l-mashriqu wa-l-maghribu*), so wherever you turn (*tuwallū*), there is God's face (*wajh*). God is indeed all-encompassing (*wāsiʿ*) and knowing.

Once again, the combination of the verb *wallā* and the noun *wajh* (even if the latter does not here function as the accusative of *wallā*) signals an evident link to the *qibla* section in Q. 2:142–52, as does the reprise of the phrase 'To God belongs the east and the west' (*li-llāhi l-mashriqu wa-l-maghribu*) later on in Q. 2:142. Thus, even before the recipient of Q. 2 has reached the *qibla* passage, she is already primed to understand that the question of where to turn in prayer is of decisively subordinate significance, however urgently the issue is then broached in v. 142, alluding to opponents criticising the Qur'anic community for discontinuing their previous *qibla* (*sa-yaqūlu l-sufahāʾu mina l-nāsi mā wallāhum ʿan qiblatihimu llatī kānū ʿalayhā*).

As shown above, Medinan passages assume a close link between communal identity and divinely mandated legislative norms, as exemplified by (but

56 On *ṣabr*, see Sinai, *Key Terms*, 464–66.

not necessarily limited to) ritual commandments, such as the commandment that the Qur'anic believers are to pray towards the Kaʿba. This nexus between community and law, when combined with the Qur'an's general recognition of the possibility of salvation outside the Qur'anic *umma*, entails a relegation of the importance of legal norms to secondary position, plainly expressed in Q. 2:177 and 5:48. It is worth adding that apart from such specific proof-texts, the general nexus between community and law is also borne out by the macrostructure of Q. 2 as a whole. According to Lowry, the text may be construed, 'from a certain altitude, primarily as a retelling of biblical narratives' – including prominently various misdeeds of the Mosaic Israelites in Q. 2:40ff. – 'and then the presentation of a set of "biblical" laws to govern the neo-biblical or neo-covenantal qur'ānic community'.[57] Lowry thus proposes a compelling answer to the question of how the miscellaneous legislative passages that are concentrated in the second half of Q. 2 cohere with the narrative and polemical material that dominates its first half: the law of Q. 2 is meant to govern and serve as a quasi-covenantal framework for the Qur'anic *umma*, who have their negative counterfoil in the Mosaic Israelites. This proposed focal point for Q. 2 as a whole matches the fact that programmatic statements in Q. 2 and 3 comment on the world-historical role of the Qur'anic *umma* (Q. 2:128, 2:143, 3:104, 3:110).[58] The Qur'an thus attaches demonstrably vital importance to the Medinan emergence of an independent community defined by allegiance to Muhammad and the Qur'anic revelations, which in practical terms entails adherence to Qur'anic law.

5 Legislative Norms as Divine Responses to Human Needs

It is worth juxtaposing the Qur'an's communitarian angle on religious law with the radical moral individualism that generally pervades the Islamic scripture.[59] It is a consistent Qur'anic theme that at the final reckoning everybody will be judged exclusively on the basis of his or her own moral track record (e.g.

57 See Lowry, 'Law, Structure, and Meaning', 148. Cf. ibid., 141.

58 On my understanding of the Qur'anic term *umma* and its role in Q. 2 and 3, see Sinai, *Key Terms*, 86–94. Other important publications on the topic are Frederick M. Denny, 'The Meaning of *Ummah* in the Qur'ān', *History of Religions* 15, no. 1 (1975): 34–70; and Hamza M. Zafer, *Ecumenical Community: Language and Politics of the Ummah in the Qur'an* (Leiden: Brill, 2020).

59 This individualism is manifest, for instance, in the way in which the Qur'an frames the notion of a divine–human covenant; see Sinai, *Key Terms*, 710–11.

Q. 53:38). In Q. 5:48 and 2:177, the basic ethico-religious criteria governing this eschatological assessment of human moral performance are signalled by terms such as 'righteousness' (*birr*) or 'good works' (*al-khayrāt*). By contrast, the 'normative practices and customs' from Q. 5:48, of which the *qibla* is one particular instance, constitute a secondary tier of norms.

Can we say more about the purpose of this secondary, legislative tier of norms, beyond the preceding observation that they somehow serve to demarcate and ensure the cohesion of religious communities? If what matters eschatologically is only one's individual moral performance, does this not ultimately make the secondary tier of 'normative practices and customs' entirely expendable? It is probably not coincidental that quite a few legislative passages in the Qur'an are cast as divine responsa to audience queries addressed to the Prophet (Q. 2:189, 2:215, 2:217, 2:219, 2:220, 2:222, 4:127, 4:176, 5:4, 8:1). A functioning human community, the Qur'an seems to presuppose, must be governed by authoritative legal norms, by 'normative practices and customs'; accordingly, human agents will themselves demand such norms, rather than merely suffering (or rejecting) their imposition from outside.[60] This being the case, it is in keeping with God's mercy to supply the Medinan *umma* with the sort of authoritative revelatory guidance that is required for the cohesion of a community defined in religious terms: the Qur'an's general portrayal of God as mercifully responsive to the needs of humans in general, and to the needs of those who believe in Him in particular, gives rise to an expectation that the deity will not simply tell bewildered believers to work out by themselves how to divide up inheritances or when and how to purify themselves for prayer or where precisely to draw the boundary between night and day, an issue that is crucial for the Qur'anic fasting regime (see Q. 2:187).[61]

In this sense, the Medinan suras' exposition of legal norms is in line with core features of the Qur'anic conception of God. Both Q. 5:48, discussed above, and the response formulae just noted indicate that the Qur'an considers Medinan law to meet concrete human needs, as does God's provision of rain or of vegetation, rather than amounting to a catalogue of arduous demands imposed for their own sake. Indeed, the *qibla* passage in Q. 2 signals much the same: the crucial verse that first mandates the Meccan *qibla*, Q. 2:144, opens with a

60 It is tempting to link this Qur'anic assumption to its critique of an ingrained human tendency towards excessive prohibitions, as described above: humans are creatures who will inevitably operate with the categories of permitted (*ḥalāl*) and forbidden (*ḥarām*; cf. Q. 10:59); in the absence of divine guidance on such matters, humans are therefore bound to fabricate dubious pseudo-proscriptions.

61 On divine responsiveness, see Sinai, *Key Terms*, 77 (which is indebted to Usman Shaikh).

description of the Qurʾan's prophetic addressee casting about for a direction of prayer: 'We certainly see how your [singular] face moves about in the sky, so We will turn you in a prayer direction (*qibla*) that will satisfy you.' It is the fact that a prayer direction needs to be authoritatively decreed that occasions the divine commandment to pray towards the Kaʿba rather than any immanent numinous quality possessed by the latter. Parenthetically, this is also in line with the fact that Qurʾanic comments on the Kaʿba's sacred status consistently foreground the human interests that are realised by God's establishment of the Meccan sanctuary and by the *ḥajj* pilgrimage. Thus, according to Q. 22:28 and 22:33, the *ḥajj* confers 'benefits' (*manāfiʿ*) upon its participants.[62]

I believe that the preceding observations warrant a generalising step, namely, to view the miscellaneous legislative norms expounded in the Medinan suras, covering such diverse domains as ritual or family law, as being generally understood to play a facilitating role with regard to the more fundamental ethico-religious virtues invoked by terms such as 'righteousness' (*birr*) and 'fear of God' (*taqwā*), and also with regard to certain basic aspects of material human flourishing (such as a measure of physical safety[63]) that are prerequisites of all further ethical and religious aspirations. From the Qurʾanic vantage point, Medinan law thus provides a communal framework of concrete rules within which an individual believer is well placed to live up to the ethico-religious demands that will determine God's verdict on the day of judgement; but legislative norms do not *themselves* form the criteria against which humans will be eschatologically assessed. This is hardly a novel insight: not only is the account just given broadly reminiscent of the post-Qurʾanic

62 See also Q. 3:97, 28:57, and 29:67, all of which underscore the divinely established security (*ʾ-m-n*) of the Meccan sanctuary. Q. 5:97 more opaquely states that God established the Kaʿba *qiyāman li-l-nāsi*. Ambros cautiously proposes that this should be taken to mean 'as a means of support for the people', in line with the use of *qiyām* in Q. 4:5; see Arne A. Ambros with Stephan Procházka, *A Concise Dictionary of Koranic Arabic* (Wiesbaden: Reichert, 2004), 232. This interpretation is further corroborated by Q. 14:37, according to which Mecca is located in an uncultivated valley whose inhabitants are provisioned by outsiders. It is true that Q. 3:97 says that 'pilgrimage to the house is an obligation that people owe to God' (*li-llāhi ʿalā l-nāsi ḥijju l-bayti*), which stresses that the pilgrimage has the character of a duty rather than appealing to its contribution to human welfare. Yet the statement just cited can be harmonised with the textual data previously catalogued by noting that after God has charged Abraham with instituting the pilgrimage rites (see Q. 22:26–27), these rites are of course mandatory. It should be noted that even though I have conveniently lumped the Kaʿba and the *ḥajj* together, the two are very likely to have been originally separate, as shown by Wellhausen (see Sinai, *Key Terms*, 208–11, with further references).

63 On the matter of safety, see the comments on Q. 3:97, 28:57, and 29:67 in the preceding note.

notion that the Sharīʿa realises certain fundamental objectives (*maqāṣid*), it also has rather specific affinity with the (equally post-Qur'anic) Muʿtazilī construal of the revealed law as a 'specification' (*tafṣīl*) or a concretisation of universally valid moral principles,[64] such that the basic rationale of adherence to the revealed law becomes an instrumental one: 'Follow this law (*sharīʿah*), so as to fulfil what is known by the intellect.'[65] Incidentally, when a Muʿtazilī theologian expressly allows that revealed laws may differ in accordance with particular circumstances,[66] this resonates with the observation above that the Qur'an recognises more than one legal framework that is in principle conducive to passing eschatological scrutiny.

My contention, then, is that Medinan legislation should be conceptualised as a divine benefaction serving independently intelligible human interests rather than as a catalogue of demands that are imposed for their own sake, as a set of demands that go above and beyond the general ethico-religious claims voiced in the Meccan suras.[67] In a way, Medinan legislation may therefore be grouped together with God's 'signs' (*āyāt*) in nature as belonging to the resources that are made available to moral agents in God's cosmic examination hall. Indeed, it is telling that there are some Medinan passages, such as Q. 2:187, 2:219, 2:221, in which the term *āyāt* is applied to legislative norms.[68]

A final corroboration for the preceding interpretation emerges from Q. 22:36–37, a passage rationalising why God exacts animal sacrifices in spite of the obvious fact that He does not require physical nourishment.[69] The explanation provided is that sacrificial rituals enable humans to give outward expression to God's majesty: God has made sacrificial animals 'subservient to you [plural] so that you may magnify God for the guidance He has granted you' (*sakhkharahā lakum li-tukabbirū llāha ʿalā mā hadākum*). Here again the Qur'an puts forward the idea that the cultic institution of sacrifice meets a human need, not a divine one. This point is also made in the immediately preceding verse Q. 22:36 with its insistence that there is 'good' (*khayr*) for the

---

64 George F. Hourani, *Islamic Rationalism: The Ethics of ʿAbd al-Jabbār* (Oxford: Clarendon Press, 1971), 135.

65 Sophia Vasalou, *Moral Agents and Their Deserts: The Character of Muʿtazilite Ethics* (Princeton: Princeton University Press, 2008), 49 (orthography modified). This instrumental function of the law was compared to medical advice; see Hourani, *Islamic Rationalism*, 135.

66 Vasalou, *Moral Agents*, 51.

67 As the Qur'anic comments on Jewish law briefly mentioned above show, the Qur'an assumes that revealed law can also be a punishment rather than a benefaction.

68 Sinai, *Key Terms*, 128 (crediting Binyamin Abrahamov and Mohsen Goudarzi).

69 On this passage, see in more detail Sinai, *Key Terms*, 305–6, as well as Sinai, 'Dietary Tetralogue', 135–36n68.

addressees in sacrificial observances (*shaʿāʾir*). Also pertinent to the present discussion is the fact that Q. 22:37 contrasts the meat and blood of sacrificial animals, which are said not to reach God, with the sacrificer's 'fear of God' (*taqwā*), which is presumably taken to be expressed in and cultivated by the act of sacrifice and which *will* reach the deity. We can discern here the same structural distinction between two normative tiers that we also saw in Q. 5:48 (normative customs and practices vs good works) and in Q. 2:177 (turning one's faces in a particular direction vs righteousness). What is distinctive about Q. 22:36–37, however, is that the latter passage suggests more clearly that the second-tier ritual of sacrifice is there to give expression to and cultivate the first-tier virtue of *taqwā*. Falling back on Muʿtazilī terminology, animal sacrifice in the context of the pilgrimage rites can perhaps quite aptly be described as a specification or concretisation of *taqwā*.

The communitarian and instrumentalist construal of legal norms just outlined makes it possible to account for the legislative shift taking place in the Medinan suras in a way that does not require positing a radical rupture in the Qur'an's epistemology or moral vision. The emergence of a sizeable body of Qur'anic legislation in Medinan texts, despite constituting a notable expansion of the Qur'an's thematic scope, is rationalised in a way that coheres with rather than disrupts the fundamentals of Meccan theology, specifically the Qur'an's basic understanding of moral norms and of humans' grasp thereof. This is so because legislatively specific norms are repeatedly presented as a second-tier concretisation of first-tier values and virtues, which latter form the ultimate benchmark of God's eschatological judgement. Legislatively specific norms operate as one among a number of equally valid communal frameworks provided by God that are meant to aid humans in living up to first-tier norms. Since legislative norms do not have first-tier status, the fact that they involve a significant portion of positive divine legislation does not mean that what humans are ultimately judged by is a plethora of divine decrees that are in principle inaccessible to human moral common sense.

It seems to me that the community-relative, functionalist understanding of religious law just reconstructed sheds useful light on the Qur'anic theme of the easiness of its legislation that I have highlighted earlier. Qur'anic law is not an end in itself, like the divine demand for righteousness, but rather a communal framework meant to realise certain objectives, in the least burdensome manner possible, which includes the function of *communally concretising* fundamental ethico-religious norms. This status of being a means to an end is precisely what opens up the possibility of exceptions, mitigations, and hardship clauses of the kind that are an important concomitant of Medinan law, just as this status gives rise to general statements stressing the easiness of Qur'anic legislation or highlighting the structural distinction between two tiers of behavioural norms.

6 Medinan Law and Moral Common Sense

As the preceding sections have tried to argue, Medinan law is viewed as the communal concretisation of more fundamental ethico-religious values. Earlier in this chapter, I also insisted that the Qur'an envisages humans as endowed with at least some degree of pre-revelatory normative insight, enabling them to appreciate that they ought to be grateful to their divine benefactor. How, then, does such moral common sense interact with divine legislation? In principle, it might be the case that moral common sense is envisaged as playing a rather limited role with regard to revelatory legislation, one that is purely propaedeutic (our realisation that we owe gratitude to our divine benefactor leads us to execute whatever commandments He imposes on us) or at most reconstructive (our moral common sense enables us to appreciate that God's commandments, once communicated to us, realise or advance certain fundamental values that are morally intelligible to us). In both cases, the role of our moral common sense would not necessarily be normatively productive, at least in those domains that are subject to explicit scriptural legislation.

Yet there is some evidence that Qur'anic legislation at times accords a more substantial role to humans' ability to make some valid distinctions between right and wrong. First, despite the fact that the Qur'an contains important legal or quasi-legal material, Qur'anic legislation by itself – i.e. without being supplemented by generous amounts of *ḥadīth* – is quantitatively far too small in order for it to be able to operate as a comprehensive divine code of the sort that was envisaged by al-Shāfiʿī (probably not entirely independently of pre-existing rabbinic conceptions of God's Torah).[70] This provides a clue that perhaps the human ability to engage in practical reasoning based on valid pre-revelatory normative intuitions is being assumed as a means of plugging the gap – at least if one is both reluctant to accept the claim that Qur'anic legislation was only ever intended to function in symbiosis with a much more extensive corpus of legal norms retrievable from the prophetic *sunna* and unwilling to consider the comparatively limited size of Qur'anic legislation as being due merely to

70 Al-Shāfiʿī's postulate of legal comprehensiveness is of course not a descriptive account of the factual reach of overt Qur'anic legislation but a programmatic statement of hermeneutical intent.

an ambitious legal project having been disastrously stunted by the death of Muhammad.[71]

A stronger and more textual piece of evidence, however, are the provisos of conformity with existing moral intuitions that are often appended to Medinan legislation, previously highlighted by Reinhart.[72] For example, the payment of compensation for a slain person and bequests are to be made 'in line what is recognised to be right' (*bi-l-maʿrūf*; Q. 2:178, 2:180). It seems quite clear that such *bi-l-maʿrūf* riders mean that the respective prescriptions are to be applied in accordance with the pre-existing and extra-scriptural moral common sense of the Qur'anic addressees. A similar role is played by the qualifier 'in line with the requirements of good conduct' (*bi-iḥsān*) in Q. 2:178 and 2:229.[73] The resulting impression is that even the Medinan suras by no means seek to furnish a closed legislative system that does not rely on antecedent moral principles and preconceptions. The relative degree of vagueness that can characterise Qur'anic law (cf. the discussion of Q. 2:280 at the beginning of this chapter) may accordingly be at least to some degree systemic and intentional. To be sure, the general admonition to 'make a bequest to parents and relatives in line with what is recognised to be right' in Q. 2:180 appears to have been subsequently superseded, in Q. 4:11–12 and 4:176, by far more precise rules about the minimum shares of an estate to which certain categories of surviving relatives are entitled. But this does not in itself settle the question whether the development towards numerical precision and a concomitant sidelining of the inherently imprecise ethical qualifier *bi-l-maʿrūf* that can be seen in the case of Qur'anic statements on inheritance should be considered paradigmatic of

71 This is not to deny the fact, much stressed by al-Shāfiʿī, that the Qur'an portrays Muhammad as an object of obedience (e.g. Q. 4:80) and of practical emulation (Q. 33:21), like Abraham (Q. 2:124, 60:4, 60:6); see Sinai, *Key Terms*, 86 (including n. 1). The Qur'anic form of legal responsa noted above certainly supports the claim that Muhammad functioned as an authority who was consulted when specific normative quandaries arose.

72 See in more detail Sinai, *Key Terms*, 518–19. A very similar point is also made in Reinhart, 'What We Know about Maʿrūf', especially 59–67. On p. 61, Reinhart additionally makes the important point that this scriptural appeal to extra-revelatory moral knowledge may be viewed as having been recognised by al-Shāfiʿī: 'The appeal to extra-textual moral knowledge was recognized, and indeed canonized, as an epistemic principle by al-Shāfiʿī in his *Risāla* when he said that understanding the Qur'ān depended upon grasping the various implications of a Qur'ānic declaration that were apparent to a speaker of the language in which the Qur'ān was revealed, but might not be apparent to a non-native.' But perhaps this is less an appeal to extra-textual moral knowledge than an attempt to implicitly fold the latter into the scriptural text.

73 Michael Cook, *Commanding Right and Forbidding Wrong in Islamic Thought* (Cambridge: Cambridge University Press, 2001), 15.

the Qur'anic understanding of divine legislation. It seems at least as likely that the evolution of Qur'anic inheritance law is an exceptional case responding to a particular need for greater specificity than initially supplied by Q. 2:180. If so, the case of inheritance law would not warrant the supposition that the governing ideal of Qur'anic legislation was to subject ever wider domains of human behaviour to a similar degree of precision. After all, there are quite a few occurrences of *maʿrūf* and *bi-l-maʿrūf* in Q. 4, too (see vv. 5, 6, 8, 19, 25, 114).

By way of a final observation, I should like to draw attention to Nora K. Schmid's recent argument that much of Medinan law is presented in a paraenetic fashion, and that this fact is explicitly articulated by the Qur'an itself, by means of the verb *waʿaẓa* and the related noun *mawʿiẓa*.[74] Schmid's article tallies with many of the features of Qur'anic legislation that have been noted throughout this chapter: not only with the recourse that some Qur'anic legal verse have open-ended ethical qualifiers like *bi-l-maʿrūf* but also with the eschatological horizon of Qur'anic legislation, often driven home by verse-final reminders, and with the claim that Qur'anic law is a behavioural concretisation of more fundamental values and virtues, laid down by a benevolent creator to whom humans owe gratitude. Divine legislation of the sort that the Qur'an portrays God as dispensing – i.e. legislation that appeals to the ethical intuitions of its audience and sometimes properly 'passes the buck' to them[75] – is quite naturally presented in exhortatory or paraenetic discourse, which builds on the existing needs and moral insights of its recipients and aims to shape and refine their internal dispositions. Thus, even the complex inheritance rules in Q. 4:11–12, arguably a peak of legal technicality in the Qur'an, are embedded in an immediate literary context (Q. 4:1–14) that has many paraenetic characteristics, beginning with a programmatic reminder of the descent of all humans from 'a single individual' (*min nafsin wāḥidatin*) and the consequent need to respect kinship ties (*al-arḥām*; Q. 4:1) and ending with a reminder of what is eschatologically at stake in adhering to the 'boundaries' (*ḥudūd*) that God has delineated (Q. 4:13–14). The paradigmatic significance of the literary register of what Schmid calls 'legal paraenesis' in the Qur'an is such that even the Mosaic tablets – surely the archetype of succinct and apodictic divine legislation in the biblical tradition – are in Q. 7:145 cast as paraenetic or hortatory discourse, as containing 'an admonition about everything and an expounding of everything' (*min kulli shay'in mawʿiẓatan wa-tafṣīlan li-kulli*

74 See Schmid, 'Exhortation'.

75 Cook, *Commanding Right*, 15: *maʿrūf* is 'the kind of ethical term that passes the buck to specific standards of behaviour already known and established'.

shay'in).[76] One may, therefore, discern a basic fit between the theology behind Qur'anic legislation, the literary form of Qur'anic legislation, and the Qur'an's own self-referential comments on divine legislation.

Bibliography

Ambros, Arne A., with Stephan Procházka. *A Concise Dictionary of Koranic Arabic.* Wiesbaden: Reichert, 2004.

Bauer, Karen, and Feras Hamza. *Women, Households, and the Hereafter in the Qur'an: A Patronage of Piety.* Oxford: Oxford University Press in association with the Institute of Ismaili Studies, 2023.

Christiansen, Johanne L. *The Exceptional Qur'ān: Flexible and Exceptive Rhetoric in Islam's Holy Book.* Piscataway: Gorgias Press, 2021.

Cook, Michael. *Commanding Right and Forbidding Wrong in Islamic Thought.* Cambridge: Cambridge University Press, 2001.

Coulson, Noel J. *A History of Islamic Law.* Edinburgh: Edinburgh University Press, 1964.

Decharneux, Julien. *Creation and Contemplation: The Cosmology of the Qur'ān and Its Late Antique Background.* Berlin: Walter de Gruyter, 2023.

Decharneux, Julien. 'The Natural Theology of the Qur'ān and Its Late Antique Christian Background: A Preliminary Outline'. In *The Study of Islamic Origins: New Perspectives and Contexts*, edited by Mette Bjerregaard Mortensen, Guillaume Dye, Isaac W. Oliver, and Tommaso Tesei, 177–99. Berlin: Walter de Gruyter, 2021.

Denny, Frederick M. 'The Meaning of *Ummah* in the Qur'ān'. *History of Religions* 15, no. 1 (1975): 34–70.

Hourani, George F. *Islamic Rationalism: The Ethics of ʿAbd al-Jabbār.* Oxford: Clarendon Press, 1971.

Hourani, George F. *Reason and Tradition in Islamic Ethics.* Cambridge: Cambridge University Press, 1985.

Hyde, Dominic, and Diana Raffman. 'Sorites Paradox'. *The Stanford Encyclopedia of Philosophy* (Summer 2018 edition), edited by Edward N. Zalta. https://plato.stanford.edu/archives/sum2018/entries/sorites-paradox/.

Loop, Jan. 'Islam and the European Enlightenment'. In *Christian–Muslim Relations: A Bibliographical History.* Vol. 13, *Western Europe (1700–1800)*, edited by David Thomas and John A. Chesworth, 16–34. Leiden: Brill, 2019.

76 Schmid, 'Exhortation', 335–41. My translation of the phrase cited is that given in Sinai, *Key Terms*, 558n2. At Q. 5:46, the term *mawʿiẓa* seems to be applied to the *injīl*; see the discussion in Schmid, 'Exhortation', 340–41.

Lowry, Joseph E. 'Exculpatory Language in the Qur'an: A Survey of Terms, Themes, and Theologies'. *Mélanges de l'Université Saint-Joseph* 66 (2015–16): 97–120.

Lowry, Joseph E. 'A Guide to the Legal Material in Sūrat al-Nisā''. In *Unlocking the Medinan Qur'an*, edited by Nicolai Sinai, 422–79. Leiden: Brill, 2022.

Lowry, Joseph E. 'Law, Structure, and Meaning in Sūrat al-Baqarah'. *Journal of the International Qur'anic Studies Association* 2, no. 1 (2017): 111–48.

Lowry, Joseph E. 'When Less Is More: Law and Commandment in *Sūrat al-Anʿām*'. *Journal of Qur'anic Studies* 9, no. 2 (2011): 22–42.

Madigan, Daniel. 'Themes and Topics'. In *The Cambridge Companion to the Qur'ān*, edited by Jane Dammen McAuliffe, 79–95. Cambridge: Cambridge University Press, 2006.

Rahbar, Daud. *God of Justice: A Study in the Ethical Doctrine of the Qur'ān*. Leiden: E.J. Brill, 1960.

Reinhart, A. Kevin. *Before Revelation: The Boundaries of Muslim Moral Thought*. Albany: State University of New York Press, 1995.

Reinhart, A. Kevin. 'What We Know about Maʿrūf'. *Journal of Islamic Ethics* 1 (2017): 51–82.

Schmid, Nora K. 'From Ethico-religious Exhortation to Legal Paraenesis: Functions of Qur'anic *Waʿẓ*'. *Islamic Law and Society* 28 (2021): 317–51.

al-Shāfiʿī. *The Epistle on Legal Theory*. Edited and translated by Joseph E. Lowry. New York: New York University Press, 2013.

Siddiqui, Sohaira Z.M. *Law and Politics under the Abbasids: An Intellectual Portrait of al-Juwaynī*. Cambridge: Cambridge University Press, 2019.

Sinai, Nicolai. *Key Terms of the Qur'an: A Critical Dictionary*. Princeton: Princeton University Press, 2023.

Sinai, Nicolai. *The Qur'an: A Historical-Critical Introduction*. Edinburgh: Edinburgh University Press, 2017.

Sinai, Nicolai. 'The Qur'ān's Dietary Tetralogue: A Diachronic Reconstruction'. *Jerusalem Studies in Arabic and Islam* 46 (2019): 113–46.

Sinai, Nicolai. 'Social Hierarchy and Inequality in the Qur'an'. Forthcoming.

Sinai, Nicolai. 'The Unknown Known: Some Groundwork for Interpreting the Medinan Qur'an'. *Mélanges de l'Université Saint-Joseph* 66 (2015–16): 47–96.

Sinai, Nicolai, ed. *Unlocking the Medinan Qur'an*. Leiden: Brill, 2022.

Sirry, Mun'im. *Scriptural Polemics: The Qur'ān and Other Religions*. Oxford: Oxford University Press, 2014.

Vasalou, Sophia. *Moral Agents and Their Deserts: The Character of Muʿtazilite Ethics*. Princeton: Princeton University Press, 2008.

Vishanoff, David R. *The Formation of Islamic Hermeneutics: How Sunni Legal Theorists Imagined a Revealed Law*. New Haven: American Oriental Society, 2011.

Weatherford, Roy C. 'Spontaneity and Indifference'. In *The Oxford Companion to Philosophy*, 2nd ed., edited by Tod Honderich. Oxford: Oxford University Press, 2005. www.oxfordreference.com.

Zafer, Hamza M. *Ecumenical Community: Language and Politics of the Ummah in the Qur'an*. Leiden: Brill, 2020.

Zellentin, Holger M. *The Qur'ān's Legal Culture: The Didascalia Apostolorum as a Point of Departure*. Tübingen: Mohr Siebeck, 2013.

CHAPTER 3

Qur'anic Morality as Qur'anic Law

Karen Bauer and Feras Hamza

This study addresses the question of how Qur'anic law is related to Qur'anic morality.[1] It was inspired by the common assumption that the Qur'an has a legal realm and a moral realm that goes beyond the merely legal. One problem with this assumption is that much of the Qur'an is taken up with commands of one sort or another, and in our view 'law' is not something easily separated from the whole body of Qur'anic commands. In other words, ought we not consider whether all commands by God constitute God's law in some sense? After all, every Qur'anic command sits within an overall moral soteriology in which right is distinguished from wrong. Ultimately, we argue that 'law', 'morality', and 'piety' cannot be considered as separate concepts in the Qur'anic frame of reference the way they might in other systems. Therefore, it is important to attend to the Qur'an's own framework of how right and wrong relate to what is licit or illicit, pious or impious, and it is important to attend to how the Qur'an relates these concepts to the aims of the scripture and of creation itself.

1 This chapter is an expansion of some points that we made initially in our book *Women, Households, and the Hereafter in the Qur'an: A Patronage of Piety* (Oxford: Oxford University Press in association with the Institute of Ismaili Studies, 2023); see especially 20–26, 35–36, 363–65. We would like to thank Mohsen Goudarzi for his thoughtful engagement with this piece; his comments improved it greatly. Any errors that remain are our own. Joseph E. Lowry has written much on Qur'anic law and we have benefitted immensely from his works, both those cited here and those not, from talks that he has given, and from our conversations with him. Holger Zellentin has also written much about the Qur'an's law and especially on its legal culture and continuities with biblical law; see Holger M. Zellentin, *The Qur'ān's Legal Culture: The Didascalia Apostolorum as a Point of Departure* (Tübingen: Mohr Siebeck, 2013); and Holger M. Zellentin, *Law beyond Israel: From the Bible to the Qur'an* (Oxford: Oxford University Press, 2022). In the latter work, he makes the important point that law is literature in these texts: 'Legal narratives, hence, are all those stories that inform the audience about the circumstances of the genesis and about the ongoing relevance of any specific set of laws, thereby establishing its validity and guiding its application ... It is this fusion [of "law" and "literature"] that necessitates our study of law *as* literature, which means that literary analysis is prerequisite to legal comprehension' (ibid., 5–6). We would also like to thank Holger Zellentin for his discussions with Karen Bauer over a number of years about the nature of Qur'anic law. As we came to the conclusion that it would be impossible to separate out 'law' from other Qur'anic commands, it was Zellentin who affirmed that he had already reached the same conclusion.

 | HTTPS://DOI.ORG/10.1163/9789004755567-005

This study concerns itself with attempting to uncover and elucidate aspects of that framework.

One underlying question concerns the nature of God's law as communal law. The Qur'an includes many rulings that regulate communal life, and it could be argued that the community of Qur'anic believers is defined by their adherence to this set of laws. When one takes into account how the Qur'an frames its own commands, it becomes clear that service to God, worship of Him, and hence affiliation with the community of believers consists partly in communal action and service to others, particularly manifested in feeding the needy, protecting the vulnerable, and being virtuous.[2] Yet, as Joseph Lowry notes, the Qur'an is not a 'law book', meaning a book of positive law that could be used to govern communal life.[3] Indeed, the Qur'an defines itself as God's guidance for the believers, and the ultimate framework for Qur'anic commands is that of belief and piety, because Qur'anic commands define what it is to be a believer (*mu'min*), to be godly (*muttaqī*), and to be virtuous (*muḥsin*); and to be these things entails an integration of one's thoughts, beliefs, and feelings with one's behaviour (see e.g. Q. 2:177). Framing this in terms of 'law', our argument is that the Qur'an's commands can be conceptualised as divine law. Yet this is not to imply that all of the Qur'an's statements or commands carry equal moral weight, or that all are equally binding. On the contrary: Qur'anic law, as a divine law, has clear moral gradations.

While the overall nature of Qur'anic commands has been debated, many scholars recognise that they have some moral elements, or that to obey these rules is to be pious. Some recognise that higher levels of moral action are often embedded within Qur'anic rulings.[4] This is commonly conceptualised as a

2 E.g. Fred Donner says, 'In short, the Believers' piety is a piety that is meant to function in, and to be a part of the world and of everyday life – not divorced from it in ascetic denial, as in the late antique Christian tradition.' Fred Donner, *Muhammad and the Believers at the Origins of Islam* (Cambridge, MA: Harvard University Press, 2012), 68; see also 80ff. More recently, see Mohsen Goudarzi, 'Worship (*Dīn*), Monotheism (*Islām*) and the Qur'ān's Cultic Decalogue', *Journal of the International Qur'anic Studies Association* 8, no. 1 (2023): 1–42.

3 Joseph E. Lowry, 'Reading the Qur'an as a Law Book: Legislation, Language, and Allusion in Islam's Scripture', in *Arabic Belles Lettres*, ed. Joseph E. Lowry and Shawkat M. Toorawa (Atlanta: Lockwood Press, 2019), 3–18. One of the key points that Lowry makes is that many of the passages in the Qur'an might have a different interpretation from that which was assigned to them by later jurists.

4 See e.g. Omaima Abou-Bakr and Mulki Al-Sharmani, 'Islamic Feminist *Tafsīr* and Qur'anic Ethics: Rereading Divorce Verses', in *Islamic Interpretive Tradition and Gender Justice: Processes of Canonization, Subversion, and Change*, ed. Nevin Reda and Yasmin Amin (Quebec: McGill-Queen's University Press, 2020), 23–66; Omaima Abou-Bakr, Asma Lamrabet, and Mulki Al-Sharmani, 'Qur'anic Ethics of Marriage', in *Justice and Beauty in Muslim Marriage:*

division between the strictly legal and the ethical: there is a minimum required action (the 'law', or what might be considered 'positive law'), and a higher level of moral action that might constitute adherence to divine wisdom or ethics. Yet it is not clear to us that higher levels of moral action are ultimately only ethical but *not* 'legal': shouldn't it be the higher levels of ethical action that are considered binding? Crucially, the Qur'an specifies that some of its commands are better than others: those who possess true understanding 'listen to the word and follow the best of it' (Q. 39:18). In effect, Qur'anic commands are morally graded, but not morally relative: there is a clear divide between right and wrong, but beyond that basic division, some actions are more correct or more incorrect than others, and this can be determined by circumstance. By attaining a higher standard of moral action, one can become *more law-abiding*, a concept that only makes sense in a salvific worldview, and which is expressed in the Qur'an as ever-increasing states of moral purity, greater levels of belief, and therefore higher degrees in the afterlife (e.g. in Q. 17:21). Fulfilling the minimum is not a virtuous aspiration. Rather, ever-increasing adherence to the fuller possibilities of these laws, and hence to greater moral purity, should be the aspiration.

The focus on moral purity and salvation means that, although the Qur'an includes regulations for the community, it is not a law that could ever be enforced fully in the community: the ultimate judge is God, and the Qur'an states repeatedly that His judgement will be enforced in the afterlife. In some legal systems, a person could be law-abiding and remain morally bankrupt; but in the Qur'an, moral bankruptcy is ultimately incompatible with law-abidingness. In Qur'anic terms, there is no categorical separation between the 'letter of the law' and the 'spirit of the law', for a moral *telos* underlies both. Because the 'law' has a moral meaning, to follow the law in the truest sense is to strive for moral excellence.

The reason that communal law, morality, piety, and salvation are inherently interconnected in the Qur'an is that the Qur'an conceptualises the life of this world as a moral test. People must attempt to discipline their actions, thoughts, and feelings: Qur'anic commands are intended to instil moral behaviour that will help humans pass that test and be saved at the Final Judgement. Some of the Qur'an's moral precepts are communicated through laws or rules that are anchored in the immediate social environment of the Qur'an's initial community, and within the very social structures of its seventh-century Arabian

---

Towards Egalitarian Ethics and Laws, ed. Ziba Mir-Hosseini, Mulki Al-Sharmani, Jana Rumminger, and Sarah Marsso (London: Oneworld Academic, 2022), 21–56; and Ramon Harvey, *The Qur'an and the Just Society* (Edinburgh: Edinburgh University Press, 2018).

milieu: male-headed households and patronage. Without a moral or legal framework, these social structures put the vulnerable at a structural disadvantage, because in patronage societies, the strong have the structural power to exploit the weak: patronage and protection come with strings attached. When the Qur'an addresses households and patronage as a part of the salvific frame, it has the effect of protecting the vulnerable from that structural disadvantage. A large part of the Qur'an's morality involves mitigating possible abuses of power; but to be among those who are truly godly requires a higher standard of doing good and foregoing immediate self-interests for the greater good. In the Qur'anic vision, believers adopt God as their ultimate patron, and a moral system of patronage facilitates acts of piety, which will be recompensed by God, rather than acts in which the patron might come to expect favours from his protégé. The vulnerable, in turn, have opportunities to exercise their piety both externally, through virtuous acts, and internally, through virtuous orientation. The fundamental message that the Qur'an imparts is that, despite living in a hierarchical society, all humans (male or female, free or slave) have equal moral agency and an equal opportunity to be saved. Social class and power have no bearing on one's spiritual status, which is earned by piety alone; in fact, according to the Qur'an those who are at a structural advantage – the elites – are often the worst offenders, morally speaking, and hence those who hold themselves exalted in this life will end up debased in the afterlife (e.g. Q. 6:124). Thus, the elision of what might, today, be called 'law' and 'morality' in the Qur'an relates directly to its hierarchical social milieu and to its ultimately egalitarian salvific message.

The Qur'anic response to its social circumstances has important consequences for how we might conceptualise Qur'anic law. One is that, occasionally, the Qur'an permits morally dubious or inferior actions in order to prevent a worse harm. It also presents a better course of action that we conceptualise as a fuller fulfilment of the law, rather than, as is common, conceptualising this as an ethical action that goes beyond the mere legal. In our view, the morally inferior action, even though it is permitted, is not a complete fulfilment of the law. This is partly because individuals become saved not solely by preventing themselves from wrongdoing, but rather also by undertaking righteous actions, and partly because the Qur'an presents its guidance as a 'straight path'. Another result of the Qur'an's pragmatism is that some Qur'anic commands are imposed for specific circumstances. In the Medinan period, the focus on protecting the vulnerable becomes intertwined with rulings that pertain to the protection of the believing community in a time of communal strife and battle. These passages have been commonly conceptualised, both in Islamic tradition and in Western scholarship, as being a development of the law. Yet we see no reason to adopt the linear, 'abrogating' model. Rather, some Qur'anic commands can be considered as contextually driven and responsive to circumstances, akin to certain secular laws that are imposed in times of national emergency (such as temporary laws imposed during war or the coronavirus pandemic).

While we cannot, due to limitations of space, fully address the complex question of the nature of Qur'anic law, the remainder of this chapter will explain these points in more detail. To summarise, the chapter makes three major arguments: (1) all Qur'anic commands can be conceptualised as divine law, which includes but is not limited to aspects of positive law. (2) However, not all commands are equally binding. Rather, Qur'anic commands are morally graded, and are often focused on preventing harm. Because of this, the Qur'an sometimes permits inferior actions to prevent a worse harm; but a higher moral choice is always available, which can be conceptualised as a fuller fulfilment of the law. (3) Some Qur'anic commands respond to current circumstances, but this does not necessarily equate with a linear development of the law in which prior commands are abrogated: it may indicate that some Qur'anic law is inherently flexible and responsive, and some is particular or circumstantial.

1 The Cultural Context: The Qur'an and Late Antique Perspectives on Divine Law

The nature of divine law was heavily debated in antiquity and late antiquity. While this is hardly the place to analyse these debates or the Qur'anic position in this discourse, it is worth noting that such debates may have influenced the Qur'an's approach to issues such as divine law, natural law, the nature of truth and rationality, and communal morality. In this section, we provide a very brief overview of these prior conceptions of divine law and address aspects of the Qur'an's position on rationality and the law.[5]

In her book *What's Divine about Divine Law? Early Perspectives* Christine Hayes describes the two major systems of thought about divine law in the ancient world. In the classical philosophical system, divine law was not a written scripture but rather a universal rational truth. In the stoics' view, 'God was nature; nature was divine. Therefore, the rational order or eternal reason

5 Saqib Hussain has drawn attention to the importance of antique theories of divine law and wisdom for the Qur'an, and he summarises the way concepts of natural law and natural morality changed over time in much more detail than we do here. See Saqib Hussain, 'Wisdom in the Qur'an' (PhD diss., University of Oxford, 2022), especially 56–58.

(*logos*) of nature is none other than the eternal reason of God.' Law, rather than being a written code, 'is reason itself'.[6] Humans are naturally aware of this law, and wise people will naturally obey it. For Plato, a code of positive law was unnecessary: good education would teach virtuous men what they should do, and the unvirtuous would not obey written law in any case.[7] The Hebrew Bible presents several different approaches to the question of whether divine law confirms natural law, or whether its decrees 'have no basis in nature'. Some elements of the scripture support an argument that the divinity of the law is located in the will of the Lawgiver: it is divine because it comes from God, rather than because it confirms a rational truth. Other texts support the view that God's law is rational and universal and that it is 'a path to wisdom'.[8]

From these initial premises about the nature of law, ancient Jewish thinkers adopted one of two major trajectories: Philo identified Mosaic law with natural law, and sought to reconcile the attributes of universality, rationality, and truth with the biblical law, whereas Paul 'represents the Mosaic Law as particular, temporary, nonrational, and not conducive to virtue.'[9] In the former view, the authority of the law lies, at least in part, in its rationality, whereas in the latter, the law's authority resides in the authority of the Lawgiver. It seems that the latter view became more prevalent. For some rabbis, the law was arbitrary and irrational, particularly in its dietary and purity requirements, and this was the very thing that showed its divinity.[10] Others applied moral reasoning to biblical law, arguing that it was particular and could change over time, thus assuming characteristics about divine law that the Greeks and Romans assumed only about human-made positive law. For these rabbis, 'the divine law's perfection is not diminished but *constituted* by the fact that it is particular, flexible, and responsive'.[11] It was the idea of divine law as irrational and temporal, put forth particularly by Paul, that laid the basis for Christian modification and rejection of some laws from the Hebrew Bible. It is important to note that not only were ideas about divine law heavily contested by both Jews and Christians, but these ideas also changed over time.

Such debates existed long before the Qur'an's emergence in seventh-century Arabia; but they are plausibly part of the cultural context of the Qur'an.[12] The

---

6 Christine Hayes, *What's Divine about Divine Law? Early Perspectives* (Princeton: Princeton University Press, 2015), 55–57.

7 Ibid., 64–65.

8 Ibid., 14–29.

9 Ibid., 3.

10 Ibid., 286.

11 Ibid., 326.

12 Stephen Shoemaker questions the extent of the Christian influence in Mecca. See Stephen J. Shoemaker, *Creating the Qur'an: A Historical-Critical Study* (Oakland: University of

Qur'an has its own approach to the relationship between nature and scripture, that is, between human rationality and divine will. It presents God's will as present both in creation and in the Qur'an itself: divine law is a natural law as well as a revealed law, and it is ultimately rational, even if the rationale may not always be immediately accessible to humans. It has elements that are eternal and elements that are particular. As noted above, in the Qur'anic view, God created the world as a moral test, the purpose of which is to see who deserves to be saved and who deserves to be damned in the afterlife. God created in humans the faculties of hearing, sight, and thought, precisely so that they might reflect and attain understanding (Q. 76:2), and He created many natural phenomena in the world as signs for people given to reflection (Q. 30:8 *et passim*). Thus, the signs of God's presence are apparent if one uses one's faculties correctly: all humans have an innate ability to recognise God (Q. 7:172–74, 91:8) and to devote (*aslama*, root: *s-l-m*) themselves to Him (Q. 3:83).

The explicit references to humans' ability to understand and reflect, and indeed the insistence that this is why they have been given those faculties, means that God has created people with innate rationality together with moral agency: the ability to recognise right and wrong and to act accordingly. Moreover, although the world was created according to God's will, it may frequently not seem fair, but the Qur'an explains any apparent unfairness by telling people that they will be tested with both the good and the bad that comes to them (Q. 21:35), that people are tests for one another (Q. 25:20), and that nobody can claim to be a believer without expecting to be tested (Q. 29:2). This message is repeated in the Qur'an many times, and it is also clear from the stories it tells; notable in this regard are the stories in Sūrat al-Kahf (Q. 18). The unfolding of the worldly test comes in the afterlife, when all worldly hierarchies based on wealth, status, and power are replaced with a hierarchy based on piety alone (Q. 49:13). At the Final Judgement God weighs and measures humans' deeds, and they are recompensed according to 'the best of what they used to do' (Q. 16:97). Thus, while the world might seem arbitrary and perhaps unjust, all events have a rational purpose, even if that purpose is known only to God.

California Press, 2022). His position has been convincingly refuted by Nicolai Sinai, 'The Christian Elephant in the Meccan Room: Dye, Tesei, and Shoemaker on the Date of the Qur'ān', *Journal of the International Qur'anic Studies Association* (2024): 1–62, https://doi.org/10.1515/jiqsa-2023-0013; Holger M. Zellentin, '*banū isrā'īl, ahl al-kitāb, al-yahūd wa-l-naṣārā*: The Qur'anic Community's Encounters with Jews and Christians', *Entangled Religions* 13, no. 2 (2023): https://doi.org/10.46586/er.13.2023.10991; and Ilkka Lindstedt, *Muhammad and His Followers in Context: The Religious Map of Late Antique Arabia* (Leiden: Brill, 2023).

In this scheme, the Qur'an itself has been revealed as a path of divine moral guidance, with a focus on encouraging people to do good and to be virtuous. In some senses, the Qur'an resembles one stream of ancient discourse in which law is conceived of as education, which is inculcated through persuasion, including exhortation, praise, and blame, with the ultimate aim of subjugating the irrational parts of the soul to the rational part.[13] Accordingly, the Qur'an lays out a system in which the soul, which is prone to greed and wrongdoing, must be exhorted (*waʿẓ*) to avoid blameworthy action (*junāḥ*) or sin (*ithm*). Thus, the Qur'an could be conceived of as a text with a message of disciplining the soul, for it is only through this self-discipline that one can attain salvation. The Qur'an's commands imply that God is able to make a fair judgement on Judgement Day, for people will have been given every opportunity to follow the 'straight path', which is, in the Qur'anic conception, a path of moral good that can be confirmed when one's thoughts, feelings, and perceptions have been properly disciplined to comprehend God's truth, which is in turn manifested in righteous action and behaviour.

In our view, the Qur'an presents all matters as morally charged, even those that, in other systems, might be considered to reside solely in the will of the Lawgiver such as dietary laws. That is because, in the Qur'anic worldview, to follow God is to adopt the patronage of good, whereas to follow Satan is to adopt the patronage of evil, and all of one's actions are considered a choice to follow one of these two patronages. Although people can choose either God or Satan as a patron (sc. Q. 2:257, 4:75–76), only God's patronage will avail them, for the path of good, light, and wholesomeness is not equal to the path of evil, which is the path of Satan, darkness, and damnation. The Qur'an repeatedly stresses that proper belief entails an understanding of the Final Judgement and bodily resurrection, when the patronages of God and Satan become embodied as actual places in which people reside in a state of bliss or suffering, though at that final moment Satan and all other false gods will desert the people who worshipped them and the damned will be left without a protector or patron because God is the only true patron (Q. 4:119–21). According to the Qur'an, it is God's judgement that will prevail over all false systems of belief, false standards of morality, and false deities (Q. 8:7–8). Ultimately, in the Qur'an's salvific moral worldview, there are standards, God is the ultimate judge, humans' choices have moral value and concrete consequences, and these choices involve internal dispositions and emotional orientations as well as righteous action.

---

13 Hayes, *Divine Law*, 64–65.

2 Qur'anic Ethics as Law

How do the concepts of the 'licit' and the 'illicit' fit into this overall moral scheme of self-discipline? To begin to answer this, we first note that not only were there multiple conceptions of law in the Qur'an's late antique milieu, but also that Qur'anic guidance is not necessarily 'law' or 'morality' as a modern, secular, audience might conceive it; this, as we shall show, has important consequences for the relationship between the 'moral' and the 'legal'. Joseph Lowry complicates how 'law' might be conceptualised in the Qur'an. He shows, for instance, that much Qur'anic legislation is imprecise: one knows one must pray, but the way this is described might refer either to praying precisely at morning, at midday, at sunset, and in the night, or to a general attitude of remembering God morning, noon, and night.[14] Importantly, he points out that the Qur'an as a whole 'adds up to a moral trajectory for the world' and that the Final Judgement is 'the master narrative against which Qur'anic legislation unfolds'.[15] Lowry proceeds from the position that there is material that can be identified as 'law' in the Qur'an, which he defines as 'binding rules meant to be adhered to by the Qur'anic community'. Yet he notes that identifying such rules is a 'serious philosophical problem'.[16] As noted above, we conceive of Qur'anic law as precepts that define what it is to be a 'believer'. The following paragraphs offer some of our own observations on the nature of the Qur'an's binding rules for the community and how these might differ from other legal systems.

2.1 Moral and Legal Language

One difference between the Qur'anic and other legal systems, such as modern secular ones, is that in other legal systems, one might determine one's own standards for living an ethical or an unethical life: there are no ultimate consequences and no ultimate standard or judge beyond the individual self. But in the Qur'an, there is an absolute standard of right and wrong, and an unequivocal judge of that standard. Some things, such as gambling and wine, can cause both benefit and harm, although only avoiding both of these things results in spiritual augmentation (Q. 2:219, 5:90–93). Such subtleties should not obscure the fact that there is a clear moral divide between several key binaries in the Qur'an: good (*khayr*) and evil (*sū'*, *sharr*), light (*nūr*) and darkness (*ẓulumāt*),

14 Lowry, 'Reading the Qur'an as a Law Book', 14–17.
15 Ibid., 8.
16 Ibid., 17.

true guidance (*hudā*) and error (*ḍalāl, ghayy*), truth (*ḥaqq*) and falsehood (*bāṭil*), what is wholesome (*ṭayyib*) and what is vile (*khabīth*).

In a secular legal system, a graver crime is recompensed with a graver punishment, and this is also true in the Qur'an. There is a clear standard of avoiding wrong in the language of boundaries (*ḥudūd*), licit acts (*ḥill, ḥalāl*), and transgression (*iʿtidāʾ*); these terms often relate to the specific social circumstances of seventh-century Arabia and the necessity to protect the vulnerable. Eleven of the twelve instances of 'God's bounds' (*ḥudūd*) in the Qur'an are used in verses where women are mentioned, and the focus is particularly on requiring men to treat women decently, to protect women's property, and not to take advantage of them. The term 'licit' (*ḥalāl*) is often used to separate out the food that may be eaten by the Qur'anic community of believers, a point by which this community is distinguished from others. However, this term is also used in several verses to indicate suitable behaviour towards women, and in the latter case there is a focus on protecting women's property (Q. 2:229, 2:230) and ensuring their ability to live as licit sexual partners in believing households (Q. 4:24, 60:10). Q. 5:5 uses the term 'licit' (*ḥill*) to refer both to food that is licit to eat and to women who are licit in marriage.

Yet language that might be considered 'legal' is bound up with concepts that might be considered 'moral', and this can be gleaned from verses such as Q. 2:230–31, which protect women's rights in divorce:

> And if he divorces her, she will not be licit for him until she marries a husband other than him, and if that husband divorces her, there is no sin upon the couple if they should remarry, if they think that they can maintain God's bounds. These are God's bounds, which He clarifies for a people who have knowledge. When you divorce women and they complete their term, then either retain them decently or release them decently, and do not retain them injuriously so that you might transgress; whoever does that certainly wrongs himself. Do not make a mockery of God's signs, and remember God's blessing upon you and what He has sent down to you of the Book and of wisdom, with which to admonish you. Be wary of God and know that God has knowledge of all things.

These verses include terms that might be considered legal and others that might be considered moral: 'licit' (*ḥalāl*), 'God's bounds' (*ḥudūd Allāh*), 'decently' (*bi-l-maʿrūf*), 'harm' (*ḍirār*), 'transgression' (*iʿtidāʾ*), 'wronging the self' (*ẓulm al-nafs*), making a 'mockery of God's signs' (*istihzāʾ*); and these verses stress the importance of remembering the 'Book' (*kitāb*) and 'wisdom' (*ḥikma*). The overarching message is that men who seek to harm their ex-wives through maltreatment and by preventing those ex-wives from remarrying are transgressing

God's bounds and making a mockery of God's signs, ultimately only harming their own souls in the afterlife, whereas men who remember the Book and wisdom treat their ex-wives decently and let them go freely, with a good provision. We shall return to these verses later; the important point to be made here is that explicitly legal language is mixed with terms such as 'decency' that might seem to be moral, rather than legal. Nevertheless, it is 'decency' that constitutes obedience to the Book and wisdom, and therefore it is 'decency' that signals compliance with Qur'anic law. The law *requires* a standard of decency in the case of divorce.[17]

The command to treat women decently establishes a clear differentiation from a secular system; for in secular law, avoiding crime is good enough: by avoiding crime, one abides by the law. In the Qur'an, the avoidance of sin and wrongdoing is not enough to be law-abiding in the fullest sense of divine law (as we understand it), because the rules regulate virtuous, as well as unvirtuous, behaviour, and it is virtuous behaviour that earns salvation. As noted earlier, higher levels of virtuous behaviour are recompensed with a higher reward (Q. 17:21). Following Qur'anic commands is not only a matter of avoiding transgression, but also of being good and doing good, which leads to ever-higher levels of moral purity (Q. 33:33). Therefore, unlike a legal code, Qur'anic rulings are not static: expectations change according to one's capacity and according to the circumstances in which believers and the whole community find themselves. One consequence is that, on the path of law-abidingness, one can be ever-more law-abiding, which in Qur'anic terms is expressed as the possibility of ever-increasing moral purity. Moreover, the focus is not only on what one ought, or ought not, to do; it is also on how to do it, how to feel, how to think, and how to train the senses to promote higher levels of moral understanding and action. Internal orientation and external action are related, and it is to this point that we now turn.

2.2 Internal Orientation and External Action

Many Qur'anic passages indicate that external action alone is not enough to be following its guidance: one must have the correct internal orientation.[18] The

17 On the ethical terms in divorce verses, see especially Abou-Bakr and Al-Sharmani, 'Islamic Feminist *Tafsīr* and Qur'anic Ethics'.

18 Lowry has also offered a simple way of categorising what might be considered as 'Qur'anic Law' for the purposes of understanding how law might act as a structuring force in Qur'anic suras: 'Legislative passages impose obligations on the qur'ānic audience to engage in specific, repeatable physical (i.e., not purely mental) conduct.' Joseph E. Lowry, 'Law, Structure, and Meaning in Surat al-Baqarah (Q. 2)', *Journal of the International*

danger of taking the Qur'an's commands as a mere set of rules is expressed in Q. 2:177, with its statement regarding the nature of Qur'anic piety, which occurs shortly after the believers are commanded to pray towards Mecca rather than Jerusalem:

> Piety (*birr*) is not that you turn your faces to the east or the west. Rather, piety is [that of] those who believe in God and the last day, and the angels, the Book, and the prophets, those who give wealth despite their love of it, to kin, orphans, the wretched (*masākīn*), the traveller, and the beggar, and to free slaves, and those who maintain the prayer and give the alms (*zakāt*), and who fulfil their covenants, and those who endure in stress and distress and in the heat of battle. Those are the ones who confirm [the truth], and it is those who are the Godwary (*muttaqūn*).

This command, first and foremost, shows that the performance of certain rituals is not enough to be constituted as a believer in the Qur'anic moral worldview: to be a pious believer (*muʾmin, muttaqī*) entails not just belief in God, prayer, and fasting; it also entails giving of one's wealth (*zakāt, nafaqa*) and a certain standard of moral conduct, particularly in one's treatment of others. This verse also shows that to be pious requires emotional discipline: one must control one's love of wealth to give charitably. This raises the question of how the Qur'an seeks to regulate the relationship between external acts and internal orientations. Many other passages indicate that emotional control is treated as an aspect of pious behaviour: in addition to the basic emotional comportment of fear of God and humility towards Him, it is also important to exercise emotional discipline towards others, as in Q. 3:133–34, where those who are saved not only spend charitably, they also restrain their rage and excuse people for their faults.[19] One cannot truly be Godwary without the combination of ritual action, social action, correct belief, and emotional control. What this means is that external actions can be rendered meaningless without the proper internal orientation, and internal orientations can be rendered meaningless without the proper action: it is the internal orientation that drives the call to action.

Qur'anic Studies Association 2, no. 1 (2017): 118. It was, in part, this simplified definition that pushed us to consider the place of the internal orientations that are intrinsic to being a believer.

19 'Hasten towards your Lord's forgiveness and a Garden as vast as the heavens and the earth, prepared for the Godwary: those who spend [charitably] in ease and adversity, restrain their rage, and excuse people, for God loves the virtuous' (Q. 3:133–34).

The importance of integrating internal orientations with external action, and with actions that could not possibly be judged by human interlocutors, is reflected in the wide semantic range of terms like Godwariness (*taqwā*), piety (*birr*), virtue (*iḥsān*), decency (*maʿrūf*), faith (*dīn*), and belief (*īmān*, root: *a-m-n*). Other scholars have noted the difficulty of comprehending these terms in English: Mohsen Goudarzi argues that the term '*dīn*' should not be translated as 'religion' or 'faith'. He notes that 'religion' is an imprecise term that might have implications to a modern audience that *dīn* does not have: *dīn* is a matter of both belief and action, predicated on one's idea of the divinity (who is worthy of being worshipped and served) and manifested in one's actions, both in the personal and communal realms; he suggests 'worship' as a better way of conveying this meaning.[20] Goudarzi's point is strengthened by the overlap in the actions performed by people who are described, variously, as the believers (*muʾminūn*), the virtuous (*muḥsinūn*), and the Godwary (*muttaqūn*): all of these terms are used to indicate what people should do to perform proper service to God, which is the reason He created them, according to Q. 51:56–58:

> I did not create the jinn and humankind except that they might serve Me; I desire no provision from them, nor do I desire that they should feed Me. Verily, it is God who is the provider, the powerful, and the strong.

These verses connect service to God with provision and feeding; but they specify that God is not the one who needs those provisions or food, for He is the provider. This language plays on patronage systems that were common in late antiquity: in the role of patron, God provides for humans. In the Qur'anic reformulation of patronage, God needs no reciprocity from humans except that they serve Him.

It was common in antiquity and late antiquity to imagine God as a master and humans as the servants. Devin Stewart points out that the use of the term 'house' (*bayt*) to indicate God's own house, or temple, 'obviously originates in an analogy between a human master's house and the house of a god ... Like the owner of a mundane estate, he or she has servants who run the household, clean the rooms, tend the grounds, prepare and serve meals, and entertain, pamper, and flatter their master or mistress.'[21] As Goudarzi notes, 'After all, the Qurʾān describes humans as slaves or servants of God (*ʿibād*, e.g., Q2:207),

---

20 Goudarzi, 'Worship', especially 4–12.

21 Devin Stewart, 'Noah's Boat and Other Missed Opportunities (2019 IQSA Presidential Address)', *Journal of the International Qur'anic Studies Association* 6, no. 1 (2021): 30.

who is in turn King and possesses all things, including humans (e.g., Q2:107, 116, 20:114, 114:2). The latter therefore owe Him service, undertaken through rituals of worship and, more generally, through a pious life lived in accordance with God's wishes and commandments.'[22] But what does this service mean, in Qur'anic terms? There is a case to be made that such service is undertaken through one's actions to others, particularly charitable giving and feeding the poor, and that in this case ritual and charity become one and the same action.

According to Sūrat al-Insān (Q. 76) and other suras, believers feed the needy not for any hope of recompense from the needy themselves, but solely for the sake of God (Q. 76:9); in Sūrat Yāsīn (Q. 36), the unbelievers attempt to dissuade believers' charity by saying that if God had wanted, He would have fed the needy Himself (Q. 36:47). Thus, Qur'anic acts of charity are related directly to the Qur'anic overturning of worldly patronage systems: one serves God by serving other people, one offers one's charity to Him by giving it to the poor and the needy. Goudarzi has emphasised that animal sacrifice was an important part of Qur'anic cultic ritual practices. Animal meat was not licit unless God's name was pronounced over it, this being a crucial and visible element of the believers' monotheistic practices as against pagan practices.[23] The scenario that we are now able to imagine is one in which believers routinely sacrifice animals in the name of God at His house (*bayt*), particularly as a part of the pilgrimage rites or maybe as a part of the Friday communal prayer,[24] and perhaps such sacrifices also take place in people's own houses (also *bayt*). However, the meat is not left as though God could consume it. Rather, it is eaten by the believers and distributed to the poor and the needy as a service to Him (Q. 22:36–37). The ritual act becomes an act of charity, which shows how service to God (or worship of Him) is frequently accomplished through service to others.

2.3 Qur'anic Law as Morally Graded

The perspective taken here, that the law itself is graded ethically rather than separable into an 'ethical' and a 'legal' realm or the 'spirit of the law' and the 'letter of the law', runs contrary to most scholars' view. However, before delving into this issue, it is important to note that some scholars of Qur'anic ethics have already pointed out the possibility of ever-increasing

22 Goudarzi, 'Worship', 36.

23 Ibid., 24–33.

24 We owe this observation, connecting the Friday prayer with feasting and sacrifice, to Mohsen Goudarzi.

moral goodness: Amira Abou-Taleb shows that the term '*iḥsān*' (moral beauty or virtue) involves going beyond mere fairness, and argues that this higher level of moral beauty is central to different types of discourse in the Qur'an, such as personal relationships, communal strife, and other matters.[25] The possibility of ever-increasing moral action that the 'straight path', as prescribed by the Qur'an, entails is a dynamic individual relationship with God's ordinances since these pertain to matters of ritual, behaviour, action, and internal orientation. A person's ability always to do better is a sign of an ever-greater capacity to comprehend God's laws and thus to consummate these in a fuller way. Therefore, although the Qur'an defines certain behaviours as transgressive, and indeed specifies communal punishment for some transgressions, the focus is not on what believers can 'get away with' to avoid punishment. Rather, to follow the Qur'an's moral path is to focus on the possibility of ever-higher levels of ethical action. It is these higher levels of action that will ensure a greater reward in the afterlife. This brings us to the question of whether, while obeying the law, one can commit a moral wrong.

The most common approach to the Qur'an's morality and its legality is that there is a 'letter of the law', and that morality goes beyond this. This approach is epitomised by Fazlur Rahman. In his influential book *Major Themes of the Qur'an*, Rahman states that it is essential to draw a distinction between 'legal enactments and moral injunctions',[26] which enables him to propose that the modern believer can apply the ethical precept that underlies the law, without necessarily adhering to the letter of the law. He gives the examples of polygamy and slavery: the Qur'an permits a man to marry up to four women in Q. 4:3, but also says that men should marry only one if they fear they will not be equitable among their wives. Thus, Rahman says, the letter of the law is that men can marry four, but only because it was not possible for the Qur'an to do away with this institution entirely 'at one stroke'. The 'moral ideal towards which the society was expected to move' is the abolition of polygamy. Similarly, since freeing a slave is a moral good and counts as an expiation from sin, the abolition of slavery entirely is a moral ideal for the society. He summarises his view as follows:

> That appears to have been the usual procedure in the Qur'ānic legislation. Generally speaking, each legal or quasi-legal pronouncement is accompanied by

25 Amira Naim Abou-Taleb, 'The Concept of *Iḥsān* (Beauty/Goodness) in the Qur'ānic Moral Worldview' (PhD diss., University of Helsinki, 2023).

26 Fazlur Rahman, *Major Themes of the Qur'an* (Chicago: University of Chicago Press, 2009; originally published in 1980 by Bibliotheca Islamica), 47. Holger Zellentin also makes the point that purity is graded in the Qur'an. See Zellentin, *Law beyond Israel*.

> a *ratio legis* explaining why a law is being enunciated. To understand a *ratio legis* fully, an understanding of the sociohistorical background (what the Qur'ānic commentators call 'occasions of revelation') is necessary. The *ratio legis* is the essence of the matter, the actual legislation being its embodiment so long as it faithfully and correctly realizes the *ratio*; if it does not, the law has to be changed. When the situation so changes that the law fails to reflect the *ratio*, the law must change. Traditional lawyers, however, while recognizing the *ratio legis*, generally stuck to the letter of the law and enunciated the principle that 'Although a law is occasioned by a specific situation, its application nevertheless becomes universal'.[27]

Rahman's contribution is significant, in part, because he recognises that the Qur'an is a pragmatic text which responded to its own society. Moreover, he recognises that there are levels of Qur'anic command, and that what was permitted was not always the ideal. To explain these different possible levels of action, Rahman distinguishes between the rationale behind the law and the 'law itself'; he argues that traditional Muslim jurisprudents recognised this distinction but followed the 'letter of the law'. This approach is intuitive if one accepts that there is a distinction between the 'legal' and the 'moral' in the Qur'anic text, perhaps because 'law' is that which is meant to be enforced in the worldly realm: in that case, one can adhere to 'the law' while recognising that a more moral course of action remains a desideratum. However, we believe that in the Qur'an, the *law itself* is morally graded: sometimes something is permitted because it prevents worse harm; but to satisfy the law more fully, one will take the better option. By fulfilling a higher moral purpose, the believer is fulfilling more of God's law, as God's purpose for humankind.

We agree with the way Rahman distinguishes between the moral precept behind the law and the 'letter of the law', and yet would add two caveats that we shall seek to demonstrate in the following pages: (1) the Qur'an itself does not make an overt distinction between the 'legal' and the 'moral', and (2) it is problematic to imply that the 'letter of the law' is represented only by the lowest possible standard of behaviour, when actually in Qur'anic terms the 'letter of the law' seems also to include the higher standards of behaviour.

The distinction between levels of moral behaviour within the law is apparent when one takes a close look at several issues. In some of these cases, such as charitable giving, there is a moral minimum and a higher standard of

27 Rahman, *Major Themes of the Qur'an*, 48. Note that some of the 'occasions of revelation' literature was produced to justify existing law and may have had nothing to do with the actual occasion on which particular verses were revealed.

behaviour, and in others, morally inadequate behaviour is permitted solely to prevent a worse harm. In this regard, it is important to note that the Qur'an itself acknowledges that its commands offer different levels of moral behaviour. The Qur'an says that people should follow the best of what has been sent down (Q. 7:145, 39:55), which shows that there is a clear hierarchy of behaviour even within what is permissible. This does not mean, however, that one can use the law for immoral ends. Rather, it is an acknowledgement that higher levels of ethical behaviour are always possible within the basic minimum of morality set by a given law, and that God is concerned with humans' moral progress along that scale. Such distinctions become clearer with a close reading of certain legislative verses, taking into account the social structures that were taken for granted in seventh-century Arabia. An obvious example of a higher path of forgiveness embedded in a ruling is the ruling on *qiṣāṣ* in Q. 2:178–79.[28] In the following paragraphs we will focus on three cases: one that has been understood as being ethically problematic (a husband's striking his wife); and two that have been used to argue for an approach that there is a 'letter of the law' and a moral sphere that goes beyond this (polygamy and divorce).

In the late antique social milieu, marriage was considered an institution that protected women; unmarried women would not have lived alone, they would have lived in the household of a male relative or patron. Moreover, a marriage was not solely a personal alliance; it was an alliance of households and hence lineages. This explains many of the verses that might otherwise be incomprehensible today, and it also, in part, explains the Qur'anic resistance to divorce. One obvious example of an ethically problematic verse is Q. 4:34, where a husband is permitted to strike his wife to avoid a worse option: her *nushūz*. *Nushūz*, in that social setting, must have been a morally worse option than hitting: desertion or rising up against the marriage, with all that implies about possible alternate liaisons that the wife may have wished to pursue. Rather than allowing the couple to separate, arbitrators from the spouses' respective birth households should come together and negotiate a way forward (Q. 4:35). This highlights that the bond between the couple was considered in fact to be a bond between families who were then to negotiate a reconciliation among themselves. In the case of the husband's *nushūz* (Q. 4:128), the couple are told that there is no sin if they reconcile, and the husband is warned against turning away from his wife and treating her unfairly. All of this presumes that *nushūz* is in some way a desertion of the marital bond, though it cannot have been adultery that was so blatant that it could be witnessed by four people (on which see Q. 24:2–10). Q. 4:34, then, presents a morally inferior action in order

28 On this verse, see Bauer and Hamza, *Women*, 228, 268, 284, 382.

to prevent what, in that society, was a greater harm: the rupture of the marital bond and the potential breakdown of the social ties – and hence communal cohesion – that came with it.[29]

The permission for a 'less bad' option is also clear in Q. 4:3, on polygamy, which Rahman uses as his example of an instance of a moral option going beyond the 'letter of the law'.[30] Here is the verse in its context:

> Give the orphans what belongs to them, exchanging not what is wholesome for what is vile, and do not consume what belongs to them with what is yours, for that is a dreadful sin. And if you fear that you will not be just (*qisṭ*) towards the orphans, then marry the women as you see fit, two, three, or four. But if you fear that you will not be equitable (*taʿdilū*), then just one or what your right hand owns, lest you become unable to provide for them. Give the women their bridal payment as a gift, so if they themselves give you any good from it, then consume it beneficially and wholesomely.

From a modern perspective, one might imagine that these verses, which are in the plural form and speak about the treatment of vulnerable members of society, might be addressed to the authorities or 'the state'. However, late antique Arabia was a tribal society, and there was no centralised state. In our view, these verses are addressed to the wealthy male heads of household who, in the absence of state structures, would have taken vulnerable members of society into their own households. Such households did not consist solely of a nuclear family. Rather, the male head of household would have had many dependants, even including his own wife or wives, who nevertheless would themselves have had a high social status and also a responsibility to look after the vulnerable.

'Orphans' are a group of vulnerable people mentioned frequently in the Qur'an. This group includes, but is not restricted to, parentless children; the Qur'anic evidence indicates that the category of 'orphan' includes women who do not have a close male relative who would be able to offer them protection and people who otherwise needed protection. Q. 4:6 mentions giving the orphans their wealth when they reach maturity, and this should certainly be understood as the under-age orphans; but in Q. 4:2–4, unmarried women are among the 'orphans' (see also Q. 4:127, where the women orphans are again mentioned). The male head of household is addressed here and is admonished that, although he has control of the orphans' property, he must not abuse this

29 Many scholars have commented on Q. 4:34. For our earlier interpretation of this verse, see Bauer and Hamza, *Women*, 270–80.

30 For a reading of this entire part of Sūrat al-Nisāʾ (Q. 4), see ibid., especially 253–56.

power, consuming the property as though it were his own, or taking the good for himself and exchanging this with inferior goods. We can assume that the 'property' (*māl*) of the orphans would have included all their possessions, money, and potentially land or other goods.

It is after the warning about the orphans' property that the fear of the head of household is invoked.[31] They are told that if they fear that they will not be just to the orphans, they may marry the women 'two, or three, or four'; they are then admonished to give the women their bridal payment so that it is the women's own property. It seems that the fear here is that they might take advantage of the dependent women in their care, either by using the women's wealth for their own purposes, or by taking advantage of them sexually. Marrying these women will protect their wealth, by ensuring they have control of their own dowry, and it will give them social status, making any sexual relationship licit. The 'fear' here, then, is a fear of grievous wrongdoing, or what we would construe as moral failure. It is only when the heads of household fear that they might do something morally abhorrent that they are permitted to marry two, or three, or four of these women. This is presented as a permission granted for something that is morally wanting to prevent a much greater wrong.

After this permission is granted, men's fear is again invoked. This second 'fear' is that if the men fear that they will not be equitable among the women or be able to provide for them, they should only marry one (free woman), or 'what your right hands possess', meaning slave women. This clause is what makes it clear that marrying more than one woman, while permissible, is not necessarily the best path: among other things, several marriages might impoverish him such that he is unable to provide for any of these women fairly. The dowry of a slave woman is presumably less than that of a free woman (see Q. 4:25), so this explains why a slave would be a good choice if he cannot marry a free woman. Another verse says that men will never be able to be fair among their wives (Q. 4:129). Although there can be no doubt that in the tribal society having many wives was a sign of power and status, the clear message is that to marry one, and to treat her properly, is the best course of action.

Although many scholars have spoken about polygamy in the Qur'an, very little has been said about the character and morality of the person being addressed in these verses. But it seems that these verses address the case of a man who has tendencies to pursue power and status, spending beyond his means, or a poor man who has many dependants. He wants to consume the property of the orphans in his care, he may wish to take advantage of

31 Our thanks to Georgina Jardim, who sent Karen Bauer an article-in-progress on men's 'fear' in the Qur'an which, although it did not deal with this case, provoked this thought.

vulnerable women, and he may wish to marry more women than he can support. The clear point to be made here is that this person probably has morally unrighteous tendencies towards the dependants over whom he has power. It is to guard against such moral delinquency that the Qur'an needs to implement some kind of boundary, lest the rights of the vulnerable be transgressed entirely. Such verses show gradation insofar as there is a moral minimum for those who are likely to overstep the basic boundaries of decency, as well as a better, more moral (and hence more law-abiding) course of action.

One Qur'anic term used to describe such a higher moral awareness is '*ḥikma*' (wisdom). As noted earlier, questions of morality and law were heavily debated in late antiquity. In an important new study of *ḥikma* in the Qur'an, Saqib Hussain argues that wisdom in the Qur'an 'stands in continuity with the evolving Near Eastern, and more specifically biblical wisdom tradition'.[32] That wisdom literature included a notion of natural law or natural morality, in which humans have an innate moral notion of right and wrong, confirmed by revelation.[33] Hussain shows that late antique Christian thinkers used the discourse of natural morality and wisdom to justify which biblical laws ought to be dispensed with. He argues that the Qur'an embraced a concept of natural morality which was also evident in Christian writings at the time but that the Qur'an goes further and 'requires that even its own laws be understood through the filter of *ḥikma*'.[34] In Hussain's reading, *ḥikma* is the moral sense which enables people to judge how to apply Qur'anic law, and this is apparent in Q. 2:31, a verse we cited and discussed earlier. He notes that men are admonished not to 'make a mockery of God's signs' by taking advantage of their right to divorce and remarry women. In his words: 'Here, [*ḥikma*] seems to be invoking the audience's moral sense to alert them to a situation in which, despite remaining within the letter of the law, they may nonetheless be guilty of wrongdoing.'[35] Thus, for Hussain, Qur'anic law must be 'understood through the audience's own moral filter'; the Qur'an contains not only law, but *ḥikma*, which involves following the law in a 'morally praiseworthy manner'.[36]

There can be no doubt that, as Hussain argues, *ḥikma* refers to moral sensibility. However, it is not clear to us that one could follow the letter of the law and be committing a moral wrongdoing. For Hussain, the law grants men the power to revoke a divorce, and it is their moral judgement (*ḥikma*) which must

32 Hussain, 'Wisdom', 33.
33 Ibid., 7.
34 Ibid., 52.
35 Ibid., 136.
36 Ibid., 137, 141. We are summarising Hussain's arguments here in a manner that does not do them full justice.

be invoked not to use this power to harm women. Our reading is that to harm women in a divorce would not be to follow the letter of the law at all. It would be to break the law, 'making a mockery of God's signs', which command men not to harm the women whom they are divorcing. The important point here is that if one conceives of the law as morally graded, then committing a moral wrong, such as harming innocent women, would go against true adherence to the law. As noted earlier, to follow the law fully in Q. 2:231 is to treat women decently. But it should be noted that this fuller fulfilment of the law may only be verifiable internally by the person who knows his own intention in the act of divorce, and by God, who will judge this internal orientation in the afterlife. Thus, what can be judged in this world ('positive law'), even when it is based on Qur'anic precepts, may not be in complete fulfilment of those precepts. If a woman can show that her husband has harmed her, a human judge could try to redress that harm. But if her ex-husband simply acts spitefully to provoke her, the judge cannot necessarily make him act nicely: only God will punish him in that case.

Why are Qur'anic laws graded? It seems that all people have the innate ability to follow Qur'anic laws: as noted earlier, the Qur'an says that God has granted all humans the faculties of sight, hearing, and hearts precisely so that they might comprehend God's signs and follow them (Q. 22:46, 76:2–3). Yet just because humans have this ability, it does not mean they use it: the Qur'an says repeatedly that most people do not understand God's signs or follow His commands. As Hussain shows, it is wisdom that enables some people to make sound moral judgements and consequently to follow God's laws morally, which we conceive as a more complete fulfillment of the law. Others are only able to maintain a moral minimum, and some remain – in Qur'anic terms – 'blind', meaning morally blind. Most people make mistakes and must repent; but some never do. The Qur'an makes it clear that wisdom is associated with true understanding and is given to some and not others (Q. 2:269); it can be passed along, as in the example of Luqmān passing wisdom to his son in Sūrat Luqmān (Q. 31); it can be revealed (Q. 2:231) and is associated with God's verses (Q. 2:151). *Ḥikma*, then, represents a higher level of spiritual awareness and moral judgement, and this relates to the sense of the word as a form of restraint from ignorant actions. Although this quality can be acquired by humans, it is ultimately godly: the Qur'an says that God is the ultimate moral judge (*khayr al-ḥākimīn*, *ḥakam*) and that He Himself is morally sound (*al-Ḥakīm*). While this subject goes well beyond the scope of this chapter, we can assume that *ḥikma*, as the higher faculty of moral judgement, is the very thing that allows some people to be more law-abiding since they are able to comprehend the moral purpose behind the laws, and thus to pursue the higher path offered by many of the Qur'an's verses.

3 Qur'anic Law as Contextual Law

Although correct ritual and social action is an important aspect of the Qur'an's laws for its believing community, it is equally noteworthy that salvation seems to be a threshold which many people can pass on the basis of their belief and righteous action. What might be called the ecumenical tent is large enough to comprehend all monotheistic believers who are doers of good. According to Q. 2:62, believers, Christians, Jews, and Sabeans can all attain salvation; and righteous people are repeatedly reassured that God sees the good that they do. This confirms the overall trajectory of Godwariness (*taqwā*) and piety (*birr*) in the Qur'an, terms which consistently describe simple actions and attitudes such as charitable giving (Q. 2:177, 76:9–10, 92:5–6, 92:17–21), gratitude (Q. 76:3), and prayer (Q. 2:177, 76:24–26). These commands, which are consistent in all periods of the Qur'anic revelation, could be considered as a baseline for salvation.

Yet there seems to be a contradiction between the overall trajectory of salvation based on a set of rather easily obtainable monotheistic beliefs, righteous actions, and ritual, with passages in Sūrat al-Tawba (Q. 9) and Sūrat al-Nisā' (Q. 4) that set a higher bar for salvation by demanding that believers be willing to sacrifice their lives in battle, and who consequently achieve a greater rank with God (Q. 9:20). In these suras, those who are reluctant to fight, who had claimed to be believers but who go back on this commitment (Q. 4:88–91), or who seek excuses not to fight even though they have the means to do so (Q. 9:93), are threatened with punishment in the afterlife. Grave threats are issued to those who renounce the correct practices of worship (*dīn*), and whose deeds will therefore be rendered futile (*ḥabiṭat aʿmāluhum*, Q. 2:217, 5:5). This is expressed most forcefully in Q. 9:53–54:

> Say, expend willingly or by coercion; it will never be accepted from you, for you are indeed a profligate people (*qawmun fāsiqūn*). Nothing stops their expenditure (*nafaqa*) from being accepted except that they deny God and His Messenger and do not perform the prayer except lazily, and do not expend except when compelled.

The profligacy of the people being addressed in this passage has the effect of nullifying deeds that might otherwise have been considered pious or of moral worth. Q. 9 is a sura that focuses on hypocrites, dissenters, and those who break their oaths; it is a sura that regulates questions of personal and communal allegiances. The people described here are enemies of the believing community, and they might even be enemies from within: they have sought to tempt the true believers away from the path and have rejoiced in the believers' affliction (Q. 9:50). Although this passage seems, therefore, to contradict other passages in which all of a person's good and bad deeds will be weighed and measured, the non-acceptance of their charity is a way of emphasising the gravity of their sins. The gravest sin is in their perception of their own self-interest: they seek to enrich themselves in this life rather than seeking God's favour for the next life, which shows that they never had genuine faith in the first place. As a result of this, God does not accept their acts of worship. The complete denial that their deeds will count is a rhetorical device that is morally instructive.

Our argument about these verses is not that there is a linear, teleological development in the Qur'an towards militancy, which has been the argument of prior scholars from within the Muslim tradition and Western academia.[37] Rather, in our view, some Qur'anic laws respond to current circumstances, particularly the danger in which the community finds itself. In this case, it is helpful to consider the 'lesser harm' principle that we outlined above: though nobody likes fighting (Q. 2:216), to fight is a lesser harm than the destruction of the community would be. Yet such provisions do not seem to abrogate all other Qur'anic commands on relations with unbelievers, because other Medinan verses normalise interactions with unbelievers. This lends weight to the hypothesis, supported by Qur'anic language, that certain Qur'anic commands refer to particular situations: 'fight them wherever you find them' (Q. 9:5) is not a command that is always meant to be acted upon, even in the Medinan period, because of the mitigating factors in this sura and elsewhere – Q. 9:4 gives exception for those pagans who do not violate their treaties; Q. 9:6 tells the believers to give asylum to the polytheists who seek asylum; the pagans are the ones who violate treaties (Q. 9:10); believers are told to fight those who aggress against them (Q. 9:13–14). In another Medinan sura, al-Mumtaḥana (Q. 60), negotiations occur between the believers and the unbelievers in cases where women wish to switch their communal allegiance. Moreover, this sura admits that believers might feel love for unbelievers (Q. 60:1); after warning the believers against the dangers of close relations with these people, the Qur'an clarifies that believers should treat them with kindness and justice (Q. 60:8) unless they have actively aggressed against the community, expelling believers from their homes and fighting them on account of their practices of worship

37 For modern Western academics taking this approach, see e.g. Mark Durie, *The Qur'an and Its Biblical Reflexes: Investigations into the Genesis of a Religion* (London: Lexington Books, 2018); and Walid A. Saleh, 'End of Hope: Sūras 10–15, Despair and a Way Out of Mecca', in *Qur'ānic Studies Today*, ed. Angelika Neuwirth and Michael A. Sells (Abingdon: Routledge, 2016), 105–23.

(Q. 60:8–9). This sura is also, like al-Tawba, situated in a time of enmity with unbelievers, but the believers are not under direct, immediate siege. In that case, relations with unbelievers seem to be fairly normalised: the believers are shown to negotiate with, rather than to kill, the unbelievers. According to some chronologies, this sura is a very late one; it has the longest mean verse length of any sura.[38] The clear implication is that, while some Qur'anic commandments are stable over time (e.g. one must believe in the One God, maintain prayer, and pay *zakāt*), other commands address particular circumstances and cannot be said to lay down a universal maxim. In moments when there is grave danger and grave harm is possible, a higher standard is required of the believers. When those moments have passed, the Qur'an seems to revert to the status quo.

4 Conclusion: Divine Law in the Social Frame

When considering why the Qur'an's commands integrate internal attitudes and external behaviours, elide the moral and the legal, and put communal action into a salvific frame, it is crucial to note that Qur'anic morality is grounded in the social realities of seventh-century Arabia. At that time, the care of the vulnerable took place through networks of patronage, and this social duty was enacted in households. The Qur'an provides clues regarding the structure of households: the male head of household was responsible not only for women and children, but also for slaves, relatives, and hangers-on (Q. 24:31). Therefore, although salvation is granted on an individual basis and nobody can intervene to save another, the righteous actions that lead to salvation are almost invariably undertaken in relation to others. One could even say that the believing community is formed of pious individuals organised in households, and wealthy households become a locus of patronage for the vulnerable and for the wider community. In turn, the community as a whole was distinguished not only by the practice of particular rites and rituals but also by its morality; and as we hope to have shown, that social morality was even enacted through rites and rituals such as slaughtering animals to feed the poor.

In a patronage society, the powerful elites have a great deal of control, but there is nobody to control them. Therefore, in the Qur'an's moral worldview, they will ultimately be judged by God. That is perhaps why so many Qur'anic commands do not specify any communal retribution, and indeed there often seems to be no possibility of enforcement within the community, even when

38 Nicolai Sinai, *The Qur'an: A Historical-Critical Introduction* (Edinburgh: Edinburgh University Press, 2017), 120.

there is a clear infringement of these commands. For instance, in the case of divorce, the ex-husband is commanded to treat his ex-wife decently, to pay her maintenance, and so forth, but there is no communal consequence specified if he does not do this. Rather, the ultimate consequence is understood as being eschatological: God will punish him in the afterlife for his moral failing. Of course, this does not necessarily mean that, in reality, he faces no communal retribution, or that he could not be forced to pay; but the mechanism for this is not discussed. Moreover, it is important to note that the exact standards of niceness and decency are themselves contextual. Decency and propriety are a constant; but what that means in exact terms may vary according to the means and situation of any household. The overall point is to protect those who might be vulnerable to exploitation, and to uphold decency even in times of strife.

This approach may help explain why there are not more instances of concrete positive law in the text. In a few cases of serious transgression (murder, theft, adultery, perjury), the Qur'an outlines a concrete standard of punishment. For example, the Qur'an specifies a hundred lashes for those whose adultery is witnessed by four people (Q. 24:2), cutting the hands of thieves (Q. 5:38), retaliation or blood money being paid in case of murder (Q. 2:178), and eighty lashes for someone who falsely accuses a chaste woman without four witnesses, in which case the accuser's testimony is never again accepted (Q. 24:4). The ultimate purpose of these commands seems to be to ensure a minimum standard of justice in the community, by controlling and punishing the most serious breaches of morality, those that infringe on others' rights, for instance, in cases of murder, theft, or false accusation, or that compromise the integrity of the community through a public display of immorality such as illicit sexual activity that is so blatant that four people could witness it. Of particular note is that the laws on fornication, which punish men and women alike, might serve to protect women, by deterring men who seek to take advantage of them. In all these cases, even unbelievers must know that there is some deterrent to egregious breaches of others' rights or of communal propriety.

Such instances show that in the Medinan period there was some law that governed all of those under the Prophet's authority, even if those people were not believers. Therefore, although the frame for Qur'anic law is belief and piety, in Medinan verses the Qur'an also establishes standards that could be applied outside of that framework. Q. 49:14 presents the scenario of people who have submitted to the Prophet's temporal authority, but who are not believers. When they say they believe, they are commanded instead to say that they have submitted to monotheism (*aslamnā*). Yet, the verse confirms, if they obey God and the Messenger, God will give them the reward for their works. Q. 49:15 affirms that the believers are only those who are willing to sacrifice their lives and possessions in God's cause; and we are probably to understand from this that they are more likely to be saved. Q. 49:17 addresses the unbelievers directly, reminding them that it is not a benefit to the Prophet (which is to say, the temporal authority governing them) that they have submitted to monotheism. Rather, God has benefitted them, in guiding them to (true) belief, if they are sincere. In other words, the Prophet is not the beneficiary of their submission; *they* are now able to benefit from God's guidance. This passage recognises that the Prophet had temporal authority over a varied community of believers, hypocrites, and unbelievers, and that a moral-eschatological *telos* underlies even the laws that they must obey. Their obedience and submission to that temporal authority might even end up doing them some eschatological good. Somewhat akin to this is the case of captives of war who are told that if God finds good in their hearts, they will be able to gain something greater than what was taken from them (Q. 8:70). They find themselves in circumstances beyond their control, but this does not undermine their moral agency. Even if that agency can be exercised only internally, their internal disposition is recognised by God.

Overall, therefore, the Qur'an's commands could be considered a moral law, rather than a code of positive law or morality, as we would understand those terms in contemporary usage. This moral law has gradations, such that fulfilling the minimum cannot be a virtuous aspiration. More can always be done: ever more virtuous adherence to these laws should be the aspiration, because morality can only be consummated by a commitment to the fuller possibilities of these laws. The Qur'an presents its law as, in some senses, both natural and guided by the will of the Lawgiver. The specific injunctions define this community as opposed to other related monotheistic communities, but even these injunctions are assumed to have a moral status, rather than being arbitrary.

Key to the Qur'anic approach is the idea that belief in God cannot result in salvation if it remains solely a feeling or an opinion. Instead, the Qur'an posits a morally driven approach to life, which includes virtuous treatment of others, especially the vulnerable; personal and communal modesty, decorum, and sexual ethics; a willingness to sacrifice one's self-interests for the greater good; submission to God and constant prayer and remembrance. This may be why it is only the most serious transgressions against others' rights, or the most blatant public transgressions of morality, for which communal punishment is specified. Rather than being bound by a set of rules to be enforced by authorities in this world, the community is instead bound by an ethical manner of conduct that underpins any enforceable rulings ('positive law' or 'communal law'). Even the most serious breaches, those that entail communal punishment, are ultimately characterised in terms of their moral wrong and the harm that these breaches will visit upon the transgressor in the afterlife, rather than solely in terms of the harm done to the victim in the life of this world.

Given that God's bounty (*faḍl*) has not been distributed according to its recipients' moral worth, but rather as a moral test, the Qur'an emphasises that believers must strive to be just to others, for individuals attain their salvation by being just and virtuous in this world, looking after the vulnerable, using their wealth for proper ends, and participating in the moral community and its rites. If everyone adhered to Qur'anic rules, the result would be communal justice; but the Qur'an proceeds from a starting point that immoral people are frequently in positions of authority and that not all people will abide by divine law. The one constant is that all people will be tested within whatever circumstances they find themselves. By providing a moral law for the believing community, the Qur'an is offering the parameters of the grand moral test of this world. This sometimes overlaps with, but is not synonymous with, a set of positive, enforceable laws.

Bibliography

Abou-Bakr, Omaima, Asma Lamrabet, and Mulki Al-Sharmani. 'Qur'anic Ethics of Marriage'. In *Justice and Beauty in Muslim Marriage: Towards Egalitarian Ethics and Laws*, edited by Ziba Mir-Hosseini, Mulki Al-Sharmani, Jana Rumminger, and Sarah Marsso, 21–56. London: Oneworld Academic, 2022.

Abou-Bakr, Omaima, and Mulki Al-Sharmani. 'Islamic Feminist *Tafsīr* and Qur'anic Ethics: Rereading Divorce Verses'. In *Islamic Interpretive Tradition and Gender Justice: Processes of Canonization, Subversion, and Change*, edited by Nevin Reda and Yasmin Amin, 23–66. Quebec: McGill-Queen's University Press, 2020.

Abou-Taleb, Amira Naim. 'The Concept of *Iḥsān* (Beauty/Goodness) in the Qur'ānic Moral Worldview'. PhD diss., University of Helsinki, 2023.

Bauer, Karen, and Feras Hamza. *Women, Households, and the Hereafter in the Qur'an: A Patronage of Piety*. Oxford: Oxford University Press in association with the Institute of Ismaili Studies, 2023.

Donner, Fred. *Muhammad and the Believers at the Origins of Islam*. Cambridge, MA: Harvard University Press, 2012.

Durie, Mark. *The Qur'an and Its Biblical Reflexes: Investigations into the Genesis of a Religion*. London: Lexington Books, 2018.

Goudarzi, Mohsen. 'Worship (*Dīn*), Monotheism (*Islām*) and the Qur'ān's Cultic Decalogue'. *Journal of the International Qur'anic Studies Association* 8, no. 1 (2023): 1–42.

Harvey, Ramon. *The Qur'an and the Just Society*. Edinburgh: Edinburgh University Press, 2018.

Hayes, Christine. *What's Divine about Divine Law? Early Perspectives*. Princeton: Princeton University Press, 2015.

Hussain, Saqib. 'Wisdom in the Qur'an'. PhD diss., University of Oxford, 2022.

Lindstedt, Ilkka. *Muhammad and His Followers in Context: The Religious Map of Late Antique Arabia*. Leiden: Brill, 2023.

Lowry, Joseph E. 'Law, Structure, and Meaning in Surat al-Baqarah (Q. 2)'. *Journal of the International Qur'anic Studies Association* 2, no. 1 (2017): 111–48.

Lowry, Joseph E. 'Reading the Qur'an as a Law Book: Legislation, Language, and Allusion in Islam's Scripture'. In *Arabi Belles Lettres*, edited by Joseph E. Lowry and Shawkat M. Toorawa, 3–18. Atlanta: Lockwood Press, 2019.

Rahman, Fazlur. *Major Themes of the Qur'an*. Chicago: University of Chicago Press, 2009. Originally published in 1980 by Bibliotheca Islamica.

Saleh, Walid A. 'End of Hope: Sūras 10–15, Despair and a Way Out of Mecca'. In *Qur'ānic Studies Today*, edited by Angelika Neuwirth and Michael A. Sells, 105–23. Abingdon: Routledge, 2016.

Shoemaker, Stephen J. *Creating the Qur'an: A Historical-Critical Study*. Oakland: University of California Press, 2022.

Sinai, Nicolai. 'The Christian Elephant in the Meccan Room: Dye, Tesei, and Shoemaker on the Date of the Qur'ān'. *Journal of the International Qur'anic Studies Association* (2024): 1–62. https://doi.org/10.1515/jiqsa-2023-0013.

Sinai, Nicolai. *The Qur'an: A Historical-Critical Introduction*. Edinburgh: Edinburgh University Press, 2017.

Stewart, Devin. 'Noah's Boat and Other Missed Opportunities (2019 IQSA Presidential Address)'. *Journal of the International Qur'anic Studies Association* 6, no. 1 (2021): 17–67.

Zellentin, Holger M. '*banū isrāʾīl, ahl al-kitāb, al-yahūd wa-l-naṣārā*: The Qur'anic Community's Encounters with Jews and Christians'. *Entangled Religions* 13, no. 2 (2023): https://doi.org/10.46586/er.13.2023.10991.

Zellentin, Holger M. *Law beyond Israel: From the Bible to the Qur'an*. Oxford: Oxford University Press, 2022.

Zellentin, Holger M. *The Qur'ān's Legal Culture: The Didascalia Apostolorum as a Point of Departure*. Tübingen: Mohr Siebeck, 2013.

CHAPTER 4

The Myth of the Elite Male Addressee and Its Implications for Regulative Verses

Abla Hasan

1 Introduction[1]

Among the firm beliefs of all Islamic schools of theology is that the Qur'an has the characteristic of *iʿjāz* (inimitability); that is, a miraculous nature. In addition to viewing the Qur'an as the unaltered speech (*kalām*) of God, revealed directly to the Prophet Muhammad through the angel Jibrīl (Gabriel), Muslims often emphasise its concision, unparalleled semantic perfection, and its grammatical and literary excellence as supporting evidence, which, for them, prove its divine origin. The Qur'an itself asserts this claim and famously addresses opponents with a *taḥaddī* (challenge) to produce anything of comparable merit as we read in Q. 2:23–24, 'If you have doubts about the revelations We have sent down to Our servant, then produce a single sura like it – enlist whatever supporters you have other than God – if you truly [think you can]. If you cannot do this – and you never will – then beware of the Fire prepared for the disbelievers, whose fuel is men and stones.'[2]

Although scholars confirm and expound upon the Qur'an's unmatched literary excellence, nevertheless they employ a range of techniques that have the effect of negating aspects of the text itself. Examples of such violations in *tafsīr* (exegesis) include, but are not limited to, an unauthorised, excessive, exegetical narrativisation of the Qur'an; the doctrine of 'abrogation' (*naskh*); occasions or circumstances of revelation (*asbāb al-nuzūl*); the use of *ḥadīth* to invalidate some Qur'anic verses; overlooking what was hastily interpreted as a mere repetition of words, phrases, and verses in the Qur'an, including the unjust characterisation of some as synonyms.[3]

---

1 I am grateful to Karen Bauer for her priceless support and valuable insights while finalising this chapter.

2 Muhammad A.S. Abdel Haleem, *The Qur'an* (New York: Oxford University Press, 2010). All Qur'anic translations, unless otherwise stated, are taken from this work.

3 For the full list I propose, and for a complete explanation, see Abla Hasan, *Decoding the Egalitarianism of the Qur'an: Retrieving Lost Voices on Gender* (Lanham, MD: Lexington Books, 2019), ch. 1.

 | HTTPS://DOI.ORG/10.1163/9789004755567-006

While a full survey of exegetical shortcomings in attempting to decode the Qur'anic text exceeds the scope of this chapter, one can say here that many interpretations were developed through local theological paradigms. Exegetes were, are, and will always be products of their time and place. In order to understand premodern exegetes, one should always refrain from simply dismissing them as misogynistic and consider 'further research into what the exegetes may have meant by their seemingly straightforward words'.[4] Aspiring for and even claiming perfection while embarking on a brave endeavour like interpreting a divine text will always be a far-fetched goal. No interpretation of the Qur'an can be perfect; therefore, while this chapter humbly offers a critique and correction of long-standing flaws in interpretation, nevertheless this is with the full recognition that it may in turn stand to be corrected by our own contemporary and future colleagues. This acknowledgement is necessary for the enhancement of what will otherwise always remain incomplete and fallible. One point that needs to be clarified even at this early stage is that the validity of our critique stems only from spotting internal inconsistencies and textual discrepancies. Our current views, shaped by modern tolerance towards gender equality, justice, and religious pluralism, cannot and should not be validated as the motivation for a wholesale rejection of classical interpretations that appear to us today as less progressive, gender biased, and exclusivist. Instead, what should lead us in our journey to understanding the Qur'an is an objective approach to the religious text that rejects current self-interests and projections in the same way that old and classical projections are rejected. In her 2009 article, '*The Male Is Not Like the Female* (Q 3:36): The Question of Gender Egalitarianism in the Qur'ān', Karen Bauer elaborates on the scholarly merit of the question of gender egalitarianism in the Qur'an:

> In order to understand most scholars' hesitance to speak of inequality in the Qur'ān, it is necessary to explore the assumptions that inform the debate. Many of the scholars who have written on the status of women in the Qur'ān are Muslims, feminists, or both. One way of assessing the scholarly merit of a work would be to judge whether it is values-driven (Muslim, or feminist, for example). A better gauge of a work's scholarly merit is whether it is selective or comprehensive. Do authors only choose evidence that fits with their theories or distort evidence to comply with those theories? Or do they make an attempt to be comprehensive, by taking into account all evidence, even that which may be morally difficult or contrary to the overall argument? On the whole, the argument for the Qur'ān's gender egalitarianism is taken by authors who have a selective

4 Karen Bauer, '"Traditional" Exegeses of Q 4:34', *Comparative Islamic Studies* 2, no. 2 (2008): 134.

> approach; authors who take a more comprehensive approach tend to acknowledge and explore the hierarchical structures of the text's treatment of men and women.[5]

A modern gender egalitarian interpretation that does not derive its scholarly merit and credibility from responding to the text and accurately reflecting its content is by no means fairer than a classical or premodern male-centred interpretation, as long as both are not committed to objectivity instead of the promotion of self-interests, prejudices, and biases of interpreters. Deficiencies and shortcomings in interpreting the Qur'an that I mention in this chapter should be characterised as flaws due to their inconsistency with what is affirmed in the rest of the Qur'an, not due to their incompatibility with our modern preferences and our ways of living and thinking. One deficiency in reading and interpreting the Qur'anic text, which I have alluded to elsewhere,[6] is what I call the fallacy of the masculine addressee. This flaw violates the applicable validity and even the same meaning of the well-established and unanimously approved doctrine of *iʿjāz* of the Qur'anic text. If the Qur'anic language is precisely codified to reveal a divinely intended reference, as schools of Islamic exegesis argue, then every word, subject pronoun, conjunction, or letter should designate a specific meaning. Unfortunately, 'the majority of verses that use the masculine plural subject pronoun, which is used in Arabic to address both a group of men or a mixed group, or to address the believing community or even to address the human community in general, were commonly interpreted one way: to suggest an exclusively male audience.'[7]

In *Qur'an and Woman,* Amina Wadud proposes a female-inclusive Qur'anic hermeneutics. She emphasises a hermeneutics of *tawḥīd* that replaces the individual reading of one verse at a time by a unified recognition of the Qur'an's coherence. As Wadud soundly observes:

> What concerns me most about 'traditional' *tafasir* is that they were exclusively written by males. This means that men and men's experiences were included, and women and women's experiences were either excluded or interpreted through the male vision, perspective, desire, or needs of woman. In the final analysis, the creation of the basic paradigms through which we examine and discuss the Qur'an and Qur'anic interpretation were generated without the

---

5 Karen Bauer, '*The Male Is Not Like the Female* (Q 3:36): The Question of Gender Egalitarianism in the Qur'ān', *Religion Compass* 3, no. 4 (2009): 639.

6 See Hasan, *Decoding the Egalitarianism of the Qur'an.*

7 Ibid., 16–17.

> participation and firsthand representation of women. Their voicelessness during critical periods of development in Qur'anic interpretation has not gone unnoticed, but it has been mistakenly equated with voicelessness in the text itself.[8]

The myth of the male addressee fallacy is one way out of a multifaceted historical process that has resulted in alienating the Qur'an, which does not read well for many today if isolated from a long history of reshaping it. In this chapter I extend the results of my investigation by applying the same methodology to three verses, namely, Q. 4:34, 4:6, and 4:3. In addition to questioning the adequacy and the accuracy of the available interpretations of the subject pronoun in each of these verses, respectively, contextual evidence supporting a new interpretation is provided. The outcome supports the argument for the community of believers at large, and not just husbands or even men, as the exclusive intended Qur'anic addressee in these three cases. As one might easily predict, this correction can have a remarkable impact in terms of dismantling the unjust portrayal of the Qur'anic text as an exclusivist and gender-biased text that allegedly argues for domestic violence, minor marriage, and unconditional polygamy.

2 The Alleged Qur'anic Endorsement of Domestic Violence: the Consequences of Applying the Myth of the Elite Male Addressee to Q. 4:34

While domestic violence exists in both Muslim and non-Muslim societies, the misinterpretation and the misrepresentation of the Qur'an as a book that provides a divine justification for it has caused (and is still causing) Muslim communities harm, embarrassment, and shame, to say the least. For this reason, it is critical we first directly address sources of confusion in the scripture itself. Many studies have already been devoted to expositing the controversy caused by Q. 4:34. Others are still to emerge, with no promise of ending the debate soon. To borrow John Andrew Morrow's words, 'The wife beating battle is not over. It is only beginning.'[9]

In his 2020 monograph, *The Most Controversial Qur'anic Verse*, Morrow expounds on the variety of exegetical choices scholars appeal to in responding

8 Amina Wadud, *Qur'an and Woman: Rereading the Sacred Text from a Woman's Perspective*, 2nd ed. (New York: Oxford University Press, 1999), 2.

9 John Andrew Morrow, *The Most Controversial Qur'anic Verse: Why 4:34 Does Not Promote Violence against Women* (Lanham, MD: Hamilton Books, 2020), 4.

to Q. 4:34. Such choices, he explains, vary from interpreting the verse independently to interpreting it on the basis of other related verses, in the context of the whole Qur'an, based on the Prophetic traditions, or according to the time and place of its revelation. He also considers reformist readings of the verse, interpretations based on 'the whole spirit of Islam',[10] Sufi readings, as well as linguistic interpretations that consider problems caused by pronunciation and vocalisation. Bauer advances this argument by exploring some of the variations in the content and methods of premodern interpretation, and by focusing on the ways in which they developed through time in the genre of Qur'anic commentary. She confirms, 'There were significant changes in the interpretations' content over time,'[11] before concluding, 'just as there was not a single uniform view of this verse in the pre-modern interpretations, nor is there in the modern interpretations.'[12] In her 2015 work, *Gender Hierarchy in the Qur'ān*, Bauer provides a practical examination of both classical and modern perspectives.[13] Each of the three parts of her book includes a chapter that examines the Qur'an and medieval interpretations of specific verses, followed by a chapter treating modern interpretations.

This diversity of scholarly approaches to Q. 4:34 reflects its problematic nature. While many scholars read the controversy as endorsing physical abuse, few tackled the issue of interpreting the verse as promoting psychological abuse in marriage. Kecia Ali soundly describes the verse as 'the clearest Qur'anic example of hierarchy between men and women'.[14] As Hadia Mubarak explains, 'The way exegetes interpret these three terms, *qawwāmūn*, *nushūz*, and *waḍribūhunna*, determines the level of authority, if any, that a husband could exercise over his wife, including the authority to potentially discipline her if she is guilty of *nushūz*.'[15] In addition to incorrectly being interpreted as promoting physical abuse, Q. 4:34 is believed to encourage husbands from withholding sex as a recommended measure for disciplining their wives. For these reasons, among many others, Nevin Reda was not exaggerating when she

10 Ibid.

11 Bauer, '"Traditional" Exegeses of Q 4:34', 130.

12 Ibid.

13 See Karen Bauer, *Gender Hierarchy in the Qur'ān: Medieval Interpretations, Modern Responses* (New York: Cambridge University Press, 2015).

14 Kecia Ali, 'Understanding a Difficult Verse, Qur'an 4:34', The Feminist Sexual Ethics Project, revised 11 February 2003, www.brandeis.edu/projects/fse/muslim/diff-verse.html.

15 Hadia Mubarak, 'Change through Continuity: A Case Study of Q. 4:34 in Ibn ʿĀshūr's *al-Taḥrīr wa'l-tanwīr*', *Journal of Qur'anic Studies* 20, no. 1 (2018): 10.

described Q. 4:34 as 'the most problematic verse for women'.[16] In *Decoding the Egalitarianism of the Qur'an*, I reject both interpretations, that is, of Q. 4:34 as an endorsement of physical or psychological abuse in marriage. I provide a full linguistic analysis of every word in the verse. Based on twenty arguments I propose a new interpretation and translation of the verse in question. In view of limited space, I provide here only the outcome of the full investigation.[17] A common pitfall, I argue, in many responses to the controversy caused by Q. 4:34 comes from failing to observe the reference to the real addressee of the verse, which can be found both in a preceding verse (Q. 4:29) and in the following verse (Q. 4:35), which is the community of believers, men and women. In fact, this single linguistic observation shifts the responsibility of applying the so-called three-step corrective method from husbands to the community, and simply by reintroducing the argument, probably as it was originally intended in the Qur'an, as an argument for legal and social correction methods that the community can use with female criminals. After all, Q. 4:34, as a careful hermeneutical investigation could prove, may have nothing to do with marriage.[18]

Among those who have notably contributed to the ongoing discussion of Q. 4:34 are Kecia Ali, Laleh Bakhtiar, Karen Bauer, Ayesha S. Chaudhry, Juliane Hammer, Celene Ibrahim, John Andrew Morrow, Hadia Mubarak, Nevin Reda, Sa'diyya Shaikh, and Laury Silvers. In my attempt to contribute to the discussion, first, I introduce the verse as it is commonly translated. I then discuss a common pitfall in many responses to the controversy (instead of providing a random survey of what has been said about the verse so far). Finally, I revisit my point of departure, namely, the myth of the male addressee, as the key to resolving Q. 4:34.

Q. 4:34 is commonly and traditionally interpreted as providing husbands with three corrective methods that they are encouraged to use in cases of marital conflict. These methods could escalate from reproaching wives to withholding sex from them and finally, a recommendation of beating them. Here is how the verse is commonly translated, including one of the best translations that I usually employ in my research:[19]

---

16 Nevin Reda, 'The Qur'an and Domestic Violence: An Islamic Feminist, Spiritually Integrative Reading of Verse 4:34', *International Journal of Practical Theology* 23, no. 2 (2019): 266.

17 For details of the arguments, see Hasan, *Decoding the Egalitarianism of the Qur'an*, ch. 3.

18 The implicit switch from addressing the community with recommendations to deal with female violators of laws in Q. 4:34 to addressing the community with recommendations on how to help couples fix broken marriages in Q. 4:35 is what causes both verses to be commonly interpreted as dealing with marriage. While they share the same addressee, i.e. the community of believers, both men and women, only Q. 4:35 deals with marriage.

19 Abdel Haleem, *The Qur'an*.

> Righteous wives are devout and guard what God would have them guard in their husband's absence. If you fear high-handedness from your wives, remind them [of the teachings of God], then ignore them when you go to bed, then hit them. If they obey you, you have no right to act against them: God is most high and great. (Q. 4:34)

Countless attempts have been made to deal with a verse that seems to be violating a basic Qur'anic right for women in marriage, namely, the right to be treated kindly and fairly (*bi-l-maʿrūf*),[20] or what I call 'the *maʿrūf* rule'.[21] A variety of methods have been adopted to respond to the challenge. Some argue for beating as a last resort, to be considered only when nothing else works to redress a collapsing marital relationship.[22] Others insist on revisiting the conditions traditional exegetes suggested be followed in order to permit beating, including administering a light beating only,[23] which includes the need to avoid the face.[24] Still others suggest a very light striking, like with a feather or a folded handkerchief. More recently, some have proposed a new meaning altogether for the Arabic word *ḍaraba* (to strike). Ayesha S. Chaudhry argues the verb *ḍaraba* is like the English 'to strike', which 'can be used in the phrases without designating one single meaning'.[25] Meanwhile, Laleh Bakhtiar interprets *ḍaraba* as the command for men 'to go away' from their wives.[26] Many seem to have hastily found in this line of argument a refuge from the ongoing humiliation associated with the traditional interpretation. This increasingly popular line of argument has been gathering support despite its clear, problematic nature. The emotional appeal of this solution does nothing to avert the scepticism of others who, like Juliane Hammer, for example, warn against 'the danger of exegetical relativism' that could eventually lead to undermining 'the authority of the text'.[27] In the following endorsement of this

---

20 See Q. 4:19.

21 Hasan, *Decoding the Egalitarianism of the Qur'an*, 70.

22 Rashīd Riḍā, *Ḥuqūq al-nisāʾ fī al-Islām* (Beirut and Damascus: al-Maktab al-Islāmī, 1984), 55.

23 ʿAbd Allāh Ibn ʿAbbās, *Tanwīr al-miqbās min tafsīr Ibn ʿAbbās* (Beirut: Dār al-Kutub al-ʿIlmiyya, 1992), 91.

24 Burhān al-Dīn al-Biqāʿī, *Naẓm al-durar fī tanāsub al-āyāt wa-l-suwar* (Cairo: Dār al-Kitāb al-Islāmī, 1984), 271.

25 Ayesha S. Chaudhry, *Domestic Violence and the Islamic Tradition* (Oxford: Oxford University Press, 2013), 14.

26 Laleh Bakhtiar, *The Sublime Quran* (Chicago: Kazi Publishers, 2007), 4:34.

27 Juliane Hammer, 'To Work for Change: Normativity, Feminism, and Islam', in 'Roundtable on Normativity in Islamic Studies', ed. Cynthia Eller, special issue, *Journal of the American Academy of Religion* 84, no. 1 (2016): 109.

interpretation, we see an example of how this line of face-saving argument has been idealised:

> The most straightforward interpretation is hence that of departure, separation, or seclusion. This arrangement, where the estranged husband deserts his wife altogether for some time, helps to bring the situation to a possible resolution because it is the final step beyond cautioning her and refusing to share her bed. Now, whilst the husband is away, the wife has ample opportunity to rethink the whole situation, to ponder the eventual consequences, and to realize the inevitable outcome of rejection, namely, divorce. At this point she must carefully decide if she would prefer to be separated permanently from her husband or be returned to the marital state. It is the moment of truth and if she is the party in the wrong, she has the choice to see reason and win back her estranged husband before it is too late.[28]

Other desperate attempts, based on comparing the conduct of the Prophet as a husband to what appears to be recommended in Q. 4:34, were made to disassociate domestic violence with the Qur'an. According to sound *ḥadīth* traditions, the Prophet did not strike a servant or a woman, and he never struck anything with his hand.[29]

The list of what has been written regarding Q. 4:34 is long indeed. However, our appreciation for these proposals does not (and should not) prevent questioning their clear problematic nature. Many of the proposed solutions entail a serious grammatical and semantic contradiction of the Qur'anic text itself. Arguing for other meanings for the verb *ḍaraba*, for example, that render physical beating into an unplausible option solves the problem only by ignoring the fact that the verb does not appear in Q. 4:34 in its root form: *wa-ḍribūhunna*, due to its morphological conjugation, designates a command given to men or a mixed-gender group to strike a group of women as the object. As I have explained elsewhere:

> All these details are embedded in the same phrase as follows: the verb is a command, and when the letter *waw* is attached to the verb, it indicates a male or a mixed group of addressees as the subject. Finally, the suffix indicates a group of

28 Abdulhamid Abusulayman, *Marital Discord: Recapturing Human Dignity through the Higher Objectives of Islamic Law*, rev. ed. (London: International Institute of Islamic Thought, 2008), 22.

29 Muslim b. al-Ḥajjāj, *Ṣaḥīḥ Muslim* (Riyadh: Dār Ṭayba, 2006), 1098 (*ḥadīth* no. 2328).

> absent women as the object.[30] In sum, considering the verb in question in isolation from its precisely conjugated Qur'anic form as it appears in 4:34 to argue for a different meaning is a tortuous route that doesn't solve the problem. Because any interpretation or translation should not ignore the fact that what we have in 4:34 is the verb in its precisely conjugated form and not the verb in isolation or the root of the verb. The verb in its conjugated form in 4:34 is clearly suggesting a command addressed to a masculine group or a mixed group and a women group as an object.[31]

Moreover, it goes without saying that in order for the verb to denote 'leaving' women instead of 'striking' them, it would require a (missing) preposition to allow for any sense of departure, separation, or seclusion ('from' them) as a plausible meaning, which is not the case here.

What is more problematic in some of these proposals is the explicit need to seek solutions external to the Qur'anic text, either by appealing to the conduct of the Prophet, which should add to our reasons to question the traditional interpretation of the verse, or by qualifying the command to beat with a light beating using a feather or a folded handkerchief, none of which is mentioned in the Qur'an. It says nothing of the intensity of beating, how it should be done, or how many times. What may be added to our list of concerns is the inadequacy of the proposed solutions. Is leaving women in cases of marital conflict even good advice? What if we imagined a gender/role reversal here – would the same advice hold? Would it still count as good advice if women were asked to simply leave their husbands? Would it help in terms of restoring the missing tranquillity in marriage? More seriously, this solution does not only seem to fail our basic common-sensical expectations but contradicts what the Qur'an adopts as a means to deal with marital conflicts. Contrary to this pseudo-advice, the Qur'an urges couples to initiate a reconciliatory dialogue in cases of conflict as we see in Q. 4:128[32] and urges their households to get involved in Q. 4:35 as it encourages spouses to engage family members and relatives, from both sides, as arbitrators, as a follow-up step in cases where high-tempered spouses would prevent any fruitful dialogues from taking place. In short, 'go away from them' as a plausible meaning of *ḍaraba* might seem like a convenient solution to avoid the shame and harm that the traditional interpretation of Q. 4:34 is associated with, but it fails to live up to what could authentically be described as Qur'anic advice to restore the missing harmony in a marriage.

---

30 Third-person pronoun.

31 Hasan, *Decoding the Egalitarianism of the Qur'an*, 75.

32 See ibid., 86–89.

Yet another problem with this new line of thinking is that the selective and apologetic manipulation of the meaning of *ḍaraba* leaves another dilemma unresolved, namely, the so-called command to ignore wives in bed by withholding sex.[33] While it might sound to some as less harmful to women, especially if compared to beating, it still violates the Qur'an by endorsing not physical but psychological abuse as a solution. This part of the verse is ignored by many, especially by proposals that focus on reinterpreting the meaning of *ḍaraba*. Unfortunately, suggesting withholding sex as a martial punishment meted out by men unjustly portrays the Qur'an as a sexist text that allows men what is forbidden to women. In addition, it contradicts the strict prohibition made in Q. 58:1–4, which forbids even announcing the mere intention to use sexual intimacy as a disciplinary tactic in marriage:

> God has heard the words of the woman who disputed with you [Prophet] about her husband and complained to God: God has heard what you both had to say, He is all hearing, all seeing. Even if any of you say to their wives, 'You are to me like my mother's back,' they are not their mothers; their only mothers are those who gave birth to them. What they say is certainly blameworthy and false, but God is pardoning and forgiving. Those of you who say such a thing to their wives, then go back on what they have said, must free a slave before the couple may touch one another again – this is what you are commanded to do, and God is fully aware of what you do – but anyone who does not have the means should fast continuously for two months before they touch each other, and anyone unable to do this should feed sixty needy people. This is so that you may [truly] have faith in God and His Messenger. (Q. 58:1–4)

Finally, basic linguistic observations in Q. 4:34 should motivate us to question the credibility of interpreting the verse as addressing marriage or the duties of husbands in cases of marital misconduct. For example, translating *rijāl* in Q. 4:34 as 'husbands' is based on an interpretive linguistic choice. Literally, *rijāl* means 'men'. Similarly, translating *nisā'* as 'wives' is based on an interpretive meaning and should be replaced by the literal sense, which is 'women'. The term *nushūz* in the verse is wrongly understood as exclusively referring to marital conflict. *Nushūz* as a Qur'anic term can refer to ways of acting differently, not confined to marriage. In Q. 58:11, we read, 'You who believe, if you are told to make room for one another in your assemblies, then do so, and God will make room for you, and if you are told to rise up (*inshizū*) do so (*inshizū*): God

33 Aḥmad b. Muḥammad Ibn ʿAjība, *al-Baḥr al-madīd fī tafsīr al-Qur'ān al-majīd* (Cairo: al-Hay'a al-Miṣriyya al-ʿĀmma li-l-Kitāb, 1999), 1:499.

will raise up, by many degrees, those of you who believe and those who have been given knowledge: He is fully aware of what you do.' *Maḍājiʿ* is better translated as bedrooms or even homes and not beds.

However, the most important step is to apply the fallacy or the myth of the male addressee to Q. 4:34. Reinterpreting and even solving the traditional problems associated with Q. 4:34 is a tenable task. To do so, we need to consider the uninterrupted Qur'anic dialogue that begins a few verses prior, from Q. 4:29, and concludes at 4:35. First, I use a common traditional translation[34] of Q. 4:29–35 and then I introduce my translation (at the end of this section).

> **You who believe**, do not wrongfully consume each other's wealth but trade by mutual consent. **Do not** kill each other, for God is merciful to you. If any of you does these things, out of hostility and injustice, We shall make him suffer Fire: that is easy for God. But **if you** avoid the great sins, you have been forbidden, We shall wipe out your minor misdeeds and let you in through the entrance of honour. **Do not** covet what God has given to some of you more than others – men have the portion they have earned and women the portion they have earned – you should rather ask God for some of His bounty: He has full knowledge of everything. We have appointed heirs for everything that parents and close relatives leave behind, including those to whom you have pledged your hands [in marriage], so give them their share: God is witness to everything. {*rijāl*} should take good care of {*nisāʾ*}, with [the bounties] God has given to some more than others and with what they spend out of their own money. Righteous {*nisāʾ*}[wives] devout and guard what God would have them guard in [their husband's absence] {when unseen}. If **you** fear high-handedness from your {*nisāʾ*}[wives], remind them [of the teachings of God], then ignore them [when you go to bed] {in bedrooms}, then hit them. If they obey you, you have no right to act against them: God is most high and great. **If you [believers]** fear that a couple may break up, appoint one arbiter from his family and one from hers. Then, if the couple want to put things right, God will bring about a reconciliation between them: He is all knowing, all aware. (Q. 4:29–35)[35]

Before offering my own translation, I should stress my commitment to staying faithful to the Qur'anic text by using *nisāʾ* and *rijāl* instead of 'husbands' and 'wives', which are not even mentioned once in Q. 4:34. As we see, the text is addressed to the community of believers – it is not addressed solely to men or husbands. This is clear from the wider context of the dialogue cited above.

34 Abdel Haleem, *The Qur'an*.

35 Emphasis added; interpolations of the original Arabic given in curly brackets.

In addition, there is no single reference to wives or husbands when we check the original Arabic text. This observation calls into question the interpretive choices that were normalised without any basis while interpreting Q. 4:34. It also eliminates the need to appeal to all those linguistic stretches of the imagination advocated by some of the responses to the controversy of Q. 4:34 as promoting domestic violence, both physical and psychological. After all, as we have shown, the verse is not addressing husbands with three corrective methods to apply in cases of marital misconduct; rather, it is addressing the community of believers with methods to consider while dealing with female criminals. Congregations and legal authorities would make use of these measures. This could escalate from reproaching the criminal or issuing a warning first, to home arrest (to be held in the woman's *maḍājiʿ*), and eventually end up with beating (corporal punishment) when nothing else works.[36]

The Qurʾanic guidance on dealing with female criminals, a vulnerable social group that could easily be exploited and wronged, indicates the following recommendations: women who insist on violating social norms and orders and who do not respond to repeated warnings could be placed under house arrest. They could be locked in their *maḍājiʿ*, a place noun for bedrooms that has been commonly but wrongly interpreted as beds.[37] If all else fails, authorities may consider physical discipline as a last resort. Now, whether authorities[38] choose to adopt or decline these methods as approved legal steps to deal with female perpetrators, or whether they need to drop some or all of these suggestions, are different questions that would require another investigation into what is considered just and fair in a legal context. It is worth noting, however, that while I dismiss the traditional interpretation of Q. 4:34 as suggesting a marital context, I do not intend to simply replace one restrictive understanding with another, one that could be narrowed down to three legal corrective methods. For, in Qurʾanic terms, humans are God's vicegerents on earth (Q. 2:30), and this itself empowers them to embrace legal creativity. Ultimately, the Qur'an's

---

36 The Qur'an is supposed to be general and flexible enough to respond to the needs of all people until the end of all times. This is how the majority of Muslims view the Qurʾan. The local and limited early understanding or applicability of some Qurʾanic teachings does not negate their assumed eternal validity. One could soundly argue for a different or a limited applicability of the legal role of the community at the time of the Prophet where there was no code of law at the time except the Qur'an itself. The verse – like many Qurʾanic rulings – seems to be responding to local needs, though not to stop there but to expand from there in all directions.

37 The same concept is confirmed in Q. 4:15.

38 The generality of the Qurʾanic language does not seem to be so concerned with a single identification of who could be classified as the legal representation of each and every community.

succinct language does not outline more than generalisations and flexible guidelines. The multifaceted application thereof should, by its nature, be variable, ongoing, and adjustable. Using the Qur'anic text as a foundation to extrapolate carefully crafted laws and rigidly refined regulations – the project which proponents of *al-tafsīr bi-l-ma'thur* (exegesis through authentic sources) have invested their time and effort in supporting – overlooks one basic linguistic character of the Qur'an, namely, generality. Treating the Qur'an as a legal document fails to reflect the fact that the Qur'an's 'legal subject matter, in the Western sense of the word, is relatively minor and does not exceed 500 verses'.[39]

What is important, however, is dismissing domestic violence as any sort of option while discussing Q. 4:34. The open-ended discussion of the three corrective methods, at the end of the day, lies in the hands of decision-makers who can decide what to adopt and how to adopt these suggestions. It is not up to husbands, let alone angry husbands, to apply these methods or to determine their validity. In a marital context, chastising, withholding sex, and beating are nothing but endorsements of verbal, psychological, and physical abuse. The three methods are not congruent with the way marriage is described in the rest of the Qur'an. On the other hand, understanding these methods as corporal punishments to deal with female criminals speaks to the need to treat women as a social category. Women who violate laws are provided repeated warnings; they are arrested in their own homes, which could save their dignity and reputation; and finally, they could be physically disciplined in accordance with what just authorities view as a final deterring punishment. The three methods have parallels in the Qur'an and could be easily defended as being coherent and consistent with the rest of the divine message.[40]

To sum up, the controversy caused by Q. 4:34 is one outcome of the myth of the elite male addressee, a premodern exegetical flaw that we see playing out next in obfuscating the legal and exegetical application of Q. 4:6. To close, Q. 4:34 could be better translated as:

> Men are the maintainers of women, those men whom God has favored some of them to others, and those who spend from their money. Righteous women are devout, they guard what God asked to be guarded, even when [they are] unseen. Those women among you [believers] from whom you fear recalcitrance,

---

39 Alexander Knysh, 'Multiple Areas of Influence', in *The Cambridge Companion to the Qur'ān*, ed. Jane Dammen McAuliffe (Cambridge: Cambridge University Press, 2006), 215.

40 For example, Q. 24:2 indicates a physical punishment, i.e. a hundred lashes in cases of publicly witnessed fornication. Likewise, Q. 4:15 prescribes house arrest as a punishment for publicly witnessed same-sex intercourse.

admonish them, and place them in house arrest, and strike them. If they obey you seek no way against them. God is most high and great.[41]

3 The Alleged Qur'anic Endorsement of Minor (Child) Marriage: the Consequences of Applying the Myth of the Elite Male Addressee to Q. 4:6

Many Muslims still believe that the Prophet Muhammad married his most beloved wife ʿĀ'isha when she was six or seven years old, and that the marriage was consummated when she was nine. While some efforts have been made to clarify this confusion and to argue that she was more likely eighteen or even twenty when she married the Prophet, the controversy still adds to the many stereotypes people have about Islam, in this case the permissibility of minor (child) marriage. The concept of minor marriage, however, remains alien to the Qur'an. As Yasmin Amin puts it, 'Rulings about child marriage in Islamic law were based on the precedent of ʿĀ'isha's marriage, though the canonized *ḥadīth* setting her age at six/nine is questionable, as demonstrated, and contradicts historical information found in the heritage books.'[42]

The Qur'an, moreover, when read in isolation from subverted readings, does not support minor marriage.[43] To the contrary, it provides guidance on the ideal age for marriage, which clearly stipulates adulthood as a prerequisite. In Q. 4:6 we read, 'test orphans until they reach marriageable age; then, if you find they have sound judgment, hand over their property to them.'[44] As is clear in this verse, the Qur'an defines the age of marriage as that when orphans can demonstrate sound judgement. Some observations are to be highlighted here. First, the specific ideal age of marriage is left unstated, to be based on what is appropriate in any given time and place, as long as the condition of demonstrating sound judgement is fulfilled. This flexibility is coherent with the

41 Hasan, *Decoding the Egalitarianism of the Qur'an*, 85.

42 Yasmin Amin, 'Revisiting the Issue of Minor Marriages: Multidisciplinary *Ijtihād* on Contemporary Ethical Problems', in *Islamic Interpretive Tradition and Gender Justice: Processes of Canonization, Subversion, and Change*, ed. Nevin Reda and Yasmin Amin (Montreal: McGill-Queen's University Press, 2020), 342.

43 For the full argument, see Hasan, *Decoding the Egalitarianism of the Qur'an*, ch. 3.

44 This chapter addresses only Q. 4:6 since the myth of the elite male addressee can have parallel outcomes when applied to 4:34, 4:6, and 4:3. More on minor marriage can be found in my discussion of Q. 65:4 in Hasan, *Decoding the Egalitarianism of the Qur'an*, 64–70.

Qur'an's open-ended legal framework, which allows ample room to adjust to the changing needs of different communities so long as the Qur'anic redlines are observed; in our case, a verifiable sound judgement. More importantly, relocating the text to its original context, by once again applying the myth of the elite male addressee to this verse, may prove a useful exercise. This could be done, first, by reintroducing the dialogue from where it starts, namely, Q. 4:1, addressing the human community, 'People, be mindful of your Lord, who created you from a single soul, and from it created its mate and from the pair of them spread countless men and women far and wide.' But what is the significance of recognising the real addressee here as the human community, which is explicitly mentioned in the Qur'an? In fact, in addressing the duty to test orphans' rational abilities and verify their sound judgement to the community, the Qur'an is clearly establishing a legal framework within which to define the parameters of what is socially considered an appropriate age for marriage. In other words, it is assigning the community the collective duty to decide what may be adopted as a legal age for marriage if the condition of proving sound judgement is fulfilled. This could entail methods each community may variably adopt to prove and document sound judgement. It could also include the diversity and variety in defining what sound judgement is in the first place, and to what degree it could vary from time to time and from community to community. What matters most, for our purpose, is the fact that this responsibility is not in any way left for potential suitors to decide.

To summarise, the apparent justification for minor marriage is based on interpretive patriarchal choices forced onto the text and not anything that can be justified within the text. Amin explains further:

> Child marriage, as discussed, is a model of male authority and female submission that contradicts two Islamic notions of justice and equity, as well as contemporary notions of human rights, and cannot be justified on religious grounds; therefore a 'decanonization' of this patriarchal interpretation that ultimately found its way into exegetical texts and laws should be considered. Respect for past precedents that were canonized in authoritative books and sources of Islamic law should not prevent future generations of Muslims from amending or setting aside prior interpretations and understandings of Islamic law that no longer respond to the changed realities of Muslim communities.[45]

45 Amin, 'Revisiting the Issue of Minor Marriages', 342–43.

4 The Alleged Qur'anic Unconditional Endorsement of Polygamy: the Consequences of Applying the Myth of the Elite Male Addressee to Q. 4:3

I argue for a distinction that needs to be made between Islamic polygamy and Qur'anic polygamy. As I have stated elsewhere:

> By 'Qur'anic polygyny', I refer to polygyny as a theoretical theological term, as it appears in the Qur'anic text: that is, as strictly conditional and precisely codified. The Qur'an, as Nevin Reda rightly observes, refers to 'monogamy as the ontological norm, hinted in the creation of a single self and from it its mate (Q 4:1), and polygamy as the exception (Q 4:3).'[46] By contrast, 'Islamic polygyny' refers to polygyny as it was practically adopted and legally by Muslim jurists throughout the history of Islamic jurisprudence; this is loosely defined and seldom soundly justified.[47]

Ahmed Souaiaia elaborates on the static status of the traditional Muslim discourse on polygamy:

> The traditional Muslim discourse on polygamy has been static. It continues to protect the interests of the elite class and ignore the rights and interests of disadvantaged women despite mounting evidence and changing circumstances that support the flexibility in interpretation. ... The rigidity and inflexibility could be the result of unyielding control exerted by an elite-dominated exegetical discourse informed by social practices. These practices defined what is proper and what is not but no original reading of the legal proofs was undertaken.[48]

Islamic polygamy is commonly justified by many exegetes due to reasons foreign to the Qur'an. Out of its many alleged positive outcomes, Ibn ʿĀshūr (d. 1973) mentions the increase of the number of Muslims, the financial support polygamy provides to women who outnumber men in all societies, and the way polygamy responds to men's innate polygamous nature.[49]

46 Reda, 'The Qur'an and Domestic Violence', 266.

47 Hasan, *Decoding the Egalitarianism of the Qur'an*, 90–91.

48 Ahmed E. Souaiaia, *Contesting Justice: Women, Islam, Law, and Society* (Albany: SUNY Press, 2008), 56.

49 Muḥammad b. al-Ṭāhir Ibn ʿĀshūr, *al-Taḥrīr wa-l-tanwīr* (Tunis: al-Dār al-Tūnisiyya, 1984), 4:226.

Contrary to Islamic polygamy, 'The Qur'an permits polygyny as a unique pro-woman, pro-family solution that is acceptable, but only as a last choice, as necessary to deal with exceptional social catastrophes.'[50] As the Qur'an states, 'And if you fear that you will not deal justly with the orphans (*yatāmā*), then marry those that please you of the women, two or three or four. But if you fear that you will not be just, then marry only one' (Q. 4:3). The conditional sentence starts by permitting polygamy only as a response to a fear of wronging displaced orphans. Also, when read carefully, the conditional permissibility is restricted to mothers of orphans.[51] The strict conditional temporary permissibility, as al-Qurṭubī (d. 672/1273) asserts, was unanimously interpreted as permitting a general unconditional ruling.[52]

However, what needs to be most stressed here and what could change the way the verse is commonly interpreted is the community and not husbands as the real addressee of the command. As we have already seen, this is clear in Q. 4:1 as the dialogue starts with 'People'. Rethinking the real addressee of Q. 4:3 may provide a paradigm shift in the way polygamy should be conceived. The fear of wronging displaced orphans should be assessed collectively by the community, not individually by husbands. The practical outcome of such an assessment could take the form of a communal declaration of an emergency that renders polygamy a plausible option.[53] Allowing polygamy as a communally determined recourse would entail assessment by community representatives and would only be allowed temporarily, contingent on the emergency case. Husbands, therefore, according to the Qur'an itself, are not authorised to make such unilateral decisions. It is a decision for the community authorities alone. This view appears to have been endorsed by Muḥammad Rashīd Riḍā (d. 1935) and Muḥammad 'Abduh (d. 1905). In addressing the harms polygamy brings to families and nations Riḍā asserted the role scholars can play in terms of calling to question the unqualified permissibility of polygamy. As he confirms, 'Abduh urged imams and scholars to change the rulings to accommodate current

50 Hasan, *Decoding the Egalitarianism of the Qur'an*, 92.

51 Not orphan girls, as is commonly but wrongly adopted by many exegetes. For the full argument, see ibid., 90–100.

52 Muḥammad b. Aḥmad al-Qurṭubī, *al-Jāmiʿ li-aḥkām al-Qurʾān* (Beirut: Mu'assasat al-Risāla, 2006), 6:26.

53 As I argue in *Decoding the Egalitarianism of the Qur'an*, other Qur'anic conditions include the permission of the first wife. Lacking such an approval could literally nullify the permissibility, even in times of nationally declared catastrophes. Adding new financial responsibilities to the family is a sacrifice that may be justified if agreed by both husband and wife, the latter also consenting to the emotional consequences entailed by sharing her husband with another wife.

needs.[54] In our times, a *fatwā* (legal edict issued by the court) could, then, be the legally sanctioned and assessed means to allow or prohibit polygamy, not the individual judgement of husbands. While many argue for reforming polygamy practices in the Arab world today, few think of this necessity as a Qur'anic argument, instead of a mere response to modernity and Westernised policies. As Barbara Freyer Stowasser soundly observers, 'That the topic of polygamy engenders a defensive reaction in modern conservative Muslims is partially due to Western criticism of that institution. While the conservative defence of polygamy is mainly directed at the West, its real target are those modern Muslims who, in accommodation to Western norms, fail to support polygamy as an intricate part of the moral Islamic social order.'[55]

The need to question polygamy as an individual decision for husbands sounds alien to many today. However, this reaction is not based on any incompatibility with the Qur'an, which literally addresses the community, not husbands, with its conditional permissibility; rather, it is due to a long history of marginalising the Qur'an and overlooking the meticulousness of its language.

5 Conclusion

Undoubtedly, the argument from the elite male addressee and its implications for regulative verses carries extensive implications not only for medieval readings of the Qur'an, dominated by a clear tendency to masculinise the divine text, but also for our modern understanding of it. The myth of the elite male addressee has created a gap, ever widening not only between the text and its medieval legal applications, but also between the text as a genderless dialogue and its common (mis)interpretation as an exclusively male-centred book.

Bibliography

Abdel Haleem, Muhammad A.S. *The Qur'an*. New York: Oxford University Press, 2010.

Abusulayman, Abdulhamid A. *Marital Discord: Recapturing Human Dignity through the Higher Objectives of Islamic Law*. Revised ed. London: International Institute of Islamic Thought, 2008.

54 Rashīd Riḍā, *Tafsīr al-manār* (Cairo: Dār al-Manār, 1947), 4:350.

55 Barbara Freyer Stowasser, *Women in the Qur'an, Traditions, and Interpretation* (New York: Oxford University Press, 1994), 121. This does not mean that polygamy is inherently Islamic, and monogamy is inherently 'Western'.

Amin, Yasmin. 'Revisiting the Issue of Minor Marriages: Multidisciplinary *Ijtihād* on Contemporary Ethical Problems'. In *Islamic Interpretive Tradition and Gender Justice: Processes of Canonization, Subversion, and Change*, edited by Nevin Reda and Yasmin Amin, 315–63. Montreal: McGill-Queen's University Press, 2020.

Bakhtiar, Laleh. *The Sublime Quran*. Chicago: Kazi Publishers, 2007.

Bauer, Karen. *Gender Hierarchy in the Qur'ān: Medieval Interpretations, Modern Responses*. New York: Cambridge University Press, 2015.

Bauer, Karen. '*The Male Is Not Like the Female* (Q 3:36): The Question of Gender Egalitarianism in the Qur'ān'. *Religion Compass* 3, no. 4 (2009): 637–54.

Bauer, Karen. '"Traditional" Exegeses of Q 4:34'. *Comparative Islamic Studies* 2, no. 2 (2008): 129–42.

al-Biqāʿī, Burhān al-Dīn. *Naẓm al-durar fī tanāsub al-āyāt wa-l-suwar*. Cairo: Dār al-Kitāb al-Islāmī, 1984.

Chaudhry, Ayesha S. *Domestic Violence and the Islamic Tradition*. Oxford: Oxford University Press, 2013.

Hammer, Juliane. 'To Work for Change: Normativity, Feminism, and Islam'. In 'Roundtable on Normativity in Islamic Studies', edited by Cynthia Eller. Special issue, *Journal of the American Academy of Religion* 84, no. 1 (2016): 98–112.

Hasan, Abla. *Decoding the Egalitarianism of the Qur'an: Retrieving Lost Voices on Gender*. Lanham, MD: Lexington Books, 2019.

Ibn ʿAbbās, ʿAbd Allāh. *Tanwīr al-miqbās min tafsīr Ibn ʿAbbās*. Beirut: Dār al-Kutub al-ʿIlmiyya, 1992.

Ibn ʿAjība, Aḥmad b. Muḥammad. *al-Baḥr al-madīd fī tafsīr al-Qur'ān al-majīd*. Cairo: al-Hay'a al-Miṣriyya al-ʿĀmma li-l-Kitāb, 1999.

Ibn ʿĀshūr, Muḥammad b. al-Ṭāhir. *al-Taḥrīr wa-l-tanwīr*. Tunis: al-Dār al-Tūnisiyya, 1984.

Knysh, Alexander. 'Multiple Areas of Influence'. In *The Cambridge Companion to the Qur'ān*, edited by Jane Dammen McAuliffe, 211–33. Cambridge: Cambridge University Press, 2006.

Morrow, John Andrew. *The Most Controversial Qur'anic Verse: Why 4:34 Does Not Promote Violence against Women*. Lanham, MD: Hamilton Books, 2020.

Mubarak, Hadia. 'Change through Continuity: A Case Study of Q. 4:34 in Ibn ʿĀshūr's *al-Taḥrīr wa'l-tanwīr*'. *Journal of Qur'anic Studies* 20, no. 1 (2018): 1–27.

Muslim b. al-Ḥajjāj. *Ṣaḥīḥ Muslim*. Riyadh: Dār Ṭayba, 2006.

al-Qurṭubī, Muḥammad b. Aḥmad. *al-Jāmiʿ li-aḥkām al-Qur'ān*. Beirut: Mu'assasat al-Risāla, 2006.

Reda, Nevin. 'The Qur'an and Domestic Violence: An Islamic Feminist, Spiritually Integrative Reading of Verse 4:34'. *International Journal of Practical Theology* 23, no. 2 (2019): 257–73.

Riḍā, Rashīd. *Ḥuqūq al-nisāʾ fī al-Islām*. Beirut and Damascus: al-Maktab al-Islāmī, 1984.

Riḍā, Rashīd. *Tafsīr al-manār*. Cairo: Dār al-Manār, 1947.

Souaiaia, Ahmed E. *Contesting Justice: Women, Islam, Law, and Society*. Albany: SUNY Press, 2008.

Stowasser, Barbara Freyer. *Women in the Qurʾan, Traditions, and Interpretation*. New York: Oxford University Press, 1994.

Wadud, Amina. *Qurʾan and Woman: Rereading the Sacred Text from a Woman's Perspective*. 2nd ed. New York: Oxford University Press, 1999.

CHAPTER 5

On the Universality of the Divine Commands versus the Casuistic Interpretation of the Regulative Verses

Gholamreza Aavani

Before embarking on a discussion of the regulative verses of the Qur'an (*āyāt al-aḥkām*), I should offer a clear definition of this term and then identify precisely the due place of such verses in the overall conspectus of the Holy Book. This, in my view, is very important considering the fact that the regulative verses comprise no more than 300–400, or at most 500, of the approximately 6,400 verses therein. They are, in sum, verses relating to the science of jurisprudence or, in other words, the science of Islamic legal theory inasmuch as they form the basis for the derivation or deduction of legal rulings which cumulatively constitute the Islamic substantive law.[1]

---

1 In his forthcoming book entitled *Āyāt al-aḥkām* (*The Regulatory Verses*), Ayatollah Mohaghegh Damad provides the following definition of this term:

"*Āyāt al-aḥkām* (regulative verses), also called *āyāt al-Qur'ān* and *fiqh al-Qur'ān*, are those verses of the Glorious Qur'an which expound the rules and regulations pertaining to the Sharīʿa, jurisprudence, and Islamic law. It is also a well-known and technical term used as a title for some books of rational jurisprudence written on the basis of the jurisprudential verses of the Holy Qur'an.

Āyāt al-aḥkām are the first and most valid source for the knowledge of the rules and regulations of Islamic legal theory and in other words (see Jaʿfarī Langarūdī, 1–46) they are the foundation of Islamic law. Muslim jurisprudents consider the knowledge of *āyāt al-aḥkām* as a necessary prerequisite for *ijtihād* (independent judgement of legal questions) (ʿAllāma Ḥillī, 3:423; Ibn ʿAllāma, 4:301–2; Shahīd Thānī, 3:62–63).

In a general purview all the subjects and problems of the Holy Qur'an can be classified into five categories:

1. The fundamental tenets of religion including topics such as demonstrating the existence of the Artificer (*Ṣāniʿ*) of the universe, His uniqueness, and His attributes of beauty and perfection; universal prophecy and the specific prophecy of the Holy Prophet; the hereafter and the conditions of the Day of Resurrection; Paradise and Hell; punishment of the sinners and the universal divine forgiveness and the like; and again the need for the existence of the inerrant Imāms, the leadership of the Muslim community, and the characteristics of such a leader.

 | HTTPS://DOI.ORG/10.1163/9789004755567-007

This chapter consists of two parts: in the first, I briefly present the views of four Muslim philosophers and thinkers, namely, Fārābī, Avicenna (Ibn Sīnā),

---

2. The canonical laws of Islam (*sharāʾiʿ*) including knowledge of issues concerning religious worship such as rules of purification (*ṭahāra*), ritual prayer, fasting, pilgrimage, Holy War, bidding the right and forbidding the wrong, alms-tax, giving a fifth of one's revenue (*khums*); legal issues such as transactions, mortgaging (*rahn*), leasing, reconciliation, debts; rules of statute law such as marriage, divorce, inheritance and laws of bequest, guardianship; the penal code such as legal punishment, blood-money, retaliation; official, political, and social affairs such as adjudication, statesmanship; rules pertaining to the Islamic community, international and intercommunal relations.
3. Events and stories about bygone religious communities, former prophets and their contentions with their contemporary tyrants such as the stories about Moses and Pharaoh, Jesus and the Apostles, Abraham and Nimrod.
4. Ethical issues elucidating and determining the exalted and sublime moral values and criteria as expounded in the Holy Qur'an as a whole.
5. Issues related to the Qur'anic cosmology such as the existence of the world, creation of the heavens and the earth, as well as the human, animal, and mineral kingdoms.

The subject of discussion in jurisprudence and its principles is exclusively restricted to the second category; I mean those legal laws and rulings which are conventionally called *āyāt al-aḥkam* (regulative verses).

The firmness and ratification of the regulative verses goes to such an extent that even those scholars who believe in the alteration of certain Qur'anic verses (*taḥrīf*) staunchly believe in the authenticity of the regulative verses (see Aghā Buzurg, 1:220–21; Mārifat et al., 90). At least this much is certain that they have not been distorted and altered in the passage of time."

I am very grateful to Professor Damad for kindly granting me access to the unpublished manuscript of his book.

The four schools of jurisprudence (Ḥanafī, Shāfiʿī, Mālikī, and Ḥanbalī) were consolidated before the middle to the end of the second century of the Islamic era. Most dogmatic theologians as well as scholars of the four schools excommunicated the philosophers (*falāsifa*) on the grounds that philosophy was an alien Greek intrusion into Islamic soil. Philosophers, on the other hand, identified philosophy with *al-ḥikma*, often mentioned and praised in the Qur'an as the basis of all divine revelations, and consequently they tried to reconcile Greek philosophy with the main tenets of the Qur'an, a fact which was very rarely or never accepted by the majority of Muslim jurisprudents and dogmatic theologians (scholars of *kalām*) who compiled many treatises against philosophers. Philosophers (*ḥukamāʾ*), on the other hand, considered the *fuqahāʾ* as reductionists who concentrated solely on the ramifications (*furūʿ*) of religion at the expense of the more fundamental principles (*uṣūl*) of faith as embodied in the Qur'an proper, both of which, according to them, are required for salvation.

It should not be forgotten that the criticisms of our authors are levelled at the jurists in the traditional Muslim community where all believed in the divine authority of the Quran and in the necessity of the regulative verses (*āyāt al-aḥkām*) as essential and indispensable for the ultimate salvation of humankind and their proximity to God. How could hundreds of such verses be totally ignored or denied by a Muslim who believed that every word of the Holy Scripture was a revelation of God? This is an undeniable fact accepted by both parties in question.

Ghazālī and Mullā Ṣadrā, about jurisprudence (*fiqh*);[2] in the second, I try as far as possible to identify the place of *fiqh* in the overall context of the Qur'an.[3]

1 Fārābī

Fārābī has two different views about *fiqh* in his two treatises, namely, the *Enumeration of Sciences* (*Iḥṣā' al-'ulūm*) and his *Book of Religion* (*Kitāb al-milla*). The *Enumeration* has five parts,[4] the fifth part of which is assigned to political philosophy and its constituents plus the sciences of jurisprudence (*fiqh*) and dogmatic theology (*kalām*). Fārābī here calls political philosophy a science (*'ilm* or certain demonstrative knowledge) and briefly discusses as to how and under what conditions it can have a scientific status,[5] but everywhere he refers to *fiqh* and *kalām* as art rather than science, both of which in addition deal with 'opinions and actions'.[6]

According to Fārābī, *kalām* at best is conducive to opinion (*ẓann*) rather than science (*'ilm*), and at worst to sophistry and in this connection he analyses briefly the views of the different groups of dialectical theologians. Some do not accept the authority of reason. If religion could be justified rationally,

2 One of the reasons for writing this chapter was my concern about the status of *fiqh* as viewed by some Muslim philosophers and distinguished thinkers such as Fārābī and Avicenna (both belonging to the Peripatetic School), Ghazālī, who in his compilations viewed all the sciences, including jurisprudence, from a gnostic perspective, and Mullā Ṣadrā, the founder of so-called Transcendent theosophy (*al-ḥikma al-muta'āliyya*), who has dealt with this problem copiously in his various books.

Even though our authors belonged to different schools of thought and manipulated different methodologies, all of them had a comprehensive view about the various branches of knowledge, such as theology, metaphysics, cosmology, angelology, eschatology, and practical philosophy, which permitted them to identify the real status of jurisprudence (*fiqh*) among the different sciences.

3 In the second part of this chapter, I try to identify the status of the regulative verses vis-à-vis the other verses of the Qur'an. Even if the regulative verses are part and parcel of the Qur'an and of paramount importance in the daily life of Muslims, especially with regard to acts of worship and public or private transactions, what happens if we over-emphasize them at the expense of the other verses of the Qur'an, which deal with the ultimate becoming of man and with the other constitutive principles of religion, especially if they overshadow or conflict with the fundamentals of religion, as it has so often happened in the past and is quite tangible in the contemporary Islamic civilisation?

4 For the other four parts of the *Enumeration*, see Charles E. Butterworth, trans., *Alfarabi, the Political Writings: Selected Aphorisms and Other Texts* (Ithaca and London: Cornell University Press, 2004), 72.

5 Ibid., 76–80.

6 Ibid., 80–81.

they argue, there would be no need for revelation.[7] Still others try to prove the validity of religion by miracles and, moreover, the faith of believers in religion in their view is due to the veracity of messengers.[8] Others resort to the most remote kinds of interpretation to resolve the supposed contradictions in religion.[9]

Yet others try to refute an adversary who finds something repulsive in their religion by seeking something as repulsive in the adversary's or in other religions.[10] Some even try to ward off their religion from the dialectical onslaught of the adversary by resorting to every kind of deceit, falsehood, slander and sophism.[11]

This negative view about the *fuqahāʾ* (sing. *faqīh*), or jurists, as well as *mutakallimūn* (dialectical theologians) might be because most of the *fuqahāʾ* of Fārābī's time were also theologians, as he states implicitly.[12]

Fārābī's approach to jurisprudence in his *Kitāb al-milla* (*Book of Religion*), where he explores the relationship between philosophy and religion, is quite different. There jurisprudence is considered as a branch of political science and he argues that if political science is to attain ultimate happiness, it should be governed by a virtuous religion[13] and a religion is virtuous if, and only if, it

---

7 Ibid., 81.

8 Ibid., 82.

9 Ibid.

10 Ibid., 83.

11 Ibid., 84.

12 'It (dialectical theology) is different from jurisprudence (*fiqh*) in that the jurist takes the opinions and actions declared by the founder of a religion as a given and sets them down as fundamentals from which he infers the things that necessarily follow from them, whereas the dialectical theologian defends the things the jurist uses as fundamentals without inferring other things from them. If it happens that there is a certain human being who has the ability to do both matters, he is a jurist and a dialectical theologian. He defends them insofar as he is a dialectical theologian and he infers them insofar as he is a jurist' (ibid., 80–81).

13 'If the first ruler is virtuous and his rulership is truly virtuous, then in what he prescribes he seeks only to obtain for himself and for everyone under his rulership the ultimate happiness that is truly happiness and that religion would be virtuous religion' (ibid.).

Practical philosophy has been variously defined as knowledge that culminates in actions or investigation into what is human or subject to volition and art. But according to Fārābī this is not a valid definition because sciences such as mathematics (geometry, arithmetic, and optics) sometimes investigate matters which are subject to human volition. They are part of theoretical philosophy and not practical or political philosophy because they do not enquire into these things from the perspective of what makes human beings happy or miserable. When, however, the object of inquiry is whether they ultimately end in human happiness or misery, then they belong to practical philosophy. Abū Naṣr al-Fārābī, 'Kitāb al-jadal', in *al-Manṭiq ʿinda al-Fārābī*, ed. Rafīq al-ʿAjam (Beirut: Dār-al Mashriq, 1985), 3:10–18. See also Miriam Galston, 'The Theoretical and Practical

is subordinated to theoretical and practical philosophy. The practical things in religion are those whose universals are demonstrated in practical philosophy. The theoretical opinions that are in religion have their demonstrative proofs in theoretical philosophy and are taken in religion without demonstrative proofs.[14]

Fārābī extensively deals with the case of a virtuous ruler of an ideal city who should possess twelve characteristic traits, the most important being *al-ḥikma*, or divine wisdom, without which the city would be ignorant. The aim of political rulership should be the attainment of ultimate happiness, which cannot be attained in this life, but only in the hereafter.[15] Only those voluntary actions which contribute to the attainment of ultimate happiness can be called virtuous and virtuous actions are only those which contribute to the ultimate happiness of man.[16]

To sum up, according to Fārābī, the establishment of a virtuous community is impossible without a common virtuous religion, bolstered by theoretical and practical wisdom. A community ruled only by *fuqāhā'* and dialectical theologians is undesirable as it leads to unnecessary limitations, which, based on 'opinions and actions', pretend to offer a complete view of the reality of revelation, but cannot in themselves without *al-ḥakma* (philosophy) provide a sound and just life in a political community.[17]

2 Avicenna

One of the great concerns of Avicenna was to reconcile religion and philosophy both in their theoretical and practical aspects.[18] In his *On the Divisions of*

Dimensions of Happiness as Portrayed in the Political Treatises of al-Fārābī', in *The Political Aspects of Islamic Philosophy: Essays in Honor of Muhsin S. Mahdi*, ed. Charles E. Butterworth (Cambridge, MA: Harvard University Press, 1992), 95–151.

In addition, in the opening paragraph of his *Taḥṣīl al-sa'āda*, Fārābī states that 'the things by means of which nations and citizens of cities attain earthly happiness and supreme happiness in the life beyond are the deliberative virtues, moral virtues and practical arts along with the theoretical virtues' (Galston, 'Dimensions of Happiness', 103).

14 Butterworth, *Alfarabi*, 97.

15 For the characteristics of an ideal ruler according to Fārābī, see Abū Naṣr al-Fārābī, *Ārā' ahl al-madīna al-fāḍila wa-muḍāddatuhā*, ed. Friedrich Dieterici (Leiden: Brill, 1895), 59–60.

16 Butterworth, *Alfarabi*, 101. See also note 13 above.

17 For further details, see ibid., 74ff.

18 Among his contemporary philosophers or those engaged in philosophy there was no serious attempt to reconcile religion and philosophy demonstratively. Ibn Miskawayh and 'Āmirī, for example, connected with the school of al-Kindī, focused on the ethical

the Rational Sciences (*Fī aqsām al-ʿulūm al-ʿaqliyya*) he lays special emphasis on the Sharīʿa, which he designates as *al-nāmūs* and, moreover, identifies with practical philosophy and claims its priority and superiority to Greek practical philosophy.[19]

---

teachings of earlier philosophers. The Ismāʿīlī Shīʿī theologians (to which Avicenna's family belonged) deployed Hellenistic intellectual heritage to justify the political claims of their party. The scholastic commentators of Aristotle in Baghdad, who were mostly Christian, had no interest in such reconciliation. Another group, exemplified by his correspondent and contemporary the famous Muslim savant and scientist al-Bīrūnī, were not concerned with philosophy and rigorous philosophical speculation. One may say therefore that Avicenna was a unique philosopher of his age who tried by rigorous apodictic proofs and logical demonstration to prove the validity of the major themes in the Islamic revelation and hence the authenticity of the Sharīʿa. He had tremendous influence even on his opponents such as Ghazālī and his attempt of reconciliation between reason and revelation was followed, perfected, and brought to fruition by later Muslim sages and speculative mystics such as Suhrawardī, the followers of Ibn al-ʿArabī (Qūnawī, Kāshānī, and Qayṣarī), and especially Mullā Ṣadrā and his school. See James W. Morris, 'The Philosopher-Prophet in Avicenna's Political Philosophy', in *The Political Aspects of Islamic Philosophy*, 153–55.

19 Muslims were not familiar with the *Politics* of Aristotle, which they most probably knew through his other works. There is common consensus among scholars that it was not translated into Arabic. But in lieu of Aristotle's *Politics* they drew copiously from Plato's *Laws* (*nomoi*), which was rendered into Arabic as *nawāmīs* as evidenced by Fārābī's *Talkhīṣ al-nawāmīs* (Epitome of Plato's *Laws*). Avicenna mentions Plato in this connection:

"By this part of practical philosophy (*nawāmīs*) is known the necessity of prophecy and why humankind is in need of the Sharīʿa both in their existence, survival, and their ultimate becoming in the hereafter. Again by *nāmūs* is known the common and universal elements in all divine laws (*sharāʾiʿ*) and that which is peculiar and specific to each single Sharīʿa in each religious community (*umma*) and in each single era. Again through *nāmūs* one can distinguish between veracious divine prophecy and all other vain claims to prophethood.

Philosophers do not mean by *nāmūs* what is conjectured by common people by which they understand artifice (*ḥīla*) and subterfuge (*khadīʿa*). But for philosophers *nāmūs* signifies eternal norms sanctioned by the *sunna* [words and deeds of the Prophet] and independent self-subsistent laws descended through revelation. Arabs again signify by this term the angel who brings down the revelation.

By the third part of practical philosophy is recognised the virtuous and the unvirtuous kinds of statesmanship and political communities and again by which is known the reason for their rise, continuance, and the cause of their decline. That part of which deals with government (*mulk*) is to be found in the works of Plato and Aristotle and that part which pertains to prophecy and the Sharīʿa is comprised in the two books of the laws (*al-nawāmīs*)."

In the above citation one can see a tinge of Plato's *Laws*, to be distinguished from more rigorous regulative verses. See M. Kadivar, 'Avicenna & the Classification of Philosophy', *The Journal of Saptiential Wisdom and Philosophy* (*Sophia Perennis*) 5, no. 9 (2009): 35–106.

In the tenth book of *al-Shifāʾ* Avicenna elaborates the same points in greater detail.

Again, in the introduction to his *Oriental Philosophy* (*al-Ḥikma al-mashriqiyya*), after treating the three branches of practical philosophy, he emphasises the fact that the legislator for these three branches should be one person and, ideally, no other than a messenger of God.[20] It is clear that for Avicenna *al-nāmūs* or the Sharīʿa in this sense has a much wider domain and extent and a broader significance than *fiqh*, because it comprises the whole gamut of practical philosophy.

The tenth book of Avicenna's *al-Shifāʾ* (*The Book of Healing*) is dedicated to practical philosophy,[21] but oddly one finds no trace of Aristotelian practical philosophy. Rather, it is an attempt to justify the principles of the Islamic Sharīʿa and especially the Prophetic revelation on the basis of his own philosophical premises.

The tenth book of *al-Shifāʾ* comprises the following topics:[22] the first principle and the procession of beings from the first principle; the ranks of intelligences or spiritual angels; the celestial souls; the four elements of the sublunary sphere; the generation of man; inspirations and veracious dreams; how supplications are answered; the nature of celestial rewards and punishments;[23] the nature of prophecy and how messengers call people to God; life in the hereafter;[24] the kinds of worship and their benefits in this life and in the next;[25] prophet as legislator; the establishment of a city and its social institutions such as households and marriage; how the Sharīʿa can be preserved through ritual acts such as canonical prayers and fasting;[26] caliphs and imams and the necessity to obey them and whether they should be chosen or appointed and the punishment of those who disobey them.[27]

Again, in his *Allusions and Remarks* (*al-Ishārāt wa-l-tanbīhāt*) in the last section on the 'Stations of Gnostics' (*maqāmāt al-ʿārifīn*), Avicenna makes a

20 According to Avicenna the necessity of a *nabī* (prophet) for the harmonisation of legislation in the three branches of practical philosophy is predicated on the fact that human beings are to achieve ultimate felicity in this world and the next. 'Of course we do not mean that it is an invented and fabricated art (*ṣanāʿa*), not being revealed by God and that every man endowed with intelligence can afford to undertake it. Such can never be the case. This kind of legislation can only come from God' (Avicenna, *Manṭiq al-mashriqiyyīn* (Qom: Marashi Najafi Library, 1984), 7–8).

21 See Michael E. Marmura, trans., *The Metaphysics of the Healing* (Provo: Brigham Young University Press, 2005), 358–78.

22 Ibid., 358–64.

23 Ibid., 364–67.

24 Ibid., 367–70.

25 Ibid., 370–74.

26 Ibid., 374–78.

27 Ibid., 378.

distinction between the ascetics (*zuhhād*, sing. *zāhid*) and the gnostics (*ʿārifīn*, sing. *ʿārif*). The ascetics worship God for some gain as if exchanging something in this world for something else in the hereafter, whereas true gnostics aim at nothing but divine satisfaction and His proximity. That is why they disdain whatever turns them away from the vision of the Real.

In the *Ishārāt*, the entire Sharīʿa, which Avicenna had exposited in his other works, especially in the tenth book of *al-Shifāʾ*, is relegated to the station of the ascetics, but the gnostics possess still a higher spiritual rank because they do not view religion as a means of transacting with God, but they worship Him out of sincere love and because for them He is essentially worthy of adoration.[28]

In sum, Avicenna tries to prove that the Sharīʿa in Islam is a perfect paragon of practical philosophy with its different branches. Hence, for him, the Sharīʿa is not equivalent to *fiqh* or jurisprudence, which at most might be its offshoot or a subsidiary.

3 Ghazālī

In the first chapter of his *Iḥyāʾ al-ʿulūm al-dīn*, Ghazālī elaborates on five critical terms which had significantly changed their meanings in his day, one of which is *fiqh*:[29]

> because nowadays it is specifically applied to the knowledge of some strange ramifications about legal verdicts and to the knowledge of their exact causes. The *fuqahāʾ* have exceeded their bounds in discussing such topics and in preserving what has been said in these matters. He who is more engaged in and delves more deeply into such subjects is said to be more learned and knowledgeable in jurisprudence (*afqah*). But *fiqh* in the first generation was absolutely applied to the knowledge of the hereafter (*ʿilm al-ākhira*) and a profound cognition of the minute details concerning the evil corruptions of the soul and the causes for the perversion of religious deeds. *Fiqh* at that time was concerned about the transitoriness and pettiness of this world and vehemently inclined to disclose the blessings of the hereafter. Fear of God overwhelmed their hearts.[30]

---

28 See Avicenna, *al-Ishārāt wa-l-tanbīhāt* (Cairo: Dār al-Maʿārif, 1957–60), 370.

29 The other four terms are 'knowledge' (*al-ʿilm*), 'unification' (*al-tawḥīd*), 'invocation' (*al-tadhkīr*), and 'philosophy' (*al-ḥikma*).

30 Abū Ḥāmid al-Ghazālī, *Iḥyāʾ ʿulūm al-dīn* (Cairo: al-Hayʾa al-Miṣriyya al-ʿĀmma li-l-Kitāb, 2018), 37–38.

According to Ghazālī, the expression *li-yatafaqqahu fī al-dīn* (Q. 9:122) mentioned in the Qur'an means a profound understanding of religion, not legal rulings such as divorce (*ṭalāq*), manumission of slaves (*ʿitq*), the oath of condemnation (*liʿān*), forward purchase (*salam*), or leasing (*ijāra*). Continuous involvement in such acts, according to our author, hardens the heart and furthers one from the fear of God.[31]

To verify his point, Ghazālī cites certain verses of the Qur'an,[32] some traditions of the Prophet, and the sayings of some Muslim Sufi saints. But in the end, Ghazālī diminishes the pungency of his attack and admits a subsidiary place for *fiqh* in the overall context of religion. 'I do not say that the word *fiqh* was not used for judicial rulings, but it was used in a much wider sense. Its usage regarding the knowledge of the hereafter was more prevalent.'[33]

4 Mullā Ṣadrā

Mullā Ṣadrā was acutely aware of all the aberrations of religion in his age. Persia had been converted to Shīʿism in the Safavid period and the *fuqahā'* from near and far had migrated to Iran and some of them had occupied the highest governmental, administrative, and religious positions, causing the emigration of many scholars, philosophers, and scientises especially to Mughal India.[34]

Ṣadrā has written extensively against some Sufis who repudiated the fundamentals of the Sharīʿa. In his *Risāleh-i seh aṣl* (*Treatise on the Three Principles*), in Persian, he has vehemently attacked the lackadaisical and lukewarm Sufis of his time who did not take the injunctions and laws of the Sharīʿa seriously.[35] In his other writings such as *Kasr al-aṣnām al-jāhiliyya* (*Breaking the Idols of Ignorance*), on the contrary, he has taken to task the *fuqahā'* of his time who have reduced the religion of Islam to a sort of juristic casuistry. There he complains that the name *faqīh* in his days is used for those who approach rulers and kings from among tyrants and high-ranking governmental officials. They

31 Ibid.

32 '"They have hearts by which they do not comprehend" (Q. 7:179) by which is meant deep faith in God and not issuing legal verdicts. Upon my life (la-ʿamrī) the words *fiqh* and *fahm* (deep understanding) are two words for the same meaning' (ibid.).

33 Ibid.

34 See, for example, Dhabīḥ Allāh Ṣafā, *Tārikh-i adabiyyāt-i Īrān*, 9th ed. (Tehran: Intishārāt-i Firdaws, Tehran, 1979), 180ff.

35 See Mullā Ṣadrā, *Risāleh-i seh aṣl*, ed. Seyyed Hossein Nasr (Tehran: Mulla Sadra Foundation, 1961).

issue long legal verdicts and unjust judgements. They are, moreover, audacious enough in demolishing the Sacred Law and even dare to perpetrate religiously forbidden acts. They lay violent hands on the property of the poor and deal high-handedly with the miserable and the downtrodden, taking possession and disposing freely of their property. They use all kinds of legal subterfuges in deducing disputative and controversial religious problems, authorising and encouraging them to actions which cause damage and are anathema to religion.[36]

In his commentary on the *Uṣūl al-kāfī* of al-Kulaynī, commenting on the Prophetic tradition that seeking knowledge is incumbent on all Muslims, Ṣadrā after elaborating on the various kinds of exoteric and esoteric sciences remarks that if a *faqīh* is asked about the meaning of one of those esoteric terms, such things as sincere devotion (*al-ikhlāṣ*) or trust in God (*al-tawakkul*) or about how to avoid hypocrisy, he would be dumbfounded, even if it is his individual religious obligation (*farḍ ʿaynihi*) to know it and neglecting it would lead to his perdition in the hereafter. But if you ask him about technical terms in jurisprudence, he will carry on a long-winded conversation which will fill volumes of precise definitions and would never be needed in all of one's lifetime. Such a person surmises that he is engaged in the true science of religion, but in fact he is fraudulently deceiving himself as well as others.[37]

From the above exposition one could say that according to Fārābī, Avicenna, Ghazālī, and Mullā Ṣadrā, one cannot dispense with the regulative verses which are necessary for the derivation and deduction of rulings inextricably

36 Mullā Ṣadrā, *Kasr al-aṣnām al-jāhiliyya*, ed. Mohsen Jahangiri (Tehran: Mulla Sadra Foundation, 1961), 54–55.

37 Mullā Ṣadrā, *Sharḥ al-Uṣūl al-kāfī*, ed. S.M. Rajai (Tehran: Mulla Sadra Foundation, 1965), 2:31. Also quoting from the *Iḥyāʾ* of Ghazālī, Ṣadrā narrates that somebody asked something from Ḥasan al-Baṣrī, the well-known ascetic of the first century, and Ḥasan gave him an answer. The questioner said: 'The *fuqahāʾ* all disagree with you,' whereupon Ḥasan rejoined: 'May your mother be bereaved of you! Have you ever seen a *faqīh* with your eyes? A real *faqīh* is one who is abstemious in this world, ever desirous of the hereafter, one who is endowed with deep insight in his religion, who perseveres in the worship of his Lord, and is God-fearing. He is the one who desists from dishonouring people, is chaste in their property, and sincere to them in his counsels' (ibid., 187–88).

Again, in his commentary on the verse 'confound not truth with falsehood nor knowingly conceal the truth' (Q. 2:42), Ṣadrā recounts a story from Ibn al-ʿArabī's *al-Futūḥāt* about a conversation between him and Malik al-Ẓāhir (Saladin's son) about the deviousness and perversion of the *fuqahāʾ* in his realm who commit abominable and atrocious things and perpetrate acts of injustice. See Mullā Ṣadrā, *Tafsīr al-Qurʾān al-karīm*, ed. Mohammad Khajavi (Qom: Bidār, 1987), 3:1118; and Ibn al-ʿArabī, *al-Futūḥāt al-Makkiyya*, ed. ʿUthmān Yaḥyā (Cairo: al-Hayʾa al-Miṣriyya al-ʿĀmma li-l-Kitāb, 1911), ch. 318.

bound to one's daily life, but they are not sufficient in themselves, if excised and taken out of the overall Qur'anic context and at the expense of the more fundamental articles of Islamic faith and especially with almost total disregard to the moral and religious virtues pertaining to all aspects of human life and much emphasised in the Holy Scripture, on the one hand, and by the ancient sages, on the other.

•••

In the final analysis there is some unanimity of opinion among the four great thinkers in that they all regard jurisprudence from a sapiential and divine viewpoint, but there are, no doubt, some differences among them as well. Both Fārābī and Avicenna look at *fiqh* from a purely philosophical perspective which takes into account metaphysical, cosmological, anthropological, political, as well as ethical and soteriological constituents, which are as significant from the religious vantage point.

Fārābī, Ghazālī, and Mullā Ṣadrā, moreover, are inclined to view *fiqh* as it was practised by the *fuqahā'* of their age. Ghazālī as well as Ṣadrā emphasise the meaning of *fiqh* as it was known and practised by the first generation of Muslims. Fārābī does the same, on the ground that *fiqh* is based on 'opinion and action' and furthermore, associated with the irrational suppositions and presumptions of the dialectical theologians, can never attain to the status of a science unless concatenated with a 'virtuous religion' subject to the universal laws of theoretical and practical philosophy (*ḥikma*) under the aegis of a wise ruler or a corporate body of rulers cumulatively having certain essential characteristics, the most important being divine wisdom.

Avicenna, on the other hand, endeavoured to deal with *fiqh* within the context of the Sharīʿa, which he designated as *al-nāmūs* (the Arabicised version of the Greek *nomos*), claiming its superiority to Peripatetic practical philosophy, perhaps approaching what is today called *maqāṣid al-sharīʿa*. Nonetheless he seldom treats of the multifarious virtues related thereto, unless we take his discussions about *maqāmāt al-ʿārifīn* (the stations of gnostics) at the end of the *Ishārāt* and the distinction he makes there between the ascetics (*zuhhād*, representing the Sharīʿa) and gnostics (*ʿārifīn*, representing the sublime divine qualities) as betokening the culmination of virtuousness.

Ṣadrā and Ghazālī, on the other hand, complain about the distancing of the *fuqahā'* from the pristine purity of Islam, exemplified by the first generation of Muslims, and again about the mundane proclivity of the *fuqahā'* who reduce the profound knowledge of religion to juristic casuistry of sorts.

5 Situating Regulative Verses in the Qur'anic Context

According to a Qur'anic verse the Prophet complains in the hereafter about those who had abandoned the Qur'an (Q. 25:30) and, on the other hand, God praises those who hold fast to the Book (Q. 7:170), and thus it is better to scrutinise the status of the regulative verses in connection with the other verses of the Qur'an.

To divide the Qur'an into fragments, moreover, is an unpardonable sin as expressed in the following verses: 'Truly I am a warner ... for those who make division, who made the Qur'an into fragments' (Q. 15:89–91); 'Do you then believe in part of the Book and disbelieve in part?' (Q. 2:85). This again means that the regulative verses should be considered within the whole context of the Sacred Book. Disregard for the other verses, in other words, would bring about the divine punishment upon the community.

6 The Fundamentals of Faith

In the very beginning of the Qur'an the basic elements of the divine guidance and hence of human salvation are stated as follows: 'those who believe in the unseen [the invisible world] and perform the prayer and spend from that which God has provided them; those who believe in what was sent down to you [O Prophet] and in what was sent [to the prophets] before you, and are certain of the hereafter – it is they who are upon guidance from their Lord and it is they who shall prosper' (Q. 2:3–5).

In the end of the same sura the principles of Islamic faith are declared to be faith in what was sent down to the Messenger and belief in God, the angels, His scriptures, and His messengers, without making any distinction between any of them (Q. 2:285). Keeping the above verses in mind one could say that the scope of religion is more extensive than what is implied by the regulative verses, and that the latter garner their meaning and significance only in the light of the above divine principles. In addition, religion comprises some more fundamental elements than what the regulative verses signify.

7 Purity of Faith

Purity of religion (*ikhlāṣ*) means devoting the entire religion to Him and to be sincere in one's devotion: 'So worship God devoting religion entirely to Him' (Q. 39:2); 'Say, "Truly I have been commended to worship God, devoting religion entirely to Him"' (Q. 39:11). Believers are again demanded to devote the religion entirely to Him and to be sincere in their devotions.

The regulative verses, no doubt, are requisite for such devotion but they do not exhaust the whole expanse of religion. Without such purity and sincerity in devotion, the regulative verses almost lose their *raison d'être* or their justification for existence.

8 Religion as the Straight Path

In every religion its messenger is the exemplar to be followed by the believers of that religion. Several verses in the Qur'an emphatically declare this fact with respect to the Prophet. 'Say, "If you love God, follow me and God will love you and forgive you your sin"' (Q. 3:31). So following the Prophet sincerely is a sign of the love of God and in other words, through following the Prophet the faithful become the beloveds of God. 'Say, "This is my Way I call unto God with clear evidence, I and those who follow me"' (Q. 12:108). This way to which all the faithful are summoned to follow is 'the Straight Path' (*al-ṣirāṭ al-mustaqīm*) mentioned in the Opening Chapter (Q. 1).

The regulative verses are no doubt a part and parcel of the Way, but they never exhaust all the possibilities which are necessary for following the Straight Path. One might even say that an over-emphasis on such verses at the expense of the rest would be a deviation from the Straight Path.

9 The Characteristic Traits of the Prophet

The Prophet Muhammad is the ultimate criterion in adjudicating all religious disputes. He is the prototype to be followed by all Muslim believers.

God, the Almighty, praises the Prophet for many of his character traits: 'And truly thou art of an exalted character' (Q. 68:4). The Prophet's wife 'Ā'isha, when asked about his character, responded: 'His character was the Qur'an.' In addition, God, addressing the Prophet, proclaimed: 'We sent thee not save as a mercy unto the worlds' (Q. 21:107), which some take as a reference to the Prophet's utterance that the first thing created was his light (*nūrī*) or his spirit (*rūḥī*).

In Sūrat al-Aḥzāb, God declared the Prophet to be a paradigm or a prototypical exemplar for all believers because of the following characteristic traits: 'Indeed you have in the Messenger of God a beautiful example for those who hope for God and the Last Day and remember God much' (Q. 33:21). The

Prophet had an incredibly vehement love for God and an ardent desire for the Last Day and was a model for those who live in constant remembrance of God.[38] He is, moreover, reported to have said: 'I was chosen [as a prophet] to bring to fruition the noble characteristic traits.'[39]

Clearly, none of the mentioned characteristic traits are the subject of discussion in the regulative verses, and hence one is not permitted to reduce the Qur'an to such so-called regulative verses.

10 All Prophets Are Teachers of the Scripture and Wisdom

In the Qur'an it is emphatically stated that all prophets are teachers of the Scripture and Wisdom (*al-kitāb wa-l-ḥikma*).[40] In the primordial covenant which God made with all the prophets, He promised to bestow the Scripture and Wisdom to all of them (Q. 3:81). In several verses mention of the Scripture and Wisdom is preceded or followed by an emphasis that such Wisdom should be coupled with purification as instructed by the Prophet.[41]

Now, the regulative verses might be partially conducive to divine wisdom and purification of the soul, if and only if they are viewed from the overall perspective of the Scripture as taught by the Prophet.

11 Fragmentation of the Qur'an Is a Grave Sin

To divide the Qur'an into fragments is a grave sin: 'Truly I am a warner … for those who make division, who made the Qur'an into fragments' (Q. 15:89–91); 'Do you then believe in part of the Book and disbelieve in part?' (Q. 2:85).

The above verses signify that the regulative verses should be considered within the whole context of the Book. In other words, utter emphasis on such verses and disregard for the rest would cause divine punishment.

In Sūrat al-Shūrā God has bidden all the prophets 'to establish the religion (*an aqīmū al-dīn*) and not to be divided in it' (Q. 42:13). Now, to uphold the

38 He is reported to have said, 'My two eyes fall asleep, but my heart never sleeps,' meaning that he was constantly remembering God even while asleep.

39 See, for example, Mullā Ṣadrā, *al-Ḥikma al-muta'āliyya fī al-asfār al-'aqliyya al-arba'a*, ed. Reza Akbarain (Tehran: Mulla Sadra Foundation, 1962), 9:118. See also Muḥammad Bāqir Majlisī, *Biḥār al-anwār* (Beirut: Dār Iḥyā' al-Turāth al-'Arabī, 1983), vol. 70, ch. 59, *ḥadīth* no. 18.

40 Q. 2:231, 3:48, 5:110.

41 Q. 2:129, 2:151, 3:164.

religion means to establish it as a whole, which would require to obey all its injunctions and prohibitions of which the regulative verses are only a part, and if taken to be the whole, without meticulous attention to the other verses, would be detrimental to religion.

12 Unity of the Islamic Community

In some verses God addressing the Muslim community says: 'Indeed this community of yours is one community and I am your Lord so worship Me' (Q. 21:92; see also 23:52). Still, another verse emphasises that at the beginning all men belonged to one single community and there arose dissension and strife among them, so God sent messengers to humankind in order to resolve those dissensions and to restore unity among them. The cause of this dissension in all the pertinent verses is declared to be *al-baghy*, which means transgression, covetousness, and a strong inclination towards injustice and iniquity.[42]

Now traditionally, jurisprudence, based on the derivation and deduction of legal rules from the regulative verses when associated with the tenets of the dogmatic theology, has often been the cause of much dissension and disunity in the Islamic world.

In several other verses to make factions in religion is categorically forbidden.[43] A believer is not permitted to make hostile factions in religion and unduly discriminate between religions or to separate God from His messengers or the messengers of God from each other. So an undue emphasis on the regulative verses might contribute to the emergence of an insidious factionalism as we are witnessing copiously in the Muslim world today.

13 The Universality of Religion in Islam

Islam proclaims the universality of religion as witnessed in the second testimony of faith (*al-nubuwwa*), and admits the validity of all previous religions based on the divine revelations, provided that the believers of each religion uphold it as it was prescribed by its messenger and its Scripture. Besides, in many verses, the Qur'an confirms and bears witness to the truth and validity of all revelations.[44] On the other hand, in at least two verses the Prophet is

42 Q. 2:213, 3:19, 42:14, 45:17.

43 For example, Q. 2:136, 3:103, 3:105, 4:150, 4:152, 6:153, 6:159, 30:32, 42:13–14, 98:4.

44 Q. 2:41, 2:97, 3:81, 4:47, 5:48, 6:92, 46:12.

declared to be sent to all the humankind.[45] Hence faith in all religions and all messengers and Scriptures is incumbent on Muslims who, moreover, are required to make no distinction between any of His messengers (Q. 2:258). Faith in all previous religions entails belief in their authenticity and disbelief in them is accounted as egregious misguidance (Q. 4:136).

Several other verses, in addition, emphasise that it has been the eternal decree of God that humankind should not belong to one single religious community.[46] In Sūrat al-Mā'ida it is specifically stated that for each community 'He has appointed a divine law and a Path. Had God willed, He would have made you one single community but His will is to test you with respect to what He has given you. So [believers in all religions are requested to] vie with one another in all good works and righteous deeds. All shall return to God and He will be the ultimate arbiter concerning that about which you differed' (Q. 5:48).

From the above verse it is clear that each religion has its own code of law and its special path of attainment to truth and its own economy of salvation. Moreover, virtuous and pious acts (good works) are common in all religions, so that devotees of all religions are required to take the lead in practising virtues and good deeds.

Still, in another verse, God addresses all mankind: 'O mankind! We created you male and female and made you nations and tribes that you may come to know each other. Indeed the noblest among you in the sight of God is the most pious [or God-wary, virtuous] among you' (Q. 49:13).

Now, it is debatable whether, from the stated verses, the regulative verses can be deduced, or on the contrary, from the regulative verses, the validity of the above premises can be demonstrated.

14 The Usage of *Fiqh* in the Qur'an

The derivatives of the root *f-q-h* are used in different verses of the Qur'an but in no case do they refer to 'jurisprudence' in the Qur'anic signification of the term. Rather, the root refers to a deep understanding and a profound knowledge and comprehension of something: 'The seven heavens and the earth and whosoever in them glorify Him and there is no thing save that it hymns His praise but you do not understand (*lā tafqahūna*) their glorification' (Q. 17:44). There is no doubt that a very deep understanding is required to comprehend the glorification of all beings.

45 Q. 7:158, 34:28.

46 Q. 5:48, 11:118, 16:94, 42:8.

To cite another exam ple, when Moses was commanded to go to Pharaoh to warn and guide him, he said, 'My lord, expand my breast; make my affair easy for me; and untie a knot from my tongue, that they may understand (*yafqahū*) my speech' (Q. 20:25–28). In these verses there is a connection between Moses' request that his breast be expanded and that a knot from his tongue be loosened so that they might comprehend his words. This might signify that the speech of a divine messenger like Moses requires a deep comprehension.

Still, in other verses, we read: '… they have hearts with which they understand not (*lā yafqahūna bihā*), they have eyes with which they see not, and they have ears with which they hear not' (Q. 7:179). In the Qur'an the heart is considered to be the locus of all revelations, inspirations, and profound comprehension.

There are some other verses to the same effect: 'What is wrong with these people that they scarcely understand (*lā yakādūna yafqahūna*) what is said' (Q. 4:78). But most important in this regard is Q. 9:122, which alludes to the real meaning of this term: 'But it is not for the believers all to go forth [to war]. And why should not a party from each group go forth to gain understanding (*li-yatafaqqahū*) in religion (*fī al-dīn*) and to warn their people when they return to them that haply they will beware.' This verse signifies that when the Prophet calls the believers to go to a Holy War it is not incumbent on all Muslims to go forth but it is the duty of some to stay in order to seek knowledge in religion. Here *fiqh* does not mean the science of jurisprudence alone because, first, what is meant is the religion in its entirety (*al-dīn*) and, second, it is clearly stated that it is their duty to warn the people when they return. It is one of the duties of all prophets to warn their community and that is why they are often called warners (sing. *nadhīr*) and givers of glad tidings (sing. *bashīr*). As we saw earlier, Ghazālī and Mullā Ṣadrā focus their attention on this verse when criticising the *fuqahā'*.

15 Three Prerequisites of Salvation

In the Qur'an three conditions are mentioned for the salvation and ultimate delivery of mankind for believers in all religions: 'Truly those who believe and those who are Jews and the Sabaeans and the Christians – whosoever believes in God and the Last Day and works righteousness, no fear shall come upon them nor shall they grieve' (Q. 5:69). These three conditions comprise staunch faith in God, the hereafter, and doing righteous deeds as prescribed in all religions. Jews, Christians, and Muslims no doubt belong to the Abrahamic religions and the Sabaeans mentioned in different verses are the devotees of all non-Abrahamic religions because, first, according to many verses of the Qur'an God has sent messengers one after another to all communities, each speaking their own language, in order to expound His message and, second, because the above verse refers more broadly to 'whosoever believes in God and the Last Day and works righteousness', thereby opening up the possibility of salvation beyond the Abrahamic faiths. There are many *fuqahāʾ* and dogmatic theologians who do not grant the possibility of salvation in religions other than Islam.

To sum up, an unnecessary emphasis on the regulative verses as encapsulating the whole message of the Qur'an would negate the validity of its message about the universality of prophecy.

16 Conclusion

The problem discussed above remains as pertinent today as it was posed by the great thinkers who were as much concerned with and anxious about the reality of religion in their age. The problem, I think, is more acute today since the jurisprudential view of religion is more paramount, while the sapiential understanding of religion, represented by the great figures above, has been weakened almost to the point of extinction, perhaps partially due to the increasingly secular currents inundating the Eastern religions and Islam in particular.

What is needed today is a synoptic and holistic view of religion as it was customary among the sages of the past who were able to reconcile reason and revelation or philosophy and religion, on the one hand, and could offer a rational defence of the injunctions of the Scripture, on the other. Too much emphasis on the regulative verses at the expense of others results in a sort of casuistry, which is an over-indulgence of reductionism, relegating religion to some of its ramifications; a reduction which, moreover, has engendered extreme sectarianism and even extremist fundamentalism which permits the extermination and eradication of rival sects and religions.

Bibliography

Avicenna. *al-Ishārāt wa-l-tanbīhāt*. Cairo: Dār al-Maʿārif, 1957–60.

Avicenna. *Manṭiq al-mashriqiyyīn*. Qom: Marashi Najafi Library, 1984.

Butterworth, Charles E., trans. *Alfarabi, the Political Writings: Selected Aphorisms and Other Texts*. Ithaca and London: Cornell University Press, 2004.

al-Fārābī, Abū Naṣr. *Ārāʾ ahl al-madīna al-fāḍila wa-muḍāddatuhā*. Edited by Friedrich Dieterici. Leiden: Brill, 1895.

al-Fārābī, Abū Naṣr. 'Kitāb al-jadal'. In *al-Manṭiq 'inda al-Fārābī*, edited by Rafīq al-'Ajam, 3:10–18. Beirut: Dār-al Mashriq, 1985.

Galston, Miriam. 'The Theoretical and Practical Dimensions of Happiness as Portrayed in the Political Treatises of al-Fārābī'. In *The Political Aspects of Islamic Philosophy: Essays in Honor of Muhsin S. Mahdi*, edited by Charles E. Butterworth, 95–151. Cambridge, MA: Harvard University Press, 1992.

al-Ghazālī, Abū Ḥāmid. *Iḥyā' 'ulūm al-dīn*. Cairo: al-Hay'a al-Miṣriyya al-'Āmma li-l-Kitāb, 2018.

Ibn al-'Arabī. *al-Futūḥāt al-Makkiyya*. Edited by 'Uthmān Yaḥyā. Cairo: al-Hay'a al-Miṣriyya al-'Āmma li-l-Kitāb, 1911.

Kadivar, M. 'Avicenna & the Classification of Philosophy'. *The Journal of Saptiential Wisdom and Philosophy* (*Sophia Perennis*) 5, no. 9 (2009): 35–106.

Majlisī, Muḥammad Bāqir. *Biḥār al-anwār*. Beirut: Dār Iḥyā' al-Turāth al-'Arabī, 1983.

Marmura, Michael E., trans. *The Metaphysics of* The Healing. Provo: Brigham Young University Press, 2005.

Morris, James W. 'The Philosopher-Prophet in Avicenna's Political Philosophy'. in *The Political Aspects of Islamic Philosophy: Essays in Honor of Muhsin S. Mahdi*, edited by Charles E. Butterworth, 142–88. Cambridge, MA: Harvard University Press, 1992.

Ṣadrā, Mullā. *al-Ḥikma al-muta'āliyya fī al-asfār al-'aqliyya al-arba'a*. Edited by Reza Akbarain. Tehran: Mulla Sadra Foundation, 1962.

Ṣadrā, Mullā. *Kasr al-aṣnām al-jāhiliyya*. Edited by Mohsen Jahangiri. Tehran: Mulla Sadra Foundation, 1961.

Ṣadrā, Mullā. *Risāleh-i seh aṣl*. Edited by Seyyed Hossein Nasr. Tehran: Mulla Sadra Foundation, 1961.

Ṣadrā, Mullā. *Sharḥ al-Uṣūl al-kāfī*. Edited by S.M. Rajai. Tehran: Mulla Sadra Foundation, 1965.

Ṣadrā, Mullā. *Tafsīr al-Qur'ān al-karīm*. Edited by Mohammad Khajavi. Qom: Bidār, 1987.

Ṣafā, Dhabīḥ Allāh. *Tārikh-i adabiyyāt-i Īrān*. 9th ed. Tehran: Intishārāt-i Firdaws, Tehran, 1979.

PART 2

The Historical Genre of *Aḥkām al-Qurʾān*

CHAPTER 6

Legal Hermeneutics and Religious Authority in *Kitāb Aḥkām al-Qurʾān* by al-Jaṣṣāṣ al-Rāzī (d. 370/981)

Devin J. Stewart

Late in his career, Ḥanafī jurist Abū Bakr Aḥmad b. ʿAlī al-Jaṣṣāṣ al-Rāzī (d. 370/981) wrote *Kitāb Aḥkām al-Qurʾān*, one of the earliest *aḥkām al-Qurʾān* works that have been preserved in complete form. Works in this genre comment on and analyse *āyāt al-aḥkām* 'the verses of legal rulings', that is, the verses of the Qurʾan that have legal content and that can serve as evidence for establishing legal rulings. While al-Jaṣṣāṣ's work fits this general description, it also addresses issues usually treated in manuals of legal hermeneutics, such as consensus (*ijmāʿ*), analogy (*qiyās*), exhaustive legal investigation (*ijtihād*), and lay Muslims' obligation to consult experts in Islamic law. Al-Jaṣṣāṣ's attention to legal hermeneutics in *Aḥkām al-Qurʾān* has been noted by Mevlüt Güngör and Safwat Khalilovich in substantial monographs devoted to the work.[1] This chapter supplements their contributions by analysing four passages that focus on these issues. After presenting an overview of the history of the genre and of al-Jaṣṣāṣ's life and works, I argue in this chapter that al-Jaṣṣāṣ aimed to include the minimum of hermeneutical scaffolding necessary to justify the main thrust of *aḥkām al-Qurʾān*, the derivation of legal rules from the Qurʾanic text itself. Moreover, I contend that al-Jaṣṣāṣ constructed his legal hermeneutics in large part in opposition to the theories of Ẓāhirīs, Muʿtazilīs, Khārijīs, and Shīʿīs and that he was strongly invested in anti-Shīʿī polemics, perhaps because of the Shīʿīs' political, social, and academic ascendancy in Iraq under the Buwayhids (334–447/945–1055). In an excursus in Appendix 1, I counter the claim, made frequently in secondary literature, that *al-Fuṣūl fī al-uṣūl* (The Chapters, on Jurisprudence), al-Jaṣṣāṣ's well-known manual of *uṣūl al-fiqh*, was written to serve as an introduction to his *Kitāb Aḥkām al-Qurʾān*. Appendix 2 includes a full translation of the passages of *Kitāb Aḥkām al-Qurʾān* that are analysed here.

---

1 Mevlüt Güngör, *Cassâs ve Ahkâmü'l-Kur'an* (Ankara: Elif Matbaası, 1989), 121–35; Safwat Mustafa Khalilovich, *al-Imām Abū Bakr al-Rāzī al-Jaṣṣāṣ wa-manhajuhu fī al-tafsīr* (Cairo: Dār al-Salām, 2008), 446–80.

 | HTTPS://DOI.ORG/10.1163/9789004755567-008

1 The *Aḥkām al-Qur'ān* Genre

One of the great ironies of Islamic law is that, while Muslim jurists admitted that the legal material in Islam's sacred text was limited, they still insisted that the Qur'an was the first, and even the main, source of the law. One modern textbook puts this principle boldly as follows: 'The entire *ummah* agreed that the Qur'ān is the primary source for the *aḥkām* of Allah.'[2] One may view the insistence on this point as theological and epistemological but statistically incorrect.[3] It came to be recognised by many jurists, including al-Māwardī (d. 450/1058), al-Ghazālī (d. 505/1111), Fakhr al-Dīn al-Rāzī (d. 606/1210), Ibn Qudāma al-Maqdisī (d. 620/1223), and many others, that the Qur'an's verses with legal content (*āyāt al-aḥkām*) numbered 500.[4] Al-Zarkashī (d. 794/1392) attributes this idea to al-Ghazālī and Fakhr al-Dīn al-Rāzī,[5] and al-Suyūṭī (d. 911/1505) to al-Ghazālī, as if to identify al-Ghazālī as the originator of this particular number. However, the number 500 must have been arrived at earlier, given that it was stated already by al-Māwardī. It is also suggested by the title *Tafsīr khamsimi'at āya* (Commentary on the Five Hundred Verses), a work attributed to Muqātil b. Sulaymān (d. 150/767), which, as will be discussed below, was probably not the original work of Muqātil. Even if the title of that work was a later invention, it was mentioned already in the *Fihrist* of Ibn al-Nadīm (d. 380/990). Other scholars report differing total numbers of legal verses. Al-Suyūṭī proposes just 150.[6] According to Muḥammad b. Ismāʿīl al-Ṣanʿānī (d. 1182/1768–69), they numbered 200.[7] Others set the number

2 Imran Ahsan Khan Nyazee, *Islamic Jurisprudence* (*Uṣūl al-Fiqh*) (Islamabad: Islamic Research Institute, 2000), 158.

3 Wael Hallaq, 'Law and the Qur'ān', *EQ*, 3:149–72, at 149–50, 155.

4 Abū al-Ḥasan ʿAlī b. Muḥammad b. Ḥabīb al-Māwardī, *al-Ḥāwī al-kabīr*, 19 vols., ed. ʿAlī Muḥammad Muʿawwaḍ and ʿĀdil Aḥmad ʿAbd al-Mawjūd (Beirut: Dār al-Kutub al-ʿIlmiyya, 1999), 16:57; Abū Ḥāmid Muḥammad b. Muḥammad al-Ghazālī, *al-Mustaṣfā min ʿilm al-uṣūl*, ed. Muḥammad ʿAbd al-Salām ʿAbd al-Shāfī (Beirut: Dār al-Kutub al-ʿIlmiyya, 1993), 342; Fakhr al-Dīn al-Rāzī, *al-Maḥṣūl*, 6 vols., ed. Ṭāhā Jābir Fayyāḍ al-ʿAlwānī (Beirut: Mu'assasat al-Risāla, 1997), 6:23; Muwaffaq al-Dīn ʿAbd Allāh Ibn Qudāma al-Maqdisī, *Rawḍat al-nāẓir wa-junnat al-munāẓir*, 2 vols., ed. Shaʿbān Muḥammad Ismāʿīl (Beirut: Mu'assasat al-Rayyān, 2002), 2:334.

5 Badr al-Dīn al-Zarkashī, *al-Burhān fī ʿulūm al-Qur'ān*, 4 vols., ed. Muḥammad Abū al-Faḍl Ibrāhīm (Beirut: al-Maktaba al-ʿAṣriyya, n.d.), 2:3; Jalāl al-Dīn al-Suyūṭī, *al-Itqān fī ʿulūm al-Qur'ān*, 2 vols. (Beirut: Dār al-Kutub al-ʿIlmiyya, 1995), 2:279–80.

6 al-Suyūṭī, *al-Itqān*, 2:280.

7 Muḥammad b. Ismāʿīl al-Ṣanʿānī, *Irshād al-nuqqād ilā taysīr al-ijtihād*, ed. Ṣalāḥ al-Dīn Maqbūl Aḥmad (Kuwait: al-Dār al-Salafiyya, 1985), 134–35.

at 600.[8] Even 600 verses represent less than one tenth of the Qur'an,[9] and 600 verses could not conceivably cover the many thousands of topics and issues that came to be addressed in Islamic legal manuals.

In contrast, a minority of authors held the view that there was no set, limited number of legal verses in the Qur'an. Al-Zarkashī states that, in the view of such scholars, the set number refers only to those verses that explicitly focus on legal topics (*al-muṣarraḥ bihi*). According to those scholars, many other verses are relevant to establishing Islamic law, 'for many legal rulings may be derived from the verses that present narratives (*qaṣaṣ*), exempla (*amthāl*), and other things.'[10] One scholar who espoused this view was Najm al-Dīn Sulaymān al-Ṭūfī (d. 716/1316), who wrote, 'The correct opinion is that the specific estimate should not to be taken into consideration and that the number of indicators of legal rulings in [the Qur'anic text] are unlimited, for just as the rulings of the sacred law may be deduced from commands and prohibitions, likewise they may be deduced from narratives (*aqāṣīṣ*), sermons (*mawāʿiẓ*), and similar texts.'[11]

Historically, proponents of the first view, that there was a relatively small number of legal verses, predominated, a principle that became the basis for the distinct genre of *aḥkām al-Qur'ān* (the legal rulings of the Qur'an), which was established by the third/ninth century. Works in this genre provided commentary on the legal verses of the sacred text, explaining the implications of the Qur'an's verses with regard to legal rulings and extracting as many points of law as possible from them through logical deduction and skilful hermeneutics.

The genre served two main functions and was characterised by two main strategies. First, it countered the possible perception that Islamic law was not solidly founded on the Qur'an, presenting tangible attestations that the specific rulings of Islamic law derived, to a large extent, from the Qur'an itself. It strove to show that the text conveys many legal rulings on diverse topics, accessible through straightforward – though thoughtful and demanding – interpretation of the text. The emphasis on the Qur'an's being the principal source of Islamic law was part of a larger strategy to claim that the Qur'an was an inexhaustible source of knowledge and scientific disciplines generally. It is no accident that al-Suyūṭī's discussion of *aḥkām al-Qur'ān* is part of a chapter devoted

8 Nyazee, *Islamic Jurisprudence*, 161.

9 The number of verses in the Qur'an is 6,236 according to the tradition of Ḥafṣ. The exact number varies according to the verse-counting system one adopts, but the difference in the total is not large; all estimates are near 6,200 or 6,300.

10 al-Zarkashī, *al-Burhān*, 2:3. The statement is repeated verbatim in al-Suyūṭī, *al-Itqān*, 2:280.

11 Najm al-Dīn Sulaymān b. ʿAbd al-Qawī al-Ṭūfī, *Sharḥ Mukhtaṣar al-Rawḍa*, 3 vols., ed. ʿAbd Allāh b. ʿAbd al-Muḥsin al-Turkī (Beirut: Mu'assasat al-Risāla, 1987), 3:577.

to the scientific disciplines that may be derived from the Qur'an (*al-ʿulūm al-mustanbaṭa min al-Qurʾān*).[12] He quotes a number of authorities who suggest that many disciplines, or even all disciplines, can be so derived, and he quotes Ibn al-ʿArabī (d. 534/1138) to the effect that they number 77,450.[13]

Second, the genre was a convenience for law students, who did not need to study the whole Qur'an or become experts in the exegesis of the entire scripture. Instead, the existence of this genre made it possible for them to bypass extraneous material. That the genre aimed to facilitate legal study is supported by the statements of al-Ghazālī and others that the number of legal verses in the Qur'an is 500 or some other finite number. Most of these statements occur in lists of requirements for *ijtihād*, and the lists are constructed to convey the message that *ijtihād* is not hopelessly difficult but rather attainable, because the material one needs to study is much more limited than one might think.

In terms of content, the genre of *aḥkām al-Qurʾān* thus sits between those of Qur'anic commentaries and Islamic legal manuals, a characteristic highlighted by the fact that some works, such as that of al-Jaṣṣāṣ, were organised according to the order of the suras of the sacred text, while others, like that of Abū Jaʿfar al-Taḥāwī (d. 321/933), were organised according to the standard order of chapters in legal manuals. The genre was adopted in various Islamic legal traditions and has continued to play an important role in Islamic legal scholarship to the present day.

The genre of *aḥkām al-Qurʾān* has been the subject of relatively limited attention in Islamic studies in comparison with studies that address Islamic law or *tafsīr*.[14] Some idea of the development of history of the genre may be gained by reconstructing a list of works based on al-Wazīr al-Maghribī's (d. 418/1027) additions to the *Fihrist al-ʿulūm* (Catalogue of the Sciences) of Ibn al-Nadīm (d. 380/990), on Badr al-Dīn al-Zarkashī's (d. 794/1392) *al-Burhān fī ʿulūm al-Qurʾān* (The Convincing Proof, on the Qur'anic Sciences), on al-Suyūṭī's

12 al-Suyūṭī, *al-Itqān*, 2:271–82.

13 Ibid., 277.

14 Muḥammad Ḥusayn al-Dhahabī, *al-Tafsīr wa-l-mufassirūn*, 3 vols. (Cairo: Maktabat Wahba, 1976), 2:319–48; Claude Gilliot, 'Exegesis of the Qurʾān: Classical and Medieval', *EQ*, 2:99–124, esp. 'special legal exegesis', 113–14; Jane Dammen McAuliffe, 'Legal Exegesis: Christians as a Case Study', in *Islamic Interpretations of Christianity*, ed. Lloyd Ridgeon (Abingdon, Oxon: Routledge, 2001), 54–77; Muṣṭafā Ibrāhīm al-Mashnī, *Ibn al-ʿArabī al-Mālikī al-Ishbīlī wa-tafsīruhu Aḥkām al-Qurʾān* (Beirut: Dār al-Jīl, 1991); Delfina Serrano Ruano, 'El Corán como fuente de legislación islámica: Abū Bakr Ibn al-ʿArabī y su obra *Aḥkām al-Qurʾān*', in *El Corán ayer y hoy: Perspectivas actuales sobre el islam – Estudios en honor al profesor Julio Cortés*, ed. Miguel Hernando de Larramendi and Salvador Peña Martín (Cordoba: Berenice, 2008), 251–75; Miklos Muranyi, 'Aus dem *Kitāb Aḥkām al-Qurʾān* des Mālikiten Ibn Ḫawāz Mandād', *Der Islam* 91, no. 2 (2014): 360–73.

(d. 911/1505) *al-Itqān fī ʿulūm al-Qurʾān* (The Masterful Work, on the Qurʾanic Sciences), and on Ḥājjī Khalīfa Kātib Çelebi's (d. 1068/1658) *Kashf al-ẓunūn ʿan asāmī al-kutub wa-l-funūn* (The Removal of Doubts, on the Titles of Works and the Names of Disciplines). The collated list follows, in chronological order by the authors' death dates:

1.1 Authors of Works in the *Aḥkām al-Qurʾān* Genre[15]

Key: * = extant, either fully or partially; WM = al-Wazīr al-Maghribī, Additions to the *Fihrist* of Ibn al-Nadīm; Z = al-Zarkashī, *al-Burhān*; S = al-Suyūṭī, *al-Itqān*; HK = Ḥājjī Khalīfa, *Kashf al-ẓunūn*.

1. Al-Shāfiʿī (d. 204/820)* [WM, Z, HK]
2. Yaḥyā b. Ādam (d. 203/818), *K. Mujarrad aḥkām al-Qurʾān* (The Plain Presentation of the Legal Rulings of the Qurʾan) [WM]
3. Hishām b. Muḥammad b. al-Sāʾib al-Kalbī (d. 204/820), transmitted from Ibn ʿAbbās (d. 68/687) [WM]
4. Abū Thawr Ibrāhīm b. Khālid (d. 240/854) [WM]
5. Yaḥyā b. Aktham (d. 243/857), *K. Ījāb al-tamassuk bi-aḥkām al-Qurʾān* (Upholding the Obligation to Adhere to the Legal Rulings of the Qurʾan) [WM]
6. Abū al-Ḥasan ʿAlī b. Ḥajar al-Saʿdī al-Marwazī (d. 244/858–59) [HK]
7. Dāwūd b. ʿAlī (Ẓāhirī, d. 270/884) [WM]
8. Ismāʿīl b. Isḥāq al-Qāḍī (d. 282/895)* [WM, Z, S, HK]
9. Abū al-Ḥasan ʿAlī b. Mūsā b. Yazdād al-Qummī al-Nīsābūrī al-Ḥanafī (d. 305/917–18)* [HK]
10. Abū Jaʿfar Aḥmad b. Muḥammad al-Ṭaḥāwī al-Ḥanafī (d. 321/933)* [HK]
11. Abū Muḥammad al-Qāsim b. Iṣbaʿ al-Qurṭubī al-Naḥwī (d. 340/951–52) [HK]
12. Bakr b. Muḥammad b. al-ʿAlāʾ al-Qushayrī (d. 344/955)* [Z, S]
13. al-Mundhir b. Saʿīd al-Ballūṭī al-Qurṭubī (d. 355/966) [HK]
14. Abū Bakr Muḥammad b. Aḥmad b. ʿAbd Allāh b. Bukayr al-Tamīmī al-Baghdādī (fl. fourth/tenth century) [Z]
15. Abū Bakr Aḥmad b. ʿAlī al-Jaṣṣāṣ al-Rāzī al-Ḥanafī (d. 370/980)* [WM, Z, S, HK]
16. Ibn Khuwayz Mindād (fl. late fourth/tenth century)* [S]

15 Ibn al-Nadīm, *al-Fihrist*, 2 vols., ed. Ayman Fuʾād Sayyid (London: Al-Furqan Islamic Heritage Foundation, 2014), 1:97; al-Zarkashī, *al-Burhān*, 2:3; al-Suyūṭī, *al-Itqān*, 2:179–80; Ḥājjī Khalīfa, *Kashf al-ẓunūn fī asāmī al-kutub wa-l-funūn*, 2 vols. (Istanbul: Milli Eğitim Basımevi, 1941–43), 1:20.

17. Abū Muḥammad Makkī b. Abī Ṭālib al-Qaysī (d. 437/1045–46), *Mukhtaṣar aḥkām al-Qurʾān* (The Abridged Work on the Legal Rulings of the Qurʾan) [Z, S, HK]
18. Al-Qāḍī Abū Yaʿlā (d. 458/1066)* [Z]
19. Abū Bakr Aḥmad b. al-Ḥusayn al-Bayhaqī (d. 458/1066)* [HK]
20. Abū al-Ḥasan ʿAlī b. Muḥammad al-Kiyā al-Harrāsī al-Shāfiʿī al-Baghdādī (d 504/1110)* [S, HK]
21. Abū Bakr Muḥammad b. ʿAbd Allāh Ibn al-ʿArabī (d. 534/1148)* [S, HK]
22. ʿAbd al-Munʿim b. Muḥammad b. Faras al-Gharnāṭī (d. 597/1201)* [Z, S, HK]
23. Jamāl al-Dīn Maḥmūd b. Aḥmad, Ibn al-Sirāj al-Qūnawī al-Ḥanafī (d. 770/1368–69), *Talkhīṣ aḥkām al-Qurʾān* (The Abridgement of the Legal Rulings of the Qurʾan)* [HK]

The list above is, however, only a preliminary record of works that would have to be considered in constructing a history of the *aḥkām al-Qurʾān* genre. Other contributions to the genre not listed here include Abū ʿAbd Allāh Muḥammad b. Aḥmad b. Abī Bakr al-Qurṭubī's (d. 671/1273) monumental *al-Jāmiʿ li-aḥkām al- Qurʾān*, which is extant.[16] In addition, several of the items in the list raise questions about date and authenticity (discussed below). Examination of the list suggests that Ḥanafīs and Mālikīs dominated the genre early on and that Mālikīs continued to be the most important contributors to it in later centuries. Several Ḥanafī jurists wrote works beginning in the late second/eighth–third/ninth century, when the genre may be said to have originated, including *K. Mujarrad aḥkām al-Qurʾān* by Yaḥyā b. Ādam (d. 203/818), *K. Ījāb al-tamassuk bi-aḥkām al-Qurʾān* by Yaḥyā b. Aktham (d. 243/857), and *Aḥkām al-Qurʾān* by Abū al-Ḥasan ʿAlī b. Mūsā b. Yazdād al-Qummī al-Ḥanafī (d. 305/917–18) and Abū Jaʿfar Aḥmad b. Muḥammad al-Ṭaḥāwī al-Ḥanafī (d. 321/933). This may be due to the important role that Ḥanafī jurists played in the Abbasid judiciary; the genre may be seen as related to the background knowledge required for judges. The most important early Mālikī work in the genre was that of Ismāʿīl b. Isḥāq al-Qāḍī (d. 282/895). Other significant Mālikī works in the genre include those of Ibn Khuwayz Mindād (fl. later fourth/tenth century), Abū Bakr Muḥammad b. ʿAbd Allāh Ibn al-ʿArabī (d. 534/1148), and al-Qurṭubī (d. 671/1273). The genre was not immediately taken up by many Shāfiʿī jurists per se, as far as is known to date, but was by other jurists loosely affiliated with al-Shāfiʿī's legacy such as Abū Thawr Ibrāhīm b. Khālid (d. 240/854) and

16 Abū ʿAbd Allāh Muḥammad b. Aḥmad b. Abī Bakr al-Qurṭubī, *al-Jāmiʿ li-aḥkām al-Qurʾān wa-l-mubayyin li-mā taḍammanahu min al-sunna wa-āy al-Furqān*, 24 vols., ed. ʿAbd Allāh b. ʿAbd al-Muḥsin al-Turkī (Beirut: Muʾassasat al-Risāla, 2006).

Dāwūd b. ʿAlī (Ẓāhirī, d. 270/884). It was not until the later jurist Abū al-Ḥasan ʿAlī b. Muḥammad al-Kiyā al-Harrāsī al-Baghdādī (d. 504/1110) that a Shāfiʿī jurist produced another major work in the genre. As for a Ḥanbalī *aḥkām al-Qurʾān* work, only al-Zarkashī mentions one, by al-Qāḍī Abū Yaʿlā al-Farrāʾ (d. 458/1066); the fact that he served as a judge seems to confirm that the genre was deemed important for acting judges.[17]

Other works on *aḥkām al-Qurʾān* from the early centuries of Islam have certainly been omitted by these authors, both works that are extant and those that have been lost to posterity. Attention to quotations and references in later works may help to fill in gaps in the history of the genre. It is accordingly not possible at present to give a full historical account of the genre, but it will be expedient to make a few observations on several significant works. Experts in Islamic law continued to produce exemplars of the genre of *aḥkām al-Qurʾān* throughout medieval, premodern, and modern times. A substantial modern work in the genre is that of the prominent Syrian Ḥanafī jurist Muḥammad ʿAlī al-Ṣābūnī (1930–2021), *Rawāʾiʿ al-bayān: tafsīr āyāt al-aḥkām min al-Qurʾān* (Splendours of Exposition: A Commentary on the Legal Verses of the Qurʾan).[18] There are even modern English works that belong to the genre.[19]

1.2 'The Five Hundred Verses' of Muqātil b. Sulaymān (d. 150/767)

One work that does not appear in any of the four lists mentioned above is ascribed to Muqātil b. Sulaymān, who died in 150/767, which appears too early for the appearance of a work in this specific genre. The full title is *Khams miʾat āya min al-Qurʾān al-karīm fī al-amr wa-l-nahy wa-l-ḥalāl wa-l-ḥarām* (Five Hundred Verses of the Noble Qurʾan on Command, Prohibition, What Is Licit, and What Is Forbidden). It is extant in one manuscript, MS British Museum, Or. 6333, which is dated 4 Jumādā II 792/20 May 1390. The work has been edited and discussed by Isaiah Goldfeld, who concludes that it was probably not written by Muqātil b. Sulaymān himself but was assembled at a later date from

17 The work is not extant but is quoted extensively by Ibn al-Jawzī (d. 597/1201) in *Zād al-masīr*. See ʿAwda ʿAbd Allāh, Sāmiḥ ʿAbd al-Ilāh ʿAbd al-Hādī, and ʿAbd al-Sattār Yūsuf Aḥmad Rayyān, 'al-Manhaj al-tafsīrī li-l-Qāḍī Abī Yaʿlā fī *Aḥkām al-Qurʾān* mustakhlaṣan min kitāb *Zād al-masīr*', *Majallat al-Mīzān li-l-Dirāsāt al-Islāmiyya wa-l-Qānūniyya* 10 (2023): 1–36.

18 Muḥammad ʿAlī al-Ṣābūnī, *Rawāʾiʿ al-bayān: tafsīr āyāt al-aḥkām min al-Qurʾān*, 2 vols. (Beirut: Muʾassasat Manāhil al-ʿIrfān, 1980).

19 See, for example, Muhammad Valibhai Merchant, *Quranic Laws* (Lahore: Sh. Muhammad Ashraf, 1947).

passages in his *Tafsīr*.[20] However, it did exist already by 377/987, for it appears in a work composed that year, the *Fihrist* of Ibn al-Nadīm, where the title is given as *Tafsīr al-khams mi'at āya* (The Exegesis of the Five Hundred Verses).[21] Although the work does not bear the title *aḥkām al-Qur'ān*, the reference to 500 verses suggests that the idea that the legal verses of the text number 500 became an important convention of the genre early on, although later authors such as al-Zarkashī and al-Suyūṭī both attribute it to al-Ghazālī (d. 505/1111).[22]

1.3 The Work of al-Kalbī (d. 204/820)

A similar work is attributed to Hishām b. Muḥammad b. al-Sā'ib al-Kalbī, in which he is reported to have presented therein the views of Ibn ʿAbbās (d. 68/687), a Companion and cousin of the Prophet who was recognised as an early authority on Qur'anic exegesis.[23] In this case as well, it appears that the work is not as early as is claimed. Al-Kalbī, an antiquarian recorder of pre-Islamic and early Islamic Arabian lore, had collected material attributed to Ibn ʿAbbās to form a commentary on the Qur'an, and a later author extracted passages therefrom to construct a work on *aḥkām al-Qur'ān*. Since the work is not extant, it is not possible to determine the identity of the probable compiler or date of the work, other than to say that it was compiled before the early fifth/eleventh century, when al-Wazīr al-Maghribī recorded his list.

1.4 Al-Shāfiʿī's *Kitāb Aḥkām al-Qur'ān*

Al-Zarkashī and Ḥājjī Khalīfa both begin their lists of works on *aḥkām al-Qur'ān* with a book by that title which is attributed to al-Shāfiʿī, and they both explicitly claim that he invented the genre: *wa-huwa awwal man ṣannafa fīhi* 'And he was the first to write on the topic.'[24] It is known that Aḥmad b. al-Ḥusayn al-Bayhaqī (d. 458/1066) collected material from *Kitāb al-Umm* and

---

20 Isaiah Goldfeld, 'Muqātil b. Sulaymān', in *Studies in Arabic and Islam*, 2 vols., ed. Jacob Mansour (Ramat-Gan: Bar-Ilan University Press, 1978), 2:1–18.

21 Ibn al-Nadīm, *al-Fihrist*, 1:641.

22 al-Zarkashī, *al-Burhān*, 2:3; al-Suyūṭī, *al-Itqān*, 2:180; al-Ghazālī, *al-Mustaṣfā*, 342; al-Rāzī, *al-Maḥṣūl*, 6:23.

23 On Ibn ʿAbbās and *tafsīr*, see Herbert Berg, *The Development of Exegesis in Early Islam: The Authenticity of Muslim Literature from the Formative Period* (Richmond, Surrey: RoutledgeCurzon, 2000).

24 Ḥājjī Khalīfa, *Kashf al-ẓunūn*, 1:20.

other works of al-Shāfiʿī on *aḥkām al-Qurʾān*.[25] The fact that such a project was undertaken by al-Bayhaqī, who was an expert on al-Shāfiʿī's life and works and had a tremendous collection of relevant sources available to him, suggests that al-Shāfiʿī's work had been irrevocably lost and that al-Bayhaqī strove to reconstruct it. In *Manāqib al-Shāfiʿī*, al-Bayhaqī writes, *qad jamaʿtu aqāwīl al-Shāfiʿī raḥimahu llāh fī aḥkām al-Qurʾān wa-tafsīruhu fī juzʾayn* 'I collected the opinions of al-Shāfiʿī – may God have mercy on him – on the legal rulings of the Qurʾan and its exegesis in two volumes.'[26] Ḥājjī Khalīfa includes this work by al-Bayhaqī in his list of *aḥkām al-Qurʾān* works and states, *laffaqahu min kalām al-Shāfiʿī* 'He patched it together from the writings of al-Shāfiʿī.'[27] Al-Bayhaqī cited passages from the master's various works and arranged them according to the *Mukhtaṣar* of al-Muzanī. He clearly did not have access to an extant work by al-Shāfiʿī titled *Aḥkām al-Qurʾān*.[28] Even al-Kiyā al-Harrāsī, who strove to create a work in the genre based on the legal doctrines of al-Shāfiʿī,[29] suggests in the introduction to his work *Aḥkām al-Qurʾān* that he was unaware of a work by al-Shāfiʿī in the same genre.

Al-Shāfiʿī certainly wrote a work titled *Aḥkām al-Qurʾān*. He mentions it in the *Risāla*, and it is cited in the *Mukhtaṣar* of al-Shāfiʿī's student, Ismāʿīl b. Yaḥyā al-Muzanī (d. 264/878).[30] Al-Rabīʿ b. Sulaymān al-Murādī (d. 270/884) reports that when al-Shāfiʿī determined to write on *aḥkām al-Qurʾān*, he read the Qurʾan one hundred times in preparation for the task.[31] As Melchert has pointed out, the *Musnad* of al-Shāfiʿī, which was compiled by the students of Abū al-ʿAbbās Muḥammad b. Yaʿqūb al-Aṣamm (d. 346/957), sheds light on the contents of *Aḥkām al-Qurʾān*. The *Musnad* includes numerous reports with the heading *wa-min Kitāb Aḥkām al-Qurʾān* 'and from the *Book of the Legal Rulings of the Qurʾan*'. After analysing the evidence from this and other works such as *Kitāb al-Umm*, Melchert suggests that *Kitāb Aḥkām al-Qurʾān* was not a comprehensive work on the legal verses of the Qurʾan but rather a more limited text that focused on the legal verses connected with just a few areas of the

25 Abū Bakr al-Bayhaqī, *Aḥkām al-Qurʾān*, ed. Abū ʿĀṣim al-Shawāmī (Cairo: Dār al-Dhakhāʾir, 2018), 59–61.

26 Abū Bakr al-Bayhaqī, *Manāqib al-Shāfiʿī*, 2 vols., ed. Aḥmad Ṣaqr (Cairo: Maktabat Dār al-Turāth, 1970), 2:368.

27 Ḥājjī Khalīfa, *Kashf al-ẓunūn*, 1:20.

28 The extant work confirms this. See al-Bayhaqī, *Aḥkām al-Qurʾān*.

29 al-Kiyā al-Harrāsī, *Aḥkām al-Qurʾān*, 4 vols. (Beirut: Dār al-Kutub al-ʿIlmiyya, 1983), 1:2–3.

30 Muḥammad b. Idrīs al-Shāfiʿī, *al-Risāla*, ed. Aḥmad Muḥammad Shākir (Cairo: Maṭbaʿat Muṣṭafā al-Bābī al-Ḥalabī wa-Awlādih, 1940; repr. Beirut, n.d.), para. 416.

31 al-Bayhaqī, *Manāqib al-Shāfiʿī*, 1:244.

law, including marriage and divorce.[32] The well-known Shāfiʿī jurist al-Rāfiʿī al-Qazwīnī (d. 623/1226) apparently had a copy of the original work at his disposal, since he reports *wa-huwa fī qadr thalāthat ajzāʾ* 'and it is the size of three volumes' (or 'three quires').[33] ʿAbd Allāh Sharaf al-Dīn al-Dāghistānī has recently published an edition of an *Aḥkām al-Qurʾān* attributed to al-Shāfiʿī that differs from al-Bayhaqī's compilation, based on a manuscript copy that he located in the Suleymaniye Library, Istanbul; according to him, it dates to the early seventh/thirteenth century.[34] The claim that this text is directly related to al-Shāfiʿī's original requires further investigation, but one may state with certainty that al-Shāfiʿī composed a work with the title *Aḥkām al-Qurʾān* and that this work did present analyses of the legal verses of the Qurʾan. It was, however, certainly shorter than comprehensive works like those of al-Jaṣṣāṣ or Ibn al-ʿArabī, and it focused on selected topics within the law.

1.5 The Work of Ismāʿīl b. Isḥāq al-Qāḍī (d. 282/895)

The twenty-two categories of Qurʾanic sciences in the *Fihrist* appear in the third chapter of Book I, devoted to scripts and scripture. However, an examination of the list of works on *aḥkām al-Qurʾān* in the manuscripts and printed editions of the *Fihrist* reveals that it does not go back to Ibn al-Nadīm himself and is the only category that has been added later to Ibn al-Nadīm's presentation of the Qurʾanic sciences. Ibn al-Nadīm did include one category of Qurʾanic scholarship that has to do with legal hermeneutics, that of *al-nāsikh wa-l-mansūkh* 'the abrogating and abrogated verses of the Qurʾan', so it is perhaps surprising that he did not include the category of works on *aḥkām al-Qurʾān*. As Valeriy Polosin explains, such interpolations in the text of the *Fihrist* likely derive from the 'additions' (*ziyādāt*) of al-Wazīr al-Maghribī (d. 419/1027).[35]

---

32 Christopher Melchert, 'The *Musnad* of al-Shāfiʿī', *Studia Islamica* 115 (2020): 9.

33 ʿAbd al-Karīm b. Muḥammad al-Qazwīnī al-Rāfiʿī, *Sharḥ Musnad al-Shāfiʿī*, 4 vols., ed. Abū Bakr Wāʾil Muḥammad Bakr Zahrān (Doha: Wizārat al-Awqāf wa-l-Shuʾūn al-Islāmiyya, 2007), 3:357. Three quires would be sixty pages.

34 Muḥammad b. Idrīs al-Shāfiʿī, *Aḥkām al-Qurʾān*, ed. Abū ʿĀmir ʿAbd Allāh Sharaf al-Dīn al-Dāghistānī (Riyadh: Āfāq al-Maʿrifa, 2020).

35 Al-Wazīr al-Maghribī possessed an autograph copy of the *Fihrist*, and he entered his interpolations into the manuscript itself. Yāqūt al-Ḥamawī (d. 623/1229) then cited that copy of the *Fihrist* when writing *Irshād al-arīb*, his biographical dictionary of literary scholars. When al-Ḥamawī referred to the autograph copy of the *Fihrist* and to a copy of the *Fihrist* with the additions of al-Wazīr al-Maghribī, he was not referring to two separate manuscripts, as Gotthelf Bergsträßer thought, one with the additions and one without, but rather to one and the same manuscript. When that autograph manuscript was copied,

FIGURE 6.1 MS arabe 4457, Bibliothèque Nationale, Paris, fol. 51r

The exact contours of al-Wazīr al-Maghribī's list deserve some attention, given its relatively early date, but here one observation regarding works in the genre by early Mālikīs seems particularly important. In my view, nos. 1–3 in al-Wazīr al-Maghribī's list designate one single work, though they are presented as three separate items. The titles are given in the manuscript as follows (Figure 6.1):

- *Kitāb Aḥkām al-Qurʾān li-Ismāʿīl b Isḥāq al-Qāḍī al-Mālikī*
- *Kitāb Aḥkām al-Qurʾān ʿalā madhhab Mālik*
- *Kitāb Aḥkām al-Qurʾān ʿan Aḥmad b. al-Muʿadhdhal*[36]

What I suspect has occurred in the transmission of the text is that three parts of a single title that had been placed underneath an elongated heading, *Kitāb*, as titles are generally presented in manuscripts of the *Fihrist*, were interpreted

later manscripts, notably Paris MS BN 4457, did not distinguish the interpolations from the original text of the *Fihrist*, and this has caused confusion for the modern editors and investigators of the text. Gotthelf Bergsträßer, 'Die Quellen von Jāqūt's *Iršād*', *Zeitschrift für Semitistik* 2 (1924): 185–86; Valeriy V. Polosin, *Fixrist Ibn an-Nadima kak istoriko-kulturniy pamyatnik X veka* (Moscow: Nauka, 1989), 31–40; Devin J. Stewart, 'Scholarship on the *Fihrist* of Ibn al-Nadim: The Work of Valeriy V. Polosin', *Al-ʿUsur al-Wusta* 18, no. 1 (2006): 10–11; Devin J. Stewart, 'Editing the *Fihrist* of Ibn al-Nadīm', *Journal of Abbasid Studies* 1 (2014): 172.

36 Ibn al-Nadīm, *al-Fihrist*, 1:97.

as three separate titles and so provided with three separate headings – *Kitāb, Kitāb, Kitāb* – on the line above. The titles refer first to al-Qāḍī Ismāʿīl b. Isḥāq, the famous Mālikī judge of Baghdad, secondly to Mālik b. Anas, the eponymous founder of the Mālikī legal school, and thirdly to Aḥmad b. al-Muʿadhdhal, the prominent Mālikī jurist and the main legal teacher of al-Qāḍī Ismāʿīl. These are out of chronological order – which is unusual in the *Fihrist* – even though they belong to the same legal school: Mālik died in 197/795, Aḥmad b. al-Muʿadhdhal in the mid-third/ninth century, and Ismāʿīl b. Isḥāq in 282/895. It is likely that these elements originally belonged to a single title that resembled the following:

> *K. Aḥkām al-Qurʾān li-Ismāʿīl b Isḥāq al-Qāḍī al-Mālikī ʿalā madhhab Mālik ʿan Aḥmad b. al-Muʿadhdhal*

In other words, it is a work of commentary on the Qurʾan's legal verses according to Mālikī legal doctrine, authored by Ismāʿīl al-Qāḍī on the basis of the lectures of his master in Islamic law, Aḥmad b. al-Muʿadhdhal (fl. third/ninth century). This hypothesis is corroborated to some extent by the next item in the list, the *Aḥkām al-Qurʾān* of Abū Bakr al-Rāzī, that is, al-Jaṣṣāṣ, which is described as 'following the legal school of the people of Iraq' (*ʿalā madhhab ahl al-ʿIrāq*), meaning the Ḥanafīs. It is similarly corroborated by an extant fragment of fourth//tenth-century Mālikī jurist Ibn Khuwayz Mindād's *Aḥkām al-Qurʾān*, in which the title page of one quire records the title as follows: *Kitāb Aḥkām al-Qurʾān ʿalā madhhab Abī ʿAbd Allāh Mālik b. Anas b. Abī ʿĀmir al-Aṣbaḥī al-Madanī.* Thus, the work of al-Jaṣṣāṣ is identified as following the legal doctrine of the Ḥanafī school, and Ibn Khuwayz Mindād's work is identified as following the legal doctrine of Mālik b. Anas, the eponymous founder of the Mālikī legal school, so it would be likely for al-Qāḍī Ismāʿīl's work to be identified as following the Mālikī legal school.[37] The work of al-Qāḍī Ismāʿīl was influential in the genre. It is mentioned prominently by al-Khaṭīb al-Baghdādī (d. 463/1071) in *Tārīkh Baghdād*, and his description corroborates the hypothesis that the three descriptions above refer to a single work. He quotes the following description of the work: *wa-huwa kitāb lam yasbiqhu aḥad min aṣḥābihi ilā mithlihi* 'It is a book the like of which none of his fellows [i.e. Mālikīs] had ever written before.' By this al-Khaṭīb al-Baghdādī means that it was the first such major work by a Mālikī jurist, with the implication that no such work had been attributed to Mālik b. Anas or to Aḥmad b. al-Muʿadhdhal. Instead, it was

37 Muranyi, 'Aus dem *Kitāb Aḥkām al-Qurʾān*', 364.

preceded only by such works authored by adherents of other legal schools.[38] A partial edition of the work has been published from fragments found in Kairouan. The edition represents only a small fraction of the original work, which was quite long.[39] According to one report, it consisted of 120 quires, that is, roughly 2,400 pages.[40]

2 Al-Jaṣṣāṣ al-Rāzī and His *Kitāb Aḥkām al-Qurʾān*

Abū Bakr Aḥmad b. ʿAlī al-Jaṣṣāṣ al-Rāzī was a prominent Ḥanafī jurist of the fourth/tenth century. Born in Rayy in 305/917, he studied law there with Abū Sahl al-Zajjāj (fl. early fourth/tenth century). In 325/937, he travelled to pursue study in Baghdad, where the leading Ḥanafī jurist Abū al-Ḥasan al-Karkhī (d. 340/952) was his main teacher in the legal sciences. Al-Jaṣṣāṣ subsequently travelled to Ahwaz and perhaps came into contact with Muʿtazilī scholars there before returning to Baghdad. He later travelled to Nishapur. While he was still studying there, in 340/952, his teacher al-Karkhī died in Baghdad, and al-Karkhī's lectures were taken up by another of his students, Abū ʿAlī Aḥmad b. Muḥammad al-Shāshī (d. 344/956). When al-Shāshī died in 344/956, al-Jaṣṣāṣ returned to Baghdad and became the leading professor of Ḥanafī law there until he passed away on 7 Dhū al-Ḥijja 370/13 June 981. He was asked to serve as judge several times but consistently refused the government post. He authored many commentaries on Ḥanafī legal works, including *Sharḥ al-Manāsik* (Commentary on the Rites of the Pilgrimage) and *Sharḥ al-Jāmiʿ al-ṣaghīr* (Commentary on the Small Summa of Law), both by Muḥammad b. al-Ḥasan al-Shaybānī (d. 189/205), *Sharḥ Mukhtaṣar al-fiqh* (Commentary on the Short Compendium) and *Mukhtaṣar Ikhtilāf al-fuqahāʾ* (Abridgement of the Disputed Opinions of the Jurists), both by al-Ṭaḥāwī (d. 321/933), *Sharḥ Adab al-qāḍī* (Commentary on the Judge's Comportment), by al-Khaṣṣāf (d. 261/874), *al-Fuṣūl fī al-uṣūl* (The Chapters, on Jurisprudence), on *uṣūl al-fiqh*, and *Kitāb Aḥkām al-Qurʾān* (The

38 al-Khaṭīb al-Baghdādī, *Tārīkh Baghdād*, 17 vols., ed. Bashshār ʿAwwād Maʿrūf (Beirut: Dār al-Gharb al-Islāmī, 2001), 6:270, 7:272.

39 al-Qāḍī Abū Isḥāq Ismāʿīl b. Isḥāq al-Mālikī, *Aḥkām al-Qurʾān*, ed. ʿĀmir Ḥasan Ṣabrī (Beirut: Dār Ibn Ḥazm, 2005).

40 Quires in the medieval Islamic world were most commonly quinions, made of five folded folios, which produces twenty pages. ʿĀmir Ḥasan Ṣabrī, introduction to ibid., 54, citing Abū Yaʿlā al-Khalīl b. ʿAbd Allāh al-Khalīlī al-Qazwīnī, *Kitāb al-Irshād fī maʿrifat ʿulamāʾ al-ḥadīth*, 3 vols., ed. Muḥammad Saʿīd b. ʿUmar Idrīs (Riyadh: Maktabat al-Rushd, 1989), 2:501.

Legal Rulings of the Qur'an). He also wrote a work on the divine epithets, *Sharḥ al-asmāʾ al-ḥusnā* (Commentary on the Most Beautiful Names).[41]

Both *Kitāb Aḥkām al-Qurʾān* and *al-Fuṣūl fī al-uṣūl* are extant and have been published. The first edition of *Kitāb Aḥkām al-Qurʾān* was printed in Istanbul in 1917–20, followed by an edition published in Cairo in 1928. Several more recent editions have been published in Beirut;[42] and the edition consulted for this study is that of Muḥammad al-Ṣādiq Qamḥāwī, published in Beirut, in five volumes in 1992.[43] The work has been the topic of several secondary studies.[44] As for *al-Fuṣūl fī al-uṣūl*, Saʿīd Allāh al-Qāḍī edited the chapters on *ijtihād* and *qiyās* in 1981, and Zuhayr Shafīq Kabbī edited the section on *ijmāʿ* (consensus) along with a study of the work in 1993.[45] A complete edition of the work was published in four volumes by ʿUjayl Jāsim Nashmī in Kuwait in 1985, and another edition by Muḥammad Muḥammad Tāmir in Beirut in 2000.[46] The extant manuscripts of *al-Fuṣūl* are incomplete, missing a section at the beginning of the work and a section at the end. The text of *Kitāb Aḥkām al-Qurʾān* refers frequently to *al-Fuṣūl fī al-uṣūl*, but the title *al-Fuṣūl* does not appear; the text refers instead to *Uṣūl al-fiqh*, as if that were the title of the book.[47] Clearly, al-Jaṣṣāṣ completed *Kitāb Aḥkām al-Qurʾān* after he wrote *al-Fuṣūl*. However, the common claim that *al-Fuṣūl fī al-uṣūl* was written to serve as an

---

41 Ibn Abī al-Wafāʾ, Abū Muḥammad ʿAbd al-Qādir b. Muḥammad al-Qurashī, *al-Jawāhir al-muḍiyya fī ṭabaqāt al-Ḥanafiyya*, 5 vols., ed. ʿAbd al-Fattāḥ Muḥammad al-Ḥulw (Cairo: Hajr, 1993), 1:220–24; Saeedullah, 'Life and Works of Abū Bakr al-Rāzī al-Jaṣṣāṣ', *Islamic Studies* 16, no. 2 (1977): 131–41; Khalilovich, *al-Imām Abū Bakr al-Rāzī al-Jaṣṣāṣ*, 27–145; Murteza Bedir, 'al-Jaṣṣāṣ (d. 370/981)', in *Islamic Legal Thought: A Compendium of Muslim Jurists*, ed. Oussama Arabi, David Powers, and Susan Spectorsky (Leiden: Brill, 2013), 147–66.

42 Abū Bakr al-Rāzī al-Jaṣṣāṣ, *Kitāb Aḥkām al-Qurʾān* (Istanbul: Maṭbaʿat al-Awqāf al-Islāmiyya, 1917–20; Cairo: al-Maṭbaʿa al-Bahiyya al-Miṣriyya, 1928; 3 vols., Beirut: Dār al-Kitāb al-ʿArabī, 1986; 3 vols., ed. Ṣiddīq Muḥammad Jamīl, Beirut: Dār al-Fikr al-ʿArabī, 2001; ed. ʿAbd al-Salām Muḥammad ʿAlī Shāhīn, Beirut: Dār al-Kutub al-ʿIlmiyya, 2007).

43 Abū Bakr al-Rāzī al-Jaṣṣāṣ, *Kitāb Aḥkām al-Qurʾān*, 5 vols., ed. Muḥammad al-Ṣādiq Qamḥāwī (Beirut: Dār Iḥyāʾ al-Turāth al-ʿArabī, 1992).

44 Antar ibn-Stanford Smith, 'Significant Features of al-Jassas' Methodology for Deriving Legal Rulings from the Qur'an' (PhD diss., University of Michigan, 1985); Güngör, *Cassâs*; Khalilovich, *al-Imām Abū Bakr al-Rāzī al-Jaṣṣāṣ*.

45 Abū Bakr al-Rāzī al-Jaṣṣāṣ, *al-Fuṣūl fī al-uṣūl: abwāb al-ijtihād wa-l-qiyās*, ed. Saʿīd Allāh al-Qāḍī (Lahore: al-Maktaba al-ʿIlmiyya, 1981); Abū Bakr al-Rāzī al-Jaṣṣāṣ, *al-Ijmāʿ: dirāsa fī fikratihi min khilāli taḥqīq bāb al-ijmāʿ*, ed. Zuhayr Shafīq Kabbī (Beirut: Dār al-Muntakhab al-ʿArabī, 1993).

46 Abū Bakr al-Rāzī al-Jaṣṣāṣ, *Uṣūl al-fiqh al-musammā al-Fuṣūl fi al-uṣūl*, 4 vols. (Kuwait: Wizārat al-Awqāf wa-l-Shuʾūn al-Islāmiyya, 1985; 2 vols., ed. Muḥammad Muḥammad Tāmir, Beirut: Dār al-Kutub al-ʿIlmiyya, 2000).

47 Khalilovich, *al-Imām Abū Bakr al-Rāzī*, 18, 133–42, 142–50, 151–65.

introduction to al-Jaṣṣāṣ's work on *aḥkām al-Qur'ān* is, in my view, incorrect; this issue is discussed in the excursus in Appendix 1.

Al-Jaṣṣāṣ was certainly conscious of writing in an established genre. He introduces quotations with such statements as *wa-dhakara ba'ḍ man ṣannafa fī aḥkām al-Qur'ān* 'one of those who authored works on the legal rulings of the Qur'an stated'.[48] In addition, it is evident that some of the works on which al-Jaṣṣāṣ drew had been written by non-Ḥanafīs, because he introduces quotations of their works as follows: *wa-qāla ba'ḍ al-mukhālifīn mimman ṣannafa fī aḥkām al-Qur'ān* 'one of our opponents among those who authored works on the legal rulings of the Qur'an said'.[49] The term 'opponents' (*mukhālifīn*) most likely designates adherents of other Sunnī legal schools besides the Ḥanafī school. Mevlüt Güngör identifies al-Jaṣṣāṣ's sources in the *aḥkām al-Qur'ān* genre as the works authored by al-Shāfi'ī, al-Ṭaḥāwī, 'Alī al-Qummī al-Ḥanafī, and al-Qāḍī Ismā'īl b. Isḥāq; his presentation suggests that the first two were al-Jaṣṣāṣ's main sources.[50] Ṣafwat Khalilovich does not include the work of al-Shāfi'ī as one of al-Jaṣṣāṣ's sources. In contrast, he assumes that al-Jaṣṣāṣ used the work of al-Ṭaḥāwī, on the grounds that al-Ṭaḥāwī's other works were thoroughly familiar to him. He also argues that al-Jaṣṣāṣ cites the works of 'Alī al-Qummī al-Ḥanafī and al-Qāḍī Ismā'īl b. Isḥāq directly, though he does not mention the titles of their works. In my view, al-Jaṣṣāṣ certainly used the latter two works; the cases for the works of al-Shāfi'ī and al-Ṭaḥāwī are not as clear.

Both Güngör and Khalilovich state that *Kitāb Aḥkām al-Qur'ān* was al-Jaṣṣāṣ's last work and represented his most mature thought and style.[51] Khalilovich poses the question whether it is merely a legal commentary on the Qur'an and answers that, while it fits the general parameters of the genre, it includes much more. He highlights the work's inclusion of theological doctrine, especially the refutation of Islamic sects and proofs of Muḥammad's prophecy, but he also reports that it includes some aspects of a general commentary on the Qur'an.[52]

A distinct feature of al-Jaṣṣāṣ's *Kitāb Aḥkām al-Qur'ān* is its inclusion of discussions of theological questions and discussions of jurisprudence or legal hermeneutics, the topic of al-Jaṣṣāṣ's larger work on jurisprudence, *al-Fuṣūl fī al-uṣūl*. The inclusion of such material is unusual; *aḥkām al-Qur'ān* works usually focus narrowly on points of law, and some, like the work of al-Ṭaḥāwī, adopt the outward form of legal manuals, presenting the standard chapters of

48 Güngör, *Cassâs*, 55.
49 Ibid.
50 Ibid., 54–55.
51 Ibid., 46; Khalilovich, *al-Imām Abū Bakr al-Rāzī al-Jaṣṣāṣ*, 153–54.
52 Khalilovich, *al-Imām Abū Bakr al-Rāzī al-Jaṣṣāṣ*, 155–65.

the law in the standard order. Güngör notes the presence of questions of legal theory or hermeneutics in al-Jaṣṣāṣ's *Kitāb Aḥkām al-Qur'ān*, and he provides a brief overview of al-Jaṣṣāṣ's discussion of legal reasoning (*ijtihād*), the laws of previous religious communities (*sharʿ man qablanā*), consensus (*ijmāʿ*), analogy (*qiyās*), and juristic preference (*istiḥsān*).[53] He also notes al-Jaṣṣāṣ's references in the work to Muʿtazilīs, whose thought on theoretical issues he engages.[54] Khalilovich also presents a substantial discussion of legal hermeneutics in al-Jaṣṣāṣ's *Kitāb Aḥkām al-Qur'ān*, including the topics of unequivocal and ambiguous verses (*al-muḥkam wa-l-mutashābih*); abrogating and abrogated verses (*al-nāsikh wa-l-mansūkh*); unrestricted and restricted verses (*al-muṭlaq wa-l-muqayyad*); unspecified and specified verses (*al-mujmal wa-l-mubayyan*); verses of general and particular scope (*al-ʿāmm wa-l-khāṣṣ*); legal reasoning (*ijtihād*); *ḥadīth*s with solitary chains of transmission (*akhbār al-āḥād*); and the status of acts according to the laws of earlier religious communities (*sharʿ man qablanā*).[55] He also presents a discussion of theological dogma, covering God's Oneness, proofs of the authenticity of Muḥammad's prophecy, torment in the grave, the refutation of Judaism and Christianity, the refutation of theological schools, the Imāmate or caliphate, and the miraculous nature of the Qur'an.[56] The opponents discussed under the rubric of theology are al-Qadariyya (Exponents of Free Will), al-Jabriyya (Predestinarians), al-Mushabbiha (Anthropomorphists), Khārijīs, and Shīʿīs.[57] Khalilovich also addresses Shīʿī views in the section devoted to the Imāmate.[58] He discusses the Muʿtazilīs in a separate section that addresses the questions to what extent al-Jaṣṣāṣ's views matched their views and whether he was a Muʿtazilī himself.[59]

3 Discourse on Legal Hermeneutics in *Kitāb Aḥkām al-Qur'ān*

I turn now to my analysis of four passages that touch on matters of legal hermeneutics: the first, on the authority of consensus, tied to Q. 2:143; the second, related to the issue of religious authority, tied to Q. 4:59, focusing on the identity of *ulū al-amr minkum* 'those of you who are in charge' or 'those of you who

53 Güngör, *Cessâs*, 121–35.
54 Ibid., 117, 126, 160, 164.
55 Khalilovich, *al-Imām Abū Bakr al-Rāzī al-Jaṣṣāṣ*, 446–80.
56 Ibid., 412–45.
57 Ibid., 428–39.
58 Ibid., 440–42.
59 Ibid., 536–50.

possess authority', the duty to obey the Messenger, and analogy as a category of legal hermeneutics; the third, discussing the meaning of *istinbāṭ* 'deduction', tied to Q. 4:83; and the fourth, discussing legal analogy and the concept of *istidlāl* 'citing evidence' or 'inference', tied to Q. 16:89. These discussions occur in isolation, following the order of their presentation in the Qur'an. However, they include topical digressions that cite verses from elsewhere in the sacred text.[60] In Appendix 2 I provide a full translation of all four passages. In selecting these passages, I have omitted consideration of issues of textual analysis that Khalilovich discusses under the rubric of *uṣūl al-fiqh*. I highlight *ijtihād*, an issue treated both by Güngör and Khalilovich, but I also stress consensus, analogy, the boundaries of the interpretive community, and the religious authority of the jurists, topics which they omit. Moreover, I pay attention to al-Jaṣṣāṣ's references, or possible references, to groups that he viewed as the proponents of deviant doctrines, including the Khārijīs and the Shīʿīs, whom Khalilovich addresses but whom Güngör ignores, as well as his references to the Ẓāhirīs, whom both leave out of consideration.

3.1 The Authority of Consensus (Q. 2:143)

Al-Jaṣṣāṣ discusses the authority of consensus in connection with Q. 2:143:

> We have made you a judicious community, so that you may bear witness [to the truth] in the presence of others and so that the Messenger may bear witness [to it] in your presence. We only made the prayer-direction the one you used to face in order to distinguish those who follow the Messenger from those who turn on their heels: that test was hard, except for those whom God has guided. God would never let your faith go to waste, for God is compassionate and merciful towards people.

Here, the text refers to the Muslim community as *ummatan wasaṭan* 'a judicious community' or 'a moderate community'. This is one of several verses commonly cited in similar discussions of the authority of consensus (*ḥujjiyyat al-ijmāʿ*) in works of jurisprudence or legal interpretation (*uṣūl al-fiqh*), including *kuntum khayra ummatin ukhrijat li-l-nās taʾmurūna bi-l-maʿrūfi wa-tanhawna ʿani l-munkari wa-tuʾminūna bi-llāhi wa-law āmana ahlu l-kitābi la-kāna khayran lahum minhumu l-muʾminūn wa-aktharuhumu l-fāsiqūn* 'You

60 On account of the frequent recourse to this method, Khalilovich reports that al-Jaṣṣāṣ's *Aḥkām al-Qur'ān* shares some of the characteristics of what has been termed *tafsīr mawḍūʿī* 'topical exegesis' in modern Islamic scholarship. Ibid., 237–44.

are the best community ever raised for humanity – you encourage good, forbid evil, and believe in God. Had the People of the Book believed, it would have been better for them. Some of them are believers, but most are rebellious' (Q. 3:110) and *wa-man yushāqiqi l-rasūla min baʿdi mā tabayyana lahu l-hudā wa-yattabiʿ ghayra sabīli l-muʾminīn nuwallihi jahannama wa-sāʾat maṣīrā* 'And whoever defies the Messenger after guidance has become clear to them and follows a path other than that of the believers, We will let them pursue what they have chosen, then burn them in Hell – what an evil end!' (Q. 4:115).[61] Of these verses, Q. 2:143 appears first in the received text of the Qur'an, and this is the main reason for al-Jaṣṣāṣ to attach his discussion of consensus to that verse in particular. He does not refer to the other verses directly.

Al-Jaṣṣāṣ endeavours to establish that Q. 2:143's reference to an *umma* 'community' ought not to be restricted to a particular era (*ʿaṣr*), especially not to the generation of the Muslims who were originally addressed by this verse. Instead, it should be understood as referring to the Muslim community throughout its existence, including both early and later generations, up until the Day of Judgement. This is necessary in order for the concept of consensus to apply to the Muslim community throughout all time and not to be restricted to a particular historical period, a view espoused by some other legal theorists such as the Ẓāhirīs.[62] Though al-Jaṣṣāṣ argues that the concept of consensus applies to all generations of the Muslim community, he nevertheless holds that the consensus of an earlier generation holds sway over later generations, for if the people of an earlier generation reached a unanimous agreement, newcomers would not be allowed to violate the pre-existing consensus.

Certain ideas regarding consensus are assumed but not stated outright in al-Jaṣṣāṣ's discussion. He assumes that consensus means unanimous agreement. This view was not universally held, since jurists such as Muḥammad b. Jarīr al-Ṭabarī (d. 310/923) espoused the opinion that 'consensus' could indicate the agreement of the overwhelming majority, against a small, dissenting minority, rather than unanimous or universal agreement.[63] In addition, for

---

61 al-Jaṣṣāṣ, *al-Fuṣūl*, 3:257–64; Bernard G. Weiss, *The Search for God's Law: Islamic Jurisprudence in the Writings of Sayf al-Dīn al-Āmidī*, rev. ed. (Salt Lake City: University of Utah Press, 2010), 194–97; Aron Zysow, *The Economy of Certainty: An Introduction to the Typology of Islamic Legal Theory* (Atlanta: Lockwood Press, 2013), 115–16.

62 ʿAlī b. Aḥmad Ibn Ḥazm, *al-Iḥkām fī uṣūl al-aḥkām*, 8 vols. in 2, ed. Iḥsān ʿAbbās (Beirut: Dār al-Āfāq al-Jadīda, 1980), 4:147–51.

63 Devin J. Stewart, 'Consensus, Authority, and the Interpretive Community in the Thought of Muḥammad b. Jarīr al-Ṭabarī', *Journal of Qur'anic Studies* 18, no. 2 (2016): 130–79, esp. 145–46.

al-Jaṣṣāṣ consensus evidently means primarily the agreement of legal experts, or those who possess legal knowledge, and not simply all Muslims.

In al-Jaṣṣāṣ's view, Q. 2:143 also provides guidance on the limits of the interpretive community. The term he uses for this is *iʿtidād* 'consideration'; it and its equivalent, *iʿtibār*, also 'consideration', are among the standard expressions used to refer to those authorities whose voices 'count' in consensus: in matters of legal interpretation those 'whose opinion is taken into consideration' (*qawluhu yuʿtaddu bihi* or *qawluhu yuʿtabaru*).[64] Like many other jurists, al-Jaṣṣāṣ interprets *wasaṭ* as meaning 'moderate' or 'judicious' and equates that quality with *ʿadāla*, the technical term referring to the good character required of official witnesses. Al-Jaṣṣāṣ's argument is that the members of the Muslim community mentioned in the verse must be able to act as witnesses on account of the explicit text, 'so that you may bear witness'. Therefore, the consensus must exclude the opinions of those who cannot legitimately serve as witnesses, that is, who do not have the requisite quality of *ʿadāla* 'judiciousness', 'moral probity', or 'good character'.[65] He mentions two groups that ought to be excluded. The first are those who are deemed theologically deviant, among whom he specifies *al-mushabbiha* 'anthropomorphists' and proponents of *jabr* 'compulsion', that is, predestination. He leaves some room for lenient application of this exclusion, stating that it applies only to those for whom these views have been reliably attested. In other words, suspicion of holding such opinions or association with others who do so would not be sufficient evidence for exclusion. The second group that al-Jaṣṣāṣ excludes from consideration in consensus are those whom he considers to be characterised by inveterate sin or transgression (*fisq*). He mentions under this category only two explicit categories, the Khārijīs and the Rāfiḍīs 'Rejectors', namely, the Shīʿīs.[66]

Comparison of this passage in *Kitāb Aḥkām al-Qurʾān* with the discussion of *iʿtidād* in *al-Fuṣūl fī al-uṣūl* reveals some interesting variation. First, in *al-Fuṣūl*, al-Jaṣṣāṣ excludes three groups of scholars, and not just two. To those who hold heretical theological opinions and the sects that are based on disagreements over the Imāmate, he adds those who do not accept standard methods of legal interpretation, particularly those who reject the use of *qiyās* or legal analogy. In *al-Fuṣūl*, he argues that only jurists who can use these methods should have

64 For a discussion of consensus and the question of who may be admitted to the interpretive community, see ibid., 133–41. See also Zysow, *The Economy of Certainty*, 122–25.

65 al-Jaṣṣāṣ, *al-Fuṣūl*, 3:257–62, 293–95. Sayf al-Dīn al-Āmidī (d. 631/1233), in contrast, interprests Q. 2:143 as indicating that Muslims are generally trustworthy, which does not guarantee the validity of consensus. Weiss, *The Search for God's Law*, 196. On witnessing in the Qur'an, see Matthias Radscheit, 'Witnessing and Testifying', *EQ*, 5:492–506.

66 See also Khalilovich, *al-Imām Abū Bakr al-Rāzī al-Jaṣṣāṣ*, 428–39.

their opinions taken into consideration for the elaboration of Islamic law. He seems to have in mind the Ẓāhirīs, but the restriction would evidently apply to most Khārijīs and Shīʿīs as well.[67]

Attention to the text of *Kitāb Aḥkām al-Qurʾān* also resolves an issue that arises in the discussion of *iʿtidād* in the text of *al-Fuṣūl*. There, he states that 'the Khārijīs and those who follow the same course (*man jarā majrāhum*)', that is, others who are similar to them, are excluded from consideration in consensus.[68] Al-Jaṣṣāṣ insists that in order for one's opinions to be considered, one must have the characteristic of moral probity, that is, to have a clean moral record (*ʿadāla*) so that one might legitimately testify in court. He explicitly states that the people of error (*ahl al-ḍalāl*) must be excluded from consideration, and he characterises those who ought to be included as the people of the truth (*ahl al-ḥaqq*). He intends the former category to exclude from consideration inveterate sinners, people whose general sinfulness has been established.[69] This presumably means that he excludes incorrigible drinkers, libertines, and so on, though he does not go into details.

Whereas al-Jaṣṣāṣ does not give additional information about the sinners in *al-Fuṣūl*, he does give other examples of the people of error, namely, heretics. He writes, 'We should not take into consideration the dissenting opinions of the Khārijīs *or of the remaining sects of error* because of their heresy that has been established.'[70] He thus excludes Khārijīs explicitly from the interpretive community. The reference to *sāʾir firaq al-ḍalāl* 'the remaining sects of error' is not defined in explicit terms. This is paired with the phrase just mentioned: 'the Khārijīs and those who follow the same course (*wa-man jarā majrāhum*)'.[71] These sects who are similar to the Khārijīs obviously cannot be other Khārijīs, and they are likely not Sunnīs, whom al-Jaṣṣāṣ would not have excluded. One is forced to conclude that they are the Shīʿīs. He probably had in mind especially the Twelver Shīʿīs, who had a substantial presence in Baghdad of his day. The interesting point for consideration here is that, whereas the readers of *al-Fuṣūl* would have had to guess at al-Jaṣṣāṣ's innuendo, the text of *Kitāb Aḥkām al-Qurʾān* confirms the supposition, explicitly stating that the Shīʿīs ought to be excluded from consensus.

67 Stewart, 'Consensus', 138–39.
68 al-Jaṣṣāṣ, *al-Fuṣūl*, 3:294; Stewart, 'Consensus', 138.
69 al-Jaṣṣāṣ, *al-Fuṣūl*, 3:294.
70 Ibid. (emphasis added).
71 Ibid.

One wonders why, when al-Jaṣṣāṣ mentioned the Khārijīs explicitly in *al-Fuṣūl*, he did not mention their counterparts, the Shīʿīs, explicitly in the same fashion and, conversely, why he mentioned both the Khārijīs and the Shīʿīs explicitly in *Aḥkām al-Qurʾān*. He must have omitted explicit mention of the Shīʿīs from *al-Fuṣūl* for a reason. Perhaps he placed them second and appended them to the Khārijīs because their asserted heresy and their political rebellion were less obvious than those of the Khārijīs. He also probably avoided explicit mention of them because the Twelver Shīʿīs represented a significant population and powerful community in Baghdad, and therefore perhaps even formed part of the audience for *al-Fuṣūl*. He may have wished to avoid the open conflicts that might result from explicit, unguarded, or direct statements and perhaps was wary of the reaction of Buwayhid officials. Indeed, one might argue that his main targets were actually the Shīʿīs rather than the Khārijīs but that he was only able to indicate this indirectly. With regard to *Kitāb Aḥkām al-Qurʾān*, the audience may have differed. It may have been less likely for the readers of this work to include Shīʿīs or their sympathisers than it was for a major work of legal theory or scriptural hermeneutics, which could be of more interest to scholars of other legal schools.

3.2 *Ulū al-Amr*: 'Those Who Are in Charge' (Q. 4:59)

In another passage devoted to a topic that does not figure directly in matters of individual legal rulings, al-Jaṣṣāṣ discusses the interpretation of Q. 4:59, which reads *aṭīʿū llāha wa-aṭīʿū l-rasūla wa-ulī l-amri minkum* 'Obey God and obey the Messenger and those among you who are in charge'. This verse, sometimes termed *āyat al-umarāʾ* 'the verse of the commanders', is an authority verse, a scriptural proof-text used to justify the authority of Muslim scholars, especially jurists. To convey this view is indeed the main aim of al-Jaṣṣāṣ's discussion. He means to justify the authority of the jurists, his own scholarly class, and to undermine the authority of other candidates for religious authority, especially the Shīʿī Imāms. In the course of this discussion, al-Jaṣṣāṣ mentions several other such authority verses, including Q. 9:122 and Q. 16:43, but Q. 4:59 occurs first in the Qurʾan's received order and so provides the occasion for the discussion of religious authority.

Authority proof-texts are an important feature of Islamic discourses generally, and they appear prominently in disparate genres, including *tafsīr*. Citations of such proof-texts have played an important role in the articulation of religious authority in Muslim communities, in negotiations over matters of orthodoxy and heterodoxy, and in the elaboration of Islamic law, theology, ritual, and practices throughout Islamic history. Scriptural proof-texts of authority like these form a major facet of Islam as a discursive tradition, the overall framework of arguments that Muslims construct regarding normative Islam.[72]

Al-Jaṣṣāṣ's discussion of Q. 4:59 may thus be recognised as part of a centrally important, widespread discourse on Islamic religious authority. Modern studies show some awareness of the discourse surrounding authority proof-texts in Islamic religious history but often present them as unique items, and do not assign them to a large category that includes many other Qurʾanic verses, Prophetic *ḥadīth* reports, and terms or slogans that are used to justify the religious authority of one or more groups in societies of the Muslim world. The most widely known of these proof-texts is the *ḥadīth* report *al-ʿulamāʾ warathat al-anbiyāʾ* 'Scholars are the heirs of the prophets', which is interpreted as suggesting that 'scholars', however one defines them, have a monopoly over religious authority after the passing of the Prophet Muḥammad. One way of interpreting such texts is as claims on the part of those who cited them to have stepped, metaphorically, into the Prophet's shoes with respect to religious authority over the Muslim community. Many discussions of the 'heirs of the prophets' *ḥadīth* report present the scholars as a single class.[73]

Modern accounts of religious authority and orthodoxy in Islam that treat the *ʿulamāʾ* 'scholars' as a monolithic group generally run roughshod over

72 On the concept of discursive tradition, see Talal Asad, *The Idea of an Anthropology of Islam*, Occasional Papers Series (Washington, DC: Center for Contemporary Arab Studies, Georgetown University, 1986); and Ovamir Anjum, 'Islam as a Discursive Tradition: Talal Asad and His Interlocutors', *Comparative Studies of South Asia, Africa and the Middle East* 27, no. 3 (2007): 656–72. The concept of a discursive tradition has the advantage of avoiding the simple dichotomies of tradition and reform that were widely adopted in earlier Islamic studies scholarship, and it allows for the complex, selective, skewed, and even deceptive use of the heritage by various Islamic groups and individual thinkers to make claims in the present about what constitutes proper Islam. While some scholars seem to think that Talal Asad has presented a comprehensive explanation of discussions of religious authority and orthodoxy in Islam, he has only taken the first step, describing the form of the explanation without delving into the content or providing illustrative examples.

73 Secondary studies that have drawn on this report include Samuel M. Zwemer's 1946 book *Heirs of the Prophets: An Account of the Clergy and Priests of Islam, the Personnel of the Mosque and 'Holy Men'* (Chicago: The Moody Bible Institute, 1946). In it, Zwemer, a Christian missionary and founder of the journal *The Moslem World* – now *The Muslim World* – likened 'the scholars' of the Islamic world to Christian clergy. Another work that uses the concept of the heirs of the prophets derived from this *ḥadīth* report is Jonathan Brockopp's account of the establishment of Muslim scholars' religious authority by the mid-tenth century, *Muhammad's Heirs: The Rise of Muslim Scholarly Communities, 622–950* (Cambridge: Cambridge University Press, 2017).

evidence indicating that several distinct groups of scholars were in competition over religious authority during various periods in Islamic history. Such groups include theologians, jurists, *ḥadīth* experts, mystic masters, philosophers, and others, not to mention Imāms or caliphs and other sovereigns. The problem that often occurs when one reads Islamic texts is that when jurists, for example, write 'scholars', they often mean 'jurists' exclusively, and the same is true of theologians, philosophers, and members of other scholarly groups. Islamic history witnessed multiple claims to be 'the heirs of the prophets' on the part of distinct classes or categories (*aṣnāf*, sing. *ṣinf*) of scholars, and these classes were in potential or real conflict on account of their competing claims to religious authority.[74]

The 'heirs of the prophets' *ḥadīth* is just one among many authority prooftexts, including Q. 4:59. While many Qur'anic verses urge the believers to obey both God and the Prophet, joining obedience to the two in a dual directive, this verse attaches to God and the Messenger a third group designated as the *ulū al-amr* 'those who possess authority' or 'those who are in charge'. Interpreters of this verse often argue that a particular group – often their own – such as the jurists or the caliphs may be identified with *ulū al-amr* mentioned in the verse and therefore possess religious authority after the demise of the Prophet Muḥammad. This reflects general contours of claims to religious authority in Islamic discourse: the religious authority of groups in Islamic societies is usually attached to and claimed to derive from that of the Prophet, and many arguments for the religious authority of one group proceed by singling out a

74 Michael Cooperson's *Classical Arabic Biography: The Heirs of the Prophets in the Age of al-Ma'mun* (Cambridge: Cambridge University Press, 2000) refers to the 'scholars are the heirs of prophets' *ḥadīth* and recognises four such categories of 'scholars': the Sunnī caliphs, the Shīʿī Imāms, *ḥadīth* scholars, and ascetic masters, represented by the Abbasid caliph al-Ma'mūn (r. 198–218/813–33), the eighth Twelver Shīʿī Imām, ʿAlī al-Riḍā (d. 203/818), the well-known *ḥadīth* expert Aḥmad b. Ḥanbal (d. 241/855), and the 'Barefoot' ascetic Bishr al-Ḥāfī (d. 227/842), respectively. Liyakat Takim points out that the disciples of the Imāms may be seen as possessing religious authority, even though they were understood to be subordinate to the Imāms. Liyakat N. Takim, *The Heirs of the Prophet: Charisma and Religious Authority in Shiʿite Islam* (Albany: State University of New York Press, 2006). See also Arthur F. Buehler, *Sufi Heirs of the Prophet: The Indian Naqshbandiyya and the Rise of the Mediating Sufi Shaykh* (Columbia: University of South Carolina Press, 1998); Ibn Rajab al-Ḥanbalī, *The Heirs of the Prophets*, trans. Zaid Shakir (Bridgeview, IL: Starlatch, 2002); William Chittick, *Ibn Arabi: Heir to the Prophets* (Oxford: Oneworld, 2005); Barnaby Rogerson, *The Heirs of Muhammad: Islam's First Century and the Origins of the Sunni-Shia Split* (New York: Little, Brown, 2006); Diego R. Sarrió, 'The Philosopher as the Heir of the Prophets: Averroes's Islamic Rationalism', *Al-Qantara* 36, no. 1 (2015): 45–68; Hadi Qazwini, 'Heir of the Prophets: Veneration of Ḥusayn b. ʿAlī and the Socio-religious Positioning of Twelver Shiism', *Islamic Studies* 60, no. 3 (2021): 267–86.

term in the Qur'an or *ḥadīth* in a context that suggests authority and then identifying that term with the contemporary group in question.

Like *warathat al-anbiyā'*, the term *ulū al-amr* has been held to refer to many groups throughout Islamic history, and several studies have called attention to such claims. Be that as it may, most of them have concentrated on the idea that *ulū al-amr* designates political rulers.[75] Al-Jaṣṣāṣ's interpretation of Q. 4:59 may be considered typical of mainstream Sunnī interpretations of this key term. In his view, *ulū al-amr* has two possible meanings, both of which may be intended simultaneously. The first is 'commanders of military expeditions', which derives from reports of *asbāb al-nuzūl* 'circumstances of revelation' that attach the verse to historical episodes when the Prophet sent out military detachments, and the members of the detachment were instructed to obey their appointed commander as long as they were away from the Prophet. The second meaning is *al-ʿulamā'* 'scholars' or, more generally, 'those who know, knowledgeable people'. These meanings were extended to refer to the caliphs/Imāms or Muslim rulers in the first case, and to specific groups of scholars, especially jurists, in the second case. This type of interpretation, which was widely shared by Sunnī jurists, arguably reflected a historical compromise of sorts regarding religious authority between the jurists and the rulers, whereby the jurisdiction of each group was divided along the lines of private law, the purview of the jurists, versus public law, the purview of the rulers. The two groups thus shared religious authority and generally granted each other mutual, reciprocal support regarding this point.[76]

75 Yusuf H.R. Seferta, 'The Concept of Religious Authority according to Muhammad ʿAbduh and Rashid Ridha', *Islamic Quarterly* 30, no. 3 (1986): 159–64; Yasuyuki Matsunaga, 'Examining the Views of ʿAllâmah Majlisî on Legitimate Political Authority (*Sulṭanat-i Mashrûʿah*) and the Guardianship of the Jurist (*Wilâyat-i Faqîh*)', *Orient* 35 (2000): 12–22; Hisseine Faradj, 'Ulu Al Amr & Authority: The Central Pillars of Sunni Political Thought' (PhD diss., City University of New York, 2014); Jennifer Thea Gordon, 'Obeying Those in Authority: The Hidden Political Message in Twelver Exegesis' (PhD diss., Harvard University, 2014); Ovamir Anjum, 'Political Metaphors and Concepts in the Writings of an Eleventh-Century Sunni Scholar, Abū al-Maʿālī al-Juwaynī (419–478/1028–1085)', *Journal of the Royal Asiatic Society* 26, no. 1–2 (2016): 7–18; Asma Afsaruddin, 'The Qur'an as a Political Programme', *Oasis* 13, no. 25 (2017): 14–21; Ovamir Anjum, 'Governance in Classical Islamic Thought', *Oxford Research Encyclopedia: Religion*, 19 December 2017, https://doi.org/10.1093/acrefore/9780199340378.013.513; Şaban Ali Düzgün, 'From De Facto Political Authority to Legitimate Power: Mâturîdî's Conceptualization of the Term Ulu'l-Amr', *Milel ve Nihal* 14, no. 1 (2017): 24–35; Mun'im Sirry, 'Who Are Those in Authority? Early Muslim Exegesis of the Qur'anic *Ulū'l-Amr*', *Religions* 12, no. 7 (2021): https://doi.org/10.3390/rel12070483.

76 Lapidus pointed out that this was something like the separation of church and state that is often denied for the Islamic case. Ira M. Lapidus, 'The Separation of State and Religion in the Development of Early Islamic Society', *International Journal of Middle East*

In addition, al-Jaṣṣāṣ rejects the opinion of an unspecified Shīʿī author that *ulū al-amr* in Q. 4:59 refers in particular to ʿAlī b. Abī Ṭālib, the cousin and son-in-law of the Prophet. He considers this interpretation wrong because ʿAlī was just one person, whereas *ulū* 'possessors of' in the phrase *ulū al-amr* is clearly a plural form and obviously refers to many people. He does not address directly the typical Shīʿī claim that *ulū al-amr* refers to the Imāms generally on the grounds that a general command to refer matters to them can only be correct if they are infallible, whereas military commanders (*umarāʾ*) and scholars (*ʿulamāʾ*) are certainly fallible and so cannot be the *ulū al-amr* intended in the verse.[77] Perhaps al-Jaṣṣāṣ intended the argument about the plural to be sufficient, since the Shīʿīs – whether Twelvers or others – hold that there is only one Imām at any given time. Like the reference to Shīʿīs in the explanation of the implications of Q. 2:143, this passage suggests that, in his legal hermeneutics, al-Jaṣṣāṣ had the particular goal of countering Shīʿī views, perhaps because he felt that their influence in the environment of Buwayhid Baghdad was growing too strong. Khalilovich notes that al-Jaṣṣāṣ assigned top priority to the Shīʿīs among the Islamic groups whose views he set out to counter, on the evidence of his frequent criticism of their views in the text.[78] Khalilovich discusses this passage as an example of al-Jaṣṣāṣ's aim to refute the Shīʿī doctrine of the infallibility (*ʿiṣma*) of the Imāms.[79]

Al-Jaṣṣāṣ was certainly aware that Q. 4:59 did not constitute the only authority proof-text. He writes of Q. 4:59, 'This is the counterpart (*naẓīr*) of God's word "So ask the people of remembrance (*ahl al-dhikr*) if you do not know" (Q. 16:43).' By this he meant that Q. 16:43 was also a *locus classicus* for the scriptural justification of religious authority, though he did not discuss that verse in detail. The term *ahl al-dhikr* 'the people of remembrance', like *ulū al-amr* 'those who are in charge', was interpreted as referring to those who possess religious authority. Both were cited frequently to justify the authority of the Imāms by Shīʿī thinkers, including the famous Ismāʿīlī Fatimid jurist al-Qāḍī al-Nuʿmān (d. 363/974), a contemporary of al-Jaṣṣāṣ, in his refutation of Sunnī jurisprudence, *Ikhtilāf uṣūl al-madhāhib*.[80] The Twelver jurist al-Shaykh al-Ṭūsī

Studies 6, no. 4 (1975): 363–85. The difference is that both the scholars and the caliphs or sultans, the rulers of the state, are claimants to *religious* authority.

77 See also Khalilovich, *al-Imām Abū Bakr al-Rāzī al-Jaṣṣāṣ*, 438–39.

78 Ibid., 435.

79 Ibid., 438–39.

80 al-Qāḍī al-Nuʿmān, *Disagreements of the Jurists*, trans. Devin J. Stewart (New York: New York University Press, 2015), 30–32.

(d. 460/1067) also identifies *ulū al-amr* and *ahl al-dhikr* with the Shīʿī Imāms in his *tafsīr*, *al-Tibyān*.[81]

A second major facet of al-Jaṣṣāṣ's discussion of this verse is the argument that it justifies the use of independent legal reasoning (*ijtihād*) and analogy (*qiyās*) as hermeneutical principles. Like many other jurists, he interprets the command to refer a disputed matter to God and the Prophet as meaning that one should consult the Qur'an and the Sunna of the Prophet. His basic reasoning is that if a matter was disputed by believers, the dispute could only have occurred if no direct, explicit answer had been available. Therefore, referring to the Qur'an and the Sunna of the Prophet cannot mean simply finding the explicit answer stated in the text. Consultation of the text must therefore refer to looking for similar, parallel cases (*naẓāʾir*) that shed light indirectly on the question at hand. The main mode of accomplishing this, in his view, is through analogy.

As a supporting argument regarding *ijtihād*, al-Jaṣṣāṣ cites the famous *ḥadīth* report about the Prophet sending the Companion Muʿādh b. Jabal (d. 18/639) to serve as a judge in Yemen. As is commonly the case, the report is adduced here in order to establish the validity of *ijtihād*.[82] The Prophet asks Muʿādh how he is going to judge, and he responds that he will judge first, by the Book of God, then by the Sunna of the Prophet, and then, 'I will do my utmost to form a considered opinion (*ajtahidu raʾyī*).' However, in this case, al-Jaṣṣāṣ uses this report primarily to critique an opponent's argument. An anonymous interlocutor objects to al-Jaṣṣāṣ's interpretation that referring a case to God and to the Prophet is tantamount to a command to exercise *ijtihād*. The interlocutor argues that since the verse commanded the Prophet's Companions to undertake this act of referral, and since it is well known that no one could perform *ijtihād* during the time of the Prophet, it could not be understood as a command to perform *ijtihād*. Al-Jaṣṣāṣ responds that this claim is false because a contemporary could do so either if he or she were absent from the Prophet for a time, as in the case of Muʿādh, or if the Prophet instructed him or her to perform *ijtihād*. Therefore, his claim that the command to refer matters to God

81 Muḥammad b. al-Ḥasan al-Ṭūsī, *al-Tibyān fī tafsīr al-Qurʾān*, 9 vols., ed. Aḥmad Ḥabīb Quṣayr al-ʿĀmilī (Beirut: Dār Iḥyāʾ al-Turāth al-ʿArabī, 1999), 3:235–37.

82 On the use of this *ḥadīth* report as a justification for *ijtihād* and/or *qiyās*, see Ignaz Goldziher, *The Ẓāhirīs: Their Doctrine and Their History: A Contribution to the History of Islamic Theology*, trans. and ed. Wolfgang Behn (Leiden: Brill, 1971), 8–10; Joseph Schacht, *The Origins of Muhammadan Jurisprudence* (Oxford: The Clarendon Press, 1950), 105–6; Zysow, *The Economy of Certainty*, 165–66; David R. Vishanoff, *The Formation of Islamic Hermeneutics: How Sunni Legal Theorists Imagined a Revealed Law* (New Haven: American Oriental Society, 2011), 257.

and to the Prophet should be understood as a directive to perform *ijtihād* is not undermined by the objection.

3.3 Deduction (*Istinbāṭ*) (Q. 4:83)

The text of the Qur'an refers to the act of deduction (*istinbāṭ*) in the following verse: 'Had they referred it to the Messenger and to those of them in charge, then those of them who could deduce it would have known it' (Q. 4:83). Al-Jaṣṣāṣ interprets the phrase *alladhīna yastanbiṭūnahu* 'those of them who could deduce it' as referring to the same groups as *ulū al-amr* in Q. 4:59, that is, both to commanders or rulers and to scholars. In other words, Q. 4:83 is another authority proof-text, and *alladhīna yastanbiṭūnahu* is another designation of the group endowed with religious authority, like *ulū al-amr* and *ahl al-dhikr*.

Deduction refers, in al-Jaṣṣāṣ's view, to the derivation of legal rulings that are not immediately evident. Not all legal rulings are established by explicit texts (*manṣūṣ*), and those that are not must be arrived at through deduction. Jurists are charged with undertaking this task, which is accomplished through such means as legal analogy (*qiyās*) and exhaustive investigation (*ijtihād*), determining the appropriate legal rulings for the specific cases that they are faced with by comparing them with other cases whose rulings are established in explicit terms. Those who are not learned in the law are obligated to consult legal experts concerning such cases and to follow the pronouncements at which they have arrived through exhaustive investigation.

Al-Jaṣṣāṣ also argues that deduction cannot be understood to mean simply finding an explicit ruling in the text, nor can it consist of the mere derivation of the text's linguistic implications. He reports an interlocutor's objection that the act of deduction mentioned in the Qur'an does not designate such rational methods as *qiyās* and *ijtihād* but rather refers instead to the citation of appropriate scriptural or textual evidence for a ruling. Al-Jaṣṣāṣ counters this objection in order to justify the validity of *qiyās*, *ijtihād*, and other methods in legal hermeneutics, arguing against scholars who claim that these methods are invalid, such as the Ẓāhirīs. As in the interpretation of Q. 4:59, al-Jaṣṣāṣ asserts that the act of deduction mentioned in Q. 4:83 could not refer to the discovery of an explicit legal ruling, since that would have been obvious to begin with and would not have required the effort involved in deduction, when the verse clearly refers to God's imposition of such effort as a religious obligation.

In this section as well, al-Jaṣṣāṣ refers to Shīʿīs, claiming that this verse also disproves their conception of the Imāmate. If all rulings of the religion were stated explicitly in the text, then the Imām would already have known them.

There would be no cause for the text to instruct anyone to employ deduction to figure them out, just as there would be no reason to refer to *ulū al-amr*. One would simply refer to the Imām, who would know the answer directly from the text. Since the verse makes deduction a clear obligation, this proves that the Qur'an does not envisage the delegation of legal questions to an omniscient Imām.

3.4 *Tibyānan li-kulli shay'* 'As an Explanation of All Things' (Q. 16:89)

Q. 16:89 states that the Qur'an has been revealed in order to serve 'as an explanation of all things'. Al-Jaṣṣāṣ interprets the verse as justifying the use of a variety of hermeneutical methods in determining the law, including independent legal reasoning or application of one's considered judgement (*ijtihād al-ra'y*), analogy (*qiyās*), juristic preference or consideration of what is best (*istiḥsān*), and resort to reports that have been received through a solitary chain of transmission (*khabar al-wāḥid*). In espousing this view, he is arguing against other jurists who take this verse as evidence that appropriate legal rulings are provided by the explicit text of the Qur'an for all necessary matters, thus obviating the need for ratiocination and resort to any other methods besides immediate consideration of the text. Shīʿī and Ẓāhirī jurists, for example, claimed that this verse proves the invalidity of *ijtihād*, *qiyās*, and other rational methods of interpretation. Al-Qāḍī al-Nuʿmān, who likely drew many of his arguments from *al-Wuṣūl ilā maʿrifat al-uṣūl* by the Ẓāhirī jurist Ibn Dāwūd (d. 297/910), cites this verse as disproving the validity of *naẓar*, *qiyās*, *istiḥsān*, and *ijtihād*.[83] The Ẓāhirī jurist Ibn Ḥazm (d. 456/1064) also cites this verse as an argument against the validity of *qiyās*, along with the Qur'anic verses *al-yawma akmaltu lakum dīnakum* 'Today I have perfected your religion for you' (Q. 5:3) and *mā farraṭnā fī l-kitābi min shay'* 'We have left nothing out of the Book' (Q. 6:38).[84] According to al-Jaṣṣāṣ's interpretation, all things – all legal rulings, that is – are indeed contained in the Qur'an, but this does not mean that the rulings are presented in explicit terms. Rather, in his view, legal rulings may be conveyed by the text in one of two ways: either explicitly and directly, in which case they may simply be identified, located, and cited, or indirectly and potentially, waiting to be discovered through use of analogy and other similar methods, based on the rulings given for other, comparable cases.

The strongest evidence that al-Jaṣṣāṣ was addressing the arguments of Ẓāhirī jurists in particular is that he critiques legal theorists who espouse the

83 al-Qāḍī al-Nuʿmān, *Disagreements of the Jurists*, 116, 130, 172, 204, respectively.

84 Ibn Ḥazm, *al-Iḥkām*, 8:3, 9, 10–11, 18, 38.

method of *istidlāl* 'inference'.[85] Here, *istidlāl* does not convey the ordinary sense of adducing proof or citing an indication or piece of evidence (*dalīl*). Rather, it is a technical term adopted by the Ẓāhirīs to describe their hermeneutics. They used *istidlāl* to mean the derivation of the implications of a verse without resort to rational operations such as legal analogy or mere opinion. In their view, *istidlāl* did not depend on extra-textual factors; it simply involved extracting what was already implied by the text and so did not involve the insertion of fallible human reasoning and judgements into the determination of the sacred law.[86] On this account, Ibn Ḥazm argues that the proponents of *qiyās* misunderstand the true meaning of *dalīl* 'indicator, evidence' and *istidlāl* 'inference from an indicator'.[87] Al-Jaṣṣāṣ, however, argues that those who claim to be using *istidlāl* are in fact employing *ijtihād* and *qiyās* while simply giving their method a different name to disguise what they are doing. He clearly directs this statement at the Ẓāhirīs, whom he criticises for violating their own stated principles of interpretation.

It is worth noting that al-Jaṣṣāṣ also uses the term *naẓar* 'speculation' or 'rational inquiry' to describe one of the methods of legal hermeneutics, along with *ijtihād* and *qiyās*, which are more ubiquitous in the genre of *uṣūl al-fiqh*. *Naẓar* was the favoured term of the theologians, especially the Muʿtazilīs, while the usual terms used by jurists for rational approaches to the law were *raʾy* 'considered opinion', *ijtihād al-raʾy* 'concerted effort to arrive at a considered opinion', *ijtihād* 'exhaustive legal reasoning', and *qiyās* 'analogy'. By al-Jaṣṣāṣ's time, *raʾy* on its own was rarely cited because it had taken on a negative connotation, being interpreted by traditionalists as 'whim' or 'baseless personal opinion', although the early Ḥanafīs had considered it a positive term designating the considered opinion of a skilled legal expert. The terms *ijtihād* and *qiyās*, however, became standard in legal discourse, while *naẓar* was touted by theologians as their primary method of analysis. For example, al-Qāḍī ʿAbd al-Jabbār (d. 415/1025) devoted one volume of his theological *summa*, *al-Mughnī fī abwāb al-tawḥīd wa-l-ʿadl* (The Indispensable Book, on the Categories of God's Oneness and Justice), to the topic of *naẓar*.[88]

The fact that *naẓar* appears together with other standard methods of legal hermeneutics in al-Jaṣṣāṣ's *Kitāb Aḥkām al-Qurʾān* suggests that he

85 al-Jaṣṣāṣ, *Aḥkām al-Qurʾān*, 5:11.

86 al-Qāḍī al-Nuʿmān, *Disagreements of the Jurists*, 181–90.

87 Ibn Ḥazm, *al-Iḥkām*, 5:105–8. For an accessible discussion of the concepts of *dalīl* 'indicator' and *istidlāl* 'inference', see Weiss, *The Search for God's Law*, 147–54, 647–71.

88 al-Qāḍī ʿAbd al-Jabbār, *al-Mughnī fī abwāb al-tawḥīd wa-l-ʿadl*, vol. 12, *al-Naẓar wa-l-maʿārif*, ed. Ibrāhīm Madkūr (Cairo: al-Muʾassasa al-Miṣriyya al-ʿĀmma, 1965).

was drawing on discussions of *naẓar* in earlier works devoted to *uṣūl al-fiqh* that belonged to, or were influenced by, the Muʿtazilī tradition. Al-Qāḍī al-Nuʿmān's *Ikhtilāf uṣūl al-madhāhib* (Disagreement among the Legal Schools' Hermeneutical Principles), a thorough refutation of Sunnī *uṣūl al-fiqh* written ca. 343–48/954–59, includes a chapter arguing that the use of *naẓar* in legal interpretation is invalid.[89] This fact suggests that he, too, was drawing on earlier manuals of *uṣūl al-fiqh* that discussed *naẓar* in an independent chapter. The one Muʿtazilī author whom al-Qāḍī al-Nuʿmān cites is Aḥmad b. ʿAlī Ibn al-Ikhshādh or Ibn al-Ikhshīd al-Baghdādī (d. 326/938), who wrote a work devoted to consensus and also *al-Maʿūna fī al-uṣūl* (The Book of Succour, on Jurisprudence [or Theology]), which may have been a manual of legal hermeneutics.[90] Al-Qāḍī al-Nuʿmān cites very few works by title or even by author, so he could have been drawing on any number of other Muʿtazilī texts in addition. The introduction to *ʿUddat al-uṣūl*, the Twelver Shīʿī al-Shaykh al-Ṭūsī's manual of *uṣūl al-fiqh*, goes against the views of al-Qāḍī al-Nuʿmān on this point. There, al-Ṭūsī also discusses *naẓar*, arguing that, under certain circumstances, rational speculation may generate certain knowledge and not simply probable knowledge.[91] These examples suggest that by the fourth/tenth century, some manuals in the genre of *uṣūl al-fiqh* came to include a distinct chapter devoted to *naẓar*. One assumes that this innovation was brought about by Muʿtazilī theologian-jurists in the late ninth or early tenth century. It so happened that a chapter on *naẓar* did not become a standard feature of the genre of *uṣūl al-fiqh* in later eras; it was limited to this particular period and then died out, leaving only scattered traces in the record of extant manuals of *uṣūl al-fiqh*.

4 Conclusion

Al-Jaṣṣāṣ's *Kitāb Aḥkām al-Qurʾān* devotes several passages to matters regarding the theory of legal hermeneutics, though it nevertheless generally conforms to the established genre to which it belongs, focusing on derivation of the points of law from the Qurʾan's legal verses. Matters of legal theory and hermeneutics are not a focus of the work throughout; al-Jaṣṣāṣ evidently wrote these sections

89 al-Qāḍī al-Nuʿmān, *Disagreements of the Jurists*, 115–34.

90 Ibid., 62.

91 Muḥammad b. al-Ḥasan al-Ṭūsī, *al-ʿUdda fī uṣūl al-fiqh*, 2 vols., ed. Muḥammad Riḍā al-Anṣārī al-Qummī (Qom: Sitāra, 1997), 1:20–24.

because he considered them of fundamental importance, since they provided the minimum necessary theoretical scaffolding for the interpretations he would present in the rest of the work. These passages justify resort to the concepts of consensus, *qiyās*, and *ijtihād* in the elaboration of Islamic law, proving, in al-Jaṣṣāṣ's view, that these methods are based on directives contained in the sacred text itself, even without recourse to extra-Qur'anic evidence. In addition, the section devoted to Q. 4:59 and to the interpretation of the crucial term *ulū al-amr* justifies the religious authority of 'the scholars' – here meaning jurists in particular – along with political authorities, whether caliphs or other rulers. Again, al-Jaṣṣāṣ may have felt that it was crucial to establish the authority of Sunnī jurists in order to support the interpretive labour he was undertaking in *Kitāb Aḥkām al-Qur'ān*. Moreover, several passages in his work show that he went out of his way to engage in anti-Shīʿī polemics in particular. This may have to do with the Buwayhid political domination of Iraq beginning in 334/945 or with the increasingly vocal presence of Shīʿīs in scholarly circles in Baghdad and other major centres.

All such passages show that al-Jaṣṣāṣ was concerned to engage with ideological challenges presented by Shīʿīs, Ẓāhirīs, and Muʿtazilī theologians, establishing what he saw as the proper boundaries of the enterprise of Islamic legal interpretation. Nevertheless, while he argues that they should be kept out of the accepted interpretive community and denounces their views as incorrect and even heretical, he nevertheless treats them as significant interlocutors. His *Kitāb Aḥkām al-Qur'ān* thus provides a view of the vigorous debates and the exuberant theories regarding the proper limits of normative Islam that ranged widely in the third/ninth and fourth/tenth centuries but subsided in the fifth/eleventh and later centuries. While later Sunnī authors and modern scholars alike may view this process as the triumph of orthodoxy, what Wael Hallaq has termed 'the Great Synthesis',[92] one may also view it as a 'Great Narrowing' of a diversity of approaches. Because so many works from this period are lost, including seminal works in the genre of *uṣūl al-fiqh*, the contours of these debates are difficult to assess directly, but fragmentary indications such as those found in al-Jaṣṣāṣ's *Kitāb Aḥkām al-Qur'ān* provide important hints for modern investigators, shedding light on the interpretive debates of this period.

92 Wael Hallaq, '*Uṣūl al-Fiqh* and Shāfiʿī's *Risāla* Revisited', *Journal of Arabic and Islamic Studies* 19 (2019): 129–83, passim.

Appendix 1: Excursus – the Relationship between *Kitāb Aḥkām al-Qur'ān* and *al-Fuṣūl fī al-uṣūl*

Many modern scholars have claimed that al-Jaṣṣāṣ wrote *al-Fuṣūl fī al-uṣūl* to serve as an introduction to his work *Kitāb Aḥkām al-Qur'ān*. Al-Nashmī, editor of *al-Fuṣūl*, and al-Qamḥāwī, editor of *Kitāb Aḥkām al-Qur'ān*, both make this claim.[93] In his monograph on *Aḥkām al-Qur'ān*, Güngör agrees that this is the case.[94] The claim has also been accepted by others, including Saeedullah in his article on the life and works of al-Jaṣṣāṣ, ʿAbd al-Ḥamīd b. ʿAlī Abū Zunayd in his introduction to al-Bāqillānī's *al-Taqrīb wa-l-irshād*, Marie Bernand in her article 'Status Questionis' on *uṣūl al-fiqh*, and Wael Hallaq in his 2019 article on the history of *uṣūl al-fiqh*.[95] Convinced that the two works are intimately related, al-Nashmī even took the odd decision to supply his own text of an introduction to the *Fuṣūl*, attempting to restore the original introduction that is missing in the acephalous manuscript by reworking the introduction to *Kitāb Aḥkām al-Qur'ān*; if one understands the *Fuṣūl* to be the introduction to *Kitāb Aḥkām al-Qur'ān*, this procedure appears illogical.[96] I believe that this interpretation is wrong: *al-Fuṣūl* was not written as an introduction to *Kitāb Aḥkām al-Qur'ān*.

In the prologue to *Kitāb Aḥkām al-Qur'ān*, al-Jaṣṣāṣ indeed describes a work that he wrote to serve as an introduction to this book on the Qur'an's legal verses. The text of this description reads as follows:

93 al-Nashmī, 'Introduction', in al-Jaṣṣāṣ, *al-Fuṣūl*, 1:30–31; al-Qamḥāwī, 'Introduction', in al-Jaṣṣāṣ, *Aḥkām al-Qur'ān*, 1:3.

94 Güngör, *Cassâs*, 43, 121–22.

95 Saeedullah, 'Life and Works', 138; Marie Bernand, 'Les *uṣūl al-fiqh* de l'époque classique status quaestionis', *Arabica* 39, no. 3 (1992): 277; Muḥammad b. al-Ṭayyib al-Bāqillānī, *al-Taqrīb wa-l-irshād al-ṣaghīr*, 3 vols., 2nd ed., ed. ʿAbd al-Ḥamīd b. ʿAlī Abū Zunayd (Beirut: Mu'assasat al-Risāla, 1998), 1:94; ʿAbd Allāh Muṣṭafā al-Marāghī, *al-Faḍl al-mubīn fī ṭabaqāt al-uṣūliyyīn*, 3 vols. (Cairo: Muḥammad ʿAlī ʿUthmān, 1947), 1:204; Hallaq, '*Uṣūl al-Fiqh* and Shāfiʿī's *Risāla* Revisited', 147.

96 al-Nashmī, 'Introduction', 1:40. Al-Nashmī's text of this contrived introduction is surprisingly an edited version of the introduction to al-Jaṣṣāṣ's *Aḥkām al-Qur'ān*. It reads as follows: 'In the name of God, the Merciful and Beneficent. After praising God and blessing the Messenger of God – may God bless him and grant him peace: This is [the work] *The Sub-chapters and Chapters on Jurisprudence*, which contains knowledge of the methods of derivation of the meanings of the Qur'an, the extraction of its proofs, the rules governing its expressions, and the ways in which the speech of the Arabs is inflected, the nouns of the lexicon, and legal terms. We beseech God to grant us success in that which brings us closer to Him, and brings us favour in His presence, for He is in control of this and able to do it.'

> We have prefaced this book with an introduction containing a summary of the bases of theology (*uṣūl al-tawḥīd*) that one cannot do without knowing and an entrée into the knowledge of the deduction of the meanings of the Qur'an, the extraction of its proofs, the rulings governing its expressions, the various modes of inflection of the speech of the Arabs, the Arabic lexicon, and legal expressions. This is because the science most deserving to be placed first is the one which declares the Oneness of God, His being beyond any semblance to His creation, and His being free of what the blasphemers among His oppressive servants have attributed to Him. Now that we have reached in our discourse mention of the legal rulings of the Qur'an and its proof-texts, we ask God to grant us guidance to what brings us close to Him and draws us near to His Presence. He is the One to whom this issue belongs, and He is the One who can bring about such guidance.[97]

The interpretation of this passage as a reference to *al-Fuṣūl fī al-uṣūl* is strained. First, the *Fuṣūl* is too large a work to have served as an introduction to *Kitāb Aḥkām al-Qur'ān*; it would be unusual to designate a book as a preface or introduction when it was equal in length to the main book or even longer. The unambiguous references in numerous passages of *Kitāb Aḥkām al-Qur'ān* to al-Jaṣṣāṣ's manual of jurisprudence, which invariably term it *Uṣūl al-fiqh*, do not match the description in the prologue, and they do not refer the reader back to the introduction or opening of the book (*ṣadr al-kitāb*).[98] For example, a typical reference to *al-Fuṣūl* reads, 'We have treated our opinion on this question in exhaustive detail in *Uṣūl al-fiqh* in a sufficient manner. Whoever wants to consult it, let him look it up there, God willing.'[99] If *al-Fuṣūl* were indeed the introduction to this same text, the reference would probably not use the term *hunāka* 'there', referring to a distant object. It seems quite unlikely that this statement could refer to the preface or introduction to the very book meant to be in the reader's hands at the moment.

Another, perhaps more convincing, argument has to do with the content described in the passage. While the prologue of *Kitāb Aḥkām al-Qur'ān* refers to some topics related to textual interpretation that could conceivably appear in a work on *uṣūl al-fiqh*, it also refers directly and unambiguously to theology. The content of the unknown introductory work is first presented in the following statement: 'a summary of the bases of theological doctrine (*uṣūl al-tawḥīd*) knowledge of which is indispensable'. The term *uṣūl al-tawḥīd*, literally 'the principles of God's Oneness', designates the fundamental principles

97 al-Jaṣṣāṣ, *Aḥkām al-Qur'ān*, 1:5.

98 Ibid., 42, 73, 73–74.

99 Ibid., 73–74.

of Islamic theology, and this is reported explicitly in the text as the topic of the introduction (*muqaddima*). A treatise on theology or creed would not usually have formed part of a manual on *uṣūl al-fiqh*, and, as far as is known, did not form part of the contents of *al-Fuṣūl*. This interpretation is corroborated farther along in the paragraph, when al-Jaṣṣāṣ writes about the science presented in that introductory work, 'The most deserving of the sciences to be placed first is that which declares the Oneness of God, His being above semblance to His creation, and His freedom from what the blasphemous among His oppressive servants have attributed to Him.' It is thus clear that al-Jaṣṣāṣ wrote an introductory work to *Aḥkām al-Qur'ān* that included a discussion of theological doctrine. It was evidently a separate but related work that was not fully incorporated into *Kitāb Aḥkām al-Qur'ān* but could stand on its own, and it was probably relatively short.

The confusion has arisen on account of the following statement, which forms part of this same descriptive passage: 'and an entrée into the knowledge of the deduction of the meanings of the Qur'an, the extraction of its proofs, the rulings governing its expressions, the various modes of inflection of the speech of the Arabs, the Arabic lexicon, and legal expressions'. This statement follows and is parallel to the opening statement in the paragraph, 'We have prefaced this book with an introduction containing a summary of the bases of theology that one cannot do without knowing.' The parallelism is evident from use of the nearly synonymous terms *muqaddima* 'introduction' in the first phrase and *tawṭi'a* 'entrée' in the second phrase. Whereas the topics listed here conceivably are included in works devoted to *uṣūl al-fiqh*, they fall far short of describing a full manual on the topic. Rather, these topics listed only have to do with textual analysis. In particular, the passage does not refer to the topics of *ḥadīth*, abrogation (*naskh*), consensus (*ijmāʿ*), analogy (*qiyās*), juristic preference (*istiḥsān*), exhaustive investigation (*ijtihād*), and so on, which represent essential components of an *uṣūl al-fiqh* manual. The passage gives no indication that this discussion is exhaustive, comprehensive, lengthy, or detailed, which one might expect on account of the length of *al-Fuṣūl* and the tremendous effort that had obviously gone into writing that book.

Khalilovich proposes a compromise in his interpretation of the evidence. He notes the obvious absence of theology from *al-Fuṣūl* and recognises that this renders unlikely the claim that the *uṣūl al-fiqh* manual was indeed the work al-Jaṣṣāṣ wrote as a prolegomenon to *Kitāb Aḥkām al-Qur'ān*. He remarks that the description of the work includes two sets of topics: theology, which ordinarily does not fit a work on *uṣūl al-fiqh*, and textual interpretation of the Scripture, which does. He suggests, however, that both may indeed refer to *al-Fuṣūl* on the supposition that *al-Fuṣūl* originally included a section at the beginning that focused on theology and was subsequently lost. Since the extant manuscripts of *al-Fuṣūl* are acephalous, missing a beginning section of unknown length, Khalilovich supposes that the missing section may have been devoted to the discussion of theology to which al-Jaṣṣāṣ refers.[100] Murteza Bedir proposes a similar interpretation, suggesting that *al-Fuṣūl* was indeed the introduction referred to in *Kitāb Aḥkām al-Qur'ān* and arguing that it probably included a major section devoted to theology that is now missing from the work.[101]

In my view, this scenario is unlikely. One possibility is that the reference to hermeneutics in this paragraph is actually a description of *Kitāb Aḥkām al-Qur'ān* itself and does not describe the introductory work. In other words, the term *al-tawṭi'a li-* 'entrée into' is followed by a description of what the introduction leads up to and not a description of the contents of the introduction itself, the theological doctrines already mentioned. This interpretation is corroborated to some extent by the statement at the end of the paragraph, 'Now that we have reached in our discourse mention of the legal rulings of the Qur'an and its proof-texts …'. This suggests a shift from the theological topics mentioned immediately before to the topics of legal interpretation that constitute the main focus of *Kitāb Aḥkām al-Qur'ān*. That very structure might be mirrored in the statement regarding the *muqaddima* and the *tawṭi'a* mentioned at the beginning of the paragraph.

An alternative possibility is that the topics having to do with hermeneutics were indeed part of the introductory work, and, in that case, Khalilovich would be partially right in arguing that the work had a dual focus, but that this work was nevertheless quite different from *al-Fuṣūl* and probably much shorter. Nevertheless, this introductory work, which presented theological and perhaps hermeneutical postulates serving as the prolegomenon to *Kitāb Aḥkām al-Qur'ān*, has yet to be identified.

It is likely that, as a student, al-Jaṣṣāṣ had engaged in significant study of theology, perhaps even with Muʿtazilī theologians. Khalilovich has addressed the question whether al-Jaṣṣāṣ could have been a Muʿtazilī himself. He concludes that even though al-Dhahabī (d. 748/1348) and other later biographers suggested that al-Jaṣṣāṣ had Muʿtazilī leanings, he was not himself a Muʿtazilī. In fact, his views went against those of the Muʿtazilīs, except for his denial of the beatific vision of God.[102] Bedir has discussed this issue thoroughly, again considering it unlikely that al-Jaṣṣāṣ was a Muʿtazilī, despite some overlap between

100 Khalilovich, *al-Imām Abū Bakr al-Rāzī al-Jaṣṣāṣ*, 135–36, 153.
101 Bedir, 'al-Jaṣṣāṣ', 151–52, 155.
102 Khalilovich, *al-Imām Abū Bakr al-Rāzī al-Jaṣṣāṣ*, 549–50.

his hermeneutical views and well-known Muʿtazilī positions. Bedir notes, however, that in the absence of a theological work by al-Jaṣṣāṣ, it will remain difficult to settle the question.[103] It hardly seems likely that al-Jaṣṣāṣ could have belonged to the Muʿtazilī school, since he makes clear in *al-Fuṣūl* that theologians ought to be excluded from consideration in consensus on legal matters.[104] However, the fact that the prolegomenon to *Kitāb Aḥkām al-Qurʾān* presented theological doctrine as fundamental background knowledge, coupled with the other references to theological positions such as predestination and anthropomorphism in the course of the work proper, suggests that al-Jaṣṣāṣ attached importance to the discipline of theology and may have been influenced significantly by contemporary Muʿtazilī thought. Indeed, this might explain why the prolegomenon has not been preserved; later Ḥanafī jurists may have suppressed it because some of the views expressed therein had become unacceptable in later periods.[105]

Appendix 2: Passages from al-Jaṣṣāṣ's *Kitāb Aḥkām al-Qurʾān*

Translator's note: Al-Jaṣṣāṣ's text exhibits many of the features typical of commentaries. It includes many ellipses and references to the text that can be understood when one is thoroughly familiar with the text being commented on but not when one is reading a translation. It also has a number of pronouns whose antecedents are less than clear. I have taken some liberties in filling in gaps, replacing pronouns with the corresponding nouns, and resorting to paraphrases in order to make the logical connections clear. My goal has been to make the text of the translation accessible to a broad audience, and in keeping with this I have tried to render most of the Arabic technical terms in English rather than retaining them in transliterated Arabic. I have also removed the standard blessings that appear after mentions of God, the Prophet Muḥammad, earlier prophets, ʿAlī b. Abī Ṭālib, and others, because in English they tend to interrupt the flow of the passages in which they occur.

103 Bedir, 'al-Jaṣṣāṣ', 156–60.

104 al-Jaṣṣāṣ, *al-Fuṣūl*, 3:296–97.

105 Murteza Bedir makes a similar suggestion. See Bedir, 'al-Jaṣṣāṣ', 155.

Consensus (Q. 2:143)[106]

[1:108] Chapter on the Validity of Consensus

God's word *ka-dhālika jaʿalnākum ummatan wasaṭan li-takūnū shuhadāʾa ʿalā l-nāsi* 'Thus, We rendered you a judicious community to be witnesses over mankind' (Q. 2:143): Experts in the Arabic lexicon have stated that *wasaṭ* means *ʿadl* 'that which is moderate or judicious', midway between one who does too little and one who does too much. It has also been said that it means 'the appropriate choice'. They amount to the same sense, because to adopt the judicious way is to choose appropriately. [The poet] Zuhayr said, **[1:109]**

hum wasaṭun yarḍā l-anāmu bi-ḥukmihim
idhā ṭaraqat iḥdā l-layālī bi-muʿaẓẓamī

They are a judicious group, whose verdict all people accept
if a certain night should witness a disastrous event.

God's word 'to be (*li-takūnū*) witnesses' means 'so that you be' (*kay takūnū*) or 'in order that you be' (*li-an takūnū*) such [witnesses]. It has been said regarding the 'witnesses' here that they bear witness against people, in both this world and the next, attesting to the deeds in which they violated what is right, as when God states, 'The prophets and witnesses were brought forward [and] judgement will be passed on all with fairness' (Q. 39:69). It has also been said [of this statement] that they witness on behalf of the prophets against their communities, who rejected them, attesting that they delivered the message to them, because the Prophet so informed them. It has also been said [that it means] 'So that you be a proof regarding what you witness', just as the Prophet is a witness, meaning a proof, standing in opposition to every one of those [communities].

Abū Bakr [al-Jaṣṣāṣ] said: The text's wording can support all these meanings, and it is possible for all these interpretations to be God's intended meaning. That is, they bear witness against the people in this world and the next regarding their deeds, and they bear witness on behalf of the prophets against their communities, attesting that these communities rejected [their prophets' messages], because God informed them of that. Furthermore, they are a proof for

106 al-Jaṣṣāṣ, *Aḥkām al-Qurʾān*, 1:108–11.

whoever comes after them with regard to the transmission of the Sacred Law and with regard to God's rulings that they adopted and believed correct.

This verse contains proof of the validity of the consensus of the Community in two respects. One respect is God's description of the Community as possessing the quality of judiciousness, and as being an appropriate choice, something which dictates that one consider them truthful or trustworthy and that one hold their opinion to be valid. This rules out the possibility of their reaching a consensus on an error. The other respect is God's word 'so that they might be witnesses against the people', meaning a proof against them [i.e. the one through whom they are held to account], just as God described the Messenger as a witness against them since he was a proof against them. The fact that God made them witnesses against others indicates that He thereby ruled that they possessed the quality of judiciousness and that their opinions ought to be accepted, because the witnesses of God cannot be unbelievers or miscreants. Therefore, the verse requires that they attest in the afterlife to the deeds of those whom they witnessed in every era but not of those who died in eras prior to their own, just as He made the Prophet a witness against those who lived in his own era.

The foregoing obtains if 'witnessing' means attesting, in the afterlife, to their former deeds. However, if 'witnessing' here means proof, then that is proof against those who witness – people of a second, later era – and against those who come after them until the Day of Resurrection, just as the Prophet was a proof against the entire Community, both early and late generations. This is because, once the proof of God is established at a point in time, it is established forever. The difference between witness of deeds in the afterlife and witness in the sense of proof is indicated to you by God's word 'What will they do when We bring a witness from every community, with you [Muḥammad] as a witness against these people?' (Q. 4:41). When God intended to refer to testimony regarding their deeds, He specified the people of [the Prophet's] era and those whom he witnessed committing them. Similarly, God said, quoting the words of Jesus, 'I was a witness against them as long as I was among them, but when You called me to You, You were the Watcher over them' (Q. 5:117). It thus becomes clear that witnessing deeds is exclusive to the time regarding which such testimony occurs but that neither the early nor the late generations of the Community are exclusively associated with the witnessing that is equivalent to proof, given that the Prophet is a proof against all generations of them. Likewise, since the people of every era are God's witnesses [1:110] in the sense of proof, they necessarily serve as proof against the people of their own era, who are included with them in their consensus, and against those who come after them, the people of all ensuing eras.

This indicates that if the people of their age agree unanimously on something, and if a certain one of them diverges from their consensus, then he is proved wrong by the preceding consensus, because the Prophet attested that the opinion of that group was valid and rendered their group a proof and convincing evidence. Therefore, anyone who leaves their group after that point has abandoned the ruling dictated by convincing evidence and proof, since it is impossible for God's indicator to be present without entailing its necessary consequence, impossible for abrogation to occur after the passing of the Prophet, and impossible for his ruling to be abandoned on account of abrogation. This indicates that consensus, no matter the circumstances under which it is established on the part of the Community, is God's proof, and no one may abandon it or depart from it. Given that the verse indicates the validity of the consensus of the first generation of the Community (*al-ṣadr al-awwal*), it also indicates the validity of the consensus of the people of all subsequent eras, since He did not single out in this regard the people of one era to the exclusion of any other era. If it were possible to interpret the ruling of the verse as being restricted to the consensus of the first generation, excluding the people of all other eras, then it would equally be possible to limit consideration to the consensus of the people of all subsequent eras, excluding that of the first generation.

If someone were to object: 'When God said, "Thus We made you a judicious community," directing an address to those who were present at the time when the verse was revealed, this indicated that they, and no one besides them, were the ones specifically addressed by it. Those others may only be included in their ruling through some additional evidence.'

One should respond to him: 'This is an error because God's word "Thus We made you a judicious community" is an address to the entire Community, both earlier and later generations, whoever of them was present at the time when the verse was revealed and those who came after them [and will continue to do so] until the arrival of the Hour. This is just like God's word "Fasting has been ordained for you, just as it was ordained for those before you" (Q. 2:183); "Retaliation has been ordained for you" (Q. 2:178); and other such verses that address the entire Community [irrespective of the generation]. Similarly, the Prophet was sent to all of the Community, those who were present during his era and those who came after him, for God stated, "We indeed send you as a witness, a conveyor of glad tidings and a warner, a caller to God by His permission and a shining beacon" (Q. 33:46) and "We have sent you only as a mercy to the generations" (Q. 21:107). I doubt that any Muslim would venture to state categorially that the Prophet was not sent to the entire Community, both earlier and later generations, that he was not a proof for them and a witness against them, and that he was not a mercy to all of them.'

If someone were to object: 'When God said, "Thus We made you a judicious community," the designation "community" applies both to those who were present in the era of the Prophet and to those who came after them until the arrival of the Hour. He ruled that the entire group of them [throughout the generations] was judicious and that their opinions should be accepted. This statement did not include a judgement indicating that the people of just one era were judicious and that only their opinions should be accepted. So how, then, could you rule that the people of each individual era are judicious to such an extent that you render them a proof against those who come after them?'

One should respond to him: 'God made those whom He judged to be judicious a proof over others regarding the rulings of God that they report or believe. It is known that this attribute applies to them in this world, and God reported [1:111] that they are witnesses over the people. Therefore, if both earlier and later generations are to be taken into consideration with regard to the Community's being a proof for God against them, then we would realise that the intended meaning is the people of each era, because the people of each era may be called a Community. This is because the word "Community" (*umma*) originally designated a group of people who all face the same direction, and the people of every era, despite their different conditions, may be subsumed under this noun. This does not preclude that the word community be used in unqualified form when the intended meaning is the people of this era. Do you not see that, when you say, "The Community has agreed unanimously that God has declared [marriage to] mothers and sisters forbidden" and "The Community has transmitted the Qur'an,"[107] those unrestricted statements would be correct?'

One should [also] respond: 'If the group (*al-qawm*) indeed has a final generation, then it is established thereby that God intended by this the people of every era.' In addition, [one should respond:] 'God stated, "We made you a judicious community," referring to them with an indefinite expression, applying this attribute to them, and making them a proof. That would necessarily refer to the people of every era, since God's word "We made you" is addressed to everyone, and the attribute applies to every subset of those who are addressed. Would you not consider God's word "And among Moses' people is a community who guides by the truth" (Q. 7:159)? All Moses' people constitute his community, but God called just some of them, on their own,[108] a community, on account of the attributes that He applied to them. Thus, it is established that the people of each era may be called a community, even if that

107 Reading *naqalat al-umma al-Qurʾān* for *naqalat al-umma wa-l-Qurʾān* in the text.
108 Reading *ʿalā al-infirād* for *ʿalā al-infirā* in the text.

designation might apply to the early generations of the community or to its later generations.

'This verse also contains an indication that all those who are manifest infidels – such as the anthropomorphists (*al-mushabbiha*) and those who explicitly avow divine compulsion (*al-jabr*), if it is proved that they harbour these views – should not be taken into consideration in consensus. Similarly, those who are manifest transgressors, such as the Khawārij and the Rawāfiḍ,[109] should not be taken into consideration in consensus. This is so whether or not the person in question sinned in act or in doctrine, because God made only those people witnesses whom He described as possessed of judiciousness and excellence,[110] and these attributes apply neither to unbelievers nor to sinners. There is no difference in this ruling between one who sins or becomes an unbeliever through allegorical interpretation and one who does so by rejecting the explicit text, since the attribute of blame applies generally[111] to all such cases, and the attribute of judiciousness or moderation cannot apply to them[112] under any circumstance. But God knows best.'

Authority and Legal Analogy (Q. 4:59)[113]

[3:177] Chapter on Obedience to Those Who Are in Charge

God said, 'O you who believe! Obey God and obey the Messenger and those of you who are in charge' (Q. 4:59): Abū Bakr [al-Jaṣṣāṣ] said: There has been disagreement over the interpretation of 'those who are in charge' (*ulū al-amr*). It has been transmitted from Jābir b. 'Abd Allāh [al-Anṣārī al-Khazrajī] (d. 78/697–98), Ibn 'Abbās (d. 68/687) – according to one report – al-Ḥasan [al-Baṣrī] (d. 110/728), 'Aṭā' (d. 114/732), and Mujāhid [b. Jabr] (d. 104/722), that *ulū al-amr* are those who possess knowledge of the law and religion (*ulū al-fiqh wa-l-'ilm*). It has been transmitted from Ibn 'Abbās – according to another report – and from Abū Hurayra (d. 58/678) that *ulū al-amr* are the commanders of military detachments. It is possible that the verse is meant to refer to both, because the verbal expression encompasses both senses. This is because commanders undertake the task of organising armies and battalions and fighting the enemy, while scholars undertake the preservation of the Sacred Law and

109 *Rāfiḍī*, pl. *Rawāfiḍ* 'deserters, rejectors', is a standard term of opprobrium for Shī'īs.

110 The reference to *khayr* 'excellence' appears to be an allusion to another Qur'anic phrase, *kuntum khayra ummatin ukhrijat li-l-nās* 'You are the best community ever raised for humanity' (Q. 3:110).

111 Reading *shamilat-hum ṣifat al-dhamm* for *shamilahum ṣifat al-dhamm* in the text.

112 Reading *lā talḥaquhum* for *lā yalḥaquhum* in the text.

113 al-Jaṣṣāṣ, *Aḥkām al-Qur'ān*, 3:177–81.

the task of distinguishing[114] what is permissible from what is illicit. For that reason, God commanded the people to obey the scholars and to accept their opinions, and this is something in which they are equivalent to commanders and rulers, as long as the scholars are judicious, reasonable people who are accepted by the public and whose piety and trustworthiness in the tasks that they carry out is a matter of confidence.

This verse is the counterpart of God's word *fa-s'alū ahl al-dhikri in kuntum lā taʿlamūn* 'So ask the people of remembrance, if you do not know' (Q. 16:43). Some people say that the most apparent meaning of *ulū l-amr* here is military commanders because God first mentioned the command to do justice, and this is an address to those who have the power to carry out verdicts, that is, commanders and rulers. God then adjoined to them the command to obey those who are in charge, the guardians (*wulāt al-amr*) who, as long as they are judicious and accepted by the public, may give rulings with regard to them. This, however, does not prevent the command in the verse from being a command to obey both groups of those who are in charge, that is, both the commanders of military detachments and the scholars, since placing the command to judge justly first does not entail in any way limiting the command to obey those who are in charge to military commanders, to the exclusion of all others. It has been transmitted from the Prophet that he said, 'Whoever obeys a commander whom I have appointed has obeyed me.'[115] [Shihāb al-Dīn] al-Zuhrī (d. 124/741–42) transmitted from Muḥammad b. Jubayr b. Muṭʿim (fl. late first/seventh century), from his father [Jubayr b. Muṭʿim] (d. 59/679), that he said: The Messenger of God stood up at al-Khayf, in the area of Minā,[116] and declaimed:

> May God reward a worshipper who has heard my speech and taken it to heart and then conveyed it to someone who has not heard it, for many a bearer of religious knowledge had no religious knowledge himself, and many a bearer of religious knowledge conveyed it to someone more knowledgeable than he. There are three things for which one should feel no rancour: the heart of the believer, the performance of a devotional act exclusively for the sake of God, and, as

114 Reading *wa-tamyīz mā yajūzu mimmā lā yajūzu* for *wa-mā yajūzu mimmā lā yajūzu* in the text.

115 The full report reads, *man aṭāʿanī fa-qad aṭāʿa llāh, wa-man ʿaṣānī fa-qad ʿaṣā llāh, wa-man aṭāʿa amīrī fa-qad aṭāʿanī wa-man aṣā amīrī fa-qad ʿaṣānī* 'Whoever obeys me, obeys God; and whoever disobeys me, disobeys God; and whoever obeys my appointed commander, obeys me; and whoever disobeys my appointed commander, disobeys me.' al-Bukhārī, *al-Ṣaḥīḥ, Kitāb al-Aḥkām, Bāb Qawl Allāh taʿālā 'wa-aṭīʿū llāha wa-aṭīʿū l-rasūla wa-ulī l-amri minkum'* [Q. 4:59], no. 1.

116 Sites near Mecca associated with the rites of the Pilgrimage.

> some have said, obedience to those who are in charge or, as some have said, giving advice to those who are in charge and adhering to the collective group of Muslims, for their supplication surrounds them with a protective shield.[117]

The most likely interpretation of this *ḥadīth* report is that, by 'those who are in charge', the Prophet meant military commanders. God's word [in the same verse] shortly after that, 'If you dispute over something, then refer it to God and to the Messenger' (Q. 4:59), indicates that the ones in charge are the jurists, because He commanded all the people to obey them, then He said, 'If you dispute over a matter, then refer it to God and the Messenger,' commanding the ones in charge to refer the disputed matter to the Book of God and the Sunna of His Prophet. This is not the station of the common people or those who do not belong among the people of knowledge, because they do not know how to refer something to the Book of God and the Sunna or how those two sources indicate the rulings of legal cases. It is therefore established that this address is directed to the scholars.

A certain scholar cited God's statement 'Obey God and obey the Messenger, and those who are in charge among you' as evidence of the invalidity of the opinion [3:178] of the Shīʿīs (*al-Rāfiḍa*) regarding the Imāmate. He said, 'The ones in charge must either be the jurists, the commanders, or the Imām that they claim. If the intended meaning is the jurists and the commanders, then it could not possibly designate the Imām, since the jurists and the commanders may commit errors or forget out of neglect, or may be substituted or changed, yet God commanded us to obey them. This invalidates the very foundation of [the Shīʿīs' conception of] the Imāmate, for, in their view, the necessary condition for the Imām is that he be infallible, such that it is impossible for him to err, commit mistakes, be substituted, or be changed. Also, the intended meaning could not possibly be the Imām because the address is connected to the following statement, "So if you dispute over a matter, then refer it to God and the Messenger" (Q. 4:59). Had an Imām whom the people were obligated to obey been present, then it would have been necessary to refer the matter to him, and he would have settled the disagreement and dispute definitively. So, when God commanded that disputed cases be referred to the Scripture and the Sunna, and not to the Imām, that indicated the invalidity of their doctrine regarding the Imāmate. Had an Imām whom it was obligatory to obey been present, then God would have stated, "So refer it to the Imām," since the Imām in their view is the one whose opinion decides the correct interpretation of the

117 Ibn Māja, *al-Sunan, Kitāb al-Manāsik, Bāb al-Khuṭba yawm al-naḥr*, no. 2 (3056); Abū Dāwūd, *al-Sunan, Kitāb al-ʿIlm, Bāb Faḍl nashr al-ʿilm*, no. 1; al-Tirmidhī, *al-Jāmiʿ al-ṣaḥīḥ, Kitāb al-ʿIlm, Bāb Mā jāʾa fī al-ḥathth ʿalā tablīgh al-samāʿ*, no. 1.

Scripture and the Sunna. Therefore, since God commanded obedience to commanders of military detachments and jurists and ordered that disputed cases be referred to the Scripture and the Sunna and not to the Imām, it is thereby established that it is not obligatory to obey the Imām with regard to the legal rulings of disputed cases and that every one of the jurists may refer those cases to similar cases that appear in the Scripture and the Sunna.

'This sect [i.e. the Shīʿīs] claimed that by God's word *wa-ulī l-amri minkum* "and those of you in charge" ʿAlī b. Abī Ṭālib (d. 40/661) is meant. That interpretation is invalid because "the ones in charge" refers to a group of people, whereas ʿAlī b. Abī Ṭālib is just one man. Also, the people were commanded to obey "the ones in charge" during the time of the Messenger of God, and it is known that ʿAlī b. Abī Ṭālib was not an Imām during the days of the Prophet. It is thus demonstrated that "those who are in charge" during the time of the Prophet were the commanders, and that those over whom they were appointed were obligated to obey them as long as they did not command them to commit a sin. Similarly, the rule concerning them in eras after the passing of the Prophet is that they must be followed and obeyed as long as it is not a sin.'

Regarding God's word 'If you dispute over a matter, then refer it to God and the Messenger', Mujāhid, Qatāda [b. Diʿāma al-Sadūsī] (d. 117/735), Maymūn b. Mihrān (d. 117/735), and al-Suddī (d. 127/745) transmitted that this meant '[… then refer it] to the Book of God and the Sunna of His Messenger'. Abū Bakr [al-Jaṣṣāṣ] said: This is a statement of general scope imposing [on Muslims] the obligation to refer to the Book of God and the Sunna of His Prophet, both during the life of the Prophet and after his death. One may refer to the Scripture and the Sunna in two ways. The first way is to refer to cases whose rulings are explicitly stated in the text and that are mentioned by name and category. The second way is to refer to such cases with regard to what they indicate[118] about the case at hand and what may be gleaned about it by way of analogy and consideration of parallels. The general expression encompasses both procedures. Therefore, it is obligatory, when we dispute over a matter, to refer to the explicit text of the Scripture and the Sunna if we find the ruling of the disputed matter mentioned explicitly in the Scripture and the Sunna. If we do not find [3:179] an explicit text mentioned there, then it is obligatory to refer it to a parallel case in either of the two, because we have been commanded to consult [the sources] under all circumstances, since God did not restrict the command to refer to those two sources to one circumstance as opposed to another. Moreover, the implication and apparent meaning of the speech dictate that one should refer to them regarding that for which there is

118 Reading *min ḥaythu al-dalāla ʿalayhi* or *min jihat al-dalāla ʿalayhi* for *min al-dalāla ʿalayhi* in the text.

no explicit text. That is because, when something is explicitly stated and no possible alternative interpretations regarding it exist, no dispute could occur over the issue among the Companions, considering their expert knowledge of the Arabic lexicon and their acquaintance with texts that support alternative interpretations, as opposed to texts regarding which there are no alternative interpretations. The verse's apparent meaning requires that one refer the disputed matter to its counterparts in the Scripture and the Sunna.

If one were to object: 'The meaning intended by this imperative statement is only a command to abandon dispute and to submit to what is contained in the Book of God and the Sunna of the Messenger of God.' One should respond: 'This verse is an address to the believers because God said, "O you who believe! Obey God and obey the Messenger." If the interpretation of this text were what you have stated, then its meaning would be "Follow the Book of God and the Sunna of His Prophet, and obey God and obey His Messenger." However, we know that every believer, by accepting faith, has already adopted as part of his creed that he believes in adhering to the ruling of God and the Sunna of the Messenger. That would lead to invalidation of the specific point of God's word, "So refer it to God and the Messenger", for since the command to do that already occurred at the beginning of the verse, in God's word, "Obey God and obey the Messenger", one cannot possibly interpret God's word "So refer it to God and the Messenger", as meaning simply that which He already conveyed plainly at the beginning of the address. It must be interpreted as conveying a separate, new piece of information (*fāʾida*): to relate a case whose ruling is not explicitly stated in the text – over which dispute has occurred – to a case whose ruling is explicitly stated. We should refer all disputed matters to the Scripture and the Sunna on account of the general scope of the text, and we should not exclude anything from this directive without a specific indication.'

If someone were to object: 'Since the ruling of this verse was addressed to the Companions when a dispute arose during the lifetime of the Prophet, and since it is known that they were not allowed to employ considered opinion (*al-raʾy*) or legal analogy in determining the legal rulings of cases in the presence of the Prophet but rather obligated to submit to his judgement and to follow his command, without undertaking the task of referring it [to other stipulated cases] by means of analogy, it is therefore established that the intended meaning is to apply rulings that are explicitly stated in the text and to abandon the burden of rational inquiry (*naẓar*) and exhaustive investigation (*ijtihād*)[119] regarding that to which no explicit text applies.'

119 I render the technical term *ijtihād* as 'exhaustive investigation' or 'legal reasoining', according to context.

One should respond to him: 'This is an error, because the application of considered opinion and exhaustive investigation and the referral of cases to their counterparts whose rulings are explicitly stated were indeed permissible during the life of the Prophet. One of two such situations occurred when Companions were absent from the Prophet's presence, such as when he sent [the Companion] Muʿādh [b. Jabal] (d. 18/639) to Yemen [to serve as a judge]. [The Prophet] asked [Muʿādh], "How will you judge when you are confronted with a case?"

He answered, "I will judge by the Book of God."

He asked, "And what if it is not in the Book of God?"

He answered, "I will judge by the Sunna of the Prophet of God."

He asked, "And what if it is neither in the Book of God nor in the Sunna of the Messenger of God?"

He answered, "I will do my utmost to form a considered opinion, and I will spare no effort."

[The Prophet] struck [Muʿādh's] breast with his hand and said, "Praise God, who granted success to the messenger of the Messenger of God in arriving at what pleases the Messenger of God."[120] That is one of the two situations in which it was permissible to adopt exhaustive independent investigation during the life of the Prophet.[121]

'The other situation occurred when the Prophet commanded someone in his presence to undertake exhaustive independent investigation [3:180] and to relate the case at hand to its counterparts. [The Prophet did this] in order to verify that Companion's ability to investigate a question independently: was he capable of doing so? If he erred and abandoned the path of rational inquiry, then [the Prophet] would inform him and guide him aright. In this fashion, he used to teach [his Companions] the obligatory nature of exhaustive investigation regarding the legal rulings for cases that would arise after his death. Thus, exhaustive investigation in his presence was permissible in this manner. As [an example of this phenomenon,] my father related to us on the authority of Ḥafṣ b. Sulaymān (d. 180/769), from Kathīr b. Shinṭīr (fl. second/eighth century), from Abū al-ʿĀliya [Rufayʿ b. Mihrān *al*-Baṣrī] (*d.* ca. 93/712), from ʿUqba b. ʿĀmir (d. 58/677–78), who said, "Two litigants came to the Messenger of God and he said, 'Judge between them, O ʿUqba.' I responded, 'O Messenger of God! Should I judge between them while you are present?!' He answered, 'Judge between them, and if you hit on the correct answer, then you will earn

120 E.g. Abū Dāwūd al-Sijistānī (d. 275/889), *al-Sunan, Kitāb al-Aqḍiya, Bāb Ijtihād al-raʾy fī al-qaḍāʾ*, no. 1.

121 On appeals to this *ḥadīth* report in manuals of *uṣūl al-fiqh*, see Weiss, *The Search for God's Law*, 634–36; Zysow, *The Economy of Certainty*, 155–56.

the reward for ten good deeds, and if you err, then you will earn the reward for one good deed.'"[122] Thus, the Prophet permitted him to perform *ijtihād* in his presence in the manner that we have explained above.'

In our opinion, the Prophet's command to Muʿādh and ʿUqba b. ʿĀmir to perform exhaustive investigation on the basis of this verse – that is, God's word 'If you dispute over a matter, then refer it to God and the Messenger' – occurs in both cases because, when we find a ruling from the Prophet that agrees in content with what the Qur'an transmits, we consider it to be a ruling that the Prophet made on the basis of the Qur'an, like his amputating the hand of the robber, flogging the adulterer, and similar things, and not a ruling initiated by the Prophet. It is incorrect to state that, since exhaustive investigation of cases' rulings was not permissible during the time of the Prophet, and since the referral of a disputed matter to the Book and the Sunna was obligatory at that time, then this indicates that the command directs one to abandon dispute and simply to accept those cases whose rulings are explicitly stated in the Book and the Sunna. It was not permissible to perform exhaustive investigation during the life of the Prophet when a Companion did so in his presence and furthermore sought to enforce the ruling, arrogating exclusively to himself the right to apply his considered opinion, as opposed to the situations that we have described above. I swear by my life! This is a rejected type of *ijtihād* that has no standing and has never been permitted to anyone. But God knows best.

Chapter on Obedience to the Messenger

God stated [the following]: 'Obey God and obey the Messenger' (e.g. Q. 5:92, 64:12); 'And We have not sent any messenger except in order that he be obeyed, by God's permission' (Q. 4:64); 'Whoever obeys the Messenger has obeyed God' (Q. 4:80); and 'Then no, by your Lord, they will not believe until they appoint you an arbiter regarding what is disputed among them. Then they did not find any discomfort in themselves from that which you judged, and they submit' (Q. 4:65). Through these verses, God confirmed the obligation to obey the Messenger of God, and He clarified that obedience to the Prophet is equivalent to obedience to God. He thus conveyed by this declaration the principle that disobedience to the Prophet is equivalent to disobedience to God. God stated, 'Those who oppose his command should take care lest a trial befall them, or a painful punishment afflict them' (Q. 24:63), threatening punishment for contradicting the command of the Messenger. Through God's word 'Then no, by your Lord! They will not believe until they appoint you an arbiter regarding

122 This *ḥadīth* report is mentioned in al-Jaṣṣāṣ, *al-Fuṣūl*, 4:45.

what is disputed among them. Then they did not find any discomfort in themselves from that which you judged, and they submit' (Q. 4:65), He rendered beyond the pale of faith those who violate the command of the Messenger, who refuse to submit to what the Messenger conveyed, and who doubt him. [3:181] One should state regarding *al-ḥaraj* 'discomfort' here that it means 'doubt'. This has been transmitted from Mujāhid. The basic meaning of *al-ḥaraj* is *al-ḍīq* 'constraint' or 'straitened circumstances'. The intended meaning may possibly be 'submission without any doubt regarding the obligation of submission and without any misgivings (*ḍīq ṣadr*) about it but rather with gladness (*inshirāḥ al-ṣadr*), insight (*baṣīra*), and certainty'.

This verse includes an indication that whoever rejects any of God's commands or the commands of His Prophet has exited the pale of Islam, whether his rejection is on account of doubt regarding it or on account of abandoning acceptance and refraining from submission. This dictates the validity of what the Companions espoused, that is, the ruling that whoever refuses to pay the alms-tax is an apostate, subject to being killed with impunity and having his offspring enslaved, because God ruled that whoever does not submit to the Prophet's judgements and his legal rulings does not belong to the people of faith.

If someone were to object: 'If obedience to the Messenger is tantamount to obedience to God, then is not the command of the Messenger tantamount to the command of God?'

One should respond to him: 'Obedience to [the Messenger] is obedience to God only because the wills or the commands[123] of each coincide. A command occurs when one utters the imperative "Do!" and it is not permissible for one imperative to issue from two commanders, just as one statement cannot issue from two speakers, or one act from two actors.'

On Deduction (*Istinbāṭ*) (Q. 4:83)[124]

[3:182] God's word 'Had they referred it to the Messenger and to those of them who are in charge, then those of them who could deduce it would have known it' (Q. 4:83): Al-Ḥasan, Qatāda, and Ibn Abī Laylā (d. 83/702–3) held that 'those of them who are in charge' are the people of knowledge and jurisprudence. [Ismāʿīl b. ʿAbd al-Raḥmān] al-Suddī (d. 127/745) stated, '[They are] the commanders and the governors.' Abū Bakr [al-Jaṣṣāṣ] said: It is possible that God

123 Reading *aw amrahu* for *awāmirahu* in the text.

124 al-Jaṣṣāṣ, *Aḥkām al-Qurʾān*, 3:182–85.

means by it both groups, the jurists and the governors, because the name applies to them both.

If one were to object: 'Those who are in charge are those who possess the command to rule over the people.' [One should respond:] 'It is possible for the jurists to be called "those who are in charge" because they know the commands and prohibitions of God and because those besides them are obligated to accept their opinions regarding legal rulings. They may thus be called "those who are in charge" on that account, just as God said in another verse, "So let them gain knowledge in the religion, and let them warn their folk when they return to them, so that they take heed" (Q. 9:122). Thus, God made caution obligatory by having them warn their folk, and He imposed the obligation on **[3:183]** those folk who were warned to accept their statements. On this account, one may apply to them the designation "those who are in charge" in unrestricted form. The commanders are also called that because their commands must be carried out by those over whom they have been appointed.'

God's word 'then those among them who were able to deduce it would know it' (Q. 4:83): Deduction (*al-istinbāṭ*) means extraction, and from this expression comes the extraction of subterranean waters (*istinbāṭ al-miyāh*) and the excavation of springs. It designates the extraction of something that was concealed so that eyes might be laid upon it and minds might perceive it. Deduction in the law is equivalent to proving by indication (*istidlāl*) or the discovery of something through inquiry (*istiʿlām*). This verse establishes the obligation to uphold the validity of legal analogy and the exhaustive application of considered judgement to the rulings of legal cases. That is because God commanded that believers refer legal cases to the Messenger during his lifetime, when they were in his presence, and to the scholars after his death and when they were not in his presence. This is absolutely necessary with regard to cases about which no explicit text exists, because, when a ruling is established by an explicit text, there is no need to deduce it. This proves that, while some of God's rulings are established by explicit texts, others are embedded in the text, and God has charged us with arriving at the latter through deduction (*istinbāṭihi*) and through the adduction of evidence (*istidlālihi*). This verse conveys several ideas (*maʿānī*). One point is that some of God's rulings are not established by explicit texts but rather only indicated thereby (*madlūl ʿalayhi*). Another point is that the scholars are obligated to deduce them and to arrive at knowledge thereof by referring them to their likes among the rulings established by explicit texts. Another point is that laymen are obligated to adopt the views of scholars regarding rulings of legal cases. Yet another point is that the Prophet was charged with deducing legal rulings and proving them on the basis of their indications, because God commanded that one refer to the

Messenger and to those who are in charge. Then God said, 'then those of them who are able to deduce them would know them.' [In this last phrase,] He did not specify in this regard the ones who are in charge (*ulū al-amr*), to the exclusion of the Messenger himself.

In this there is evidence that everyone can undertake deduction and arrive at knowledge of legal rulings by citing evidence. If someone were to object: 'What is discussed here is not deduction regarding the rulings on legal cases. Rather, it refers to security and fear of the enemy, on the grounds of God's word "If a matter comes to them of security or fear, they spread it abroad, but if they had referred it to the Messenger and to those of them who were in charge, then those of them who were capable of deduction would have known it" (Q. 4:83). The verse refers to deduction only with regard to matters such as false rumours mongered by the hypocrites. God commanded the believers to cease putting store in such rumours and to refer them to the Messenger to avoid sapping the strength of the Muslims, if they contained something that caused fear, and if they contained something that suggested safety, to avoid allowing them to be lulled into a false sense of security and so leave off preparing for war and exercising caution against the unbelievers. The verse provides no indication that the use of deduction regarding the rulings of legal cases is permitted.'

One should respond to him: 'God's word "If a matter comes to them of security or fear" is not limited to the matter of the enemy, because security and fear may occur regarding that which they adopt as their religion, including the rulings of the Sacred Law: what is licit, what is forbidden, what is permissible, and what is not permissible. All this constitutes part of security and fear. Therefore, God's mention of security and fear conveys no indication of the obligation to restrict consideration to false rumours that engender a sense of **[3:184]** security from or incite fear of the enemy. Rather, the ruling applies to all cases in general. By this statement, God forbade laymen from saying, regarding any cases subject to legal rulings, what they should be: that such-and-such is forbidden, permitted, made obligatory, or otherwise. God required them to refer such cases to the Messenger and to those who are in charge so that they might deduce their rulings by citing as evidence thereof parallel examples, cases whose rulings are established by explicit texts. In addition, if we concede to you that the revelation of the verse was restricted to security and fear from the enemy, then its indication of what we have mentioned would still stand. One may declare such a thing for the following reason: One may deduce the conduct of war and deceptions of the enemy – by exercising caution sometimes, advancing boldly in one circumstance and holding back in another circumstance. However, since God imposed all such matters on us as our religion, and since He entrusted command over those matters to the considered judgement and exhaustive investigation of the ones who are in charge, then there is no distinction between the obligation to perform exhaustive investigation regarding the rulings of cases that have to do with the conduct of battles, setting traps for the enemy, or fighting the unbelievers, and exhaustive investigation and the adduction of evidence (*istidlāl*) regarding all other legal matters, including acts of devotion and the various branches of the Sacred Law, since they all belong to the rulings of God. Whoever disallows the performance of exhaustive investigation and deduction regarding such things is like one who permits deduction in the chapter of sales exclusively but disallows it in the chapter of marriage or who permits it in prayer but disallows it in the rites of the pilgrimage, and that would be a contradiction.'

If someone were to object: 'Deduction is not limited to analogy and the exhaustive application of considered judgement, to the exclusion of citing evidence in the Arabic lexicon that only supports one interpretation.'

One should respond to him: 'Lexical evidence that only supports one sense does not settle something that is disputed among experts in the Arabic lexicon, if it is something that may be comprehended from the verbal expression. That is not deduction. Rather, it is an implication of the address (*mafhūm al-khiṭāb*). In our view, making such an argument would be like saying that God's word "Do not say to them 'Uff!'" (Q. 17:23) provides no indication that beating one's parents, insulting them, killing them, and so forth, are prohibited. There is no dispute regarding this. If by evidence you mean that which supports only one meaning, then these are types of implication (*dalāʾil al-khiṭāb*). There is no dispute over this, and there is no need for deduction. If by evidence you mean the mention of something in an exclusive, contrastive manner, such that the statement indicates that other things besides require a ruling that is the opposite of the explicit ruling for the first case, then that is likewise not an indication. [Rather, it is a negative implication.] We have explained this in [our book] *Uṣūl al-fiqh*.[125] If this were a type of evidence, then the Companions would not have neglected it, and they would have cited it[126] as evidence for the rulings of legal cases. And if they had done that, then it would have been widely reported about them and would have become well-known. Since no such things have been reported about them, this indicates that your opinion is invalid.

'In addition, if that were a type of citation of evidence, it would not rule out considering deduction obligatory with regard to matters at which one can arrive only through use of considered opinion and analogy, since that type of

125 al-Jaṣṣāṣ, *al-Fuṣūl*, 1:289–323; Weiss, *The Search for God's Law*, 473–93; Zysow, *The Economy of Certainty*, 96–109.

126 Reading *wa-la-stadallat bihi* for *wa-lā stadallat bihi* in the text.

indication does not occur in every case. God commanded us to deduce the rulings of all cases regarding which there is no explicit text, so when we do not find that type of evidence, we must then deduce their legal rulings through use of analogy and exhaustive interpretation, **[3:185]** since we have no means to do so otherwise.'

If someone were to object: 'When God stated, "Then those of them who are capable of deduction would know it," the evidence of legal analogy does not lead us to knowledge of what was indicated. One who performs analogy considers that he may err and does not consider it possible to arrive at a definitive answer, whereby that to which his analogy and legal interpretation led him is the very truth according to God. Therefore, we know that, here, God did not intend deduction by means of analogy and legal interpretation.'

One should respond to him: 'Your statement that one who performs analogy is not decisively certain that his analogy is the truth according to God is an error that we do not accept. That is because, when something is known by way of exhaustive investigation, one performing legal interpretation must have decisive certainty that to which his exhaustive investigation led him is the truth according to God. In our view, this means certainty on his part that it is God's ruling on the matter. Deduction of cases' rulings through legal interpretation necessarily produces knowledge of the validity of that at which he arrived and that to which his exhaustive investigation led him.

'This verse also indicates the invalidity of the opinion of those who espouse the Imāmate, because, if all rulings of the religion had been stated explicitly in the text, then the Imām would have known them. There would be no occasion for deduction, and there would be no point in referring cases to those who are in charge. Rather, the obligation would have been to refer to the Imām, who would have known what is valid versus what is invalid from the explicit text.'

Tibyānan li-kulli shay' 'An Explanation of All Things' (Q. 16:89)[127]

God's word 'We sent the Scripture down to you as an explanation of all things' (Q. 16:89). This means – and God knows best – an explanation of all things that are matters of religion through explicit text and through indication. No new case arises, whether of tremendous gravity or of paltry importance, without God's having pronounced a ruling regarding it that He made clear in the Scripture, either by stating it explicitly in the text or by presenting an indication of it. That which the Prophet made clear derived only from the Scripture, on account of God's word 'Whatever the Messenger produces for you, then take

127 al-Jaṣṣāṣ, *Aḥkām al-Qur'ān*, 5:10–11.

it, and whatever he forbids you from doing, then desist' (Q. 59:7); 'You indeed lead to a straight path, the path of God' (Q. 42:52); and 'Whoever obeys the Messenger has obeyed God' (Q. 4:80). So, that which the Messenger made clear derives from God and belongs to the Scripture's explanation of it, on account of God's command that we obey him and submit to his command. That which is established as consensus also has its source in the Scripture, because the Scripture indicates the validity and incontrovertible authority of consensus and indicates that [the Muslim Community] will never agree unanimously on an error. That which is established by analogy (*al-qiyās*), the exhaustive application of judgement (*ijtihād al-ra'y*), and all other types of inference, including consideration of what is best (*al-istiḥsān*) and the acceptance of solitary-chain *ḥadīth* reports – all that belongs to the Scripture's clarification, because the Scripture refers to all of those methods. There is no legal ruling but that its clarification may be found in the Scripture by one of the methods that we have mentioned.

This verse indicates the validity of espousing legal analogy, for the following reason. When we do not find an explicit ruling for a particular case [5:11] in the text of the Scripture, in the Sunna, or in consensus, given that God reported that there is an explanation of all things that are matters of religion in the Scripture, it is established that the path thereto is to adopt the method of rational inquiry (*al-naẓar*)[128] and to derive indications of the case's ruling through analogy. After all, there remains no way to arrive at the ruling of a case except in this manner. Those who state that there is a hidden explicit text or who espouse 'inference'[129] have adopted different expressions that are nevertheless equivalent [to these] in meaning. They cannot escape forming a considered judgement through exhaustive investigation and the application of rational speculation and analogical argument, though they do not realise it.

Bibliography

'Abd Allāh, 'Awda, Sāmiḥ 'Abd al-Ilāh 'Abd al-Hādī, and 'Abd al-Sattār Yūsuf Aḥmad Rayyān. 'al-Manhaj al-tafsīrī li-l-Qāḍī Abī Ya'lā fī *Aḥkām al-Qur'ān mustakhlaṣan* min

128 Reading *thabata anna ṭarīqahu al-naẓar* ... for *thabata anna ṭarīqat al-naẓar* ... in the text.

129 This is a reference to the Ẓāhirīs. See Devin J. Stewart, 'Muḥammad b. Dā'ūd al-Ẓāhirī's Manual of Jurisprudence, *al-Wuṣūl ilā ma'rifat al-uṣūl*', in *Studies in Islamic Legal Theory*, ed. Bernard G. Weiss (Leiden: Brill, 2002), 119–20, 127–28, 153–54; Zysow, *The Economy of Certainty*, 108–9.

kitāb Zād al-masīr'. *Majallat al-Mīzān li-l-Dirāsāt al-Islāmiyya wa-l-Qānūniyya* 10 (2023): 1–36.

Afsaruddin, Asma. 'The Qur'an as a Political Programme'. *Oasis* 13, no. 25 (2017): 14–21.

Anjum, Ovamir. 'Islam as a Discursive Tradition: Talal Asad and His Interlocutors'. *Comparative Studies of South Asia, Africa and the Middle East* 27, no. 3 (2007): 656–72.

Anjum, Ovamir. 'Political Metaphors and Concepts in the Writings of an Eleventh-Century Sunni Scholar, Abū al-Maʿālī al-Juwaynī (419–478/1028–1085)'. *Journal of the Royal Asiatic Society* 26, no. 1–2 (2016): 7–18.

Asad, Talal. *The Idea of an Anthropology of Islam*. Occasional Papers Series. Washington, DC: Center for Contemporary Arab Studies, Georgetown University, 1986.

al-Khaṭīb al-Baghdādī. *Tārīkh Baghdād*. 17 vols. Edited by Bashshār ʿAwwād Maʿrūf. Beirut: Dār al-Gharb al-Islāmī, 2001.

al-Bāqillānī, Muḥammad b. al-Ṭayyib. *al-Taqrīb wa-l-irshād al-ṣaghīr*. 3 vols. 2nd ed. Edited by ʿAbd al-Ḥamīd b. ʿAlī Abū Zunayd. Beirut: Muʾassasat al-Risāla, 1998.

al-Bayhaqī, Abū Bakr. *Aḥkām al-Qurʾān*. Edited by Abū ʿĀṣim al-Shawāmī. Cairo: Dār al-Dhakhāʾir, 2018.

al-Bayhaqī, Abū Bakr. *Manāqib al-Shāfiʿī*. 2 vols. Edited by Aḥmad Ṣaqr. Cairo: Maktabat Dār al-Turāth, 1970.

Bedir, Murteza. 'al-Jaṣṣāṣ (d. 370/981)'. In *Islamic Legal Thought: A Compendium of Muslim Jurists*, edited by Oussama Arabi, David Powers, and Susan Spectorsky, 147–66. Leiden: Brill, 2013.

Berg, Herbert. *The Development of Exegesis in Early Islam: The Authenticity of Muslim Literature from the Formative Period*. Richmond, Surrey: RoutledgeCurzon, 2000.

Bergsträßer, Gotthelf. 'Die Quellen von Jāqūt's *Iršād*'. *Zeitschrift für Semitistik* 2 (1924): 184–218.

Bernand, Marie. 'Les *uṣūl al-fiqh* de l'époque classique: status quaestionis'. *Arabica* 39, no. 3 (1992): 273–86.

Brockopp, Jonathan. *Muhammad's Heirs: The Rise of Muslim Scholarly Communities, 622–950*. Cambridge: Cambridge University Press, 2017.

Buehler, Arthur F. *Sufi Heirs of the Prophet: The Indian Naqshbandiyya and the Rise of the Mediating Sufi Shaykh*. Columbia: University of South Carolina Press, 1998.

Chittick, William. *Ibn Arabi: Heir to the Prophets*. Oxford: Oneworld, 2005.

Cooperson, Michael. *Classical Arabic Biography: The Heirs of the Prophets in the Age of al-Ma'mun*. Cambridge: Cambridge University Press, 2000.

al-Dhahabī, Muḥammad Ḥusayn. *al-Tafsīr wa-l-mufassirūn*. 3 vols. Cairo: Maktabat Wahba, 1976.

Düzgün, Şaban Ali. 'From De Facto Political Authority to Legitimate Power: Mâturîdî's Conceptualization of the Term Ulu'l-Amr'. *Milel ve Nihal* 14, no. 1 (2017): 24–35.

Faradj, Hisseine. 'Ulu Al Amr & Authority: The Central Pillars of Sunni Political Thought'. PhD diss., City University of New York, 2014.

al-Ghazālī, Abū Ḥāmid Muḥammad b. Muḥammad. *al-Mustaṣfā min ʿilm al-uṣūl*. Edited by Muḥammad ʿAbd al-Salām ʿAbd al-Shāfī. Beirut: Dār al-Kutub al-ʿIlmiyya, 1993.

Goldfeld, Isaiah. 'Muqātil b. Sulaymān'. In *Studies in Arabic and Islam*, 2 vols., edited by Jacob Mansour, 2:1–18. Ramat-Gan: Bar-Ilan University Press, 1978.

Goldziher, Ignaz. *The Ẓāhirīs: Their Doctrine and Their History: A Contribution to the History of Islamic Theology*. Translated and edited by Wolfgang Behn. Leiden: Brill, 1971.

Gordon, Jennifer Thea. 'Obeying Those in Authority: The Hidden Political Message in Twelver Exegesis'. PhD diss., Harvard University, 2014.

Güngör, Mevlüt. *Cassâs ve Ahkâmü'l-Kur'an*. Ankara: Elif Matbaası, 1989.

Ḥājjī Khalīfa. *Kashf al-ẓunūn fī asāmī al-kutub wa-l-funūn* 2 vols. Istanbul: Milli Eğitim Basimevi, 1941–43.

Hallaq, Wael. '*Uṣūl al-Fiqh* and Shāfiʿī's *Risāla* Revisited'. *Journal of Arabic and Islamic Studies* 19 (2019): 129–83.

Ibn Abī al-Wafā', Abū Muḥammad ʿAbd al-Qādir b. Muḥammad al-Qurashī. *al-Jawāhir al-muḍiyya fī ṭabaqāt al-Ḥanafiyya*. 5 vols. Edited by ʿAbd al-Fattāḥ Muḥammad al-Ḥulw. Cairo: Hajr, 1993.

Ibn Ḥazm, ʿAlī b. Aḥmad. *al-Iḥkām fī uṣūl al-aḥkām*. 8 vols. in 2. Edited by Iḥsān ʿAbbās. Beirut: Dār al-Āfāq al-Jadīda, 1980.

Ibn al-Nadīm. *al-Fihrist*. 2 vols. Edited by Ayman Fu'ād Sayyid. London: Al-Furqan Islamic Heritage Foundation, 2014.

Ibn Qudāma al-Maqdisī, Muwaffaq al-Dīn ʿAbd Allāh. *Rawḍat al-nāẓir wa-junnat al-munāẓir*. 2 vols. Edited by Shaʿbān Muḥammad Ismāʿīl. Beirut: Mu'assasat al-Rayyān, 2002.

Ibn Rajab al-Ḥanbalī. *The Heirs of the Prophets*. Translated by Zaid Shakir. Bridgeview, IL: Starlatch, 2002.

al-Jaṣṣāṣ, Abū Bakr al-Rāzī. *Kitāb Aḥkām al-Qur'ān*. Istanbul: Maṭbaʿat al-Awqāf al-Islāmiyya, 1917–20; Cairo: al-Maṭbaʿa al-Bahiyya al-Miṣriyya, 1928; 3 vols., Beirut: Dār al-Kitāb al-ʿArabī, 1986; 5 vols., edited by Muḥammad al-Ṣādiq Qamḥāwī, Beirut: Dār Iḥyā' al-Turāth al-ʿArabī, 1992; 3 vols., edited by Ṣiddīq Muḥammad Jamīl, Beirut: Dār al-Fikr al-ʿArabī, 2001; edited by ʿAbd al-Salām Muḥammad ʿAlī Shāhīn, Beirut: Dār al-Kutub al-ʿIlmiyya, 2007.

al-Jaṣṣāṣ, Abū Bakr al-Rāzī. *al-Fuṣūl fī al-uṣūl: abwāb al-ijtihād wa-l-qiyās*. Edited by Saʿīd Allāh al-Qāḍī. Lahore: al-Maktaba al-ʿIlmiyya, 1981.

al-Jaṣṣāṣ, Abū Bakr al-Rāzī. *al-Ijmāʿ: dirāsa fī fikratihi min khilāli taḥqīq bāb al-ijmāʿ*. Edited by Zuhayr Shafīq Kabbī. Beirut: Dār al-Muntakhab al-ʿArabī, 1993.

al-Jaṣṣāṣ, Abū Bakr al-Rāzī. *Uṣūl al-fiqh al-musammā al-Fuṣūl fi al-uṣūl*. 4 vols. Kuwait: Wizārat al-Awqāf wa-l-Shu'ūn al-Islāmiyya, 1985; 2 vols., edited by Muḥammad Muḥammad Tāmir, Beirut: Dār al-Kutub al-ʿIlmiyya, 2000.

Khalilovich, Safwat Mustafa. *al-Imām Abū Bakr al-Rāzī al-Jaṣṣāṣ wa-manhajuhu fī al-tafsīr*. Cairo: Dār al-Salām, 2008.

Lapidus, Ira M. 'The Separation of State and Religion in the Development of Early Islamic Society'. *International Journal of Middle East Studies* 6, no. 4 (1975): 363–85.

al-Mālikī, al-Qāḍī Abū Isḥāq Ismāʿīl b. Isḥāq. *Aḥkām al-Qurʾān*. Edited by ʿĀmir Ḥasan Ṣabrī. Beirut: Dār Ibn Ḥazm, 2005.

al-Marāghī, ʿAbd Allāh Muṣṭafā. *al-Faḍl al-mubīn fī ṭabaqāt al-uṣūliyyīn*. 3 vols. Cairo: Muḥammad ʿAlī ʿUthmān, 1947.

al-Mashnī, Muṣṭafā Ibrāhīm. *Ibn al-ʿArabī al-Mālikī al-Ishbīlī wa-tafsīruhu Aḥkām al-Qurʾān*. Beirut: Dār al-Jīl, 1991.

Matsunaga, Yasuyuki. 'Examining the Views of ʿAllâmah Majlisî on Legitimate Political Authority (*Sulṭanat-i Mashrûʿah*) and the Guardianship of the Jurist (*Wilâyat-i Faqîh*)'. *Orient* 35 (2000): 12–22.

al-Māwardī, Abū al-Ḥasan ʿAlī b. Muḥammad b. Ḥabīb. *al-Ḥāwī al-kabīr*. 19 vols. Edited by ʿAlī Muḥammad Muʿawwaḍ and ʿĀdil Aḥmad ʿAbd al-Mawjūd. Beirut: Dār al-Kutub al-ʿIlmiyya, 1999.

McAuliffe, Jane Dammen. 'Legal Exegesis: Christians as a Case Study'. In *Islamic Interpretations of Christianity*, edited by Lloyd Ridgeon, 54–77. Abingdon, Oxon: Routledge, 2001.

Melchert, Christopher. 'The *Musnad* of al-Shāfiʿī'. *Studia Islamica* 115 (2020): 1–16.

Merchant, Muhammad Valibhai. *Quranic Laws*. Lahore: Sh. Muhammad Ashraf, 1947.

Muranyi, Miklos. 'Aus dem *Kitāb Aḥkām al-Qurʾān* des Mālikiten Ibn Ḫawāz Mandād'. *Der Islam* 91, no. 2 (2014): 360–73.

Nyazee, Imran Ahsan Khan. *Islamic Jurisprudence* (*Uṣūl al-Fiqh*). Islamabad: Islamic Research Institute, 2000.

Polosin, Valeriy V. *Fixrist Ibn an-Nadima kak istoriko-kulturniy pamyatnik X veka*. Moscow: Nauka, 1989.

al-Qāḍī ʿAbd al-Jabbār. *al-Mughnī fī abwāb al-tawḥīd wa-l-ʿadl*. Vol. 12, *al-Naẓar wa-l-maʿārif*. Edited by Ibrāhīm Madkūr. Cairo: al-Muʾassasa al-Miṣriyya al-ʿĀmma, 1965.

al-Qāḍī al-Nuʿmān. *Disagreements of the Jurists*. Translated by Devin J. Stewart. New York: New York University Press, 2015.

al-Qazwīnī, Abū Yaʿlā al-Khalīl b. ʿAbd Allāh al-Khalīlī. *Kitāb al-Irshād fī maʿrifat ʿulamāʾ al-ḥadīth*. 3 vols. Edited by Muḥammad Saʿīd b. ʿUmar Idrīs. Riyadh: Maktabat al-Rushd, 1989.

Qazwini, Hadi. 'Heir of the Prophets: Veneration of Ḥusayn b. ʿAlī and the Socio-religious Positioning of Twelver Shiism'. *Islamic Studies* 60, no. 3 (2021): 267–86.

al-Qurṭubī, Abū ʿAbd Allāh Muḥammad b. Aḥmad b. Abī Bakr. *al-Jāmiʿ li-aḥkām al-Qurʾān wa-l-mubayyin li-mā taḍammanahu min al-sunna wa-āy al-Furqān*. 24 vols. Edited by ʿAbd Allāh b. ʿAbd al-Muḥsin al-Turkī. Beirut: Muʾassasat al-Risāla, 2006.

al-Rāfiʿī, ʿAbd al-Karīm b. Muḥammad al-Qazwīnī. *Sharḥ Musnad al-Shāfiʿī*. 4 vols. Edited by Abū Bakr Wāʾil Muḥammad Bakr Zahrān. Doha: Wizārat al-Awqāf wa-l-Shuʾūn al-Islāmiyya, 2007.

al-Rāzī, Fakhr al-Dīn. *al-Maḥṣūl*. 6 vols. Edited by Ṭāhā Jābir Fayyāḍ al-ʿAlwānī. Beirut: Muʾassasat al-Risāla, 1997.

Ruano, Delfina Serrano. 'El Corán como fuente de legislación islámica: Abū Bakr Ibn al-ʿArabī y su obra *Aḥkām al-Qurʾān*'. In *El Corán ayer y hoy: Perspectivas actuales sobre el islam – Estudios en honor al profesor Julio Cortés*, edited by Miguel Hernando de Larramendi and Salvador Peña Martín, 251–75. Cordoba: Berenice, 2008.

Rogerson, Barnaby. *The Heirs of Muhammad: Islam's First Century and the Origins of the Sunni-Shia Split*. New York: Little, Brown, 2006.

al-Ṣābūnī, Muḥammad ʿAlī. *Rawāʾiʿ al-bayān: tafsīr āyāt al-aḥkām min al-Qurʾān*. 2 vols. Beirut: Muʾassasat Manāhil al-ʿIrfān, 1980.

Saeedullah. 'Life and Works of Abū Bakr al-Rāzī al-Jaṣṣāṣ'. *Islamic Studies* 16, no. 2 (1977): 131–41.

al-Ṣanʿānī, Muḥammad b. Ismāʿīl. *Irshād al-nuqqād ilā taysīr al-ijtihād*. Edited by Ṣalāḥ al-Dīn Maqbūl Aḥmad. Kuwait: al-Dār al-Salafiyya, 1985.

Sarrió, Diego R. 'The Philosopher as the Heir of the Prophets: Averroes's Islamic Rationalism'. *Al-Qantara* 36, no. 1 (2015): 45–68.

Schacht, Joseph. *The Origins of Muhammadan Jurisprudence*. Oxford: The Clarendon Press, 1950.

Seferta, Yusuf H.R. 'The Concept of Religious Authority according to Muhammad ʿAbduh and Rashid Ridha'. *Islamic Quarterly* 30, no. 3 (1986): 159–64.

al-Shāfiʿī, Muḥammad b. Idrīs. *Aḥkām al-Qurʾān*. Edited by Abū ʿĀmir ʿAbd Allāh Sharaf al-Dīn al-Dāghistānī. Riyadh: Āfāq al-Maʿrifa, 2020.

al-Shāfiʿī, Muḥammad b. Idrīs. *al-Risāla*. Edited by Aḥmad Muḥammad Shākir. Cairo: Maṭbaʿat Muṣṭafā al-Bābī al-Ḥalabī wa-Awlādih, 1940. Reprint, Beirut, n.d.

Sirry, Munʾim. 'Who Are Those in Authority? Early Muslim Exegesis of the Qurʾanic *Ulūʾl-Amr*'. *Religions* 12, no. 7 (2021): https://doi.org/10.3390/rel12070483.

Smith, Antar ibn-Stanford. 'Significant Features of al-Jassas' Methodology for Deriving Legal Rulings from the Qur'an'. PhD diss., University of Michigan, 1985.

Stewart, Devin J. 'Consensus, Authority, and the Interpretive Community in the Thought of Muḥammad b. Jarīr al-Ṭabarī'. *Journal of Qurʾanic Studies* 18, no. 2 (2016): 130–79.

Stewart, Devin J. 'Editing the *Fihrist* of Ibn al-Nadīm'. *Journal of Abbasid Studies* 1 (2014): 159–205.

Stewart, Devin J. 'Muḥammad b. Dāʾūd al-Ẓāhirī's Manual of Jurisprudence, *al-Wuṣūl ilā maʿrifat al-uṣūl*'. In *Studies in Islamic Legal Theory*, edited by Bernard G. Weiss, 99–158. Leiden: Brill, 2002.

Stewart, Devin J. 'Scholarship on the *Fihrist* of Ibn al-Nadim: The Work of Valeriy V. Polosin'. *Al-ʿUsur al-Wusta* 18, no. 1 (2006): 8–13.

al-Suyūṭī, Jalāl al-Dīn. *al-Itqān fī ʿulūm al-Qurʾān*. 2 vols. Beirut: Dār al-Kutub al-ʿIlmiyya, 1995.

Takim, Liyakat N. *The Heirs of the Prophet: Charisma and Religious Authority in Shiʿite Islam*. Albany: State University of New York Press, 2006.

al-Ṭūfī, Najm al-Dīn Sulaymān b. ʿAbd al-Qawī. *Sharḥ Mukhtaṣar al-Rawḍa*. 3 vols. Edited by ʿAbd Allāh b. ʿAbd al-Muḥsin al-Turkī. Beirut: Muʾassasat al-Risāla, 1987.

al-Ṭūsī, Muḥammad b. al-Ḥasan. *al-Tibyān fī tafsīr al-Qurʾān*. 9 vols. Edited by Aḥmad Ḥabīb Quṣayr al-ʿĀmilī. Beirut: Dār Iḥyāʾ al-Turāth al-ʿArabī, 1999.

al-Ṭūsī, Muḥammad b. al-Ḥasan. *al-ʿUdda fī uṣūl al-fiqh*. 2 vols. Edited by Muḥammad Riḍā al-Anṣārī al-Qummī. Qom: Sitāra, 1997.

Vishanoff, David R. *The Formation of Islamic Hermeneutics: How Sunni Legal Theorists Imagined a Revealed Law*. New Haven: American Oriental Society, 2011.

Weiss, Bernard G. *The Search for God's Law: Islamic Jurisprudence in the Writings of Sayf al-Dīn al-Āmidī*. Revised ed. Salt Lake City: University of Utah Press, 2010.

al-Zarkashī, Badr al-Dīn. *al-Burhān fī ʿulūm al-Qurʾān*. 4 vols. Edited by Muḥammad Abū al-Faḍl Ibrāhīm. Beirut: al-Maktaba al-ʿAṣriyya, n.d.

Zwemer, Samuel M. Heirs of the Prophets" An Account of the Clergy and Priests of Islam, the Personnel of the Mosque and 'Holy Men'. Chicago: The Moody Bible Institute, 1946.

Zysow, Aron. *The Economy of Certainty: An Introduction to the Typology of Islamic Legal Theory*. Atlanta: Lockwood Press, 2013.

CHAPTER 7

The Imāmī Reception of the Qur'an's Regulative Verses (*Āyāt al-Aḥkām*)

Seyed Mohammad G.S. Fatemi and Syed Wajee ul-Hasan Shah

1 Introduction

Āyāt al-aḥkām (regulative verses) refers to the Qur'anic verses through which Islamic rulings can be explained, extrapolated, and inferred by an astute jurist (*mujtahid*) through *ijtihād* (exerting one's utmost effort to extrapolate a ruling from the relevant evidence). The *āyāt al-aḥkām* explain certain rules regarding prayer (*ṣalāt*), fasting (*ṣawm*), rules of war (*jihād*), paying alms/financial dues (*zakāt*/*khums*), pilgrimage (*ḥajj*), rules regarding permissible (*ḥalāl*) and impermissible (*ḥarām*) food and drink, marriage, divorce, and so on. Although the topic of *āyāt al-aḥkām* has major implications for the elaboration of Islamic law (*fiqh*), it is a subject which has been understudied in Western academia. According to certain reported traditions of the Prophet and Imāms, one-third or one-fourth of the Qur'an is concerned with the rulings of Sharīʿa, while many Sunnī and Shīʿī jurists claim that there are approximately 500 verses regarding legal rulings.[1]

It has been claimed by the grand-jurist Shihāb al-Dīn al-Marʿashī al-Najafī (d. 1990) that the first book written on *āyāt al-aḥkām* in the Imāmī circles was that of Abū al-Naṣr Muḥammad b. al-Sā'ib b. Bishr al-Kalbī, a companion of Imāms al-Bāqir and al-Ṣādiq who lived in the second/eighth century, titled *Kitāb aḥkām al-Qur'ān*.[2] ʿAlī Aṣghar Nāṣiḥiyān, in his paper 'Aḥkām al-Qur'ān', discusses the attribution of the work to al-Kalbī. Nāṣiḥiyān suggests that Abū al-Faraj Muḥammad b. Isḥāq al-Nadīm (d. 380/990), the renowned tenth-century bibliographer and historian, can be traced as the earliest source to mention al-Kalbī's *Aḥkām al-Qur'ān*. Despite Ibn al-Nadīm's historical reference to this work, Naṣiḥyān himself remains undecided about attributing

1 Muḥammad b. Yaʿqūb al-Kulaynī, *al-Kāfī*, ed. Muḥammad Jaʿfar Shams al-Dīn (Tehran: Dār al-Kutub al-Islāmiyya, 1987), 2:627–28.

2 Shihāb al-Dīn al-Marʿashī al-Najafī, 'Risālat manhaj al-rashād fī tarjamat al-fāḍil al-Jawād', in his short essay prefaced to Fāḍil Jawād al-Kāẓimī, *Masālik al-afhām ilā āyāt al-aḥkām*, 4 vols., ed. Muṣṭafā Murtazawī (Qom: al-Maktaba al-Murtazawiyya, 1986), 1:8.

such a work to al-Kalbī.[3] Whether this book existed and later went missing, or did not exist at all, remains a matter of ongoing historical academic research, which is beyond the scope of the present study.

Among the most significant and welcomed Imāmī books on *āyāt al-aḥkām* that are currently extant, inter alia, are (1) *Fiqh al-Qurʾān* by Quṭb al-Dīn al-Rāwandī (d. 573/1178); (2) *Kanz al-ʿirfān fī fiqh al-Qurʾān* by al-Miqdād b. ʿAbd Allāh al-Suyūrī (d. 826/1423); (3) *Zubdat al-bayān fī aḥkām al-Qurʾān* by al-Muqaddas al-Ardabīlī (d. 993/1585); (4) *Masālik al-afhām ilā āyāt al-aḥkām* by Fāḍil Jawād al-Kāẓimī (d. 1065/1654); and (5) the more recent *Tafsīr āyāt al-aḥkām fī al-Qurʾān* by the contemporary Imāmī jurist Muḥammad Bāqir al-Īrawānī (b. 1368/1949).

Although both Shīʿī and Sunnī scholars have produced books on the topic of *āyāt al-aḥkām*, the way they tackle this topic differs greatly. The organisation of Shīʿī books on *āyāt al-aḥkām* follows the pattern of texts devoted to the points of law. In legal texts, the chapters begin with ritual purity and then continue to the acts of worship and transactional and inheritance law. Al-Rāwandī organised his text on *āyāt al-aḥkām*, *Fiqh al-Qurʾān*, in this manner, and subsequent scholars followed his arrangement.

The following is the list of al-Rāwandī's chapters in his legal work *Fiqh al-Qurʾān* in order: *kitāb al-ṭahāra* (Chapter on Ritual Purity), *kitāb al-ṣalāt* (Chapter on Ritual Prayer), *kitāb al-ṣawm* (Chapter on Fasting), *kitāb al-zakāt wa-jāmiʿ al-ʿibādāt al-māliyya* (Chapter on Alms and All Financial Dues), *kitāb al-ḥajj* (Chapter on Pilgrimage), *kitāb al-jihād* (Chapter on Holy War), *kitāb al-duyūn wa-l-kifālāt wa-l-ḥawālāt wa-l-wikālāt* (Chapter on Loans, Debt, Sponsorships, Transfers, and Types of Agency), *kitāb al-shahādat* (Chapter on Testimony), *kitāb al-qaḍāyā* (Chapter on Court Cases), *kitāb al-makāsib* (Chapter on Trade), *kitāb al-matājir* (Chapter on Transaction and Trade), *kitāb al-nikāḥ* (Chapter on Marriage), *kitāb al-ṭalāq* (Chapter on Divorce), *kitāb al-ʿitq wa-anwāʿihi* (Chapter on Manumission and Its Different Types), *kitāb al-aymān wa-l-nudhūr wa-l-kaffārāt* (Chapter on Oaths, Vows, and Acts of Atonement), *kitāb al-ṣayd wa-l-dhabāʾiḥ* (Chapter on Hunting and Slaughter), *kitāb al-aṭʿima wa-l-ashriba* (Chapter on Food and Drink), *kitāb al-wuqūf wa-l-ṣadaqāt* (Chapter on Endowments and Charity), *kitāb al-waṣāyā* (Chapter

3 ʿAlī Aṣghar Naṣiḥyān, 'Aḥkām al-Qurʾān-e Muḥammad b. Sāʾib al-Kalbī', in *Jarayān-shināsī-ye tafāsīr fiqhī, tārīkh, taṭavvur va namuneh-hā*, ed. Muḥammad ʿAlī Mahdavī Rād (Mashhad: Dāneshgāh-e ʿUlūm-e Islāmī Razavī, 1970), 1:35–44.

on Wills), *kitāb al-mawārīth* (Chapter on Inheritance), *kitāb al-ḥudūd* (Chapter on Fixed Punishments), *kitāb al-diyāt* (Chapter on Blood Money).[4]

By contrast, most Sunnī books on *āyāt al-aḥkām* are organised in accordance with the order of the Qur'anic chapters. *Aḥkām al-Qur'ān* by Aḥmad b. Muḥammad b. Salāma al-Ṭaḥāwī (d. 321/943) diverges from the conventional approach adopted by mainstream Sunnī scholars in this genre.[5] The implications of these contradistinctive approaches vary between the Shīʿī and Sunnī schools. The Shīʿī scholars examined the *āyāt al-aḥkām* predominantly from a legal point of view and therefore referred to the reported traditions (*aḥādīth*, sing. *ḥadīth*) of the Prophet and Imāms in conjunction with other legal sources such as reason (*ʿaql*) and consensus (*ijmāʿ*) to derive an Islamic legal ruling from certain verses considered to be *āyāt al-aḥkām*. In comparison, Sunnī scholars, such as the famous Ḥanafī jurist Abū Bakr Aḥmad b. ʿAlī al-Rāzī al-Jaṣṣāṣ (d. 380/970) in his celebrated work *Aḥkām al-Qur'ān*, examined the *āyāt al-aḥkām* from a predominantly exegetical angle. In his process of exegesis, he strove to determine whether a particular verse entailed a legal ruling.[6]

Notably, a comprehensive chronological analysis of *āyāt al-aḥkām* remains a significant gap in existing scholarship and has yet to be produced. Such an analysis would yield valuable insights into the progressive development of normative aspects within Islam, revealing the chronological order in which various norms were introduced within the Qur'anic discourse. This would facilitate a deeper understanding of the historical progression of obligatory practices such as prayer and religious pilgrimage, as well as the prohibition of alcohol, for instance.

Crucially, however, this raises an important question: is it even feasible to have a chronological analysis of *āyāt al-aḥkām*? Conducting such an analysis undoubtedly poses considerable challenges. The available exegetical literature lacks clarity regarding the chronological sequence of normative rules in Islam, that is, the chronological appearance of legal rulings within the history of revelation of the Qur'an. Moreover, the majority of *asbāb al-nuzūl* (causes/incidents of revelation) narrations explaining the context and reasons for the revelation of Qur'anic verses are historically inadequate and lack hermeneutical precision. This renders these narrations epistemically unreliable sources

4 Quṭb al-Dīn Saʿīd b. Hibat Allāh al-Rāwandī, *Fiqh al-Qur'ān* (Qom: Mu'assasat Āl al-Bayt li-Iḥyā' al-Turāth, 2003).

5 Aḥmad b, Muḥammad b. Salāma al-Ṭaḥāwī, *Aḥkām al-Qur'ān al-karīm* (Istanbul: Markaz al-Buḥūth al-Islāmiyya, 1998).

6 Abū Bakr Aḥmad b. ʿAlī al-Rāzī al-Jaṣṣāṣ, *Aḥkām al-Qur'ān* (Beirut: Dār al-Iḥyā' al-Turāth al-ʿArabī, 1992).

for constructing a chronology of Qur'anic legislation. Further research drawing on early historical sources is needed in order to establish the progression of normative principles in the Qur'an. Any chronological framework must be approached with caution because of the scarcity of sound reports definitively dating the revelation of specific verses.

Recently, however, several attempts have been made to reconstruct and then (re)interpret the Qur'an in the chronological order of revelation, mainly based on orthodox reports of that order.[7] For example, ʿAbdulkarīm Bahjatī, a contemporary Imāmī author, has attempted to offer a chronological exegesis of the Qur'an.[8] Additionally, Richard Bell, a scholar of Arabic and Islam, renowned for his 1937 English translation of the Qur'an, categorised the suras into three major periods – early Meccan, later Meccan (after the *hijra* to Medina), and the main Medinan period. Within each period, he arranged the passages from earliest to latest revelations, drawing from both internal textual evidence and the accounts of traditional Muslim scholars. Notably, Bell's rearrangement included explanatory notes and cross-references that linked related verses across different chapters. His work aimed to illustrate how Islamic doctrines and regulations evolved over time in response to changing circumstances in the early Muslim community.[9]

This study will present a brief introduction to al-Rāwandī's work, as the earliest extant Imāmī comprehensive book on *āyāt al-aḥkām*, and then examine five key areas of contention regarding the authority of the apparent indication of Qur'anic verses. The first discussion of a contentious area scrutinises the Akhbārī challenge to the apparent indication of the Qur'an, questioning the very legitimacy of Qur'anic interpretation without reliance on reported traditions of the Imāms. Herein, diverse viewpoints of Akhbārī scholars such as Muḥammad Amīn al-Astarābādī (d. 1033/1623–24 or 1036/1626–27), Muḥammad b. al-Ḥasan b. ʿAlī b. al-Ḥusayn al-Ḥurr al-ʿĀmilī (d. 1104/1693), and Yūsuf al-Baḥrānī (d. 1186/1772) are presented and juxtaposed with counter-arguments by leading Uṣūlī figures like Muḥammad Mahdī al-Narāqī (d. 1209/1795), Murtaḍā al-Anṣārī (d. 1281/1864), and Muḥammad Kāẓim al-Khurāsānī (d. 1329/1911).

The second discussion of a central area of contention involves a linguistic and philosophical investigation into whether the Qur'an's scope – as a

7 See, for instance, 'Welcome to Qur'anic Warners', Qur'anic Warners, https://quranicwarners.org/quran.

8 ʿAbdulkarīm Bahjatī, *Hamgām bā waḥy: tafsīr-e tanzīlī* (Qom: Mu'assase-yi Tamhīd, 2019).

9 Richard Bell, *The Qur'ān: Translated, with a Critical Re-arrangement of the Surahs* (Edinburgh: T&T Clark, 1937).

historical text revealed in a particular context – extends beyond its immediate audience. A comparative analysis of similar epistemologies from two different schools of thought, one by Sunnī jurist Ibrāhīm b. ʿAlī al-Fayrūzabādī al-Shīrāzī (d. 476/1083) and the other by the Shīʿī jurist al-Mīrzā Abū al-Qāsim b. Muḥammad Ḥasan al-Shaftī (commonly referred to as Mīrzā Qummī or Ṣāḥib al-Qawānīn) (d. 1231/1815–16), illustrates the ways in which scholars navigate the question of the Qur'an's universality.

The third and fourth discussions of areas of contention are bifurcated into two segments: an examination of the (possible) occurrence of distortion (*taḥrīf*) in the Qur'an and its impact on its regulative verses, followed by an exploration of different recitations (*qirāʾāt*) and their potential effects on the regulative verses.

The fifth and, according to the authors of this study, arguably the most crucial challenge requires focused consideration of both Shīʿī and Sunnī jurists. It revolves around ascertaining the level of epistemic authority that can be attributed to the apparent indication of the Qur'an. This is particularly crucial, given that most verses related to norms are already supported by accompanying explanations, narrations, or established consensus on interpretation.

Concluding the discussion is an exploration of the Qur'an's status in Shīʿī discourse: whether it is viewed as a primary or secondary source, alongside perspectives from adherents of both the primary source camp and the secondary source camp. The epistemological implications of their stances and their direct influence on regulative verses are scrutinised through a case study of the highly disputed obligation of offensive *jihād*.

2 Al-Rāwandī: Transmitter of al-Ṭūsī's Paradigm

Al-Tibyān fī tafsīr al-Qurʾān[10] by the most influential Imāmī jurists and theologian Abū Jaʿfar Muḥammad b. al-Ḥasan al-Ṭūsī (known as Shayk al-Ṭāʾifa, d. 460/1067) historically appears to be the earliest known comprehensive Imāmī exegesis that systematically addresses all verses of the Qur'an. This influential work established an exegetical framework that subsequent Imāmī scholarship followed. In addition to inclusion of all the verses of the Qur'an, for the first time in the history of Imāmī exegesis, *al-Tibyān* inaugurated the method of multidisciplinary exegesis of the Qur'an, discussing various aspects

10 Abū Jaʿfar Muḥammad b. al-Ḥasan al-Ṭūsī, *al-Tibyān fī tafsīr al-Qurʾān*, 10 vols. (Qom: al-Nashr al-Islāmī, 1992).

of its verses, including linguistic, hadithic, historical, theological, and legal perspectives.

Fiqh al-Qurʾān by Quṭb al-Dīn Abū al-Ḥusayn Saʿīd b. ʿAbd Allāh b. Ḥusayn b. Hibat Allāh al-Rāwandī al-Kāshānī (known as al-Quṭb al-Rāwandī, d. 573/1178) is the earliest extant contribution to the study of *āyāt al-aḥkām*. Al-Rāwandī was a distinguished jurist, theologian, and Qur'anic exegete of the sixth/twelfth century. His work pioneered the examination of Qurʾanic verses related to legal rulings, making it the first known surviving Imāmī text on this subject. Its content shares similarities and thematic parallels with al-Ṭūsī's *al-Tibyān*. Al-Rāwandī's work echoes al-Ṭūsī's ideas, showing a connection between them, despite the fact that he does not refer to al-Ṭūsī explicitly. This connection pays homage to *al-Tibyān* and is a way of honouring or acknowledging al-Ṭūsī's scholarship which was normal in past scholarly writings/publications, indicating an underlying connection between the two. This interplay between the two works is interesting for scholars as *Fiqh al-Qurʾān* mirrors many of the ideas and thoughts of al-Ṭūsī in *al-Tibyān*.

On the one hand, one can argue that al-Rāwandī's work is not a copy of *al-Tibyān*, but a way to continue al-Ṭusī's contribution and indeed his legacy. This connection between the works has a significant impact, as *Fiqh al-Qurʾān* becomes a bridge for *al-Tibyān*'s ideas to reach later generations. On the other hand, Alizade contends that although al-Rāwandī lived during a period commonly referred to by historians of Shīʿī Islamic law as the era of al-Ṭūsī's dominance, a period during which the vast majority of Shīʿī jurists unwaveringly adhered to his teachings and scholarly methods, al-Rāwandī's work stands apart as more than a mere repetition or emulation of al-Ṭūsī's teachings. In certain cases, he demonstrates a distinct and respectful departure from the latter's doctrinal path. This is especially noteworthy given al-Ṭūsī's extraordinary influence and universally acknowledged authority in Imāmī thought and legal theory in an era when wavering or differing from al-Ṭūsī's predominance was exceedingly rare because of his esteemed status as a pre-eminent scholar.[11]

3 Authority of the Apparent Indication of the Qur'an: Preliminary Notes

To clarify the concept of the authority of the apparent indication (or meaning) of the Qur'an, it is essential to define key terms within the framework of Shīʿī legal theory: *naṣṣ* (explicit), *ẓāhir* (apparent), *mujmal* (ambiguous), *muḥkam*

11 Mīrzā ʿAlīzādeh, 'Fiqh al-Qur'ān Rāwandī', in *Jarayān-shināsī-yi tafāsīr-i fiqhī*, 149.

(clear/decisively strong), *mutashābih* (unclear/allegorical), and *mu'awwal* (interpreted).

(a) *Naṣṣ* (explicit): A word for which it is not possible to have multiple meanings. Rather, there is only one clear meaning, a fact which acts as a barrier against contradictory interpretations.

(b) *Ẓāhir* (apparent): If a word can encompass various meanings but retains its primary interpretation, it assumes the status of *ẓāhir* or the apparent indication/meaning. The fundamental similarity between *naṣṣ* and *ẓāhir* lies in their shared quality as definitive and predominant interpretations of a particular expression.

(c) *Muḥkam* (clear/decisively strong): In the parlance of the legal theorists, both *naṣṣ* and *ẓahir* are considered *muḥkam* (decisively clear) within the realm of Qur'anic terminology.

(d) However, when a word equally indicates two or more distinct meanings, it is categorised as *mujmal* (ambiguous).

(e) Since the *ẓāhir* holds dominance as the prevailing interpretation, it implicitly acknowledges the existence of a secondary, less preferred meaning. This secondary meaning is termed *mu'awwal* or interpreted. A shared characteristic between ambiguous words and less preferred meanings is their propensity to be *mutashābih*, unclear or obscure.[12]

Moreover, Mīrzā Qummī highlights the presence of these terms within the Qur'an:

> He it is who has revealed the Book to you; some of its verses are clear (*muḥkamāt*), and they are the basis of the Book, while others are allegorical (*mutashābihāt*). Then, as for those in whose hearts there is perversity, they follow the part of it which is unclear/allegorical, seeking to mislead and seeking to give it [their own] interpretation (*ta'wīl*). But none knows its interpretation except God and those who are firmly rooted in knowledge. Say: 'We believe in it. It is all from our Lord, and none take heed except those who possess understanding.'[13]

Having laid the foundation of this study by introducing the terminology and concepts related to the examination of the apparent indication of the Qur'an, we shall now address the contentious issue of its normative authority (*ḥujjiyya*) within the Shīʿī legal school. This is a contentious issue, largely because of

12 Mīrzā Abū al-Qāsim al-Jīlānī al-Qummī, *al-Qawānīn al-muḥkama fī uṣūl al-mutqana* (Beirut: Dār al-Murtaḍā, 2009), 1:378.

13 Q. 3:7.

the scarcity, if not the absence altogether, of explicit textual references (*naṣṣ*) within the normative legal verses of the Qur'an.

4 The Akhbārī Challenge

As mentioned above, the main point of dispute initiated by the Akhbārī scholars pertains to the concept of *ḥujjiyyat ẓawāhir al-Qur'ān* (normative authority of the apparent indication of the Qur'an).[14] The central focus of the Akhbārīs has been whether the Qur'an can be interpreted – or even comprehended – without any reference to the statements of the infallible Imāms.[15] Such a dispute emerges as a consequence of the existence of number of traditions which have had an impact on Imāmī scholars' approach to the Qur'an. For example, some traditions attributed to the Prophet and the Imāms speak about the reprehensibility of interpreting the Qur'an through mere personal opinion (*ra'y*). A tradition attributed to the Prophet, for example, states:

> Whoever interprets the Qur'an according to his own opinion and is correct has erred (*faqad akhṭa'a*).[16]

In another tradition attributed to Imām al-Ṣādiq (d. 148/765), he states:

> Whoever interprets the Qur'an according to his own opinion and his interpretation just so happens to be correct, he will not be rewarded for it; and if his interpretation is incorrect, then he bears the sin for it.[17]

---

14 For further information on the Akhbārī/Uṣūlī debates, dialogue, and differing methodologies, see Andrew J. Newman, 'The Nature of the Akhbārī/Uṣūlī Dispute in Late Ṣafawid Iran. Part 1: 'Abdallāh al-Samāhijī's "*Munyat al-Mumārisīn*"', *Bulletin of the School of Oriental and African Studies* 55, no. 1 (1992): 22–51; and Andrew J. Newman, *Twelver Shiism: Unity and Diversity in the Life of Islam, 632 to 1722* (Edinburgh: Edinburgh University Press, 2021), chs. 6–8.

15 al-Muqaddas al-Ardabīlī, *Zubdat al-bayān fī aḥkām al-Qur'an*, ed. Muḥammad al-Bāqir al-Bahbūdī (Tehran: al-Maktaba al-Murtaḍawiyya, n.d.), 1; Fāḍil al-Jawād al-Kāẓimī, *Masālik al-afhām ilā āyāt al-aḥkām*, ed. Muḥammad Bāqir Sharīf Zādeh (Tehran: Intishārāt-e Murtaḍawī, 1945), 1:3–12.

16 al-Faḍl b. al-Ḥasan al-Ṭabrisī, *Majma' al-bayān fī tafsīr al-Qur'ān* (Beirut: Mu'asassat al-A'lamī li-l-Maṭbū'āt, 1995), 1:39. Al-Ṭabrisī cites this tradition from Sunnī sources.

17 Muḥammad b. Mas'ūd al-'Ayyāshī, *Tafsīr al-'Ayyāshī: A Fourth/Tenth Century Shī'ī Commentary on the Qur'an*, trans. Nazmina Dhanji, ed. Wahid M. Amin (Birmingham: AMI Press, 2020), 1:52–53. For other traditions in this vein, see ibid., 1:50–54.

Secondly, other traditions speak about the Family of the Prophet (*ahl al-bayt*) as being the key to understanding the content of the Qur'an.[18] The most widely cited tradition in this regard is the famous tradition attributed to the Prophet known as the 'Tradition of the Two-Weighty Matters' (*ḥadīth al-thaqalayn*) in which he states, during his final sermon:

> You will not go astray if you cling to two things which I have left you: the Book of God – the Mighty, the Great – and my family/household (*ahl baytī*).[19]

Another tradition attributed to Imām al-Ṣādiq states:

> I do not claim that we [the Imāms of the *ahl al-bayt*] possess knowledge of the unseen (*ʿilm al-ghayb*), but I do say that we know the Book of God – a book which encompasses everything within it. God has taught us things which none besides us know, things which He taught only to His angels and His prophets. Whatever is known to His angels and His messengers is also known to us.[20]

The existence of such traditions may explain why early Imāmī commentaries on the Qur'an primarily engage in tradition-based exegesis (*al-tafsīr bi-l-ma'thūr*). Commentaries such as those of ʿAlī b. Ibrāhīm al-Qummī (fl. third/ninth century),[21] Furāt b. Ibrāhīm al-Kūfī (d. early fourth/tenth century),[22] and Muḥammad b. Masʿūd al-ʿAyyāshī (d. 320/932–33) primarily rely on traditions to make sense of Qur'anic verses. If a tradition cannot be found which speaks

18 On the Imāms as interpreters of the Qur'an, see Meir M. Bar-Asher, *Scripture and Exegesis in Early Imāmī Shiism* (Leiden: Brill, 1999), 98–101.

19 Muḥammad b. Yaʿqūb al-Kulaynī, *al-Kāfī*, ed. Muḥammad Ḥusayn al-Darāyatī (Qom: Dār al-Ḥadīth, 2008), 2:25. The term '*thaqalayn*' appears in a different version of the tradition in Abū Jaʿfar Muḥammad b. ʿAlī b. al-Ḥusayn b. Mūsā al-Qummī, *ʿUyūn akhbār al-Riḍā*, ed. Ḥusayn al-Aʿlamī (Beirut: Mu'asassat al-Aʿlamī li-l-Maṭbūʿāt, 1984), 1:34. The tradition also appears in different versions in numerous Sunnī collections; for example: Muslim b. al-Ḥajjāj, *Kitāb Ṣaḥīḥ Muslim*, ed. Muḥammad Fu'ād ʿAbd al-Bāqī (Beirut: Dār Iḥyā' al-Turāth al-ʿArabī, 1955), 4:1874; Aḥmad b. Shuʿayb al-Nasā'ī, *al-Sunan al-kubrā*, ed. Ḥasan ʿAbd al-Munʿim Shalabī (Beirut: Mu'asassat al-Risāla, 2001), 7:310. On this tradition in Imāmī commentaries, see Bar-Asher, *Scripture*, 93–98.

20 al-ʿAyyāshī, *Tafsīr*, 1:48. For related traditions, see ibid., 40–50.

21 ʿAlī b. Ibrāhīm al-Qummī, *Tafsīr al-Qummī* (Qom: Mu'assasat Dār al-Kitāb li-l-Ṭibāʿa wa-l-Nashr, 1984).

22 Furāt b. Ibrāhīm b. Furāt al-Kūfī, *Tafsīr Furāt al-Kūfī* (Tehran: Vizārat-e Irshād, 1988).

about a particular verse, then they usually avoid offering any substantive interpretation of the given verse of the Qur'an.[23]

This approach is indicative of a broader trend of thought among Imāmīs, later identified and categorised as Akhbārism, conceived of in opposition to Uṣūlism. The history of Akhbārism has been a topic of much dispute in the secondary literature. Some historians such as Wilferd Madelung, Etan Kohlberg, and Andrew J. Newman argue that the fact that there were Imāmīs who adhered to such an approach as far back as these early commentators indicates that Akhbārism has been a constant theme in Imāmī thought.[24] On the other hand, historians such as, Norman Calder, Rula Jurdi Abisaab, Robert Gleave, Ehsan Gheisari, and Mahdī ʿAlī Pūr hold that the Akhbārī movement emerged out of the response of Muḥammad Amīn al-Astarābādī to the dominant legal methodology of the time.[25]

While acknowledging that there did exist what can be described as proto-Akhbārīs in the pre-Astarābādī period, we are inclined to adopt the latter theory of Akhbārism's origins. Nevertheless, there does seem to have been some influence of proto-Akhbārī thinking prior to al-Astarābādī, given evidence of the presence of anti-Akhbārī positions, such as those taken by al-Muqaddas al-Ardabīlī (d. 993/1585). These Uṣūlī scholars saw the need to respond to potential arguments that would come to be core tenets of Akhbārī doctrine, such as whether the Qur'an can be interpreted without any reference to the statements of the Prophet or the Imāms. What this essentially boils down to is the question over the apparent meaning of the Qur'an in the eyes of Akhbārī scholars, such as Muḥammad Amīn al-Astarābādī and Yūsuf b. Aḥmad al-Baḥrānī. Also, a critique of these scholars shall be presented by illustrious

---

23 On the characteristics of this early school of Imāmī Qur'an commentary, see Bar-Asher, *Scripture*, 71–86; and Mohammad Ali Amir-Moezzi, 'The *Tafsīr* of al-Ḥibarī (d. 286/899): Qur'anic Exegesis and Early Shiʿi Esotericism', in *The Study of Shiʿi Islam: History, Theology and Law*, ed. Farhad Daftary and Gurdofarid Miskinzoda (London: I.B. Tauris in association with the Institute of Ismaili Studies, 2014), 113–34.

24 Wilferd Madelung, 'Akhkhbāriyya', in *EI*²; Etan Kohlberg, 'Ak̲bārīya', in *EIr*; Andrew J. Newman, 'The Nature of the Akhbārī/Uṣūlī Dispute in Late Ṣafawid Iran. Part 2: The Conflict Reassessed', *Bulletin of the School of Oriental and African Studies* 55, no. 2 (1992): 252.

25 211–50; Norman Calder, 'Doubt and Prerogative: The Emergence of an Imāmī Shīʿī Theory of *Ijtihād*', *Studia Islamica* 70 (1989): 68; Rula Abisaab, *Converting Persia: Religion and Power in the Safavid Empire* (London: I.B. Tauris, 2004), 105–12; Robert Gleave, *Scripturalist Islam: The History and Doctrines of the Akhbārī Shīʿī School* (Leiden: Brill, 2007), 10–30. Gleave has provided the most sustained argument in support of this position, critiquing many of the arguments put forward by those upholding the opposing view. Ehsan Gheisari, 'Akhbāriyya', trans. Jawad Qasemi, in *EI*; Mahdī ʿAlī Pūr, *Tārīkh ʿilm al-uṣūl*, trans. ʿAlī Ẓāhir (Beirut: Dār al-Walāʾ, 2010), 191–92.

Uṣūlī scholars such as Muḥammad Mahdī al-Narāqī, Murtaḍā al-Anṣārī, and Muḥammad Kāẓim al-Khurāsānī.

Muḥammad Amīn al-Astarābādī, a staunch proponent of Akhbārism, argues that the best approach when dealing with the Qur'an and the Sunna is to imitate and adopt the approach of the early Akhbārī scholars. Their doctrine was that God has clearly conveyed everything the Muslim community will need until Judgement Day, even with regards to the slightest norm. Much of what the Prophet taught regarding the Qur'an and the knowledge of the Sunna which includes abrogation (*naskh*), restriction (*taqyīd*), specification (*takhṣīṣ*), and personal/subjective interpretation (*ta'wīl*) can only be accessed through the interpretations and teachings which are preserved by the pure infallible Imāms. He believes,

> The Qur'an, in most instances, is presented in a general manner in relation to the publics' minds, and this holds true for many of the Prophetic traditions. When it comes to matters of non-self-evident religious rulings (*al-aḥkām al-sharʿiyya al-naẓariyya*), be they fundamental principles or subsidiary issues, we have no recourse other than to seek guidance from the truthful ones, i.e., the Imāms.[26]

Al-Astarābādī goes on the offensive against the Uṣūlī methodology and strongly argues that it is impermissible to deduce and infer non-self-evident rulings solely from the apparent indications found in the Qur'an or the Sunna, unless we are aware of their context as explained by the Imāms. Without such insight from the Imāms, one should refrain from making any assumptions; only the Imāms possess the necessary understanding to explain the religious rulings, and the sole authority to elucidate on matters regarding the Qur'an and the Sunna. To him, it is obligatory to exercise caution and restraint when dealing with the outward meaning of the Qur'an and the apparent aspects of the Sunna, and this is known as *tawaqquf* (abstaining from judgement) and *iḥtiyāṭ* (precaution) in religious matters, especially when the full context is not known and clarified by the Imāms. Al-Astarābādī states, 'Whoever exercises personal reasoning regarding His rulings, if they err, then they have lied against God and fabricated, but if they are correct, then they receive no reward.'[27]

Al-Ḥurr al-ʿĀmilī, another renowned scholar of the Akhbārī persuasion, similarly adhered to the view that it is impermissible to rely solely upon the apparent indication of the Qur'an without recourse to the narrations of the Imāms.

26 Muḥammad Amīn al-Astarābādī, *al-Fawā'id al-madaniyya* (Qom: Mu'assasat al-Nashr al-Islāmī al-Tābiʿ li-Jamāʿat al-Mudarrisīn, 2005), 104.

27 Ibid.

This viewpoint is evident in his celebrated compilation of *ḥadīths*, where he emphasised his perspective in a chapter titled 'On the Inadmissibility of Deducing Non-self-evident Rulings from the Apparent Meaning of the Qur'an, except after Knowing Their Interpretation from the Imāms'.[28] Moreover, in his other work, *al-Fawā'id al-Ṭūsiyya*, al-ʿĀmilī stated that:

> I saw in some of the works of [my] contemporaries arguments for the permissibility of acting on the non-self-evident rulings according to the apparent indication of the Qur'an which is open to multiple possibilities such as abrogation, qualification, and specification and allegorical interpretation, etc., even if there is no explicit text in the approval of their content, nor their interpretation from the Imāms. When I saw that this view was in conflict with mass-transmitted reports (*mutawātir*), I thought it best to report those arguments and to give my answer to them.[29]

He then mentioned numerous arguments offered by those who advocate the permissibility of relying upon the apparent indication of the Qur'an and rebutted each point. Al-ʿĀmilī's main argument centred on the fact that all the proofs given for the permissibility of reliance on the apparent indication of the Qur'an, without recourse to narrations, are circular in nature. Adducing such proofs amounts to using the apparent indication of the Qur'an to prove the normative authority (*ḥujjiyya*) of the Qur'an's apparent indication. He argues that proponents of this view provide no external evidence to substantiate their claim that the apparent indication of the Qur'an can be used independently to derive rulings.[30]

The eighteenth-century scholar Yūsuf al-Baḥrānī, who expressed a more moderate form of Akhbārism in his distinguished compendium of Shīʿa law entitled *al-Ḥadā'iq al-nāḍira*, reported that Akhbārīs were divided into two camps. Some Akhbārīs held an extreme view that no part of the Qur'an, even unequivocal verses such as 'Say: He is God, the One' (Q. 112:1), could be properly understood without interpretation from the Imāms. In opposition, some other Akhbārīs advocated the view that Imāmī scholars may share the authority to interpret the Qur'an with the Imāms, particularly in explaining its ambiguous

28 Muḥammad b. Ḥasan al-Ḥurr al-ʿĀmilī, *Tafṣīl wasā'il al-shīʿa ilā taḥṣīl masā'il al-sharʿiyya* (Mu'assasat Āl al-Bayt li-Iḥyā' al-Turāth, 2008), 27:176.

29 Muḥammad b. al-Ḥasan al-Ḥurr al-ʿĀmilī, *al-Fawā'id al-Ṭūsiyya* (Qom: Maktabat al-Maḥallātī, 2002), 163–68.

30 Ibid., 163–68.

texts. Al-Baḥrānī's own position seems to fall somewhere between these two stances.[31]

He explains that the rationale given by proponents of the extreme view was the numerous Qur'anic verses and reports prohibiting drawing on personal opinion (*ra'y*) in order to interpret the Scripture. According to these scholars, the narrations rejecting personal opinion were more explicit and required absolute reliance on *ḥadīth* in which the infallible Imāms explain the Qur'an.

5 Critiques of the Akhbārī Challenge

Akhbārism's influence decreased because of the efforts of al-Waḥīd al-Bihbihānī (d. 1205/1791), but an examination of the works of legal theory (*uṣūl al-fiqh*) by his first- and second-generation students shows that the challenges posed by the Akhbārīs remained issues of concern to the Uṣūlīs, who thought they warranted being addressed. Muḥammad Mahdī al-Narāqī, a prominent Shīʿī Uṣūlī scholar, summarised the Akhbārī framework of this issue as follows:

> The Akhbārīs have claimed that it is not permissible to interpret the Qur'an without a narration from the Imāms and that any verse the interpretation of which has not been provided by the Imāms should not be acted upon, whether it is an explicit (*naṣṣ*), clear (*muḥkam*), apparent (*ẓāhir*), or ambiguous (*mutashābih*) text. They also said, 'All of the Qur'an is ambiguous to us.' Their statement can be interpreted as denying the authority of the Qur'an altogether, because any verse for which the infallible [Imāms] did not provide the interpretation cannot be interpreted or acted upon, and those verses for which they did provide an interpretation can only be used as evidence with their help.[32]

Therefore, according to the Akhbārīs' epistemological framework, only reported narrations issued from the Imāms are reliable without doubt. These narrations are the sole epistemic tool to infer legal rulings from the Qur'an, meaning that if a narration specifies, limits, or restricts (*takhṣīṣ*) the apparent indication of a specific Qur'anic verse then Akhbārī interpreters accept this restriction of the verse by the *ḥadīth* report. Additionally, if a narration provides an allegorical explanation of a verse which is not apparent, then the

---

31 Yūsuf al-Baḥrānī, *al-Ḥadā'iq al-nāḍira fī aḥkām al-ʿiṭra al-ṭāhira* (Qom: Mu'assasat al-Nashr al-Islāmī, n.d.), 1:28–35. For further information, see Chapter 9 of the present volume.

32 Muḥammad Mahdī al-Narāqī, *Anīs al-mujtahidīn* (Qom: Mu'assasat Būstān-i Kutub, 2009), 1:195–96.

explanation of the verse based solely on the narration is accepted. Ultimately, the normative authority (*ḥujjiyya*) of any verse of the Qur'an relies solely on reported narrations.[33]

Al-Narāqī responded to the Akhbārī view by asserting that the people of *ijtihād* unanimously agreed that *naṣṣ*, *muḥkam*, and *ẓāhir* of the Qur'an, as previously defined, can be interpreted and acted upon without the need to refer to the interpretive narrations of the infallible Imāms. According to this view, anyone who is proficient in the Arabic language and who possesses knowledge of its nuances may understand clear verses of the Qur'an and act according to their own interpretation.

In other words, the Qur'an enjoys a normative legal authority (*ḥujjiyya*) for its recipients. Epistemically, the nature of *ḥujjiyya* is two-sided. God can employ the Qur'anic text as evidence conveying clear instructions on His postulated norms that everyone must adhere to, holding them accountable for their actions. Simultaneously, the Qur'an also acts as proof for its recipients allowing them to answer to God for their actions and omissions, even if they might in reality (*nafs al-amr*) have erred because of their interpretation of the Qur'an's apparent indications.

To support this stance, al-Narāqī argues that God revealed the Qur'an in clear Arabic, making it a comprehensive source and decisive evidence for all. He describes it as a source of light and guidance, an elaborative statement, and a source of healing. The Qur'an contains evidence of monotheism, knowledge of God's perfect attributes, foundational principles for legal rulings, and guidance on what is permissible and impermissible. God instructed His servants to ponder it, derive insights from it, and He warned them not to neglect contemplating it. The Qur'an also includes sermons and advice, urging people to adhere to it and to act in accordance with its teachings. Al-Narāqī contends that, from the Akhbārī perspective, none of these benefits of the Qur'an could be appreciated, and their view might even entail that it was impermissible to derive any benefit from it at all.[34]

Furthermore, al-Narāqī argues that it is impossible that God could address mankind in a manner which indicates something different from what He meant, since doing so would contradict the consensus of the Muslim community. Such a discrepancy would also entail assigning responsibilities to people beyond their capacity and issuing deceptive statements. Al-Narāqī cited numerous narrations indicating that, when conflicting narrations arise, they must be compared to the Qur'an and that the one in agreement with the Qur'an

33 Ibid.
34 Ibid.

must be accepted, while those which contradict the Qur'an should be rejected. In addition, he cited the narration of *thaqalayn*, which was mentioned earlier, and argued that, according to the Akhbārī view, only one of them would be a reference and the weightier epistemic source – in other words, the Qur'an would be abandoned as an authoritative source, lacking normative authority.[35]

Murtaḍā al-Anṣārī, one of the most influential and leading legal theorists of the modern period, similarly discusses the issue of the apparent indication of the Qur'an at length. He closely considered the core of the Akhbārī challenge, which essentially posited that the hermeneutical understanding of the Qur'an be subject to interpretation and that only the infallible Imāms have the authority to engage in such interpretation. In response to this challenge, al-Anṣārī carefully summarises their argument as follows:

> The summary of this [Akhbārī's] argument refers to the view that the Lawgiver (*al-Shāriʿ*) prohibited [acting according to the apparent indication of the Qur'an]. This would entail that the purpose of the speaker was not to convey content of his messages with this statement, and thus, [God's communication] would not be like ordinary, conventional conversation.[36]

Al-Anṣārī offers two responses to the arguments of the Akhbārīs. Firstly, he contends that adhering to the apparent indication of the Qur'an, even after an exhaustive search for potential abrogators (*nāsikh*) and specifiers (*mukhaṣṣiṣ*), is not considered interpretation but rather a reliance on the literal meaning conveyed by the text. Al-Anṣārī further elaborates that:

> Even if one accepts that applying the apparent meaning of a word is an act of interpretation, but what is meant by personal view (*raʾy*) is a speculative subjective interpretation, thus it does not include applying the apparent indication of the Qur'an to their conventional ordinary language.[37]

In other words, al-Anṣārī assumes that God's communication through His messenger is conveyed in the same natural language used by ordinary people.

Secondly, even if one were to regard the practice of acting according to the apparent indication of the Qur'an as a form of interpretation, it is essential to note that it does not fall under the category of prohibited interpretation.

35 Ibid., 196–97.
36 Murtaḍā al-Anṣārī, *Farāʾid al-uṣūl* (Qom: Muʾassasat al-Nashr al-Islāmī, 1986), 57–58.
37 Ibid., 57.

Prohibited interpretation is a subjective and personal form of interpretation, known as *tafsīr bi-l-raʾy*, rather than interpretation per se.

Muḥammad Kāẓim al-Khurāsānī, a prominent Shīʿī scholar whose seminal work *Kifāyat al-uṣūl* is still taught in Shīʿī seminaries as an advanced text of legal hermeneutics today, cites four main criticisms of the Akhbārī rejection of the authority of the apparent meaning of the Qur'an. Following the lead of his mentor al-Anṣārī, al-Khurāsānī posits that the communication of the Lawgiver is conveyed through the apparent indication in the same everyday language used by ordinary people. Consequently, unlike the Akhbārīs, who differentiate between the apparent indications of the Qur'an and those of the Sunna, al-Khurāsānī perceives no distinction in terms of authority between these sources.

Furthermore, he rejects the core Akhbārī idea that the profound concepts in the Qur'an are beyond the comprehension of ordinary humans who lack divine wisdom. Al-Khurāsānī also categorically disagrees with the Akhbārīs' claim that because the Qur'an contains several allegorical expressions, this makes the whole content of the Qur'an ambiguous (*mutashābih*) and unfathomable for deriving legal norms. Moreover, he disputes the Akhbārī contention that the many specifications (*takhṣīṣ*) and restrictions (*taqyīd*) of general Qur'anic maxims leave one with only a vague summary, such that its propositions are unclear and confusing.[38]

For al-Khurāsānī, although the Qur'an contains profound truths and sophisticated messages, it is ultimately a book of guidance meant for humanity at large, and therefore its essential message can be comprehended by fallible individuals. He contends that the existence of allegorical verses does not negate the possibility of deriving legal norms from clear (*muḥkam*) verses. Al-Khurāsānī further states that the specifications and restrictions placed on some verses do not make the entirety of the Qur'an ambiguous, but rather help qualify their legal implications – as is the case for any legal text. In sum, he firmly upholds the authority of the apparent indication of the Qur'an against Akhbārī arguments that it cannot be used as a source for legal reasoning. He maintains that the Qur'an is accessible, comprehensible, and suitable for the derivation of legal rulings, provided that proper interpretive principles are followed. This allows the Uṣūlī school to rely on the Qur'an as an authoritative legal text, contrary to the Akhbārī position.

38 Muḥammad Kāẓim al-Khurāsānī, *Kifāyat al-uṣūl* (Qom: Muʾassasat Āl al-Bayt li-Iḥyāʾ al-Turāth, n.d.), 280–81.

6 The Transhistorical Applicability Challenge

Some Muslim jurists have advanced a semantic-philosophical challenge that questions the Qur'an's authority to broaden its message beyond its immediate audience. This theory questions whether the obligations outlined in Islamic law were exclusively intended for the specific audience during the time of revelation. This has a significant impact on whether and how the regulative verses and the obligations they stipulate can be extended to people beyond the immediate audience of the Qur'an.

The issue that could potentially attract more acceptance from contemporary religious reformists is the historical context of legal obligations. Asserting and proving the historical circumstances surrounding legal rulings plays a crucial role in religious understanding and interpretation. Contemporary religious thinkers explain historicity by referring to the intellectual, cultural, social, political, economic, and customary conditions of the era when revelations occurred. They determine that many legal topics have historical dimensions – certain duties were specific to the direct audience of the Qur'an, and those belonging to later eras/contexts may have different responsibilities. Orthodox Muslim jurists refer to certain principles in legal theory to ascertain that all legal obligations apply uniformly to all Muslims in all contexts.

One fascinating semantic argument forwarded by the distinguished Shāfiʿī Uṣūlī scholar Ibrāhīm b. ʿAlī al-Fayrūzabādī al-Shīrāzī posits that the Qur'an's direct speech and calls are exclusively directed towards its immediate audience at the time of revelation. He argues that verses containing phrases like 'O people' and 'O you who believe' are specifically addressing the contemporaneous audience of the Qur'an's initial revelation. To substantiate his point, he presents the following argument:

> Regarding God Almighty's statements to creation couched in direct address such as His word 'O people' and 'O you who believe', those who have not yet been created are not included in this address in terms of wording and phrasing. This is because such an address is only suitable for one who already exists in the audience when the statement is uttered. Regarding those not yet created, this address does not apply to them. Also, if the Messenger of God directly addresses someone, the call linguistically does not include others, because that direct call to him does not include others besides him, and other people may fall under the same ruling of the address by an [other] evidence, that is: my verdict for one is my verdict for all, and also by way of analogy (*qiyās*).[39]

39 Ibrāhīm b. ʿAlī al-Fayrūzabādī al-Shīrāzī, *al-Lumaʿ fī uṣūl al-fiqh* (Rabat: Dār al-Ḥadīth al-Kattāniyya, 2013), 107–8.

Al-Fayrūzabādī's argument focuses on linguistic aspects and pertains specifically to Qur'anic verses that include phrases such as 'O people' and 'O you who believe'. In essence, although he does not make claims regarding the historical or contextual nature of these Qur'anic verses, limiting them linguistically to historical applications can shed light on the notion of the historical contextuality of the regulative verses within the Qur'an.

Al-Fayrūzabādī's argument found a favourable reception among certain Imāmī scholars. For instance, Mīrzā Qummī – in a more theo-philosophical rather than mere linguistic discussion of the matter – comments on the irrationality of including Muslims after the revelation within the direct audience of the Qur'an. Al-Qummī, fully conscious of different scholarly views regarding the scope of audience addressed by the Qur'an, states that:

> The well-known view of the Imāmī scholars is that whatever is postulated in the Qur'an for addressing a verbal audience in the Qur'an, such as 'O you who believe' and 'O people', and the like, does not extend to later generations, after the communication took place. Some writers even claim *the existence* of consensus of our Imāmī scholars on that. This view is considered the predominant one among the scholars of Sunnī Islam. Some other scholars take a more inclusive approach (suggesting that these verses apply to all Muslims, regardless of the time period). The former view is the true, justified one. Our argument in favour of the first view is that addressing those who did not exist during the revelation of the Qur'an is deemed rationally and religiously unacceptable (*qabīḥ ʿaqlan wa-sharʿan*).[40]

In his theo-philosophical approach, al-Qummī contends that the Ashʿarī position, which permits the inclusion of subsequent generations of Muslims within the Qur'anic address, is grounded in their belief in the primacy of private mental speech (*kalām nafsī*). He then echoes a view closely aligned with the Muʿtazilī/Imāmī tradition, categorically rejecting the concept of private mental speech as entirely irrational. Al-Qummī's argument against this view is particularly intriguing and may resonate with contemporary philosophies of language.

Over a hundred years before Wittgenstein highlighted the irrationality of private mental speech due to its inherently relational (*iḍāfī*) nature, al-Qummī articulated a similar view. This perspective emphasises that any linguistic communication is contingent upon relevant parties, namely, the speaker and the

40 al-Qummī, *al-Qawānīn*, 1:517.

recipient. Consequently, when a required party is absent, the need for communication ceases to exist.[41]

In other words, according to al-Qummī, an obligation in the Qur'an is essentially a form of demand, and a demand inherently involves a relational aspect that requires the existence of the parties involved. Since the required element – i.e. future generations – is absent during the revelation, there is no connection between the request and its fulfilment. Al-Qummī argues that, just as individuals who are insane or unaware cannot be considered as subjects of a legal/religious demand and therefore cannot be primary obligation holders, the same logic applies to non-existent individuals. Consequently, the request loses its validity, since it pertains exclusively to the contemporaneous audience of the Prophet, not those who will come later and did not exist during the time of revelation.[42]

Muḥammad Ḥasan al-Najafī (d. 1265/1849), a highly eminent Imāmī jurist, also argues that it is a well-established principle in the Imāmī school of thought that the Qur'anic calls and addresses are specifically directed to its immediate audience and context.[43]

However, many of those who claim that the Qur'an's address extends beyond its direct audience and thus applies to all people irrespective of time base their argument on the juristic maxim of 'the primacy of inclusion' (*qāʿidat al-ishtirāk*). This primacy is based on narrations such as the Prophetic saying 'My verdict for one is my verdict for all', and Imām Jaʿfar al-Ṣādiq's narration, 'Whatever the Prophet made permissible (*ḥalāl*) is permissible until the Day of Judgement, [and whatever] the Prophet made impermissible (*ḥarām*) is impermissible until the Day of Judgement.'[44] Therefore, the laws that were stipulated by the Prophet are applicable to all Muslims in all periods.[45] Thus, the primacy of inclusion acts as a supplementary hermeneutical tool to extend the authority of the Qur'an from the direct audience to later audiences who were absent during the initial act of communication. As a result, the subsequent generations of Muslims after the Prophet share the same religious duties, the regulative verses apply to Muslims beyond its immediate audience, and the

41 Ibid.

42 Ibid.

43 Muḥammad Ḥasan b. Bāqir b. ʿAbd al-Raḥīm al-Najafī, *Jawāhir al-kalām fī sharḥ Sharāʾiʿ al-Islām* (Beirut: Dār Iḥyāʾ al-Turāth al-ʿArabī, 1983), 41:16.

44 Muḥammad b. Yaʿqūb al-Kulaynī, *Uṣūl al-Kāfī*, ed. ʿAlī Akbar al-Ghaffārī, 5th ed. (Qom: Dār al-Kutub al-Islāmiyya, 1944), 1:57.

45 al-Sayyid Muḥammad Kāẓim al-Muṣṭafawī, *al-Qawāʿid: miʾat qāʿida fiqhiyya maʿnan wa-madrikan wa-mawridan* (Qom: Muʾassasat al-Nashr al-Islāmī, 2015), 43.

laws regarding permissible and prohibited acts are equally applicable, since all Muslims are included in the same normative system instated by the Prophet.

If rationally and linguistically communicating the demand to non-existing individuals is impossible, then what would cause one to hold them responsible for the Islamic norms when they come into existence? Al-Qummī replies that God informed His messenger that when they come into existence, they will become addressees and bearers of responsibility for those norms. This is in fact what some Shīʿī jurists intended by their claim of consensus based on the primacy of inclusion. Al-Qummī succinctly summarised his argument as follows:

> We do not say that non-existing individuals are the addressees of those Qur'anic calls, either in a real sense or metaphorically. We rather say that they are under the same obligation on account of another set of evidence, such as consensus, necessity, and mass-transmitted reports.[46]

A pertinent question now arises: if all Muslims – in one way or another – are addressees of these textual demands, then what would be the implications of al-Qummī's claim? His response is that the implications become evident when one considers the historical messages. In other words, since the message of God contains apparent indications, then it would be inappropriate to interpret them in a different sense from what they apparently indicate. More importantly, al-Qummī believes if the latter generations are addressees of the message in the same way as of the direct audience, then they do not have to investigate the original meaning of the words during the time of revelation. Rather, they can rely on their own contemporary understanding of the text.[47]

However, it is worth noting that many scholars who came after al-Qummī did not endorse his view. For example, al-Khurāsānī, in a concise response that seemingly represents the opposing perspective, contends that rational agents normally rely on the apparent indication of words to convey their messages. The Lawgiver did not disapprove of this ongoing established human practice, nor did He introduce an alternative method for conveying His message to humanity.[48]

46 al-Qummī, *al-Qawānīn*, 1:521.

47 Ibid.

48 al-Khurāsānī, *Kifāyat al-uṣūl*, 313.

7 The Distortion Challenge

Distortion (*taḥrīf*) is a controversial term used to refer to the claim that the Qur'an has been subject to alterations or distortions. This claim has been historically debated among Muslim jurists and theologians. While most Muslims firmly believe that the Qur'an has been preserved as it was revealed to the Prophet, some individuals and sects have proposed the notion of *taḥrīf*, asserting that certain verses have been changed or removed from the original text. For instance, Aḥmad b. ʿAlī b. Abī Ṭālib al-Ṭabrisī (d. 599/1202) recounted an incident in his work *al-Iḥtijāj*. In a reported tradition – which would have been considered weak because it was *mursal*, i.e. it had gaps in its chain of transmission – a heretic approached Imām ʿAlī and voiced his scepticism by stating: 'If it were not for the contradictions and inconsistencies in the Qur'an, I would have embraced your religion.' He specifically mentioned Q. 4:3, which reads, 'If you fear that you might not treat the orphans justly, then marry the women that seem good to you.' He contended that marrying women does not equate to justice for orphans, because not all women are orphans. In response, Imām ʿAlī reportedly explained that this apparent contradiction was a consequence of what he previously mentioned regarding the hypocrites' omissions of passages from the Qur'an. He pointed out that between the Qur'an's discussions on orphans and the subject of marrying women various passages and narratives encompassing more than a third of the Qur'anic content had been omitted.[49]

As al-Ṭabrisī's report demonstrates, the potential implications of the *taḥrīf* claim upon the regulative verses in Islamic law can be significant. If one were to accept the notion of *taḥrīf*, particularly concerning regulative verses, it would raise fundamental questions regarding the authenticity and applicability of Qur'anic legal principles.

Within the Imāmiyya sect there are two schools of thought with regard to the claim of distortion or tampering of the Qur'an: those who affirm *taḥrīf* and those who reject it. Many early classical Shīʿī scholars acknowledged and affirmed the belief in *taḥrīf* and used specific narrations as the basis for their belief, as shall be explained below. However, the majority of Shīʿī scholars deny that the Qur'an has been altered in any way, such as that additions have been made or that verses or chapters have been removed. Among this camp are the likes of the twentieth-century grand-jurist Sayyid Abū al-Qāsim al-Mūsawī

49 Aḥmad b. ʿAlī al-Ṭabrisī, *al-Iḥtijāj ʿalā Ahl al-Lujāj* (Mashhad, 1983), 1:254.

al-Khūʾī (d. 1992), who held the view that reliable narrations denied the alteration of the Qurʾan in any such way.

Amir Moezzi categorised studies of *taḥrīf* in the Imāmī school into three groups:[50]

1. The first group argues that doubts raised about the authenticity of the ʿUthmānic codex have no historical basis and are driven by dogmatic and political-theological views. They believe that Imāmī Shīʿism is primarily a political movement seeking temporal power and that claims of falsification are merely attempts to assert the superiority of ʿAlī over other companions of the Prophet. However, this perspective overlooks the doctrinal and historical accounts supporting the notion of falsification found in various sources.
2. The second group acknowledges some discrepancies in the ʿUthmānic codex but believes that it nevertheless contains most of the revelation. They criticise ʿUthmān for rejecting other recensions, particularly ʿAlī's commentary.[51] Some suggest that views regarding falsification originated from non-Shīʿī groups aiming to discredit Shīʿī *ḥadīth*.[52]
3. The third group contends that the early Imāmī Shīʿīs openly questioned the integrity of the ʿUthmānic codex and accused non-Shīʿīs of falsifying the Qurʾan, adducing proof in the form of utterances of their Imāms reported in early Shīʿī *ḥadīth*. This early Imāmī position is supported by historical accounts and Imāmī tenets, mainly before the Buwayhid period.

However, during the Buwayhid period, starting from the mid-fourth/tenth century, the majority of Twelver scholars, including Muḥammad b. ʿAlī b. Bābawayh (d. 381/991), shifted to adopt the Sunnī viewpoint, abandoning the idea of *taḥrīf*. In summary, these studies present varying perspectives on *taḥrīf* in Shīʿī Islam, ranging from outright rejection to acknowledgement of early Imāmī Shīʿīs' questioning of the ʿUthmānic codex.[53]

It is important to highlight that in the study of abrogation in the Qurʾan, the Sunnī scholars believe in the validity of the 'abrogation of the recitation while preserving the norm', due to the existence of such a concept in Sunnī *ḥadīth*

50 Mohammad Ali Amir-Moezzi, *The Silent Qurʾan & the Speaking Qurʾan: Scriptural Sources of Islam between History and Fervor*, trans. Eric L. Ormsby (New York: Columbia University Press, 2016), 62–65.

51 S. Husain M. Jafri, *Origins and Early Development of Shiʿa Islam* (London: Longman, 1979), 311–12.

52 Mohammad Ali Amir-Moezzi, *The Divine Guide in Early Shiʿism: The Sources of Esotericism in Islam*, trans. David Streight (New York: State University of New York Press, 1994), 6–19.

53 Ibid., 77–91.

literature. According to a well-known narration, ʿUmar b. al-Khaṭṭāb insisted that a verse in the chapter of al-Nūr (Q. 24) stipulated that if an elderly man and woman engaged in adultery, they should be punished by stoning (*rajm*). This verse, however, is not found in the current written compilation of the Qur'an. The Sunnī explanation is that the verse was abrogated in recitation but not ruling, meaning the recitation of the verse was abolished but the legal ruling of stoning as punishment remained valid.[54]

Furthermore, al-Zarkashī (d. 794/1392), a reputed Sunnī scholar specialising in Qur'anic studies, reported additional instances that indicate the potential existence of chapters in the Qur'an that are presently absent from the known compilation.[55]

The existence of reports about the distortion of the Qur'an has been considered by Muḥammad Sharīf Māzandarānī (Sharīf al-ʿUlamāʾ) (d. 1245/1830–1), a notable scholar and teacher of Murtaḍā al-Anṣārī, as a serious epistemic impediment against normative authority of the apparent indication of the Qur'an. A pressing question which arises is why Akhbārīs who believed in the distortion of the Qur'an – palatable to them because of the references to *taḥrīf* found in narrations attributed to the Imāms – have not resorted to this idea to substantiate their rejection of the apparent indication of the Qur'an. One reply offered by Mūsā Tabrīzī in his commentary on al-Anṣārī's *Rasāʾil* is that the Akhbārīs' rejection is based solely on the belief that the interpretation of the Qur'an's apparent indication is an exclusive privilege belonging to the Prophet and Imāms. This holds true whether distortion occurred or not. Fallible jurists and interpreters of the Qur'an do not share this privilege and authority with the Prophet/Imāms.[56]

However, Māzandarānī's student Murtaḍā al-Anṣārī found the argument presented by his mentor unsatisfactory. Al-Anṣārī's epistemic critique of his teacher focuses on the assertion that even if the concept of *taḥrīf*, assuming it to be valid, were accepted, this would not be an impediment for the authority of the apparent indication of the Qur'an. Al-Anṣārī's reasoning stems from the fact that *taḥrīf* does not lead to summary knowledge (*ʿilm ijmālī*) that would affect the apparent indication of other verses. This is because the proposed or alleged distorted verses may not necessarily pertain to the regulative verses. Al-Anṣārī articulates this viewpoint by stating, 'The occurrence of alleged

54 Badr al-Dīn Muḥammad b. ʿAbd Allāh al-Zarkashī, *al-Burhān fī ʿulūm al-Qurʾān* (Cairo: Maktabat Dār al-Turāth, 1984), 35.

55 Ibid., 37.

56 al-Mīrzā Mūsā al-Tabrīzī, *Awthaq al-wasāʾil fī sharḥ al-rasāʾil* (Qom: Muʾassasat Āl al-Bayt, 1949), 92.

distortion (*taḥrīf*) in the Qur'an does not prevent adherence to its apparent meaning on account of the lack of summary knowledge regarding the distortion of regulative verses.'[57]

Muḥammad Kāẓim al-Khurāsānī, an outstanding disciple of al-Anṣārī, aligns with his teacher against Māzandarānī regarding this topic. While al-Khurāsānī does not endorse *taḥrīf* outright, he acknowledges certain narrations that advocate for it. Additionally, his rational analysis lends some support to the concept of distortion. Though not directly stating his approval, al-Khurāsānī admits there is basis for *taḥrīf* in textual sources and logical deliberation. His indirectness implies a nuanced stance – neither fully accepting nor rejecting the idea of corruption in religious texts. Nonetheless, al-Khurāsānī proceeds to present his own arguments in response to this matter:

> The claim of a summary knowledge (*ʿilm ijmālī*) regarding the occurrence of tampering in the Qur'an, either through omission or distortion, although not far-fetched, as some reports testify and rational deliberation supports, does not invalidate the authority of its apparent indications. This is because of the lack of knowledge regarding any inherent flaws in those indications in the first place. Even if it is accepted, there is no knowledge of its occurrence in the regulative verses.[58]

Despite its novelty and historical as well as epistemic appeal, Māzandarānī's unprecedented argument challenging the normative authority of the apparent indication of the Qur'an has not gained serious acceptance, either among Uṣūlī scholars or among Akhbārīs.

8 The Recitations' Challenge

Although there are variant readings of the Qur'an (*qirāʾāt*), they do not greatly affect the regulative verses.[59] In the examination of variant styles of recitations, it seems that few verses related to legal rulings. For instance, Q. 2:222 can be read in two different ways. The verse states:

---

57 Murtaḍā al-Anṣārī, *Farāʾid al-uṣūl*, ed. Muḥammad Bāqir al-Bihbūdī (Qom: Majmaʿ al-Fikr al-Islāmī, 1998), 1:158.

58 Muḥammad Kāẓim al-Khurāsānī, *Kifāyat al-uṣūl*, ed. ʿAbbās ʿAlī al-Zāriʿī al-Sabzawārī (Qom: Muʾassasat al-Nashr al-Islāmī, 1997), 2:295.

59 Amir-Moezzi, *The Silent Qur'an*, 70–74.

> They ask you concerning [the rules of] menstruation, say it is a discomfort, therefore keep aloof from the woman during the menstrual discharge and do not approach them until they have become clean [*yaṭhurna* or *yaṭṭahharna*].

The reading *yaṭhurna* may be translated as 'until they become clean', while the reading with *tashdīd*, *yaṭṭahharna*, translates to 'until they cleanse themselves [by bathing or *ghusl*]'. This now gives rise to two distinct legal norms.

Legal norm (a): The word *yaṭhurna*, meaning 'until they become clean', is prevalent in the majority of readings. Therefore, the legal ruling permits intercourse with one's spouse after her menstrual cycle has ended, and she is not obligated to perform the major ritual ablution (*ghusl*).

Legal norm (b): However, in other readings, when read as *yaṭṭahharna*, which means 'until they cleanse themselves', the legal ruling is that after the menstrual cycle ends, the wife is obligated to perform the major ritual ablution before engaging in intercourse. The addition or omission of a single vowel or change in the verb form thus significantly impacts the legal ruling of the verse.

The second example in the Qur'an which is affected by varying styles of recitation involves Q. 5:6, the verse on ablutions (*wuḍū'*). Because of the difference, a historical legal dispute arose between Shī'ī and Sunnī Muslims. The verse states, 'When you rise up for prayer, wash your faces and your hands up to the elbows, wipe your heads, and wash/wipe your feet to the ankles.'[60]

The focal point of contention resides in the nuanced interpretation of the phrase 'and your feet' within the Qur'anic context. This interpretive variance has consequential implications for Muslims, specifically pertaining to the obligation of either washing or wiping their feet as part of the ritual purification preceding obligatory prayers. The crux of the dispute revolves around the pivotal role played by the conjunction 'and', and the verbs 'wash' and 'wipe' within the verse. The question arises whether this conjunction is linked to the preceding directive, which enjoins the act of wiping the head, thus suggesting a continuation of that instruction, or whether it is linked to the original verb of command, which pertains to the act of washing.

The discrepancy of either washing or wiping arises from the nuances of Arabic grammar. The reading of Ḥafṣ, which is used in the most widely available printed versions of the Qur'an, states: 'wash your feet'. However, a slight change in declension of the noun 'feet' – a vowel change from *i* in *arjulikum* to *a* in *arjulakum* – alters the meaning. Many Sunnī scholars interpret the verse as *arjulakum*, which obligates them to 'wash their feet', the 'and' referring to the command verb 'wash'. Whereas Imāmī scholars argue that linguistically, it

60 Q. 5:6.

should be 'wipe your feet', although this is not the only reason for Shīʿī jurists for their respective juristic edicts.[61] This subtle difference leads to distinct legal norms, highlighting the intricate nature of Qur'anic recitations and their impact on legal understandings within Islamic law.[62]

The existence of two different readings for these two verses relating to menstruation and *wuḍū'*, respectively, which entail different legal rulings, raises a question regarding the conflict of evidence (*taʿāruḍ al-amārāt*). According to mainstream Shīʿī legal theorists, in cases when conflicting pieces of evidence are equally strong, that is, when there is no epistemic preponderating factor allowing one piece of evidence to be favoured over the other, the hermeneutical principle is to abandon or disregard both pieces of evidence. In such cases, a jurist is unable to use these two aforementioned Qur'anic verses as a reference to make a ruling. This is based on the hermeneutical theory of instrumentality (*ṭarīqiyya*), according to which, evidence act as an instrument to help ascertain reality or the correct Islamic legal ruling. Therefore, neither reading of the verse is taken as an authoritative source, and hence the verse itself is no longer used as a referent for the ruling either on washing vs wiping, or on bathing after menstruation prior to intercourse. However, according to the alternative hermeneutical school of thought, that is, the causality theory (*sababiyya*), when dealing with equally conflicting evidences, a jurist must act according to one of the conflicting pieces of evidence, in this case, variant readings, at their discretion (*takhyīr*).[63] In this case, a jurist is able to choose one reading of the aforementioned Qur'anic verses when issuing an edict on washing or wiping or on whether it is necessary to bathe after menstruation and prior to intercourse or not.

9 Redundancy Challenge

The task of qualifying the generality of Qur'anic rules with the assistance of *ḥadīth* reports has assumed heightened significance in the contemporary era. This pertinence arose because of the prevalence of a substantial number of contentious and potentially problematic legal rulings, particularly those pertaining to human rights issues, which find their roots in the *ḥadīth* rather

61 Bāqir al-Īrawānī, *Durūs tamhīdiyya fī fiqh al-istidlāl* (Qom: al-Markaz al-ʿĀlamī li-l-Dirāsāt al-Islāmiyya, 2004), 1:54.

62 For the Sunnī–Shīʿī debate on this topic, see al-Miqdād b. ʿAbd Allāh al-Suyūrī, *Kanz al-ʿirfān fī fiqh al-Qur'ān*, 2 vols. (Tehran: Intisharāt-i Murtaḍawī, 1964), 1:12–14.

63 al-Khurāsānī, *Kifāyat al-uṣūl*, 285.

than in the Qur'an itself. Against the backdrop of a rapidly evolving modern context, characterised by shifting societal norms and emerging ethical and legal challenges, there is an increasing demand for a nuanced and contextually sensitive interpretation of Islamic law. Issues such as human rights, gender equality, and social justice necessitate careful deliberation and a judicious approach in order to harmonise traditional Islamic teachings with evolving societal values and international human rights standards. Consequently, the critical examination of the hermeneutical relationship between the Qur'an and *ḥadīth* assumes a pivotal role in shaping the ethical and legal framework that guides Muslim communities in addressing complex contemporary issues. This dynamic process underscores the adaptability and resilience of Islamic law, allowing it to meet the multifaceted challenges of the modern world while steadfastly upholding its foundational principles and values.

The degree to which the Qur'an's apparent indication is considered authoritative in Islamic legal hermeneutics is a matter of profound importance. Some Muslim scholars, however, perceive this matter as an inconsequential, trivial issue, arguing that most verses related to norms already have clarifications, accompanying narrations, or established consensus on interpretation.

However, al-Anṣārī mounts a challenge to this prevailing perspective. He discerns that while this assertion may hold some validity about acts of worship (*ʿibādāt*), it finds its limits when applied to general legal principles enshrined in verses addressing commercial transactions (*muʿāmalāt*); for instance, verses instructing believers to fulfil contracts, permitting trade, mandating mutual consent in business transactions, cautioning against giving wealth to fools, warning against taking an orphan's property, and emphasising the importance of verifying news from wicked people, as al-Anṣārī discusses.[64]

In fact, al-Anṣārī's reply does not address the root of the challenge. Most Muslim jurists consider an authentic narration not just an interpretive tool clarifying the ambiguity of Qur'anic verses. For them, more importantly, the narrations enjoy the hermeneutical advantage of restricting the generality of Qur'anic norms by qualifying or specifying their scope. Al-Khurāsānī's stance, for example, is a hermeneutical view typical of most Muslim orthodox jurists:

> Undoubtedly, it is permissible to specify a Qur'anic verse using a reliable singular report, just as it is permissible to do so through the Qur'an itself, or a *mutawātir* report, or a singular report supported by decisive evidence. This practice is evident in the interpretive method of Shīʿī scholars, who consistently relied on singular narrations over the general rulings of the Qur'an [from the present

64 al-Anṣārī, *Farāʾid al-uṣūl* (ed. al-Bihbūdī), 1:155.

> time] until the time of the Imāms, peace be upon them. It is not plausible at all to suggest that this practice could be due to the existence of certain contextual evidence.[65]

According to al-Khurāsānī, disregarding the role of *ḥadīth* reports in specifying and qualifying the generality of Qur'anic verses would inevitably lead to the wholesale rejection of *ḥadīth*, given how rarely a *ḥadīth* report aligns with the general meaning of a Qur'anic verse. The fact that the authenticity of Qur'anic general rules is firmly established, while singular narrations are epistemically uncertain, should not deter one from interpreting non-definitive indications of Qur'anic generality. Otherwise, it would not have been permissible to specify such an indication, even through a mass-transmitted narration.[66]

This issue becomes further exacerbated when the restriction of the generality of the Qur'an by solitary narrations leads to serious implications in the modern context. For instance, a case in point involves the rulings on apostasy in Islam. Many Shīʿī jurists who favour lesser epistemic sources such as solitary reports over more authoritative sources like the Qur'an impose the death penalty in cases of apostasy, despite the absence of explicit Qur'anic injunctions to that effect. This is so even though the Qur'an solely mentions eschatological, not worldly, consequences for apostasy, thereby relegating its punishment to the hereafter, without specifying any temporal repercussions. However, delving into the *ḥadīth* literature, one finds a small number of narrations that mention that the punishment for leaving Islam is death. Nonetheless, in the framework of Uṣūlī jurists like al-Anṣārī and al-Khurāsānī, the solitary narrations will restrict the generality of the Qur'an and impose the death penalty for apostasy, notwithstanding the absence of such a punishment within Qur'anic penal verses.[67]

10 Conclusion

In the hierarchy of sources for Islamic law, the Qur'an is prima facie considered by most Muslims to be the highest and most authoritative source, followed by

65 al-Khurāsānī, *Kifāyat al-uṣūl*, 1:326.

66 Ibid.

67 For further information on this issue, see Mohsen Kadivar, *Blasphemy and Apostasy in Islam: Debates in Shi'a Law*, trans. Hamid Mavani (Edinburgh: Edinburgh University Press, 2021); and Hashim Bata, *Exploring the Mind of God: An Introduction to Shiʿite Legal Epistemology* (Leiden: Brill, 2023), 107–13.

the Sunna which, for most Muslims, seems to serve as a complementary source of guidance to the Qur'an. The regulative verses cover a wide range of subjects, including matters related to personal conduct, family law, inheritance, contracts, commerce, criminal law, and more. The Qur'an, however, often provides general principles and guidelines, and it is the task of jurists to interpret and apply these principles to specific situations.

Nevertheless, the multifaceted discourse surrounding the role and authoritative position regarding the apparent indications of the Qur'an within Imāmī Shīʿī thought has produced a spectrum of perspectives. Within this spectrum, divergent viewpoints emerge, with some scholars apparently positing the Qur'an as a primary epistemic source that underpins a jurist's *ijtihād*, while others do not refer to the apparent indications of the Qur'anic verses as a primary normative source to be used for extrapolating legal norms. For such scholars, the Sunna is considered the primary epistemic source when deciphering Sharīʿa rulings.

Among the jurists who view the Qur'an as a primary source for Islamic rulings, one example is Sayyid Khū'ī. He held the apparent indications of the Qur'an in high regard, something evident in his elucidation of the role these apparent indications played in his *ijtihād* or legal interpretation. His view regarding the authority of the apparent indications of the Qur'an occupies a significant place within his legal methodology and legal reasoning. An illustrative context for Khū'ī's stance emerges in his discourse on the concept of *jihād*. In contrast to the majority of Shīʿī jurists, who primarily derive their conclusions from two sources – the *ḥadīth* and consensus – Khū'ī advocates for the permissibility of *jihād* even in the absence of an infallible Imām. This contention underscores the primacy he accords to Qur'anic edicts vis-à-vis *ḥadīth*. Khū'ī's rationale for endorsing *jihād* during the absence of an infallible Imām rests on his conviction that the Qur'an assumes a foundational role in shaping Islamic law, thereby transcending the confines of *ḥadīth*-based prohibitions. By elevating the Qur'an to the status of a primary source, he endeavours to justify the permissibility of *jihād* – a stance that sets him apart from his contemporaries and predecessors. According to Khū'ī:

> Indeed, *jihād* against the infidels is one of the pillars of the Islamic religion, and Islam has been strengthened and its command has spread throughout the world through the call to monotheism under the banner of the Noble Prophet. It has been mentioned in many verses that it is obligatory for Muslims to fight and [engage in] *jihād* with the polytheistic infidels until they surrender or are killed, and with the People of the Book until they surrender or pay *jizya* while they are submissive. Naturally, allocating this ruling to a temporary time, which was the

> time of presence [of the infallible Imāms], is not consistent with the concern of the Qur'an and its command to do it without timing in its many texts.[68]

However, for the majority of Imāmī Shīʿī jurists, the apparent indication of the Qur'an seems to play a subsidiary role to the *ḥadīth* and consensus when deriving legal rulings and norms. According to this dominant trend of thought within Imāmī Shīʿism, the apparent indication of the Qur'an is viewed as a complementary source, while *ḥadīth* and consensus, the latter necessarily involving an infallible Imām, are the primary sources for extrapolating Islamic legal norms. For instance, al-Rāwandī, a pioneering author of works on the regulative verses of the Qur'an, explains that the delay among Imāmī scholars in authoring books on the regulative verses stems from the Shīʿī community's access to an infallible Imām to explicate divine law and the meaning of the Qur'an. As al-Rāwandī states:

> Our excuse is clear, because the argument and the evidence of the Shīʿī school of thought, in truth and correctness of what they particularly believe in it, of the indication of normative reports and textual obligations, as well as what they share with the jurists of other schools of thought, is their consensus. Because their consensus is a decisive evidence and it is an indicator which causes certainty that the infallible who is immune from mistakes is part of that consensus. If added to that, the Book of God or any other way which causes certainty and produces surety, it is an indicator added to another indicator. Otherwise, their consensus is sufficient.[69]

This seems to be the practical position of the majority of Imāmī jurists, according to which, the primary sources are the narrations, supported by consensus. The Qur'an, thus, according to al-Rāwandī, merely confirms the narrations and consensus.

Moreover, the generality of Qur'anic verses are typically specified or qualified by the narrations and/or consensus in Imāmī law. Khū'ī's position on issues like offensive *jihād* therefore appears incongruous in comparison with mainstream practice, since he privileges the general apparent indication of the Qur'an on *jihād* over the particular injunctions of the narrations. Nonetheless, one may plausibly characterise Khū'ī's stance on offensive *jihād* as inconsistent with his broader legal methodology, since in most of his legal works, he allows narrations and consensus to specify and qualify the universal indications of Qur'anic verses.

68 al-Sayyid Abū al-Qāsim al-Mūsawī al-Khū'ī, *Minhāj al-ṣāliḥīn* (Qom: Mehr, 1981), 1:363–64.
69 al-Rāwandī, *Fiqh al-Qur'ān*, 1:60.

Some Muslim reformists appeal to the Qur'an as a means of reconciling traditional Islamic law with contemporary human rights norms, revisiting Qur'anic verses and foregrounding principles of justice, equality, and compassion, endeavouring to reinterpret Islamic teachings in alignment with evolving modern values. This exegetical approach has catalysed valuable discussions of women's rights, religious liberty, and individual freedoms within an Islamic framework, as seen in the work of scholars such as Amina Wadud.[70] However, the complex hermeneutics of scriptural interpretation and the diverse historical contexts in which Qur'anic verses were revealed render such undertakings challenging. Despite well-intentioned efforts, the issue of *jihād* as discussed by Khū'ī illuminates potential risks associated with reformist approaches. Khū'ī's novel perspective on *jihād* underscores the potential for reinterpretations to drift into a new form of political Islam with fundamentalist overtones, characterised by absolutist claims to truth. This highlights the delicate balance between updating Islamic jurisprudence and avoiding the unintended consequences of radical exegesis with adverse sociopolitical implications.

The hermeneutical implications of examining challenges to the apparent indication of the Qur'an seem applicable to the Sunna as well. Scrutinising all three challenges invites analogous investigation into the Sunna's authority. The striking resemblance between the Qur'an and Sunna, as historical texts, underlines interconnected hermeneutical implications. Moreover, concerns over the Sunna's transmission authenticity highlight the significance of textual variations and alterations during transmission. This challenge underscores the need for critical textual analysis and comparing versions to discern the most authentic content. In short, implications arising from challenges to the Qur'an's reliability exhibit congruence when applied to the Sunna. This intersection reinforces the importance of a critical, contextual approach to interpreting both, and underscores universal challenges that can compromise reliability.

Bibliography

Abisaab, Rula. *Converting Persia: Religion and Power in the Safavid Empire*. London: I.B. Tauris, 2004.

Amir-Moezzi, Mohammad Ali. *The Divine Guide in Early Shi'ism: The Sources of Esotericism in Islam*. Translated by David Streight. New York: State University of New York Press, 1994.

70 Amina Wadud, *Qur'an and Woman: Rereading the Sacred Text from a Woman's Perspective* (Oxford: Oxford University Press, 1999).

Amir-Moezzi, Mohammad Ali. *The Silent Qur'an & the Speaking Qur'an: Scriptural Sources of Islam between History and Fervor*. Translated by Eric L. Ormsby. New York: Columbia University Press, 2016.

Amir-Moezzi, Mohammad Ali. 'The *Tafsīr* of al-Ḥibarī (d. 286/899): Qur'anic Exegesis and Early Shiʿi Esotericism'. In *The Study of Shiʿi Islam: History, Theology and Law*, edited by Farhad Daftary and Gurdofarid Miskinzoda, 113–34. London: I.B. Tauris in association with the Institute of Ismaili Studies, 2014.

al-Anṣārī, Murtaḍā. *Farāʾid al-uṣūl*. Qom: Muʾassasat al-Nashr al-Islāmī, 1986.

al-Anṣārī, Murtaḍā. *Farāʾid al-uṣūl*. Edited by Muḥammad Bāqir al-Bihbūdī. Qom: Majmaʿ al-Fikr al-Islāmī, 1998.

al-Astarābādī, Muḥammad Amīn. *al-Fawāʾid al-madaniyya*. Qom: Muʾassasat al-Nashr al-Islāmī al-Tābiʿ li-Jamāʿat al-Mudarrisīn, 2005.

al-ʿAyyāshī, Muḥammad b. Masʿūd. *Tafsīr al-ʿAyyāshī: A Fourth/Tenth Century Shīʿī Commentary on the Qurʾan*. Translated by Nazmina Dhanji. Edited by Wahid M. Amin. Birmingham: AMI Press, 2020.

Bahjatī, ʿAbdulkarīm. *Hamgām bā waḥy: tafsīr-e tanzīlī*. Qom: Muʾassasa-yi Tamhīd, 2019.

al-Baḥrānī, Yūsuf. *al-Ḥadāʾiq al-nāḍira fī aḥkām al-ʿiṭra al-ṭāhira*. Qom: Muʾassasat al-Nashr al-Islāmī, n.d.

Bar-Asher, Meir M. *Scripture and Exegesis in Early Imāmī Shiism*. Leiden: Brill, 1999.

Bata, Hashim. *Exploring the Mind of God: An Introduction to Shiʿite Legal Epistemology*. Leiden: Brill, 2023.

Bell, Richard. *The Qurʾān: Translated, with a Critical Re-arrangement of the Surahs*. Edinburgh: T&T Clark, 1937.

Calder, Norman. 'Doubt and Prerogative: The Emergence of an Imāmī Shīʿī Theory of *Ijtihād*'. *Studia Islamica* 70 (1989): 55–78.

Furāt b. Ibrāhīm b. Furāt al-Kūfī. *Tafsīr Furāt al-Kufī*. Tehran: Vizārat-i Irshād, 1988.

Gleave, Robert. *Scripturalist Islam: The History and Doctrines of the Akhbārī Shīʿī School*. Leiden: Brill, 2007.

al-Ḥurr al-ʿĀmilī, Muḥammad b. Ḥasan. *al-Fawāʾid al-Ṭūsiyya*. Qom: Maktabat al-Maḥallātī, 2002.

al-Ḥurr al-ʿĀmilī, Muḥammad b. Ḥasan. *Tafṣīl wasāʾil al-shīʿa ilā taḥṣīl masāʾil al-sharʿiyya*. Qom: Muʾassasat Āl al-Bayt li-Iḥyāʾ al-Turāth, 2008.

al-Īrawānī, Bāqir. *Durūs tamhīdiyya fī fiqh al-istidlāl*. Qom: al-Markaz al-ʿĀlamī li-l-Dirāsāt al-Islāmiyya, 2004.

Jafri, S. Husain M. *Origins and Early Development of Shiʿa Islam*. London: Longman, 1979.

al-Jaṣṣāṣ, Abū Bakr Aḥmad b. ʿAlī al-Rāzī. *Aḥkām al-Qurʾān*. Beirut: Dār al-Iḥyāʾ al-Turāth al-ʿArabī, 1992.

al-Jawād al-Kāẓimī, Fāḍil. *Masālik al-afhām ilā āyāt al-aḥkām*. Edited by Muḥammad Bāqir Sharīf Zādeh. Tehran: Intishārāt-e Murtaḍawī, 1945.

Kadivar, Mohsen. *Blasphemy and Apostasy in Islam: Debates in Shi'a Law*. Translated by Hamid Mavani. Edinburgh: Edinburgh University Press, 2021.

al-Khū'ī, al-Sayyid Abū al-Qāsim al-Mūsawī. *Minhāj al-ṣālihīn*. Qom: Mehr, 1981.

al-Khurāsānī, Muḥammad Kāẓim. *Kifāyat al-uṣūl*. Edited by 'Abbās 'Alī al-Zāri'ī al-Sabzawārī. Qom: Mu'assasat Āl al-Bayt li-Iḥyā' al-Turāth, n.d.

al-Kulaynī, Muḥammad b. Ya'qūb. *al-Kāfī*. Edited by Muḥammad Ja'far Shams al-Dīn. Tehran: Dār al-Kutub al-Islāmiyya, 1987.

al-Kulaynī, Muḥammad b. Ya'qūb. *al-Kāfī*. Edited by Muḥammad Ḥusayn al-Darāyatī. Qom: Dār al-Ḥadīth, 2008.

al-Kulaynī, Muḥammad b. Ya'qūb. *Uṣūl al-Kāfī*. Edited by 'Alī Akbar al-Ghaffārī. 5th ed. Qom: Dār al-Kutub al-Islāmiyya, 1944.

al-Mar'ashī al-Najafī, Shihāb al-Dīn. 'Risālat manhaj al-rashād fī tarjamat al-fāḍil al-Jawād'. In Fāḍil Jawād al-Kāẓimī, *Masālik al-afhām ilā āyāt al-aḥkām*, 4 vols., edited by Muṣṭafā Murtazawī, 1:8. Qom: al-Maktaba al-Murtazawiyya, 1986.

Mīrzā 'Alīzādeh. 'Fiqh al-Qur'ān Rāwandī'. In *Jarayān-shināsī-yi tafāsīr-i fiqhī: tārīkh, taṭavvur va-namuneh-hā*, edited by Muḥammad 'Alī Mahdavī Rād, 149. Mashhad: Dāneshgāh-e 'Ulūm-e Islāmī Razavī, 1970.

al-Muqaddas al-Ardabīlī. *Zubdat al-bayān fī aḥkām al-Qur'ān*. Edited by Muḥammad al-Bāqir al-Bahbūdī. Tehran: al-Maktaba al-Murtaḍawiyya, n.d.

Muslim b. al-Ḥajjāj. *Kitāb Ṣaḥīḥ Muslim*. Edited by Muḥammad Fu'ād 'Abd al-Bāqī. Beirut: Dār Iḥyā' al-Turāth al-'Arabī, 1955.

al-Muṣṭafawī, al-Sayyid Muḥammad Kāẓim. *al-Qawā'id: mi'at qā'ida fiqhiyya ma'nan wa-madrakan wa-mawridan*. Qom: Mu'assasat al-Nashr al-Islāmī, 2015.

al-Najafī, Muḥammad Ḥasan b. Bāqir b. 'Abd al-Raḥīm. *Jawāhir al-kalām fī sharḥ Sharā'i' al-Islām*. Beirut: Dār Iḥyā' al-Turāth al-'Arabī, 1983.

al-Narāqī, al-Mawlā Muḥammad Mahdī. *Anīs al-mujtahidīn*. Qom: Mu'assasat Būstān-i Kutub, 2009.

al-Nasā'ī, Aḥmad b. Shu'ayb. *al-Sunan al-kubrā*. Edited by Ḥasan 'Abd al-Mun'im Shalabī. Beirut: Mu'assasat al-Risāla, 2001.

Naṣiḥyān, 'Alī Aṣghar. 'Aḥkām al-Qur'ān-i Muḥammad b. Sā'ib al-Kalbī'. In *Jarayān-shināsī-yi tafāsīr-i fiqhī: tārīkh, taṭavvur va-namuneh-hā*, edited by Muḥammad 'Alī Mahdavī Rād, 35–44. Mashhad: Dānishgāh-i 'Ulūm-i Islāmī-i Razavī, 1970.

Newman, Andrew J. 'The Nature of the Akhbārī/Uṣūlī Dispute in Late Ṣafawid Iran. Part 1: 'Abdallāh al-Samāhijī's "*Munyat al-Mumārisīn*"'. *Bulletin of the School of Oriental and African Studies* 55, no. 1 (1992): 22–51.

Newman, Andrew J. 'The Nature of the Akhbārī/Uṣūlī Dispute in Late Ṣafawid Iran. Part 2: The Conflict Reassessed'. *Bulletin of the School of Oriental and African Studies* 55, no. 2 (1992): 250–61.

Newman, Andrew J. *Twelver Shiism: Unity and Diversity in the Life of Islam, 632 to 1722*. Edinburgh: Edinburgh University Press, 2021.

Pūr, Mahdī ʿAlī. *Tārīkh ʿilm al-uṣūl*. Translated by ʿAlī Ẓāhir. Beirut: Dār al-Walāʾ, 2010.

al-Qummī, Abū Jaʿfar Muḥammad b. ʿAlī b. al-Ḥusayn b. Mūsā. *ʿUyūn akhbār al-Riḍā*. Edited by Ḥusayn al-Aʿlamī. Beirut: Muʾassasat al-Aʿlamī li-l-Maṭbūʿāt, 1984.

al-Qummī, ʿAlī b. Ibrāhīm. *Tafsīr al-Qummī*. Qom: Muʾassasat Dār al-Kitāb li-l-Ṭibāʿa wa-l-Nashr, 1984.

al-Qummī, Mīrzā Abū al-Qāsim al-Jīlānī. *al-Qawānīn al-muḥkama fī uṣūl al-mutqana*. Beirut: Dār al-Murtaḍā, 2009.

al-Rāwandī, Quṭb al-Dīn Saʿīd b. Hibat Allāh. *Fiqh al-Qurʾān*. Qom: Muʾassasat Āl al-Bayt li-Iḥyāʾ al-Turāth, 2003.

al-Shīrāzī, Ibrāhīm b. ʿAlī al-Fayrūzabādī. *al-Lumaʿ fī uṣūl al-fiqh*. Rabat: Dār al-Ḥadīth al-Kattāniyya, 2013.

Stewart, Devin J. *Islamic Legal Orthodoxy: Twelver Shiite Responses to the Sunni Legal System*. Salt Lake City: University of Utah Press, 1998.

al-Suyūrī, al-Miqdād b. ʿAbd Allāh. *Kanz al-ʿirfān fī fiqh al-Qurʾān*. 2 vols. Tehran: Intisharāt-i Murtaḍawī, 1964.

al-Ṭabrisī, Aḥmad b. ʿAlī. *al-Iḥtijāj ʿalā Ahl al-Lujāj*. Mashhad, 1983.

al-Ṭabrisī, al-Faḍl b. al-Ḥasan. *Majmaʿ al-bayān fī tafsīr al-Qurʾān*. Beirut: Muʾasassat al-Aʿlamī li-l-Maṭbūʿāt, 1995.

al-Tabrīzī, al-Mīrzā Mūsā. *Awthaq al-wasāʾil fī sharḥ al-rasāʾil*. Qom: Muʾassasat Āl al-Bayt, 1949.

al-Ṭaḥāwī, Aḥmad b. Muḥammad b. Salāma. *Aḥkām al-Qurʾān al-karīm*. Istanbul: Markaz al-Buḥūth al-Islāmiyya, 1998.

al-Ṭūsī, Abū Jaʿfar Muḥammad b. al-Ḥasan. *al-Tibyān fī tafsīr al-Qurʾān*. 10 vols. Qom: al-Nashr al-Islāmī, 1992.

Wadud, Amina. *Qurʾan and Woman: Rereading the Sacred Text from a Woman's Perspective*. Oxford: Oxford University Press, 1999.

al-Zarkashī, Badr al-Dīn Muḥammad b. ʿAbd Allāh. *al-Burhān fī ʿulūm al-Qurʾān*. Cairo: Maktabat Dār al-Turāth, 1984.

PART 3

Interpretation of Regulative Verses

CHAPTER 8

Āyāt al-Aḥkām in Early Ibāḍī Thought

Nora K. Schmid

1 Introduction

This chapter discusses the role of *āyāt al-aḥkām*, the Qur'an's legal verses, in Ibāḍī doctrine and theology during the formative period of Ibāḍī thought (second/eighth and third/ninth centuries).[1] I ask how early Ibāḍīs imagined the implementation of the *aḥkām* verses and what doctrinal importance they attributed to their enactment. I argue that early Ibāḍīs were committed to the idea that Qur'anic regulations could be applied by the believers directly to their own lives, based on an unmediated literal understanding of the text. As Robert Gleave has pointed out, the 'literal meaning' is effectively a construct.[2] Believing in the literal meaning of a text is tantamount to believing that the text 'has a meaning which is ingrained in its structure'.[3] When I argue that the Ibāḍīs strove to enact the Qur'anic text according to its literal meaning, I understand this to refer to 'whatever is immediate in the mind of the hearer'.[4] While this idea has intuitive appeal, it needs also to be recognised that detecting the literal meaning 'requires a series of interpretative acts'.[5] Despite this caveat, a belief in the existence of an unmediated understanding of the Qur'an's meaning and in the possibility of its full enactment informs the approach of the Ibāḍī texts analysed in this chapter. Early Ibāḍī scholars believed that, for the individual to remain a believer, and, in the same vein, for

---

1 This chapter is based on a paper I delivered in the framework of the 'Inaugural Qur'anic Conference: Regulative Verses of the Qur'ān (*āyāt al-aḥkām*)', convened at the Al-Mahdi Institute in Birmingham, UK (27 April 2023), and it reflects the state of research in 2023/early 2024. I am grateful to Dr Seyed Fatemi and the members of the AMI for their invitation. The research and writing of this chapter were carried out in the framework of the project Qur'anic Commentary: An Integrative Paradigm, funded by the European Research Council (ERC) under the European Union's Horizon 2020 research and innovation programme (grant agreement no. 771047). I would like to thank Robert Gleave, Joseph Lowry, Devin Stewart, and Shawkat Toorawa for their helpful comments on earlier drafts of this chapter.

2 Robert Gleave, *Islam and Literalism: Literal Meaning and Interpretation in Islamic Legal Theory* (Edinburgh: Edinburgh University Press, 2012), 25 and ch. 1, passim.

3 Ibid., 1.

4 Ibid., 10.

5 Ibid., 16.

 | HTTPS://DOI.ORG/10.1163/9789004755567-010

the ruler to remain legitimate, Qur'anic verses needed to be implemented to the letter.

My exploration focuses on three case studies covering three different genres: sermons, epistles, and exegesis. I first focus on the ideas about *aḥkām* verses expressed in the 'sermons' or 'orations' (*khuṭab*, sing. *khuṭba*) that Abū Ḥamza (Yaḥyā b. al-Muhktār, or al-Mukhtār b. ʿAwf, d. 130/748) addressed to the people of the Hijaz. They have been preserved in various historical and philological works, among them al-Ṭabarī's *Tārīkh* and al-Jāḥiẓ's *al-Bayān wa-l-tabyīn*.[6] Abū Ḥamza, who originated from Majazz, close to Sohar in what is now Oman, but whose tribe had moved to Basra, was one of the leaders of the first Ibāḍī revolt against the Umayyads, in the years 747–48.[7] The different versions of Abū Ḥamza's sermons display a great deal of variety, and the question of authenticity has accordingly been repeatedly raised by scholars.[8] Attribution of the ser-

6 al-Jāḥiẓ, *al-Bayān wa-l-tabyīn*, 4 vols., ed. ʿAbd al-Salām Muḥammad Hārūn (Cairo: Maktabat al-Khānjī, 1998), 2:122–25; al-Ṭabarī, *Tārīkh al-rusul wa-l-mulūk*, ed. as *Annales quos scripsit Abu Djafar Mohammed Ibn Djarir at-Tabari*, prima series, 6 vols., secunda series, 3 vols., tertia series, 4 vols., ed. Michael Jan de Goeje (Leiden: Brill, 1879–1901), [secunda series] 3:2008, 2009, 2009–11; trans. as *The History of al-Ṭabarī (Taʾrīkh al-rusul waʾl-mulūk)*, vol. 27, *The ʿAbbāsid Revolution*, trans. John Alden Williams (Albany: State University of New York Press, 1985), 113–14, 115, 115–17. I have modified Williams' translations where it seemed necessary. Further versions of some of Abū Ḥamza's sermons are also transmitted in Ibn ʿAbd Rabbihi's (d. 328/940) *al-ʿIqd al-farīd*, Abū al-Faraj al-Iṣfahānī's (d. 356/967) *Kitāb al-Aghānī*, and Ibn Abī al-Ḥadīd's (d. 655/1257) *Sharḥ Nahj al-balāgha*. Besides Sunnī works, the sermons have been preserved in Abū al-ʿAbbās Aḥmad b. Saʿīd al-Darjīnī's (d. ca. 670/1271–72) *Kitāb Ṭabaqāt al-mashāʾikh bi-l-Maghrib*.

7 On Abū Ḥamza and his political activities, see al-Ṭabarī, *Tārīkh*, [secunda series] 3:1981–84, 2006–14. On the uprising in south-west Arabia, see John C. Wilkinson, *Ibâḍism: Origins and Early Development in Oman* (Oxford: Oxford University Press, 2010), 177–83.

8 Abū Ḥamza's sermons have garnered considerable scholarly interest. See Stephan Dähne, *Reden der Araber: Die politische ḫuṭba in der klassischen arabischen Literatur* (Frankfurt am Main: Peter Lang, 2001), 17–19, 102–7, 212–28, and passim; Stephan Dähne, 'Zu den *ḫutab* des Abū Ḥamza aš-Šārī in der klassischen arabischen Literatur', in *Erlesenes: Sonderheft der Halleschen Beiträge zur Orientwissenschaft anläßlich des 19. Kongresses der Union Européenne d'Arabisants et Islamisants*, ed. Walter Beltz and Sebastian Günther (Halle: Institut für Orientalistik, 1998), 30–45; Stephan Dähne, 'Qur'anic Wording in Political Speeches in Classical Arabic Literature', *Journal of Qur'anic Studies* 3, no. 2 (2001): 1–13; Sergueï A. Frantsouzoff, 'Les Ibaḍites du Ḥaḍramawt: Quelques suggestions généalogiques et historiographiques', in *L'Ibadisme dans les sociétés de l'Islam médiéval: Modèles et interactions*, ed. Cyrille Aillet (Berlin: De Gruyter, 2018), 63–71; Tahera Qutbuddin, *Arabic Oration: Art and Function* (Leiden: Brill, 2019), 361–62 and passim. Since I submitted the final version of this chapter, two studies on Abū Ḥamza's sermons have appeared that could not be considered in the following analysis: Andrew Marsham, 'Wealth and the Image of the Umayyads in the Sermons Attributed to Abū Ḥamza (d. 748)', in *Between Rebels and Rulers in the Early Islamicate World: Power, Contention and Identity*, ed. Hannah-Lena Hagemann and Alasdair

mon fragments to the historical Abū Ḥamza is, however, of little importance in the present context. For my purposes here, it is sufficient that they were credibly attributed to an early Ibāḍī historical figure and recorded at an early date – by the third/ninth century at the latest.

I compare the perspective on *aḥkām* verses that emerges from Abū Ḥamza's sermons with that of Sālim b. Dhakwān, as expressed in his 'Epistle' or *Sīra*.[9] The *sīra* was an important genre through which Ibāḍī thought was articulated, and recent research has made available further, albeit slightly later, specimens.[10] Sālim b. Dhakwān's 'Epistle' displays intriguing parallels with Abū Ḥamza's sermons, although it is fundamentally an attack on radical Khārijism (to which Abū Ḥamza is still close), especially the views of Azraqīs and Najadāt. Crone and Zimmermann have described Sālim b. Dhakwān as a 'shadowy figure' of the second/eighth century.[11] Indeed, barely anything is known about him. He might be a local boy captured in Sīstān by the Arabs in the year 30/650, but the Ibāḍī biographer al-Shammākhī (d. 928/1522) assigns him to an altogether different generation. According to him, Sālim b. Dhakwān would have flourished in the second half of the second/eighth century. Later Ibāḍī authors even mention that he flourished in the fourth/tenth or fifth/eleventh century.[12] While Sālim b. Dhakwān's identity and the time when he lived cannot be established with any certainty, it is plausible to assume that the 'Epistle' encapsulates an early stage of Ibāḍī identity formation. The dates of the 'Epistle' that have been proposed by scholars so far range from 72/691 to the period between 133/750 and 185/800; most scholars suggest a date in the first half of the second/eighth century.[13]

Grant (Edinburgh: Edinburgh University Press, 2024), 265–90; Enki Baptiste, 'La *khuṭba* d'Abū Ḥamza al-Shārī: soulèvement ibāḍite et rhétorique de la contestation en péninsule Arabique au second siècle de l'Islam. Traduction commentée d'une version inédite du sermon', *Al-ʿUṣūr al-Wusṭā* 32 (2024): 165–249.

9 For an edition, translation, and study of the 'Epistle', see Patricia Crone and Fritz Zimmermann, *The Epistle of Sālim ibn Dhakwān* (Oxford: Oxford University Press, 2001). The work is also studied in Michael Cook, *Early Muslim Dogma: A Source-Critical Study* (Cambridge: Cambridge University Press 1981), 1–106; and Wilkinson, *Ibâḍism*, 205–10.

10 See, for example, the three epistles to the people of Mansura, Khwarazm, and Khurasan, composed in the fourth/tenth and fifth/eleventh centuries, edited and translated by Abdulrahman Al-Salimi in *Ibāḍism East of Mesopotamia: Early Iran, Central Asia and India* (Berlin: Klaus Schwarz, 2016).

11 Crone and Zimmermann, *Epistle*, 11.

12 Ibid. The dating is also discussed by Adam R. Gaiser, 'Ibn Dhakwān, Sālim', in *Encyclopaedia of Islam, THREE*, ed. Kate Fleet, Gudrun Krämer, Denis Matringe, John Nawas, and Devin J. Stewart (Leiden: Brill, 2020), http://dx.doi.org.ezproxy-prd.bodleian.ox.ac.uk/10.1163/1573-3912_ei3_COM_32133; and Wilkinson, *Ibâḍism*, 205–6.

13 Gaiser, 'Ibn Dhakwān'.

Abū Ḥamza can be considered an earlier intermediary figure between the Khārijī *shurāt* or 'sellers' (as they called themselves) and the Ibāḍīs;[14] Sālim b. Dhakwān rejects militant Khārijism, as mentioned above, but still pushes for active warfare, *jihād*, instead of quietism, *quʿūd*. John Wilkinson has argued that this indicates that the 'Epistle' was composed at a time before the Ibāḍīs had first 'gone out', that is, before the revolt in southern Arabia in which Abū Ḥamza was involved.[15] This conclusion, however, is not certain, and it is difficult to establish whether the 'Epistle' predates or postdates Abū Ḥamza's sermons. What we can observe is that there are noteworthy parallels between the sermons and the 'Epistle'. Above all, Abū Ḥamza's and Sālim b. Dhakwān's approaches to the *aḥkām* verses are comparable in that both demand absolute and uncompromising commitment to the letter of scripture, and specifically to Qur'anic regulations.

Ibāḍī exegesis (*tafsīr*) displays similar tendencies to the ideas expressed in the sermons and 'Epistle', as demonstrated in the third, later case study: Ibāḍī *tafsīr* works emphasise the link between faith and acts, and they define righteous acts in light of Qur'anic *aḥkām* verses. Not many complete exegetical works by Ibāḍīs exist – Ibāḍīs mainly used Sunnī *tafsīr* works, and only very few Ibāḍī exegetes produced complete *tafsīr* works before the twentieth century.[16] One of them, however, dates to the third/ninth century: Hūd b. Muḥakkam's (more rarely: Muḥakkim or Muḥkim, d. ca. 290/903) *Tafsīr Kitāb Allāh al-ʿazīz*.[17] It is based on the *tafsīr* of the Basran scholar Yaḥyā b. Sallām (d. 199/815). Hūd, a Berber from north-eastern Algeria, came to know the work because nearly a century earlier, Ibn Sallām had taught exegesis in Qayrawān for a time. His work may have been transmitted orally until Hūd's time.[18] Hūd's own *tafsīr*

14 On the ambiguous relation of the Ibāḍīs to the *shurāt*, see Adam R. Gaiser, *Shurāt Legends, Ibāḍī Identities: Martyrdom, Asceticism, and the Making of an Early Islamic Community* (Columbia: University of South Carolina Press, 2016). Modern Ibāḍīs do not acknowledge links to the Khārijīs, but throughout history, Ibāḍīs looked back favourably on some early *shurāt* and fashioned their identity around them.

15 Wilkinson, *Ibâḍism*, 208.

16 For a historical survey of Ibāḍī exegesis, see İsmail Albayrak, *Approaches to Ibāḍī Exegetical Tradition* (Wiesbaden: Harrassowitz, 2020), 1–64.

17 Hūd b. Muḥakkam al-Hawwārī, *Tafsīr Kitāb Allāh al-ʿazīz*, ed. Bālḥājj b. Saʿīd al-Sharīfī (Beirut: Dār al-Gharb al-Islāmī, 1990). On Hūd b. Muḥakkam's *tafsīr*, see Albayrak, *Approaches*, 27–31; Josef van Ess, 'Untersuchungen zu einigen ibāḍitischen Handschriften', *Zeitschrift der Deutschen Morgenländischen Gesellschaft* 126, no. 1 (1976): 42–43; and Claude Gilliot, 'Le Commentaire Coranique de Hūd b. Muḥakkam/Muḥkim', *Arabica* 44, no. 2 (1997): 179–233.

18 On Yaḥyā b. Sallām, see the comments in the introduction of the editor of the *tafsīr*, Hūd b. Muḥakkam, *Tafsīr*, 1:21–22n3. Also commented on by Karen Bauer, *Gender Hierarchy in*

may well be an abridgement of Ibn Sallām's work, but it has important Ibāḍī elaborations and is characterised by noteworthy omissions.[19] This is especially true where doctrinal points are concerned, such as the relation between faith and works. Where these topics arise, Hūd himself has added to the *tafsīr*. An examination of some interpretations of *aḥkām* verses to which Abū Ḥamza and Sālim b. Dhakwān refer that appear in the *tafsīr* work yields significant continuities, although Hūd's *tafsīr* draws its own specific conclusions about the unbelief of those who do not successfully enact the commandments of Islamic Scripture.

The theological and doctrinal engagement with specific *aḥkām* verses and the notion of the 'judgement' or 'ruling' (*ḥukm*) of Islamic Scripture are pervasive in early Ibāḍī thought. The idea that Islamic Scripture can be directly enacted may be traced back to the birth hour of Khārijism. The Khārijīs who seceded from ʿAlī b. Abī Ṭālib (d. 40/661) after the Battle of Ṣiffīn (37/657) are said to have uttered the slogan 'Judgement belongs to God alone!' (*lā ḥukma illā li-llāh*). For this reason, they became known as the 'Muḥakkima'. The secession occurred in reaction to ʿAlī's decision to allow arbitrators to settle the dispute between him and Muʿāwiya b. Abī Sufyān (d. 60/680). The Khārijī rebels demanded that the conflict be settled on the basis of scripture alone, and in so doing insisted on the authority of the Qur'an.[20] Despite obvious continuities relating to the ideal of a literal enactment of what scripture says, shifts and accommodations can be observed over the course of time, as Ibāḍī identity formation progressed. The observations that follow are relevant not only to the study of early Ibāḍī religious thought but also to the early development of Ibāḍī legal ideas, a field of study that has only recently started to flourish.[21]

---

the Qurʾān: Medieval Interpretations, Modern Responses (Cambridge: Cambridge University Press, 2015), 113.

19 See Miklos Muranyi, 'The *Tafsīr* of Hūd b. Muḥakkim al-Hawwārī (d. in the 2nd Half of the 3rd/9th Century) and Yaḥyā b. Sallām al-Baṣrī (124/742–200/815): A Synoptical and Intertextual Approach', in *Local and Global Ibadi Identities*, ed. Yohei Kondo and Angeliki Ziaka (Hildesheim: Georg Olms Verlag, 2019), 41–56. Some examples are also given by Bālḥājj b. Saʿīd al-Sharīfī, the editor of Hūd's *tafsīr*. See Hūd b. Muḥakkam, *Tafsīr*, 1:32–38.

20 On the slogan and scriptural authority, see Gerald R. Hawting, 'The Significance of the Slogan *Lā Ḥukm^{a} Illā Lillāh* and the References to the *Ḥudūd* in the Traditions about the Fitna and the Murder of 'Uthmān', *Bulletin of the School of Oriental and African Studies* 41, no. 3 (1978): 453–63.

21 For an overview of the early development of Ibāḍī law and a discussion of previous scholarship, see Ersilia Francesca, 'Constructing an Identity: The Development of Ibadi Law', in *On Ibadism*, ed. Angeliki Ziaka (Hildesheim: Georg Olms Verlag, 2014), 109–33; Ersilia Francesca, 'Tracing the History of Ibāḍī Law and Jurisprudence', *Journal of Islamic Law* 2 (2021): 204–11; Knut S. Vikør, 'Ibadism and Law in Historical Contexts', *Oñati Socio-Legal*

New legal texts continue to be discovered, and in recent years, critical editions have made existing material available.[22]

2 *Āyāt al-Aḥkām* and *Ḥukm al-Qurʾān* in Abū Ḥamza's Sermons[23]

Abū Ḥamza revolted in the last years of Umayyad rule, specifically during the reign of Marwān II (r. 127–32/744–50). The revolt broke out in southern Arabia under the leadership of ʿAbd Allāh b. Yaḥyā al-Kindī, also named Ṭālib al-Ḥaqq ('Seeker of Truth/Right/Justice'[24]). It had a very strong tribal dimension but was conducted with the backing of Basran Ibāḍīs. Abū Ḥamza was one of the major figures who supported Ṭālib al-Ḥaqq in his uprising, another important supporter being Balj b. ʿUqba. They conquered Mecca and then Medina. After an occupation that lasted only three months, Abū Ḥamza and his men were defeated by an Umayyad military detachment under the command of ʿAbd al-Malik b. Muḥammad b. ʿAṭiyya. All three leaders of the uprising, Ṭālib al-Ḥaqq, Balj b. ʿUqba, and Abū Ḥamza, were killed.

In sermon fragments and in historical reports, Abū Ḥamza and his followers appear as literal interpreters of Qurʾanic *aḥkām* verses. A historical report preserved in al-Ṭabarī's *Tārīkh* is particularly telling. The report concerns a confrontation between Abū Ḥamza and his men and the Umayyad commander Ibn ʿAṭiyya shortly before Abū Ḥamza's final defeat. Abū Ḥamza asks his men to conduct a veritable inquisition on their Umayyad opponents:

> When Abū Ḥamza and Ibn ʿAṭiyya met [i.e. on the battlefield], Abū Ḥamza told his people, 'Don't fight them until you have questioned them.' They called out to Ibn ʿAṭiyya's men, 'What do you have to say about the Qurʾan and acting according to it (*mā taqūlūna fī l-qurʾāni wa-l-ʿamali bihi*)?' Ibn ʿAṭiyya shouted back, 'We put it deep into the saddlebag (*fī jawfi l-juwāliq*)!' They called out, 'What do you say about the property of the orphan?' He replied, 'We consume

Series 10, no. 5 (2020): 963–65. See also the contributions in Barbara Michalak-Pikulska and Reinhard Eisener, eds., *Ibadi Jurisprudence: Origins, Developments and Cases* (Hildesheim: Olms, 2015).

22 See, for example, Abdulrahman Al-Salimi, *Early Islamic Law in Basra in the 2nd/8th Century* (Leiden: Brill, 2018). Further references are mentioned in Francesca, 'Tracing the History', 207n4.

23 The following discussion of Abū Ḥamza's sermons is based on Nora K. Schmid, *The Ascetic Qurʾan and Its Kharijite Readers* (Leiden: Brill, 2026), ch. 8.

24 Wilkinson, *Ibâḍism*, 178.

> his property (*na'kulu mālahu*) and we engage in debauchery with his mother (*nafjuru bi-ummihi*)!' These are only some of the things I have heard that they questioned them about. When they had heard their answers, they fought with them until evening. Then they called out, 'Woe to you, Ibn 'Aṭiyya, God has made the night for rest (*qad ja'ala al-layla sakanan*), so you rest and we'll rest!' But he refused and fought them until he had killed them.[25]

The story contrasts two groups of men: one group follows the Qur'an and enacts it, namely, the followers of Abū Ḥamza. The Umayyads, in contrast, continually and brazenly transgress clear and well-known scriptural injunctions and *aḥkām*.

First, Abū Ḥamza's men ask whether their opponents act according to scripture (literally, *al-'amal bi-*), that is, whether they do as it says. The answer they receive is that the Umayyad men keep the Qur'an in their saddlebags. To understand this transgression of scripture, it is important to know that the Qur'an severely criticises the 'People of Scripture' in the Prophet's audience for superficial modes of engagement with their own scripture, the Torah. This is reflected in the simile or 'likeness' of the donkey in Q. 62:5:

> The likeness of those who have been loaded (*ḥummilū*) with the Torah and then have not carried it (*lam yaḥmilūhā*), is as the likeness of an ass carrying books. Evil is the likeness of the people who deny the truth of God's signs. God does not guide people who do wrong.[26]

The verse criticises the Jews for carrying the Torah around without acting according to it. The simile has been understood by exegetes to mean that the Jews failed to keep the commandments. Mujāhid, for example, adduces the simile to explain the reference in Q. 2:65 to the Jews who ignored the Sabbath and whom God tells, 'Be apes, despised' (*kūnū qiradatan khāsi'īn*).[27] Both verses linked in this interpretation deal with scriptural transgressions. The implication of the story about Abū Ḥamza is that his and his men's enemies carry the Qur'an around without truly having it in mind and acting in accordance with it, just like the Jews in Q. 62:5.

---

25 al-Ṭabarī, *Tārīkh*, [secunda series] 3:2013; Williams, *History*, 27:119. Translation modified.

26 Qur'an translations here and in the following are based on Alan Jones, trans., *The Qur'ān* (Cambridge: Gibb Memorial Trust, 2007). I have modified Jones' translations where it seemed necessary to me.

27 See Gleave, *Islam and Literalism*, 77–78. I thank Robert Gleave for alerting me to this discussion.

The next scriptural transgression is devouring what belongs rightfully to orphans. One thinks of *aḥkām* verses such as Q. 4:2, in which the root *ʾ-k-l* is used in the context of rulings concerning the property of orphans – indeed, the admonition not to devour the property of orphans is prominent in the Qurʾan:

> Give orphans their property; and do not substitute the bad for the good, nor devour their property by adding it to your own. That is a great sin (*wa-ātū l-yatāmā amwālahum wa-lā tatabaddalū l-khabītha bi-l-ṭayyibi wa-lā taʾkulū amwālahum ilā amwālikum innahu kāna ḥūban kabīrā*).

Abū Ḥamza's reference to sexual relations with the mother may reflect Q. 4:15–16, which discuss illicit sexual relations. However, the root *f-j-r* is not used in the Qurʾan in this context.[28]

The Umayyad soldiers commit yet another transgression of scripture when they decline to stop fighting at night and rest because God 'made the night a rest' (*wa-jaʿala l-layla sakanan*) in Q. 6:96:

> He splits the sky in the morning, and He has made the night a rest (*wa-jaʿala l-layla sakanan*), and the sun and moon as a reckoning. That is what the Mighty and the Knowing has determined.

The account here refers to the hymnic passage in Q. 6:95–99, specifically to Q. 6:96. By not resting, the Umayyad soldiers go against what God has determined through His intervention in creation. Abū Ḥamza thus calls them to follow a Qurʾanic principle, and they choose to violate it.

Al-Ṭabarī's account clearly contrasts the enactment of scriptural injunctions and regulations on the part of Abū Ḥamza's men with failure to do so on the part of the Umayyad military detachment sent against them. Each group stands for one of these behaviours. The story is carefully constructed to illustrate precisely this difference between the groups it purports to depict. Regardless of the historicity of this episode, the way the story is narrated suggests an awareness of the importance of scriptural enactment among early Ibāḍīs. This impression is confirmed by the sermons attributed to Abū Ḥamza.

Abū Ḥamza's sermons display ideas similar to those present in the encounter narrated by al-Ṭabarī: they reflect a relentless striving for the enactment of the Qurʾan's injunctions and regulations. In one of his sermons, Abū Ḥamza describes a situation of lawlessness and injustice as the background to the *khurūj* ('going out', whence the designation 'Khārijīs') that he and his

28 I am grateful to Joseph Lowry for pointing out this potential parallel.

companions performed. In this context, he brings up the notion of *ḥukm al-qurʾān* ('the judgement of the Qurʾan'):

> You know, people of Medina, that we did not go out (*lam nakhruj*) from our homes and leave behind our possessions arrogantly, recklessly, or foolishly, or in order to rule a kingdom with which we wish to enter into war, or out of an old blood revenge that impinged on our honour. When we saw that the lamps of truth had been extinguished, that the speaker of truth had been chastised, and that the one who stood up for justice was slain (*qutila al-qāʾimu bi-l-qisṭi*), the earth in all its breadth became too narrow for us. We heard a summoner calling us to obey the Merciful and the judgement of the Qurʾan (*ḥukm al-qurʾān*). We responded to the summoner of God: 'Those who do not answer God's summoner will not frustrate [Him] on earth' [Q. 46:32]. … Then we met your [i.e. the Medinan] men at Qudayd, and we summoned them to obey the Merciful and the judgement of the Qurʾan (*ḥukm al-qurʾān*). They, however, summoned us to obey Satan and the judgement of the clan of Marwān (*ḥukm Āl Marwān*). By God, how different is guidance from transgression![29]

Abū Ḥamza describes his men's calling to obey 'the judgement of the Qurʾan' (*ḥukm al-qurʾān*).[30] Once again, two groups are contrasted: Abū Ḥamza's followers summon their opponents to enact scriptural law, while their opponents in turn summon Abū Ḥamza's men to follow the Umayyad caliph Marwān's law.

Scriptural enactment is clearly also an important factor in determining political legitimacy for Abū Ḥamza. This can be gleaned from his longest sermon, in the version preserved by al-Jāḥiẓ. Starting with the Prophet, Abū Ḥamza goes through the caliphs, one by one, lauding or criticising them, in accord with the degree to which they did or did not adhere to scripture. This has been identified as a *topos* in Ibāḍī literature. Sālim b. Dhakwān, discussed below, introduces the same 'caliphs *topos*'.[31] This *topos*, according to Crone and Zimmermann, 'takes the form of a survey of Muslim sovereigns from the Prophet onwards; it is always done reign by reign, and it is characterized by

29 al-Ṭabarī, *Tārīkh*, [secunda series] 3:2009–10; Williams, *History*, 27:115. The translation I offer here is only very loosely based on Williams'.

30 Alternative translations into English would be 'authority of the Qurʾan', in the sense of scriptural authority, or 'rule of the Qurʾan', but 'judgement of the Qurʾan' seems more appropriate because Abū Ḥamza clearly has the *aḥkām* verses in mind when he summons his listeners to obey scripture.

31 On the 'caliphs *topos*', see Crone and Zimmermann, *Epistle*, 17. I am grateful to Hannah Hagemann for drawing my attention to the *topos*.

transition phrases. ... its precise form depends on the agenda of the speech or epistle in which it is found.'[32]

Abū Ḥamza says about Abū Bakr and ʿUmar:

> He [Abū Bakr] killed the apostates, and he acted according to the Scripture and the *sunna* (*ʿamila bi-l-kitābi wa-l-sunnati*). He passed away – may God have mercy on him. Then ʿUmar b. al-Khaṭṭāb came into power – may God have mercy on him – and he followed the model of his predecessor and acted according to the Scripture and the *sunna* (*ʿamila bi-l-kitābi wa-l-sunnati*).[33]

The sermon about Abū Ḥamza's *khurūj* discussed above focused on the enactment of the Qurʾan alone. In this sermon, Abū Ḥamza mentions 'scripture' (*al-kitāb*) alongside the *sunna*. This might seem surprising at first, given that Khārijīs and early Ibāḍīs are often said to have rejected *ḥadīth* and to have adhered to what Josef van Ess calls 'fundamental scripturalism'.[34] A century after Abū Ḥamza, al-Shāfiʿī (d. 204/820) in his short treatise *Jimāʿ al-ʿilm* would refer to one group of Muslims who outright rejected *ḥadīth*. Al-Shāfiʿī does not specify their identity, but Hüseyin Hansu has argued that he likely referred to Khārijīs, not Muʿtazilīs as scholars have long held.[35] There is also evidence which stems from within the Ibāḍī tradition: a letter to Caliph ʿAbd al-Malik b. Marwān (d. 86/705) which ʿAbd Allāh b. Ibāḍ is said to have written in 76/695, but which is arguably an eighth-century apocryphal composition,[36] similarly rejects the authority of *ḥadīth*.[37] As Aisha Musa has observed, the letter, likely composed before al-Shāfiʿī's *Risāla*, vehemently criticises the use

---

32 Crone and Zimmermann, *Epistle*, 17. In Sālim b. Dhakwān's 'Epistle', another *topos*, the 'mission *topos*', precedes the 'caliphs *topos*'. This *topos*, in turn, became a standard feature of doctrinal 'epistles' by the late Umayyad period. See ibid., 16, 290; and Cook, *Early Muslim Dogma*, 7.

33 al-Jāḥiẓ, *al-Bayān*, 2:122–23.

34 See notably Josef van Ess, *Theologie und Gesellschaft im 2. und 3. Jahrhundert Hidschra: Eine Geschichte des religiösen Denkens im frühen Islam* (Berlin: De Gruyter, 1991), 1:38 ('neigten zu einem grundsätzlichen Skripturalismus').

35 Hüseyin Hansu, 'Debates on the Authority of Hadith in Early Islamic Intellectual History: Identifying al-Shāfiʿī's Opponents in *Jimāʿ al-ʿIlm*', *Journal of the American Oriental Society* 136, no. 3 (2016): 520–23. Hansu argues that al-Shāfiʿī may have held debates against Khārijīs and Ibāḍīs, among them a scholar named Maslak b. Ibāḍ. Ibid., 520n32.

36 Cook, *Early Muslim Dogma*, 66–67.

37 For this debate, see Josef van Ess, *Zwischen Ḥadīṯ und Theologie: Studien zum Entstehen prädestinatianischer Überlieferung* (Berlin: De Gruyter, 1975), 56; Aisha Y. Musa, *Ḥadīth as Scripture: Discussions on the Authority of Prophetic Traditions in Islam* (New York: Palgrave Macmillan, 2008), 37; and Hansu, 'Debates', 522.

of *ḥadīth*. It says about the Kufans that 'they abandoned the judgement of their Lord and took *ḥadīth* for their religion; and they claim that they have obtained knowledge from other than the Qur'an' (*wa-kharajū min ḥukmi rabbi-him wa-ttakhadhū l-aḥādītha dīnan wa-zaʿamū anna ʿindahum ʿilman aṣābūhu min ghayri l-qurʾāni*).[38]

Despite this evidence, the *sunna* and *ḥadīth* were not categorically rejected by all early Ibāḍīs who emphasised the 'judgement of the Qur'an' and enjoined their audience to act in accordance with the Qur'an. Abū Ḥamza's sermons and the texts discussed in this chapter illustrate this. However, it is noteworthy that the *sunna* mentioned in the sermon – however we may choose to interpret the term, for it may just be a reference to a form of communal memory – plays no role beyond being mentioned. When Abū Ḥamza discusses the successors of the first two caliphs, he only adduces Qur'anic verses and measures the caliphs' actions solely against Qur'anic injunctions. For example, he accuses the Umayyads of scriptural transgressions and of ruling and judging by 'that which has not been sent down by God':

> As for the Umayyads, they are an erring sect (*firqatu l-ḍalāli*). When they strike, they strike like tyrants. They take [people's property] on the basis of uncertain rulings in religious law (*yaʾkhudhūna bi-l-ẓanni*),[39] they pass judgement whimsically (*yaqḍūna bi-l-hawā*), they kill in anger (*yaqtulūna ʿalā l-ghaḍabi*), they judge through intermediates, and they take alms from places they should not be taken from and give them to people who have no right to them (*yaʾkhu-dhūna al-farīḍata min ghayri mawḍiʿihā wa-yaḍʿūnahā fī ghayri ahlihā*). God made clear to whom they are owed, and He established eight categories [of legitimate recipients]. He said, 'The alms are for the poor and the destitute, for those who work to collect them, and those whose hearts are to be reconciled, to free slaves, and debtors, for God's cause, and for the traveller – a duty imposed by God, and God is Knowing and Wise' [Q. 9:60]. The Umayyads invented a ninth category which is not among these and then took all the shares. They are a sect that judges by that which has not been sent down by God (*tilkumu l-firqatu al-ḥākimatu bi-ghayri mā anzala llāhu*) [cf. Q. 5:48, 49: *fa-/wa-ani ḥkum bayna-hum bi-mā anzala llāhu*].[40]

38 Cited by Musa, *Ḥadīth as Scripture*, 38. Translation slightly modified.

39 The phrase *yaʾkhudhūna bi-l-ẓanni* designates the failure of the Umayyads to have certain knowledge of what God's law allows believers to do or not do. *Ẓann* is an invalid basis for religious rulings. I am grateful to Joseph Lowry and Robert Gleave for their suggestions regarding the interpretation of this term.

40 al-Jāḥiẓ, *al-Bayān*, 2:124.

Q. 9:60 mentions eight categories of recipients of alms (*ṣadaqāt*). Abū Ḥamza condemns the Umayyads for transgressing this scriptural ruling and believes that they have therefore forfeited political legitimacy.

Aḥkām verses play an important role in Abū Ḥamza's thought world. The commitment to enact them is what serves to distinguish believers from unbelievers and legitimate rulers from tyrants. He repeatedly brings up the notion of *ḥukm al-qur'ān* as a shorthand for the doctrinal importance of *aḥkām* verses in shaping the believers' actions and beliefs.

3 Scripture as a Judge and Imam: the 'Epistle' of Sālim b. Dhakwān

The ideas that human acts should be based on scripture and that humans should accordingly also be judged by their implementation of scripture remained important in Ibāḍī religious thought and doctrine. In this regard, the *Sīra* or 'Epistle' of Sālim b. Dhakwān offers some interesting parallels to early Ibāḍī sermons like the ones discussed above. Crone and Zimmermann have detected some concrete phraseological parallels between the 'Epistle' and Abū Ḥamza's sermons.[41] The affinity of both genres, *khuṭba* and *sīra*, goes beyond similar phrasing and individual theological points: Crone and Zimmermann have called Sālim b. Dhakwān's 'Epistle' a 'pulpit manifesto', suggesting that it was originally intended for oral delivery. In its final, transmitted form, however, it is too long and theologically involved for it to have actually served as an oration.[42]

The 'Epistle' opens with exhortations such as the following:

> Take, then, the Scripture of God as your guideline, and heed what God has asked you to heed (*fa-'tammū bi-kitābi llāhi wa-ḥāfiẓū ʿalā mā staḥfaẓakum Allāhu*). God sent His Messenger to be obeyed and sent down His Scripture to be followed and to judge between people in their disagreements (*wa-anzala kitābahu li-yuttabaʿa wa-li-yaḥkuma bayna l-nāsi fīmā khtalafū fīhi*). ... Those who follow

41 Crone and Zimmermann, *Epistle*, 251–54 (passim – Abū Ḥamza's sermons are adduced alongside other Ibāḍī texts).

42 Ibid., 23–24. Other Ibāḍī epistles display a similar proximity to the oratory genre. For example, Al-Salimi has observed that Rāshid b. Saʿīd al-Yaḥmadī's (elected to the imamate in 425/1034) 'Epistle to the People of Mansura' is a 'manifesto', which occasionally addresses its readers as listeners and which displays a 'style characteristic of sermons'. See Al-Salimi, *Ibāḍism East of Mesopotamia*, 88–89.

> this Qur'an are dispensed by God from everything else; and from those who neglect it He will accept nothing else.[43]

Sālim b. Dhakwān exhorts the believers not merely to display a Qur'an-based piety. Rather, he infuses scripture itself with a surprisingly strong agency, the agency to judge. Crone and Zimmermann have pointed to one passage in the 'Epistle' which appears particularly 'scripturalist':

> So let yourselves be advised and guided by the Scripture of God, for he who is not guided by it will not be guided by anything else. It is through this Qur'an alone that you have been commanded (*fa-innakum lam tu'marū illā bi-hādhā l-qur'āni*), by it alone that your Prophet let himself be guided (*wa-lam yahtadi nabiyyukum illā bihi*), about it alone that you will be questioned (*wa-lan tus'alū illā ʿanhu*), and according to it alone that you will be exhorted (*wa-lan tūʿaẓū illā bihi*). Those who make the Scripture of God their judge and imam today (*fa-innahu man ḥakkama al-yawma kitāba llāhi wa-jaʿalahu imāman*), attending to its firm argument and clear command, will be confirmed by God 'with the firm word in this life and the next'.[44]

Crone and Zimmermann define a scripturalist as 'a person who regards the scripture as the only authoritative source of law and doctrine, everything else being fallible human reasoning or custom'.[45] The Prophetic model is de-emphasised in this passage insofar as Prophetic authority itself is scripture-based. Despite this statement, according to Crone and Zimmermann Sālim b. Dhakwān was not a scripturalist; he clearly acknowledged the authority of the *sunna*. It must be noted that the term *sunna* in the 'Epistle' does not always designate the Prophetic *sunna*. The term often refers to what Crone and Zimmermann, following Calder, call 'community *sunna*', the customs adopted and validated by the Muslims. Accordingly, one should probably not imagine a dichotomy between a position that accepts scripture alone as a source of authority and one that is based on the Qur'an and the *sunna*. Despite Sālim b. Dhakwān's references to and acknowledgement of the *sunna*, the entire 'Epistle' never cites even a single *ḥadīth* verbatim, and it endorses only one or two ideas and rulings derived from Prophetic *sunna* instead of the Qur'an.[46] The 'Epistle' abounds

43 Crone and Zimmermann, *Epistle*, 42–45 (at §§ 4–5). Translation slightly modified.
44 Ibid., 44–45 (at § 5). Translation slightly modified.
45 Ibid., 292.
46 Ibid.

with Qur'anic quotations and allusions.[47] Wilkinson accordingly argued that the Qur'an in the 'Epistle' is similar to the *Kitāb Allāh* of the Muḥakkima, in that it is 'virtually the whole basis' for the argument.[48] The Qur'an appears, as the passage quoted above states, as the judge and imam.

A similar scriptural agency emerges from other epistles, such as the 'Epistle to the People of Khurasan', a fourth/tenth-century work by an unknown author, which likely cites an earlier epistle by Wā'il b. Ayyūb al-Ḥaḍramī, who, in turn, flourished in the second/eighth century.[49] The 'Epistle to the People of Khurasan' reminds the addressees that 'the Qur'an is our imam' (*al-qur'ān imāmunā*) and advises that 'faith is not achieved through disobedience to God's obligations or through persisting in doing what God has made unlawful' (*wa-lā yathbutu l-īmānu bi-ntiqāṣi farā'iḍi llāhi wa-lā bi-l-muqāmi 'alā ḥarāmi llāhi*).[50]

Returning to the 'Epistle' of Sālim b. Dhakwān, the Prophet here appears primarily as a bequeather of scripture:

> The Messenger of God proceeded in the best manner of the previous prophets, may the blessings and the mercy of God be upon them. He bequeathed to you the Scripture (*awrathakum al-kitāba*).[51]

This is a noteworthy view of the Prophet, a very functional one, in a period when the Prophetic model and his normative practice became increasingly important in Sunnī legal discourse. To some degree, one may see how this normative model gains a greater importance in Sālim b. Dhakwān's thought than before. The 'Epistle' includes a discussion of previous rulers that parallels the survey found in Abū Ḥamza's sermons:

> 37 … He [Abū Bakr] took the Qur'an as an imam (*fa-ttakhadha l-qur'āna imāman*), followed the *sunna* of God's Prophet, and knew that when he would meet his Lord, who had put him in charge of the community of Muḥammad, may God's blessings and peace be upon him, He would question him about the state in which he had left it. So he acted rightly and adhered to justice (*al-'adl*) among them. …

47 On the 'dense Qur'anicity' of the 'Epistle', see ibid., 26–31.
48 Wilkinson, *Ibâḍism*, 207.
49 Al-Salimi, *Ibāḍism East of Mesopotamia*, 41.
50 'Epistle to the People of Khurasan', §9, ed. and trans. in Al-Salimi, *Ibāḍism East of Mesopotamia*, 49, 68. Translation slightly modified.
51 Crone and Zimmermann, *Epistle*, 72–73 (at §33). Translation slightly modified.

> 38 After consulting with the Muslims, he appointed ʿUmar b. al-Khaṭṭāb to succeed him as caliph. ʿUmar acted according to the Scripture of God (*fa-ʿamila bi-kitābi llāhi*), followed the *sunna* of God's Messenger, and adopted the *sunna* of Abū Bakr. But he was also confronted with cases which were not covered by Qurʾanic pronouncements or prior *sunna*, whether [received] from the Messenger of God, may God's blessing and peace be upon him, or instituted by Abū Bakr. He was the first to settle some matters of inheritance law; and when his governor in Syria wrote to him that many people were about to fall under the sway of wine and would not give it up without a strong deterrent, he [prescribed] eighty lashes as a deterrent. For many other problems, too, ʿUmar b. al-Khaṭṭāb instituted precedents (*sanna sunan*) as they arose after consulting with the Muslims and his independent reasoning (*ḥīna nazalat bihi ʿan mushāwarati l-muslimīn wa-ijtihādi raʾyihi*); and it is the duty of every Muslim to endorse them and enact them (*ḥaqqan ʿalā kulli muslimin an yarḍā bihā wa-yaʿmala bihā*). For God says, 'Obey God and obey the Messenger and those of you who have authority. If you quarrel with one another about anything, refer it to God and the Messenger if you believe in God and the Last Day. That is better, and fairer as a course' [Q. 4:59].[52]

The passage highlights the interplay between Qurʾanic scriptural authority, Prophetic *sunna*, and a cumulative 'community *sunna*'. Scripture is again attributed significant agency in that the Qurʾan functions as 'imam' to Abū Bakr. The belief in the importance of committed scriptural enactment remains unbroken from Abū Ḥamza to Sālim b. Dhakwān. Despite this, the 'Epistle' acknowledges – somewhat 'inconsistently', as Wilkinson observed[53] – that some legal cases could not be solved based on a direct and unmediated enactment of Qurʾanic *aḥkām* alone, because Islamic Scripture (and the *sunna* of the Prophet, for that matter) did not cover every possible scenario. Consequently, ʿUmar set out to create legal precedents for these cases in two ways: through consultation (*mushāwara*) with the Muslims and through 'independent legal reasoning' (*ijtihād*). The legal precedents were then accepted and enacted (*an yarḍā bihā wa-yaʿmala bihā*) by Muslim believers. Despite the complex picture that emerges from this section of the 'Epistle', the idea of scriptural enactment remained pervasive. In Abū Bakr's case, literal adherence to the *aḥkām* verses in the 'Epistle' is seen as tantamount to his taking the side of 'justice' (*ʿadl*).

---

52 Ibid., 76–77 (at §37–38). Translation significantly modified; Crone and Zimmermann have omitted *ijtihādu raʾyihi* in their translation.

53 Wilkinson, *Ibâḍism*, 207.

While references to the *sunna* should be acknowledged, the 'Epistle' evaluates the actions of the individual caliphs and groups like the Azraqīs and Murji'a only in light of Qur'anic injunctions and commandments, never in light of Prophetic *ḥadīth*. Sālim b. Dhakwān takes issue with individual caliphs and sects when they ignore and neglect Qur'anic verses, take Qur'anic passages out of context, or misinterpret Qur'anic injunctions and rulings. Failure to act according to scriptural rulings has the same significant consequences for the question of political legitimacy as those which emerge from Abū Ḥamza's sermons. Sālim b. Dhakwān portrays 'Uthmān as transgressing *aḥkām* verses, pertaining, once again, to alms (*ṣadaqāt*):

> He ['Uthmān] made [God's] property (*al-māl*) something to be taken in turns among his relations: he gave Marwān the *khums* of Ifrīqiya, al-Ḥārith b. al-Ḥakam the *ṣadaqa* of Baḥrayn, al-Walīd b. 'Uqba the *ṣadaqa* of Kalb, and he wrote [an order] for 300,000 dirhams in favour of al-Ḥakam to al-Ḥārith b. Nawfal, who was governor of Mecca and its environs. In so doing, he transgressed against the judgement of God and judged by other than what God has sent down (*fa-ta'addā fī hādhā ḥukma llāhi wa-ḥakama fīhi bi-ghayri mā anzala llāhu*). God says, 'Those who do not judge according to what God has sent down – they are the unbelievers' [Q. 5:44].[54]

The role played by *aḥkām* verses, specifically those touching on the state's or ruler's distribution of property, in Abū Ḥamza's sermons and in the 'Epistle' is noteworthy. Judging by other than what God has sent down is tantamount to going against God's judgement by misappropriating property of God held in trust for the community.

Abū Ḥamza's and Sālim b. Dhakwān's conception of the *aḥkām* verses was similar: they both demanded a rigorous application of scriptural regulations by believers, those with and without political power. To them, the transposition of Islamic Scripture into life was what distinguished the believer from the unbeliever, and the legitimate ruler from the tyrant. One significant difference is that Sālim b. Dhakwān's 'Epistle' does allow for slightly greater accommodation of normative practice, by mentioning the *sunna* repeatedly, and by admitting that the unmediated enactment of scripture was not possible in every case. This may simply be due to the fact that the 'Epistle' has survived in its entirety, whereas of Abū Ḥamza's sermons only fragments survive. Another, perhaps likelier possibility is that the sermons represent a slightly earlier stage of Ibāḍī thought. However, in light of the authenticity debate about the sermons and

54 Crone and Zimmermann, *Epistle*, 78–79 (at §41). Translation slightly modified.

the murky picture of the origins and dating of the 'Epistle', no definitive conclusions can currently be drawn.

4 Following Scripture in Its Entirety: Hūd b. Muḥakkam's *Tafsīr Kitāb Allāh al-ʿAzīz*

The tendencies described above remained pervasive in early Ibāḍī *tafsīr*, which developed relatively late. Hūd b. Muḥakkam's *tafsīr* bears witness to the ongoing process of 'hadithication' in Ibāḍī religious scholarship.[55] *Ḥadīth* over which there was consensus among Ibāḍīs were increasingly incorporated into various genres alongside Ibāḍī oral dicta. This process culminated in the sixth/twelfth century when Abū Yaʿqūb Yūsuf b. Ibrāhīm al-Warjlānī (d. 570/1174–75) arranged (*tartīb*) a *ḥadīth* collection attributed to the Ibāḍī imam al-Rabīʿ b. Ḥabīb al-Farāhīdī (d. 170/786). This *Musnad Rabīʿ*, also known as *al-Jāmiʿ al-ṣaḥīḥ*, developed out of al-Rabīʿ's *āthār* and included traditions of the Prophet and the Companions transmitted by the Ibāḍī imams.[56] It is the product of an attempt at a closer alignment with Sunnī-Ashʿarī norms.

Hūd b. Muḥakkam's *tafsīr*, according to Wilkinson, reflects the 'assimilation of *ḥadîth* into the *âthâr*'. This 'essentially occurred through a process of dialysis, filtering through study of non-Ibâḍi sources'.[57] Hūd cites al-Kalbī, Mujāhid, al-Ḥasan al-Baṣrī, Ibn ʿAbbās, Ibn Masʿūd, Abū Hurayra, and others. He only cites two Ibāḍī authorities, namely, Jābir b. Zayd and Abū ʿUbayda.[58] He tends to omit *isnād*s or replace references to authorities with the phrase *qāla baʿḍuhum* ('a certain authority said').[59] Even so, the work bears witness to the increasing importance of the Prophetic *sunna* and *ḥadīth* in Ibāḍī literature and thought. However, it also reflects continuity in religious commitments by including and developing ideas similar to those expressed by Abū Ḥamza and Sālim b. Dhakwān, especially relating to an exhaustive and literal enactment of the Qur'an.

Valerie Hoffman and Claude Gilliot have pointed out that a doctrine of major importance which emerges from Ibāḍī exegesis is that fulfilling religious

55 Francesca, 'Tracing the History', 206.

56 Ibid., 211. On Ibāḍī *ḥadīth* and al-Warjlānī's compilation, see Wilkinson, *Ibâḍism*, 432–36.

57 Wilkinson, *Ibâḍism*, 378.

58 Ibid.

59 This is discussed under the rubric of *ḥadhf* by Bālḥājj b. Saʿīd al-Sharīfī, the editor of Hūd's *tafsīr*. See Hūd b. Muḥakkam, *Tafsīr*, 1:37.

obligations is essential to faith[60] – only those who fulfil these obligations are believers. To more radical sects like the Azraqīs, grave sinners were unbelievers. Ibāḍīs adopted a somewhat more moderate stance in this regard by distinguishing two types of infidelity: *kufr shirk*, infidelity of idolatry, that is, the unbelief of those outside the pale of the Islamic *umma*, and *kufr nifāq*, infidelity of hypocrisy among Muslims, or *kufr niʿma*, infidelity through ingratitude towards God's blessings.[61] This distinction is already visible in Sālim b. Dhakwān's 'Epistle' – he refers to the *munāfiqūn* among his people.[62] The differentiation of types of infidelity has to be understood in light of doctrinal developments that occurred after the second/eighth century, such as the emergence of the concepts of 'affiliation' (*walāya*) and 'dissociation' (*barāʾa*). 'Affiliation' and 'dissociation' regulated the comportment of individuals in a religious group towards those who, in their view, did not carry out religious precepts satisfactorily – a distinction that served to reinforce group identity and to establish communal boundaries more clearly.[63] The distinction remains an essential one in modern Ibāḍī thought.[64]

Different forms of *kufr* are also distinguished in Hūd b. Muḥakkam's *Tafsīr Kitāb Allāh al-ʿazīz* when the text addresses the enactment of *aḥkām* verses. An example is Q. 5:44, the verse cited by Sālim b. Dhakwān in his engagement with ʿUthmān's transgressions of specific *aḥkām*, 'Those who do not judge according to what God has sent down – they are the unbelievers'. When commenting on the verse, Hūd b. Muḥakkam states that it refers to the Jews, but he then proceeds to generalise:

> Anyone who does not follow the rules of their Scripture in their entirety (*man lam yaḥkum minhum jamīʿan bi-mā fī kitābihi*), and God's covenant, and what His Prophet Muḥammad – may God's blessings and peace be upon him – has ordered him to do, is an infidel, a wrongdoer, and a sinner. Nonetheless, the unbelief (*kufr*) of the People of Scripture is idolatry (*shirk*), whereas the unbelief

60 Gilliot, 'Le Commentaire Coranique', 183–87; Valerie J. Hoffman, 'Ibāḍī *Tafsīr* Literature', in *The Oxford Handbook of Qur'anic Studies*, ed. Mustafa Shah and Muhammad Abdel Haleem (Oxford: Oxford University Press, 2020), 741. On Ibāḍī doctrine in general, see Valerie J. Hoffman, 'Ibāḍism: History, Doctrines, and Recent Scholarship', *Religion Compass* 9, no. 9 (2015): 300–4.

61 See Hoffman, 'Ibāḍī *Tafsīr* Literature', 741.

62 See the discussion in Crone and Zimmermann, *Epistle*, 198–203.

63 On *walāya* and *barāʾa*, see Francesca, 'Constructing an Identity', 121–22.

64 Valerie J. Hoffman, *The Essentials of Ibāḍī Islam* (Syracuse: Syracuse University Press, 2012), 156–211 (based on the primer *al-ʿAqīda al-wahbiyya*, 'The *Wahbī* Creed').

> (*kufr*) of the people who confess faith in God and the Prophet is an infidelity of hypocrisy (*kufr nifāq*).[65]

The passage stresses that any transgression of the Qur'an and Prophetic *sunna* turns a believer into an infidel. Hūd b. Muḥakkam does distinguish different kinds of unbelief (*kufr*), but the basic assumption is that a direct and literal scriptural enactment is the basis of righteous action as a matter of Ibāḍī dogma. Additionally, this scriptural enactment is not carried out satisfactorily if it is carried out only occasionally or even most of the time; it needs to be carried out without fail, and Islam's Scripture needs to be enacted in its entirety.

Hūd b. Muḥakkam's interpretation of the *mathal* of the donkey in Q. 62:5, which I adduced above to explain the exchange between Abū Ḥamza and the Umayyads shortly before Abū Ḥamza's final defeat, heavily stresses the exhaustive literal approach to the enactment of Qur'anic verses just described:

> The word of the Mighty and Exalted One 'The likeness of those who have been loaded (*ḥummilū*) with the Torah', meaning the Jews, 'and who then have not carried it (*lam yaḥmilūhā*)', that is, they denied some of it (*kadhdhabū bi-baʿḍihā*). Whosoever disbelieves even a single letter of God's Scripture (*man kafara bi-ḥarfin min kitābi llāhi*) is in disbelief of all of it (*fa-qad kafara bihi ajmaʿa*). This is their rejection of Muḥammad and Islam and what they changed of the Torah, for they permitted what they wanted of what God forbade in it and they forbade what they wanted to forbid of what God permitted them in it.[66]

Enactment of *aḥkām* (and other verses, for that matter) in this context means that the true believer cannot deviate by as much as a single letter.[67] Scriptural obligations have to be fulfilled with absolute exactitude, as though the believer had innate knowledge of precisely how to do this in all situations arising in daily life. This idea is consonant with what Abū Ḥamza and Sālim b. Dhakwān described as *ḥukm al-qur'ān*. Failure to enact scriptural verses and obligations without fail constitutes a form of unbelief.

---

65 Hūd b. Muḥakkam, *Tafsīr*, 1:473–74 (at Q. 5:44). On this verse in Ibāḍī theology, see also Hoffman, 'Ibāḍī *Tafsīr* Literature', 741–42. Translation modified. On Q. 5:44, see furthermore Wilferd Madelung, 'Early Ibāḍī Theology', in *The Oxford Handbook of Islamic Theology*, ed. Sabine Schmidtke (Oxford: Oxford University Press, 2016), 245.

66 Hūd b. Muḥakkam, *Tafsīr*, 4:352 (at Q. 62:5).

67 The term *ḥarf* is ambiguous here. I have translated it as 'letter', but 'word' is possible as well. The translation does not affect the sense of the passage: the one who disbelieves small chunks of scripture is in disbelief of all of it.

There are numerous other instances in Hūd b. Muḥakkam's *tafsīr* in which acts and their relation to faith are emphasised. It is such a prominent topic that Claude Gilliot in his 1997 article 'Le Commentaire Coranique de Hūd b. Muḥakkam/Muḥkim' discusses it first among the theological and doctrinal characteristics of this *tafsīr* work. Acting as one should is, in most cases, tied to fulfilling Qur'anic legal obligations. Hūd b. Muḥakkam's commentary on Q. 2:8 illustrates that a verbal profession is not enough. The believer is required to perform acts to enact scripture properly:

> Then God mentioned another category of people, namely, the hypocrites (*munāfiqūn*), saying, There are some people who say, 'We believe in God and the Last Day,' but they are not believers. He says, They profess [their faith to] God with their tongues, but their acts contradict [their profession of faith] (*wa-khālafat aʿmāluhum*). They are not believers (*wa-mā hum bi-muʾminīna*), that is, until they perfect God's religion and fulfil the obligations (*farāʾiḍahu*) that He imposed, like 'Abraham who fulfilled (*waffā*)' [Q. 53:37].[68]

Hūd b. Muḥakkam equates hypocrites with unbelievers. He stresses the contradiction between their words and their acts. They can only become believers once they start fulfilling religious obligations (*farāʾiḍ*) by enacting scripture, thus perfecting religion.

It is noteworthy that Hūd b. Muḥakkam has a very expansive view of what constitutes *aḥkām* verses and how they relate to other parts of Islamic Scripture. This is visible in modifications he introduced in Ibn Sallām's commentary, some of which Miklos Muranyi has detected.[69] One such modification concerns the commentary on Q. 22:16:

> Thus We have sent it down as clear signs (*wa-ka-dhālika anzalnāhu āyātin bayyinātin*), and because God guides those whom He wishes.

Ibn Sallām, whose commentary has survived independently, comments that the 'clear signs' (*bayyināt*) are 'the lawful and the unlawful things' (*al-ḥalāl wa-l-ḥarām*). To this, Hūd b. Muḥakkam adds 'and religious duties and the legal

68 Hūd b. Muḥakkam, *Tafsīr*, 1:83 (at Q. 2:8). Wilkinson also comments on the crucial link between words and actions in Ibāḍī thought. See Wilkinson, *Ibâḍism*, 217. Note that Jones translates Q. 53:37 as 'and Abraham who paid his debt in full'. I diverge here from his translation.

69 Muranyi, '*Tafsīr*'.

rulings' (*al-ḥalāl wa-l-ḥarām wa-l-farāʾiḍ wa-l-aḥkām*).[70] It is noteworthy that the Qur'anic verse is not embedded in a legal context in Q. 22. Instead, it forms part of a polemical opening, and the preceding and following verses emphasise God's power and the eschatological fate of believers and different other religious groups. The equation of *bayyināt* with terms that have legal dimensions, among them most notably *aḥkām*, is therefore striking. *Aḥkām* are consequently conceptualised as inherently 'clear' and, in turn, 'clear verses' are by implication necessarily legally relevant.

A similar example is the interpretation of the word *furqān* in Q. 25:1:

> Blessed is He who has sent down the *furqān* to His slave, for him to be a warner to all created beings.

To explain the word *furqān*, Ibn Sallām cites a tradition:

> Qatāda said, 'It is the Qur'an, its *furqān* is what is lawful and unlawful in it' (*wa-huwa al-qurʾān, furqānuhu ḥalāluhu wa-ḥarāmuhu*).

Hūd b. Muḥakkam omits the mention of Qatāda and adds again 'religious duties and the legal rulings' (*farāʾiḍuhu wa-aḥkāmuhu*).[71] This interpretation of the somewhat opaque word *furqān*, just like the interpretation of the word *bayyināt*, suggests a potentially expansive understanding of what precisely *aḥkām* verses are in the Qur'an. Muranyi has suggested that the insertion of juridical topics in Hūd b. Muḥakkam's *tafsīr* has to do with the development of the genre of *aḥkām al-qurʾān*,[72] the earliest preserved fragments of which date back to the second half of the third/ninth century. Hūd b. Muḥakkam's insertions might accordingly have been influenced by the exegetical and legal developments of his time.[73]

5 Conclusion

Legal verses, in the widest possible sense, figure prominently in texts produced during the gestation period of Ibāḍī thought. The orator Abū Ḥamza cites legal verses in his sermons to contrast believers and unbelievers for political

70 Hūd b. Muḥakkam, *Tafsīr*, 3:104 (at Q. 22:16). See Muranyi, '*Tafsīr*', 45.
71 Hūd b. Muḥakkam, *Tafsīr*, 3:200 (at Q. 25:1). See Muranyi, '*Tafsīr*', 49.
72 See Devin Stewart's chapter in this volume.
73 Muranyi, '*Tafsīr*', 49; note 72 includes references to such works.

purposes. Unbelievers are depicted as constantly ignoring scriptural injunctions and regulations whereas believers are those who fulfil them to the letter and follow them as a guideline for political action.

There are many features that link religio-political orations such as Abū Ḥamza's to Ibāḍī 'epistles', among them hortatory passages, similar *topoi* like the 'caliphs *topos*', and, most importantly for the present context, a comparable deployment of Qur'anic legal verses to legitimise and delegitimise rulers, on the one hand, and to draw identitarian boundaries around the group of (Ibāḍī) believers, on the other. The 'Epistle' of Sālim b. Dhakwān, as perhaps the most prominent and well-researched example of an Ibāḍī epistle, shares with Abū Ḥamza's sermons a distinct focus on scripture-mindedness and scriptural enactment as aspects crucial to belief – despite generally acknowledging authoritative Prophetic and community *sunna*. Scripture acquires a significant agency when it is conceptualised and personified as a 'judge' or an 'imam'. One important distinction is that the 'Epistle' recognises that, historically, situations arose in which Islamic Scripture could not be directly applied, or in which no *sunna* (Prophetic or otherwise) existed. Notwithstanding these complexities, the basis remains, as much as possible, the unmediated transposition of scriptural rulings into life by both believers and legitimate rulers.

Ibāḍī exegesis, specifically the one early work that has been preserved in its entirety, Hūd b. Muḥakkam's *tafsīr*, is characterised by tendencies comparable to those found in sermons and epistles regarding the topic discussed here. The work as it has been preserved, as well as Hūd b. Muḥakkam's alterations to Ibn Sallām's *tafsīr* on which it is based, point to an important juridical layer of understanding that characterises the work. *Aḥkām* verses are all clear and clearly intended to be applied by God, Hūd b. Muḥakkam's additions seem to suggest. Depending on people's willingness and ability to enact such verses, different degrees of unbelief are distinguished from belief. Someone who professes faith in God and His Messenger might still be an unbeliever of the *kufr nifāq* category if he or she does not also enact the regulations. Belief is only belief when it is accompanied by scripture-based actions, more specifically *aḥkām*-based actions, always and without fail.

One cannot draw definitive conclusions about the understanding and role of *aḥkām* verses in the formative period of Ibāḍī thought solely on the basis of the three case studies discussed here. As more and more early Ibāḍī texts are discovered and edited, a more coherent picture of the thought of this period will emerge. For now, one may tentatively conclude that Ibāḍīs who flourished in the second/eighth and third/ninth centuries approached *aḥkām* verses as a tool to define their own position vis-à-vis those outside of their community. When Ibāḍīs speak of the 'judgement of the Qur'an' (*ḥukm al-qur'ān*), a frequent notion in Ibāḍī works of different gernes, they mean this quite literally: the Qur'an is not only 'authoritative', it quite literally 'judges' believers on the basis of their words and actions.

Bibliography

Primary Sources

Crone, Patricia, and Fritz Zimmermann, eds. and trans. *The Epistle of Sālim ibn Dhakwān*. Oxford: Oxford University Press, 2001.

Hūd b. Muḥakkam al-Hawwārī. *Tafsīr Kitāb Allāh al-ʿazīz*. Edited by Bālḥājj b. Saʿīd al-Sharīfī. Beirut: Dār al-Gharb al-Islāmī, 1990.

al-Jāḥiẓ, Abū ʿUthman ʿAmr b. Baḥr. *al-Bayān wa-l-tabyīn*. 4 vols. Edited by ʿAbd al-Salām Muḥammad Hārūn. Cairo: Maktabat al-Khānjī, 1998.

Jones, Alan, trans. *The Qurʾān*. Cambridge: Gibb Memorial Trust, 2007.

al-Ṭabarī. *Tārīkh al-rusul wa-l-mulūk*, edited as *Annales quos scripsit Abu Djafar Mohammed Ibn Djarir at-Tabari*. Prima series, 6 vols. Secunda series, 3 vols. Tertia series, 4 vols. Edited by Michael Jan de Goeje. Leiden: Brill, 1879–1901; translated as *The History of al-Ṭabarī (Taʾrīkh al-rusul waʾl-mulūk)*. Vol. 27, *The ʿAbbāsid Revolution*. Translated by John Alden Williams. Albany: State University of New York Press, 1985.

Secondary Literature

Albayrak, İsmail. *Approaches to Ibāḍī Exegetical Tradition*. Wiesbaden: Harrassowitz, 2020.

Al-Salimi, Abdulrahman. *Early Islamic Law in Basra in the 2nd/8th Century*. Leiden: Brill, 2018.

Al-Salimi, Abdulrahman. *Ibāḍism East of Mesopotamia: Early Iran, Central Asia and India*. Berlin: Klaus Schwarz, 2016.

Baptiste, Enki. 'La *khuṭba* d'Abū Ḥamza al-Shārī: soulèvement ibāḍite et rhétorique de la contestation en péninsule Arabique au second siècle de l'Islam. Traduction commentée d'une version inédite du sermon'. *Al-ʿUṣūr al-Wusṭā* 32 (2024): 165–249.

Bauer, Karen. *Gender Hierarchy in the Qurʾān: Medieval Interpretations, Modern Responses*. Cambridge: Cambridge University Press, 2015.

Cook, Michael. *Early Muslim Dogma: A Source-Critical Study*. Cambridge: Cambridge University Press, 1981.

Dähne, Stephan. 'Qur'anic Wording in Political Speeches in Classical Arabic Literature'. *Journal of Qurʾanic Studies* 3, no. 2 (2001): 1–13.

Dähne, Stephan. *Reden der Araber: Die politische ḫuṭba in der klassischen arabischen Literatur*. Frankfurt am Main: Peter Lang, 2001.

Dähne, Stephan. 'Zu den *ḫutab* des Abū Ḥamza aš-Šārī in der klassischen arabischen Literatur'. In *Erlesenes: Sonderheft der Halleschen Beiträge zur Orientwissenschaft anläßlich des 19. Kongresses der Union Européenne d'Arabisants et Islamisants*, edited by Walter Beltz and Sebastian Günther, 30–45. Halle: Institut für Orientalistik, 1998.

Ess, Josef van. *Theologie und Gesellschaft im 2. und 3. Jahrhundert Hidschra: Eine Geschichte des religiösen Denkens im frühen Islam*. Vol. 1. Berlin: De Gruyter, 1991.

Ess, Josef van. 'Untersuchungen zu einigen ibāḍitischen Handschriften'. *Zeitschrift der Deutschen Morgenländischen Gesellschaft* 126, no. 1 (1976): 25–63.

Ess, Josef van. *Zwischen Ḥadīṯ und Theologie: Studien zum Entstehen prädestinatianischer Überlieferung*. Berlin: De Gruyter, 1975.

Francesca, Ersilia. 'Constructing an Identity: The Development of Ibadi Law'. In *On Ibadism*, edited by Angeliki Ziaka, 109–33. Hildesheim: Georg Olms Verlag, 2014.

Francesca, Ersilia. 'Tracing the History of Ibāḍī Law and Jurisprudence'. *Journal of Islamic Law* 2 (2021): 204–11.

Frantsouzoff, Sergueï A. 'Les Ibaḍites du Ḥaḍramawt: Quelques suggestions généalogiques et historiographiques'. In *L'Ibadisme dans les sociétés de l'Islam médiéval: Modèles et interactions*, edited by Cyrille Aillet, 63–71. Berlin: De Gruyter, 2018.

Gaiser, Adam R. 'Ibn Dhakwān, Sālim'. In *Encyclopaedia of Islam, THREE*, edited by Kate Fleet, Gudrun Krämer, Denis Matringe, John Nawas, and Devin J. Stewart. Leiden: Brill, 2020. http://dx.doi.org/10.1163/1573-3912_ei3_COM_32133

Gaiser, Adam R. *Shurāt Legends, Ibāḍī Identities: Martyrdom, Asceticism, and the Making of an Early Islamic Community*. Columbia: University of South Carolina Press, 2016.

Gilliot, Claude. 'Le Commentaire Coranique de Hūd b. Muḥakkam/Muḥkim'. *Arabica* 44, no. 2 (1997): 179–233.

Gleave, Robert. *Islam and Literalism: Literal Meaning and Interpretation in Islamic Legal Theory*. Edinburgh: Edinburgh University Press, 2012.

Hansu, Hüseyin. 'Debates on the Authority of Hadith in Early Islamic Intellectual History: Identifying al-Shāfiʿī's Opponents in *Jimāʿ al-ʿIlm*'. *Journal of the American Oriental Society* 136, no. 3 (2016): 515–33.

Hawting, Gerald R. 'The Significance of the Slogan *Lā Ḥukm[a] Illā Lillāh* and the References to the *Ḥudūd* in the Traditions about the Fitna and the Murder of 'Uthmān'. *Bulletin of the School of Oriental and African Studies* 41, no. 3 (1978): 453–63.

Hoffman, Valerie J. *The Essentials of Ibāḍī Islam*. Syracuse: Syracuse University Press, 2012.

Hoffman, Valerie J. 'Ibāḍī *Tafsīr* Literature'. In *The Oxford Handbook of Qur'anic Studies*, edited by Mustafa Shah and Muhammad Abdel Haleem, 734–45. Oxford: Oxford University Press, 2020.

Hoffman, Valerie J. 'Ibāḍism: History, Doctrines, and Recent Scholarship'. *Religion Compass* 9, no. 9 (2015): 297–307.

Madelung, Wilferd. 'Early Ibāḍī Theology'. In *The Oxford Handbook of Islamic Theology*, edited by Sabine Schmidtke, 242–51. Oxford: Oxford University Press, 2016.

Marsham, Andrew. 'Wealth and the Image of the Umayyads in the Sermons Attributed to Abū Ḥamza (d. 748).' In *Between Rebels and Rulers in the Early Islamicate World: Power, Contention and Identity*, edited by Hannah-Lena Hagemann and Alasdair Grant, 265–90. Edinburgh: Edinburgh University Press, 2024.

Michalak-Pikulska, Barbara, and Reinhard Eisener, eds. *Ibadi Jurisprudence: Origins, Developments and Cases*. Hildesheim: Olms, 2015.

Muranyi, Miklos. 'The *Tafsīr* of Hūd b. Muḥakkim al-Hawwārī (d. in the 2nd Half of the 3rd/9th Century) and Yaḥyā b. Sallām al-Baṣrī (124/742–200/815): A Synoptical and Intertextual Approach'. In *Local and Global Ibadi Identities*, edited by Yohei Kondo and Angeliki Ziaka, 41–56. Hildesheim: Georg Olms Verlag, 2019.

Musa, Aisha Y. *Ḥadīth as Scripture: Discussions on the Authority of Prophetic Traditions in Islam*. New York: Palgrave Macmillan, 2008.

Qutbuddin, Tahera. *Arabic Oration: Art and Function*. Leiden: Brill, 2019.

Schmid, Nora K. *The Ascetic Qur'an and Its Kharijite Readers*. Leiden: Brill, 2026.

Vikør, Knut S. 'Ibadism and Law in Historical Contexts'. *Oñati Socio-Legal Series* 10, no. 5 (2020): 960–84.

Wilkinson, John C. *Ibâḍism: Origins and Early Development in Oman*. Oxford: Oxford University Press, 2010.

CHAPTER 9

The Irrelevance of 'Qur'anic Meaning': Akhbārī Shīʿī Interpretive Techniques and the Legal Verses of the Qur'an

Robert Gleave

The extent to which the legal content of the Qur'an was (historically speaking) a 'source' for the post-Qur'anic elaboration of the law by Muslim jurists has been a point of disagreement in the secondary literature. Some academics have argued that the edifice of the Muslim legal system was, in large part, constructed without extensive influence of the Qur'an.[1] This has spawned yet further debates around which extra-Qur'anic source was the most significant: the laws of the Umayyads, the pre-Islamic Arabs, the Jews, the Byzantines, and the Romans have all been proposed as alternative sources of both the whole Islamic legal system and specific individual laws. Sometimes, the spur for these investigations is the question of whether the Qur'an can really be said to be the 'the first source' of Islamic law as the Muslim jurists, almost unanimously, say it is. They appear as answers to the question 'Whence Islamic law?' because it does not come from the Qur'an.[2]

Alongside this, there has more recently been renewed scholarly attention on whether or not the Qur'anic text postulates (or assumes) an ethical/legal

1 See Joseph Schacht, *The Origins of Muhammadan Jurisprudence* (Oxford: Clarendon, 1967), 224: 'Muhammadan law did not derive directly from the Koran but developed, as we saw, out of popular and administrative practice under the Umaiyads, and this practice often diverged from the intentions and even the explicit wording of the Koran'; and Norman Calder, *Studies in Early Muslim Jurisprudence* (Oxford: Clarendon, 1993), 219: 'Here it is only necessary to acknowledge that the Qur'ān was an influence on the law, usually secondary and intrusive.'

2 Patricia Crone, 'Jāhilī and Jewish Law: The *Qasāma*', *Jerusalem Studies in Arabic and Islam* 4 (1984): 153–201; Patricia Crone and Martin Hinds, *God's Caliph: Religious Authority in the First Centuries of Islam* (Cambridge: Cambridge University Press, 1986), 43–57; Patricia Crone, *Roman, Provincial and Islamic Law* (Cambridge: Cambridge University Press, 1987); Patricia Crone, 'Two Legal Problems Bearing on the Early History of the Qur'ān', *Jerusalem Studies in Arabic and Islam* 18 (1994): 1–37; Benjamin Jokisch, *Islamic Imperial Law: Harun al-Rashid's Codification Project* (Berlin: Walter de Gruyter, 2007), passim; Michael Cook, 'Early Islamic Dietary Law', *Jerusalem Studies in Arabic and Islam* 7 (1986): 218–77.

 | HTTPS://DOI.ORG/10.1163/9789004755567-011

system, and if so, what might that system be.[3] To an extent, this line of enquiry might also be said to be generated by a perceived disjuncture between later Muslim jurisprudence (*fiqh*) and the legal context (and content) of the Qur'an. However, the main intellectual drive has most recently come from treating the Qur'an as a text of late antiquity which contains (and reveals) elements of the legal world of that time.[4] What it came to mean for Muslims is viewed as outside the scope of such an enquiry. This methodological stance does not preclude Muslim exegesis of the Qur'an (whether in formal works of *tafsīr* or more ad hoc interpretations in other genres of Muslim literature) from being a potential source for understanding why the Qur'an is as it is. The overall approach, though, is to avoid allowing later tradition a controlling role on the contextual understanding of Qur'anic law.[5]

3 John Burton, *The Sources of Islamic Law: Islamic Theories of Abrogation* (Edinburgh: Edinburgh University Press, 1990); Hallaq has emphasised the centrality of the Qur'an to the early development of Islamic law. See Wael B. Hallaq, *The Origins and Evolution of Islamic Law* (Cambridge: Cambridge University Press, 2004), 8–28. On the *āyat al-aḥkām* specifically, he writes: 'The traditional count of all the legal verses comes to about five hundred – a number that at first glance seems exiguous, considering the overall size of the Quran. However, as Goitein has perceptively remarked, these verses represent a larger weight than the number may indicate. It is common knowledge that the Quran repeats itself both literally and thematically, but this tendency of repetition is absent in the legal subject matter. The proportion of the legal verses, therefore, is larger than that suggested by an absolute number. And if we consider the fact that the average length of the legal verses is twice or even thrice that of the non-legal verses, it is not difficult to argue, following Goitein, that the Quran contains no less legal material than does the Torah, which is commonly known as "the Law"' (ibid., 21). The reference at the end is to S.D. Goitein, 'The Birth-Hour of Muslim Law: An Essay in Exegesis', *The Muslim World* 50, no. 1 (1960): 23–29.

4 Angelika Neuwirth can be considered the pioneer in this field – see generally her *The Qur'an and Late Antiquity* (Oxford: Oxford University Press, 2019). See also Lena Salaymeh, *The Beginnings of Islamic Law: Late Antique Islamicate Legal Traditions* (Cambridge: Cambridge University Press, 2016). On the literary qualities of Qur'anic law, see e.g. Joseph E. Lowry, 'When Less Is More: Law and Commandment in *Sūrat al-An'ām*', *Journal of Qur'anic Studies* 9, no. 2 (2007): 22–42. See also Holgar Michael Zellentin, *The Qur'an's Legal Culture: Didascalia Apostolorum as a Point of Departure* (Tübingen: Mohr Siebeck, 2010); and his various articles (including the one presented in this volume).

5 Ignoring how later 'Muslim tradition' (as articulated by *tafsīr*, *fiqh*, and other genres) presents its understanding of the Qur'an is, of course, a methodological choice. See e.g. G.R. Hawting, *The Idea of Idolatry and the Emergence of Islam: From Polemic to History* (Cambridge: Cambridge University Press, 1999), 1n1, where he outlines his attempt to analyse the Qur'an distinct from the 'Muslim tradition': 'The expression "Muslim tradition" refers to the mass of traditional Muslim literature, such as lives of the Prophet (*sīras*), commentaries on the Koran (*tafsīrs*), and collections of reports (*ḥadīths*) about the words and deeds of the Prophet ... The tradition is extensive and, within certain boundaries, diverse. The Koran is a work *sui generis* and is usually regarded as distinct from the traditional literature.'

Notwithstanding this ever-expanding body of scholarship, the religious belief in the Qur'an as the primary source of Islamic jurisprudence is a given.[6] It is worth remembering that when Muslim jurists assert this stance, they are not usually making an historical point. Given the doctrine of the serial nature of the Qur'anic revelation (i.e. occurring over many years and happening alongside Prophetic practice), they are not saying that the law of the Qur'an came chronologically first. The general theory is that there are many elements of Prophetic Sunna which, on most accounts, predate related Qur'anic revelations. Rather, the assertion of Qur'anic primacy as a legal source is an expression of the theological doctrine of God being the author of the Sharīʿa.[7] The doctrine also comes out of Muslim juristic discussions as to the procedure a jurist should follow when attempting to uncover God's ruling on a particular issue (later formalised in the procedure of *ijtihād*). Given this, the academic debates are first over whether the Qur'an was the source of Islamic law, and second whether Qur'anic law is different from Islamic law. These debates have very little to do with discussions over the position of *al-kitāb* ('the Book') in works of Islamic legal theory (*uṣūl al-fiqh*). In the discussions of legal theory, the aim is to lay out the link between *fiqh* and the Qur'an in a coherent manner.

That the Qur'an is the first source of the Sharīʿa is so widely held that when a Muslim movement, such as the Akhbāriyya of the Twelver Shīʿites, appears which argues differently, it is particularly noteworthy.[8] In the rest of this chapter, I outline the Akhbārī positions on the irrelevance of the Qur'an for Islamic law. This was not necessarily linked to a belief in the corrupted nature of the Qur'an (i.e. the belief that the text 'between one's hands' is deficient).[9] This is a view which has been expressed (in many different forms) in Shīʿī circles from the earliest times, and remains a minority position today. It can range from the assertion that individual words in the text have been altered, to the belief that God's revelation was larger (by several times over) than the surviving Qur'an.

6 Robert Gleave, 'The "First Source" of Islamic Law: Classical Muslim Legal Exegesis of the Qur'an', in *Law and Religion: Current Legal Issues, Volume 4*, ed. Richard O'Dair and Andrew Lewis (Oxford: Oxford University Press, 2001), 145–61.

7 Wael B. Hallaq, 'The Primacy of the Qur'ān in Shāṭibī's Legal Theory', in *Islamic Studies Presented to Charles J. Adams*, ed. Wael B. Hallaq and Donald P. Little (Leiden: Brill, 1991), 69–90.

8 On the other hand, when a movement (like that of the so-called Qur'āniyyūn) advocates a sole reliance on the Qur'an (and a rejection of the *ḥadith* as a legal reference, or the Sunna as a legal source), they are highly controversial. For example, on the Ahl al-Qur'ān in the early modern Punjab, see Usman Qasmi, *Questioning the Authority of the Past: The Ahl al-Qur'an Movements in the Punjab* (Oxford: Oxford University Press, 2012).

9 On *taḥrīf* and the Akhbārī movement, see Rainer Brunner, *Die Schia und die Koranfälschung* (Stuttgart: Deutsche Morgenländische Gesellschaft, 2001), and particularly the discussion of Ḥusayn al-Nūrī al-Ṭabarsī (d. 1320/1902).

One can see how this belief may fit nicely with the assertion that the Qur'an cannot be counted as a source when investigating legal rulings. Indeed, some of the Akhbārīs discussed in this chapter may well have held that the Qur'an in circulation is not identical with 'the Book' as revealed.[10] Any argument around the textual reliability of the Qur'anic document, though, does not feature, to my knowledge, in their arguments for its legal irrelevance. Instead, these arguments are primarily based on who, if anyone, has the authority to interpret the Qur'an.

•••

Categorising certain verses as being 'regulative' (i.e. the *āyāt al-aḥkām*) was a common feature of Islamic legal discussions and, as this collection demonstrates, it spawned in the early period a genre of literature which has been continuously popular through the centuries. At first blush, the genre seems incongruous. Declaring that certain verses are 'legal', and placing a specified number (be it 500 or otherwise) in the category seems unnecessary. Why restrict the primary source in the juristic enterprise in this way? Interpretation needs all the evidence it can lay its hands on, and by saying some verses are 'legal', one implicitly excludes others as 'non-legal' – and therefore unavailable for legal argumentation. Precisely why the genre was established and became popular is probably linked, primarily, to demonstrating that the Qur'an is a legally relevant source against those who were frustrated with its legal limitations. Five hundred is a high enough number to demonstrate (but not overstate) its utility. Furthermore, limiting the number of verses may, once again, reflect the need to make the process of legal derivation manageable. In the definitions of *ijtihād*, there is almost always mention of the *mujtahid* needing to 'know' the Qur'an, but the conditional restriction is often added that he only need know the 'legal' verses and that these are limited in number.[11] Sometimes he only needs to be able to find the verses in a Qur'an copy (*muṣḥaf*) – he need

10 B.T. Lawson, 'Note for the Study of a "Shīʿī Qurʾān"', *Journal of Semitic Studies* 36 (1991): 279–95.

11 For example, Abū Ḥāmid al-Ghazālī (d. 505/1111) states, 'It is not a condition that [the *mujtahid*] know all the Book – rather, he needs to know these [elements] which relate to rulings – and these number 500 verses. Secondly, he does not have to know them by heart – he only needs to know where they are, so he can seek out the verse which is required at the time of need.' Abū Ḥāmid al-Ghazālī, *al-Mustaṣfā fī uṣūl al-fiqh* (Beirut: Dār al-Kutub al-ʿIlmiyya, 1998), 2:342–43.

not even know them by rote. The idea of there being *āyāt al-aḥkām* proved handy when elaborating on the necessary qualifications of the jurist.[12]

The Akhbārī movement in Twelver Shīʿism, as I and others have explained, rejected *ijtihād*. If one is to speak with dangerous generality, the Akhbārīs saw the process of a (supposedly) qualified scholar, searching for evidence among the various sources and then coming up with his opinion (*ẓann*) as to God's ruling on a legal matter, to fall short of the epistemological rigour required by the Imāms themselves. Certainty (*ʿilm, qaṭʿ*) is required. The Imāms, according to the Akhbārīs, stipulated that their Shīʿa should act on knowledge not mere opinion, and that interpretive processes (*qiyās*/analogy, etc.) which produce *ẓann* are practices of the deviant Sunnīs. By permitting *ẓann*, Akhbārīs argued, the Twelver Shīʿī jurists (i.e. their opponents – the Uṣūlīs) were denying the very foundations of the true (i.e. Twelver Shīʿite) religion. These ideas came to be the bedrock of the Akhbārī movement, and became popular in the seventeenth century, initially through the work of Muḥammad Amīn al-Astarābādī (d. 1036/1626–27). Al-Astarābādī was an Iranian Shīʿī scholar whose book *al-Fawāʾid al-madaniyya* was subsequently taken by many to lay out the foundations of the Akhbārī approach. His position on whether the Qurʾan is a source of our legal understanding is summarised nicely in that work:

> The correct position – in my view – is the opinion and method of the early Akhbārīs. They upheld the doctrine that everything which the community needs until the Day of Resurrection – even the compensatory payment for a scratch – has a clear, definitive proof from God.
>
> Most of the legal rules brought by the Prophet, and matters concerning abrogation, specification, particularisation, and interpretation in relation to the Book of God and the Sunna of his Prophet – have been preserved by the Holy Family.
>
> It is not permitted to deduce speculative rules from the apparent meanings of the Book of God, or from the apparent meanings of the Prophetic Sunna when their statuses, in the view of the *ahl al-dhikr* (upon them be peace) ['the People of Remembrance', i.e. Imāms], are as yet unknown – instead [in such circumstances] one must suspend making a judgement (*tawaqquf*) and act cautiously (*iḥtiyāṭ*).[13]

12 A similar 'manageability clause' is often added to the requirement to know the 'Sunna', with a limit on the number of *ḥadīth* the *mujtahid* is required to know, and how he need only be able to find them in the *ḥadīth* books, and not know them off by heart. Al-Ghazālī says, again, that though the *ḥadīth*s he needs to know are numerous 'they are limited in number' and he does not have to know them by heart. Ibid., 343.

13 Muḥammad Amīn al-Astarābādī, *al-Fawāʾid al-madaniyya* (Qom: Muʾassasat al-Nashr al-Islāmī, 2006), 1:104.

The texts of the two principal sources of Islamic law – *kitāb* and *sunna* – cannot be used as legal sources on their own, al-Astarābādī argues. What they appear to mean (*fī al-ẓāhir*) may not be God's intended meaning (whether it is directly in the Qur'an or indirectly through the recorded actions and words of the Prophet). That language is sometimes used in an allusive rather than literal manner is a known and accepted fact: intended meaning is not always deduced from the apparent (or literal) meaning of the text. Here, an accepted element of rhetorical analysis and scriptural exegesis is used to undermine the practice of direct consultation with (and derivation from) the legal sources. Revelation is, therefore, cryptic (*ʿalā wajh al-taʿmiyya* – literally 'blindness', or concealing, mystifying – in relation to scripture's meaning). However, revelation's intended meaning has been lodged with the descendants of the Prophet through his daughter Fāṭima (i.e. the *ahl al-bayt* or *ahl al-dhikr*). In fact, for al-Astarābādī, it was to them that revelation was delivered and 'addressed', not to all people at all times, and also not to the specific Prophetic community.

This position was taken up by subsequent Akhbārīs; it was modified and refined, but the fundamental, polemical, element remained the same. The opponents of the Akhbārīs (i.e. the *mujtahids*) argued that it was a perfectly justified exegetical manoeuvre to identify the Qur'an's apparent meaning as a strong contender for God's intended meaning. Qur'anic apparent meanings have legal probative force (*ḥujjiyyat ẓawāhir al-Qur'ān*). However, even the *mujtahids* agreed that a verse's apparent meaning regularly deviated from the Lawgiver's intended meaning. Apparent meaning, therefore, did not bring certainty regarding a verse's true, intended meaning; it only brought a justified assumption (or opinion, *ẓann*) of the verse's true meaning. It was to this epistemological compromise – from certain knowledge (*ʿilm/yaqīn/qaṭʿ*) to supposedly justified presumption (*ẓann*) – that the Akhbārīs objected. The Qur'an is not gibberish for the Akhbārīs – meaning can be derived from the words on the page. What cannot be known is what the true referent of these words might be.

The Akhbārī position (as outlined by al-Astarābādī) was clearly a point of heated debate. There are records of actual debates between Akhbārīs and their opponents. For example, an early follower of al-Astarābādī, Sayyid Niʿmat Allāh al-Jazāʾirī (d. 1112/1701), relates a story which illustrates the Akhbārī doctrine on this point:

> I was in the congregational mosque in Shiraz, and my teacher, the *mujtahid* al-Shaykh Jaʿfar al-Baḥrānī,[14] and my shaykh, the *muḥaddith*, the author of

---

14 Jaʿfar b. Kamāl al-Dīn al-Baḥrānī (d. 1088/1678). See Muḥsin Amīn, *Aʿyān al-Shīʿa* (Dār al-Maṭbūʿāt, 1983), 4:136.

Jawāmiʿ al-kalim,[15] were arguing on this question [of *ḥujjiyyat al-Qurʾān* – the probative force of the Qurʾan]. Their discussion went on and on until the honourable *mujtahid* said:

'What do you say of [the verse] "*qul huwa Allāh aḥad*" ["Say that God is singular", Q. 112:1]? In order to understand its meaning, do you need to resort to *ḥadīth*?'

He replied:

> 'Yes. We do not know the meaning of *aḥadiyya* (singularity); nor the differences between *aḥad* (singular) and *wāḥid* (one), along with other things.'[16]

The view that the Qurʾan was totally cryptic was the subject of some ridicule and criticism. An almost immediate objection can be found in *al-Shawāhid al-Makkiyya* by Nūr al-Dīn ʿAlī al-ʿĀmilī (d. 1068/1657). His work was a commentary on, and refutation of, al-Astarābādī's text. On the question of the *ḥujjiyyat al-Qurʾān*, he writes:

> There is no doubt that in the Qurʾan there are hidden secrets, and concealed wisdom which only the Imāms can access after the Prophet. In matters of legal requirement and the pronouncement thereof, however, it would not be justifiable to conceal and not reveal them in any way. This would contradict the intended purpose of the Qurʾan. To confirm this, there is [God's] statement 'We only send a prophet using the language of his people' [Q. 14:4] – i.e. so that they can understand each other. If they do not understand, then there is no point [to the Qurʾan].[17]

This argument against the Akhbārī position is based around Muʿtazilī stipulations concerning the perspicuity of revelatory speech. God must speak clearly when He addresses His servants. Not only does He promise that He will do this (in Q. 14:4) but He is required to do so by reason. It would be rationally unjustifiably for the just Lawgiver to speak in an unclear manner. Given that the Lawgiver will punish disobedience to His law, He must (when delivering it)

---

15 Mīrzā Ibn Sharaf al-Dīn ʿAlī b. Niʿmat Allāh al-Jazāʾirī (d. eleventh/seventeenth century) – who apparently died in Hyderabad. Aghā Buzurg al-Ṭiḥrānī, *Ṭabaqāt aʿlām al-Shīʿa* (Beirut: Dār Iḥyāʾ al-Turāth al-ʿArabī, 2009), 8:602–3.

16 al-Sayyid Niʿmat Allāh al-Jazāʾirī, *Manbaʿ al-ḥayāt wa-ḥujjiyyat qawl al-mujtahid min al-amwāt* (Qom: Muʾassasat al-Aʿlamī li-l-Maṭbūʿāt, n.d.), 48.

17 al-ʿĀmilī, *al-Shawāhid al-Makkiyya* [printed with al-Astarābādī's *al-Fawāʾid al-madaniyya*, 269–70].

make the content of the law clear to those whom He expects to be loyal servants. There is a burden of clarity on the Lawgiver, and the Akhbārī doctrine of *taʿmiyya* undermines this.[18]

That there was debate among the Akhbārīs is confirmed by the discussion of al-Ḥurr al-ʿĀmilī (d. 1104/1693). In his *al-Fawāʾid al-Ṭūsiyya*, he discusses the doctrine of an unnamed Uṣūlī 'contemporary' opponent:

> We say: Our contemporary first defines [the term] *naṣṣ* as 'an utterance which indicates a preponderant meaning without the possibility of contradiction'. He defines [the term] *ẓāhir* as 'an utterance which indicates one of its possible meanings through a preponderant indicatory method, which does not eliminate the fact that there are alternative possibilities'. Then he sets about demonstrating that it is permitted to act on the basis of the *ẓāhir* using various arguments.[19]

Al-Ḥurr al-ʿĀmilī goes on to attempt to demolish the opinion that it is acceptable to act on the *ẓāhir* meaning (as the term is defined in this citation) even though its referent is uncertain. In this way the debate around the *ḥujjiyyat ẓāhir al-Qurʾān* becomes part of the wider Akhbārī–Uṣūlī epistemological debate around whether it is acceptable to act on the basis of *ẓann* not *ʿilm*. In the course of his refutation of this position, he admits, however, that there is intra-Akhbārī debate on whether one accept the *ẓāhir* of the Qur'an when that may be all that is available:

> The fifth of [our replies]: There is no dispute that it is obligatory to act on the basis of the Qur'an. There is only discussion around the permissibility of acting on the basis of [the Qur'an] when there is no unambiguous statement from the Imāms interpreting it in accordance with its *ẓāhir*, and thereby eliminating [the possibility of] abrogation, conditionality, particularisation, interpretation, and the like.[20]

While there was debate and discussion among Akhbārīs about whether the *ẓāhir* of a Qur'anic verse might be considered the intended meaning, there was general agreement that if it were to be acceptable, it was not for any 'rational'

---

18 See Robert Gleave, 'Delaying the Elucidation (*Taʾḫir al-Bayān*) in Early Muslim Legal Theory', in *Theological Rationalism in the Medieval Islam: New Sources and Perspectives*, ed. Gregor Schwarb and Lukas Muehlethaler (Leuven: Peters, 2018), 59–80.

19 Muḥammad b. al-Ḥasan al-Ḥurr al-ʿĀmilī, *al-Fawāʾid al-Ṭūsiyya* (Qom: Maktabat al-Maḥallātī, 2002), 163.

20 Ibid., 169.

reason. A crucial Uṣūlī argument was that accepting the probative force of the apparent meaning of the Qurʾan was rationally demonstrated. That is, reason (*ʿaql*) dictates that the *ẓāhir* meaning of any speech act was a justified inference on the part of the hearer; and since revelatory discourse follows the same pragmatic principles as everyday speech, it must be justified to accept the *ẓāhir* meaning of the Qurʾan also (providing there is no evidence to the contrary). Akhbārīs did not accept that there was a rational justification for taking the *ẓāhir* meaning of a Qurʾanic verse: it was, though, possible in the view of some Akhbārīs that there could be a transmitted (*manqūl*) reason to take the *ẓāhir* – namely, if the Imām had said so for either a specific verse, or the Imām had stipulated that one can take the *ẓāhir* of the Qurʾan as part of a general exegetical procedure. Al-Jazāʾirī himself appears to tend towards this view when he concludes that

> taking rulings from the unambiguous pronouncements of the Qurʾan, or its apparent meaning, or its implied meaning, and the like is permitted – just as the *mujtahid*s do.[21]

Yet other Akhbārīs argued that the *ẓāhir* of Qurʾanic verses could be confirmed as the intended meaning by both the Imāms and 'direct' confirmatory experience. Muḥsin Fayḍ al-Kāshānī (d. 1091/1680), famous as a philosopher-mystic, but also as an Akhbārī, was perhaps most explicit in asserting this view, and in holding this view, he claimed that he was following the stipulations laid down by the Imāms themselves:

> In *al-Kāfī*, transmitted from al-Ṣādiq from his father [i.e. Imām al-Bāqir]: No one pits one part of the Qurʾan against another except someone who disbelieves. I say: What is meant here by 'pitting one part against another' is interpreting the ambiguous elements of [the Qurʾan] by referring to another element, in accordance with one's whim without referring to [1] any revelation from [the Qurʾan's] People [i.e. the Imāms], or [2] inspiration and guidance from God.[22]

Here 'inspiration and guidance' from God sit alongside the sources for the statements of the Imāms (i.e. the *akhbār*) as a possible means of interpreting the ambiguous verses in the Qurʾan. Opposition to this 'mystical' approach was not restricted to the Uṣūlīs. The later Akhbārī Yūsuf al-Baḥrānī (d. 1186/1772)

---

21 al-Jazāʾirī, *Manbaʿ al-ḥayāt*, 52.

22 Muḥsin Fayḍ al-Kāshānī, *al-Ṣāfī* (Qom: Muʾassasat al-Hādī, 1995), 1:37.

describes Muḥsin Fayḍ as 'following the principles of the Sufis who claim to be at the same level at the Imāms in these lofty issues'.[23]

Even 'Abd Allāh al-Tūnī (d. 1071/1660–61), considered (by later writers) an Uṣūlī with Akhbārī leanings, is unhappy with accepting the *ẓawāhir al-Qur'ān*:

> We accept that the possibility that there are general statements in the Qur'an which, when they were revealed, had contextual indicators which made the intended meaning clear to the audience at the time. If we accept that, then the probative force of 'apparent' meanings [of the Qur'anic verses] as they appear to us cannot be acknowledged. [Accepting the *ẓawāhir al-Qur'ān* as having *ḥujjiyya*] would necessarily entail rejecting most of the reports transmitted in books of *akhbār* which have been revealed as interpretations of verses and rulings. This is obvious to anyone who looks at the Four Books and the others – especially *al-Kāfī*[24] and the *Tafsīr* of 'Alī b. Ibrāhīm [al-Qummī, d. 217/919], and the *'Uyūn akhbār al-Riḍā*[25] – two thirds of them – maybe four fifths of them – contradict the apparent meaning when understood linguistically. For example, *al-shams* is understood to mean the Prophet, and *al-nahār* is 'Alī b. Abī Ṭālib, and *al-layl* is 'He Who Shall Not Be Named'.[26]

By the early to mid-twelfth/eighteenth century, then, the Akhbārī position on accepting the *ẓāhir* of the Qur'an had become complicated and nuanced. The straightforward rejection one encounters in al-Astarābādī's writings had been modified in the face of Uṣulī criticism, and numerous 'Akhbārī' positions could not be identified – from the mystical (such as that of Muḥsin Fayḍ) to the purely scriptural (such as al-Jazā'irī).

Perhaps the most explicit modification of al-Astarābādī's position can be found in the writings of the later Karbala-based scholar Shaykh Yūsuf b. Aḥmad al-Baḥrānī, who is sometimes labelled a 'moderate' Akhbārī. He ties the permissibility of direct legal derivation from the Qur'an to the doctrine of the legally 'regulative verses' (*āyāt al-aḥkām*), when he writes:

> Concerning the Holy Book: There is no dispute among our Uṣūlī colleagues concerning acting on the basis of it [i.e. the Book] in legal rulings, and relying upon

23 Yūsuf b. Aḥmad al-Baḥrānī, *al-Durar al-Najafiyya* (Manama: Dār al-Muṣṭafā li-Iḥyā' al-Turāth, 2007), 340.

24 A reference to the work with this title by Muḥammad b. Ya'qūb al-Kulaynī (d. 329/941).

25 A reference to the work with this title by al-Shaykh al-Ṣadūq Ibn Bābawayh (d. 380/991).

26 'Abd Allāh al-Tūnī, *al-Wāfiya fī uṣūl al-fiqh* (Qom: Majma' al-Fikr al-Islāmī, 1992), 136.

> it – some of them have even written books on the verses which are related to legal rulings – them being 500 verses in their opinion.[27]

The employment of the Qur'an as a legal source in which the *āyāt al-aḥkām* are identified and used in legal argumentation is seen by al-Baḥrānī as a distinctly Uṣūlī approach. It is not an approach associated with the Akhbārīs. Later, when he discusses the difference between Akhbārīs and Uṣūlīs, the probative force of the Qur'an is seen as one of the major differences between the two groups – but he identifies differences among the Akhbārīs:

> Among [the differences] that they mention is that legal deduction from the Book and the Sunna alone is a distinctive doctrine of the Akhbārīs. However, there is dispute among the Akhbārīs about this.
>
> Among them is the *muḥaddith* ('traditionalist') al-Astarābādī, who was the reviver of the Akhbārīs' school in the contemporary period. He explicitly states in his book *al-Fawā'id al-madaniyya* that it is impossible to know[28] anything from it [i.e. the Qur'an] without referring to the interpretation provided by the Sinless Ones [i.e. the Imāms].
>
> Others limit any action to the *muḥkamāt* ('unambiguous verses') [of the Qur'an].
>
> Yet others go even further, such that they virtually share the same position as the Imāms in understanding its [i.e. the Qur'an's] *mutashābihāt* ('ambiguous verses').[29]

The description of al-Astarābādī's position offered here by al-Baḥrānī appears an exaggeration. Al-Astarābādī's point was not that one cannot deduce anything at all from the revelatory text, but rather that it was that the text's meaning remained undetermined (or ambiguous) until the Imām's interpretation (*tafsīr*) was known. However, before we unjustly accuse al-Baḥrānī of exaggerating al-Astarābābādī's position here, it is worth noting an edition variant. In the most recent edition, the sentence reads:

> He explicitly states in his book *al-Fawā'id al-madaniyya* that it is impossible to know anything (*al-ʿilm bi-shay'*) from it without referring to the interpretation provided by the Sinless Ones.[30]

---

27 Yūsuf b. Aḥmad al-Baḥrānī, *al-Ḥadā'iq al-nāḍira*, ed. Yūsuf al-Biqāʿī (Beirut: Dār al-Adwā' li-l-Ṭibāʿa wa-l-Nashr wa-l-Tawzīʿ, 1993), 1:27.

28 This reads *al-ʿilm bi-shay'* – but see below as this is problematic.

29 al-Baḥrānī, *al-Ḥadā'iq al-nāḍira* (ed. al-Biqāʿī), 1:185.

30 Ibid.

In the earlier edition, which accords with the manuscripts I have consulted, the sentence reads:

> He explicitly states in his book *al-Fawā'id al-madaniyya* that it is not permitted to act on anything (*al-ʿamal bi-shay'*) from it without referring to the interpretation provided by the Sinless Ones.[31]

Not being permitted to act on our apparent understanding of the Qur'an is quite different from not being able to know anything about what the Qur'an might mean. It would appear that a popular caricature of the Akhbārī position (i.e. that the Qur'anic text was meaningless) has influenced the most recent edition of al-Baḥrānī's text. Al-Baḥrānī appears to give al-Astarābādī's critique some merit. In a rather convoluted statement he says:

> It is not certain that it is obligatory to follow unconditionally [... generally speaking ...] what is understood as the 'apparent' meaning of the Qur'an.

That is, the Uṣūlīs have not proven *with certainty* that an individual (be they jurist or otherwise) is obligated to follow what they understand to be the apparent meaning of a verse of the Qur'an.

Perhaps the second opinion enumerated by al-Baḥrānī (where the *muḥkamāt* can be followed) is a position close to that of al-Jazā'irī (see above). The third Akhbārī position (i.e. those who consider themselves equal to the Imāms) would appear to be a reference to Muḥsin Fayḍ's position. There are no explicit references to the Akhbārīs who held these three views in al-Baḥrānī's text, so it would be adventurous to assert these identities. What is significant is al-Baḥrānī's own position – which he claims is that of Imām ʿAlī himself, and which was confirmed by Muḥammad b. al-Ḥasan al-Ṭūsī (d. 460/1067, 'Shaykh al-Ṭā'ifa'):

> The precise opinion and the accurate position on this matter is what Shaykh al-Ṭā'ifa says in his *Tibyān*, and is accepted by many of our notable scholars, when he says, after recounting various reports from the two perspectives (in summary): Qur'anic meaning is divided into four categories.[32]

31 Yūsuf b. Aḥmad al-Baḥrānī, *al-Ḥadā'iq al-nāḍira*, ed. Muḥammad Taqī al-Īrwānī (Qom: Mu'assasat al-Nashr al-Islāmī, 1957), 1:169.

32 al-Baḥrānī, *al-Ḥadā'iq al-nāḍira* (ed. al-Biqāʿī), 1:185.

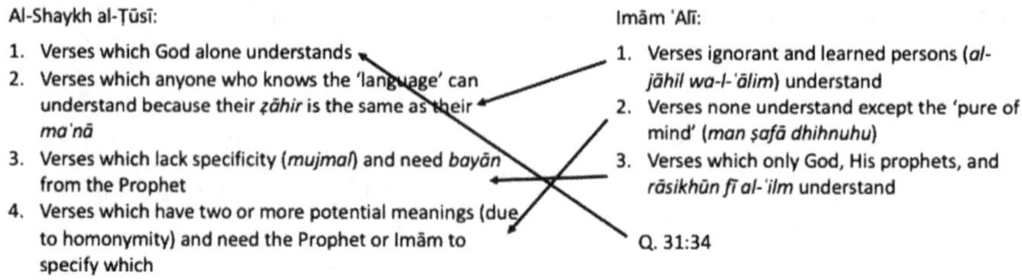

FIGURE 9.1 The correspondence between the verse classification schemas attributed to al-Shaykh al-Ṭūsī and Imām ʿAlī

His discussion is complicated, and I have discussed it elsewhere,[33] but it can be summarised as follows:

1. Imām ʿAlī himself mentions three different categories of Qur'anic verses.
2. Shaykh al-Ṭā'ifa mentions four different categories.
3. These two categorisation schemes can be married together according to the following matrix:

Crucially for al-Baḥrānī, Imām ʿAlī himself affirms that there are some Qur'anic verses which can be understood and treated as 'proofs' through direct understanding – so the Qur'an is not entirely cryptic (i.e. al-Astarābādī's *taʿmiyya* doctrine does not apply universally). However, there remain parts of the Qur'an (perhaps a significant proportion) which cannot be understood directly, and therefore any understanding relies on the *tafsīr* of the Imāms (in line with other Akhbārī positions). The debate did not end with al-Baḥrānī. Perhaps the most influential, and best-known, Akhbārī after him is Mīrzā Muḥammad al-Akhbārī (d. 1233/1818). In his refutation of Uṣūlī views on the probative force of *ẓawāhir al-Qur'ān*, he opens up a new line of argument. First, he reiterates the Akhbārī position that the Qur'an is, in fact, not addressed to the general population, but specifically to the Imāms. His *Bughyat al-fuḥūl* is a refutation the *Asās al-uṣūl* of the Indian *mujtahid* Sayyid Dildār ʿAlī (d. 1235/1820). The *Asās al-uṣūl* is itself a refutation of al-Astarābādī's *al-Fawā'id al-madaniyya*; Mīrzā Muḥammad continues the chain with a text which condemns Sayyid Dildār (and all Uṣūlism) for religious deviancy and illogicality. For example:

> [Sayyid Dildār says:] It is impossible for God to issue an address in which its *ẓāhir* [prima facie meaning] indicates something other than the intended meaning without there being a contextual indicator.

33 Robert Gleave, *Inevitable Doubt: Two Theories of Shīʿī Jurisprudence* (Leiden: Brill, 2000), 48–55.

> [Mīrzā Muḥammad replies:] Agreed – but this does not refute us because the addressee is the Sinless One, and the ones who are made legal obliged by [the announcement] are the people after having asked them [i.e. the Imāms] and them having explained it to them.[34]

Recognising that the true meaning of the Qur'an is intended to be understood only by the Imāms is the key to locating the real source of legal understanding.

Sayyid Dildār argues that the Akhbārī method of solving *ḥadīth* contradictions violates their principle that the Qur'an cannot be understood directly:

> The conclusion of these deductions are:
> To know whether a report is true depends on comparing it to the Book of God.
> Comparing it to the Book of God depends on understanding the meaning.
> Understanding the meaning depends on knowing the truth of the report (according to what our opponents – the Akhbārīs – claim).
> This is a circular argument.[35]

Mīrzā Muḥammad tackles this argument face on:

> Not all the reports are of uncertain provenance or indication such that they need to be compared [to the Book]. This is obvious to anyone who considers [on the one hand] the reports which need to be interpreted by the Imāms, and [on the other] the reports that stipulate comparison with the Book and the Sunna. So, in the reports relating to the two topics, there is no overlap or intersection at all – so where is the circulatory which the author [i.e. Sayyid Dildār] claims? No one says that the whole Book – including even the unequivocal statements (*nuṣūṣ*) – are cryptic. Yes, to compare something to the Book and Sunna requires one to understand them; and for us, understanding the *ẓawāhir* relies on the explanation of al-Quwwām [i.e. the Imāms].[36]

This complexly worded passage appears to rely on a distinction between the hermeneutic categories of *naṣṣ* (an unequivocal statement) and *ẓāhir* (a prima facie meaning). A statement which is unequivocal can only ever bear a single interpretation, and there are such statements in the Qur'an. However, they do not appear to be numerous in Mīrzā Muḥammad's view. What is more relevant

34 Sayyid ʿAlī Dildār and Mīrzā Muḥammad al-Akhbārī, *Asās al-uṣūl/Bughyat al-fuḥūl* (Karbala: Manshūrāt Dār al-Ḥusayn, 2018), 47.

35 Ibid., 59.

36 Ibid., 57.

for legal interpretation is the *ẓāhir* meaning of equivocal verses (i.e. verses which can bear more than one interpretation). Here *ẓāhir* does not mean something 'obvious' which appears in the mind of the reader. Instead, it is the term for the selected possible meaning revealed by the Imāms. Now, when two reports from the Imāms appear to contradict one another, they should be compared to the Qur'an, and since there are very few unequivocal verses, the comparison will in the vast majority of cases be to the *ẓāhir* meaning of the equivocal verses, and these *ẓāhir* meanings are determined by the Imāms' *tafsīr*. There is, then, no circularity in the Akhbārī position at all, for Mīrzā Muḥammad. Contradictory *ḥadīth*s are compared not with the Qur'an directly, but to the *ẓāhir* meaning of the Qur'an which is supplied by the Imāms.

For Mīrzā Muḥammad, determining what the *ẓāhir* meaning of a Qur'anic verse might be is not a straightforward matter:

> Understanding the *ẓawāhir* relies on the explanation of al-Qawwām [i.e. the Imāms] in our view, and upon the *mujtahid* making known his opinion in the view of the opponent [i.e. Sayyid Dildār].[37]

What is and what is not 'apparent' is not obvious – the question for Mīrzā Muḥammad is who determines that this *ẓāhir* might be. The Uṣūlīs place this interpretive power in the hands of the *mujtahid*s; for Mīrzā Muḥammad, it can only belong to the Imāms:

> It is amazing that, on the one hand, the opponent's view does not [in his view] lead to denying [the *ẓawāhir al-Qur'ān*] any probative force – and yet, on the other hand, the view of the *muḥaddith*s [i.e. the Akhbārīs] does lead to denying them probative force. How on earth did you arrive at that position?[38]

For Mīrzā Muḥammad, both Akhbārīs and Uṣūlīs effectively deny the probative force of apparent meanings – if 'apparent meaning' here means the meaning which is 'obvious' to an ordinary reader. For Akhbārīs, this is because the obvious meanings of the Qur'an are not authoritative – but the Imāms' selected meaning (which, once they have selected it, becomes the *ẓāhir*) is. However, for Uṣūlīs, he argues, the *ẓawāhir* are defined not by the ordinary readers but by the *mujtahid*s. The notion that there are unmediated obvious meanings of the Qur'anic text is an Uṣūlī myth, in Mīrzā Muḥammad's view. In Uṣūlī theory, what is *ẓāhir* is only so because the *mujtahid*s have described it as such.

37 Ibid.
38 Ibid.

Busting this myth is the principal objective of Mīrzā Muḥammad Akhbārī, and his position returns the central interpretive role to the words of the Imām.

Conclusions

All this does not mean, of course, that the apparent meaning of the Qur'anic text is disconnected with the Imām's *tafsīr* for Akhbārīs. At times, the meaning apparent to the reader can, for Akhbārīs, be confirmed by the Imām as the correct reading; the possibility that it may not, though, is what makes the Imām's *tafsīr* essential. When the Imāms provide a *tafsīr*, it is not entirely unrelated to the Qur'anic text for Akhbārīs. In legal terms, it is one of a number of possible readings of a Qur'anic verse which confirms a particular legal rule. The Imāms inform the community what the correct reading is.

In fairness, there were Akhbārīs who did not want to abandon completely the notion of direct access to Qur'anic meaning, and in this they moved close to their Uṣūlī opponents. Al-Baḥrānī appears to formulate a theory in which the Imāms permit the use of the Qur'anic text directly for legal deduction providing there is no explicit alternative meaning proposed (on another occasion) by the Imāms. Critically, though, this methodology is based on the testimony of the Imāms (specifically Imām 'Alī). It is not established by 'reason', and al-Baḥrānī does not appear to have much time for the Uṣūlī notion that taking the obvious or apparent meaning of the Qur'anic text is the rationally justified course of action. In this way, Akhbārīs maintained the legal supremacy of the Imāms' *tafsīr* while controlling direct interpretation of the Qur'an. Al-Baḥrānī's position may appear as a moderate Akhbārī one, but in fact it contains no fundamental compromise with the Akhbārī view that all legal interpretation must flow through the Imāms.

A methodological distinction needs to be drawn, then, between the legal verses of the Qur'an (*āyāt al-aḥkām*) and their interpretation, on the one hand, and interpretation of the Qur'an for the purposes of establishing the law, on the other. The former relies on there being a simple distinction between verses which have legal relevance, and those which are legally irrelevant. This might be alternatively expressed as verses for which the primary intended meaning by the Lawgiver is of legal relevance, and those where the intended meaning concerns something else. Even given this re-expression, the Akhbārī theory of Qur'anic exegesis, generally speaking, does not recognise this distinction. Akhbārī jurists just did not consider it possible, from the Qur'anic text alone, to make a distinction between verses of legal and non-legal content. In theory, this makes the entire Qur'anic text potentially relevant for legal interpretation and the *āyāt al-aḥkām* category is seen as an artificial Uṣūlī hermeneutic device. The distinction between 'regulative' and 'non-regulative verses' may be ingrained in Muslim legal interpretation generally; the Akhbārīs, though, were unconvinced that it was relevant, that it could be meaningfully made, and ultimately that it made much sense.

Bibliography

al-Amīn, Muḥsin. *Aʿyān al-Shīʿa*. Beirut: Dār al-Maṭbūʿāt, 1983.

al-Astarābādī, Muḥammad Amīn, and Nūr al-Dīn al-ʿĀmilī. *al-Fawāʾid al-Madaniyya wa-bi-dhaylihi al-Shawāhid al-Makiyya*. Qom: Muʾassasat al-Nashr al-Islāmī, 2006.

al-Baḥrānī, Yūsuf b. Aḥmad. *al-Durar al-Najafiyya*. Manama: Dār al-Muṣṭafā li-Iḥyāʾ al-Turāth, 2007.

al-Baḥrānī, Yūsuf b. Aḥmad. *al-Ḥadāʾiq al-nāḍira*. Edited by Muḥammad Taqī al-Īrwānī. Qom: Muʾassasat al-Nashr al-Islāmī, 1957.

al-Baḥrānī, Yūsuf b. Aḥmad. *al-Ḥadāʾiq al-nāḍira*. Edited by Yūsuf al-Biqāʿī. Beirut: Dār al-Adwāʾ li-l-Ṭibāʿa wa-l-Nashr wa-l-Tawzīʿ, 1993.

Brunner, Rainer. *Die Schia und die Koranfälschung*. Stuttgart: Deutsche Morgenländische Gesellschaft, 2001.

Burton, John. *The Sources of Islamic Law: Islamic Theories of Abrogation*. Edinburgh: Edinburgh University Press, 1990.

Calder, Norman. *Studies in Early Muslim Jurisprudence*. Oxford: Clarendon, 1993.

Cook, Michael. 'Early Islamic Dietary Law'. *Jerusalem Studies in Arabic and Islam* 7 (1986): 218–77.

Crone, Patricia. 'Jāhilī and Jewish Law: The *Qasāma*'. *Jerusalem Studies in Arabic and Islam* 4 (1984): 153–201.

Crone, Patricia. 'Two Legal Problems Bearing on the Early History of the Qurʾān'. *Jerusalem Studies in Arabic and Islam* 18 (1994): 1–37.

Crone, Patricia. *Roman, Provincial and Islamic Law*. Cambridge: Cambridge University Press, 1987.

Crone, Patricia, and Martin Hinds. *God's Caliph: Religious Authority in the First Centuries of Islam*. Cambridge: Cambridge University Press, 1986.

Dildār, Sayyid ʿAlī, and Mīrzā Muḥammad al-Akhbārī. *Asās al-uṣūl/Bughyat al-fuḥūl*. Karbala: Manshūrāt Dār al-Ḥusayn, 2018.

al-Ghazālī, Abū Ḥāmid. *al-Mustaṣfā fī uṣūl al-fiqh*. Beirut: Dār al-Kutub al-ʿIlmiyya, 1998.

Gleave, Robert. 'Delaying the Elucidation (*Taʾḫir al-Bayān*) in Early Muslim Legal Theory'. In *Theological Rationalism in the Medieval Islam: New Sources and Perspectives*, edited by Gregor Schwarb and Lukas Muehlethaler, 59–80. Leuven: Peters, 2018.

Gleave, Robert. 'The "First Source" of Islamic Law: Classical Muslim Legal Exegesis of the Qur'an'. In *Law and Religion: Current Legal Issues, Volume 4*, edited by Richard O'Dair and Andrew Lewis, 145–61. Oxford: Oxford University Press, 2001.

Gleave, Robert. *Inevitable Doubt: Two Theories of Shīʿī Jurisprudence*. Leiden: Brill, 2000.

Goitein, S.D. 'The Birth-Hour of Muslim Law: An Essay in Exegesis'. *The Muslim World* 50, no. 1 (1960): 23–29.

Hallaq, Wael B. *The Origins and Evolution of Islamic Law*. Cambridge: Cambridge University Press, 2004.

Hallaq, Wael B. 'The Primacy of the Qur'ān in Shāṭibī's Legal Theory'. In *Islamic Studies Presented to Charles J. Adams*, edited by Wael B. Hallaq and Donald P. Little, 69–90. Leiden: Brill, 1991.

Hawting, G.R. *The Idea of Idolatry and the Emergence of Islam: From Polemic to History*. Cambridge: Cambridge University Press, 1999.

al-Ḥurr al-ʿĀmilī, Muḥammad b. al-Ḥasan. *al-Fawāʾid al-Ṭūsiyya*. Qom: Maktabat al-Maḥallātī, 2002.

al-Jazāʾirī, al-Sayyid Niʿmat Allāh. *Manbaʿ al-ḥayāt wa-ḥujjiyyat qawl al-mujtahid min al-amwāt*. Qom: Muʾassasat al-Aʿlamī li-l-Maṭbūʿāt, n.d.

Jokisch, Benjamin. *Islamic Imperial Law: Harun al-Rashid's Codification Project*. Berlin: Walter de Gruyter, 2007.

al-Kāshānī, Muḥsin Fayḍ. *al-Ṣāfī*. Qom: Muʾassasat al-Hādī, 1995.

Lawson, B.T. 'Note for the Study of a "Shīʿī Qurʾān"'. *Journal of Semitic Studies* 36 (1991): 279–95.

Lowry, Joseph E. 'When Less Is More: Law and Commandment in *Sūrat al-Anʿām*'. *Journal of Qurʾanic Studies* 9, no. 2 (2007): 22–42.

Neuwirth, Angelika. *The Qurʾan and Late Antiquity*. Oxford: Oxford University Press, 2019.

Qasmi, Usman. *Questioning the Authority of the Past: The Ahl al-Qurʾan Movements in the Punjab*. Oxford: Oxford University Press, 2012.

Salaymeh, Lena. *The Beginnings of Islamic Law: Late Antique Islamicate Legal Traditions*. Cambridge: Cambridge University Press, 2016.

Schacht, Joseph. *The Origins of Muhammadan Jurisprudence*. Oxford: Clarendon, 1967.

al-Ṭiḥrānī, Āghā Buzurg. *Ṭabaqāt aʿlām al-Shīʿa*. Beirut: Dār Iḥyāʾ al-Turāth al-ʿArabī, 2009.

al-Tūnī, ʿAbd Allāh. *al-Wāfiya fī uṣūl al-fiqh*. Qom: Majmaʿ al-Fikr al-Islāmī, 1992.

Zellentin, Holgar Michael. *The Qurʾan's Legal Culture: Didascalia Apostolorum as a Point of Departure*. Tübingen: Mohr Siebeck, 2013.

CHAPTER 10

Arguments for the Conditional Variability of *Ḥudūd* Punishments

M. Ashraf Adeel

1 Introduction

The term *ḥudūd* is used in Islamic jurisprudence to refer to fixed punishments for certain crimes like adultery, theft, and consumption of alcohol.[1] This chapter aims to emphasise the variability[2] of Qur'anic *aḥkām*, or legal rulings, under changed conditions for the following reasons. (1) The term *ḥudūd* is not used in the Qur'an with the meaning of 'fixed punishment' anywhere, and its connotations are primarily moral that can vary. Generally, the Qur'anic *aḥkām* vary with change in the conditions of the responsible person. (2) Under the *maqāṣid al-sharīʿa*, or the higher objectives of Islamic law, the changed conditions call for relevant change in the law to ensure meeting these objectives. (3) Ismāʿīl al-Fārūqī has argued that the Qur'anic value system must form a hierarchy on pain of contradiction and values in this system cannot be treated as all falling on the same level. Some are higher, and others are lower in the hierarchy. In case of conflict between the higher and the lower values, the lower must be held in abeyance and the higher must be implemented. Hence,

1 The consensus among jurists is that adultery, false accusation of adultery, theft, drinking alcohol, and highway robbery are *ḥadd* crimes with fixed punishments.

2 Juridical tradition throughout history has held *ḥadd* punishments as fixed, although jurists on both Sunnī and Shīʿī sides canonised what Intisar A. Rabb characterises as 'doubt canon': 'Muslim jurists made doubt – and avoidance of punishment on its basis – a central pillar of Islamic criminal law'. Intisar A. Rabb, *Doubt in Islamic Law: A History of Legal Maxims, Interpretation, and Islamic Criminal Law* (New York: Cambridge University Press, 2015), 4. The severity of *ḥadd* punishments and resulting moral concerns have been always on the minds of the jurists of Islam. This avoidance of punishments in view of doubt in the elements of a given legal case (twenty-five such cases from early history are listed in appendix B by Rabb) is a feature of Islamic criminal law history that shows that conditions of a case were allowed to figure in the judgements related to whether a *ḥadd* punishment should be applied. Variability in application of these punishments, therefore, has always existed. Rabb's work is a comprehensive source for details about the development of 'doubt canon' and its use through the centuries.

 | HTTPS://DOI.ORG/10.1163/9789004755567-012

if the literal interpretation of a text conflicts with some higher objectives of the Lawgiver, the literal meaning must be held in abeyance to protect the higher objective(s). (4) Qur'anic epistemology is a *taqwā*-based or virtue epistemology and requires interpretations that do not violate any of the intellectual virtues. The intellectual conscientiousness required by the Qur'anic epistemology implies taking the changed conditions of a society into account before implementing a law. The Qur'anic view of the epistemic state of understanding lends support to hierarchical view of propositions in the Qur'an.

2 The First Argument: the Qur'anic Use of the Term *Ḥudūd*

The term *ḥudūd Allāh* is used fourteen times in ten verses of the Qur'an. Below, I examine these passages to understand the connotations with which the Qur'an uses this term in all these contexts.

While ordaining certain matters related to diet and sex during the fasting month, the Qur'an states the following:

> It has been made permissible for you the night preceding fasting to go to your wives [for sexual relations]. They are clothing for you, and you are clothing for them. God knows that you used to deceive yourselves, so He accepted your repentance and forgave you. So now, have relations with them and seek that which God has decreed for you. And eat and drink until the white thread of dawn becomes distinct to you from the black thread [of night]. Then complete the fast until the sunset. And do not have relations with them as long as you are staying for worship in the mosques. These are the limits [set by] God, so do not approach them. Thus does God make clear His ordinances to the people that they may become righteous. (Q. 2:187)

Prohibition of food from dawn to dusk and of sex even at night during *iʿtikāf*, in the course of which one generally confines oneself to the mosque for prayers and remembrance of God, are described in this verse as *ḥudūd Allāh* or limits set by God. But, in the same context of fasting, the following verses occurs prior to this one:

> O you who have believed, decreed upon you is fasting as it was decreed upon those before you that you may become righteous –
>
> [Fasting for] a limited number of days. So, whoever among you is ill or on a journey [during them] – then an equal number of days [are to be made up]. And

> upon those who are able [to fast, but with hardship] – a ransom [as substitute] of feeding a poor person [each day]. And whoever volunteers excess – it is better for him. But to fast is best for you if you only knew. (Q. 2:183–84)[3]

When read in conjunction, these three verses clearly indicate that the term *ḥudūd Allāh* as used here does not imply completely fixed obligation regarding the fast and *iʿtikāf*. Under varied conditions, the obligations placed on a person are allowed to vary. It may also be noted that Q. 2:187 connects the concept of *ḥudūd Allāh* with righteousness or *taqwā*. This shows that the concept of *ḥudūd* is a moral one, because *taqwā* is the central moral concept in the Qur'an and signifies a natural human ability to distinguish right from wrong.[4]

The second context in which the term *ḥudūd Allāh* is used is that of divorce, where once again there is variability:

> Divorce is twice. Then, either keep [her] in an acceptable manner or release [her] with good treatment. And it is not lawful for you to take anything of what you have given them unless both fear that they will not be able to keep [within] the limits of God. But if you fear that they will not keep [within] the limits of God, then there is no blame upon either of them concerning that by which she ransoms herself. These are the limits of God, so do not transgress them. And

3 According to Ibn Kathīr, 'These are the limits [set] by God' in Q. 2:187 means, 'This is what We have explained, ordained, specified, allowed and prohibited for fasting. We also mentioned the fast's objectives, what is permitted during it, and what is required of it. These are the set limits that Allah has legislated and explained, so do not come near them or transgress them.' Ibn Kathīr, *Tafsīr Ibn Kathīr*, trans. Safiur-Rahman Al-Mubarakpuri, 2:20, https://archive.org/details/TafsirIbnKathirVolume0110English_201702/page/n1213/mode/2up. However, about Q. 2:184 he says that it has been abrogated by Q. 2:185, i.e., 'The month of Ramadhan [is that] in which was revealed the Qur'an, a guidance for the people and clear proofs of guidance and criterion. So, whoever sights [the new moon of] the month, let him fast in it; and whoever is ill or on a journey – then an equal number of other days. Allah intends for you ease and does not intend for you hardship and [wants] for you to complete the period and to glorify Allah for that [to] which He has guided you; and perhaps you will be grateful.' Before the revelation of this verse, people either fasted or fed a poor person instead. After Q. 2:185 the situation changed. Healthy people did not have such an option; only the old and the sick did. Ibid., 1:519. It may be added here that *al-Mīzān fī tafsīr al-Qur'ān* by ʿAllāma Ṭabāṭabāʾī does not speak of the abrogation of Q. 2:184 by Q. 2:185 and treats Q. 2:183–85 as a unit revealed together. See the English translation by ʿAllāma Sayyid Saʿīd Akhtār Rizvī at https://almizan.org/.

4 See Fazlur Rahman, 'Some Key Ethical Terms of the Qur'ān', *The Journal of Religious Ethics* 11, no. 2 (1983): 170–85; M. Ashraf Adeel, *Epistemology of the Quran: Elements of a Virtue Approach to Knowledge and Understanding* (Cham: Springer, 2019), ch. 4.

> whoever transgresses the limits of God – it is those who are the wrongdoers. (Q. 2:229)[5]

The verse points to two different ways of staying within the limits of God. Here staying within the limits of God seems to mean staying within recognised moral limits. But the point from our perspective is variability of *ḥudūd Allāh*. The verse points to different ways of staying within God's limits. It connects the violation of these moral limits with *ẓulm* or injustice. Since injustice is both a legal and moral concept, it follows that husband and wife are expected to stay within the framework of what is legally and morally good or right. In that case, given that there are varying ways of staying within the legal and moral limits according to this verse, the term *ḥudūd Allāh* cannot designate a single, fixed legal or moral meaning.

Next, the Qur'an uses the term *ḥudūd Allāh* in Q. 2:230 and 4:13–14 in the context of divorce and inheritance. It is determined that after the third time, divorce becomes effective. Similarly, inheritance is fixed in Q. 4:12 for the wife and husband and other relatives, and then it is referred to as *ḥudūd Allāh* in Q. 4:13–14.[6] These are primarily socio-economic limits fixed by the Qur'an in the context of divorce and inheritance. However, even in these contexts, variation in the situation or circumstances of the concerned people leads to variation in *ḥudūd Allāh*.

Next, the Qur'an uses the term in the context of Bedouin psychology:

> The Bedouins are stronger in disbelief and hypocrisy and more likely not to know the limits of what [laws] God has revealed to His Messenger. And God is Knowing and Wise. (Q. 9:97)

This is an epistemic verse insofar as it points out that because of the strength of their unbelief and hypocrisy, Bedouins are more likely not to have knowledge of the revealed limits. There is no implication here that these limits are invariable even if the circumstances change.

---

5 Ibn Kathīr comments on *ḥudūd Allāh* mentioned here in these words: 'This means that the laws that Allah has legislated are His set limits, so do not transgress them.' Ibn Kathīr, *Tafsīr Ibn Kathīr*, 2:174. *Al-Mīzān* contains a similar statement: '"Limits of Allāh" are His commands and prohibitions, the things prohibited or made obligatory by Him.' Tabatabai, *Al-Mizan*, ch. 2.

6 *Al-Mīzān* states that '*al-ḥadd* means a barrier between two things which prevents their mixing together and keeps their mutual distinction and differentiation intact, like the limit or boundary of a house or a garden. The word, as used here, refers to the inheritance laws and the decreed shares.' Ibid., ch. 4.

Then the Qur'an explicitly places *ḥudūd Allāh* in the context of religious life and moral right and wrong:

> [Such believers are] the repentant, the worshippers, the praisers [of God], the travellers [for His cause], those who bow and prostrate [in prayer], those who enjoin what is right and forbid what is wrong, and those who observe the limits [set by] God. And give good tidings to the believers. (Q. 9:112)

Once again, there is no pointing to any fixedness of these limits of God under changed circumstances.

Next the term is used in the Qur'an after condemnation of the reprobate custom of *ẓihār* in the then Arab society where a husband would call his wife his mother in order to divorce her. Q. 58:3–4 note *kaffāra* or atonement for such a reprehensible act:

> And those who pronounce *ẓihār* from their wives and then [wish to] go back on what they said – then [there must be] the freeing of a slave before they touch one another. That is what you are admonished thereby; and God is Acquainted with what you do.
>
> And he who does not find [a slave] – then a fast for two months consecutively before they touch one another; and he who is unable – then the feeding of sixty poor persons. That is for you to believe [completely] in God and His Messenger; and those are the limits [set by] God. And for the disbelievers is a painful punishment. (58:3–4)

Here the term *ḥudūd Allāh* is explicitly linked with *kaffāra* or atonement for a vice. However, the *kaffāra* punishment is also made clearly variable depending on the circumstances of the sinner. The sinner must free a slave but if he does not have the capacity, then he must fast for sixty days consecutively. But if he does not have the ability to do so, he must feed sixty poor persons. As Fazlur Rahman notes, a further implication is clear here that if he is unable to feed sixty people, then some other punishment might be proposed.[7] So, the concept of fixed punishment is not a part of the concept of *ḥadd* in the Qur'an. Indeed, it is clear that *ḥadd* varies with the change in the circumstances of the perpetrator of a sin or crime.

The Qur'an again explicitly links *ḥudūd Allāh* with *taqwā* in the following verse:

---

7 Fazlur Rahman, 'The Concept of *Ḥadd* in Islamic Law', *Islamic Studies* 4, no. 3 (1965): 241.

> O Prophet, when you [Muslims] divorce women, divorce them for [the commencement of] their waiting period and keep count of the waiting period, and fear God, your Lord. Do not turn them out of their [husbands'] houses, nor should they [themselves] leave [during that period] unless they are committing a clear immorality. And those are the limits [set by] God. And whoever transgresses the limits of God has certainly wronged himself. You know not; perhaps God will bring about after that a [different] matter. (Q. 65:1)

The phrase translated as 'fear God' is '*wattaqū Allāh*', which means 'have *taqwā* of God'. *Taqwā* for the Qur'an is part of the human ability to distinguish right from wrong as implied by the use of the term by in Q. 91:7–8: 'And by the soul and the One Who fashioned it, then with the knowledge of right and wrong inspired it!' In short, *taqwā* is human conscience.[8] So, the verse exhorts the husband and wife in the eventuality of a divorce to behave according to *taqwā*. It is this which keeps them from transgressing the limits of God. Hence, the primary sense in which the term *ḥudūd Allāh* is used in this verse is also moral. Such a sense of the term becomes further clearer when the verse declares transgression of God's limits to be an 'injustice against oneself' or *ẓalama nafsah*. It is an injustice against oneself because it violates one's conscience.

The analysis above of all the verses of the Qur'an in which the term *ḥudūd Allāh* occurs brings out two things clearly about the concept of *ḥadd* or 'limit of God' in the Qur'an:

1. *Ḥudūd Allāh* are variable conditionally. Changes in the circumstances of the people concerned bring variation in the *ḥadd* to be implemented in relation to them.
2. *Ḥudūd Allāh* are linked with moral right and wrong and, hence, exercise of one's conscience in different situations of life. They need to be understood and implemented in the light of the requirements of *taqwā* or conscientiousness.[9] Their violation is a form of injustice because it involves violation of one's conscience, be it in a moral or legal context.

---

8 See Fazlur Rahman, *Major Themes of the Qur'an* (Chicago: University of Chicago Press, 2009), 29.

9 Commenting on *ḥudūd Allāh* Rahman says: 'First, these sanctions are not properly legal but constitute *kaffārah* or atonement. In fact, this question is to be raised generally about all Qur'anic "legislation" and punishments connected with them, since it is obvious throughout the Qur'an that its real concern is with the religio-moral health of the Community. The employment of such concepts as *tawhah* even where specific punishments are mentioned makes the character of the Qur'anic "legislation" all the more religious rather than legal. This means once again that law proper has to be deduced from the Qur'an rather than this law being found there ready-made.' Ibid.

3 The Second Argument: *Maqāṣid al-Sharīʿa* or the Higher Objectives of Islamic Law

Maqāṣid al-Sharīʿa or the higher objectives of Islamic law is an important genre in Islamic jurisprudence that first garnered attention in the fourth/tenth century. It was made prominent in the works of Imām al-Ghazālī (d. 505/1111).[10] These higher objectives are derived from the texts of the Qur'an and Sunna, and they are normally considered to be an expression of *maṣlaḥa* or public good.[11] Al-Ghazālī's teacher Imām al-Juwaynī (d. 478/1085), and after him al-Ghazālī himself, identified the *maqāṣid* of Islamic law, as derived from the Qur'an and Sunna, to be five, namely, protection of religion, life, reason, lineage, and property.[12] Jurists assert that these are the protections provided by law in every human society. They are primary to public good or interest and need to be preserved in the society as essential.

After al-Ghazālī, Imām al-Shāṭibī (d. 790/1388) is an important figure who contributed to the evolution of the theory of *maqāṣid*. His position can be summed up as follows:

10 Mohammad Hashim Kamali sums up the early history of *maqāṣid* as follows: 'It was not until the early fourth century that the term "*maqāṣid*" was used in the juristic writings of Abu 'Abd Allah al-Tirmidhi al-Hakim (d. 320/932) and recurrent references to it appeared in the works of Imam al-Haramayn al-Juwayni (d. 478/1085) who was probably the first to classify the *maqāṣid al-Sharīʿah* into the three categories of essential, complementary and desirable (*ḍarūriyyāt, ḥājiyyāt, taḥsīniyyāt*) which has gained general acceptance ever since. Juwayni's ideas were then developed further by his pupil, Abū Ḥāmid al-Ghazālī who wrote at length on public interest (*maṣlaḥah*) and ratiocination (*taʿlīl*) in his works, *Shifāʾ al-Ghalīl* and *al-Mustaṣfā*. Al-Ghazālī was generally critical of *maṣlaḥah* as a proof but validated it if it promoted the *maqāṣid* of the *Sharīʿah*. As for the *maqāṣid* themselves, al-Ghazālī wrote categorically that the *Sharīʿah* pursued five objectives, namely those of faith, life, intellect, lineage and property which were to be protected as a matter of absolute priority.' Mohammad Hashim Kamali, '"*Maqāṣid al-Sharīʿah*": The Objectives of Islamic Law', *Islamic Studies* 38, no. 2 (1999): 199.

11 For a scholarly overview, see Felicitas Opwis, Maṣlaḥa *and the Purpose of the Law: Islamic Discourse on Legal Change from the 4th/10th to 8th/14th Century* (Leiden: Brill, 2010). This study looks at the concept of *maṣlaḥa* (public good) in the writings of leading legal theorists from al-Jaṣṣāṣ (d. 370/980) to al-Shāṭibī (d. 790/1388). For a useful collection of papers on *maqāṣid* in Arabic, see Muhammad Salim 'Awwa, ed., *Maqāṣid al-sharīʿa al-Islāmiyya: Dirāsat fī qaḍāyā al-manhaj wa-majallāt al-taṭbīq* (*Studies in the Philosophy of Islamic Law, Theory and Applications*) (London: Al-Furqan Islamic Heritage Foundation, 2010). The first part of this collection includes papers on the beginnings and development of *maqāṣid*.

12 Felicitas Opwis, 'New Trends in Islamic Legal Theory: *Maqāṣid al-Sharīʿa* as a New Source of Law?', *Welt des Islams* 57, no. 1 (2017): 10.

1. Imām al-Shāṭibī, a key theorist of Islamic jurisprudence, argues for Islamic law to be understood in terms of the higher objectives and the intent of the Lawgiver.
2. He divides the higher objectives into three categories: essential, exigencies, and embellishments.
3. Exigencies, or objectives arising from needs, presuppose the essential objectives of the law while embellishments presuppose the exigencies.
4. There are five essential higher objectives or interests of law: religion, human life, progeny, material wealth, and human reason. The intent of the law is to protect all of them.[13] (In some places he adds 'honour' as a sixth higher objective.[14])
5. Al-Shāṭibī argues that Islamic law protects the essential interests as well as exigencies and embellishments through legislation and perpetuation of the laws and, also, by protecting them from annihilation. For example, protection of religion is undertaken through its fundamental doctrines and practices such as prayer and *zakāt* while its preservation is ensured through *jihād*, punishment for apostates, and prohibition of innovations.[15]
6. The most important thing for interpretation of the law for al-Shāṭibī is to understand the higher objectives of the Lawgiver regarding the concerned law. If the objectives of the Lawgiver are not being met, then the law cannot be applied in the current form. ʿUmar b. al-Khaṭṭāb, for example, suspended the punishment for theft during the time of famine. The intent of the Lawgiver in the prescribed punishment is to punish the transgressor and to deter others from such transgression. But during famine someone may steal out of necessity. Such a person would not constitute a transgressor. Hence, the prescribed punishment cannot be applied in such changed conditions.[16]
7. Al-Shāṭibī strikes the middle course between literalism and *taʿlīl* or cause-based interpretation when it comes to understanding the Qur'anic rulings and prohibitions. He says, 'Slavish, excessive adherence to texts' apparent meaning is a far cry from the Lawgiver's intention; however, disregard for these meanings is likewise a type of immoderation. Thus,

13 Ahmad al-Raysuni, *Imam al-Shatibi's Theory of the Higher Objectives and Intents of Islamic Law* (London and Washington, DC: The International Institute of Islamic Thought, 2005), 109.

14 Ibid., 142. However, as noted by Kamali, 'Objectives of Islamic Law', 199, 'honor' was originally added to the list by the Mālikī jurist Shihāb al-Dīn al-Qarāfī (d. 1285/1868).

15 al-Raysuni, *Higher Objectives*, 109.

16 Ibid., 334.

> if one conducts himself in accordance with what he understands to be the basis for this or that command or prohibition, he will be proceeding along the right path and be in harmony with the Lawgiver's intention in every respect.'[17]

The essential objectives of Islamic law constitute public interest or public good, normally referred to as *maṣlaḥa* (pl. *maṣāliḥ*).[18] The central idea of *maqāṣid* theorists is that Islamic law is based on *maṣāliḥ*, that is, public interests or public good. For example, 'Izz al-Din b. 'Abd al-Salām al-Sulami' (d. 660/1262) underscored the benefit of people, *maṣlaḥa*, as the greatest objective of the Sharīʿa.[19] Hence, the criterion for the legitimacy of a law or its interpretation, according to *maqāṣid* theorists, is whether the said law or its interpretation can help fulfil one or more of the higher objectives or purposes of the Sharīʿa. Al-Ghazālī, for example, held that if a new analogically derived law meets one of the objectives of the Sharīʿa, it would be legitimate even if it is not based on the text of the Qur'an or *ḥadīth*.[20]

A more recent author, Muḥammad al-Ṭāhir Ibn ʿĀshūr (1879–1973), who in his *Treatise on Maqāṣid al-Sharīʿa* modernised the terminology of *maqāṣid* discourse, connects the higher objectives of Islamic law with *fiṭrah* or the natural human disposition. Islamic beliefs and legislation are based on reason and preserve reason in civilisation. Islamic law seeks to do so through legislations whose objectives seek ease rather than hardship for humanity. His own words are worth quoting here:

> Moderation constitutes the backbone of all virtuous qualities. *Samāḥah* is commendable ease in matters where people tend toward sternness and does not cause harm or corruption. Qur'an and the *Sunnah* confirm Islam's magnanimity. The underlying wisdom is that God has made Islam the religion of the *fiṭrah* and matters of the *fiṭrah* pertain to humankind's constitution and inborn disposition. As a result, the *Sharīʿa* brings comfort to both individuals and societies.[21]

---

17 Ibid., 270.

18 For an overview, see Felicitas Opwis, '*Maṣlaḥa* in Contemporary Islamic Legal Theory', *Islamic Law and Society* 12, no. 2 (2005): 182–223.

19 Kamali, 'Objectives of Islamic Law', 200.

20 Asifa Qureshi, 'Interpreting the Qur'an and the Constitution: Similarities in the Use of Text, Tradition, and Reason in Islamic and American Jurisprudence', University of Wisconsin Law School, Legal Studies Research Paper Series Paper No. 1036, February 2007, 103.

21 Muhammad al-Tahir Ibn Ashur, *Treatise on* Maqāṣid al-Shariʿah, trans. Mohamed El-Tahir El-Mesawi (London and Washington, DC: The International Institute of Islamic Thought, 2006), 7–8.

Ibn ʿĀshūr's emphasis on ease and comfort of individuals and societies as an overall objective of the Islamic law is also present in the writings of al-Shāṭibī and earlier classical scholars. Al-Shāṭibī, for example, in his discussion of the occasion-based analysis of Islamic law, refers both to the general and specific textual principles of the Qur'an regarding the human good and ease being the goal of the Sharīʿa. He refers to Q. 21:107, where the Qur'an notes that the Prophet has been sent as a mercy to all the worlds, and to Q. 5:6, where the Qur'an says regarding the ritual ablution that God does not want to impose any hardship on human beings.[22]

We can say, therefore, that fulfilment of one or more of the higher objectives, to secure the benefit of the people ensuring ease and comfort for them, is what needs to be kept in view in understanding Islamic laws and their application. This is the perspective of the *maqāṣid* approach to Islamic law and its interpretation. Let us investigate the limitations of this perspective.

In a useful comparison of Islamic and American jurisprudence, Asifa Qureshi has argued that both juridical traditions have the *maqāṣid* perspective (understanding a law through its underlying purpose or spirit) along with literalism (understanding a law based on the plain literal meaning of the text) and originalism (understanding the text as interpreted historically by the founders) for the interpretation of their respective laws. All three approaches to the interpretation of Islamic law as well as the American Constitution have their limitations. Here we are concerned with the *maqāṣid* approach only.

Since the *maqāṣid* approach interprets the law in the light of *maṣlaḥa* (public interest in view of which a law has been revealed), it becomes a controversial issue as to whether the *maṣlaḥa* not mentioned in the text can be made a part of the relevant interpretations of the law. This type of *maṣlaḥa* is called *maṣlaḥa mursala* in the Islamic juridical tradition and was a matter of controversy between Mālikī and Shāfiʿī schools of Islamic jurisprudence. Shāfiʿīs insisted that the text of the Qur'an and *ḥadīth* covers all that is to be covered in relation to the public good or *maṣlaḥa* and, hence, going beyond the text to include *maṣlaḥa mursala* is unjustified. Mālikī jurists, however, did not believe that only the textually mentioned public interests need to be considered in interpreting the Sharīʿa. As Qureshi puts it:

> Malik himself insisted that when an approved *Maṣlaḥa* is not upheld, the likely result is the infliction of hardship on the people, which is contrary to the purposes of God's Law. In this light, Malikis believe *Maṣlaḥa* to be itself a norm of the *shari'a*, not extraneous to it. From here, it is not a leap for Malikis to incorporate

22 al-Raysuni, *Higher Objectives*, 107.

> *Maṣlaḥas* that have no textual source into their jurisprudence. The idea is that anything that is in the public good can be legally determinative, since *Maṣlaḥa* is the ultimate purpose of the Law in the first place.[23]

The problem that textualists like Shāfiʿīs saw with this kind of *maṣlaḥa*-based approach to the interpretation of the Sharīʿa was that it may be informed by the subjective thinking of the interpreter, be it an individual or a community. With the passage of time, such an approach can lead to all sorts of views of public interest to be incorporated into the Sharīʿa. This can result in dilution of the real text-based understanding of the law. Similar objections are raised against purpose-based interpretations of the American Constitution by those who want to confine the interpretations to the text of the Constitution.[24]

While al-Ghazālī and al-Shāṭibī considered a nod to the text, even if indirect, as necessary in interpreting the Sharīʿa, Najm al Dīn al-Ṭūfi (d. 716/1316) boldly suggests that the purpose of divine law is the benefit of the society and jurists should try to determine *maṣlaḥa* or public good by use of reason and by looking at what the society considers to be its *maṣlaḥa*. In this process the jurists should interpret the text to make it compatible with the public interest.[25]

In the context of our concerns in this chapter, the most important point is that al-Ghazālī, al-Shāṭibī, al-Ṭūfī, and others look at *maqāṣid* or the higher objectives of Islamic law as significant for interpretations of the Sharīʿa. The overall public good is what the higher objectives aim at. This includes avoidance of hardship for the public. Hence, it appears that, we need to find an interpretation of *ḥadd* punishments that protects the public good as understood in contemporary societies and that ensures comfort and ease for the people. This needs to be achieved without doing any disservice to the text of the Qur'an, of course. How is this possible?

Let us take the punishment for theft as enshrined in the following verse:

> [As for] the thief, the male and the female, amputate their hands in recompense for what they committed as a deterrent [punishment] from God. And God is Exalted in Might and Wise. (Q. 5:38)

The question from the *maqāṣid* perspective is what the purpose of the Lawgiver is when it comes to this punishment. The verse itself states that the purpose is 'deterrence'. The *maṣlaḥa* or interest of the thief as well as the society from

23 Qureshi, 'Interpreting the Qur'an', 104–5.
24 Cf. ibid., 115.
25 Ibid., 110.

a deterrence point of view will be met by amputating the hand of the thief. However, while he or she will surely be deterred from stealing again, is not amputation going to create hardship for the thief? If one of the higher objectives of Islamic law is to create ease and comfort rather than hardship for the people, then amputation is not going to facilitate fulfilment of this objective. The person thus punished will suffer extreme hardship for the rest of their life. It appears, therefore, that there is a tension between the overall *maṣlaḥa* of the Islamic law (avoidance of hardship for people) and the specific purpose of deterrence through literal application of this punishment. A *maqāṣid* theorist will look for a way to resolve this conflict. Such resolution can be achieved by carefully understanding the socio-economic conditions of the thief and their society and deciding as to how they (and other members of the society) can be deterred from stealing in the changed contemporary conditions without encroaching upon the overall objectives of Islamic law. This will have to be done in the light of the best available knowledge about the socio-economic conditions of the society as well as human knowledge in general. In other words, reason will have to play a crucial role in such a determination. In addition, the contemporary understanding of that society regarding its public interests must be taken into account. The formula constitutes reason plus what is *maʿrūf* or customary good.

Once such a determination has been made a deterrent punishment can be proposed for the crime of theft such that there is no conflict between the *maqāṣid* of the Sharīʿa and deterrence required by Q. 5:38. As discussed under the next argument, Ismāʿīl al-Fārūqī also noted that the values in the Qur'an form a hierarchy and the higher values need to be protected before the ones that fall lower in the hierarchy.[26] Not all Qur'anic values are at the same level of significance. Making such an assumption regarding the Qur'anic values can be detrimental to proper understanding of the revelation.

It follows, therefore, that punishment for stealing need not be fixed and invariable in changed socio-economic conditions and contemporary societal understanding of what is *maʿrūf* (generally accepted) as *maṣlaḥa* or public interest. This proposal does not violate the text of the Qur'an and simply places the text in the context of higher objectives to interpret it anew in the changed societal conditions and understanding of what is public good. The Qur'an, for example, itself allows for variation in *kaffāra* for *ẓihār* under changed condition as noted in the previous section.

26 Ismāʿīl al-Fārūqī, 'Towards a New Methodology for Qur'ānic Exegesis', *Islamic Studies* 1, no. 1 (1962): 35–52.

4 The Third Argument: the Axiological Hierarchy in the Qur'an

Ismāʿīl al-Fārūqī in his 'Towards a New Methodology for Qur'ānic Exegesis' develops an approach which somewhat resembles those who support the *maqāṣid* approach to the interpretation of Islamic law. His overall idea is based on three propositions: (1) The Qur'an is comprehensive and complete as an embodiment of the principles of the ideal values rather than as a list of 'real existents'. (2) Taking various values enshrined in the Qur'anic principles as equally important and at a level with each other and real existents lays the Qur'an open to 'pernicious charges of incompleteness, imperfection, out-of-datedness and self-contradiction'.[27] It is a 'betrayal of its holiness' and is 'nothing short of moral apathy'.[28] (3) Hence, there is an urgent need for an 'axiological systematization' of the Qur'an.

Al-Fārūqī's basic idea is that once we understand the hierarchy in which the Qur'an arranges different values, we will understand the levels of values. The values at the higher level will have priority over the values at the lower levels. In case of any apparent conflict between the higher and the lower values, we will stick to the higher values. The lower values will continue to remain a part of the Qur'anic system but will not be implemented at the cost of the higher. 'The higher lays a greater claim than the lower member of the hierarchy and where it conflicts with the lower, it legitimately demands the lower to be forsaken for the sake of the higher.'[29] We can literally accept every word of the Qur'an as divine and still implement only the higher value in case of its conflict with the lower value. Implementing the higher value only does not logically imply rejection of the conflicting lower value.

After a discussion of *naskh* or abrogation as undertaken by scholars from al-Suyūṭī (d. 911/1505) through Fakhr al-Dīn al-Rāzī (d. 606/1210) and Muhammad 'Abduh[30] (d. 1905) to Shāh Walī Ullāh (d. 1176/1762) for resolving

27 Ibid., 39–40.

28 Ibid., 41.

29 Ibid., 40.

30 Muhammad 'Abduh is one of the earliest and most influential of the modernist thinkers of Islam who strongly advocates that a nation's laws should change with changes in its conditions. In an article titled 'Laws Should Change in Accordance with the Conditions of Nations and Theology of Unity', he says: 'Since the conditions of nations depend on their collective stores of information, and the two are related in terms of cause and effect, each nation adopts rules for its activities and chooses laws for its circumstances in accordance with its power of theoretical investigation and its level of thought' (in *Modernist Islam, 1840–1940: A Sourcebook*, ed. Charles Kurzman (Oxford: Oxford University Press, 2002), 51). He goes on to contend that with changes in the circumstances, a nation's earlier laws

apparent conflicts between the verses of the Qur'an, al-Fārūqī concludes that any contradictions were found by these scholars to be only apparent. His contention is that such contradictions are effectively resolved and even the datedness of some of the concrete *aḥkām* of the Qur'an is effectively addressed if we properly understand the levels in the hierarchy of values in the Qur'an. He shows this by analysing Q. 5:38 cited above. Al-Fārūqī's analysis is as follows:

> Literally, the verse commands the realization of a real-existent state, *viz*, having the hands cut off in the case of the proven thief. The values this verse seeks to realize are purification through penitence, education through example, and retribution. These are all values: but they do not all stand on the same level. A cutting off of the hand that realizes retribution but violates the other two cannot be deemed obligatory.[31]

Al-Fārūqī goes on to add that all the three values embodied in this verse are not meant to be ends in themselves. They are meant to realise the higher ends/values of social justice and felicitous existence of the community.

It appears, therefore, that the net result of al-Fārūqī's claim of a structure of values with levels in the Qur'an is that we can continue to hold the 'retribution' part of the said verse as 'authoritative' without making it 'obligatory' upon us as long as we are in the process ensuring realisation of the higher level value of 'just distribution of wealth' in our society. Without a just distribution of wealth, how can the other two values of purification through penitence and education through example be realised effectively? In an unjust dispensation, amputating a hand is not going to help purify a thief or educate others who are suffering under injustice. Not to pay attention to different levels of values in the Qur'an, al-Fārūqī contends, is 'un-Islamic' and amounts to 'moral blindness'.[32] In a nutshell, amputating a thief's hand is not an Islamic punishment on al-Fārūqī's reading if we keep the higher values of Islamic law. Religion cannot be unjust, al-Fārūqī says, by referring to Q. 22:78. Al-Fārūqī takes this position, it appears, without having to reject the literal meaning of the concerned verse of the Qur'an.

I conclude, therefore, that other verses that are claimed by the *fiqh* tradition to embody *ḥadd* punishments can be similarly interpreted by allowing levels

---

can become even harmful for it (ibid., 52). 'Abduh's approach to law, therefore, implies that verses about *ḥadd* punishments may not be interpreted once for all times and circumstances.

31 Ibid., 48.

32 Ibid., 46.

to the values of the Qur'an or, in the *maqāṣid* language, by looking at the higher objectives of the Legislator.

5 The Fourth Argument: Intellectual *Taqwā* or the Virtue Epistemology of the Qur'an

A careful analysis of the epistemic concepts of the Qur'an shows that the Qur'anic verses presuppose a virtue approach in relation to knowledge and understanding.[33] That means that knowledge and understanding result from the exercise of intellectual virtues or intellectual conscientiousness. If that is the case, then interpretations of the Qur'anic verses, themes, and principles will have to be carried out within the framework of intellectual virtues that the Qur'an advocates in relation to the pursuit of epistemic goals in all other areas. In other words, the Qur'anic epistemic principles will have to be applied to the interpretation of the Qur'an as well. This idea is supported by one of the classical principles of *tafsīr* or Qur'anic exegesis that the Qur'an must be interpreted in the light of the Qur'an itself.[34] This, I believe, should be applied not only across verses of the Qur'an, as has been the practice throughout, but also at the conceptual and epistemological level. The epistemic concepts presupposed by the verses of the Qur'an should be applied to the verses of the Qur'an for gaining knowledge and understanding of their meaning and applicability.

An analysis of the concept of *taqwā* in all its Qur'anic contexts shows that it comprehensively covers all aspects of life, particularly moral and intellectual.[35] Intellectual *taqwā* or conscientiousness is explicitly connected by the Qur'an with the exercise of a number of intellectual virtues. This particularly comes into sharp focus if we examine all those verses where the Qur'an uses the etymological variants of the root *j-h-l*, denoting Arabic terms related to ignorance. In all these contexts the Qur'an characterises someone as displaying ignorance because of their violation of some intellectual virtue. Let us look at the details.

There are twenty-four verses in the Qur'an that use words with the root letter *j-h-l* to characterise 'ignorance' in the following ways: refusal to accept (even overwhelming) evidence in favour of an idea (Q. 6:111), adopting others' customs thoughtlessly (7:138), inability/refusal to see the worth of people because of their (lowly) station (11:29), satisfying desires unnaturally (27:55),

---

33 See Adeel, *Epistemology of the Quran*.

34 See Hafiz Zulfiqar Ali and Muhammad Farooq Haider, 'Principles of Qur'ānic Commentary by Shāh 'Abd al-'Azīz: An Applied Study of *Tafsīr Fatḥ al-'Azīz*' [in Urdu], *Al-Adwa/Al-Aẓvā* 33, no. 50 (2018): 117.

35 See Adeel, *Epistemology of the Quran*, ch. 4, for a detailed discussion on *taqwā*.

lack of openness to evidence combined with arrogance (46:23), thinking other than the truth about God (3:154), false vanity (of tribalism) (5:50), showy behaviour (33:33), zealotry (for wrong causes) (48:26), accepting reports of unrighteousness without investigation (49:6), taking unprecedented moral risk beyond one's capacities (at the time of creation) (33:72), lying on behalf of God (2:67), taking the poor to be self-sufficient, i.e., social insensitivity (2:273), misplaced impatience for results (6:35), asking for a favour for your family (from God) without knowing its real meaning (11:46), falling prey to temptation (12:33), harming your brother out of jealousy (12:89), aggressive attitude and arrogance towards the humble (25:63), vain talk or ill speech (28:55), and attributing partners to God (39:64). Four other verses that employ variants of the root *j-h-l* have only indirect relevance for the concept of ignorance in the Qur'an because one exhorts us to keep away from the company of the ignorant (Q. 7:199) and the other three speak about the acceptability of repentance for actions done in ignorance (4:17, 6:54, 16:119).

Now, if we look at these Qur'anic characterisations of ignorance, we realise that each one of them results from a failure to exercise some intellectual or epistemic virtue. There is a failure of the following virtues that the Qur'an criticises in the above contexts: epistemic responsibility of being open to evidence, rational responsibility to evaluate ideas before adopting them, epistemic fairness, avoidance of epistemic lapse or failure to exercise some relevant epistemic virtue or epistemic vigilance, epistemic humility, fairness in regard to oneself or reasonable self-respect, caring for what is right, responsibility of accepting only trustworthy testimony, knowing the proper extent of one's capacities, responsibility for a rational analysis of ideas, patience to get all the facts right, avoiding prejudice by being open to relevant facts, and openness to the truth (of revelation).

Contemporary epistemologists consider exercise of these virtues and similar intellectual virtues as intellectual or epistemic conscientiousness.[36] The key point for the Qur'an seems to be exercise of epistemic conscientiousness while forming beliefs. For example, we no longer can remain epistemically conscientious in case we ignore overwhelming evidence for an idea or fail to rationally evaluate it before adopting it. Similarly, if we violate epistemic or intellectual fairness or fail to exercise some other relevant epistemic virtue in a given situation, we cannot remain conscientious. The same goes for all the other virtues mentioned above. However, this is not meant to be an exhaustive list of the epistemic virtues mentioned in the Qur'an. These are the virtues presupposed by the verses that mention ignorance in various ways. There are

36 See, for example, James A. Montmarquet, *Epistemic Virtue and Doxastic Responsibility* (Lanham: Rowman & Littlefield, 1993), 23.

many other epistemic virtues mentioned in the Qur'an in different contexts.[37] My basic point here is that any judgement in any area of enquiry that violates intellectual conscientiousness is going to be marred by ignorance as per the Qur'anic epistemology.

Let us turn now to the Qur'anic concept of understanding.[38] This concept is displayed in verses that talk about 'people of understanding' or *ulū al-albāb*. Understanding, according to the concept presupposed or implied by these verses, seems to function at least in the following ways: an insight into deeper aspects of a principle (Q. 2:179), a kind of a cognitive state that contributes to or facilitates our special ability or disposition to distinguish right from wrong in all situations (2:197, 5:100, 65:10), cognitive state or ability to grasp the significance of wisdom for human life (2:269), special aptitude or disposition to seeing natural phenomena as pointing towards God or deeper meaning (3:190), ability to see a story as a connected whole and draw a moral/lesson from it (12:111), comprehending an entire system of ideas and values, such as revealed message, and grasping their interrelations (13:19, 14:52, 38:29, 40:54), seeing a higher dimension to worldly blessings or trials (38:43), paying heed to the difference between devout and un-devout, knowledgeable and ignorant (39:9), and mastery of a language and following the best of its meaning in different situations (39:18).

There seem to be three basic ideas in these functions of understanding mentioned in the Qur'an: understanding is gained by grasping the deeper logical or interpretive implications of principles or phenomena or stories; understanding is involved in grasping the ethical and the wiser course; understanding is involved in mastery of a language. All three functions presuppose grasp of interrelations between parts and wholes. Hence, in understanding a subject or a system or a language, we come to grasp the interrelations between their parts and wholes. In other words, we come to grasp what has been characterised as dependence relations – logical, causal, or conceptual – between parts and wholes of a system or a subject in understanding it.[39]

---

37 See *EOQ*, ch. 4, for some additional intellectual virtues mentioned in the Qur'an.

38 Contemporary epistemology takes knowledge to be propositional in character. We 'know' individual propositions of bioethics, for example. We can also 'understand' individual propositions, but such understanding is not distinct from knowledge. However, holistic or objectual understanding is 'understanding' of a system of propositions with the interrelations between them. Such holistic understanding presupposes knowledge of individual propositions. That is the Qur'anic position on this matter. For further discussion, see *EOQ*, ch. 5.

39 See John Greco, 'Episteme: Knowledge and Understanding', in *Virtues and Their Vices*, ed. Kevin Timpe and Craig A. Boyd (Oxford: Oxford University Press, 2014), 293.

It is this kind of comprehensive understanding, which if put to its best practical use in a relevant situation, that the Qur'an calls *ḥikma* or wisdom. According to the Qur'an, wisdom is the abundant moral and intellectual good, *khayran kathīran* (Q. 2:269), and a knowledge that can be taught and learned (2:151), is involved with making the best argument on a subject (16:125), involves understanding (2:269), discernment of speech (38:20), and the ability to clarify contentious issues (43:63), and leads to moral and spiritual rectitude or overall righteousness (62:2). The elements of this abundant moral and intellectual good are knowledge, understanding, and best possible arguments that should jointly lead to overall righteousness. Hence, for the Qur'an wisdom is a form of knowledge as well as understanding that produces comprehensive righteousness in one's life. It is a virtue that the Qur'an seems to take to be a product of knowledge and understanding that involves best argument or reasoning. Hence wisdom, being a virtue, does appear to be an ability to act righteously. Although it is an epistemic or cognitive state, it is a state that produces overall righteousness. Since it is applied or practical understanding, that is, understanding put to best practical use, it can be said that in wise decisions our understanding reflets upon itself to find its own best practical use. It becomes a reflective understanding or meta-understanding.[40]

This view of the Qur'ānic concept of understanding and wisdom takes wisdom to require a holistic understanding of a given field of concern for us and then find the best way to use this understanding in action or practice related to that field. Our field of concern here is interpretation of the legal verses of the Qur'an, including those related to *ḥadd* punishments. What will the application of the Qur'anic epistemology amount to in this context? It is obvious that the first step is to develop a holistic understanding of the Qur'anic legal verses and concepts. This itself is a huge undertaking. It must be emphasised, though, that such an undertaking will involve not only the knowledge of individual legal verses and their objectives and implications but also the so-called dependence relations between all the verses as well as concepts. What that means is that we will have to subsume particularised concrete applications of principles under the more general verses or principles. The goal will be to see the logical, causal, and social inter-dependence relations between the principles and their concrete applications. This will give us a holistic understanding of the legal verses.[41]

40 See *EOQ*, ch. 7.

41 Cf. Fazlur Rahman's two-tiered methodology for the interpretations of the Qur'an for contemporary times in the introduction of his *Islam and Modernity: Transformation of an Intellectual Tradition* (Chicago: University of Chicago Press, 1982).

The second step will be to find the best way to apply such an understanding to our contemporary relevant situations in the society. That obviously requires understanding of the contemporary situations in the light of the current state of our knowledge of society through social sciences. Unless we clearly understand the contemporary relevant situations, we will not be able to decide whether we are making the best use of legal verses. In other words, we have to act wisely in using our holistic understanding of the Qur'anic legal verses. Otherwise, we will be violating the Qur'anic requirement of intellectual conscientiousness. This would mean that our judgements would be tainted by ignorance.

Now, if we take all the verses designated as *ḥadd* punishment verses and look at them along with all the legal verses of the Qur'an and relevant legal and moral concepts in the Qur'an, we end up with a picture in which *ḥadd* punishments will have to be viewed as part of a system of propositions or ideas. The interrelations between them will have to be grasped, and some propositions/ideas will be logically prior to others. Similarly causal relations will place some propositions as effects of others. This immediately introduces levels between propositions in the system. But there will be multiple such levels because of different levels of generality that various propositions will have. Hence, in order to understand the Qur'anic laws with intellectual conscientiousness, we will need to subsume propositions embodying lower values to the ones that embody higher values. Therefore, the position of *maqāṣid* theorists, outlined above, is supported by the virtue epistemology of the Qur'an as well.

6 Conclusion

My first argument has shown that variation in the conditions of an agent or their circumstances leads to changes in the Qur'anic legal and religious requirements on them. The contexts in which the Qur'an uses the term *ḥudūd Allāh* have variations in orders under changed circumstances. In other words, conditional variability is implied by the text as far as *ḥadd* punishments are concerned. Additionally, the Qur'an connects *ḥudūd Allāh* with *taqwā*, which makes them primarily moral limits.

This inference is reinforced by the *maqāṣid* argument, which allows for not adhering to the literal interpretation of the text in case such an interpretation conflicts with one or more of the higher objectives of Islamic law. *Ḥudūd* punishments can be reinterpreted to make them consistent with the higher objectives of the Lawgiver, which aim at ease and comfort for humanity and protect its interests. This also implies conditional variability of these punishments because, with changes in society and human knowledge, older interpretations may come to conflict with our understanding of public good or *maṣlaḥa*, which it is the aim of the Sharīʿa to protect.

My third argument, based on Ismāʿīl al-Fārūqī's idea of axiological hierarchy in the Qur'an, means that a value lower in the Qur'anic hierarchy can be held in abeyance in order to protect or promote a higher value in case there is conflict between them. This does not mean rejection of the lower value or text embodying it. It only means that under changed circumstances the lower value, or the text embodying it, remains unapplied for the sake of protecting the higher value or text embodying it. This argument from axiological hierarchy lends support to the *maqāṣid* argument, which also asks for adjustment in interpretation under changed circumstances in view of the higher objectives of the law that protect public good.

Finally, my fourth argument from the virtue epistemology of the Qur'an showed that an intellectually conscientious understanding of the legal verses, including *ḥadd* punishments, would also lead to higher and lower propositions in the concerned system of verses. In the Qur'anic view the epistemic state of understanding is systematic and holistic. As such it involves understanding of interrelations or dependence relations between parts and wholes. Some propositions are logically prior to others, and some are causally and conceptually prior to others. As this layering happens at multiple levels in a system of proposition, like all the legal verses of the Qur'an, there can be multiple levels of propositions in the understanding that one would develop of these verses. As a result, there will have to be higher and lower levels. Hence, the Qur'anic view of understanding, as a product of intellectual conscientiousness, lends support to the idea of propositional/axiological hierarchy in the Qur'an and thereby the *maqāṣid* argument.

Overall, the Qur'anic worldview, with the higher objectives of Islamic law embodied in it, supports a flexible and conditionally variable interpretation of the *ḥadd* punishments.

Bibliography

'Abduh, Muhammad. 'Laws Should Change in Accordance with the Conditions of Nations and Theology of Unity'. In *Modernist Islam, 1840–1940: A Sourcebook*, ed. Charles Kurzman, 50–60. Oxford: Oxford University Press, 2002.

Adeel, M. Ashraf. *Epistemology of the Quran: Elements of a Virtue Approach to Knowledge and Understanding*. Cham: Springer, 2019.

Ali, Hafiz Zulfiqar, and Muhammad Farooq Haider. 'Principles of Qur'ānic Commentary by Shāh 'Abd al-'Azīz: An Applied Study of *Tafsīr Fatḥ al-'Azīz*'. [In Urdu.] *Al-Adwa/Al-Aẕvā* 33, no. 50 (2018): 117–40.

'Awwa, Muhammad Salim, ed. *Maqāṣid al-sharīʿa al-Islāmiyya: Dirāsat fī qadāyā al-manhaj wa-majallāt al-taṭbīq* (*Studies in the Philosophy of Islamic Law, Theory and Applications*). London: Al-Furqan Islamic Heritage Foundation, 2010.

al-Fārūqī, Ismāʿīl. 'Towards a New Methodology for Qur'ānic Exegesis'. *Islamic Studies* 1, no. 1 (1962): 35–52.

Greco, John. 'Episteme: Knowledge and Understanding'. In *Virtues and Their Vices*, edited by Kevin Timpe and Craig A. Boyd, 284–301. Oxford: Oxford University Press, 2014.

Ibn Ashur, Muhammad al-Tahir. *Treatise on* Maqāṣid al-Shariʿah. Translated by Mohamed El-Tahir El-Mesawi. London and Washington, DC: The International Institute of Islamic Thought, 2006.

Ibn Kathīr. *Tafsīr Ibn Kathīr*. Translated and abridged by a group of scholars under the supervision of Sheikh Safiur-Rahman Al-Mubarakpuri. 10 vols. https://archive.org/details/TafsirIbnKathirVolume0110English_201702/page/n1213/mode/2up.

Kamali, Mohammad Hashim. '"*Maqāṣid al-Sharīʿah*": The Objectives of Islamic Law'. *Islamic Studies* 38, no. 2 (1999): 193–208.

Montmarquet, James A. *Epistemic Virtue and Doxastic Responsibility*. Lanham: Rowman & Littlefield, 1993.

Opwis, Felicitas. Maṣlaḥa *and the Purpose of the Law: Islamic Discourse on Legal Change from the 4th/10th to 8th/14th Century*. Leiden: Brill, 2010.

Opwis, Felicitas. '*Maṣlaḥa* in Contemporary Islamic Legal Theory'. *Islamic Law and Society* 12, no. 2 (2005): 182–223.

Opwis, Felicitas. 'New Trends in Islamic Legal Theory: *Maqāṣid al-Sharīʿa* as a New Source of Law?'. *Welt des Islams* 57, no. 1 (2017): 7–32.

Qureshi, Asifa. 'Interpreting the Qur'an and the Constitution: Similarities in the Use of Text, Tradition, and Reason in Islamic and American Jurisprudence'. University of Wisconsin Law School, Legal Studies Research Paper Series Paper No. 1036, February 2007.

Rabb, Intisar A. *Doubt in Islamic Law: A History of Legal Maxims, Interpretation, and Islamic Criminal Law*. New York: Cambridge University Press, 2015.

Rahman, Fazlur. 'The Concept of *Ḥadd* in Islamic Law'. *Islamic Studies* 4, no. 3 (1965): 237–51.

Rahman, Fazlur. *Islam and Modernity: Transformation of an Intellectual Tradition*. Chicago: University of Chicago Press, 1982.

Rahman, Fazlur. *Major Themes of the Qur'an*. Chicago: University of Chicago Press, 2009.

Rahman, Fazlur. 'Some Key Ethical Terms of the Qur'ān'. *The Journal of Religious Ethics* 11, no. 2 (1983): 170–85.

al-Raysuni, Ahmad. *Imam al-Shatibi's Theory of the Higher Objectives and Intents of Islamic Law*. London and Washington, DC: The International Institute of Islamic Thought, 2005.

Tabatabai, Allamah. *Al-Mizan: An Exegesis of the Qur'an*. Translated by 'Allāma Sayyid Sa'īd Akhtār Rizvī. https://almizan.org/.

CHAPTER 11

Metaphysical and Legal Implications of the Earliest Instance of *Āyāt al-Aḥkām*

The Prophet Muḥammad's Spiritual Journey in Light of the Obligatory Nature of the Night Prayer Vigil (*Ṣalāt al-Layl*) in Sūrat al-Muzzammil

Imranali Panjwani

Sūrat al-Muzzammil is often designated the third Meccan chapter revealed to the Prophet Muḥammad in order of revelation, but Qur'anic commentators consider its last verse to have been revealed in Medina, signalling the obligatory nature of the daily prayers and thereby abrogating the initial obligation to perform the night vigil or night prayer (*ṣalāt al-layl*) rendering it merely 'recommended' (*mustaḥabb*) instead. The discussion revolves around whether the night prayer vigil described in Q. 73 was abrogated and why it arguably represents the earliest historical case of *āyāt al-aḥkām*, the regulatory verses of the Qur'an.

This study aims to explore critically the relationship between the night prayer vigil and the daily prayers, with specific reference to the circumstances of their revelation (*asbāb al-nuzūl*) amid the challenges the Prophet Muḥammad faced in preparing himself to receive the revelation of *qawl thaqīl* ('a weighty word', Q. 73:5). I argue that the concept of *āyāt al-aḥkām* should first be examined through the lens of the developing soul of the Prophet as opposed to being considered legal regulations imposed upon himself or Muslims generally. This lens brings into focus the metaphysical and spiritual reasons behind prayer itself.

Secondly, there is evidence from oral narrations cited in Qur'anic commentaries that those who prayed the night prayer vigil with the Prophet found it difficult to perform the prayer – either because of its stipulated time or because of its duration. However, it appears those who found it difficult to perform did not later make up their lapsed prayers. This may have distinct juristic implications concerning the necessity of performing a make-up prayer, which is applicable to those adjusting to new rites in Islam such as converts new to the faith and children who have just attained maturity. Thirdly, analysis of this issue may suggest an expansion of the dimensions of legal capability (*istiṭāʿa*) for the

 | HTTPS://DOI.ORG/10.1163/9789004755567-013

performance of ritual obligations to take into consideration one's psychological, spiritual, and physical capacity.

1 The Subject Matter of the Regulatory Verses (*Āyāt al-Aḥkām*)

Āyāt al-aḥkām may be defined comprehensively as follows: 'The verses of regulations are those verses that are concerned with clarifying legal rulings and indicating them, whether the rulings have to do with belief, practical actions, individual actions, behaviour, or ethics.'[1] However, the majority of scholars have viewed the regulative verses in the context of Islamic law, and that is why this subject may also be known as *fiqh al-Qur'ān* (law based on the Qur'an). Hence, traditionally, *āyāt al-aḥkām* refer to 'the verses that clarify the legal rulings and indicate them by explicit text or deduction'.[2] Common legal examples derived from the Qur'an have to do with ablution (*wuḍū'*), prayer (*ṣalāt*), alms (*zakāt*), fasting (*ṣiyām*), and pilgrimage (*ḥajj*). For example, the verse of ablution states, 'O you who have faith! When you stand up for prayer, wash your faces and your hands up to the elbows, and wipe a part of your heads and your feet, up to the ankles' (Q. 5:6). Such verses indicate the clear, practical legal duty of the legally responsible believer (*mukallaf*) to perform ablution as a requirement for daily prayer.

It is important to note also that the term '*sharī'a*' (path to God) is broader than law. Law is defined in English legal dictionaries (and in the Western conception of the word) as

> the regime that orders human activities and relations through systematic application of the force of politically organised society, or through social pressure, backed by force, in such a society.[3]

Law therefore pertains to commands and enforcement within the context of a state. However, the Sharī'a's five categories of obligatory (*wājib*), prohibited (*ḥarām*), recommended (*mustaḥabb*), reprehensible (*makrūh*), and permitted

1 Walīd al-'Umarī, *Muqaddimāt fī al-āyāt al-aḥkām*, https://tafsīr.net/article/5397/mqdmt-fy-aayat-al-ahkam#_ftn2.

2 Ibid. See also 'Alī b. Sulaymān al-'Ābid, *Tafasīr āyāt al-aḥkām wa-manāhijihā* (Riyadh: Dār al-Tadmuriyya, 2010).

3 Bryan A. Garner, ed., *Black's Law Dictionary*, 9th ed. (Saint Paul, MN: West – Thomson Reuters, 2009), 962.

(*mubāḥ*) may all be ethical and spiritual in nature rather than just strictly legal.[4] For example, it is obligatory to pray five times a day to God, but a state cannot enforce this against an individual. At the same time, it is obligatory to pay the alms (*zakāt*), and payment may be enforceable in a Muslim state but will not be enforceable in a non-Muslim state. It is also recommended for Muslims to greet one another with *salām* ('peace'), but this customary practice is purely ethical in nature.

At this point, the definition of *āyāt al-aḥkām* becomes broader in scope and more open to interpretation. There is disagreement on the number of *āyāt al-aḥkām*; some authorities set the number of such verses at 500, others at only 100, and others still at 150.[5] In fact, while many classical books in the genre of *āyāt al-aḥkām* or *aḥkām al-Qur'ān* traditionally present the typical chapters of the law in their standard order – ritual purity, prayer, alms, fasting, and pilgrimage, and so on[6] – some contemporary works include numerous spiritual and ethical matters under the title of *āyāt al-aḥkām*.[7] Moreover, contrary to the common idea that Meccan suras prima facie do not contain verses with

4 See the analysis by Fatemi, 'by labelling *fiqhi* norms as "law", however, he contributes to the confusion about the nature of *fiqh*, a confusion created by previous scholars such as Schacht in their introductions to the discipline (Schacht, 1964). As I have concluded elsewhere, *fiqh* should not be confused either with "law" in the modern sense or with a "moral system" in modern philosophical terms (Fatemi, 2005a, p. 298). *Fiqhi* norms are a set of religious ethical commands and precepts with rare legal sanctions that are a product of jurists' argumentation from primary sources of Sharīʿah (Fatemi, 2005b, p. 194).' S. Mohammad Ghari S. Fatemi, 'Autonomy and Equal Right to Divorce with Specific Reference to Shiʿi *Fiqh* and the Iranian Legal System', *Islam and Christian–Muslim Relations* 17, no. 3 (2006): 281, 282–83.

5 al-ʿUmarī, *Muqaddimāt*. See also Bāqir al-Īrwānī, *Durūs tamhīdiyya fī tafsīr āyāt al-aḥkām min al-Qur'ān*, 1st ed. (Beirut: Dār Kumayl, 2004), 1:19.

6 For the traditional categorisation of *āyāt al-aḥkām* through the lens of jurisprudential books, see, for example, Abū Jaʿfar Aḥmad al-Ṭaḥāwī, *Aḥkām al-Qur'ān al-karīm*, https://archive.org/details/FP45899FP/00_45899/. See also 'Tafsir Ayat al-Ahkam', Irshad, https://irshad.org.uk/library/tafsīr-ayat-al-ahkam/. Muḥammad Ibrāhīm Jannatī lists the core works of *āyāt al-aḥkām* under each school of thought, the earliest of which are: Shiʿa: *Āyāt al-aḥkām*, by Muḥammad b. Sā'ib al-Kalbī (d. 146/763). Besides this book, he had written a complete *tafsīr* of the Qur'an; Zaydī: *Sharḥ āyāt al-aḥkām*, by Yaḥyā b. Ḥamza al-Yamanī (d. 749/1348); Ḥanafī: *Aḥkām al-Qur'ān*, by ʿAlī b. Ḥajar al-Saʿdī al-Marwazī al-Khurāsānī (d. 244/858); *Mālikī: Aḥkām al-Qur'ān*, by Aḥmad b. al-Muʿadhdhal (d. 240/854); *Shāfiʿī: Aḥkām al-Qur'ān*, compiled by Muḥammad b. Idrīs al-Shāfiʿī, the leader of the Shāfiʿī school of law (d. 204/819); Ḥanbalī: *Āyāt al-aḥkām*, compiled by Qāḍī Abū Yaʿlā al-Kabīr (d. 458/1066); Ẓāhirī: *Aḥkām al-Qur'ān*, compiled by Dāwūd b. ʿAlī al-Ẓāhirī al-Iṣfahānī (201–70/816–83); Muḥammad Ibrāhīm Jannatī, *Manābiʿ-e ijtihād az dīdgāh-e mazāhib-e islāmī* (Tehran: Intishirāt-e-Kayhān, 1991), 7–12.

7 Al-Īrwānī includes wide-ranging topics in his textbook on *āyāt al-aḥkām* such as *tawba*, *ṣabr*, *istiqāma*, *al-tafaqquh*, *iftā'*, *taqlīd*, *tablīgh* of *aḥkām*, *tawakkul*, *dhikr Allāh*, and how to recite the Qur'an, among many others. See al-Īrwānī, *Durūs tamhīdiyya fī tafsīr āyāt al-aḥkām*, vols. 1–2.

legal content, while Medinan suras do, this example involving the obligation to perform night prayer or vigils serves as an instance of *āyāt al-aḥkām* revealed in Mecca.[8] Two important points may be made here. Firstly, *āyāt al-aḥkām* may comprise all the standard chapters of Islamic legal manuals but may also sometimes include the ethical and spiritual dimensions of those legal topics, such as intention and forgiveness.[9] Secondly, regardless of one's conception of *āyāt al-aḥkām*, the common thread here is that whether the act is performative as a ritual, financial, or societal obligation or as an ethical or spiritual act – all of them are in the end *practical acts* to seek nearness to God through *what we perceive* as obligations, prohibitions, recommendations, dissuasions, or permissions emanating from God.

It is here that I can now begin my argument. Night prayer vigil, according to my research, constitutes the first performative and practical act that the Prophet was commanded to do himself, but the command took due consideration of his own spiritual, moral, and practical circumstances. It therefore represents the earliest case of the presentation of *āyāt al-aḥkām*, or verses with legal implications, in the Qur'an. Examination of this topic may provide a holistic model indicating how to interpret *āyāt al-aḥkām* consistently and may make it possible to review existing approaches to this topic while also providing solutions to new jurisprudential challenges.

2 My Methodological Approach to *Āyāt al-Aḥkām*: Exegesis according to the Historical Order of Revelation (*Tafsīr al-Qur'ān Ḥasab Tartīb al-Nuzūl*)

The most obvious question is why begin with night vigils and not with ritual purity, prayer, or alms, following the dominant scholarly approach in the genre of works on *āyāt al-aḥkām*. I will justify this in three stages. Firstly,

8 Muḥammad Ibrāhīm Jannatī summarises the division between Meccan and Medinan verses with regard to *āyāt al-aḥkām*: 'a significant number of Qur'anic verses constitute *āyāt al-aḥkām* (legally relevant verses). These verses have been, and are, the basis for deriving *ahkam*. Their number totals approximately 500. These were gradually revealed on various occasions during the years following the Prophet's Hijra. Accordingly, the *āyāt al-aḥkām* are to be sought in the Medinan verses. The *āyāt al-aḥkām* lay down the Islamic laws and rules concerning social, penal, and economic matters. In contrast, the Meccan verses mostly describe and prescribe doctrinal and ethical principles.' Jannatī, *Manābiʿ-e ijtihād*, 6.

9 See Bāqir al-Īrwānī, *Durūs tamhīdiyya fī al-fiqh al-istidlālī ʿalā al-madhhab al-Jaʿfarī*, 3 vols. (Qom: Mu'assasat al-Fiqh, 2005). As an example, al-Īrwānī and many jurists discuss the role of intention (*niyya*) in fasting and whether a fast was broken intentionally or not and the corresponding level of recompense. See ibid., 1:192.

my approach in understanding the trajectory and historical context of the Qur'an is in the chronological order it was revealed, not compiled. We know as a matter of historical fact that the Qur'an was not revealed in its current order of compilation.[10] According to the majority view of the chronological order of revelation, the first five verses of Sūrat al-ʿAlaq were revealed to the Prophet, then verses of Sūrat al-Qalam, then verses of Sūrat al-Muzzammil, and then verses of Sūrat al-Muddaththir.[11] You will note that I have used the term 'verses' and not chapters, as initially no chapter was revealed in full. Sūrat

10 Muḥammad Hādī Maʿrifa, in citing several scholars from the Sunnī and Shīʿī traditions in order to show consensus on this issue, lists the chapters of the Qur'an in the order they were revealed and divides them into Meccan and Medinan. See Muḥammad Hādī Maʿrifa, *Talkhīṣ al-tamhīd: mūjaz dirāsāt mubassaṭāt ʿan mukhtalif shuʾūn al-Qurʾān al-karīm* (Qom: Muʾassasat al-Nashr al-Islāmī, 2009), 89–92. Furthermore, Ṭabāṭabāʾī states, 'in 17:106 we read: "And it is a Qur'an that we have divided that you may recite it to mankind at intervals and we have revealed it by (successive) revelations." As further proof there are abrogating and abrogated verses which are directly related to events from different periods and circumstances and which obviously were not revealed at one time. At this point we should note that the chapters and verses were not revealed in the order in which they are set out; that is the first chapter "al-Fātiḥah" (The Opening) was revealed after "The Cow", "The Family of ʿImrān", "Women" and "The Table Spread". This is true also for the order of the verses which do not necessarily follow chronologically. The content of a Qur'anic text may for example show that the content of some chapters and verses concord with the first period of the Prophet's mission – like the chapters "The Clot" and "Nūn" but are recorded at the end of the Qur'an.' Muḥammad Ḥusayn Ṭabāṭabāʾī, *The Qur'an in Islam: Its Impact and Influence on the Life of Muslims*, 1st ed. (India: World Islamic Network, 1998), pt. 5, www.al-islam.org/quran-islam-its-impact-and-influence-life-muslims-sayyid-Muḥammad-husayn-tabatabai/part-5-order.

11 Ibn Nadīm quotes the following narration in this regard: 'Abū al-Ḥasan b. Yūsuf (al-Nāqiṭ) transmitted to me, saying that Abū ʿAbd Allāh Muḥammad b. Ghālib transmitted to us, saying that Abū Muḥammad ʿAbd Allāh b. al-Ḥajjāj al-Madanī arrived in the year 99 ah, saying that Bakr b. ʿAbd al-Wahhāb al-Madīnī said that Muḥammad b. ʿUmar al-Wāqidī transmitted to me, saying that Maʿmar b. Rāshid reported, on the authority of al-Zuhrī, on the authority of Muḥammad b. Nuʿmān b. Bashīr, that the first of what was revealed of the Qur'an to the Prophet was *Iqraʾ bi-smi rabbika* to *ʿallama l-insāna mā lam yaʿlam* (Q. 96), then *Nūn wa-l-qalam* (Q. 68), then *Yā ayyuhā al-muzzammil* (Q. 73) ... It has further been narrated on the authority of Mujāhid that he said: Sūrat al-Masad (Q. 111), al-Takwīr (Q. 81), then al-Aʿlā (Q. 87), then *a-lam nashraḥ laka ṣadrak* (Q. 94), then al-ʿAsr (Q. 103), then al-Fajr (Q. 89), then al-Ḍuḥā (Q. 93), then al-Layl (Q. 92), then al-ʿĀdiyāt (Q. 100), then al-Kawthar (Q. 108), then al-Takāthur (Q. 102), then Māʿūn (Q. 107), then al-Kāfirūn (Q. 109), etc.' I am adopting the chronology from the aforementioned narration that Ibn Nadīm quotes which goes back to Abū al-Ḥajjāj Mujāhid b. Jabr al-Qārī (who studied under ʿAlī b. Abī Ṭālib and Ibn ʿAbbās) and states the order of revelation of the Qur'an. Abū al-Faraj Muḥammad b. Isḥāq al-Nadīm, *Kitāb al-fihrist*, ed. Ayman Fuʾād Sayyid, 2nd ed. (London: Al-Furqan Foundation, 2014), 1:62.

al-Fātiḥa is regarded as the first sura to have been revealed in complete form, after the aforementioned suras.[12]

The fact that verses and not chapters were initially revealed to the Prophet is of course crucial to understand his personal, spiritual, psychological, moral, practical, social, and cultural circumstances at the time of revelation. These verses specifically responded to the inner and outer state of the Prophet, as I will demonstrate through examination of the case of night prayer vigils in Sūrat al-Muzzammil. It is this multifaceted process of communication and reception, involving the personality of the Prophet and God's messages to him, that constitutes the primary lens by which we should view *āyāt al-aḥkām*. *Āyāt al-aḥkām* are not necessarily first about the law; rather, they are about the Prophet's personal journey within himself and the society in which he lived, which must be critically examined to understand why a practical duty arose in that instance as well as what its current scope is. These instances are deeper than the circumstances of revelation (*asbāb al-nuzūl*), which Muḥammad Hādī Maʿrifa defines as occurring 'if there had been a current problem that did not have a clear solution'.[13] They are 'more specific'[14] than the background of the revelation (*sha'n al-nuzūl*), which 'clarify or explain a verse or sura ... such as stories and information of past peoples and ancient nations, the situations of earlier prophets that may have been distorted and nearly affected their dignity and degraded their sanctity'.[15] What I am advocating is a critical examination of the Prophet's spiritual journey of revelation, which may be termed as *sulūk al-nuzūl*.

Secondly, the approach of understanding the Qur'an according to its revelatory descent has been attempted by Muslim scholars, albeit by an extremely small minority.[16] There is a gradual, although slow, contemporary awareness

12 See Maʿrifa, *Talkhīṣ al-tamhīd*, 93–97.

13 Ibid., 112.

14 Ibid.

15 Ibid., 113.

16 The exegetical works based on the revelatory sequence of the Qur'an I could find are: Muḥammad ʿIzzat Darwaza al-Nāblusī, *al-Tafsīr al-ḥadīth tartīb al-suwar ḥasab al-nuzūl*; ʿAbd al-Qādir b. Sayyid Muḥammad Ḥuwaysh b. Maḥmūd al-Ghāzī al-ʿĀnī (known as Mulla Ḥuwaysh), *Bayān al-maʿānī murattab tartīb al-nuzūl*; ʿAbd al-Raḥmān Ḥasan Ḥabbanaka al-Maydānī, *Maʿārij al-tafakkur wa-daqā'iq al-tadabbur*; Asad Aḥmad ʿAlī, *Tafsīr al-Qur'ān al-murattab manhaj li-l-yusr al-tarbawī*; Muḥammad ʿĀbid al-Jābirī, *Fahm al-Qur'ān al-ḥakīm: al-tafsīr al-wāḍiḥ ḥasab tartīb al-nuzūl*. For an explanation of the nature of these works, see Muḥammad Mujlī Aḥmad Rabābiʿa, *Tafsīr al-Qur'ān al-karīm ʿalā tartīb al-nuzūl: manbaʿuhu wa-fawā'iduhu*, https://arabicpdfs.com/تفسير-القرآن-الكريم-على-ترتيب-النزول-م/.

of the need to fulfil this scholarly void.[17] The significant majority of exegeses begin their interpretation of the Qur'an with Sūrat al-Fātiḥa, then Sūrat al-Baqara, Sūrat Āl 'Imrān, and so on, in the order in which the suras were compiled, known as sequential or ordinal exegesis (*al-tafsīr al-tartībī* or *al-tafsīr al-tajzīʾī*).[18] However, this approach does not consider the historical narrative of the Qur'an, nor does it help us understand the Prophet's own personal spiritual journey. There are also disagreements among scholars as to the

17 Haydar Hobbollah comments that the smaller chapters of the Qur'an have been neglected by exegetes: 'The short chapters are often neglected in the works of Muslim commentators since the ordinal commentator [i.e. the one who conducts exegeses according to the compilation of the Qur'an] reaches the end of the Holy Book and he has researched most of the topics or his powers have exhausted. As such, the short chapters receive little research compared to the long chapters – especially the chapters that precede Sūrat Maryam. There has been a need to revive these chapters, as some scholars did, such as the martyr Muḥammad Bāqir al-Ṣadr, may God be pleased with him, in his exegesis (*Mannat al-Mannān*), for in these chapters there are many subtleties and beautiful concepts that deserve to be examined.' See Haydar Hobbollah's official Facebook page: www.facebook.com/HaidarHobbollah/posts/818356611545971/. Secondly, in Western academia, Alan Godlas acknowledges Mulla Ḥuwaysh's exegesis according to the sequence of revelation, not compilation: "Abd al-Qādir b. Sayyid Muḥammad Ḥuwaysh b. Maḥmūd al-Ghāzī al-ʿĀnī, known as Mulla Ḥuwaysh – the author of the Qur'ān commentary, *Bayān al-maʿānī murattab tartīb al-nuzūl* ("The Elucidation of the Meanings according to the Order of Revelation"). Mulla Ḥuwaysh, an Ashʿarī Ḥanafī, did not compose this Arabic *tafsīr* in accordance with the traditional ordering of the suras. Instead, he arranged his *tafsīr* according to the chronological order of revelation. The *tafsīr*, written in 1936–37, includes both exoteric and Sufi material, though Sufi material only plays a very minor role (Ḥuwaysh 1964–65).' Alan Godlas, 'Sufism', in *The Blackwell Companion to the Qur'ān*, ed. Andrew Rippin (Oxford: Blackwell Publishing, 2006), 350–62, esp. 360.

18 For example, Jaʿfar Subḥānī divides exegesis into *ʿaql* (intellect) and *naql* (transmission). Under the first category, exegesis can be based on pure intellect (*al-ʿaql al-ṣarīḥ*), theological schools (*al-madāris al-kalāmiyya*), social norms (*al-sunan al-ijtimāʿiyya*), the science of *ḥadīth* (*al-ʿilm al-ḥadīth*), esoteric interpretation (*taʾwīlāt al-bāṭiniyya*), or Sufi interpretation (*taʾwīlāt al-ṣūfiyya*). The second category includes interpretation of the Qur'an through the Qur'an (*tafsīr al-Qurʾān bi-l-Qurʾān*), rhetorical interpretation of the Qur'an (*al-tafsīr al-bayānī li-l-Qurʾān*), interpretation through language and the rules of Arabic (*bi-l-lugha wa-l-qawāʿid al-ʿarabiyya*), and interpretation through narrations from the Prophet and the Imāms (*bi-l-maʾthur ʿan al-nabī wa-l-aʾimma*). Jaʿfar Subḥānī, *al-Manāhij al-tafsīriyya fī ʿulūm al-Qurʾān* (Qom: Muʾassasat al-Imām al-Ṣādiq, 2010), 4–5. In addition to this list there is also thematic exegesis (*al-tafsīr al-mawḍūʿī*). See, for example, Muḥammad Bāqir al-Ṣadr, *al-Tafsīr al-mawḍūʿī wa-l-falsafa al-ijtimāʿiyya fī al-madrasa al-Qurʾāniyya* (Beirut: al-Dār al-ʿĀlamiyya, 1989); ʿAbd al-Ḥamīd Maḥmūd Ṭahmāz, *al-Tafsīr al-mawḍūʿī li-suwar al-Qurʾān al-ʿaẓīm* (Beirut: al-Dār al-Shāmiyya, 2014).

order of the compilation of the suras depending on the codex (*muṣḥaf*) of the Qur'an referred to.[19]

Thirdly, one major historical reason for adopting the sequential rather than revelatory exegetical approach is due to only looking at the traditional narrative on the compilation of the Qur'an in order to understand its meanings. It is commonly understood that Abū Bakr instructed Zayd b. Thābit to compile the Qur'an as he felt he was an intelligent, devoted person. Zayd acknowledged the huge weight upon him but undertook the task by collecting various fragments of the Qur'an. Once compiled, his copy passed from Abū Bakr to ʿUmar to the latter's daughter Ḥafṣa.[20] During his own caliphate, ʿUthmān b. ʿAffān sensed that the nation (*umma*) would differ about the recitation of the Qur'an like the Jews and Christians did about their books so he sent for Ḥafṣa to bring her copy of the Qur'an and rejected the other copies.[21]

However, another important narrative cited by Ibn Nadīm appears under the title *Tartīb suwar al-Qur'ān fī muṣḥaf amīr al-mu'minīn ʿAlī b. Abī Ṭālib – karrama Llāhu wajhahu*, concerning the codex of ʿAlī b. Abī Ṭālib. He cites the following narration:

> Ibn al-Munādī said that al-Ḥasan b. al-ʿAbbās transmitted to me, saying on the authority of ʿAbd al-Raḥmān b. Abī Ḥammād, who was informed on the authority

---

19 In the codex (*muṣḥaf*) of ʿAbd Allāh b. Masʿūd, the order of chapters is al-Baqara, al-Nisā', Āl ʿImrān, al-Aʿrāf, al-Anʿām, al-Mā'ida, Yūnus, al-Barā'a (or al-Tawba). In this *muṣḥaf*, he did not include the *muʿawwidhatān* ('the two suras of refuge'), meaning Sūrat al-Falaq and Sūrat al-Nās, or Sūrat al-Fātiḥa. Ibn al-Nadīm, *Kitāb al-fihrist*, 1:64. In the *muṣḥaf* of Ubayy b. Kaʿb, the order was as follows: al-Fātiḥa, al-Baqara, al-Nisā', Āl ʿImrān, al-Anʿām, al-Aʿrāf, al-Mā'ida, Yūnus, al-Anfāl, Tawba, Hūd, Maryam. Ibid., 65. This also means there are variations of the number of chapters and verses in the Qur'an: 116 chapters in the codex of Ubayy vs 111 or 112 chapters in the codex of Ibn Masʿūd.

20 Ibid., 60. Ṭabāṭabā'ī also comments, 'Just about a year after the death of the Prophet, the war of Yamāmah took place in which seventy of the reciters were killed and the Caliphs conceived the idea of collecting the different chapters and verses into one volume. They feared that should a future battle take place and the rest of the *qurrā'* be killed, the whole Qur'an would disappear with them. Thus, on the orders of the Caliph, a group of the *qurrā'* from amongst the companions including Zayd ibn Thābit, collected the chapters and verses (written on tablets, bones and date palm fronds and kept in the Prophet's house or the houses of reciters), and produced several hand-written copies of the complete Book. They then sent copies of this compilation to all areas of the Muslim domain. That the chapters and verses were not revealed in one place but rather in stages over a period of twenty-three years during the Prophet's mission is authenticated not only by historical evidence but also from evidence from the various verses.' Ṭabāṭabā'ī, *The Qur'an in Islam*, pt. 5.

21 Ibn al-Nadīm, *Kitāb al-Fihrist*, 1:61.

> al-Ḥakam b. Ṭāhir al-Sadūsī, on the authority of ʿAbd Khayr, on the authority of ʿAlī – peace be upon him – that, 'He saw a commotion/agitation (*ṭayra*) among the people after the death of the Prophet, so he swore that he would not put his robe on his back until he had collected the Qur'an. So he sat in his house for three days until he had compiled the Qur'an.' This was the first *muṣḥaf* that was gathered of the Qur'an from what he had memorised. And this is the *muṣḥaf* according to the descendants of Jaʿfar.[22]

Ṭabāṭabā'ī further states, 'After the death of the Prophet, ʿAlī, who (according to a tradition of absolute authority) was more knowledgeable about the Qur'an than any other man, retired to his house and compiled the Qur'an in one volume in the order corresponding to the order of revelation. Before six months had elapsed after the death of the Prophet, the volume was completed and carried by camel to show to other people.'[23] Lalani also explains:

> Scholars are unanimous regarding the fact that ʿAlī possessed his own transcript of the text of the Qur'ān that he had collected himself, and his version, although not available, is therefore the first compilation ever of the Qur'ān. This is recorded in numerous traditions reported in both Sunni and Shiʿi sources. The unique aspect about this version was that it had been collected in the order it was sent and Companions such as Ibn Sīrīn, among others, have regretted the loss of this text. Evidence of this is to be found in sources such as Ibn Saʿd's *Ṭabaqāt*, al-Balādhurī's *Ansāb* and al-Suyūṭī's *Itqān*. Frequently, ʿAlī is known to have reminded people to 'ask me before you lose me … there is not a single verse of which I do not know whether it was sent down at night or during the day, or whether it was revealed on a plain or on a mountain.'[24]

If we examine the meaning of the Qur'an through the lens of ʿAlī b. Abī Ṭālib's codex, even if it is not extant, we may come to appreciate why he compiled it

---

22 Ibid., 70. Maʿrifa also comments on ʿAlī b. Abī Ṭālib's codex stating that this codex arranged the chapters of the Qur'an in the chronological order they were revealed without any words or verses omitted; verses were recorded in the manner the Prophet recited them; in the margins of the codex were explanations about the circumstances, reasons, place, time, and audience of the verse, and finally, comments about the general application of the verses that may not have been restricted to a particular time, place, or people. Maʿrifa, *Talkhīṣ al-tamhīd*, 1:148–56. See also Seyfeddin Kara, *In Search of ʿAlī ibn Abī Ṭālib's Codex: History and Traditions of the Earliest Copy of the Qur'ān* (Berlin: Gerlach Press, 2018).

23 Ṭabāṭabā'ī, *The Qur'an in Islam*, pt. 5.

24 Arzina Lalani, "Ali ibn Abi Talib', in *The Qur'an: An Encyclopaedia*, ed. Oliver Leaman (Abingdon: Routledge, 2006), 30.

in the order it was revealed – it helps us understand the Qur'an's own history chronologically. This enables us to understand why specific events, interactions, laws, and norms unfolded in the way they did. We may therefore adopt the method of 'Alī b. Abī Ṭālib even if we do not have his official copy with us.[25]

Fourthly, different approaches to exegesis are natural within Muslim scholarship precisely for this reason: a scholar intends to bring out an aspect of the Qur'an that he believes has not been examined before. The few authors who have attempted to tackle exegesis according to the chronological sequence of revelation have emphasised the reception of revelation (*waḥy*) into the Prophet's heart, which they argue traditional exegeses do not examine. For example, Muḥammad 'Izzat Darwaza al-Nāblusī (d. 1984), in his *al-Tafsīr al-ḥadīth tartib al-suwar ḥasab al-nuzūl*, which he started writing while imprisoned in Damascus, highlights the following themes as key parts of his methodology: the revelation of the Qur'an; its environment; the biography (*sīra*) and character traits of the Prophet; the Prophet's reception of revelation – his capability, heart, and visions according to suras such as al-Takwīr (Q. 81), al-Najm (Q. 53), al-Naḥl (Q. 16), and al-Qiyāma (Q. 75); and the order of revelation, whether or not scholars accounted for when specific verses were revealed. He begins his exegesis with Sūrat al-Fātiḥa (Q. 1), then al-'Alaq (Q. 96), al-Qalam (Q. 68), al-Muzzammil (Q. 73), al-Muddaththir (Q. 74), and so on, according to the general order of revelation, not the order of the compiled codex.[26]

Perhaps an apt paragraph from his exegesis may summarise his methodology. In his explanation of Sūrat al-Muzzammil, Darwaza states that the Prophet's

> immersion in God in solitude and the silence of most of the night resulted in the purity of his soul and strengthened his spirit – especially by virtue of retreats and spiritual retreats before his mission – may God's blessings and peace be upon him. This is based on what has been related in the narration of al-Bukhārī on the authority of 'Ā'isha – may God be pleased with her – which we mentioned in

25 Seyfuddin Kara argues that Western academia and Sunnī scholarship in general do not place importance on the codex of 'Alī b. Abī Ṭālib (despite the fact that his codex is cited in Sunnī books) because of the 'widespread assumption that Shi'ism is a heretic interpretation of Islam, and the only way to study Islam is to rely on the Sunnī sources'. As a result, his codex was suppressed in the history of the Qur'an. See Seyfeddin Kara, 'The Suppression of 'Alī ibn Abī Ṭālib's Codex: Study of the Traditions on the Earliest Copy of the Qur'ān', *Journal of Near Eastern Studies* 75, no. 2 (2016): 268.

26 Muḥammad 'Izzat Darwaza al-Nāblusī, *al-Tafsīr al-ḥadīth tartib al-suwar ḥasab al-nuzūl*, 1st ed. (Cairo: Dār Iḥyā' al-Kutub al-'Arabiyya, 196), vol. 1, https://shamela.ws/book/23603/395#p1.

> the interpretation of al-ʿAlaq, wherein it is stated: 'He loved solitude, so he used to be alone in the Cave of Ḥirāʾ and engage in devotional exercises (*taḥannuth*) for many nights.' This undoubtedly had an effect on his willingness to receive the revelation of his Lord, and it was one of the reasons why God chose him for that task.[27]

Darwaza's efforts, and that of other scholars such as ʿAbd al-Qādir b. Sayyid Muḥammad Ḥuwaysh b. Maḥmūd al-Ghāzī al-ʿĀnī, known as Mullā Ḥuwaysh (d. 1978), are to be commended for highlighting the potential of re-examining the meanings of the Qurʾan through its sequence of revelation. However, upon reading through their works, I still found a fundamental area of exegetical methodology that had not been dealt with. They did not generally conceive of how this methodology of Qurʾanic interpretation could critically impact our existing understanding of doctrine, law, mystical knowledge (*ʿirfān*), and other notable classical Islamic disciplines.

For example, regarding the subject matter of this article, does it make a difference to our understanding of what an obligation (*wājib*) is in law (particularly in relation to one's spiritual and general capability) if we consider that the night prayer vigil was revealed to the Prophet as the first obligatory prayer in Islam but that it was based on his spiritual, psychological, and physical capacity at the time? How and why was this prayer amended, and does the manner of this amendment affect the way we may amend other obligations in Islamic law? Was *ṣalāt al-layl* an extension of *taḥannuth* or a direct result of the verbal and physical abuse the Prophet received, according to what is recorded in Sūrat al-Qalam (Q. 68)? If the Prophet engaged in *taḥannuth* before revelation, then surely there was a personal means and freedom by which he not only received revelation but also applied revelation to his own life and to others' lives? These are the questions which highlight the benefit of producing a commentary on the Qurʾan that follows the historical order of revelation and which I will try to answer in this study. In sum, the benefits of this approach are:

- understanding the Qurʾan as it was revealed in its own historical timeline;
- understanding the mystical, moral, and socio-political experience of the Prophet;
- tracing the goals or spirit of revelation as it unfolded, which guides the scope of regulative verses;
- paying attention to the early revelations and shorter suras which are often overlooked in *tafsīr*.

27 Ibid., 1:107.

3 The Nature and Context of the Night Prayer Vigil

> O one who is wrapped up in a cloak! Stand in the night except a little, half of it or reduce a little from that or add to it and recite the Qurʾan in a measured tone. (Q. 73:1–4)

Q. 73:1–4 describe the nature of the night prayer vigil with which God instructed the Prophet. The standing in the night as well as recitation of the Qurʾan demonstrates that this is a worshipful or spiritual standing that has a particular form and extent. One may call it a prayer since 'the watch of the night is firmer in tread and more upright in speech' (Q. 72:6). Verses that were revealed later explicitly show that God should be glorified in the night and that the night vigil (*tahajjud*) should be observed as a supererogatory prayer, since God may 'raise you to a praiseworthy position' (Q. 17:79).[28]

The majority of Shīʿī and Sunnī exegetes argue that the first nineteen verses of Sūrat al-Muzzammil – including the first four, clearly – were revealed in Mecca but that the last verse (Q. 73:20) was revealed in Medina.[29] The last verse established the obligation to pray the five daily prayers and to give alms, and it rendered the night prayer vigil supererogatory on account of people's circumstantial and physical difficulties in performing it.[30]

---

28 See Q. 17:79, 25:64, 65:3.

29 Al-Shawkānī states, 'It is Meccan. All of it is Meccan according to the statement of al-Ḥasan al-Baṣrī, 'Ikrima, and Jābir. However, Ibn 'Abbās and Qatāda say that two of its verses are Medinan: *wa-ṣbir 'alā mā yaqūlūn* and the last verse.' Muḥammad 'Alī b. Muḥammad al-Shawkānī, *Fatḥ al-Qadīr* (Cairo: Dār Ibn al-Jawzī, 2012), 511. And al-Anṭākī states that the chapter is Meccan except the last verse, which was revealed in Medina according to most scholars. However, there are differences of opinion in relation to four verses of the sura. The Kufans, Medinans, and Syrians count *Yā ayyuhā al-muzzamil* as a verse, but others do not accept this; the Meccans consider *innā arsalnā ilaykum rasūlan* as a verse and others do not count it as such. The phrase *ilā Firʿawn rasūlan* – the Meccans do not count it as a verse, while others count it as such. Wildāna Shayān –the Medinan – does not count it as a verse but others count it as such. Abū al-Ḥasan 'Alī b. Muḥammad b. Ismāʿīl b. Bushrā al-Tamīmī al-Anṭākī, *Kitāb 'add āy al-Qurʾān – li-l-Makkī wa-l-Madaniyyayn wa-l-Kūfī wa-l-Baṣrī wa-l-Shāmī – al-muttafiq 'alayhi wa-l-mukhtalaf fīhi* (Cairo: Mu'assasat al-Saʿūdiyya, 2011), 546–48.

30 See Abū 'Alī al-Faḍl b. al-Ḥasan b. al-Faḍl al-Ṭabrisī, *Majmaʿ al-bayān fī tafsīr al-Qurʾān*, Q. 73:1, www.altafsīr.com/Tafasir.asp?tMadhNo=4&tTafsīrNo=3&tSoraNo=73&tAyahNo=1&tDisplay=yes&UserProfile=0&LanguageId=1; Muḥammad Ḥusayn Ṭabāṭabāʾī, *al-Mīzān fī tafsīr al-Qurʾān*, Q. 73:1, www.altafsīr.com/Tafasir.asp?tMadhNo=4&tTafsīrNo=56&tSoraNo=73&tAyahNo=1&tDisplay=yes&UserProfile=0&LanguageId=1; 'Abd al-Raḥmān b. 'Alī b. Muḥammad Abū al-Faraj Ibn al-Jawzī, *Zād al-masīr fī 'ilm al-tafsīr*, Q. 73:1, www.altafsīr.com/Tafasir.asp?tMadhNo=2&tTafsīrNo=15&tSoraNo=73&tAyahNo=1&tDisplay=yes

There is a range of grammatical opinions on how to interpret the phrase *niṣfahu* ('half of it') – specifically asking what the antecedent of the pronoun *-hu* in *niṣfahu* is. Is the antecedent the night, or is it merely a short part of the night? The first opinion is that it is an appositive that 'substitutes a part for the whole' (*badal al-baʿḍ min al-kull*) of the word *al-layl* ('the night'). So the Prophet should pray half of the night in the first instance. Therefore, *illā qalilā* ('except a little') is a grammatical exception (*istithnāʾ*) from *niṣfahu* ('half of it'). The second opinion is that *niṣfahu* is an appositive to *qalīl* ('a little'), and therefore 'half of it' refers not to the entire night but rather only to short portion of the night from which the rest of Q. 73:4 follows logically. This is because the Prophet may 'reduce a little from that or add to it'.[31] Other interpretations of Q. 73:2–4 show that 'a little' (*qalīl*) is 'smaller than a half and what is less than one sixth; or it is said "that which is less than one tenth"; Muqātil and al-Kalbī said the intended meaning of "a little" is one third[32] … and that the phrase "except a little" (*illā qalīlā*) means "pray the prayer that is easy for you to do".'[33] These grammatical interpretations are significant because the Prophet was given flexibility by God in the performance of the night prayer vigil according to his capability and circumstances. He could choose the timings and length of his vigils as long as he performed them during the night.

Regarding the occasions of revelation, all Sunnī and Shīʿī exegetes agree that the night prayer vigil was revealed for two reasons – firstly, to comfort the Prophet and to make him more patient at a time when he was being verbally abused, being called a poet (*shāʿir*), soothsayer (*kāhin*), or madman (*majnūn*), according to Q. 73:10; and secondly, to prepare him for the weighty revelation of the Qur'an that was being revealed to him, according to Q. 73:5.[34] Mystical exegetes emphasise God's intention to train the Prophet spiritually. For example, in relation to Q. 73:10, which states, 'Be patient at what they say, and keep away from them in a graceful manner', Ibn al-ʿArabī interprets this as a divine spiritual order propelling the Prophet to develop his soul, meaning, 'And restrain your soul (*wa-ḥbis nafsaka*) from recklessness (*al-ṭaysh*) and disturbance (*al-iḍṭirāb*), but rather move towards seeking sustenance and attention in relation to what is whispered to you – strengthen your soul (*qawwi*

&UserProfile=0&LanguageId=1; Abū ʿAbd Allāh Muḥammad b. Shihāb al-Dīn Jalāl al-Dīn al-Maḥallī and Jalāl al-Dīn al-Suyūṭī, *Tafsīr al-Jalālayn* (Karachi: al-Bushrā, 2018), 3:596.

31 Muḥibb al-Dīn Abū al-Baqāʾ al-ʿUkbarī, *al-Tibyān fī iʿrāb al-Qurʾān* (Beirut: Dār Ibn Ḥazm, 2017), 603.

32 al-Shawkānī, *Fatḥ al-Qadīr*, 512.

33 Ibid., 511.

34 Ibid., 511–12. See also al-Ṭabrisī, *Majmaʿ al-bayān*, Q. 73:1.

nafsaka).'[35] The night prayer vigil, therefore, was a personal instruction from God to the Prophet to withstand the abuse and rejection he was facing from the polytheists and to prepare his spiritual, mental, and psychological capacity to receive further revelation.

The meaning and historical context of the Prophet's being addressed as *muzzammil* confirms the anxiousness and internal disturbance he felt at the time he was receiving the abuse. The term *muzzammil* ('wrapped up in a cloak') has been interpreted in various ways – 'wrapped up in the cloak of prophethood'; 'wrapped up in God's message'; 'wrapped up in the Qur'an'; and 'wrapped up in a cloak (*dithār*), seeking comfort in God from the polytheists'.[36] In all of these senses, there is one common theme – turning to God for strength to continue on in his prophetic mission. This is also why many exegetes comment that this could be the first time that the Prophet heard the voice of Gabriel after his constant practice of spiritual devotions (*taḥannuth*) and that when he heard the angel's voice or saw his figure, he was trembling and approached his wife, Khadīja, saying 'Cover me' (*zammilīnī* or *daththirīnī*).[37] Most, however, say that the first five verses of Sūrat al-ʿAlaq constitute the first revelation of the Qur'an, since the verses of Sūrat al-Muzzammil appear to have been revealed a little later on in the Prophet's mission on account of the historical context of these verses.[38] Sūrat al-Muzzammil is generally considered to be the second or third chapter to be revealed after Surat al-ʿAlaq.[39]

---

35 Muḥammad b. ʿAlī Ibn al-ʿArabī, *Tafsīr al-Qur'ān al-karīm* (Beirut: Dār al-Kutub al-ʿIlmiyya, 2001), 2:360.

36 al-Shawkānī, *Fatḥ al-Qadīr*, 511; al-Ṭabrisī, *Majmaʿ al-bayān*, Q. 73:1.

37 al-Shawkānī, *Fatḥ al-Qadīr*, 511.

38 Al-Wāḥidī cites the oft-quoted narration from *Ṣaḥīḥ al-Bukhārī* and *Ṣaḥīḥ Muslim* in which the Prophet states the following (after Gabriel instructs him to 'recite' three times): '"I cannot recite." He seized me a third time and pressed me so hard that I felt exhausted and then he released me, saying: "Read: In the name of thy Lord who created ..." until he reached "... that which he knew not".' Al-Wāḥidī argues from narrations such as the above that the beginning five verses of Sūrat al-ʿAlaq constitute the first revelation of the Qur'an to the Prophet. He also cites seemingly contradictory narrations such as the one from Jābir b. ʿAbd Allāh al-Anṣārī, who states that the first revelation was 'O one who is wrapped up in a cloak', which is Sūrat al-Muddaththir (Q. 74). He reconciles both sets of narrations stating that Jābir did not hear the first report from the Prophet concerning the first five verses of Sūrat al-ʿAlaq. As a result, he considered Sūrat al-Muddaththir to be the first revelation of the Qur'an. Al-Wāḥidī further argues there was a gap in the period of revelation between the verses of Sūrat al-ʿAlaq and Sūrat al-Muddaththir due to the difference in the initial and later descriptions of Gabriel by the Prophet. See al-Ḥasan ʿAlī b. Aḥmad al-Wāḥidī, *Asbāb al-nuzūl* (Cairo: Dār al-Furqān, 2015), 71–78.

39 See Maʿrifa, *Talkhīṣ al-tamhīd*, 93–97.

4 The Traditional Interpretation of Reference to the Night Prayer Vigil as an Instance of *Āyāt al-Aḥkām*

The majority of Sunnī and Shīʿī exegetes accept that the night prayer vigil was obligatory upon the Prophet but differ as to how much he prayed during the night, what he prayed, and for how long he prayed it, in terms of months and years. The obligatory nature of the night prayer vigil was extended to his followers, but again there is dispute as to whether it was immediately obligatory or recommended for them to perform it. Most exegetes, however, agree that Q. 73:20, which was revealed in Medina, signalled the beginning of the five daily prayers and abrogated the night prayer vigil as an obligation, rendering it as a recommended practice – whether for the Prophet or for him and his community.[40]

The reasons for the disputes among exegetes as to the extent of the night prayer vigil, upon whom it was obligatory, and how long the Prophet and his followers prayed it are intriguing. Al-Ṭabrisī states that the Prophet and his followers prayed the night prayer vigil as soon as God instructed him to do so, until 'a man among them did not know how much he had prayed and how much of the night remained, so he used to pray all night for fear that he might not observe the obligatory extent until God lightened the burden for them at the end of this sura'.[41] There are similar narrations in the *Muwaṭṭa'* of Imām Mālik with Ibn al-Faras al-Andalusī emphasising one narration in his analysis of why the obligation of the night prayer vigil was abrogated. In quoting the *Muwaṭṭa'*, he states:

> The Messenger of God – peace and blessings be upon him – stood for the night prayer vigil in Ramadan on the rear part of a mat that he had retained and subsequently performed the prayer. The people prayed along with his prayer. Then they [the number of people the next night] increased from the preceding night, so he chose the mosque [for the prayer] on the third or fourth night. However, the Messenger of God – peace and blessings be upon him – did not come out to them when they had thrown pebbles against his door [to draw his attention], so he emerged angrily and said, 'I only refrained from departing [my house] because I feared to impose [the prayer] upon all of you.' According to the text

40 See al-Ṭabrisī, *Majmaʿ al-bayān*, Q. 73:1; Ṭabāṭabāʾī, *al-Mīzān*, Q. 73:1.

41 al-Ṭabrisī, *Majmaʿ al-bayān*, Q. 73:1.

of the narration, he [the Prophet] only spoke to them again after the morning had arrived.[42]

The above narrations demonstrate that some people, eventually a majority, it seems, found it difficult to observe the night prayer vigil as an obligation. Al-Ṭabrisī cites a narration from ʿĀʾisha confirming that the Prophet and his Companions prayed the night prayer vigil for a year until God lightened the obligation and made it voluntary. He cites another narration on the authority of Saʿīd b. Jubayr that ten years had passed between the revelation of the beginning of the sura and the revelation of its last verse. Then, on the authority of Ibn Kaysān, Muqātil, al-Ḥasan al-Baṣrī, and ʿIkrima, the night prayer vigil was abrogated by the five daily prayers.[43] Ṭabāṭabāʾī concludes by citing three possible modes of abrogation for the night prayer vigil: first, that it was obligatory for the Prophet and the believers; second, that it was recommended for all; or third, that it was obligatory for the Prophet but only recommended for others.[44] The current status of the night prayer vigil, according to the majority of Muslim jurists, is that it was an obligatory prayer but that it has now been abrogated yet remains a highly recommended prayer. They may differ, however, regarding which portions of the prayer were initially obligatory or recommended and for how long. I have listed their opinions in Tables 11.1 and 11.2, which I constructed by summarising Ibn al-Faras al-Andalusī's analysis of whether or not the night prayer vigil is endorsed (*muḥkam*) or abrogated (*mansūkh*), respectively.[45]

The reader may observe from Table 11.1 that there are Muslim jurists who never considered the night prayer vigil to have been abrogated, because either it was always a recommend prayer only directed to the Prophet; it was obligatory upon the Prophet until his death, and so there was no need for abrogation to occur; or it was obligatory upon both the Prophet and his community at the time but only to a minimum or specified extent, while the rest of the prayer, whether in terms of the duration of its recitation or the number of its units (*rakʿas*), was recommended.

In contrast, Table 11.2, which represents the popular juristic opinion, demonstrates that either the night prayer vigil was only obligatory upon the

42 ʿAbd al-Munʿim b. Muḥammad Ibn al-Faras al-Andalusī, *Aḥkām al-Qurʾān*, 3 vols. (Beirut: Dār Ibn Ḥazm, 2019), 3:599. He states this narration is from *al-Muwaṭṭaʾ* by Imām Mālik, *kitāb al-ṣalāt, bāb al-targhīb fī al-ṣalāt fī Ramaḍān*, 113/1.

43 al-Ṭabrisī, *Majmaʿ al-bayān*, Q. 73:1.

44 Ṭabāṭabāʾī, *al-Mīzān*, Q. 73:1.

45 Opinions summarised from Ibn al-Faras al-Andalusī, *Aḥkām al-Qurʾān*, 3:599–602.

TABLE 11.1 The night prayer vigil as endorsed (*muḥkam*)

Jurisprudential status of the ruling	Subject of the ruling	Extension of subject of the ruling	Scope of the ruling
Recommended	Prophet	Community	
Obligatory	Prophet		Until his death
Obligatory	Prophet	Community	Not the whole night
Obligatory	Prophet	Community	Minimum performance: 'only to the measure of milking sheep' (*ʿalā qadr ḥalb shāh*)
Obligatory	Prophet	Community	Necessary to recite fifty verses of the Qurʾan
Obligatory and recommended	Prophet	Community	Two *rakʿa*s with *witr* after the first third of the night obligatory, but after that, only recommended

TABLE 11.2 *Ṣalāt al-layl* as abrogated (*mansūkh*)

Jurisprudential status of the ruling	Subject of the ruling	Extension of subject of the ruling	Scope of the ruling
Obligatory	Prophet		Abrogated but the Prophet prayed it voluntarily
Obligatory	Prophet	Community	Abrogated but difference of opinion on period of obligation: a year, eighteen months, ten years, or twenty years
Obligatory	Prophet	Community	Abrogated by Q. 73:20 because of lack of physical capacity of people to perform it

TABLE 11.2 *Ṣalāt al-layl* as abrogated (*mansūkh*) (*cont.*)

Jurisprudential status of the ruling	Subject of the ruling	Extension of subject of the ruling	Scope of the ruling
Obligatory	Prophet	Community	Abrogated by Q. 73:20 with the five daily prayers
Obligatory	Prophet	Community	Abrogated but then became permissible
Obligatory	Prophet	Community	Abrogated with a lighter obligation
Obligatory	Prophet	Community	Abrogated with a lighter, perhaps recommended act

Prophet, but then it was abrogated and he decided to pray it voluntarily; it was obligatory upon the Prophet and his community at the time, but then it was abrogated and replaced by the five daily prayers because some or many of his followers found it physically difficult to perform, so that it remained only as a recommended act; or finally, that it was abrogated and replaced with a lighter obligation, so that it remained only as a permissible act of devotion, as opposed to recommended.

Both tables show that there is in fact scholarly disagreement, based on divergent narrations, as to when and how the night prayer vigil shifted from an obligatory to recommended status. While the majority view is apparently that the night prayer vigil is currently a recommended prayer – and an extremely meritorious one – especially since the imposition of the five daily prayers along with the alms (*zakāt*) in Q. 73:20, an argument may be made according to the minority juristic opinion that the night prayer vigil continues to be obligatory upon all believers but only to a minimum extent – for example, only lasting as long as it would take to milk a sheep – because of the hardship involved in consistently praying it every night.

5 The Issue of the Night Prayer Vigil in Commentaries That Adopt the Order of Revelation

A re-examination of the traditional jurisprudential and exegetical interpretation of the night prayer vigil from the perspective of the historical order of revelation may help broaden the metaphysical and practical foundations of Islamic prayer, providing a hermeneutical model for the interpretation of other regulative verses.

The starting point is the question why the verses referring to the night prayer vigil were revealed at that particular historical point in the Prophet's life, even if there is scholarly disagreement as to exactly what date and for how long Sūrat al-Muzzammil (Q. 73) was revealed. If we follow the order of revelation of the first five verses of Sūrat al-ʿAlaq (Q. 96) and then the first seventeen verses of Sūrat al-Qalam (Q. 68), we know that the Prophet was being called 'mad' or 'possessed by a demon' (*majnūn*) by the polytheists and disbelievers. Hence, Q. 68:2 states, 'You are not, by your Lord's blessing, mad.' The verbal abuse the Prophet was facing appears to have gone on for some time, to the extent that specific verses were revealed personally to him to strengthen his soul and remove the distress he was feeling. In fact, Ṭabāṭabāʾī, in his interpretation of Q. 96:4 ('He who taught by the pen'), states that this verse is 'an expression sent to strengthen the soul of the Prophet (*li-taqwiyat nafs al-nabī*) and to remove distress and disturbance from it (*izālat al-qalaq wa-l-iḍṭirāb*) in such a manner that he is commanded to recite while he was unlettered (*ummī*)'.[46] We then find God further strengthening and reassuring the Prophet through Q. 68:3–4, which state, 'And yours indeed will be an everlasting reward, and indeed you possess a great character.' The revelatory order of the verses of Sūrat al-ʿAlaq and Sūrat al-Qalam are perfectly in line with the psychological and spiritual journey of the Prophet, which reflect a natural human reaction to the verbal abuse he was facing.

It is the aforementioned psychological and spiritual context that ushers in the first nineteen verses of Sūrat al-Muzzammil. Now was the time for the Prophet to direct his physical, mental, and spiritual energies into a performative act – the night prayer vigil, which would not only heighten his metaphysical capacity to receive further revelation from God but also reassure him in the face of any verbal and physical abuse from his enemies in the long term. Even without going to the various exegeses, Sūrat al-Muzzammil itself answers why it was revealed to the Prophet. It states:

> Indeed, soon We shall cast on you a weighty word. Indeed, the watch of the night is firmer in tread and more upright in respect to speech, for indeed during the day you have drawn-out engagements. So celebrate the Name of your Lord and dedicate yourself to Him with a total dedication, Lord of the East and the West,

46 Ṭabāṭabāʾī, *al-Mīzān*, Q. 96:4, www.altafsīr.com/Tafasir.asp?tMadhNo=4&tTafsīrNo=56&tSoraNo=96&tAyahNo=4&tDisplay=yes&Page=2&Size=1&LanguageId=1.

> there is no god except Him, so take Him for your trustee, and be patient over what they say, and keep away from them in a graceful manner. Leave Me to deal with the deniers, the opulent, and give them a little respite. Indeed, with Us are heavy fetters and a fierce fire. (Q. 73:5–12)

God clearly wanted to prepare the Prophet for further verses to be revealed to him ('a weighty word'). The night was the best spiritual preparation to 'celebrate the Name of your Lord ... with a total dedicate' as during the day the Prophet would be occupied with 'drawn-out engagements'. The Prophet had to increase his level of 'patience' and to leave God to deal with the 'deniers, the opulent'. These verses demonstrate that the night vigil was a multifaceted prayer that served to prepare the Prophet psychologically, morally, and spirituality for the tasks he faced.[47] The metaphysical purpose of the night prayer vigil may be summed up by the statement of Ibn al-ʿArabī who reports that God was telling the Prophet, 'Take God as your trustee, which means stripping off your action, so that He might govern you with the sight of all actions, so that your affairs be entrusted to Him. He governs your affairs and does for you what He wills.'[48]

One therefore may formulate the first principle guiding us to understand *āyāt al-aḥkām* from the context of the night prayer vigil: legal acts are first and foremost based on adjusting our souls towards God in the manner the Prophet did to heighten our spiritual and moral capacities, which may be driven by an original goal of seeking nearness to God (*qurbatan ilā Llāh*). The legal compliance of the act is secondary.

Secondly, the Prophet's performance of the prayer in terms of its extent and duration was based on his physical and spiritual capability at that time in his life, his engagements during the day, and the portion of the night he was able

47 Ṭabāṭabāʾī interprets 'a weighty word' as having two meanings: 'it is the speech of God from the expanse of His greatness that cannot be received by anyone except a pure soul that is free from impurity and cut off from every cause except God; and it is a Mighty Book with apparent and hidden layers, revelation, and esoteric interpretation clarifying everything. And it is weighty because what was witnessed in the state of the Prophet of perspiring and resembling fainting as per what is stated in extensive reports.' Ṭabāṭabāʾī, *al-Mīzān*, Q. 73:5, www.altafsīr.com/Tafasir.asp?tMadhNo=4&tTafsīrNo=56&tSoraNo=73&tAyahNo=1&tDisplay=yes&UserProfile=0&LanguageId=5. Al-Fayḍ al-Kāshānī states the Qur'an is a moral burden which is weighty upon legally responsible believers, and it is also called weighty because of the revelation which changed the Prophet's state and caused him to perspire. al-Fayḍ al-Kāshānī, *al-Tafsīr al-ṣāfī*, Q. 73:5, www.altafsīr.com/Tafasir.asp?tMadhNo=4&tTafsīrNo=41&tSoraNo=73&tAyahNo=4&tDisplay=yes&UserProfile=0&LanguageId=1.

48 Ibn al-ʿArabī, *Tafsīr al-Qurʾān al-karīm*, 2:360.

to devote to God, either on account of his weariness or on account of the natural process of adjusting to the new guidance God was giving to him. This is why Q. 73:2–4 give the Prophet options to perform the night prayer vigil during various portions of the night. The second principle one may therefore formulate is that the performance of a legal act is fundamentally dependent on one's spiritual, psychological, and practical ability at the time.

Thirdly, when the Prophet attempted to extend the performance of the night prayer vigil to his community, some found it difficult to perform. This is why Q. 73:20 was revealed. There, God states:

> Indeed *your* Lord knows that *you* stand vigil nearly two thirds of the night – or [at times] a half or a third of it – along with a group of those who are with *you*. Allah measures the night and the day. He knows that you cannot calculate it [exactly], and so He was lenient towards you. So recite as much of the Qur'an as is feasible. He knows that some of you will be sick, while others will travel in the land seeking God's grace, and yet others will fight in the way of God. So recite as much of it as is feasible, and maintain the prayer and pay the alms and lend God a good loan. Whatever good you send ahead for your souls you will find it with God [in a form] that is better and greater with respect to reward. And plead to God for forgiveness; indeed God is Forgiving, Merciful. (Q. 73:20)

This verse, which is likely to have been revealed in Medina, clearly demonstrates that God understood the difficulty for the community to perform the night vigil and therefore lightened the performance of the prayer into what the majority of scholars argue is a recommended act. The third principle that one may formulate is that *āyāt al-aḥkām* are directed to the barometer of capability of the Prophet, but for the community, that barometer must be adjusted due to their differing capability. Indeed, the people who performed the night prayer vigil were a nascent group of believers who had converted to Islam in Mecca, which adds a psychological dimension to their barometer of capability, since they were not used to worshipping God at night or to performing any other act which the Prophet would instruct them to do.

Fourthly, the Prophet himself made his own human judgement to extend the night prayer vigil to his community, but he later realised himself, according to the narrations cited above, that the prayer was difficult for them to perform on a consistent basis. It was at this point that Q. 73:20 was revealed to him, making the five daily prayers obligatory along with the alms and rendering the night prayer vigil a recommended act. This is also why there is dispute among Muslim scholars regarding to whom this prayer was obligatory and for how long. One may ask, why wouldn't the five daily prayers have been revealed first, if the Prophet or God knew that the human community could not perform the night prayer vigil? Why should the Prophet and his community go through this trial and experience? A common answer is that it was not the Prophet who was making his own human judgement since, according to Sūrat al-Najm, 'nor does he speak out of desire. It is nothing but revelation that is revealed' (Q. 53:3–4). Secondly, God, in His wisdom, knew what verses were appropriate for the Prophet and the community at the time and so it does not matter that the night prayer vigil was presented in revelation as an obligatory prayer before the five daily prayers became obligatory.

The argument made above, however, is contradictory. There are several examples in the Qur'an of the Prophet's being corrected by God or God's changing the status of a performative act in response to the Prophet's experience with his community. For example, Q. 9:43 states, 'God forgive you! Why did you give them leave until those who spoke the truth had become manifest to you and you had known the liars?' The context of this verse is that prior to the Battle of Tabūk, some people came to the Prophet and asked him if they could stay back and not go out to fight. The Prophet gave them permission to do so, but after he had done this, Q. 9:43 was revealed, since the very people who had asked the Prophet were in fact hypocrites. Here God rebukes the Prophet, though with forgiveness first, since their request was not genuine.[49] Here, if the Prophet is not speaking out of his desire, how can God reveal to or enable the Prophet to give the hypocrites permission to stay back but when the Prophet did, he is rebuked by God? This would mean God has either contradicted his initial action or that He does not possess the necessary knowledge of the unfolding events in the Prophet's life. Both would be illogical for an omnipotent and omniscient God.[50]

It is more accurate to say that the Prophet made a personal judgement which did not turn out as expected and then sought further guidance from God.[51] The

49 See Abū Jaʿfar Muḥammad b. Jarīr b. Yazīd al-Ṭabarī, *Jāmiʿ al-bayān ʿan taʾwīl āy al-Qurʾān*, Q. 9:43, www.altafsīr.com/Tafasir.asp?tMadhNo=1&tTafsīrNo=1&tSoraNo=9&tAyahNo=43&tDisplay=yes&UserProfile=0&LanguageId=1.

50 See other examples from the Qur'an in the same vein: Q. 8:67–69, 66:1.

51 There are, of course, distinct implications for the Shīʿī doctrine of *ʿiṣma* (infallibility) in how we categorise incorrect personal judgements of the Prophet which are then corrected by God. In order to reconcile these two positions, Ṭabāṭabāʾī, in reference to Q. 66:1, states that the verse is addressed to the Prophet (*al-nabī*) rather than him as a messenger (*al-rasūl*) and that it is addressed to himself besides anyone else. Ṭabāṭabāʾī, *al-Mīzān*, Q. 66:1, www.altafsīr.com/Tafasir.asp?tMadhNo=4&tTafsīrNo=56&tSoraNo=66&tAyahNo=1&tDisplay=yes&UserProfile=0&LanguageId=1. Kamāl al-Ḥaydarī in his *durūs al-khārij* lectures, entitled 'Fiqh al-mar'a: ḍarūrat al-tamyīz bayn al-sīra al-nabawiyya wa-l-sunna al-nabawiyya', states that the Prophet made individual or personal judgements in the

course of events that evidently occurred also show that he experimented with what type and level of worship would be appropriate for people by applying both the conceptual and practical parameters of the verses revealed to him – in this case, the time, duration, and content of the night prayer vigil. Revelation is a two-pronged process, combining the Prophet's natural human experience and judgement with God's own guidance. Therefore, the fourth principle one may formulate is that a legal obligation may be presented, tested, and adjusted in the Muslim community before it is implemented on a consistent level. This may apply to a range of legal rulings concerning devotional practices (*ʿibādāt*) and transactions (*muʿāmalāt*), such as the rulings pertaining to moon-sighting, pilgrimage, eating and drinking, interacting with non-Muslims, and so on, whereby in a globalised and technological world all legal acts can be periodically reviewed in order to ensure that there be not only no hardship in the performance of that act but also that its spiritual purpose be preserved.

Fifthly, a legal question arises as to whether or not the community at the time when the night prayer vigil was imposed as an obligation performed make-up prayers (*qaḍāʾ*) when they missed the night prayer vigil. From my reading of both Sunnī and Shīʿī narrations, I could not find narrations specifically pertaining to the obligation of performing a make-up prayer for a missed session of the night prayer vigil *during that revelatory period* if a believer missed it. There are, of course, numerous narrations about making up the five daily prayers and other prayers, but these narrations came about when the Prophet had already instituted the five daily prayers and established his Medinan community. One may argue that as a concept, the performance of make-up prayers was not instituted for the community at the time when the night prayer vigil was regularly performed, or if it was, it appears that only the Prophet could have practised it on a personal level.

When one examines, for example, the chapter devoted to lapsed prayer in al-Ḥurr al-ʿĀmilī's *Wasāʾil al-Shīʿa*, we find several narrations such as, on the authority of Abū Jaʿfar Muḥammad al-Bāqir, the fifth Shīʿī Imām, 'that he was asked about a man who prayed without purification or forgot the [five daily] prayers and did not pray them or slept. He replied, "He should make it up when he remembers it, at any time of the day or night."'[52] With specific regard to

instances of Q. 8:67–9, 9:43, and 66:1, and that these were not the definitive rulings according to the sacred law (*ḥukm al-shāriʿ*); rather, these were the Prophet's *madhāq*, meaning the result of his personal taste or view, trying out something. See his lecture: www.youtube.com/watch?v=lDfsZHBIIHA&t=2196s.

52 al-Ḥurr al-ʿĀmilī, *Wasāʾil al-Shīʿa*, 2nd ed. (Qom: Muʾassasat Āl al-Bayt li-Iḥyāʾ al-Turāth, 1993), vol. 8, ch. 1, *ḥadīth* no. 10565, https://ar.lib.eshia.ir/11025/8/253.

capability of performing a prayer, examination shows that there are essentially two categories of narrations. The first has to do with the circumstances one can control such as neglecting purification (*ṭahāra*), as one sees in the narration above, forgetfulness (*nisyān*), and sleep (*nawm*). In all these instances, a make-up prayer for any missed obligatory prayer must be performed, since these circumstances are within the believer's control, so he must take personal responsibility for missing the obligation.

The second category of narrations includes those that deal with circumstances beyond the individual believer's control, such as not having reached the age of maturity (*bulūgh*) when one is too young, not having control of one's mind because one is insane (*majnūn*), or suddenly losing one's physical senses when, for example, one has a fainting spell (*ighmāʾ*). In these circumstances, the believer does not have to make up the obligatory prayer since one cannot be held liable by God for circumstances beyond one's control. This is why Shīʿī *ḥadīth* compilations contain narrations such as the following: on the authority of Abū ʿAbd Allāh Jaʿfar, the sixth Shīʿī Imām: 'I asked him about a man who passed out for days and did not pray but then came to his senses: "Should he complete the prayers that he missed?" He replied, "There is nothing for him [to pray]."'[53]

What is important when one analyses the way in which the night prayer vigil was observed by the Prophet's followers is that there clearly was an adjustment period for these new converts to observe this prayer. There appears to have been gradual interest in the prayer until people found it difficult to perform on account of its timing or duration, or because of their own capacity. This is to be expected since they were not used to performing this ritual. What one has, therefore, is an intriguing early case in which it appears that there was no obligation to make up prayers for sessions of night prayer that one missed. The new converts (*muhtadūn*) apparently had difficulty adjusting to the performance of this prayer ritual. In this regard, forgetfulness or sleep may be exceptional instances that a convert cannot control initially but later may be in a position to do so. Therefore, the fifth principle one may formulate to guide an understanding of *āyāt al-aḥkām* is that the duration, extent, and obligation to make up for the non-performance of any legal act should be reviewed to allow converts to adjust to them. This could plausibly extend to the case in which a boy or a girl reaches maturity and requires some days, months, or even a year to adjust to the new legal acts that he or she must now perform. The reviewing of the specific requirements of these obligatory legal acts should depend on the legal responsible believer's physical, mental, and spiritual capacity.

53 Ibid., *ḥadīth* no. 10593.

In sum, the five principles that one may formulate from the case study of the night prayer are the following:

(1) Legal acts are primarily based on adjusting our souls towards God in the manner the Prophet did, in order to heighten our spiritual and moral capacities. The legal compliance of the act is a secondary consideration.

(2) The performance of a legal act is fundamentally dependent on one's spiritual, psychological, and practical ability at the time.

(3) *Āyāt al-aḥkām* are first directed to the barometer of the capability of the Prophet, but for the community that barometer must be adjusted on account of their differing capability.

(4) A legal obligation, whether constituting legal rulings to do with *ʿibādāt* or *muʿāmalāt*, may be presented, tested, and adjusted first in the Muslim community before being implemented on a consistent level. This is to ensure that there be no hardship in its performance and that the spiritual purpose of the act be preserved.

(5) A legal act's duration and extent, and the obligation to make up for missed performance, should be reviewed to allow converts and believers who have just attained maturity to adjust to these acts and rituals.

6 Conclusion

One may argue that some of the aforementioned principles may be found in books of jurisprudential rules or legal maxims (*al-qawāʿid al-fiqhiyya*) and that later verses of the Qur'an have discussed issues of hardship or ease for the believers.[54] This is of course true, but the purpose of analysing the case study of the night prayer vigil is to identify why, from a metaphysical standpoint, this particular prayer was revealed to the Prophet, how he adjusted himself to it, and the sort of judgement he made in extending its practice to the community. These principles may provide a consistent model for approaching *āyāt al-aḥkām* through the developing soul of the Prophet himself, who is regarded as the best model for Muslims.

We may therefore conclude by stating that exegesis according to the chronological sequence of revelation (*tafsīr al-Qurʾān ḥasab tartīb al-nuzūl*) helps ascertain the metaphysical goals of regulative verses through consideration of the Prophet's reception of *waḥy* and his experience of the historical

54 Principles such as *qāʿidat nafy al-ḥaraj*, *qāʿidat lā ḍarar*, and *qāʿidat al-tanāfur*. See, for example, Bāqir al-Īrwānī, *Durūs tamhīdiyya fī al-qawāʿid al-fiqhiyya*, 2 vols. (Qom: Intishārāt Naṣāyiḥ, 2014).

circumstances or the time. Secondly, the notion of capability (*istiṭāʿa*) may be broadened in law and legal hermeneutics through focus on the Prophet as the primary subject, paying attention to his psychological and spiritual dimensions, which then extends to the rest of the legally responsible believers (*mukallafūn*). Thirdly, we can review Muslim juristic approaches to collective worship through the Prophet's own experience of his community and allow trial and error in the application of jurisprudence.

Bibliography

al-ʿĀbid, ʿAlī b. Sulaymān. *Tafāsīr āyāt al-aḥkām wa-manāhijihā*. Riyadh: al-Dār al-Tadmuriyya, 2010.

al-Anṭākī, Abū al-Ḥasan ʿAlī b. Muḥammad b. Ismāʿīl b. Bushrā al-Tamīm. *Kitāb ʿadd āy al-Qurʾān – li-l-Makkī wa-l-Madaniyyayn wa-l-Kūfī wa-l-Baṣrī wa-l-Shāmī – al-muttafaq ʿalayhi wa-l-mukhtalaf fīhi*. Cairo: Muʾassasat al-Saʿūdiyya, 2011.

Fatemi, S. Mohammad Ghari S. 'Autonomy and Equal Right to Divorce with Specific Reference to Shiʿi *Fiqh* and the Iranian Legal System'. *Islam and Christian–Muslim Relations* 17, no. 3 (2006): 281–94.

Garner, Bryan A., ed. *Black's Law Dictionary*. 9th ed. Saint Paul, MN: West – Thomson Reuters, 2009.

Godlas, Alan. 'Sufism'. In *The Blackwell Companion to the Qurʾān*, edited by Andrew Rippin, 350–62. Oxford: Blackwell Publishing, 2006.

al-Ḥurr al-ʿĀmilī, Muḥammad b. al-Ḥasan. *Wasāʾil al-Shīʿa*. 2nd ed. Qom: Muʾassasat Āl al-Bayt li-Iḥyāʾ al-Turāth, 1993. https://ar.lib.eshia.ir/11025/8/253.

Ibn al-ʿArabī, Muḥammad b.ʿAlī. *Tafsīr al-Qurʾān al-karīm*. Beirut: Dār al-Kutub al-ʿIlmiyya, 2001.

Ibn al-Faras al-Andalusī, ʿAbd al-Munʿim b. Muḥammad. *Aḥkām al-Qurʾān*. 3 vols. Beirut: Dār Ibn Ḥazm, 2019.

Ibn al-Jawzī, ʿAbd al-Raḥmān b. ʿAlī b. Muḥammad Abū al-Faraj. *Zād al-masīr fī ʿilm al-tafsīr*. www.altafsīr.com/Tafasir.asp?tMadhNo=2&tTafsīrNo=15&tSoraNo=73&tAyahNo=1&tDisplay=yes&UserProfile=0&LanguageId=1.

Ibn al-Nadīm, Abū al-Faraj Muḥammad b. Isḥāq. *Kitāb al-fihrist*. Edited by Ayman Fuʾād Sayyid. 2nd ed. London: Al-Furqan Foundation, 2014.

al-Īrwānī, Bāqir. *Durūs tamhīdiyya fī al-fiqh al-istidlālī ʿalā al-madhhab al-Jaʿfarī*. 3 vols. Qom: Muʾassasat al-Fiqh, 2005.

al-Īrwānī, Bāqir. *Durūs tamhīdiyya fī al-qawāʿid al-fiqhiyya*. 2 vols. Qom: Intishārāt Naṣāyiḥ, 2014.

al-Īrwānī, Bāqir. *Durūs tamhīdiyya fī tafsīr āyāt al-aḥkām min al-Qurʾān*. 1st ed. Beirut: Dār Kumayl, 2004.

Jannatī, Muḥammad Ibrāhīm. *Manābiʿ-e ijtihād az dīdgāh-e mazāhib-e islāmī*. Tehran: Intishirāt-e-Kayhān, 1991.

Kara, Seyfeddin. *In Search of ʿAlī ibn Abī Ṭālib's Codex: History and Traditions of the Earliest Copy of the Qurʾān*. Berlin: Gerlach Press, 2018.

Kara, Seyfeddin. 'The Suppression of ʿAlī ibn Abī Ṭālib's Codex: Study of the Traditions on the Earliest Copy of the Qurʾān'. *Journal of Near Eastern Studies* 75, no. 2 (2016): 267–89.

al-Kāshānī, al-Fayḍ. *al-Tafsīr al-ṣāfī*. www.altafsīr.com/Tafasir.asp?tMadhNo=4&tTafsīrNo=41&tSoraNo=73&tAyahNo=4&tDisplay=yes&UserProfile=0&LanguageId=1.

Lalani, Arzina. "Ali ibn Abi Talib'. In *The Qur'an: An Encyclopaedia*, edited by Oliver Leaman, 28–32. Abingdon: Routledge, 2006.

al-Maḥallī, Jalāl al-Dīn Muḥammad b. Aḥmad, and Jalāl al-Dīn al-Suyūṭī. *Tafsīr al-Jalālayn*. Karachi: al-Bushrā, 2018.

Maʿrifa, Muḥammad Hādī. *Talkhīṣ al-tamhīd: mūjaz dirāsāt mubassaṭāt ʿan mukhtalaf shuʾūn al-Qurʾān al-karīm*. Qom: Mu'assasat al-Nashr al-Islāmī, 2009.

al-Nāblusī, *Muḥammad ʿIzzat* Darwaza. *al-Tafsīr al-ḥadīth tartīb al-suwar ḥasab al-nuzūl*. 1st ed. Cairo: Dār Iḥyāʾ al-Kutub al-ʿArabiyya, 1963. https://shamela.ws/book/23603/395#p1.

Rabābiʿa, Muḥammad Mujlī Aḥmad. *Tafsīr al-Qurʾān al-karīm ʿalā tartīb al-nuzūl: manbaʿuhu wa-fawāʾiduhu*. https://arabicpdfs.com/تفسير-القرآن-الكريم-على-ترتيب-النزول-م/.

al-Ṣadr, Muḥammad Bāqir. *al-Tafsīr al-mawḍūʿī wa-l-falsafa al-ijtimāʿiyya fī al-madrasa al-Qurʾāniyya*. Beirut: al-Dār al-ʿĀlamiyya, 1989.

al-Shawkānī, Muḥammad ʿAlī b. Muḥammad. *Fatḥ al-Qadīr*. Cairo: Dār Ibn al-Jawzī, 2012.

Subḥānī, Jaʿfar. *al-Manāhij al-tafsīriyya fī ʿulūm al-Qurʾān*. Qom: Mu'assasat al-Imām al-Ṣādiq, 2010.

al-Ṭabarī, Abū Jaʿfar Muḥammad b. Jarīr b. Yazīd. *Jāmiʿ al-bayān ʿan taʾwīl āy al-Qurʾān*. www.altafsīr.com/Tafasir.asp?tMadhNo=1&tTafsīrNo=1&tSoraNo=9&tAyahNo=43&tDisplay=yes&UserProfile=0&LanguageId=1.

Ṭabāṭabāʾī, Muḥammad Ḥusayn. *al-Mīzān fī tafsīr al-Qurʾān*. www.altafsīr.com/Tafasir.asp?tMadhNo=4&tTafsīrNo=56&tSoraNo=73&tAyahNo=1&tDisplay=yes&UserProfile=0&LanguageId=1.

Ṭabāṭabāʾī, Muḥammad Ḥusayn. *The Qurʾan in Islam: Its Impact and Influence on the Life of Muslims*. 1st ed. India: World Islamic Network, 1998. www.al-islam.org/quran-islam-its-impact-and-influence-life-muslims-sayyid-Muḥammad-husayn-tabatabai/part-5-order.

al-Ṭabrisī, Abū ʿAlī al-Faḍl b. al-Ḥasan b. al-Faḍl. *Majmaʿ al-bayān fī tafsīr al-Qurʾān*. www.altafsīr.com/Tafasir.asp?tMadhNo=4&tTafsīrNo=3&tSoraNo=73&tAyahNo=1&tDisplay=yes&UserProfile=0&LanguageId=1.

al-Ṭaḥāwī, Abū Jaʿfar Aḥmad. *Aḥkām al-Qurʾān al-karīm*. https://archive.org/details/FP45899FP/00_45899/.

Ṭahmāz, ʿAbd al-Ḥamīd Maḥmūd. *al-Tafsīr al-mawḍūʿī li-suwar al-Qurʾān al-ʿaẓīm*. Beirut: al-Dār al-Shāmiyya, 2014.

al-ʿUkbarī, Muḥibb al-Dīn Abū al-Baqāʾ. *al-Tibyān fī iʿrāb al-Qurʾān*. Beirut: Dār Ibn Ḥazm, 2017.

al-ʿUmarī, Walīd. *Muqadimmāt fī al-āyāt al-aḥkām*. https://tafsīr.net/article/5397/mqdmt-fy-aayat-al-ahkam#_ftn2.

al-Wāḥidī, al-Ḥasan ʿAlī b. Aḥmad. *Asbāb al-nuzūl*. Cairo: Dār al-Furqān, 2015.

PART 4

Contemporary Philosophical Perspectives

CHAPTER 12

Making Sense of Obligatory Faith in the Qur'an

Hamid Vahid

In the Qur'an, God is represented as prizing faith so highly as to make it the most important virtue of humankind.[1] We are told that our highest goal is to be in a loving relationship with God and that faith (in conjunction with other virtues like *taqwā* or God-fearingness) is the means of achieving this goal.

> Say, 'If you love Allah, then follow me; Allah will love you and forgive your sins, and Allah is all-forgiving, all-merciful. (Q. 3:31)[2]

It is, thus, no exaggeration to say that faith plays a, or perhaps *the*, central role in the Qur'an when characterising humanity's optimal response to God. There is, however, a central feature of faith, namely, the fact that it is not under one's voluntary control, which renders its role in the God–human relationship puzzling and mysterious. The idea is that, at first glance, religious faith does not appear to be something that can be gained voluntarily. Nevertheless, it is represented in the Qur'an as a standard that must be attained by individuals, whose achievement is regarded as commendable and whose absence is blameworthy. Many passages in the Qur'an explicitly state that one must have faith. Here are some typical samples:

> O you who have faith! Have faith in Allah and His Apostle. (Q. 4:126)
>
> So have faith in Allah and His Apostle, the untaught prophet, who has faith in Allah and His words, and follow him so that you may be guided. (Q. 7:158)
>
> Have faith in Allah and His Apostle, and spend out of that of which He has made you heirs. (Q. 57:7)
>
> Why should you not have faith in Allah when the Apostle invites you to have faith in your Lord, and He has certainly made a covenant with you, if you are [genuinely] faithful? (Q. 57:8)

---

1 For helpful comments and discussion of the ideas in this chapter, I am grateful to Muhammad Legenhausen, Yaser Mirdamadi, two anonymous reviewers, and the audience at the conference on the regulative verses of the Qur'an at Al-Mahdi Institute (Birmingham).

2 All the quotations from the Qur'an are taken from its translation by Ali Quli Qarai.

 | HTTPS://DOI.ORG/10.1163/9789004755567-014

In these verses, people are required to attain faith just as they are required to, say, give in charity. But how are we expected to acquire faith when entering such a state is not under our direct control, like giving in charity? To deal with this question, we need, however, to discuss a number of related issues at the heart of this debate, such as an investigation of the concept of faith and a description of doxastic freedom and agency. In this article, I shall suggest two distinct solutions to the puzzle of obligatory faith. One, less basic solution derives from the plausibility of a specific analysis of faith, and so its fate very much depends on whether the analysis in question can withstand critical scrutiny. However, the second, more fundamental solution is an outgrowth of the larger discussion of whether epistemic norms are hypothetical or categorical in nature. In the first section, I introduce the first solution to the puzzle, which begins with a discussion of a well-known analysis of faith. The second section begins by providing an account of doxastic freedom to show why the involuntary nature of belief poses no threat to epistemic agency. This paves the way for the second solution to the puzzle, which also addresses the question of whether epistemic reasons are categorical and binding. Finally, I briefly discuss how the Qur'anic perspective on faith acquisition can be made sense of in light of the conceptual framework provided. Let us begin, then, with the first response to the puzzle that appeals to a particular understanding of the notion of faith.

1 Voluntary Faith: the Cognitive Aspects of Faith

Despite the centrality of the notion of faith in both religious and non-religious contexts, there is no consensus on how this notion is to be understood, not least because 'faith' can appear in different locutions such as 'faith in' and 'faith that'. I will be here concerned with the 'faith that' locution, often known as 'propositional faith', as it is used in religious contexts. While the 'faith in' locution signifies 'trust' in somebody or some object, propositional faith is an expression of a positive attitude towards a proposition as when one professes to have faith that God exists. Despite the lack of consensus on the analysis of the concept of faith, it is generally agreed that 'faith' is a complex concept incorporating conative as well as cognitive aspects. The conative aspect involves a conative orientation towards the truth of a particular proposition (p). The idea is that to have faith that p, one must consider the truth of p to be desirable and want it to be true. Faith is more than a mere agreement to follow a set of practical rules or regulations. Rather, it also involves a positive emotional orientation. It appears that it is about this aspect of faith that the Qur'an admonishes some of the faithful not to use 'faith' lightly.

> The Bedouins say, 'We have faith.' Say, 'You do not have faith yet; rather, say, "We have embraced Islam," for faith has not yet entered into your hearts.' (Q. 49:14)

An unbiased or unsympathetic orientation towards the truth of p cannot be consistent with having the propositional faith that p. This is what undermines the identification of faith with belief for one can believe that p while finding the truth of p abhorrent as when, say, a cancer patient believes that she will die soon. Another function of the conative aspect is to allow faith to affect our character as well as our behaviour. After all, the acquiring of faith is supposed to have a transforming effect on one's life.

This leaves us with the cognitive aspect of faith that has traditionally been identified with belief. However, many philosophers have argued that the notion of 'belief' is inadequate to describe the different layers of our cognitive lives and that we need to invoke additional attitudes when trying to understand people's cognitive behaviour. For some philosophers, this is especially true in the realm of religion where 'belief' does not appear to be an adequate term to capture the kinds of commitments that religious individuals find themselves with 'in these secular, scientistic, intellectually unsettled times'.[3] William Alston, for example, has argued that an attitude like 'acceptance' is more adequate for such purposes. In his book *An Essay on Belief and Acceptance*, Jonathan Cohen explored the distinction between belief and acceptance in depth. He singled out several features that he took to distinguish belief from acceptance. For example, he took the 'belief that p' to be a disposition such that, when considering whether p, one often tends to feel it to be the case that p (with some degree of confidence). Moreover, if one believes that p, then one will tend to use p as a premise in theoretical and practical reasoning. More importantly, he considered belief to be an involuntary disposition that is constitutively linked to the truth of its contents.

According to Cohen, 'acceptance' is also a positive attitude towards a proposition. To accept that p is to 'take on board', to adopt a policy of including p among one's premises 'for deciding what to do or think in a particular context'.[4] Acceptance, however, differs from belief in, at least, two important respects. Accepting that p does not include a tendency to feel that p is the case when the question of whether p is raised. Moreover, reasons for accepting a proposition can include practical considerations. As an example, Cohen gives the case of an attorney who believes that his client is not innocent but, to plead before a jury, accepts that he is. Finally, unlike belief, acceptance is under one's direct

3 William P. Alston, 'Belief, Acceptance, and Religious Faith', in *Faith, Freedom, and Rationality*, ed. Jeff Jordan and Daniel Howard-Snyder (Lanham: Rowman & Littlefield, 1996), 16.

4 Ibid.

voluntary control. It aims at utility but not truth, which is why one can accept certain things that one believes are false. There are, of course, cases where one cannot accept a proposition (p) regardless of one's epistemic situation as when things are not so clear one way or another. Here, given the pressure of our situation, one can resort to less positive attitudes towards p, such as 'assumption' or 'working hypothesis', to guide one's action.[5]

Indeed, some philosophers have contended that the very same reasons that necessitated a weaker cognitive attitude like acceptance to stand for the cognitive aspect of faith, namely, the volatile commitments of the modern religious life, would push us towards still weaker or more inclusive attitudes such as 'propositional trust', 'propositional hope', or 'beliefless assumption'. Howard-Snyder, for example, has argued for the attitude of (beliefless) assumption.[6] We assume things, he says, that we neither believe (disbelief) nor accept (reject). 'Assuming that the p' still represents a positive cognitive attitude because it is inconsistent with disbelieving that p. It also differs from both belief and acceptance because, unlike the case of the latter attitudes, when we assume that p, we lack a tendency to accept p or to feel that p to be the case when considering whether p. Understood thus, we seem to be facing a plethora of cognitive attitudes all standing for the cognitive aspect of faith. There need not, however, be a competition between such states. After all, faith is a matter of degree. There is the faith of ordinary believers and there is the faith of the mystics whose cognitive attitudes presumably involve something like flat-out belief or knowledge.

Here is one way of thinking about the preceding analysis of 'faith'. We can see the different attitudes that stand for the cognitive aspect of faith (hope, assuming, acceptance, etc.) as denoting different stages of acquiring faith that end with flat-out belief. To give an analogy, imagine a large marathon race with many participants who want to reach the finish line. However, as it happens, only some will be able to achieve that feat. Others will retire after covering certain distances on the route to the finish line. We can see the aforementioned cognitive attitudes (belief, acceptance, etc.) as standing for the various distances that people cover in their attempt to reach the finish line (knowledge of God).

There is much to be said about this 'picture' of faith, but what is relevant to our discussion about the puzzle of obligatory faith is as follows. If it is true that acceptance or assuming are the correct representations of the cognitive

5 Ibid.

6 Daniel Howard-Snyder, 'Propositional Faith: What It Is and What It Is Not', *American Philosophical Quarterly* 50, no. 4 (2013): 357–72.

aspect of faith, then our puzzle dissolves because such attitudes are under our voluntary control. Of course, in our case, the resolution of the puzzle crucially depends on whether the Qur'an takes such attitudes, rather than belief, to be the proper cognitive component of faith. Some might argue that nowhere in the Qur'an is there an explicit statement to the effect that only belief can play such a role.[7] If so, one would be able to make sense of those verses in the Qur'an that implicate faith as an obligation by thinking of faith as involving cognitive attitudes, such as acceptance and assuming, that are under our voluntary control.

But what if it is 'belief' that the Qur'an takes to be the cognitive constituent of faith? In that case, the possibility of obligatory faith would require a different line of explanation. So far, our discussion has been run on the premise that we do not have epistemic agency on the ground that beliefs are not under our voluntary control as are our actions. But maybe freedom of action is not the correct model for doxastic freedom. In the following section, I am going to argue that epistemic agency is consistent with our lack of voluntary control over our beliefs. Assuming that it is possible to clear space for doxastic freedom, we may then be able to make sense of having obligations involving belief. In that case, the idea of obligatory faith, with belief as its cognitive ingredient, may not be as improbable as we first thought. So, let us begin by reflecting on the question of doxastic freedom.

2 Faith as Belief: Doxastic Freedom and Epistemic Agency

We regulate our beliefs in the course of forming, retaining, reasoning, and revising them. And it does look as if we are exercising freedom in doing so, especially in the cases which involve reflective reasoning. But what sort of freedom is at issue here? As we have seen, belief regulation does not follow the same pattern that the regulation of action does. Free action requires intention. Even when actions are habitual and automatic, there is still a dispositional involvement of intentions where we exercise a capacity to do what we intend to do. But doxastic states are not intentions-reactive. This may not, however, impede the exercise of doxastic agency. After all, intentions themselves, despite being free, do not, on pain of an infinite regress, require prior

7 Indeed, Ali Qarai almost consistently translates the Arabic word *'īmān'* as 'faith' rather than 'belief', clearing space for the possibility of taking other attitudes to represent the cognitive aspect of faith.

intentions.[8] There is, however, another model for the freedom of action that appears to be more congenial to doxastic states. The idea is that free action involves the capacity to act in light of what one judges to be the most reasons to act. This is true even in the case of habitual and automatic actions for even in such cases we would react differently were we to judge that there are reasons that tell against the action.[9]

Although the 'reasons-reactivity' model seems a more apt option for doxastic freedom, the fit is not perfect because while actions can be performed on account of moral, prudential, and in general, practical reasons, that is not the case with beliefs. We cannot directly *believe* for practical reasons just as we cannot *intend* for such reasons as when we are, say, offered some reward to form an intention while recognising that we have no reason to perform the relevant action. A natural way out of this impasse is to distinguish between state-given and object-given reasons.[10] Object-given reasons for attitudes are those considerations that bear on the object (content) of the attitudes, while state-given reasons are those that bring about or cause the attitudes themselves as when one is threatened to be put to death unless one admires, say, a tyrant. State-given reasons are the 'wrong kind' of reasons for attitudes.[11] However, while in the case of actions, freedom is exercised by regulating our reactions

8 See, for example, Nishi Shah, 'Clearing Space for Doxastic Voluntarism', *The Monist* 85, no. 3 (2002): 436–45.

9 See, for example, Conor McHugh, 'Epistemic Responsibility and Doxastic Agency', *Philosophical Issues* 23, no. 1 (2013): 132–57.

10 Ibid.

11 Derek Parfit, *On What Matters*, 2 vols. (Oxford: Oxford University Press, 2011). According to evidentialism, the position assumed in this chapter, the only considerations that can bear on a belief's correctness are those that bear on its truth. This rules out practical considerations as normative reasons for belief. It also gives rise to a distinction between the 'wrong' and 'right' kinds of reasons. What underlies this distinction is the observation that reasons for valuing an object do not always reflect the value of that object. One way of cashing out the idea behind this distinction is to discriminate between state-given and object-given reasons. The thought is that reasons for an attitude are either grounded in the features of the attitude itself or they pertain to the features of the object of that attitude. Object-given reasons count in favour of a subject's holding an attitude by bearing on its object or content. They are, thus, the right kind of reasons for that attitude. For example, in the case of belief, since to believe that p is to take its content to be true, anything that does not bear on p must bear on the belief qua a state. This means that state-given reasons merely reflect the benefits (costs) of being in a particular attitude and are therefore reasons of the wrong kind for (or against) having that attitude. This allows us to differentiate between believing a proposition p and bringing about (or causing) that one has the belief in question. Accordingly, on an evidentialist account, the potential benefits of a belief can be regarded as the normative reasons for *bringing about* one has the belief in question rather than as reasons for the belief itself.

to any kind of reason, doxastic freedom requires being responsive only to object-given reasons. In general, epistemic agency and doxastic freedom only require being responsive to the right kinds of reasons where to be responsive to a reason is to correctly appreciate and react to that reason's normative force.

The preceding observations show that there is a kind of doxastic freedom that can underwrite our epistemic agency when we are regulating our beliefs. Beliefs need not be under our voluntary control to be assessed as rational, irrational, epistemically responsible, and so on. They only need to have been formed and guided in response to reasons that determine what is demanded in a particular domain. So, if there is an 'ought' that can be applied to beliefs, that 'ought' must stem from reasons to which our beliefs are sensitive. This means that one can coherently countenance the possibility of cognitive obligations despite beliefs not being under our voluntary control. The involvement of reasons, however, raises another complication. On some accounts, reasons and evidence, on their own, lack normative force. At best, they *permit* the forming of certain beliefs. So, there are no positive epistemic obligations that can be directly generated by evidence alone. If true, this would pose another threat to the possibility of obligatory faith that involves belief. To address this issue, we need to make some quick incursions into the epistemological territory. As I shall argue below, the threat can be averted once we are clear as to what we are talking about when we mention having reason or evidence.

2.1 Epistemic Normativity: Hypothetical or Categorical

A fundamental question in epistemology concerns the conditions under which beliefs are rational or justified. According to the traditional Cartesian–Lockean conception of justification, it is to be construed in terms of the fulfilment of epistemic duty or obligation. Many find the notion of justification as somehow devoid of content when 'cut loose from considerations of obligation and blame'.[12] On this approach, justification is taken to be a function of how an agent has formed her beliefs vis-à-vis the fulfilment or violation of her epistemic obligations and duties. Despite its illustrious history, this view of justification has, in recent years, come under attack primarily on the grounds of presupposing the implausible thesis of doxastic voluntarism and for failing to respect the truth conductivity of epistemic justification. We have, however, already argued that there are conceptions of doxastic freedom that do not undermine our doxastic agency, so we need not bother about this problem.

12 William P. Alston, 'Concepts of Epistemic Justification', reprinted in *Epistemic Justification: Essays in the Theory of Knowledge* (Ithaca: Cornell University Press, 1989), n21.

A more fundamental objection to this conception, however, concerns the very coherence of positive epistemic obligations or duties. We shall address this question independently of the viability of its associated conception of justification. The question is whether there are both positive and negative duties, things that we ought to do and those we ought not to do. As far as actions are concerned such obligations seem to be unproblematic. Our moral, prudential, and, in general, practical reasons require us to do certain things and avoid others. But are there things we ought or ought not to believe on purely epistemic grounds? These epistemic obligations usually pertain to epistemological policies, such as, 'one ought to proportion one's belief to one's evidence', or 'one ought to consider all the available evidence before forming a belief', or 'one ought to maintain consistency in one's stock of beliefs', and so on.

In opposition to such claims, some epistemologists have argued that there are *no* positive epistemic obligations, that there are only negative ones such as 'you ought *not to* believe things in the absence of evidence', or 'you ought *not to* believe things more than what your evidence suggests', and so on.[13] On such views, evidence is permissive in that it only specifies the range of propositions that one is permitted or warranted to believe. It is only when evidence is conjoined with non-epistemic considerations that obligations are generated. There are, however, several ways that the permissive view has been defended.

On a traditional approach, it is the instrumentalist nature of epistemic rationality or justification that undermines the claim that evidence can, on its own, ground epistemic obligations. Instrumental rationality is the sort of rationality that is involved when one takes the means to one's ends.[14] Suppose I intend to attend a conference in another part of the world, and I know that I will only be able to do that by travelling to that place, then it is instrumentally rational for me to make the necessary travel arrangements. When our goals happen to be epistemic, epistemic rationality turns out to be a species of instrumental rationality. But what are such goals? For the instrumentalist, this is the universal goal of having true beliefs and not having false beliefs (the 'truth goal'). It follows from this that epistemic reasons are not categorical. Rather, they are hypothetical reasons contingent on one's having the truth goal. This means that the facts that underlie the rationality of our beliefs are dependent on our having the goal in question.

---

13 See, for example, Mark T. Nelson, 'We Have No Positive Epistemic Duties', *Mind* 119, no. 473 (2010): 83–102.

14 See, for example, Richard Foley, *The Theory of Epistemic Rationality* (Cambridge, MA: Harvard University Press, 1987).

In response, opponents of instrumental rationality have claimed that whether one has reason to hold a belief depends entirely on one's epistemic circumstances regardless of what goals one has. So, epistemic reasons have to be viewed as categorical. These theorists deny the instrumentalists' claim that we have the universal goal of truth. After all, it is not the case that people proceed to form beliefs about every state of affairs that they come across in their daily engagements. That would be a psychologically outrageous claim. We indeed have a preference for having true beliefs about particular matters as when we consult a phone book to contact a particular person or consult dictionaries to find the meaning of words. But, as Thomas Kelly observes,[15] such specific concerns are a far cry from the universal concern for truth. Moreover, there are many truths, such as whether there are an even or odd number of stars in the universe, that serve none of our goals, and, in fact, there are cases where we intentionally try to avoid knowing the truth of a particular matter (e.g. a movie's ending). Nevertheless, were we to come across evidence for such propositions, we would be required to form appropriate beliefs, which speak in favour of the view that epistemic reasons are categorical. In response, the instrumentalists distinguish between 'having evidence' for some proposition (p) and 'having reason' to believe that p. They claim that the cases just mentioned merely show the obtaining of some evidence for a proposition p. However, for that evidence to be a reason for believing p, one must have the appropriate goals.

A different line of attack on the possibility of epistemic obligations has been taken by Mark Nelson.[16] Nelson's main reason for defending permissivism is, what he calls, the 'infinite justificational fecundity' of evidence. The idea, in a nutshell, is that every single piece of evidence potentially epistemically justifies an infinite number of different beliefs. This may seem innocuous at first, but, when combined with positive epistemic obligations, it requires that we believe everything that our evidence supports or justifies. Suppose, for example, that I see my colleague's car in the car park of our institute. This gives me good evidence that he is in his office. But this piece of evidence equally justifies such beliefs as 'I have a colleague', that 'there are car parks', that 'there are cars', that 'there are tiers', and so on. Surely, I lack the psychological capacity to believe an infinite number of such propositions, some of which will be too complex for me to even grasp. Nelson, thus, concludes that which proposition one should believe depends not only on one's epistemic situation but also on one's needs,

15 Thomas Kelly, 'Epistemic Rationality as Instrumental Rationality: A Critique', *Philosophy and Phenomenological Research* 66, no. 3 (2003): 612–40.

16 Nelson, 'We Have No Positive Epistemic Duties'.

interests, and preferences. So, although he grants that there are negative epistemic obligations, he concludes that 'epistemic ought' is not wholly grounded in one's epistemic circumstances but is conditional on one's non-epistemic considerations that may include one's needs, desires, moral duties, and so on.

Still, a different strategy to deny the categorical nature of epistemic normativity exploits an idea of Gilbert Harman that we should, on pain of wasting our cognitive resources, avoid cluttering our minds by believing trivialities, pointless matters, and matters in which we have no interest.[17] An example of such matters is the trivial consequences of one's beliefs. For example, if one believes that p, this belief also implies 'p or q', 'p or p', 'p and either p or r', and so on. Jane Friedman has labelled propositions that are of no interest to us 'junk propositions', and belief in such propositions 'junk beliefs'.[18] She then turns Harman's thought that one should not clutter one's mind with junk into a meta-normative principle (CA) to the effect that 'if p is junk for S at world (w) and time (t), then S ought not to believe p at w, t'. She thinks that (CA) can come into conflict with epistemic obligations that require S to form belief (with content p) in response to having sufficient evidence (r) on the ground that p might well be junk for S. She takes this argument to favour an interest-driven epistemology where the norms of belief revision are largely hypothetical and depend on our local interests in particular matters in addition to our epistemic or evidential circumstances.

The above debates have generated a lot of ongoing discussions among their disputants. I think what fuels these discussions, thus, making the disputants often talk past each other, is rooted in the ambiguity of the notion of 'evidence' as employed in them. To see this, we need to distinguish between three senses of evidence, namely, 'evidence there is', 'known evidence', and 'possessed evidence'. For example, in the debate over instrumental rationality, the instrumentalists' concern is mainly with 'known evidence' whereas their opponents have 'possessed evidence' in mind when talking about epistemic normativity. As we saw, the instrumentalists distinguish between 'having good evidence' and 'having reason', arguing that what bridges the divide is the subject's having appropriate goals. To explain, Adam Leite gives an example where a subject (S) is idly noticing that all of the people who exit the park are accompanied

17 Gilbert Harman, *Change in View: Principles of Reasoning* (Cambridge, MA: MIT Press, 1986).

18 Jane Friedman, 'Junk Beliefs and Interest-Driven Epistemology', *Philosophy and Phenomenological Research* 97, no. 3 (2018): 568–83.

by dogs.[19] S is not irrational, he says, if S fails to believe that the next person coming out is likely to have a dog, if S's mind is fully occupied with, say, his job interview in the afternoon. It is clear that, in this example, to say that S *has* evidence is merely to say that he is *aware* of that evidence without being concerned with how it bears on the proposition that <the next person coming out of the park has a dog>.

By contrast, the anti-instrumentalist conception of 'having evidence' goes beyond the mere awareness of the fact that constitutes the evidence. This is clear from the various examples that Kelly gives in his attack on instrumentalist rationality, and, more pointedly, from his critique of what he calls the 'indicator' theory of evidence. He considers the case of Koplik spots which at some point in time were found to be strongly correlated with measles. However, for Kelly, whether the (known) proposition (r) that <the patient has Koplik spots on her skin> is evidence to believe (p) <the patient has measles> 'depends crucially on whether [one] is aware of the correlation between Koplik spots and measles'.[20]

The same thing is true about Nelson's examples in support of his permissive view. Nelson, as we saw, begins his argument against the possibility of positive obligations by asking whether 'I really have a duty to believe everything for which I have evidence'. But the answer to this question depends on whether 'having evidence' is supposed to go beyond the mere awareness of the evidence. In fact, his 'fecundity' argument does not seem to require more than 'known evidence' for it involves an infinite number of propositions that the subject cannot entertain, and a fortiori fails to see whether they are favoured by the evidence of which he is aware. So, unlike Kelly's gloss on 'having evidence', which also requires awareness of the evidence favouring or supporting the relevant proposition, Nelson's conception of evidence is lacking in this respect.

Finally, Friedman's account of junk belief, and the (meta-normative) principle (CA) to which it gives rise, are equally vulnerable to the problem just mentioned. When she says 'evidence alone does not demand belief, and it cannot even, on its own, permit or justify belief', she seems to have merely 'known evidence' in mind. This is because junk propositions are those propositions that are of no interest to the subject to consider them. A fortiori, they are not

19 Adam Leite, 'Epistemic Instrumentalism and Reasons for Belief: A Reply to Tom Kelly's "Epistemic Rationality as Instrumental Rationality: A Critique"', *Philosophy and Phenomenological Research* 75, no. 2 (2007): 456–64.

20 Thomas Kelly, 'Evidence and Normativity: Reply to Leite', *Philosophy and Phenomenological Research* 75, no. 2 (2007): 471.

the sort of propositions that one would be interested to see if one's evidence supports them.

So far, I have tried to show how different uses of 'evidence' have been responsible for the disputants within the preceding debates talking past each other. But this discussion has been conducted only at an intuitive level without a principled account of what 'having evidence' is supposed to consist of. To provide such an account, we should look into the structure of reasons in general and epistemic reasons in particular.

2.2 The Dispositional Structure of Epistemic Reasons

Normative reasons are standardly understood in terms of considerations that objectively favour (or disfavour) certain actions and beliefs. They are reasons that explain why one ought to perform certain acts or form certain beliefs. Motivating (or possessed) reasons, on the other hand, are those in the light of which an agent acts or forms beliefs. It is highly controversial how normative reasons bear on the rationality of actions and beliefs if, as is widely believed, rationality requires that we correctly respond to our perspectival (or 'apparent') reasons, that is, reasons that we possess which may or may not coincide with the objective reasons that are out there in the world.[21] But what is it to possess a reason? Here I will be concerned only with the possession conditions of epistemic reasons, that is, reasons that are expected to justify attitudes such as beliefs. In other words, our question concerns what it is to possess a reason (r) for holding a belief in a proposition p.

An obvious initial condition (the 'epistemic requirement') would be for r to be available or cognitively accessible to the subject where 'availability' can be understood either in normative terms as involving knowledge or justified belief or in non-normative terms involving presentational states such as seemings or merely doxastic states such as beliefs. For my purposes here, I shall leave open the exact nature of the epistemic requirement, and only take it to minimally require that one's reasons be cognitively accessible to the subject. It is obvious that, understood thus, the availability of reasons is not sufficient for their possession, assuming that only possessed reasons rationalise beliefs.

To see this, consider a scenario in which a subject is told that the fish she is going to have for lunch contains salmonella.[22] The fact that (r) <the fish

---

21 Maria Alvarez, *Kinds of Reasons: An Essay on the Philosophy of Action* (Oxford: Oxford University Press, 2010).

22 This example is adapted from John Broome, 'Does Rationality Consist in Responding Correctly to Reasons?', *Journal of Moral Philosophy* 4, no. 3 (2007): 349–74.

contains salmonella> is a normative reason for not eating the fish. But, reasonably believing that it is harmless, she forms the belief that it is safe to eat the fish. Here, even though she is aware of the reason, r fails to impact the epistemic status of her belief. What explains the subject's predicament is that, despite being aware of r, she still fails to *possess* it as a reason for believing that it is unsafe to eat the fish. It is generally thought that what is missing here is that she fails to 'see' or 'treat' r as a reason for holding the belief in question. In other words, she fails to appreciate that r bears on or supports that belief. What this means is that, to possess r as an epistemic reason for believing that p, one should not only have some sort of cognitive access to r but should also *treat* it as a reason for p (the 'treating requirement'). This raises the obvious question of what it is to treat some considerations as reasons. There are several accounts of the treating requirement in the literature but I shall focus on what I take to be the correct approach to this question.[23]

Consider a subject (S) who knows that the presence of salmonella in a fish is a reason for not eating the fish. Accordingly, S acquires the information that the presence of salmonella in a fish is positively relevant to the question of whether to believe that it is safe to eat the fish. We may view the gaining of this information by S as endowing her with an epistemic potential to possess a reason about whether to believe that it is safe to eat a particular fish that turns out to contain salmonella. This potential (but real) epistemic property manifests itself as S's *possessing a reason* when she is given the information (r) that the fish she is going to have for lunch contains salmonella. By possessing r as a reason to believe that (p) <it is unsafe to eat the fish>, S comes to have propositional justification to believe that p.

A different way of describing this scenario is that, before learning about the presence of salmonella in the fish, S has an epistemic disposition (to possess r as a reason for believing that p) very much like when we ascribe the disposition to dissolve in water to a lump of sugar (in virtue of its molecular structure) while denying it to a piece of paper (on the ground that it lacks that molecular structure). This epistemic disposition then manifests itself when evidence r is made available to S. In other words, just as the molecular structure of the lump of sugar grounds its disposition to dissolve in water, we can view the satisfaction of the treating requirement by S as grounding her epistemic disposition to possess r as a reason for believing that p in response to (the available) r.

23 For a full defence of this view, see Hamid Vahid, *The Dispositional Architecture of Epistemic Reasons* (New York: Routledge, 2020). For the purposes of this chapter, it does not matter which account of 'possession' one should adopt. For other views, see, for example, Errol Lord, *The Importance of Being Rational* (Oxford: Oxford University Press, 2018).

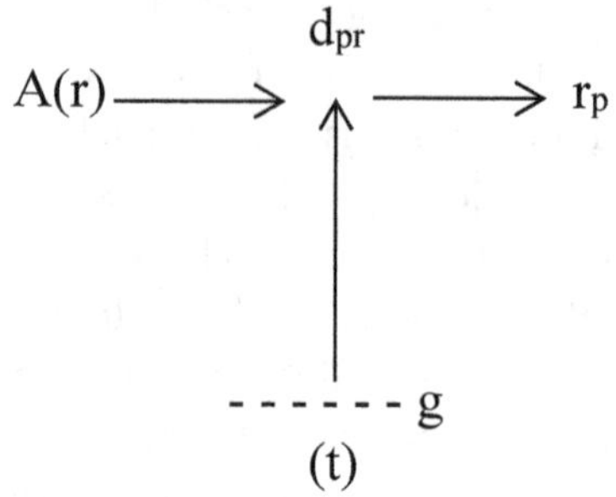

FIGURE 12.1
Possessing a reason: 'A(r)' – stimulus – denotes 'being aware of reason r', 't' denotes 'being in a treating-state' functioning as the ground (g) of disposition (d_{pr}), 'd_{pr}' denotes 'having disposition to possess r as a reason to believe p', 'r_p'– response – denotes 'possessed reason'.

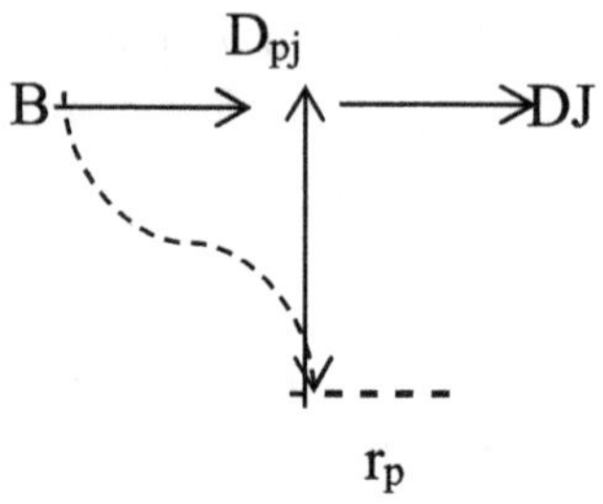

FIGURE 12.2
'B'– stimulus – stands for 'belief', 'r_p' denotes 'possessed reason r' grounding the disposition D_{pj}, 'D_{pj}' denotes 'having propositional justification', 'DJ' – response – denotes 'being doxastically justified', and the dotted line represents the basing of B on r_p

Let us say of a subject that meets the treating requirement that she is in a mental state, a 'treating state', whereby she appreciates that a particular reason (r) favours or supports a particular proposition (p). Whether this state involves belief or other attitudes does not concern us at this stage. All that matters is that we can understand the possession of a reason (r) by a subject in terms of the subject being in a relevant treating-state such that to be in that state in regard to the propositions r and p is to have a disposition to possess r (as a reason for believing that p) in response to (the available) r. When r is made available to the subject, the disposition manifests itself in the subject's coming to possess r as a reason for p, thus, having propositional justification to believe that p. So, our dispositional account of reason-possession construes it as the manifestation of an epistemic disposition, grounded in a treating-state, when the relevant reason is made available to the agent (Figure 12.1).

Finally, when S comes to possess the reason r to believe that p, the possession of r, in turn, grounds in him an epistemic disposition (propositional justification) to believe p with doxastic justification. When S forms the belief that p, the belief is said to be doxastically justified as it is now *based* on r (Figure 12.2).

2.3 Making Sense of Positive Epistemic Obligations

As the above account shows, to possess evidence (r) to believe a proposition (p), one should not only be aware of r (the epistemic requirement) but should also be in a treating-state vis-à-vis r and p (the treating requirement). The important thing is that it is only when evidence is possessed by the subject that it acquires its normative force. Prior to this stage, the evidence is either not known or not treated as a reason by the subject. Furthermore, commensurate with the non-binding and binding levels of evidence, we can distinguish between two stages of epistemic normativity, namely, the possession stage and the justification stage. The former pertains to the stage where, by satisfying the epistemic and the treating requirements, the subject comes to possess evidence. The justification stage is where the evidence exercises its justifying force. Positive epistemic obligations are grounded in the justification stage where evidence is binding.

Of the two stages, it is the possession stage that is crucial for it is at this stage that the subject acquires epistemic agency by responding to evidence. As noted earlier, however, evidence has the potential to support and justify an infinite number of propositions. This raises the question of how the subject places herself in an appropriate treating relation vis-à-vis her evidence and some of the propositions in the infinite set. In other words, what is it that prompts the subject to select both the evidence (r) and the proposition (p) for which r is the evidence? On our account, it is here that non-epistemic, practical considerations (interests, desires, commitments, moral considerations, etc.) play their normative role. There are, at least, three ways that practical considerations can help the subject to enter a treating-state in regard to some evidence r and proposition p.

To begin with, they can help the subject select a particular proposition from the set of propositions that are supported by the evidence of which she is aware. Here the subject is guided by her interests, goals, and needs. Consider the car example again. As we saw, my evidence of seeing my colleague's car in the car park can support an infinite number of propositions. So, I can enter a treating-state vis-à-vis my evidence and each of those propositions. However, given my particular interest on that day, say, giving a joint seminar with him, I am prompted to select the proposition that he is now in his office. Accordingly, by satisfying the epistemic and treating requirements, I come to possess the evidence as a reason to believe that my colleague is in his office. This is when I enter the justification stage where my possessed evidence grounds a disposition (propositional justification) in me to believe that my colleague is in his office with doxastic justification. The possessed evidence is, at this stage, categorical and binding. In the event that I fail to form the belief in question, I would be judged for not believing as I should.

Sometimes, however, it is not a particular proposition about which we are in the dark. Rather, while entertaining the content of a potential belief, we lack the necessary evidence to enter a treating-state with respect to that content.

Here, practical considerations can help us locate the relevant evidence. To explain, a long-standing tradition in epistemology, 'pragmatism', holds that practical considerations justify belief in the same way that epistemic considerations do. Pragmatism's major handicap, however, has been getting around the well-known problem that practical considerations, on their own, are unable to motivate belief. In response, some recent proponents of pragmatism have suggested seeing such considerations as (motivating) reasons whose role is to cause the subject to be more responsive to her apparent normative reasons. Since there is no problem with normative reasons causing belief, the motivation objection can easily be bypassed.

I do not think that this strategy is of any help to the pragmatists. But I shall not argue for it here. Instead, I shall put an alternative gloss on the pragmatists' new strategy. When explaining their strategy, the new pragmatists take its strength to consist of incorporating the advantages of evidentialism without compromising pragmatism: 'if there are moral or prudential reasons to believe p, you might do so by *selectively focusing your attention* on the evidence supporting p, and ignoring evidence against it.'[24] Here, it seems that the main function of practical considerations is taken to consist in facilitating attentional shifts on the part of the subject. They make the subject aware of the relevant evidence that she would have missed in the absence of such considerations. This role is not unlike one of the roles that emotions are said to play in our cognitive lives. Emotions are said to have epistemic value by alerting us to the presence of objects in our environment quickly and without much mental effort – objects that we would have otherwise missed.[25] Without emotions, we would normally fail to notice what we ought to notice. By means of attentional shifts, emotions help make important things salient to us. In their current role, practical considerations also seem to function as sources of salience 'illuminating' part of our epistemic environment by motivating us to look for those normative reasons that bear on the entertained propositions.

Finally, another way that non-epistemic, practical considerations can operate in the possession stage is by manipulating the conditions under which one can enter or exit a treating-state. As we saw, to be in a treating-state vis-à-vis evidence r and a proposition p is for the subject to appreciate that r favours or supports p. As it turns out, however, the level of the support relation depends on practical factors or stakes. On this theory, known as 'pragmatic

24 Susanna Rinard, 'No Exception for Belief', *Philosophy and Phenomenological Research* 94, no. 1 (2017): 121–43.

25 See, for example, Julien Deonna and Fabrice Teroni, *The Emotions: A Philosophical Introduction* (New York: Routledge, 2012).

encroachment',[26] if the stakes are high, that is, if the cost of a belief being false is high, this raises the threshold of the evidence needed to justify belief so that the evidence is no longer able to justify that belief. The reverse can also happen, as when the potential benefits of a belief lower the threshold of the evidence necessary for justification. The thesis of pragmatic encroachment thus depicts another way in which practical considerations can operate at the possession stage. The preceding observations mean that by confining the role of practical considerations to the possession stage, I am denying that they are the inhabitants of the justification stage, as pragmatists are keen to claim.

3 Obligatory Faith in the Qur'an

To sum up, our previous discussions have demonstrated that, when properly understood, epistemic reasons are categorical and binding, justifying the coherent possibility of positive epistemic obligations. But how do these conclusions bear on the central question of this chapter? If, as assumed previously, belief is to represent the cognitive aspect of faith, then, given the coherent possibility of positive epistemic obligations, the obligation to acquire faith should be equally coherent. Indeed, our two-tier account of epistemic normativity seems quite congenial to the Qur'anic perspective of multiple phases of faith acquisition. One of the most noticeable aspects of the Qur'an is the dual character of its call on people to have (propositional) faith. It emphasises the advantages (costs) of belief (disbelief) in God, on the one hand, and draws emphasis to the countless indications and signs (*āyāt*) that are presented as reasons to believe in God, on the other.

> But those who have faith and do righteous deeds, We will admit them into gardens with streams running in them, to remain in them forever – a true promise of Allah, and who is truer in speech than Allah? (Q. 4:122)
>
> As for those who have faith and do righteous deeds, He will pay them in full their rewards, and He will enhance them out of His grace. But those who are disdainful and arrogant, He will punish them with a painful punishment, and they will not find besides Allah any guardian or helper. (Q. 4:172)
>
> Allah has promised those who have faith and do righteous deeds forgiveness and a great reward. (Q. 5:9)

26 Jeremy Fantl and Matthew McGrath, 'Evidence, Pragmatics, and Justification', *Philosophical Review* 111, no. 1 (2002): 67–94.

Here, the potential benefits of belief in God operate at the possession stage of epistemic normativity drawing and shifting the attention of people towards the signs of God. They help people enter appropriate treating-states vis-à-vis the signs and the proposition that God exists, signs which they would have otherwise ignored. By being placed in appropriate treating-states, people are expected to appreciate the normative force of the signs (evidence) for the existence of God. In numerous verses in the Qur'an, people are encouraged to reflect on the signs in heaven and earth.

> Indeed in the creation of the heavens and the earth, and the alternation of night and day, and the ships that sail at sea with profit to men, and the water that Allah sends down from the sky – with which He revives the earth after its death, and scatters therein every kind of animal – and the changing of the winds, and the clouds disposed between the sky and the earth, there are surely signs for a people who exercise their reason. (Q. 2:164)
>
> You are vindictive toward us only because we have believed in the signs of our Lord, when they came to us.' 'Our Lord! Pour patience upon us, and grant us to die as Muslims.' (Q. 7:126)
>
> Indeed in the alternation of night and day, and whatever Allah has created in the heavens and the earth, there are surely signs for a people who are Godwary. (Q. 10:6)
>
> Have they not regarded the birds disposed in the air of the sky: no one sustains them except Allah. There are indeed signs in that for a people who have faith. (Q. 16:79)

This shows that the acquisition of faith, like all other examples of belief regulation, will contain the twin stages of possession and justification. The acquisition of faith involves as much epistemic agency as does that of belief. Being responsive to evidence, there is no compulsion in acquiring either. This is also in tune with the Qur'an expressly stating that 'there is no compulsion in the religion' (Q. 2:256).

> Had your Lord wished, all those who are on earth would have believed. Would you then force people until they become faithful? (Q. 10:99)

Indeed, it seems that the mission of the Prophet is confined only to the possession stage where his role is described as being only that of a 'warner' and a 'bearer of good news', that is, to properly dispose people to appreciate the various signs of God.

> Indeed, We have sent you with the truth, as a bearer of good news and as a warner, and you will not be questioned concerning the inmates of hell. (Q. 2:119)
>
> We did not send you except as a bearer of good news and warner to all mankind, but most people do not know. (Q. 34:28)

The Qur'an's emphasis on the role of practical considerations in securing faith is something that has also been shared in the philosophical literature. Indeed, this is how some philosophers have understood practical arguments for the existence of God, such as Pascal's wager, which seek to ground belief in God on the incentives for such a belief, like having a blissful life for eternity in heaven. The wager, they say, is 'an enabling device prompting persons to situate themselves so as properly to appreciate the evidence ... just as training in microscopic techniques has a legitimate epistemic function of enabling one into the proper position to evaluate the evidence'.[27] To put it in our terminology, the idea is that to believe in God, people need to possess evidence for such a belief. To possess such evidence, however, they are required to appreciate the force of evidence, that is, how signs signify a creator's existence. But only properly disposed hearts are able of such appreciation. Those whose hearts have been sealed are unable to believe even if they see all the signs.

> Have you seen him who has taken his desire to be his god and whom Allah has led astray knowingly, set a seal upon his hearing and heart, and put a blindfold on his sight? So who will guide him after Allah [has consigned him to error]? Will you not then take admonition? (Q. 45:23)

It is, however, the job of non-epistemic, practical considerations to bring about such a disposition. Only when people pass this stage and come to possess evidence (i.e. appreciate the signs) that belief in God (faith) will be required of them. Obligatory faith strikes us as mysterious because we expect it to obtain at the possession stage. But without first passing through the possession stage, it is not possible for evidence to be binding and for the beliefs to be required.

> How many a sign there is in the heavens and the earth that they pass by while they are disregardful of it! (Q. 12:105)

---

27 Jeff Jordan, *Pascal's Wager: Pragmatic Arguments and Belief in God* (New York: Oxford University Press, 2006), 173.

4 Conclusion

We began with the question of how to make sense of certain verses in the Qur'an that seem to require or demand people to acquire faith. It was noted that a response to this question depends on whether we take the cognitive aspect of faith to be a doxastic state like belief or some other mental states such as 'assuming' or 'acceptance' that are under our voluntary control. It was argued that the latter option is quite consistent with obligatory faith. The belief option, however, presented a serious challenge to the coherence of obligatory faith. In response, we began to clear some space for doxastic freedom by rejecting the action model of such freedom. It was argued that the reasons-responsiveness model can secure both doxastic freedom as well as epistemic agency. Next, we turned to the feasibility of positive epistemic obligations based on this conception of epistemic agency. It was argued that a proper account of possessing evidence or reason can provide us with the necessary conceptual resources to show why epistemic reasons can be categorical and binding. Finally, we showed how such a model of epistemic normativity might adequately make sense of the Qur'anic demand on people to have propositional faith in God.

Bibliography

Alston, William P. 'Belief, Acceptance, and Religious Faith'. In *Faith, Freedom, and Rationality*, edited by Jeff Jordan and Daniel Howard-Snyder, 3–27. Lanham: Rowman & Littlefield, 1996.

Alston, William P. 'Concepts of Epistemic Justification'. Reprinted in *Epistemic Justification: Essays in the Theory of Knowledge*, 81–115. Ithaca: Cornell University Press, 1989.

Alston, William P. 'The Deontological Conception of Epistemic Justification'. Reprinted in *Epistemic Justification: Essays in the Theory of Knowledge*, 115–53. Ithaca: Cornell University Press, 1989.

Alston, William P. *Epistemic Justification: Essays in the Theory of Knowledge*. Ithaca: Cornell University Press, 1989.

Alvarez, Maria. *Kinds of Reasons: An Essay on the Philosophy of Action*. Oxford: Oxford University Press, 2010.

Broome, John. 'Does Rationality Consist in Responding Correctly to Reasons?'. *Journal of Moral Philosophy* 4, no. 3 (2007): 349–74.

Cohen, L. Jonathan. *An Essay on Belief & Acceptance*. Oxford: Clarendon Press, 1992.

Deonna, Julien, and Fabrice Teroni. *The Emotions: A Philosophical Introduction*. New York: Routledge, 2012.

Fantl, Jeremy, and Matthew McGrath. 'Evidence, Pragmatics, and Justification'. *Philosophical Review* 111, no. 1 (2002): 67–94.

Foley, Richard. *The Theory of Epistemic Rationality*. Cambridge, MA: Harvard University Press, 1987.

Friedman, Jane. 'Junk Beliefs and Interest-Driven Epistemology'. *Philosophy and Phenomenological Research* 97, no. 3 (2018): 568–83.

Harman, Gilbert. *Change in View: Principles of Reasoning*. Cambridge, MA: MIT Press, 1986.

Howard-Snyder, Daniel. 'Propositional Faith: What It Is and What It Is Not'. *American Philosophical Quarterly* 50, no. 4 (2013): 357–72.

Jordan, Jeff. *Pascal's Wager: Pragmatic Arguments and Belief in God*. New York: Oxford University Press, 2006.

Kelly, Thomas. 'Epistemic Rationality as Instrumental Rationality: A Critique'. *Philosophy and Phenomenological Research* 66, no. 3 (2003): 612–40.

Kelly, Thomas. 'Evidence and Normativity: Reply to Leite'. *Philosophy and Phenomenological Research* 75, no. 2 (2007): 465–74.

Leite, Adam. 'Epistemic Instrumentalism and Reasons for Belief: A Reply to Tom Kelly's "Epistemic Rationality as Instrumental Rationality: A Critique"'. *Philosophy and Phenomenological Research* 75, no. 2 (2007): 456–64.

Lord, Errol. *The Importance of Being Rational*. Oxford: Oxford University Press, 2018.

McHugh, Conor. 'Epistemic Responsibility and Doxastic Agency'. *Philosophical Issues* 23, no. 1 (2013): 132–57.

Nelson, Mark T. 'We Have No Positive Epistemic Duties'. *Mind* 119, no. 473 (2010): 83–102.

Parfit, Derek. *On What Matters*. 2 vols. Oxford: Oxford University Press, 2011.

Rinard, Susanna. 'No Exception for Belief'. *Philosophy and Phenomenological Research* 94, no. 1 (2017): 121–43.

Schroeder, Mark. 'Having Reasons'. *Philosophical Studies* 139, no. 1 (2008): 57–71.

Shah, Nishi. 'Clearing Space for Doxastic Voluntarism'. *The Monist* 85, no. 3 (2002): 436–45.

Sylvan, Kurt. 'What Apparent Reasons Appear To Be'. *Philosophical Studies* 172, no. 3 (2015): 587–606.

Vahid, Hamid. *The Dispositional Architecture of Epistemic Reasons*. New York: Routledge, 2020.

CHAPTER 13

A Decision-Theoretic Approach to the *Ḥujjiyya* of Regulative Qur'anic Verses

Mahmoud Morvarid

1 Introduction

There is a consensus among the various schools of classical Islamic jurisprudence that the Qur'an is the main source of Islamic law. Nevertheless, apart from the ongoing disputes about the interpretations of Qur'anic verses, there is also a great deal of controversy as to under what conditions an alleged interpretation is *ḥujja* in the sense that it can be relied upon in the course of *istinbāṭ* (i.e. deriving divine rulings).[1]

This article largely focuses on a specific approach to the *ḥujjiyya* of the 'apparent meaning' (*ẓāhir*) of the regulative Qur'anic verses, which has been prevalent in the late Shīʿī *uṣūl al-fiqh*.[2] Drawing on ideas from the contemporary decision theory, I will challenge this approach and put forth an alternative theory of *ḥujjiyya* in general, exploring some of its implications for the *ḥujjiyya*

1 The Arabic term '*ḥujja*' means authority, proof, and evidence, and the term '*ḥujjiyya*' is an abstract noun derived from *ḥujja*. These are two pivotal technical terms in the late Shīʿī principles of jurisprudence (*uṣūl al-fiqh*). In general, the attribute of being *ḥujja* (referred to as '*ḥujjiyya*') is ascribed either to specific kinds of mental states (like a subject's certainty concerning a divine ruling), or to specific types of evidence (such as an apparent meaning of a Qur'anic verse which indicates a particular divine ruling). Put very roughly, a mental state or a specific piece of evidence is regarded as *ḥujja* when it leads to either liability or exemption from blame before the divine legislator. For example, in accordance with the late Shīʿī *uṣūl* perspective, when an individual becomes certain that God has mandated the performance of a specific action, A, they bear the responsibility for executing A. In other words, failing to carry out A will render them blameworthy. Conversely, if the individual attains the certainty that A is not obligatory, they won't be held accountable for omitting A, even if, in reality, A is indeed obligatory. I'll delve further into the concept of *ḥujjiyya* in the course of the article.

2 When referring to the late Shīʿī *uṣūl al-fiqh*, I am specifically addressing the period from the nineteenth century to the present. While certain aspects of the approach in question have historical precedents, its full development took place predominantly within this specified period. Moreover, when I mention the Uṣūlīs, I am referring to Shīʿī scholars of *uṣūl al-fiqh* from this particular era.

 | HTTPS://DOI.ORG/10.1163/9789004755567-015

of the *ẓāhir* (or the *ẓuhūr*) of regulative verses.[3] One significant offshoot of this theory is its ability to address the issue concerning those regulative verses which appear to conflict with our moral intuitions. The proposed theory offers a principled way to neutralise the normative force of (or at least of some) such regulative verses, without requiring radical modifications of the classic theological theories regarding revelation and divine speech. It is important to point out that even though this article initially centres around the standard framework of later Shīʿī *uṣūl al-fiqh*, the alternative theory presented at the end is independent of that framework.

2 An Outline of the Prevalent View of *Ḥujjiyya* in Later Shīʿī *Uṣūl al-Fiqh*

Shīʿī (as well as Muʿtazilī) theologians believe that it is obligatory to follow the rulings validly deduced from the Qurʾan and *ḥadīth*s, as these rulings are supposedly God's commands. According to their assumptions, since God is the creator and provider of blessings, it is morally incumbent upon us to follow His commands (or fulfil His desires). Thus, the normativity of all jurisprudential rulings is traced back to the normativity of moral requirements. To this extent, there is no particular predicament in terms of Shīʿī-Muʿtazilī theology. However, the challenge arises where God's commands and desires are not often discernible. To address this challenge, the Uṣūlīs have tried to develop a systematic rendering of the rules for deducing jurisprudential rulings.

In later Shīʿī principles of jurisprudence (after al-Shaykh Murtaḍā al-Anṣārī, 1214–81/1781–1864), a formal structure has been introduced for this purpose. The structure is roughly as follows: when a subject examines a specific action, A, and dedicates sufficient time and effort to explore its jurisprudential ruling, he either becomes certain that the action falls under one of the five religious

3 The Arabic word '*ẓuhūr*' lexically means appearance, and '*ẓāhir*' is an adjectival form derived from it, meaning apparent. As we shall see in section 2, according to the Uṣūlīs' terminology, when a speaker's utterance, S, provides inconclusive evidence that he has intended P by uttering S, then it is said that S is *ẓāhir* in P (or that S has a *ẓuhūr* in P). In such cases, even though the speaker might have meant something other than P, based on the relevant linguistic data, his having intended P remains more likely than any other alternatives. The technical term '*ẓāhir*' can be thus translated as 'apparent meaning' or 'prima facie meaning', yet throughout this chapter, I prefer to adhere to the original term '*ẓāhir*' (and its nominal form, '*ẓuhūr*'). We will also see that the late Shīʿī Uṣūlīs typically hold that if a Qur'anic verse is *ẓāhir* in a divine ruling, then one should adhere to that ruling. This idea is commonly known as 'the *ḥujjiyya* of *ẓāhir* of Qur'anic verses' or 'the *ḥujjiyya* of *ẓuhūr* of Qur'anic verses'. I will use these two phrases interchangeably in this chapter.

rulings (i.e. *wujūb*, *istiḥbāb*, *ibāḥa*, *karāha*, and *ḥurma*) or not. If he does, then he is obliged to act in conformity to his certainty, as certainty about jurisprudential rulings is *ḥujja*, to use the Uṣūlīs' terminology. While a detailed explanation of the technical concept of *ḥujjiyya* is not necessary here, it is worth noting that certainty is considered *ḥujja* in that it leads to liability or exemption from blame before the divine legislator. That is, if an individual is certain that action, A, is obligated by God, then he is rationally obligated to perform A. Similarly, if he is certain that A is forbidden by God, then he is rationally obligated to refrain from performing it. And in case he fails to comply with his certainty and hence breaches the religious ruling of obligation or forbiddance, he will be deemed blameworthy. However, if he becomes certain that A is not obligatory, he may omit it. Then, even if A is indeed obligatory, he will not be considered blameworthy. Likewise, if he becomes certain that A is not forbidden, he may perform it. Then, even if A is indeed forbidden, he will not be deemed blameworthy.[4]

In contrast, if one does not attain certainty about the religious ruling, then there are two possibilities: either he acquires a 'credible indication' (*al-amāra al-muʿtabara*) about the jurisprudential ruling of A or not. In the jargon of Shīʿī Uṣūlīs, an *amāra* (or indication) for a proposition is inconclusive evidence for the proposition, which lays some support for its truth without rendering it certain. An example of an *amāra* is a report that acts as evidence for the truth of the reported event, without yielding certainty because the reporter might have made an error or lied. Nevertheless, the report is still evidence that the event occurred. Another example, again using the Uṣūlīs' terminology, is

4 There are several issues that may arise here, but for the purposes of this article, we will not delve into them. Some of these issues include:

(1) What is the exact definition of 'certainty' in this context, considering the diverse conceptions of certainty found within contemporary epistemology?

(2) Using the Uṣūlīs' terminology, is the *ḥujjiyya* of certainty 'essential' to it? That is, can the divine legislator cancel its *ḥujjiyya* under certain circumstances?

(3) If one becomes certain that A is obligatory, while A is not actually obligatory, will he be blameworthy if he omits A?

For the thesis that certainty is *ḥujja*, and related issues, see, for example, Murtaḍā al-Anṣārī, *Farāʾid al-uṣūl*, vol. 1 (Qom: Majmaʿ al-Fikr al-Islāmī, 1998), 29–35; Muḥammad Kāẓim al-Khurāsānī, *Kifāyat al-uṣūl* (Qom: Muʾassasat Āl al-Bayt li-Iḥyāʾ al-Turāth, 1996), 257–58; Abū al-Qāsim al-Khūʾī, *Ajwad al-taqrīrāt*, vol. 2 (Sidon: Maktabat al-ʿIrfān, 1933), 2–7; Muḥammad ʿAlī al-Kāẓimī, *Fawāʾid al-uṣūl*, vol. 3 (Qom: Muʾassasat al-Nashr al-Islāmī, 1988), 3–9; Ḍiyāʾ al-Dīn al-ʿArāqī, *Maqālāt al-uṣūl*, vol. 2 (Qom: Majmaʿ al-Fikr al-Islāmī, 1999), 10–13; Muḥammad Taqī al-Burūjirdī, *Nihāyat al-afkār*, vol. 3 (Qom: Muʾassasat al-Nashr al-Islāmī, 1984), 6–9; Muḥammad al-Bihsūdī, *Miṣbāḥ al-uṣūl*, vol. 1 (Qom: Maktabat al-Dāvarī, 1996), 15–17; Maḥmūd al-Hāshimī, *Buḥūth fī ʿilm al-uṣūl*, vol. 4 (Qom: al-Majmaʿ al-ʿIlmī li-l-Shahīd al-Ṣadr, 1984), 27–34.

the *ẓāhir* (i.e. the apparent meaning) of an utterance as an *amāra* or indication of the speaker's real intention. To elucidate the idea, imagine someone who utters an indicative sentence with P as its literal linguistic meaning. In this case, the utterance is an *amāra*, or indication, that the speaker is asserting that P. Similarly, if the speaker utters a sentence with the literal linguistic meaning of commanding an action, A, then it is an *amāra* that the speaker is commanding A. In each case, the relevant *amāra* is not conclusive evidence, among other things because of the possibility that the speaker used the sentence metaphorically.

Speaking of indications or *amārāt*, some are credible, so to speak, while others are not. A credible indication is one that, notwithstanding its failure to confer certainty, is authorised by the divine legislator as reliable for deducing jurisprudential rulings. In other words, the divine legislator has established *ḥujjiyya* for it. For the Uṣūlīs, non-conclusive indications lack *ḥujjiyya* by default and can only be relied upon when we become certain or find valid evidence that the divine legislator has established *ḥujjiyya* for an indication. Many Uṣūlīs maintain that the divine legislator has established *ḥujjiyya* for the report by a single reliable person and for the apparent meanings of the Qur'an and the sayings of the Prophet and Infallible Imāms. Accordingly, if a Qur'anic verse apparently indicates that a certain action is obligatory for the subject (and he is certain or has credible evidence for the *ḥujjiyya* of the apparent meanings of the Qur'an), he must perform the act in question and will be blameworthy if he does not. On the other hand, if a Qur'anic verse apparently indicates that an action is permissible for the subject (and he is certain or has credible evidence for the *ḥujjiyya* of the apparent meanings of the Qur'an), he may perform the act and will not be blameworthy even if the action is actually forbidden.

In the next stage, if one fails to obtain a credible indication about an action, A, then there are two possibilities: either he has a *sharʿī* procedural principle (*al-uṣūl al-ʿamaliyya al-sharʿiyya*) about A, or he does not. A *sharʿī* procedural principle is a principle established by the divine legislator to determine the practical stance the subject should adopt when he is uncertain about the religious ruling and lacks credible indications that settle the issue.[5]

Finally, if there are no applicable *sharʿī* procedural principles for A, then the subject must adhere to primary (or rational) procedural principles (*al-uṣūl*

5 There are significant controversies within the late Shīʿī *uṣūl* regarding the genuine distinction between a credible indication and a Sharīʿa procedural principle, which we need not delve into here. For a useful discussion of this issue, see Maḥmūd al-Hāshimī, *Buḥūth fī ʿilm al-uṣūl*, vol. 5 (Qom: al-Majmaʿ al-ʿIlmī li-l-Shahīd al-Ṣadr, 1984), 11–16.

al-ʿamaliyya al-ʿaqliyya). These principles are supposed to determine the practical stance one should adopt in the absence of the following conditions: (1) certainty about the real divine ruling, (2) credible indications that settle the issue, and (3) a *sharʿī* procedural principle which determines the proper practical stance. Allegedly, human beings can comprehend these principles through their rational faculties, hence their appellation as 'rational procedural principles'. There are disagreements, of course, among the Uṣūlīs as to what rational procedural principles are in force in different doxastic conditions the subject has. Most of them subscribe to 'the principle of rational exemption' (*al-barāʾa al-ʿaqliyya*). According to this principle, if a subject knows that A is not forbidden, but is undecided whether it is obligatory or not, without there being credible indications or *sharʿī* procedural principles regarding A, then the subject is not required to perform A, even if A is indeed obligatory. Some Uṣūlīs, however, instead subscribe to 'the principle of rational caution' (*al-iḥtiyāṭ al-ʿaqlī*). According to the latter principle, in the situation just depicted, the subject must remain cautious and perform A[6] (likewise, the two alleged principles have opposite verdicts in cases where the subject knows that A is not obligatory, but is undecided as to whether it is forbidden).[7]

The above was a rough presentation of the general structure of *ḥujjiyya* in later Shīʿī *uṣūl*. The same structure applies to deriving divine rulings from the Qurʾanic regulative verses (in particular, the two issues of *ḥujjiyya* of certainty and, more importantly, *ḥujjiyya* of credible indications are pertinent here). To illustrate, let us begin with a distinction introduced by Uṣūlīs in their discussion of textual evidence (*al-dalīl al-lafẓī*). Normally, a speaker's utterance, S, provides some evidence for the hearer as to what the speaker has intended by S. Sometimes such evidence is certain, that is, given the linguistic conventions, the rules of conversation, and the context of the utterance, it is not likely that the speaker has meant anything but, say, P. In such cases, to use the Uṣūlīs' jargon, S is *naṣṣ* about P. But sometimes S provides only inconclusive evidence that the speaker has intended P. That is, although the speaker might have meant something other than P, given the linguistic data (i.e. the linguistic conventions, the rules of conversation, and the context of the utterance) his having intended P is still more probable than all other alternatives. In these latter cases it is said that the utterance S is *ẓāhir*, or has a *ẓuhūr*, in P,

6 For an illuminating survey of this debate, see ibid., 23–29.

7 For simplicity's sake, in formulating these principles I ignored situations in which the subject has 'non-specific knowledge' (*al-ʿilm al-ijmālī*) of an obligation, that is, where the subject knows that one of the actions, A_1, …, and A_n, is obligatory, without knowing which of them specifically is.

meaning roughly that S provides inconclusive and defeasible evidence that the speaker has intended P by uttering S.[8] An example of this is the Qur'anic verse 'maintain the prayer', which is *naṣṣ* that performing prayers is desired by God, but it is only *ẓāhir* in its being obligatory. This is because, considered by itself, an imperative utterance is only inconclusive evidence for obligation, as the imperative form could be used when the speaker just intends to recommend (and not to obligate) an action.

Now, since it is assumed that the text of the Qur'an is *certainly* God's word, when a Qur'anic verse is *naṣṣ* about a specific divine ruling, it will provide certainty about that ruling. Thus, according to the Uṣūlīs, we must comply with the ruling in question because, as noted before, they maintain that certainty about a divine ruling is *ḥujja*. Moreover, the Uṣūlīs usually hold that if a Qur'anic verse is not *naṣṣ*, but only has a *ẓuhūr* in a divine ruling, then it will still be necessary to adhere to that ruling. The reason is that, according to the Uṣūlīs, the divine legislator has considered the *ẓuhūr* of an utterance in P as a credible indication (*al-amāra al-muʿtabara*) that the speaker has intended that P. This idea is sometimes put forward by the slogan that the divine legislator has established *ḥujjiyya* for the *ẓāhir* or *ẓuhūr* (of the Qur'anic verses and credible *ḥadīth*s).[9]

Since there are few regulative verses that are *naṣṣ* about respective rulings, recourse to the Qur'anic verses often depends on the idea of the *ḥujjiyya* of the *ẓuhūr*. The crucial question then concerns the conditions under which the *ẓuhūr* of Qur'anic verses is *ḥujja*. I will briefly address this question in the third section. But before that, we shall see in the next section that the Uṣūlīs have adopted a too lenient approach towards the *ḥujjiyya* of the *ẓuhūr*.

8 As previously noted, '*ẓuhūr*' lexically means *appearance*, and '*ẓāhir*' is its adjectival form, meaning *apparent*. Roughly speaking, a *ẓuhūr* (of a token utterance S in a content C) is the property of being an inconclusive evidence for the speaker's having intended P by uttering S. In some contexts, however, the word '*ẓuhūr*' refers to the content P itself, that is, the very content that the utterance provides an inconclusive evidence for the speaker's having intended that content.

9 As we shall briefly see in section 4, the primary argument put forth by the Uṣūlīs in favour of the *ḥujjiyya* of the *ẓuhūr* can be outlined as follows. Within their interpersonal interactions, rational individuals are inclined to rely on the *ẓuhūr* of each other's statements. Furthermore, the divine legislator has not prohibited this customary behaviour, indicating His approval for adopting the same approach when interpreting His own words. For a detailed discussion of this kind of argument for the *ḥujjiyya* of the *ẓuhūr*, see al-Hāshimī, *Buḥūth*, vol. 4, 249–66. See also al-Anṣārī, *Farāʾid al-uṣūl*, 137; al-Khurāsānī, *Kifāyat al-uṣūl*, 281; al-Kāẓimī, *Fawāʾid al-uṣūl*, 135; al-Burūjirdī, *Nihāyat al-afkār*, 90; al-Bihsūdī, *Miṣbāḥ al-uṣūl*, 117–18.

3 The Traditional Approach to the *Ḥujjiyya* of the *Ẓuhūr*

The majority of the Uṣūlīs have (explicitly or implicitly) endorsed two main theses regarding the *ḥujjiyya* of the *ẓuhūr*:

(a) The *ḥujjiyya* of a *ẓuhūr* is not conditional upon having *ẓann* to the effect that the *ẓuhūr* in question corresponds to reality.

(b) The *ḥujjiyya* of the *ẓuhūr* (of a Qur'anic verse) in a ruling is independent of the amount of the stake involved in complying with that ruling.

These theses comprise what I call the 'traditional approach to the *ḥujjiyya* of the *ẓuhūr*'. In this section, I provide a brief exposition of these theses and their implications, beginning with (a). Suppose that a Qur'anic verse is *ẓāhir* in that God has made a certain action, A, obligatory. Does the *ḥujjiyya* of this *ẓuhūr* depend on the subject's assigning a rather high probability (e.g. more than 50 per cent) to A's being in fact obligatory? In later Shīʿī *uṣūl* literature, this question is sometimes put forward as whether or not the *ḥujjiyya* of a *ẓuhūr* depends on the subject's having '*ẓann*' (i.e. a high degree of credence) to the effect that the *ẓuhūr* corresponds to reality.[10] The overwhelming majority of Uṣūlīs give a negative response to this question (they even go further, holding that having *ẓann* to the effect that the *ẓuhūr* in question is not veridical does not undermine its *ḥujjiyya*).[11] This common view is occasionally articulated in a somewhat cryptic manner, stating that the *ḥujjiyya* of a *ẓuhūr* does not depend on having an 'actual *ẓann*' (*al-ẓann al-fiʿlī*) to the effect that the *ẓuhūr* is veridical, but rather hinges solely on having a 'typical *ẓann*' (*al-ẓann al-nawʿī*) to that effect.[12] This debate, along with the notions of 'actual *ẓann*' and 'typical *ẓann*', can be interpreted in various manners, which I cannot elaborate on here. It seems, nevertheless, that the main idea in (a) can be articulated more clearly as follows.

As mentioned previously, when the Uṣūlīs say that a Qur'anic verse is *ẓāhir* in that God has made action A obligatory, they should be understood as saying that, relative to the linguistic data (i.e. linguistic conventions, the rules of conversation, and the context of the utterance), it is highly probable that God

---

10 The term '*ẓann*' is occasionally translated as *conjecture*. However, in *uṣūl* context, when it is said that a subject holds a *ẓann* to the effect that P, it signifies that the individual has a higher level of confidence in the truth of P than in its negation. To put it differently, having a *ẓann* to the effect that P is tantamount to having a level of confidence greater than 0.5 but less than 1 in the truth of P.

11 See, for example, al-Anṣārī, *Farāʾid al-uṣūl*, 170; al-Khurāsānī, *Kifāyat al-uṣūl*, 281; al-Khūʾī, *Ajwad al-taqrīrāt*, 94; al-Kāẓimī, *Fawāʾid al-uṣūl*, 145–46; al-Bihsūdī, *Miṣbāḥ al-uṣūl*, 118.

12 See, for example, al-ʿArāqī, *Maqālāt al-uṣūl*, 61; al-Burūjirdī, *Nihāyat al-afkār*, 89–90. See also al-Hāshimī, *Buḥūth*, vol. 4, 275–76.

has made A obligatory. However, the probability assigned to any proposition is always relative to a body of evidence. *Ex hypothesis*, relative to the body of linguistic evidence, the probability of A being obligatory is high, say, more than 50 per cent. Now, suppose that relative to our *total evidence*, the probability of A being obligatory is rather low, say, less than 50 per cent. In this case, is the *ẓuhūr* of the Qur'anic verse still *ḥujja* so that we are obliged to perform A? According to many Uṣūlīs, the answer is yes. This is indeed what they mean when they say that having (actual) *ẓann* about the veridicality of a *ẓuhūr* is not required for the *ḥujjiyya* of that *ẓuhūr*.

Let us now turn to (b). Arguably, some Qur'anic verses have a *ẓuhūr* in rulings which are highly risky, in the sense that compliance with such rulings involves high stakes. Consider, for example, the verses expressing the rulings of *qiṣāṣ* and *ḥudūd*. Let us assume that these verses have a *ẓuhūr* in that under circumstances C, a specific action (revenge of a murderer or corporal punishment of a guilty party) must be performed. Needless to say, if such an action is executed, while God has not actually obligated it under circumstances C (i.e. if the *ẓuhūr* of those verses does not correspond to reality), then a significant repercussion will ensue: an individual's life will be unjustly taken, or he will be unrightfully harmed. Now the question is whether such a *ẓuhūr* (i.e. a *ẓuhūr* in a ruling complying with which involves a considerable amount of risk) is still *ḥujja*. As far as I know, nearly all Uṣūlīs tend to answer in the affirmative. That is, according to them, the *ḥujjiyya* of a *ẓuhūr* of a verse is independent of the amount of the stake involved in complying with that *ẓuhūr*.

The traditional approach to the *ḥujjiyya* of *ẓuhūr* has several consequences. One of them is that it tends to be too lenient in attributing *ḥujjiyya* to cases of *ẓuhūr*. For, according to this approach, the *ḥujjiyya* of a *ẓuhūr* in a specific ruling depends neither on the degree of the probability the subject assigns to its veridicality, nor on the level of risk associated with adhering to that ruling.

Another major implication is that when the *ẓuhūr* of a verse conflicts with any other kind of inconclusive evidence, it is the former that will take precedence in almost all cases. Consider, for instance, a case where a Qur'anic verse has a *ẓuhūr* in that an action, A, is obligated by God, while at the same time, there is a moral intuition to the effect that A is wrong (at least under present circumstances). Suppose further that this intuition, like almost all instances of moral intuitions, does not provide us with certainty regarding its content. The moral intuition, in the view of Shīʿī Uṣūlīs, would serve as evidence for A's not being obligated by God, as they believe that divine rulings are constrained by morality. Thus, there are two opposing pieces of evidence here: the *ẓuhūr* of the Qur'anic verse, which suggests that performing A is obligated by God, and the moral intuition, which implies that it is not. Consequently, taking all the evidence into consideration, the probability of A being obligatory may not be high, and in some cases, may be very low. That said, the traditional approach to *ḥujjiyya* still treats such a *ẓuhūr* (in A's being obligatory) as *ḥujja*. This is because, on the one hand, the moral intuitions are not *ḥujja* in their own right, as they are typically uncertain, and hence, the default judgement about them (as in other cases of uncertain indications) is that they are not *ḥujja*. Furthermore, there is allegedly no reason to think that they are authorised as *ḥujja* by the divine legislator. On the other hand, even though the conflict between the *ẓuhūr* of the Qur'anic verse and our moral intuitions may lead to a low probability of A being obligatory relative to the overall evidence at our disposal, this does not undermine, given (a) above, the *ḥujjiyya* of the *ẓuhūr* of the verse. By the same token, in cases where the *ẓuhūr* of a verse is inconsistent with empirical evidence, the traditional approach still holds that the *ẓuhūr* retains its *ḥujjiyya*.[13]

So far, I have provided a brief exposition of the traditional approach and some of its implications. In the next section, I will suggest an alternative approach to the *ḥujjiyya* of *ẓuhūr*.

4 Towards a Decision-Theoretic Approach to the *Ḥujjiyya* of *Ẓuhūr*

While the Uṣūlīs have introduced the notion of *ḥujjiyya* in the context of the relationship between humans and God (vis-à-vis the human responsibility or lack thereof towards God), the underlying intuitive idea is not confined to this particular case. To illustrate, the core idea of the *ḥujjiyya* of certainty may apply to cases beyond the human–God relationship. It could be argued that certainty

13 Needless to say, empirical sciences do not directly say anything about divine rulings. However, since divine rulings are subject to considerations of benefits (*maṣāliḥ*) and disadvantages (*mafāsid*), empirical evidence may bear upon the *ẓuhūr* of regulative verses. For instance, some argue that Qur'anic verses have a *ẓuhūr* in that *qiṣāṣ* ought to be performed in all circumstances, regardless of time, location, or community. Now, *suppose* that there are compelling reasons to think that the benefit (*maṣlaḥa*) behind the legislation of *qiṣāṣ* was to serve as a deterrent (let us call this the 'auxiliary assumption'). Moreover, suppose that the sociology of crime has indicated that under circumstances C, *qiṣāṣ* has no deterrent effect. Of course, those sociological findings (like the findings of other empirical sciences) are uncertain. Nevertheless, taken together, those findings and the auxiliary assumption provide us with an uncertain reason to believe that under circumstances C, *qiṣāṣ* is no longer desired by the divine legislator. This reason conflicts with the relevant Qur'anic *ẓuhūr*. Here again, the traditional approach (as explained above) entails that the *ẓuhūr* in question is still *ḥujja*.

about (the presence or the absence of) moral obligations can be deemed *ḥujja* in an intuitive sense. For example, if I am certain that performing a specific action can save someone's life, then it is incumbent upon me to perform that action. If I fail to do so, then I will be morally blameworthy (at least, in situations where my omission results in the person's death). Similarly, if I am certain that a particular action does not involve an infringement of any moral obligations, then I am excused from performing that action, even if it does in fact violate some moral obligations. What is more, the idea of the *ḥujjiyya* of certainty can also extend beyond the moral domain. For example, if I intend to reach point A, and I am certain that performing action B leads me to A, then I am rationally required to perform B.

In this way, the concept of *ḥujjiyya* seems to be closely tied to that of practical rationality. A key issue concerning practical rationality is to determine the rational course of action for a subject when he has goals (of varying degrees of importance) and assigns different probabilities to each goal being achieved by different alternative actions. The issue of *ḥujjiyya* in *uṣūl al-fiqh* is simply a specific instance of this broader topic, with the goal here being to fulfil the intents of the divine legislator. Thus, the Uṣūlīs' slogan 'certainty about divine obligations is *ḥujja*' can be roughly construed as follows: 'assuming that the subject's goal is to adhere to the rulings of the divine legislator, then if he is certain about a divine obligation, he is rationally obliged to act on his certainty'. Likewise, the statement 'the *ẓuhūr* of the Qur'an is *ḥujja*' can be roughly understood as follows: 'assuming that the subject's goal is to act in accordance with the rulings of the divine legislator, then he is rationally required to act on the *ẓuhūr* of the Qur'an'. And other Uṣūlīs' theses regarding *ḥujjiyya* can be construed in a similar manner.

Viewed through this lens, the concept of *ḥujjiyya* in *uṣūl al-fiqh* can be understood as operating within the broader framework of practical rationality. In this way, insights from contemporary philosophical discussions of rationality can help provide a more precise rendering of the issues surrounding *ḥujjiyya*. In particular, a common contemporary view of rational choice, which could have important bearings upon the issue of *ḥujjiyya*, is the so-called normative decision theory. In what follows, I briefly explore the implications of framing the notion of *ḥujjiyya* within the decision theory framework.

In decision theory, the main problem is what the subject should rationally choose relative to his preferences and the probabilities he assigns. While a detailed exposition of the technical aspects of this theory is far beyond the scope of this article, the basic idea can be summarised as follows. Suppose someone is faced with several alternative courses of actions: O_1 ... O_n, such that he can only perform one of those actions. Now, each of the alternative actions has an *expected utility*, which is a function of the person's preferences and the degree of rational probabilities he assigns to each preference being fulfilled by that action. Next, the person is rationally required to choose the alternative that has the greatest expected utility. The following simple example can illustrate the main idea: suppose that a person, S, faces a choice between two actions: A and B. If S performs A, there is a 30 per cent chance that S gains $1,000, but there is a 70 per cent chance that S loses $100. If S performs B, then there is a 40 per cent chance that S gains $500, and there is a 60 per cent chance that S loses $200. Which course of action is more rational: A or B?

> The expected utility of A: $(1000 \times 0.3) - (100 \times 0.7) = 230$
> The expected utility of B: $(500 \times 0.4) - (200 \times 0.6) = 80$

So, if the person's goal is just to gain more money, performing A will be more rational than performing B, and if there are no other considerations, he is rationally required to perform A.[14]

Let us apply the same model to the issue of *ḥujjiyya*. A Muslim has the goal of adhering to the true divine rulings. According to the prevalent view among the Uṣūlīs, divine obligations and prohibitions are legislated by God in virtue of true benefits (*maṣāliḥ*) and disadvantages (*mafāsid*) involved in obligated and prohibited actions, respectively. Accordingly, a Muslim's goal (as a Muslim) is to gain the benefits and avoid the disadvantages considered by the divine legislator in the rulings He enacts, where those benefits and disadvantages are of varying degrees of gravity or importance. Now consider a Muslim agent who wants to determine the practical stance he should rationally adopt vis-à-vis an action, A. Suppose he assigns the probability of α to A being obligated by God, and knows that if A is in fact obligatory then a benefit with the magnitude of s inherits in performing A. Moreover, he assigns the probability of β to A being prohibited, and knows that if A is indeed forbidden by God then it involves a disadvantage with the magnitude of t. On the other hand, suppose that the person knows that there are no separate benefits or disadvantages involved in omitting A. (This scenario is rather general. A more specific scenario would be where β is zero; that is, cases in which the prohibition of A is unlikely, and there exists only a suspicion regarding its obligation. Another specific scenario is a case where there is just a suspicion about the action being prohibited, in which case α is zero.) As a preliminary step, let's outline two methods for

14 There is a plethora of literature on normative decision theory. For a useful entry, see Katie Steele and H. Orri Stefánsson, 'Decision Theory', *Stanford Encyclopedia of Philosophy Archive* (Winter 2020 Edition), https://plato.stanford.edu/archives/win2020/entries/decision-theory/.

calculating the expected utility of carrying out action A or omitting it in our envisaged scenario. The first method, although flawed, will help set the stage for introducing the second, more accurate one.

The first method: Given that disadvantages are indeed negative values, the expected utility of performing A is equal to $\alpha \times s - \beta \times t$. Moreover, since it is assumed that the person knows that no separate benefits or disadvantages are involved in omitting A, the expected utility of omitting A will be zero. We can therefore conclude that if $\alpha \times s - \beta \times t > 0$, then the agent ought to perform A; if $\alpha \times s - \beta \times t < 0$, then he ought to omit A; and finally, if $\alpha \times s - \beta \times t = 0$, then it will be up to the agent to perform or omit A.

The first method does not seem plausible, however. It entails that in almost all cases it is rationally obligatory either to perform A or to omit it, and cases in which it is up to the agent to do or omit A will be rare. For example, if there exists a modest probability that A is mandated by God, with the possibility of it being forbidden being excluded, it will become imperative for the agent to execute A. Conversely, when there is a marginal probability that A is prohibited by God, and its being obligated by God is excluded, it becomes incumbent upon the agent to refrain from doing A. This is implausible, and so, the first method seems problematic.

The second method: The problem with the first method was that it left out a major influential benefit: that of *ibāḥa* (permissibility; i.e. neither being obligatory nor forbidden). It seems that there might be some benefit to the very state of not having any requirements with respect to performing or omitting the action in question. To determine the rational course of action, this benefit should also be taken into consideration.[15] In the above example, suppose that

15 The idea that the very state of permissibility of an action might carry its own benefit (*maṣliḥa*) has been proposed by some *uṣūlīs* as well. According to these scholars, divine permissibility can be categorized into two types: *al-ibāḥa al-lāʾiqtiḍāʾiyya* and *al-ibāḥa al-iqtiḍāʾiyya* (which can be loosely translated as *negative permissibility* and *positive permissibility*, respectively). An action is *negatively permissible* when God has legislated it as such solely because either the action holds no benefits or disadvantages at all, or its benefits or disadvantages are insufficient to warrant its obligation or prohibition. In these cases, the action is permissible simply due to the absence of compelling reasons for its obligation or prohibition. Sometimes, however, the very permissibility of an action carries its own benefits, and it is this benefit that serves as the reason for God legislating it as permissible; such actions are considered *positively permissible* (see, e.g. al-Hāshimī, *Buḥūth, Vol. 4*, 204–205). There is a crucial question regarding the precise nature of this kind of benefit (that is, the benefit of the very state of legislative freedom), and the types of actions it resides. Cursory references to these issues can be found when the Uṣūlīs discuss the topic of *al-ibāḥa al-iqtiḍāʾiyya*. One might argue that the benefit of legislative freedom

the subject knows that the benefit of the absence of any requirements with regards to performing A is equal to m, and the benefit of the absence of any requirements with regards to omitting A is equal to n. Now, for A to be rationally obligatory, it is not enough that the expected utility of performing A (i.e. $\alpha \times s - \beta \times t$) is greater than the expected utility of omitting A (i.e. zero); rather, it must also be greater than the benefit of the absence of any requirements with respect to performing A (i.e. m). In the same vein, for refrainment from A to be rationally obligatory, it is not enough that the expected utility of performing A (i.e. $\alpha \times s - \beta \times t$) is smaller than zero, but it is also necessary that its absolute value (i.e. $\alpha \mid \times s - \beta \times t \mid$) is greater than the benefit of the absence of any requirements with respect to the omission of A (i.e. n). The intermediate state is where $\alpha \mid \times s - \beta \times t \mid$ is neither greater than m, nor greater than n. In that case, it will be up to the person to do or to omit A. In this way, we arrive at the following principle, which I call the 'principle of maximising expected divine intents' (MEDI).

> (MEDI) Suppose that (i) the subject assigns the probability of α to the proposition that a benefit with the magnitude of s inherits in performing A, (ii) he assigns the probability of β to A's involving a disadvantage with the magnitude of t, (iii) the subject knows that the benefit of the absence of any requirements with respect to performing A is equal to m, and (iv) the subject knows that the benefit of the absence of any requirements with respect to omitting A is equal to n. In that case,
>
> (1) If $\alpha \times s - \beta \times t > m$, then performing A is rationally required.
>
> (2) If $\alpha \times s - \beta \times t < - n$, then refraining from doing A is rationally required.
>
> (3) Otherwise, it is up to the person to do or to refrain from doing A.

It seems that the primary principle of *ḥujjiyya* is MEDI or something in that line, rather than the principle of rational exemption or that of rational caution, as the Uṣūlīs have asserted.[16] Thus, as far as the primary principle of *ḥujjiyya* in

is inherent in all actions, including those that are obligatory or forbidden. However, in the case of the latter actions, a more significant advantage or drawback surpasses the benefit of permissibility, leading to divine obligation or prohibition. If this holds true, then the likelihood of there being some benefit in the permissibility of a given action can be deemed 1 in all cases. Thus, for the sake of simplicity, the subsequent text will only introduce variables (i.e. m and n) to represent the magnitude of the benefit of permissibility, without introducing a variable for its probability.

16 It is noteworthy that MEDI serves merely as an initial formulation of the primary principle of *ḥujjiyya*, and it requires further refinement in at least three respects. First, it might be the case that the subject assigns the probability α to A involving a benefit of magnitude

concerned, the *ḥujjiyya* of *ẓuhūr* of the regulative verses and other indications (*amārāt*) will be subject to the above principle. The role played by (*ẓuhūr* of) the regulative verses is just that they provide evidence that determines (along with other pieces of evidence) the probability rationally assigned to various divine rulings. It is in light of these probabilities that MEDI determines the course of action one is rationally required to take.[17]

The preceding remarks suggest a decision-theoretic approach to *ḥujjiyya* in general, and to the *ḥujjiyya* of *ẓuhūr* in particular. On this approach, different verdicts regarding the *ḥujjiyya* of *ẓuhūr* of regulative verses will ensue, which I shall briefly outline in the remainder of this section. One implication of the decision-theoretic approach (as illustrated in MEDI) is that none of the two components of the traditional approach to the *ḥujjiyya* of *ẓuhūr* (sketched in section 2 above) will be plausible any longer. According to the first component, what matters for the *ḥujjiyya* of a *ẓuhūr* in P is just that the probability of the speaker's having intended P is high relative to the overall linguistic evidence (i.e. the linguistic conventions, the rules of conversations, and the context of the speech), even though it is not high relative to the subject's total evidence. MEDI, however, implies that what is crucial is the rational probability the subject assigns relative to his total evidence. This being the case, if a Qur'anic verse has a *ẓuhūr* in A's being obligatory, but other pieces of evidence (including moral intuitions and empirical discoveries) indicate that A is not obligatory, then the overall probability of A being obligatory will diminish, and performing A may no longer be rationally required, in which case the *ẓuhūr* of the verse will cease to be *ḥujja* (more on this later).

---

s, and simultaneously assigns the probability α* to A inhering a benefit of magnitude s*. MEDI, in its current form, does not incorporate such cases, but it can be adjusted in a natural and familiar way to accommodate scenarios of this kind. Second, clauses (iii) and (iv) in MEDI are framed in terms of *knowledge* rather than probabilistic terms, unlike the other two clauses, (i) and (ii). This choice was partly for simplicity and partly based on what has been discussed in note 15, where it is suggested that the probability of there being some benefit in the permissibility of a given action might be considered 1 in all cases. Nevertheless, MEDI can be naturally refined to accommodate instances where the subject assigns probabilities other than 1 to the presence of a specific amount of benefit in the permissibility of the action in question, by rephrasing (iii) and (iv), too, in probabilistic terms. Third, MEDI needs further modifications to handle situations involving vague and indeterminate probabilities, as pointed out in section 4.

17 Given that MEDI serves as the primary principle of *ḥujjiyya*, a natural question arises: has God authorised *ḥujjiyya* for *ẓuhūr* of the regulative verses, and if so, does the scope of this authorised *ḥujjiyya* diverge from the requirements of decision theory as illustrated in MEDI? I will turn to this issue in section 4.

The second component of the traditional approach suggests that the *ḥujjiyya* of the *ẓuhūr* of a Qur'anic verse in a particular ruling remains unaffected by whether the implementation of the ruling carries a substantial level of risk. This is contrary to what MEDI suggests. Consider the Qur'anic verse of *qiṣāṣ*, for instance. At most, the verse merely has a *ẓuhūr* (and fails to be *naṣṣ*) in the permissibility of *qiṣāṣ* in our age and time. Suppose that, given this verse, we assign a rather high probability to *qiṣāṣ* being permissible. But if *qiṣāṣ* is not in fact permissible in our time and age, then performing *qiṣāṣ* will involve tremendously great harm, namely, unjust murder of someone. In virtue of such a high risk in performing *qiṣāṣ*, one might say that performing *qiṣāṣ* is no longer rationally permissible. To illustrate, the *ẓuhūr* of the verse of *qiṣāṣ* might justify us in assigning a high probability for α, but since human lives extremely matter, it is necessary to assign a high magnitude to t as well. Ultimately, the magnitude of the expected utility of performing *qiṣāṣ* (i.e. $\alpha \times s - \beta \times t$) might be low, and hence, performing *qiṣāṣ* might be rationally forbidden.[18]

It is noteworthy that some Shīʿī Uṣūlīs have proposed a similar idea in the case of the *ḥujjiyya* of the report of a trustworthy person (*khabar al-thiqa*). In their view, while such reports are *ḥujja* in the case of ordinary rulings, their *ḥujjiyya* does not extend to cases involving punitive rulings that result in taking a person's life. The reason they adduce for the claim is that the *ḥujjiyya* of such reports is grounded in the manner of rational agents (*banāʾ al-ʿuqalāʾ*) and they do not rely on such reports where stakes are high.[19] This presents an intriguing and pivotal observation. However, curiously, the *uṣūlī* scholars do not extend this idea to the *ḥujjiyya* of *ẓuhūr* of regulative verses. For the Uṣūlīs,

18 It is worth noting that the formula $\alpha \times s - \beta \times t$ is inadequate for accurately calculating the expected utility of enacting *qiṣāṣ*. This is due to the fact that even though *qiṣāṣ* may be deemed a religious obligation, it inherently involves negative value, as taking a person's life, whether they are guilty or innocent, carries *pro tanto* badness. The only thing is that the divine legislator has presumably weighed the benefits against these harms, ultimately mandating its practice. In light of this, it becomes crucial to consider the intrinsic negative value associated with *qiṣāṣ* when evaluating the expected utility of its implementation. Consequently, the value of β should be set at 1 to appropriately incorporate this negative aspect. As a result, the expected utility of executing *qiṣāṣ* would be $\alpha \times s - t$. This adjustment implies that enforcing the *qiṣāṣ* ruling would prove to be more challenging than suggested in the text.

19 See, for example, Aḥmad al-Khunsārī, *Jāmiʿ al-madārik fī sharḥ Mukhtaṣar al-Nāfiʿ*, vol. 7 (Tehran: Muʾassasat Ismāʿīliān, 1984), 35–36, 166, 179, 247. See also al-Muḥaqqiq al-Ḥillī, *Sharāʾiʿ al-Islām fī masāʾil al-ḥalāl wa-l-ḥarām*, vol. 4 (Tehran: Istiqlāl, 1988), 910; Zayn al-Dīn al-ʿĀmilī, *al-Rawḍa al-bahiyya fī sharḥ al-Lumʿa al-Dimashqiyya*, vol. 3 (Qom: Dāwarī, 1989), 126; al-Fāḍil al-Ābī, *Kashf al-rumūz fī sharḥ Mukhtaṣar al-Nāfiʿ*, vol. 2 (Qom: Muʾassasat al-Nashr al-Islāmī, 1987), 411; ʿAlī al-Ṭabāṭabāʾī, *Riyāḍ al-masāʾil fī taḥqīq al-aḥkām bi-l-dalāʾil*, vol. 2 (Qom: Muʾassasat Āl al-Bayt, 1983), 465.

the *ḥujjiyya* of *ẓuhūr* is also grounded in the manner of rational agents. But arguably, just as rational individuals do not trust uncertain reports when the stakes are high, they likewise refrain from relying on an uncertain *ẓuhūr* that carries potentially risky implications.[20]

Furthermore, the significance of the stakes in relation to a ruling is not solely confined to situations where the ruling directly imperils human life. It extends to rulings that encompass the imposition of physical and psychological distress upon individuals, or their curtailment of personal freedoms. In all of these instances, a considerable weight should be attributed to the parameter *t*, albeit to varying extents. This *may* pose a challenge for the *ḥujjiyya* of *ẓuhūr* concerning the pertinent divine decrees.[21]

Another crucial ramification of the decision-theoretic approach is that it underscores the role of non-transmitted evidence (*al-adilla ghayr al-naqliyya*) in the process of *istinbāṭ*. We can easily see that, according to MEDI, the example discussed towards the end of section 2 might well have another fate. As you recall, we supposed that there was a Qur'anic verse that has a *ẓuhūr* in that an action, A, is obligatory, while our moral intuitions or empirical findings provide evidence to the contrary. Under these circumstances, the rational probability assigned to A's being obligatory relative to our total evidence will be low, in which case performing A may cease to be rationally required.[22] Put

20 As pointed out in the next section, it can be argued that the manner of rational people in acting on reports by trustworthy persons and on the *ẓuhūr* of their statements is indeed a rational behaviour arising from an implicit alignment with the principles of the decision theory.

21 This potential challenge is particularly pressing, considering my earlier point in note 18. In these cases, it might be justifiable to assign a value of 1 to β, as inflicting physical and psychological harm on individuals and depriving them of their freedoms involve *pro tanto* negative value, even though the divine legislator may have made such actions obligatory due to more significant benefits. Having said this, it should be noted that MEDI does not imply that the *ḥujjiyya* of the relevant *ẓuhūr* will be automatically undermined in all these cases. Instead, MEDI merely opens the door to the possibility that the significance of the stakes involved, influenced by the magnitude of the relevant probabilities, could potentially prevent the *ẓuhūr* in question from being *ḥujja*. The crucial inquiry into when a particular *ẓuhūr* loses or retains its *ḥujjiyya* must be approached on a case-by-case basis, involving a thorough evaluation of all pertinent evidence available (more on this below in the main text).

22 It goes without saying that the Qur'an's being certainly authentic (i.e. its being *qaṭʿī al-ṣudūr*) does not, on its own, ensure that the rational probability assigned to A's being obligatory, relative to our total evidence, will always be high – let's say, greater than 0.5. As long as the verse in question is not explicit (*naṣṣ*) but only has a *ẓuhūr* in A's being obligatory, the probability of the veracity of this *ẓuhūr* could diminish when confronted with conflicting evidence. This is a concession that the traditional approach might readily make. What this approach will reject, but MEDI allows, is the idea that such a decrease in

differently, non-transmitted evidence, even if not certain, could potentially undermine the *ḥujjiyya* of the *ẓuhūr* of the verse in question.

In general, the decision-theoretic approach provides a model of how inter-religious (revelation-based) and extra-religious (non-revelation-based) evidence can interact and jointly contribute to the process of *istinbāṭ*. In this model, *istinbāṭ* is a holistic procedure in which not only the *ẓuhūr* of the Qur'an and *ḥadīth*s (and other traditional sources of *istinbāṭ*), but also moral intuitions and argumentations as well as empirical studies (albeit tentative and non-certain), could play a crucial role. All this constitutes the total evidential base that determines the relevant probabilities and, thereby, the course of actions one must rationally take before God.

Finally, the decision-theoretic approach provides us with a principled way to treat (at least some of) those regulative verses that seem problematic today (verses pertinent to *qiṣāṣ*, *ḥudūd*, beating women, etc.). Overall, according to MEDI, there are two possible obstacles in the way of the *ḥujjiyya* of the *ẓuhūr* of these verses. First, given our moral intuitions, the overall probability of the veridicality of the *ẓuhūr*s in question (i.e. α) will diminish. Second, the rulings indicated by those verses often involve high stakes (i.e. a high magnitude should be assigned to parameter t). In this way, the expected utility of the relevant action effectively decreases in these cases, potentially causing the *ḥujjiyya* of the *ẓuhūr* in question to be compromised. Interestingly, the success of my proposed treatment of these verses is not owed to their reinterpretation; suffice it to show that their *ẓuhūr*s are not *ḥujja* for us. In that case, without any radical modifications of the classic theological views regarding the nature of revelation, divine speech, and divine legislation (and even within the framework of those traditional theological theories) the normative force of such Qur'anic verses can be neutralised.[23]

---

probability can potentially undermine the *ḥujjiyya* of the *ẓuhūr* in question, even in cases where the conflicting evidence falls short of certainty.

23 The approach presented here to the theory of *ḥujjiyya* shares certain similarities with the views of some scholars, such as Abū al-Qāsim Fanāyī and Amir Saemi (see Abū al-Qāsim Fanāyī, *Akhlāq-i Dīn-Shināsī* (Tehran: Nigāh-i Muaʿsir, 2015), chs. 1 and 4; Amir Saemi, *Morality and Revelation in Islamic Thought and Beyond* (Oxford: Oxford University Press, 2024), ch. 6). However, significant differences also exist, the discussion of which goes far beyond the scope of this chapter. I aspire to explore and discuss these views on other occasions in the future.

5 Two Objections and Replies

First objection: The advocate of the traditional approach to the *ḥujjiyya* of *ẓuhūr* might mount a defence of his position by arguing that while MEDI holds promise as the primary principle of *ḥujjiyya*, its precise articulation requires further refinement. A more precise formulation of MEDI, according to this viewpoint, should involve a condition to the effect that the subject has not obtained a credible indication or *sharʿī* procedural principle concerning the action in question. The underlying idea here is that the primary principle of *ḥujjiyya* (whether it be rational exemption, rational caution, or MEDI) is supposed to determine one's responsibility towards God when one is uncertain about the divine ruling. But God Himself can establish a kind of 'secondary ruling' (in terms of an indication or a *sharʿī* procedural principle) regarding one's responsibility under such circumstances. Once one is aware of such a ruling, then he is required to act accordingly. Thus, whatever the primary principle of *ḥujjiyya*, it will be automatically conditional upon the agent not having obtained a credible indication or *sharʿī* procedural principle about the action in question.[24]

The advocate of the traditional approach might go on to say that this condition is not fulfilled, because we have sufficient reason to the effect that God has established *ḥujjiyya* for *ẓuhūr* of the Qur'an and *ḥadīth*s, where the scope of the established *ḥujjiyya* is as extended as the traditional approach claims. That is, firstly, every *ẓuhūr* is considered as *ḥujja* by the divine legislator, even though the probability of its veridicality is low relative to the subject's total evidence, and secondly, the *ḥujjiyya* of a *ẓuhūr* is not contingent upon the insignificance of the stakes involved.

Reply: Let's assume (for the purpose of our discussion) that the precise rendition of MEDI should involve a condition to the effect that the subject has not acquired a credible indication or a *sharʿī* procedural principle regarding the action in question. However, what reason is there to think that the divine legislator has established *ḥujjiyya* for the *ẓuhūr* of the Qur'an as extensively as depicted in the traditional approach? Fortunately, the key point here is provided by the Uṣūlīs themselves. The main (and perhaps the only) argument they propose for the *ḥujjiyya* of the *ẓuhūr* makes an appeal to *banāʾ al-ʿuqalāʾ* (the manner or practice of rational people). The idea is that in their interpersonal interactions, rational people tend to trust the *ẓuhūr* of each other's

24 See, for example, al-Hāshimī, *Buḥūth*, vol. 4, 152, vol. 5, 176, 180.

statements. Furthermore, the divine legislator has not banned this practice, which implies His consent to comply with this same practice in understanding His own rulings. That is to say, the divine legislator has established *ḥujjiyya* for the *ẓuhūr* of Qurʾanic verses.

Of course, it is out of the question that rational agents *do* often trust the *ẓuhūr* of each other's statements. What is crucial, however, is whether the scope of such a practice is as extensive as depicted in the traditional approach. Arguably, the answer is negative. In a nutshell, it seems that people's reliance on the *ẓuhūr* of their statements is governed by the same general rules of practical rationality that are formulated in decision theory. It goes without saying that ordinary people cannot formulate the rules of the decision theory, but this is not to deny that their behaviours often conform to such rules. This is comparable to the fact that people's beliefs often conform to the rules of logic, although they are sometimes unable to articulate those rules, or the fact that their speeches conform to grammatical rules, even though they fail to formulate the rules. Even if we do not have sufficient reason to believe that the ordinary practice of acting on *ẓuhūr* conforms to the rules of the decision theory, at least we can say that there is no reason to believe the contrary. And this is just enough for our being rationally bound to comply with the initial formulation of MEDI. The reason is that the condition incorporated into the refined formulation of MEDI was that one should *not have obtained* a credible indication concerning the action in question. And since there is no reason to think that the rational people's habitude to act on the *ẓuhūr*s diverges from the requirements of the decision theory, we do not obtain a credible indication that might have a verdict inconsistent with the decision-theoretic requirements.[25]

25 A similar verdict applies to the alleged *ḥujjiyya* of the report from a trustworthy individual (*khabar al-thiqa*). In this case as well, the primary argument supporting the *ḥujjiyya* of such reports points to the manner of rational people who rely on them – a manner purportedly sanctioned by the divine legislator. However, it is essential to note that while rational people *do* possess such a habitude, its scope is arguably constrained by the general principles of practical rationality, or, at the very least, there is no compelling reason to assume otherwise. Therefore, even if we acknowledge that the accurate articulation of MEDI includes a 'no-contrary-secondary-ruling' condition, the practical stance one should rationally take upon receiving a report from a trustworthy individual remains governed by the original formulation of MEDI. Another crucial question to be explored elsewhere is in which cases, if any, we have sufficient reason to believe that the divine legislator has established a secondary ruling contrary to what MEDI dictates, thereby rendering the 'no-contrary-secondary-ruling' condition unsatisfied – specifically, a ruling such as the purported principle of *sharʿī* exemption (*al-barāʾa al-sharʿiyya*).

It is worthwhile to consider a pertinent objection that might be raised against the framework I proposed for the role of non-certain, non-transmitted evidence (or *al-ẓann*

Second objection: A notable objection that may be raised against MEDI as the primary principle of *ḥujjiyya* is that we almost never are in a position to assign a precise numerical probability to divine rulings (and to the benefits and harms that ground their legislation). For this reason, even if MEDI is theoretically acceptable, its practical applicability remains severely limited in the vast majority of cases.

Reply: A comprehensive treatment of this objection lies beyond the confines of this article. What holds weight, however, is that this objection not only poses a challenge to the applicability of MEDI but also casts doubt on the broader applicability of decision theory in general. With the exception of specific cases like dice-throwing, there are hardly any other scenarios where we can ascribe precise numerical probabilities to pertinent propositions. In most ordinary cases, the assigned probabilities tend to be ambiguous or indeterminate. Advocates of normative decision theory have put forth a range of solutions and refinements to surmount this challenge, and the dispute on this subject remains ongoing.[26] I tentatively suggest that the solutions proposed to address

al-ʿaqlī in *uṣūlī* jargon) in the process of *istinbāṭ*. The objection can be summarised as follows:

(1) While MEDI can be in principle considered as the primary principle of *ḥujjiyya*, its precise formulation includes a 'no-contrary-secondary-ruling' condition.

(2) There are compelling textual reasons for the divine legislator's prohibition of exploiting *any* form of non-certain, non-transmitted evidence in the process *istinbāṭ* (one might attempt to support this premise by appealing to various reports from the Infallible Imāms that explicitly forbid the application of *qiyās* and *raʾy*).

(3) If the divine legislator has forbidden the exploitation of non-certain, non-transmitted evidence, this prohibition serves as a secondary ruling that nullifies the otherwise effective role of such evidence in determining the expected utility of actions within the framework of MEDI.

(4) Consequently, it becomes imperative to completely disregard non-certain, non-transmitted evidence when calculating relevant probabilities during the application of MEDI.

The assessment of this objection exceeds the intended scope of this chapter. What I wish to emphasise here is that the second premise can be robustly contested on the basis that it is not clear at all whether the concept of 'acting upon *qiyās* and *raʾy*' (in the relevant *ḥadīths*) is applicable to cases where the subject adequately reflects on all relevant evidence (both transmitted and non-transmitted) to determine which action is rationally required according to the general principles of practical rationality.

26 See, for example, Peter Klibanoff, Massimo Marinacci, and Sujoy Mukerji, 'A Smooth Model of Decision Making under Ambiguity', *Econometrica* 73 (2005): 1849–92; Matthias C.M. Troffaes, 'Decision Making under Uncertainty Using Imprecise Probabilities', *International Journal of Approximate Reasoning* 45 (2007): 17–29; Teddy Seidenfeld, Mark J. Schervish, and Joseph B. Kadane, 'Coherent Choice Functions under Uncertainty', *Synthese* 172

this challenge could potentially be applicable within the context of the theory of *ḥujjiyya*, thereby allowing for the development of more refined versions of MEDI. Nevertheless, this remains an open question, to be explored on a separate occasion.

Let us recap. A central idea of this article was that the concept of *ḥujjiyya* in *uṣūl al-fiqh* should be understood as functioning within the wider framework of practical rationality. Accordingly, I proposed a decision-theoretic approach to the *ḥujjiyya* in general, exploring some of its implications for the *ḥujjiyya* of the *ẓuhūr* of regulative verses. In particular, this approach provides a model for the interaction between inter-religious and extra-religious evidence in the process of *istinbāṭ*, allowing for a principled treatment of those regulative verses which conflict with our moral intuitions. Of course, the approach suggested herein was only a rudimentary sketch, leaving numerous significant inquiries for future explorations.[27]

Bibliography

al-Ābī, Ḥasan (al-Fāḍil al-Ābī). *Kashf al-rumūz fī sharḥ Mukhtaṣar al-Nāfiʿ*. Vol. 2. Qom: Mu'assasat al-Nashr al-Islāmī, 1987.

al-ʿĀmilī, Zayn al-Dīn. *al-Rawḍa al-bahiyya fī sharḥ al-Lumʿa al-Dimashqiyya*. Vol. 3. Qom: Dāwarī, 1989.

al-Anṣārī, Murtaḍā. *Farā'id al-uṣūl*. Vol. 1. Qom: Majmaʿ al-Fikr al-Islāmī, 1998.

al-ʿArāqī, Ḍīyā' al-Dīn. *Maqālāt al-uṣūl*. Vol. 2. Qom: Majmaʿ al-Fikr al-Islāmī, 1999.

al-Bihsūdī, Muḥammad. *Miṣbāḥ al-uṣūl* [transcript of the *uṣūl* class of al-Khū'ī]. Vol. 1. Qom: Maktabat al-Dāvarī, 1996.

Bradley, Richard. *Decision Theory with a Human Face*. Cambridge: Cambridge University Press, 2017.

al-Burūjirdī, Muḥammad Taqī. *Nihāyat al-afkār* [transcript of the *uṣūl* class of al-ʿArāqī]. Vol. 3. Qom: Mu'assasat al-Nashr al-Islāmī, 1984.

Fanāyī, Abū al-Qāsim. *Akhlāq-i Dīn-Shināsī*. Tehran: Nigāh-i Muaʿsir, 2015.

(2010): 157–76; J. Robert G. Williams, 'Decision-Making under Indeterminacy', *Philosophers' Imprint* 14 (2014): 1–34; Nathan Huntley, Robert Hable, and Matthias C.M. Troffaes, 'Decision Making', in *Introduction to Imprecise Probabilities*, ed. Thomas Augustin, Frank Coolen, Gert de Cooman, and Matthias C.M. Troffaes (New York: John Wiley and Sons, 2014), 190–206; Richard Bradley, *Decision Theory with a Human Face* (Cambridge: Cambridge University Press, 2017), pt. IV.

27 I am grateful to the participants of the AMI conference 'Regulative Verses of the Qur'ān', and, in particular, to three anonymous reviewers for their valuable comments on earlier drafts of this chapter.

al-Hāshimī, Maḥmūd. *Buḥūth fī ʿilm al-uṣūl* [transcript of the *uṣūl* class of al-Ṣadr]. Vol. 4. Qom: al-Majmaʿ al-ʿIlmī li-l-Shahīd al-Ṣadr, 1984.

al-Hāshimī, Maḥmūd. *Buḥūth fī ʿilm al-uṣūl* [transcript of the *uṣūl* class of al-Ṣadr]. Vol. 5. Qom: al-Majmaʿ al-ʿIlmī li-l-Shahīd al-Ṣadr, 1984.

al-Ḥillī, Najm al-Dīn Jaʿfar (al-Muḥaqqiq al-Ḥillī). *Sharāʾiʿ al-Islām fī masāʾil al-ḥalāl wa-l-ḥarām*. Vol. 4. Tehran: Istiqlāl, 1988.

Huntley, Nathan, Robert Hable, and Matthias C.M. Troffaes. 'Decision Making'. In *Introduction to Imprecise Probabilities*, edited by Thomas Augustin, Frank P.A. Coolen, Gert de Cooman, and Matthias C.M. Troffaes, 190–206. New York: John Wiley and Sons, 2014.

al-Kāẓimī, Muḥammad ʿAlī. *Fawāʾid al-uṣūl* [transcript of the *uṣūl* class of al-Nāʾīnī]. Vol. 3. Qom: Muʾassasat al-Nashr al-Islāmī, 1988.

al-Khūʾī, Abū al-Qāsim. *Ajwad al-taqrīrāt* [transcript of the *uṣūl* class of al-Nāʾīnī]. Vol. 2. Sidon: Maktabat al-ʿIrfān, 1933.

al-Khunsārī, Aḥmad. *Jāmiʿ al-madārik fī sharḥ Mukhtaṣar al-Nāfiʿ*. Vol. 7. Tehran: Muʾassasat Ismāʿīliān, 1984.

al-Khurāsānī, Muḥammad Kāẓim. *Kifāyat al-uṣūl*. Qom: Muʾassasat Āl al-Bayt li-Iḥyāʾ al-Turāth, 1996.

Klibanoff, Peter, Massimo Marinacci, and Sujoy Mukerji. 'A Smooth Model of Decision Making under Ambiguity'. *Econometrica* 73 (2005): 1849–92.

Saemi, Amir. *Morality and Revelation in Islamic Thought and Beyond*. Oxford: Oxford University Press, 2024.

Seidenfeld, Teddy, Mark J. Schervish, and Joseph B. Kadane. 'Coherent Choice Functions under Uncertainty'. *Synthese* 172 (2010): 157–76.

al-Ṭabāṭabāʾī, ʿAlī. *Riyāḍ al-masāʾil fī taḥqīq al-aḥkām bi-l-dalāʾil*. Vol. 2. Qom: Muʾassasat Āl al-Bayt, 1983.

Troffaes, Matthias C.M. 'Decision Making under Uncertainty Using Imprecise Probabilities'. *International Journal of Approximate Reasoning* 45 (2007): 17–29.

Williams, J. Robert G. 'Decision-Making under Indeterminacy'. *Philosophers' Imprint* 14 (2014): 1–34.

CHAPTER 14

The Existential Perspective on the Regulative Verses (*Āyāt al-Aḥkām*) of the Qur'an

Arif Abdul Hussain

A case of domestic violence was brought before the blessed Prophet by the father of the beaten woman.[1] The Prophet advised that his daughter respond in kind to the husband, that is, as per *lex talionis*, which was the principle underlying the regulative norm in Q. 2:178 revealed previously. Upon issuing this judgement, Q. 4:34 was revealed stipulating a regulation or regulative form affording men the right to castigate their unruly spouses; the verse also supplied the rationale for this regulative form, namely, that 'men were the governors of their womenfolk' (*al-rijālu qawwāmūna ʿalā al-nisāʾ*) for two reasons: firstly, because 'God bestowed them with existential merit' (*bi-mā faḍḍala Allāhu baʿḍahum ʿalā baʿḍ*) and not the latter, and hence secondly, because of 'the wealth they expended as provision' (*bi-mā anfaqū min amwālihim*) for the latter's upkeep.[2] Clearly, the initial judgement of the Prophet was more egalitarian than the regulative form of Q. 4:34, and yet the latter was more equitable considering the context of revelation; this is because the latter was formulated in light of the principle of justice, the prevailing views and norms regarding gender-specific societal roles and spousal relations, rights and responsibilities, and the existential aptitudes of men and women generally at that time.[3] The contextuality of this regulative form ensured that it was just, relevant to the people it was formulated for, and hence contributed to the functionality of a just community, which in turn was fundamental insofar as a just community

1 The author is grateful to Riaz Walji for kindly editing and referencing the chapter, and colleagues at Al-Mahdi Institute for organising the workshop in which an early draft of this chapter was presented and for their efforts in getting it to publication.

2 For reference to the context of Q. 4:34, see the exegeses of Faḍl b. Ḥasan al-Ṭabarsī, *Majmaʿ al-bayān fī tafsīr al-Qurʾān* (Beirut: Muʾassasat al-Aʿlamī li-l-Maṭbūʿāt, 1995), 3:79; Muḥammad Sayyid al-Ṭanṭāwī, *al-Tafsīr al-wasīṭ li-l-Qurʾān al-karīm* (Cairo: Maṭbaʿat al-Saʿāda, 1983), 3:176; Ismāʿīl Ibn Kathīr, *Tafsīr al-Qurʾān al-ʿaẓīm* (Beirut: Dār wa-Maktabat al-Hilāl, 1990), 2:70.

3 For the existential perspective and reading of this verse, see Arif Abdul Hussain, 'The Existential Perspective on "God's Bestowal of *Faḍl* upon Men" and Its Implication on *Qiwāma*', in *Islam and the Institution of Marriage: Legal and Sociological Approaches*, ed. Katherine Lemons and Laurens de Rooij (Birmingham: AMI Press, 2023), 9–32.

is conducive to the rational, moral, and spiritual growth of both its individuals and collectivities. The aforementioned information about this regulative form, its revelation, and context demonstrates the centrality of the principle of justice; it also demonstrates the appreciation of the existential aptitudes and context of individuals and collectivities in the methodology of the Lawgiver of the Sharīʿa apropos shaping the forms of regulative essences.[4] Accordingly, they are pivotal in the formulation of regulative forms in the existential framework.

Traditional *uṣūlī*s (legal theorists) generally accept the aforementioned features of regulative forms but maintain that the contextuality of any given regulative form of the Qur'an or the Prophet does not affect or curtail its infallibility, immutability, and universality. Thus, all such regulative forms are to be enforced in all times and places.[5] The contextuality of such regulative forms are overlooked due to their being 'Qur'anic' and/or 'prophetic'; hence they are presumed to be the 'best' regulative forms irrespective of whether they are 'just' and/or rational in other contexts.[6] The *uṣūlī* paradigm maintains that the regulative forms of the Qur'an or the Prophet are based on the following considerations: (a) that the relations of things to humans qua humans are value laden in terms of 'benefit' and 'harm'; and (b) that all such relations (of things to humans qua humans) and their respective values of 'harm' and 'benefit' are

4 For information on the notions of 'form' and 'essence' in the legal methodology of the existential framework, see Arif Abdul Hussain, 'A Functional Interpretation of *Zakāt* and the Inclusion of Contemporary Taxation as Its Legitimate Form', in *The Efficacy of Financial Structures for Islamic Taxes and Dues: Proceedings of the 7th AMI Contemporary Fiqhī Issues Workshop*, ed. Wahid M. Amin (Birmingham: AMI Press, 2020), 8–31; Arif Abdul Hussain, 'The Existential Perspective on the Meaning and Implication of Impure Substances within Shīʿī Jurisprudential Discourse', in *The Regulations of Purity in Islam: Proceedings of the 8th AMI Contemporary Fiqhī Issues Workshop*, ed. Hashim Bata (Birmingham: AMI Press, 2022), 81–84; Arif Abdul Hussain, 'The Conflict between the Actual and Apparent Regulations – Part 2: The Solution of "the Existential Framework"', Shaykh Arif (blog), www.shaykharif.com /blog/the-conflict-between-the-actual-and-apparent-regulations, 9–13.

5 For the *uṣūlī*s, the notion of the infallibility, immutability, and universality of the regulative forms of the Qur'an and the Prophet is corroborated by religious reports (*aḥādīth*), e.g. 'The permissible of Muḥammad is permissible forever till the Day of Judgement, and his prohibition is prohibited forever till the Day of Judgement.' See reports in Muḥammad b. Yaʿqūb al-Kulaynī, *Uṣūl al-kāfī* (Beirut: Manshūrāt al-Fajr, 2007), 1:34–35. It should be noted that the notions of constant (*thawābit*) and variable (*mutaghayyirāt*) regulations have been discussed by *uṣūlī*s in the modern period; however, in summary, they maintain that the regulative forms of the Qur'an and those of the Prophet that are not known to have been issued in his capacity as 'the head of state' or an adjudicator are 'constant', and hence infallible, immutable, and universal. See the views of Muḥammad Ḥusayn Ṭabāṭabāʾī, Muḥammad Ḥusayn Gharavī Nāʾīnī, and Muḥammad Bāqir Ṣadr in Mohsen Kadivar, 'From Traditional Islam to Islam as an End in Itself', *Die Welt des Islams* 51, no. 3–4 (2011): 462–71.

6 See references in previous note.

known by God and hence have normative statuses in accordance with those values.[7] *Uṣūlīs* classify regulative forms contained within certitude-bearing sources of normativity, such as the Qur'an, as 'actual regulations' (*aḥkām wāqiʿiyya*, sing. *ḥukm wāqiʿī*), that is, regulative forms that correspond to the statuses of the relations of things to humans qua humans in terms of 'benefit' and 'harm' in the mind of God.[8] Therefore, all the regulative forms of the Qur'an classify as 'actual regulations' irrespective of whether they pertain to devotional practices, human interactions, or consumables.

This chapter demonstrates that the *uṣūlī* view of the infallibility, immutability, and universality of Sharīʿa regulative forms generally and the regulative forms of the Qur'an in particular is premised on the untenable assumption of the fixed and immutable nature of the statuses of the relations of things to humans qua humans vis-à-vis the values of 'benefit' and 'harm'. The result is a conflation between the notions of 'the actual' (*al-wāqiʿī*) and 'actuality' (*al-wāqiʿ*); strictly speaking, the former refers to the regulative forms of the Qur'an or the Prophet that correspond to the existential statuses of the relations of things to humans qua 'the immediate audience of the Qur'an and the Prophet' in the mind of God, whereas the latter refers to the mind of God in which the existential statuses of the relations of things to humans qua 'humans of every possible context' is known; to reiterate, 'the actual' refers to regulative forms that corresponded to regulative forms in the knowledge of God during the revelatory era only and not beyond, whereas 'actuality' refers to God's knowledge of the regulative forms of every conceivable context (in other words, it refers to God's knowledge of the existential statuses of the relations of things to humans of differing existential aptitudes and contexts).[9]

---

7 Arif Abdul Hussain, 'The Conflict between the Actual and Apparent Regulations – Part 1: The Theoretical Foundations of *Uṣūl al-Fiqh* and the *Uṣūlī* Resolutions', Shaykh Arif (blog), www.shaykharif.com/blog/the-conflict-between-the-actual-and-apparent-regulations, 4, 6; Muḥammad Bāqir al-Ṣadr, *Durūs fī ʿilm al-uṣūl* (Qom: Markaz al-Abḥāth wa-l-Darāsāt al-Takhaṣṣuṣiyya li-l-Shahīd al-Ṣadr, 2005), 1:176–77.

8 Muḥammad Ṣanqūr ʿAlī, *al-Muʿjam al-uṣūlī* (Qom: Dār al-Mujtabā, 2001), 535–36. Note that since the statuses assigned to the relations of things to humans are based on the considerations of the 'benefit' and 'harm' of things vis-à-vis the rational, moral, and spiritual growth of humans, they are 'existential'. Thus, the phrase 'the *existential* statuses of the relations of things to humans in the mind of God' is used predominantly henceforth instead of 'the statuses of relations of things to humans in terms of "benefit" and "harm" in the mind of God'.

9 The notion of *al-wāqiʿ* (actuality or the realm of actuality) in *uṣūl al-fiqh* is termed *nafs al-amr* (factuality or the realm of factuality) in Islamic philosophy. It signifies the realm of facts to which propositions that do not correspond to things in 'manifested existence qua this observable, contingent universe' (such as certain moral, legal, logical, and philosophical propositions) have correspondence. For *uṣūlīs*, regulative forms pertaining to every aspect of human life exist in the mind of God. The truth of legal propositions, or regulative forms, lies in their correspondence to the regulative forms (or 'the *existential* statuses of the relations

An implication of this distinction is that the 'actual' regulative forms of the revelatory era cannot be deemed to be 'the actual' regulative forms for contexts differing from the revelatory and other similar contexts. The failure to distinguish between these two notions has caused the ascription of 'finality', 'universality', and 'infallibility' to the regulative forms of the verses of the Qur'an.

This chapter argues that the difference between the notions of 'the actual' and 'actuality' is rooted in the dynamic nature of manifested existence qua this observable, contingent universe.[10] It demonstrates that the principles of 'justice', 'ease', and 'non-hardship' mentioned in the Qur'an are existential, fundamental, and meta-legal, and hence the regulative forms of the Qur'an were formulated in light of the contexts and existential aptitudes of the individuals and collectivities they were addressing.[11] The conclusions of this chapter include (a) that the formulation and issuance of the regulative forms of the Qur'an were based on the existential statuses of the relations of things to humans qua 'the immediate audience of the Qur'an' in actuality, which in turn were based on the considerations of the existential aptitudes and contexts of its immediate audience and the principles of 'justice', 'ease', and 'non-hardship'; (b) the regulative forms of the Qur'an are not accurate depictions of 'actuality' beyond their own contexts, and hence are not optimal vis-à-vis the rational, moral, and spiritual growth of individuals and collectivities in different contexts and with diverse existential aptitudes; (c) however, they do yield the 'general' and 'specific' essences or growth values that they encapsulated, safeguarded, and upheld; and (d) thus, newer regulative forms can be formulated

of things to humans') in *al-wāqiʿ* or *nafs al-amr*. See Ṣanqūr ʿAlī, *al-Muʿjam al-uṣūlī*, 369–70; Muḥammad Ḥusayn Ṭabāṭabāʾī, *Bidāyat al-ḥikma* (Qom: Muʾassasat al-Nashr al-Islāmī, 2018), 24–25.

10 This chapter is concerned with the relationship between the notions of 'the actual', 'actuality', and 'manifested existence qua this observable, contingent universe'. Henceforth, the phrase 'manifested existence' is employed as shorthand to refer to 'manifested existence qua this observable, contingent universe'.

11 The principles of 'ease' and 'non-hardship' in the existential framework should not be confused with similar precepts among the normative precepts (*qawāʿid fiqhiyya*) that are used by legists at the level of, or within the domain of, the current corpus of Sharīʿa regulative forms, that is, at the 'horizontal' level (this notion is explained in the chapter later). In the existential framework, these principles, together with that of 'justice', are existential, fundamental, and meta-legal; hence they are influential at the level of the formulation and modification of regulative forms in the mind of God, the legist's modifications of regulative forms in extenuating circumstances, and the legist's formulation of regulative forms in and for contexts differing from those of the revelatory and other similar contexts. Although *uṣūlīs* agree that the principles of 'ease' and 'non-hardship' were instrumental at the level of the appreciation of regulative forms of the Sharīʿa in actuality, they restrict their utility within the domain of existing Sharīʿa regulative forms only, that is, as 'normative precepts'.

in light of (i) the 'general' and 'specific' essences or growth values of the regulative forms of the Qur'an and the Prophet, (ii) the existential aptitudes and contexts of the individuals and collectivities of newer contexts, (iii) the principles of 'justice', 'ease', and 'non-hardship', thereby ensuring that regulative forms continue to facilitate the growth of individuals and collectivities in different contexts and with diverse existential aptitudes optimally.

Therefore, this chapter presents the following:

i. An overview of the *uṣūlī* position and theory on Sharīʿa regulative forms generally and the regulative verses of the Qur'an in particular.
ii. The *uṣūlī* perspective on the regulative forms of the Qur'an, the underlying assumption of the fixed nature of the existential statuses of the relations of things to humans qua humans in 'actuality', and the resulting equivalence of the notions of 'the actual' and 'actuality'.[12]
iii. A critique of the assumption of the fixed nature of the existential statuses of the relations of things to humans qua humans in 'actuality', its underlying assumption of the fixed nature of the relations of things to humans qua humans in manifested existence, and its implications on the 'optimality' of the regulative verses of the Qur'an vis-à-vis the rational, moral, and spiritual growth of individuals and collectivities in different contexts and with diverse existential aptitudes.
iv. The existential reading of the regulative forms of the Qur'an in light of the dynamic nature of the relations of things to humans qua humans in manifested existence and their existential statuses in 'actuality', and the hermeneutical dichotomy of 'form' and 'essence'.

1 The *Uṣūlī* Position and Theory on Sharīʿa Regulative Forms Generally and the Regulative Verses of the Qur'an in Particular

The regulative verses (*āyāt al-aḥkām*) of the Qur'an can be divided into the following three categories based on the degree of their directness or indirectness vis-à-vis normative instruction:[13]

a. Theological regulative verses
b. Ethical and virtuous regulative verses
c. Normative regulative verses

---

12 The *uṣūlī* perspective and position is going to be explained throughout the discussions in this chapter.

13 See Ḥaydar Ḥubbullāh, 'Introduction to Qur'anic Jurisprudence' [in Arabic], Hobbollah, 19 September 2015, https://hobbollah.com/p/44657/المدخل-إلى-الفقه-القرآني.

The verses of the last category, which directly address human behaviour, are the subject of this chapter. They are classified as follows:[14]

i. Regulative verses about devotional practices
ii. Regulative verses about human interactions
iii. Regulative verses about consumables

Two types of regulative forms can be derived from the two main sources of normativity in the Sharīʿa, namely, the Qur'an (an ordained, scriptural source) and the Sunna (an ordained, non-scriptural source):

a. The actual regulation (*al-ḥukm al-wāqiʿī*); this is a regulative form in which there is no doubt regarding the normative status of its subject; this category of regulative forms is divided further into 'the primary actual regulation' (*al-ḥukm al-wāqiʿī al-awwalī*), which is active vis-à-vis the subject ordinarily, and 'the secondary actual regulation' (*al-ḥukm al-wāqiʿī al-thānawī*), which is active in extenuating circumstances.[15]
b. The apparent regulation (*al-ḥukm al-ẓāhirī*); this is a regulative form in which there is doubt regarding the normative status of its subject;[16] an example is the precept of purity (*qāʿidat al-ṭahāra*), which confers the status of 'purity' to things whose purity-status is unknown;[17] such precepts, from which individual regulative statuses stem, are derived from the more basic principles of 'ease' and 'non-hardship';[18] it should be noted that all such precepts are 'actual' in themselves insofar as no doubt exists regarding their issuance from the Lawgiver of the Sharīʿa and their respective contents; the qualification 'apparent' refers to the regulative statuses that such precepts confer to their respective subjects, for doubt subsists regarding the conferred regulative statutes.

The categories of normative regulative forms (*aḥkām taklīfiyya*) are 'obligation', 'prohibition', 'encouragement', 'discouragement', 'permissibility in the specific sense', and 'permissibility in the general sense', which comprises the latter three categories.[19]

14 This category includes both normative regulative forms (*aḥkām taklīfiyya*) and status-based regulative forms (*aḥkām waḍʿiyya*).
15 Ṣanqūr ʿAlī, *al-Muʿjam al-uṣūlī*, 529–30, 531–32, 535–36.
16 Ibid., 533–34.
17 For information on the precept of purity, see Muḥammad Kāẓim al-Muṣṭafawī, *al-Qawāʿid* (Qom: Mu'assasat al-Nashr al-Islāmī, 2014), 156–58.
18 The bases of these existential, fundamental, and meta-legal principles are the following verses of the Qur'an: 'God desires ease for you, and He does not desire hardship for you' (Q. 2:185), 'God does not desire to put on you any difficulty' (Q. 5:6), and 'He has chosen you and has not laid upon you [any] hardship in religion' (Q. 22:78).
19 al-Ṣadr, *Durūs fī ʿilm al-uṣūl*, 1:177–78.

There are two fundamental assumptions regarding Sharīʿa regulative forms, which include the regulative forms of the Qurʾan:

a. An ontological assumption: Sharīʿa regulative forms are based on the values of 'benefit' and 'harm' vis-à-vis the relations of things to humans qua humans in the realm of actuality (*al-wāqiʿ*). These values are the existential bases or the theoretical criteria of regulative forms (*milākāt aḥkām*).[20]
b. An epistemic assumption: the legist's knowledge/derivations of the Sharīʿa regulative forms may correspond to those in 'actuality', or the correspondence may be probable, which is known as the *uṣūlī* position of fallibilism (*takhṭiʾa*).[21] Due to the possibility of non-correspondence to 'actuality', all the regulative forms of the Sharīʿa derived by legists (*fuqahāʾ*) classify as 'apparent' because of the probable nature of their extrapolations from Sharīʿa sources.[22]

Thus, regulative forms extrapolated by legists from the textual sources of the Sharīʿa are 'apparent regulations', strictly speaking, on account of the probable nature of the meanings of texts in addition to the possibility of error regarding the authenticity of most the textual sources.[23] (It should be noted that the word 'apparent' in this context refers to 'the lack of certitude about the intent of the Lawgiver', and not 'the lack of certitude about the regulative status of a given subject' mentioned above.) This means that despite (the few) authentic textual sources containing regulative forms that correspond to the existential statuses of the relations of things to humans in actuality, the legist's knowledge vis-à-vis the correspondence is probable. The *uṣūlī*s circumvent the lack of certitude about the authenticity of most textual sources and the probable nature of the meanings of textual sources by establishing that such sources and 'the apparent meaning' of texts are 'Sharīʿa-ordained' and hence probative.[24] Thus, they have exhaustive discourses in their literature on 'the principiality of the apparent meaning' (*aṣālat al-ẓuhūr*) – including its justifications as a hermeneutical device, its probativity generally, and the probativity of its linguistic instances and applications – as the means of disclosing the intent of the Lawgiver in textual sources carrying regulative forms.[25] By establishing the

20 Ibid., 176–77.

21 Ṣanqūr ʿAlī, *al-Muʿjam al-uṣūlī*, 369–72.

22 Hence, the epistemological position of *uṣūlī* jurists and legists is 'fallibilism' (*al-takhṭiʾa*) vis-à-vis the correspondence of their extrapolated regulative forms to 'actuality' (*al-wāqiʿ*), as opposed to 'the infallibilism' (*al-taṣwīb*) in Sunnī *uṣūl al-fiqh*. Ibid.

23 Muḥammad Riḍā al-Muẓaffar, *Uṣūl al-fiqh* (Qom: Intishārāt Ismāʿīliyān, 2004), 3:45–46, 59–61, 113–14.

24 Ibid., 59–80, 113–31.

25 Ibid., 1:30–33, 3:113–31.

probativity of both the apparent meaning and Sharīʿa-ordained sources (that is, in spite of the probable nature of the former vis-à-vis correspondence to actuality and the latter vis-à-vis authenticity), regulative forms derived on the basis of the former and/or from the latter are to be regarded as 'actual' (*wāqiʿī*) regulations, that is, as regulative forms derived from sources whose authenticity are certain and significations explicitly clear (*nuṣūs ṣarīḥa*).[26] To reiterate, *uṣūlī*s regard apparent regulations (or 'probable' – *ẓannī* – regulative forms) as epistemically equivalent to actual regulations (or 'certain' – *qaṭʿī* – regulative forms) that correspond to actuality as long as:

i. the sources of derivation are Sharīʿa ordained, and
ii. the apparent meaning of the text is ascertained.

The next section summarises the *uṣūlī* outlook on the regulative forms of the Qur'an and the underlying assumption of the fixed nature of the existential statuses of the relations of things to humans qua humans in actuality.

2 The *Uṣūlī* Outlook on the Regulative Forms of the Qur'an and the Assumption of the Fixed Nature of the Existential Statuses in Actuality

The *uṣūlī* perspective on the regulative forms of the Qur'an is based on the doctrinal belief that the Qur'an is the final communication of God, who is Perfect and Omniscient, and that He has declared the religion of Islam to be complete;[27] thus, it concludes that the regulative forms of the Qur'an are:

a. final, namely, they cannot be superseded by others,
b. universal, which means they are applicable in all times and places, and
c. infallible, that is, they encapsulate, safeguard, and uphold their respective essences or growth values perfectly.[28]

The argument for this perspective is as follows: (i) the regulative forms of God are based on His knowledge of the statuses of the relations of things to humans qua humans in terms of 'benefit' and 'harm' in the realm of actuality, and hence they are absolutely accurate; (ii) the Qur'an is the final communication of God; and so (iii) the regulative forms of the Qur'an are based on the knowledge of God in actuality and hence are absolutely accurate for humans qua humans;

26 Ibid., 3:14–19.
27 This is based on theological reasoning, a verse of the Qur'an (discussed in the next section), and religious reports. For examples of reports, see al-Kulaynī, *Uṣūl al-kāfī*, 1:34–35.
28 See Munīr Khabbāz, 'Constancy and Change in the Textual Evidences' [in Arabic], al-Moneer, 3 October 2019, www.almoneer.org/?act=av&action=view&id=4124.

therefore (iv) they are final, universal, and infallible regulative forms. To reiterate, the regulative forms of the Qur'an are immutable and unchanging because they are based on His knowledge of the existential statuses of the relations of things to humans qua humans, and hence they are applicable in all times and places. The implication of this is that the existential statuses – by which is meant the growth-promoting and growth-impeding statuses, or in other words, the valuation of the relations in terms of 'benefit' and 'harm' – of the relations of things to humans qua humans are stable and not subject to change, that is, from the time of revelation till the end of the terrestrial history of humankind. This assumption of the fixed nature of the existential statuses of the relations of things to humans qua humans in 'actuality', and hence of their relations in manifested existence, means that the distinction between the notions of 'the actual' (*al-wāqiʿī*) regulation and 'actuality' (*al-wāqiʿ*) is superfluous, and hence they can be used interchangeably as synonyms for each other. Thus, the *uṣūlī* perspective on the regulative forms of the Qur'an has the following two implicative assumptions:

1. the fixed nature of the existential statuses of the relations of things to humans qua humans in 'actuality' (and hence of their relations in manifested existence), and
2. the equivalence of the notions of 'the actual' and 'actuality'.

It is these assumptions that underlie the *uṣūlī* position of strictly adhering to 'the principiality of the apparent meaning qua conventional word-meaning association' as the method of ascertaining the meaning intended by the Lawgiver (the Author of the textual sources of Sharīʿa normativity). The theory of 'the principiality of the apparent meaning qua apparent meaning' in *uṣūl al-fiqh* is based on the analysis of the phenomenon of communication between any speaker and listener and the assumptions therein. Hence, as a theory of understanding audible communication, 'the apparent meaning qua apparent meaning' was the means of understanding the Qur'an generally and its regulative forms in particular for its immediate audience. In brief, 'the apparent meaning qua apparent meaning' of any given speech assumes the speaker's usage of (a) the rules of language and (b) the language's conventional word-meaning association in any given context.[29] However, whenever 'the apparent meaning qua apparent meaning' of the Qur'an (that is, the meaning as understood by its immediate audience) cannot be discerned due to the absence of context, the legist is to adhere to and utilise 'the principiality of the apparent meaning qua conventional word-meaning association' to

29 al-Muẓaffar, *Uṣūl al-fiqh*, 3:113–14.

establish the apparent meaning.[30] Simply put, in cases where the context of the verses of the Qur'an is unknown, 'the principiality of the apparent meaning qua conventional word-meaning association' instructs the legist to assume that the Lawgiver intended to convey the meanings associated with words in the minds of the people of that time irrespective of their existential context and aptitudes, or in other words, the Lawgiver intended to convey the meaning as per the conventional word-meaning associations in the minds of the immediate audience of the Qur'an devoid of the consideration of their existential contexts and aptitudes. The consequences of applying 'the principiality of the apparent meaning qua conventional word-meaning association' to the regulative verses of the Qur'an in light of the aforementioned assumptions is the following:

a. The resultant meanings are not contextual and holistic, and hence classify as 'literal'.
b. These literal meanings are considered as corresponding to the existential statuses of the relations of things to humans qua humans in the mind of God at present and in the future.
c. Hence, they are considered as 'the actual' regulations that are final, universal, and infallible.
d. This is the case for all the regulative verses of the Qur'an, that is, those pertaining to devotional practices, human actions and interactions, and consumables.

In view of this and the preceding section, the *uṣūlī* outlook is that:

i. The regulative forms of the Qur'an are to be adhered to as per 'the apparent meaning qua conventional word-meaning association' and as though they are 'primary actual regulations', all things being equal; thus, for instance, the duration of a fast in the month of Ramaḍān is fixed as commencing at dawn and ending at sunset in all times and places irrespective of the extreme hours (both too long and too short) that this entails in many regions of the world, all things being equal; likewise the norms of possessing slaves, concubines, and amputating the hands of thieves are fixed and applicable in all times and places, all things being equal.
ii. In extenuating circumstances, the duties of such 'primary actual regulations' are either laxed or absolved on account of the activity of the general normative precepts (*qawāʿid fiqhiyya*) of 'ease' and 'non-hardship' and hence superseded by 'secondary actual regulations';[31] for instance, persons unable to perform the extremely lengthy fasts in certain regions

30 Ibid., 123–25.

31 Ṣanqūr ʿAlī, *al-Muʿjam al-uṣūlī*, 531–32.

of the world are absolved of the obligation of fasting; and a starving person is obliged to consume the flesh of swine assuming it is the only consumable available; likewise Muslim collectivities residing in non-Islamic contexts are exempt from amputating the hands of thieves and flogging those who consume alcohol.

iii. The regulative forms of the Qur'an governing human interactions are to be viewed as 'primary actual regulations' due to their being formulated in light of the principle of justice; thus, for instance, its regulative form stating that men can discipline their insubordinate wives is a primary actual regulation.

The *uṣūlīs* accept the phenomenon of the modification of regulative forms vis-à-vis the Qur'an in the following contexts: (a) the abrogation of some of the regulative forms of former scriptures by the regulative forms of the Qur'an,[32] (b) the abrogation of earlier regulative forms of the Qur'an by later ones,[33] (c) the modification of the regulative forms of the Qur'an by the normative precepts of 'ease' and 'non-hardship', and (d) the modification of the regulative forms of the Qur'an pertaining to devotional practices in abnormal circumstances. The *uṣūlīs* maintain that the 'abrogated' regulative forms of the former scriptures and those of the Qur'an itself were non-final, particular/contextual, and fallible, whereas the 'abrogating' regulative forms of the Qur'an were final, universal, and infallible.[34] As for the modification of the regulative forms of the Qur'an by the normative precepts of 'ease' and 'non-hardship', the *uṣūlīs* interpret the relationship between them in the following two ways:

1. The precepts are informative, instructive, and causally prior to the regulative forms. This means the regulative forms are issued by God in light of the precepts of 'ease' and 'non-hardship'; consequently, their formulations, which are based on 'the apparent meanings qua conventional word-meaning association', are intrinsically 'bearable'.[35] Obviously, God understands human nature, is aware of human aptitudes, and knows what is bearable for them. Thus, the precepts are viewed in the same manner as in the existential framework, which is as meta-legal principles that are informative and instructive at the stage of the consideration of Sharīʿa regulative forms (*iʿtibār al-ḥukm fī marḥalat al-thubūt*), prior to

32 Ibid., 136; al-Sayyid Abū al-Qāsim al-Mūsawī al-Khūʾī, *The Prolegomena to the Quran*, trans. Abdulaziz A. Sachedina (Qom: Ansariyan Publications, 1992), 191.

33 Ibid., 188–92.

34 Ibid., 192–94.

35 See Jaʿfar al-Subḥānī, 'Islamic Beliefs in Light of the School of Ahl al-Bayt' [in Arabic], Shia Online Library, https://shorturl.at/NwcUJ, 166–67.

the stage of their formulation and issuance logically speaking (*marḥalat al-ithbāt wa-l-ibrāz*). Accordingly, the relationship between such precepts and the regulative forms is vertical causally speaking, for they are formulated in light of the precepts of 'ease' and 'non-hardship'.

2. The precepts are modificatory after the formulation and issuance of regulative forms; this is in addition to being informative, instructive, and causally prior to them.[36] When adherence to regulative forms, which are 'bearable' all things being equal, is difficult for individuals due to extenuating circumstances, such as ill health, the duties of regulative forms are either laxed or absolved for such individuals due to the activity of the precepts.[37] Thus, 'primary actual regulations' are replaced by 'secondary actual regulations' stipulating the lack of duties for those unable to discharge the duties, for instance. Accordingly, the relationship between the precepts and the regulative forms is horizontal in terms of effecting modifications (as well as being vertical as discussed in the previous interpretation), for they can affect the latter after the latter's formulation and issuance by God in individual cases of hardship and difficulty.

The bases of the normative precepts of 'ease' and 'non-hardship' are the principles of 'ease' and 'non-hardship' in the Qur'an. These principles stem from and hence are subsumed under the principle of justice, which is presupposed throughout the Qur'an and is defined theologically as 'putting things in their rightful places'. The principle of justice is alluded to in verses of the Qur'an such as, 'God is never oppressive to His creatures' (Q. 3:182, 8:51, 22:10) and 'God does not task a soul beyond its capacity' (Q. 2:228).[38] Finally, as for the modification of the regulative forms of the Qur'an pertaining to devotional practices, such as shortening prayers during battle or praying while fleeing on foot or horseback, *uṣūlīs* are likely to agree that such formal changes are effected in order to convey and secure (or perpetuate, preserve, and accommodate) the essence of prayers in those circumstances; however, they would confine the process of modifying the devotional regulative forms of the Qur'an to the causes and instances of modification listed in the textual sources, which in this example is 'fear of the enemy's attack'; they would not extend it to the other genres of regulative forms.[39] To reiterate, the process of modifying devotional regulative

36 al-Muṣṭafawī, *al-Qawāʿid*, 9–11.

37 See ibid., 296–98.

38 For examples of verses exhorting 'justice', see Q. 3:18, 4:58, 4:135, 5:8, 5:42, 7:29, 7:181, 10:47, 10:54, 11:85, 16:90, 42:15, 49:9, 57:25, 60:8.

39 This is clear upon a cursory reading of any *fiqh istidlālī* work; moreover, extending the process of regulative formal modification beyond the instances cited in religious texts is liable to be attributed with the designation of 'unwarranted analogy' (*qiyās*).

forms cannot be extended and applied beyond those instances listed in the Qur'an and/or other textual sources and other very similar cases pertaining to the same genres of devotional practices, that is, it cannot be extended and applied to other devotional practices whose forms have not undergone such modifications during the revelatory era and hence are not listed in the Qur'an and/or other textual sources.[40] This reluctance, in *uṣūl al-fiqh*, to consider applying the process of formal regulative modification to regulative forms whose forms were not modified during the revelatory period and hence are not listed in the Qur'an and/or other textual sources is indicative of the influence of the assumptions of 'finality', 'universality', and 'infallibility' of the Qur'an qua a communication of God on the *uṣūlī* outlook apropos the regulative forms of the Sharīʿa generally and the regulative forms of the Qur'an in particular; and as discussed previously, these assumptions ensue from the more fundamental assumption of the fixed nature of the existential statuses of the relations of things to humans qua humans in the realm of actuality and its corollary assumption of the equivalence of the notions of 'the actual' and 'actuality'.

In conclusion, the *uṣūlī* perspective on the regulative forms of the Qur'an is that they are intrinsically 'just' and 'bearable' and hence applicable in all times and places. Instances of difficulty are viewed as exceptions to the rule and hence would be modified or absolved for the duration of their unbearability.

The next section critiques the fundamental *uṣūlī* assumptions of the fixed nature of the existential statuses of the relations of things to humans qua humans in actuality, and the equivalence of the notions of 'the actual' and 'actuality'.

3 Critique of the *Uṣūlī* Assumptions: the Fixed Nature of the Existential Statuses in Actuality, and the Equivalence of 'the Actual' and 'Actuality'

There are two fundamental components underlying the *uṣūlī* outlook on the regulative forms of the Qur'an: a theological commitment or presupposition and an implicative philosophical assumption, where the latter both consolidates and is consolidated by the former as discussed in the previous sections:

a. The theological commitment or presupposition: God, who is Perfect and Omniscient, has declared the religion of Islam to be complete.[41]

---

40 A case in point is the aversion of *uṣūlīs* to modifying the length of fasts in regions where the fasts are either abnormally long or short.

41 See note 4 for allusions to other evidences.

b. The implicative philosophical assumption: the fixed nature of the existential statuses of the relations of things to humans qua humans in actuality.

The theological premise is evinced from the following verse of the Qur'an: 'This day have I perfected your religion for you and completed My favour unto you, and have approved Islam as a religion for you' (Q. 5:3). Despite the declaration of the completion and perfection of 'your' religion in this verse, regulative verses continued being revealed after its revelation chronologically. Thus, the assertion of the completion and perfection of 'your' religion in this verse did not mark the point of the completion of the issuance of the regulative forms of the Qur'an and the Prophet.[42] Based on this and the fact that the verse was revealed immediately after the Prophet and Muslims finished performing their first major pilgrimage (*ḥajj*), it can be surmised that the completion and perfection of 'your' religion mentioned in this verse marked the completion of the religion as a distinct, formal, and an organised religion with established devotional practices and a religious and spiritual identity.[43] To reiterate, the verse merely referred to the completion of the religion as an organised religion with a religious and spiritual identity and the establishment of its devotional practices, namely, the five daily prayers, fasting during the month of Ramaḍān, and the pilgrimage of *ḥajj*; the notion of the 'completion' of 'your' religion in the verse did not signify the immutability of its religious and spiritual identity

42 It could be claimed that the completion and perfection of 'your' religion mentioned in this verse included the regulative forms that had been issued up until that point. However, one then has to explain the phenomenon of issuance of regulative forms after the revelation of this verse, and hence the meaning of 'completion' and 'perfection' therein.

43 The usage of the second-person plural pronoun as the direct objects and possessive pronouns in the verse ('I perfected your religion for you', 'completed My favour unto you', and 'approved Islam as a religion for you') signifies the perfection and completion of the religion vis-à-vis the existential aptitudes and contexts of its immediate audience; for had the religion of Islam qua 'the organised religion of all Muslims' been completed, then the verse would have stated unequivocally, 'I have perfected Islam and I have completed My favours'. Furthermore, it should be noted that the Qur'an states that the prophets conveyed the same one religion – Islam – on the one hand, and yet on the other, it refers to each of the previous Abrahamic faiths by its distinct spiritual identity marker and name. This means all the Abrahamic faiths were regarded as 'Islam' by God and hence declared to be 'perfect' and 'complete' as distinct, formal, and organised religions with established devotional practices and religious and spiritual identities for their respective adherents at particular moments in history, and yet their societal and interactional regulations continued to be modified by subsequent prophets. This is evidence that the regulative aspect of every religion, whose function is to regulate humans, cannot be deemed to be 'perfect' or 'complete' beyond its original existential context and other similar contexts due to the dynamic nature of human existence.

markers or even its regulative forms pertaining to the devotional practices in every time and region.[44]

In any case, the *uṣūlī* presumptions of the infallibility, eternality, and universality of the regulative forms of the Qur'an, all of which are encapsulated in the notion of 'finality' vis-à-vis the regulative forms of the Sharīʿa generally, follow on naturally from the acceptance of the assumptions of the fixed nature of the existential statuses of the relations of things to humans qua humans in actuality and the equivalence of the notions of 'the actual' and 'actuality'. However, if these assumptions are inaccurate, then the consequent presumptions are inaccurate too. In other words, if the relations of things to humans qua humans in manifested existence are dynamic, and hence their respective existential statuses subject to flux in actuality, then the regulative forms of the Qur'an can only be deemed to be 'infallible' and 'universal' with respect to the individuals and collectivities of the existential contexts they were formulated in and for and the individuals and collectivities of other similar contexts; this is because it is only in these contexts that one can be certain of the correspondence between 'the actual' (regulations of the Qur'an) and (the existential statuses of the relations of things to humans qua 'the individuals and collectivities comprising the immediate audience of the Qur'an' in) 'actuality'; for beyond these contexts, one cannot be certain of the said correspondence; and hence it is necessary to distinguish between 'actuality' and 'the actual' regulative forms of the Qur'an.

The assumption of the fixed nature of the existential statuses of the relations of things to humans qua humans in actuality is untenable because the nature of manifested existence, which includes human beings and their

44 Evidently, the regulative forms of the five daily prayers and fasting during Ramaḍān are in need of modification vis-à-vis Muslims residing in regions with abnormally long or short days and nights. Change due to differences and/or growth in the existential aptitudes and contexts of individuals and collectivities necessitates change in the forms of regulations in order to continue to facilitate the optimal growth of individuals and collectivities, irrespective of whether regulative forms are devotional, societal, or pertain to consumables. Obviously, novel challenges require minds to conceive of regulative forms afresh in all these categories of regulative forms, such as Muslims residing on the International Space Station for a few months or the rights of artificially intelligent workers; a Muslim astronaut is in need of regulative forms instructing on the rules of prayers in zero gravity and environments in which terrestrial sunrises and sunsets are not experienced. In view of this, the claim that Islam is complete and comprehensive vis-à-vis its current corpus of regulative forms is inaccurate both with respect to unprecedented future challenges and conveying their respective essences or values in differing contexts and hence facilitating growth therein.

contexts, is one of constant flux and change.[45] This flux necessitates change vis-à-vis the relations of things to humans and hence their existential statuses too in actuality.[46] In view of this, then, the regulative forms of the Qur'an were formulated for their original contexts primarily, given they were revealed in and for particular contexts, and other similar existential contexts secondarily. Thus, they are 'actual' regulative forms corresponding to the existential statuses of the relations of things to humans qua 'humans who were the immediate audience of the Qur'an in seventh-century Arabia' in actuality. To uphold the assumption of the finality of the regulative forms of the Qur'an today is to claim that they are 'the actual' regulative forms corresponding to the existential statuses of the relations of things to humans qua 'humans today' in actuality; this assumes that there has been no change in the existential aptitudes and contexts of humans since the revelatory era, which is patently absurd, for it ignores the dynamic nature of manifested existence and hence of the existential statuses of the relations of things to other things in the realm of actuality. The result is the conflation and equivalence of the notions of 'the actual' and 'actuality', the consequence of which is that it is not possible to distinguish between the essences or growth values of regulations and their context-based forms. The essences of the regulative forms of the Qur'an are final, acontextual/universal, and infallible, for they pertain to and are perpetually in line with the existential property and telos of growth, but their original forms are temporal, contextual, and fallible, and hence may be rendered obsolete as humankind grows (rationally and morally) and contexts change.

In light of the dynamic nature of manifested existence, the following two points ensue vis-à-vis 'actuality' and 'the actual':

a. The condition of humans and other things in manifested existence is one of evolution and dynamism; hence their relations to things and each other in manifested existence are subject to flux, which means their existential statuses in the realm of actuality are also subject to change. Flux in human aptitudes and contexts can result in either unprecedented challenges requiring the formulation of novel regulative forms or significant changes over time necessitating the modification of existing regulative

45 Arif Abdul Hussain, 'The Primacy of the Freedoms of Thought and Expression within the Existential Framework: Implications on Sharīʿa Regulations, Rights, and Freedoms', in *Free Speech, Scholarly Critique and the Limits of Expression in Islam: Proceedings of the 9th AMI Contemporary Fiqhī Issues Workshop*, ed. Wahid M. Amin (Birmingham: AMI Press, 2022), 14–16.

46 Abdul Hussain, 'The Conflict between the Actual and Apparent Regulations – Part 2', 7–9, 11–14.

forms in order to safeguard and facilitate the attainment of the essences or growth values in the original forms.

b. The regulative forms of the Qur'an correspond with 'actuality' in their original contexts and other similar contexts only; accordingly, they qualify as 'the actual' regulative forms therein only and not other differing contexts. This means the regulative forms of the Qur'an were never intended to be efficacious in facilitating the growth of individuals and collectivities in every possible existential context, and hence they were never required to convey the intended essences or values beyond their immediate and similar contexts.

In summary, the regulative forms of the Qur'an do not correspond to actuality, and hence do not classify as 'the actual' (regulations) beyond their own and other similar existential contexts; and they were never meant to be deemed as eternal or universal regulative forms to be applied in all times and places. Thus, there is 'no finality' with respect to the 'forms' of the regulations of the Qur'an, but there is 'finality' (which includes its subsidiary notions of 'eternality', 'universality', and 'infallibility') with respect to the 'essences' or 'growth values' inherent in the 'forms' of the regulations of the Qur'an, which is elaborated upon in the next section.

The next section delineates the outlook of the existential framework on the regulative forms of the Qur'an.

4 The Existential Outlook on the Regulative Forms of the Qur'an

Manifested existence is dynamic as per 'the principiality of substantial motion' (*aṣālat al-ḥaraka al-jawhariyya*) therein; it is in constant motion, moving to completion by actualising its innate potential gradually. Thus, motion is both the principal norm and the telos of manifested existence on account of the existential property of growth, for manifested existence is imbued with the property of growth, and hence its raison d'être is to grow and complete itself.[47] It is not merely the bodies of the individuals and collectivities of the human species that are subject to evolutionary motion and growth but also their minds and souls. Technically, growth is said to occur along the vertical and horizontal axes of the existence of things; growth along the vertical axis

47 Growth, or motion to completion, is an existential property on account of 'the principiality of existence' (*aṣālat al-wujūd*) and 'the principiality of substantial motion' (*aṣālat al-ḥaraka al-jawhariyya*) and as such, manifested existence cannot be devoid of it.

refers to the motion of the individuals and collectivities of any given species from potentiality to actuality, and growth vis-à-vis the horizontal axis refers to the degrees of growth of individuals and collectivities relative to one another either within the same or differing eras.[48]

In view of this, since 'the actual' (*al-wāqiʿī*) regulative forms are the formulations and issuances of the existential statuses of the relations of things to humans qua humans in 'actuality' (*al-wāqiʿ*) or the mind of God, then perpetual flux vis-à-vis manifested existence necessitates that there will be change in those relations in manifested existence and hence in the existential statuses in 'actuality'. If regulative forms do not reflect such changes in the existential statuses in 'actuality', then they will be suboptimal vis-à-vis growth at best or outrightly unjust at worst. Moreover, the phenomenon of perpetual flux vis-à-vis manifested existence affects every type of regulative form: those pertaining to devotional practices, human interactions, and consumables. This means 'the actual' regulative forms qua God's considerations of the existential statuses of the relations of things to humans qua humans in 'actuality' (*iʿtibār al-ḥukm fī marḥalat al-thubūt li-l-ḥukm*) are in a constant state of flux. Thus, it is inaccurate to claim equivalence between the notions of 'the actual' and 'actuality' given that 'the actual' regulative forms of the Qur'an corresponded to 'actuality' only during the revelatory and other similar contexts. To reiterate, the regulative forms of the Qur'an were formulations and issuances of God's considerations of the existential statuses of the relations of things to humans qua 'the immediate audience of the Qur'an' in actuality; in other words, they were formulated in light of God's consideration of the vertical and horizontal axes of existential growth of the individuals and collectivities that comprised the immediate audience of the Qur'an.

This section discusses (a) the existential features of the regulative forms of the Qur'an; (b) the implications of the non-equivalence of the notions of 'the actual' and 'actuality' on the presumption of the 'finality', 'universality', and 'infallibility' of the regulative forms of the Qur'an; (c) the worth of 'the apparent meaning qua conventional word-meaning association' of the regulative verses of the Qur'an beyond the revelatory and other similar contexts and the method of formulating regulative forms in the absence of such 'apparent meaning'; and (d) the role of the notions of 'essence' and 'form' in the formulation of new *societal* regulative forms in the existential framework.

---

48 For information on the notions of the vertical and horizontal axes of existential growth, see Abdul Hussain, 'The Conflict between the Actual and Apparent Regulations – Part 2', 7–9.

4.1 The Existential Features of the Regulative Forms of the Qur'an

The purpose of the regulative forms of the Qur'an was to regulate the lives of humans qua 'the immediate audience of the Qur'an' in their individual and collective capacities, and thereby facilitate the actualisation of their innate potential and hence their rational, moral, and spiritual growth. The fulfilment of this purpose (the growth of individuals and collectivities) is contingent upon regulative forms that address the needs of both the body and spirit of the individuals and collectivities of any given society. Congruence between regulative forms and the bodily and spiritual needs of individuals and collectivities results in balance (between these two aspects of the humans), and hence peace, harmony, and the fulfilment of the needs of individuals and collectivities without infringing upon the rights of the 'other'. Accordingly, the regulative forms of the Qur'an were formulated in light of the existential aptitudes and contexts of its immediate audience, as is evinced in all its regulative verses including the example of Q. 4:34 cited at the beginning of this chapter (the context of which was the case of domestic violence brought before the blessed Prophet). A chronological reading of the verses of the Qur'an reveals that regulative forms were few and minimalistic during the Meccan period of the revelatory era, that is, prior to the Prophet's migration to Medina, after which they increased gradually both in number and sophistication to accommodate the increasing aptitudinal and contextual needs of the individuals and collectivities of Medina.[49]

As discussed in previous sections, the regulative forms of the Qur'an were formulated in light of existential principles. They include the principles of 'justice', 'ease', and 'non-hardship' in religion. These were instrumental in the formulation and issuance of the forms of the essences or growth values of the regulations of the Qur'an. They contributed to ensuring that the regulative forms were formulated and issued in light of the existential aptitudes and contexts of the immediate audience of the Qur'an. In this way, the regulative forms addressed and catered for their bodily and spiritual needs, thereby facilitating optimal growth. The principles of 'justice', 'ease', and 'non-hardship' were not only influential during the process of formulating the regulative forms of the Qur'an, but rather they were also contributory in the process of modifying regulative forms in extenuating circumstances and thereby accommodating,

49 This is evinced from a chronological reading of the chapters of the Qur'an.

safeguarding, and continuing the applicability of the essences or values of those regulative forms in differing contexts.[50]

Other meta-legal principles that (a) are subsidiary, subordinate, and stem from the principles of 'justice', 'ease', and 'non-hardship', and (b) were influential in the formulation of the societal regulative forms of the Sunna specifically (alongside the existential aptitudes and contexts of the immediate audience of the Qur'an), include the precepts of 'the accuracy of testimonies' and 'just trade'.[51]

In view of the above, the *uṣūlī* assertion of the intrinsic 'bearability' and 'justness' of the regulative forms of the Qur'an is true with respect to the contexts (and existential aptitudes) they were formulated in and for and other similar contexts (and existential aptitudes) only; it is not true with respect to contexts (and existential aptitudes) differing from those of the revelatory era and other similar contexts.

---

50 See Q. 22:78: 'He has not laid upon you [any] hardship in religion'. This verse conveys the fact that the norm of God is to formulate and issue regulative forms in light of the principles of 'ease' and 'non-hardship' vis-à-vis individuals and collectivities. Examples of regulative verses offering alternative regulative forms when existing ones became 'unbearable' and in which the principles of 'ease' and 'non-hardship' are either explicitly stated or presupposed include (a) Q. 2:185, in which travellers and sick persons are exempted from fasting during Ramaḍān for the duration they are travelling or ill, respectively, and instructed to make up the missed days after the month has ended; the verse also provides the rationale for the modification, which is that 'God desires ease for you, and He does not desire hardship for you'; (b) Q. 2:239, in which those in danger are instructed to perform their prayers on foot or while riding and hence are to forego the acts of bowing and prostrating and the requirement of the direction of prayers; and (c) Q. 4:101–4, in which soldiers are instructed to shorten their prayers during battle.

Similarly, see Q. 16:90 vis-à-vis the principle of justice: 'Indeed, God commands justice and the doing of good'. Such verses exhort individuals and collectivities comprising the immediate audience of the Qur'an to abide by the principle of justice. Interestingly, such verses never define 'justice' on account of it being self-evident, existential, and contextual in its applications. 'Justice' is to give each thing its rightful due in accordance with its existential aptitude and context. Thus, in the case of Q. 4:34, cited at the beginning of this chapter, pertaining to the case of domestic violence brought before the Prophet, the egalitarian judgement of the Prophet was superseded by the said regulative verse based on the existential aptitudes of men and women generally at that time and the prevailing views and norms regarding gender-specific societal roles and spousal relations, rights, and responsibilities. The same is the case regarding the regulative verses pertaining to the shares of inheritance, divorce, and child maintenance.

51 These subsidiary and subordinate meta-legal principles (that is, the precepts of 'the accuracy of testimonies' and 'just trade') can be derived from Q. 2:282 and 4:29.

To summarise, the following are the main points vis-à-vis the existential and meta-legal principles that are either stated explicitly or presupposed in the regulative verses of the Qur'an:

1. In addition to the considerations of the existential aptitudes and contexts of the immediate audience of the Qur'an, the principles of 'justice', 'ease', and 'non-hardship' are the fundamental guiding principles in the formulation of regulative forms, the assignment of rights, and the modification of regulative forms.
2. The precepts of 'the accuracy of testimonies' and 'just trade' are examples of subsidiary guiding principles in the formulation of regulative forms, the assignment of rights, and the modification of regulative forms, in the domain of societal human interactions and trade.
3. The fundamental guiding principles also serve as means of absolving the duties of individuals who are unable to discharge them and for which there is no alternative.

This existential understanding of these fundamental guiding principles differs radically from the *uṣūlī* appreciation of them. The latter regard them mainly as referential precepts that legists appeal to and invoke in order to absolve individuals from adhering to the duties of the Sharīʿa regulative forms in extenuating circumstances; this means the relationship between them and regulative forms is horizontal, for they effect modifications in them after their issuance by God in individual cases of hardship.[52] In the existential framework, however, these guiding principles are meta-legal and hence instrumental at the level of (a) God's considerations of the regulative forms and rights in 'actuality', and hence His initial formulations of them as regulative forms and rights in the textual sources, and (b) God's considerations of modified regulative forms and rights in 'actuality', and hence His formulations of them as such in the textual sources.

4.2 The Implications of the Non-equivalence of the Notions of 'the Actual' and 'Actuality' on the Presupposition of the 'Finality', 'Universality', and 'Infallibility' of the Regulative Forms of the Qur'an

The existential property of growth means that everything in manifested existence is subject to existential flux. The implication of this is that the regulative forms of the Qur'an are not 'final', 'universal', and 'infallible' in (a) conveying and securing their essences or growth values in and for contexts (and

52 al-Muṣṭafawī, *al-Qawāʿid*, 9–15.

existential aptitudes) differing from those of the immediate audience of the Qur'an and hence (b) in facilitating growth in such contexts. However, their non-infallibility in fulfilling their purpose (which is to convey and secure their respective essences or growth values in order to facilitate the maximum possible growth) extends to the revelatory contexts themselves. This is because the regulative forms of the Qur'an qua 'regulative forms' could never achieve the ideal of being 'the best forms' (that is, apropos conveying and securing their essences and values, and hence in facilitating the maximum possible growth) with respect to every individual of the collectivities of the immediate audience of the Qur'an. This incapacity (to convey and secure their essences and values vis-à-vis every individual of the collectivity and hence facilitate the maximum possible growth) is an essential feature of regulative forms qua regulative forms due to their being formulated in light of 'the lowest common denominator' or 'the average' among any given collectivity in terms of existential aptitudes. Thus, it is more appropriate to state that the regulative forms of the Qur'an were 'optimal' in conveying and securing their essences and values in the contexts they were formulated for, rather than stating that they were 'final', 'universal', and 'infallible'.

The impossibility of the regulative forms of the Qur'an to be 'infallible' – with respect to every individual of the collectivities comprising the immediate audience of the Qur'an – can be evinced from the following examples of the verses of the Qur'an pertaining to the Sharīʿa-ordained regulative forms of testimony: (a) Q. 4:111–13 was revealed warning the Prophet of deceit on the part of witnesses after he had adjudicated a case based on their testimonies; he subsequently revised his judgement in light of new evidence; (b) Q. 5:106–8 affirms that the testimonies of two male witnesses is undermined when two other credible witnesses offer counter-testimonies; and (c) the tonality of Q. 2:282, which implies that the testimonies of two female witnesses are to be counted as a single testimony (of a male witness) judicially, affirms the fallibilistic nature of the process of establishing the facts and hence by extension the regulative forms governing it. Thus, it is clear that the Qur'an's regulative forms were formulated for its immediate audience within the limitations of their context and in accordance with the existential aptitudes of either 'the lowest common denominator' or 'the average' among them. Hence, its regulative forms could not be more than 'optimal', that is, they could never claim to be 'infallible' with respect to all the individuals they addressed in any genre of regulative forms (devotional practices, human actions and interactions, and consumables) let alone all the individuals of every possible and conceivable context.

Undoubtedly, the regulative forms of the Qur'an are 'infallible' in terms of their being formulated in accordance with the existential aptitudes and needs of either 'the lowest common denominator' or 'the average' among its immediate audience. They were 'the actual' regulative forms insofar as they did correspond to the existential statuses of the relations of things to humans qua 'the immediate audience of the Qur'an' in 'actuality'. However, they cannot be considered 'the actual' regulative forms, and hence 'infallible', vis-à-vis other individuals and collectivities of different existential aptitudes and contexts of (i) the same era, that is, along the horizontal axis, or (ii) different eras, that is, along the vertical axis; at most, its regulative forms could be claimed to be 'optimal' with respect to them too. Inevitably, as individuals and collectivities actualise their innate potential and grow over time, past regulative forms lose not only their 'infallibility' within the same region but also their 'optimality' in the same and other regions too. This is corroborated by the fact that successive scriptures were revealed periodically, and some earlier regulative forms of the Qur'an were abrogated by later ones. Past regulative forms lose their 'optimality' due to changes in the existential aptitudes and contexts of individuals and collectivities, and so they no longer convey and secure their essences or growth values, and hence facilitate the maximum possible growth, with respect to individuals and collectivities with different existential aptitudes in differing contexts. Therefore, it is clear that the forms of regulations are 'non-final' essentially.

In summary, the main points vis-à-vis the 'infallibility' of the regulative forms of the Qur'an are as follows:

1. The correctness of the attribution of the statuses of 'infallibility' and 'optimality' to the regulative forms of the Qur'an is restricted to the revelatory and other similar contexts only.
2. Beyond the revelatory and other similar contexts, the regulative forms of the Qur'an lose their 'optimality' along both the horizontal and vertical axes of the existential growth of individuals and collectivities.
3. Therefore, the regulative forms of the Qur'an are not 'final', 'universal', or 'infallible' in conveying and securing their essences and growth values, and hence facilitating the maximum possible growth, with respect to all people of every possible, conceivable context.

4.3 'The Apparent Meaning qua Conventional Word-Meaning Association' of the Regulative Verses of the Qur'an beyond the Revelatory and Other Similar Contexts, and the Formulation of Regulative Forms in the Absence of Such 'Apparent Meaning'

Given that there is 'change in actuality' and hence 'the actual' regulative forms of the Qur'an do not correspond with 'actuality' beyond their own and other similar contexts, no certitude-based sources or evidences exist from which 'the actual' regulative forms pertaining to contexts differing from the revelatory and other similar contexts can be extrapolated. This means 'the apparent meaning qua conventional word-meaning association' of the regulative verses of the Qur'an (which is the basis of the legists' extrapolations of the regulative forms of the Qur'an) do not yield regulative forms that correspond to the existential statuses of the relations of things to humans qua 'individuals and collectivities with different aptitudes and in differing contexts to those of the revelatory and other similar contexts' in 'actuality'. Inevitably, such regulative forms will be suboptimal in conveying and securing their essences or growth values, and hence facilitating the maximum possible growth, with respect to individuals and collectivities with different existential aptitudes and in differing contexts to those of the immediate audience of the Qur'an. Thus, it is untenable to regard the regulative forms of the Qur'an as 'infallible' regulative forms beyond the revelatory and other similar contexts on the basis of the presumptions that (a) the regulative verses of the Qur'an carry regulative forms that correspond to 'actuality' vis-à-vis humans qua humans, and hence (b) their appreciation via 'the apparent meaning qua conventional word-meaning association' yields God's intended regulative forms for all individuals and collectivities in every possible and conceivable context. In light of this inefficacy (of 'the apparent meaning qua conventional word-meaning association' of the regulative verses of the Qur'an to yield regulative forms corresponding to 'actuality' beyond the revelatory and other similar contexts), the question is how and by what means are regulative forms to be reformulated so that they convey and secure the essences or growth values of the original regulative forms of the Qur'an and hence continue to facilitate the maximum possible growth for individuals and collectivities of different existential aptitudes and contexts.

Legists are able to extrapolate the intended essences or growth values inherent in the regulative forms of the Qur'an on account of the fact that the regulative forms corresponded to the existential statuses of relations of things to humans qua 'the immediate audience of the Qur'an' in 'actuality' and hence were optimal vis-à-vis the rational, moral, and spiritual growth of the individuals and collectivities they were formulated for. As discussed in previous sections, the regulative forms of the Qur'an were formulated, and modified occasionally, in light of the fundamental guiding principles of 'justice', 'ease', and 'non-hardship' to ensure that they were optimal in conveying and securing the intended essences or growth values. Thus, the regulative forms of the Qur'an provide valuable insights into the process of their own formulation. In some of its regulative verses, the essences of its regulative forms are stated explicitly, and in the rest, the essences are implied and become manifest upon reading them existentially, that is, in light of the existential property and telos of growth. Once the particular growth facet or essence of any given regulative form of the Qur'an is known, then a newer regulative form can be conceived of in light of (i) the aforementioned guiding principles, (ii) an appreciation of the existential aptitudes and contexts of the individuals and collectivities it is being formulated for, (iii) the existential telos of growth, and (iv) all other means that assist in the reformulation of its particular growth facet or essence.[53] The justification for resorting to such means and sources, which are liable to be attributed with the charge of 'lying beyond the text of the Qur'an', is that the regulative forms of the Qur'an are themselves a reading of the existential contexts and aptitudes of the individuals and collectivities that comprised its immediate audience, and hence they are not extraneous means and sources in the least. Therefore, the means of formulating regulative forms on account of not being able to rely upon 'the apparent meaning qua conventional word-meaning association' of the regulative verses of the Qur'an is to determine the essences or growth values of the regulative forms of the Qur'an primarily and then to formulate befitting forms that convey and secure those essences.

4.4 The Role of the Notions of 'Essence' and 'Form' in the Formulation of New Societal Regulative Forms in the Existential Framework

Despite the diversity of genres, the regulative forms of the Qur'an can be reduced to two types from the perspective of their essences:

1. Those formulated on the basis of 'the general essence' or 'the generic existential facet of growth'; these comprise the societal regulative forms of the Qur'an mainly.
2. Those formulated on the basis of 'particular essences' or 'particular facets of growth' contained within the regulative forms of the Qur'an; they comprise regulative forms pertaining to devotional practices, consumables, and 'marriable/unmarriable persons'.

The societal regulative forms of the Qur'an were either endorsed or modified forms of pre-Qur'anic norms, and as such they were not novel introductions. Such pre-Qur'anic norms pertained to transactions, the marriage contract, divorce, retributive justice, inheritance, and so on. Norms requiring modification were presented in the regulative verses of the Qur'an as norms that had undergone modification in light of the principles of 'justice', 'ease', and 'non-hardship', 'human dignity and nobility', and the existential contexts and

53 Other means include knowledge from the humanities and sciences.

aptitudes of the people.[54] Since the principle of justice was the basis of the modifications of pre-Islamic societal norms in the Qurʾan, it is the yardstick in the existential framework to (a) judge whether the societal regulative forms of the Qurʾan are optimal in facilitating the growth of individuals and collectivities, and (b) modify them if they are not.[55]

As discussed in previous sections, the existential property of growth means there is constant flux in manifested existence. In the human domain, this translates as growth in existential aptitudes as a result of humans actualising their potential gradually. The principle of justice demands that such growth be met by modifying societal regulative forms so that they continue to be optimal in facilitating the rational, moral, and spiritual growth of individuals. Similarly, 'human dignity and nobility' dictates that such growth be mirrored by changes in the methods of punishments; thus, regulative forms instructing that the limbs of thieves be decapitated in order to deter theft and protect society can be replaced by regulative forms stipulating imprisonment and/or moral education, therapy, and community service so long as they achieve the same results, namely, deterring theft and protecting society.[56]

Generally, societal regulative forms can be conceived of and hence formulated independently of the textual sources of the Sharīʿa. The more demanding and detailed areas vis-à-vis the modification of the regulative forms of

54 Joseph Schacht, *An Introduction to Islamic Law* (Oxford: Clarendon Press, 1982), 6–14. Even the devotional practices of Islam had antecedent forms in pre-Islamic Arabia; for instance, the pilgrimage of *ḥajj* was a norm in pre-Islamic Arabia, as were the devotional practices of prayers and fasting, which were practised by pre-Islamic, Arabian Jews and Christians (see Q. 2:125, 22:26–27, 2:183; Abdul Hussain, 'A Functional Interpretation of *Zakāt*', 9). Similarly, norms pertaining to diet and 'marriable/unmarriable persons' were established and listed in the Bible (see Lev. 20:10 onwards). All such pre-existing norms were either endorsed or modified and supplemented in the regulative verses of the Qurʾan.

55 For instance, Q. 4:34 designated 'men' as 'the governors of women' and supplied the rationale for the designation, which was 'God's bestowal of existential merit upon men'; in other words, the superior rights conferred upon men were due to their existential state. It follows from this that if the existential aptitudes of women are equal to those of men in any given context (such as those that facilitate the actualisation of their potential), then the principle of justice demands that regulative forms are modified to be egalitarian vis-à-vis rights and responsibilities within the familial, marital, and societal domains. Consequently, men would not have the right to castigate their spouses, the unilateral right to divorce, double shares of inheritance, nor privileged societal positions, in such contexts. See Abdul Hussain, 'The Existential Perspective on "God's Bestowal of *Faḍl* upon Men"', 12–32.

56 In the context of such growth in existential aptitudes, 'human dignity and nobility' will necessitate the formulation of regulative forms that abrogate the regulative forms pertaining to slavery, concubinage, and 'the othering' of non-Muslims too.

the Qur'an in the existential framework are those pertaining to non-societal norms, that is, regulative forms in the domains of the devotional practices, consumables, and some areas of societal regulative forms. The methodology of determining the essences and values of such regulative forms is complex and requires lengthy expositions; and as such its delineation is beyond the scope of this chapter.[57]

5 Conclusion

Uṣūlīs consider the regulative forms of the Qur'an (*āyāt al-aḥkām*) to be infallible, immutable, and universal. This means they are applicable and enforceable vis-à-vis individuals and collectivities irrespective of their existential aptitudes and contexts. This position assumes the fixed and immutable nature of the statuses of the relations of things to humans qua humans vis-à-vis the values of 'benefit' and 'harm' in the mind of God. This is because they maintain that the regulative forms of the Qur'an are instances of 'the actual' (*al-wāqiʿī*) till the Day of Reckoning, which means they correspond to the existential statuses of the relations of things to humans qua humans in the mind of God (or 'actuality' – *al-wāqiʿ*) for the remainder of human existence upon this earth.

57 For an introduction to the application of the notions of 'essence' and 'form' as per the existential framework generally and in the domains of regulative forms pertaining to the devotional practices and consumables in particular, see Arif Abdul Hussain, *Islam and God-Centricity: Plurality and Mutability of Religion* (Birmingham: Sajjadiyya Press, 2022), 57–173; Abdul Hussain, 'A Functional Interpretation of *Zakāt*'; Abdul Hussain, 'The Existential Perspective on "God's Bestowal of *Faḍl* upon Men"'. The following is an example of the essence of a regulative form in the domain of devotional practices: based on the verses of the Qur'an on fasting (Q. 2:183–85, 2:187) and the *ḥadīth* literature (the narrations of the Prophet and his blessed family), the legist is able to discern that the essence of the obligatory practice of fasting during the month of Ramaḍān is 'to abstain from sexual activity and the consumption of food and drink for the majority of the waking hours of each day of the month in accordance with what is "bearable" for the "average" person and for the sake of the refinement of the soul'. With respect to the immediate audience of the Qur'an, this essence was conveyed and secured by the regulative form of the Qur'an stipulating that each fast commenced at dawn and terminated at sunset, that is, a conventional day of twelve and a half to sixteen hours depending on which season the month of Ramaḍān fell in any given year in the Hejaz. In regions of the earth with abnormally long or short periods of daylight, the regulative form would not stipulate the duration of each fast in terms of 'sunrise' and 'sunset', for that would entail contravening the 'essence'; rather, the duration would be defined in terms of the conventional meaning of 'day' and 'night'. Additionally, recourse would be made to the medical sciences to ascertain what constitutes 'a fast' that is 'bearable' vis-à-vis the body and given that it is to be performed daily for a month.

The result is a conflation in their discourse between the notions of 'the actual' (*al-wāqiʿī*) and 'actuality' (*al-wāqiʿ*).

However, the Qur'an is emphatic that its regulative forms were based on the principles of 'justice', 'ease', and 'non-hardship'. This means they were formulated in light of the contexts and existential aptitudes of the individuals and collectivities they were addressing, which proves that the regulative forms of the Qur'an were contextual and not acontextual, and hence they were not infallible, immutable, and universal; it also is demonstrative of the existential, fundamental, and meta-legal nature of the principles of 'justice', 'ease', and 'non-hardship' in the formulation of its regulative forms. Moreover, the dynamic nature of manifested existence as per 'the principiality of substantial motion' (*aṣālat al-ḥaraka al-jawhariyya*) means that the relations of things to humans are in flux, and hence their existential statuses in 'actuality' are subject to change. Consequently, the notions of 'the actual' and 'actuality' must be distinguished from each other. This is because the regulative forms of the Qur'an classify as instances of 'the actual' during the revelatory and other similar contexts only and not for other differing contexts; hence, they only correspond to the existential statuses of the relations of things to humans qua 'the immediate audience of the Qur'an' in 'actuality' and not to the existential statuses of the relations of things to humans qua 'humans of differing existential aptitudes and contexts to those of the revelatory era' in 'actuality'.

The following are the conclusions of this chapter: (a) the formulation and issuance of the regulative forms of the Qur'an were based on the existential statuses of the relations of things to humans qua 'the immediate audience of the Qur'an' in 'actuality', which in turn were based on the considerations of the existential aptitudes and contexts of its immediate audience and the principles of 'justice', 'ease', and 'non-hardship'; (b) the regulative forms of the Qur'an do not correspond to 'actuality' beyond their own and other similar contexts, and hence are not optimal vis-à-vis the rational, moral, and spiritual growth of individuals and collectivities in different contexts and with diverse existential aptitudes; (c) despite this non-correspondence with 'actuality', the regulative forms of the Qur'an do yield the 'general' and 'specific' essences or growth values that they encapsulated, safeguarded, and upheld; and (d) accordingly, it is possible to formulate new regulative forms in light of (i) the 'general' and 'specific' essences or growth values of the regulative forms of the Qur'an and the Prophet, (ii) the existential aptitudes and contexts of the individuals and collectivities of newer contexts, and (iii) the principles of 'justice', 'ease', and 'non-hardship'. In this way, legits will ensure that regulative forms continue to facilitate the growth of individuals and collectivities in different contexts and with diverse existential aptitudes optimally.

Finally, based on the distinction between the notions of 'the actual' and 'actuality', it is clear that the regulative forms of the Qur'an were never meant to be deemed as eternal or universal regulative forms that are to be applied in all times and places. Therefore, there is 'no finality' with respect to the 'forms' of the regulations of the Qur'an; however, there is 'finality' (and hence 'eternality', 'universality', and 'infallibility') with respect to the 'essences' or 'growth values' inherent in the 'forms' of the regulations of the Qur'an.

Bibliography

Abdul Hussain, Arif. 'The Conflict between the Actual and Apparent Regulations – Part 1: The Theoretical Foundations of *Uṣūl al-Fiqh* and the *Uṣūlī* Resolutions'. Shaykh Arif (blog). www.shaykharif.com/blog/the-conflict-between-the-actual-and-apparent-regulations.

Abdul Hussain, Arif. 'The Conflict between the Actual and Apparent Regulations – Part 2: The Solution of "the Existential Framework"'. Shaykh Arif (blog). www.shaykharif.com/blog/the-conflict-between-the-actual-and-apparent-regulations.

Abdul Hussain, Arif. 'The Existential Perspective on "God's Bestowal of *Faḍl* upon Men" and Its Implication on *Qiwāma*'. In *Islam and the Institution of Marriage: Legal and Sociological Approaches*, edited by Katherine Lemons and Laurens de Rooij, 9–32. Birmingham: AMI Press, 2023.

Abdul Hussain, Arif. 'The Existential Perspective on the Meaning and Implication of Impure Substances within Shīʿī Jurisprudential Discourse'. In *The Regulations of Purity in Islam: Proceedings of the 8th AMI Contemporary Fiqhī Issues Workshop*, edited by Hashim Bata, 79–110. Birmingham: AMI Press, 2022.

Abdul Hussain, Arif. 'A Functional Interpretation of *Zakāt* and the Inclusion of Contemporary Taxation as Its Legitimate Form'. In *The Efficacy of Financial Structures for Islamic Taxes and Dues: Proceedings of the 7th AMI Contemporary Fiqhī Issues Workshop*, edited by Wahid M. Amin, 8–31. Birmingham: AMI Press, 2020.

Abdul Hussain, Arif. *Islam and God-Centricity: Plurality and Mutability of Religion*. Birmingham: Sajjadiyya Press, 2022.

Abdul Hussain, Arif. 'The Primacy of the Freedoms of Thought and Expression within the Existential Framework: Implications on Sharīʿa Regulations, Rights, and Freedoms'. In *Free Speech, Scholarly Critique and the Limits of Expression in Islam: Proceedings of the 9th AMI Contemporary Fiqhī Issues Workshop*, edited by Wahid M. Amin, 10–39. Birmingham: AMI Press, 2022.

Ḥubbullāh, Ḥaydar. 'Introduction to Qur'anic Jurisprudence'. [In Arabic.] Hobbollah, 19 September 2015. https://hobbollah.com/p/44657/المدخل-إلى-الفقه-القرآني.

Ibn Kathīr, Ismāʿīl. *Tafsīr al-Qur'ān al-ʿaẓīm*. Beirut: Dār wa-Maktabat al-Hilāl, 1990.

Kadivar, Mohsen. 'From Traditional Islam to Islam as an End in Itself'. *Die Welt des Islams* 51, no. 3–4 (2011): 462–71.
Khabbāz, Munīr. 'Constancy and Change in the Textual Evidences'. [In Arabic.] al-Moneer, 3 October 2019. www.almoneer.org/?act=av&action=view&id=4124.
al-Khū'ī, al-Sayyid Abū al-Qāsim al-Mūsawī. *The Prolegomena to the Quran*. Translated by Abdulaziz A. Sachedina. Qom: Ansariyan Publications, 1992.
al-Kulaynī, Muḥammad b. Ya'qūb. *Uṣūl al-kāfī*. Beirut: Manshūrāt al-Fajr, 2007.
al-Muṣṭafawī, Muḥammad Kāẓim. *al-Qawā'id*. Qom: Mu'assasat al-Nashr al-Islāmī, 2014.
al-Muẓaffar, Muḥammad Riḍā. *Uṣūl al-fiqh*. Qom: Intishārāt Ismā'īliyān, 2004.
al-Ṣadr, Muḥammad Bāqir. *Durūs fī 'ilm al-uṣūl*. Qom: Markaz al-Abḥāth wa-l-Darāsāt al-Takhaṣṣuṣiyya li-l-Shahīd al-Ṣadr, 2005.
Ṣanqūr 'Alī, Muḥammad. *al-Mu'jam al-uṣūlī*. Qom: Dār al-Mujtabā, 2001.
Schacht, Joseph. *An Introduction to Islamic Law*. Oxford: Clarendon Press, 1982.
al-Subḥānī, Ja'far. 'Islamic Beliefs in Light of the School of Ahl al-Bayt.' [In Arabic.] Shia Online Library. https://shorturl.at/NwcUJ.
al-Ṭabarsī, Faḍl b. Ḥasan. *Majma' al-bayān fī tafsīr al-Qur'ān*. Beirut: Mu'assasat al-A'lamī li-l-Maṭbū'āt, 1995.
Ṭabāṭabā'ī, Muḥammad Ḥusayn. *Bidāyat al-ḥikma*. Qom: Mu'assasat al-Nashr al-Islāmī, 2018.
al-Ṭanṭāwī, Muḥammad Sayyid. *al-Tafsīr al-wasīṭ li-l-Qur'ān al-karīm*. Cairo: Maṭba'at al-Sa'āda, 1983.

PART 5

Contemporary Legal and Ethical Trajectories

CHAPTER 15

Rules and Rituals in the Qurʾan: Is There a Role for Reasons?

Oliver Leaman

It is often difficult to find reasons for religious rituals. Some look as though they have obvious purposes, but others less so, and this has led to a lively discussion about how to ground the rules of religion in something other than divine fiat. The argument here is that there is nothing else one can ground them on, and certainly not on the idea of defining a role for the *maqāṣid al-sharīʿa,* the intentions behind Islamic law. Trying to explain rules of ritual in terms of human welfare is replete with problems, and some of these will be explored here. A better source for explanation of the rules is represented by God. God tells believers how He wants them to act without necessarily explaining the reason, and this might be objectionable in a human being but is appropriate for a deity. It does not follow from this argument that our rules are based on no reasons at all, only that the reasons are not always if ever available to us. The language of the Qurʾan renders any other conclusion implausible.

When should a law tell us why we should obey it? This issue arises in religious ethics, and especially in those religions that are law based like Islam and Judaism. Here we will limit ourselves to talking mainly about Islam, but comparisons will be made with other legal and religious systems.

A good place to start is with the distinction between civil and divine law. When a government enacts legislation it is normal to explain the point of it. Even if citizens disagree with the law, they still understand why it is there. They may disagree with its purpose and rationale, yet they should be able to understand it. We should qualify this by acknowledging that a lot of law is too complex to understand, which is why presumably there is work for lawyers. Yet if we set ourselves the task of understanding it, we could in principle do so – there is nothing mysterious about it. It may be that it has a malign intention, and that intention can be devised and grasped. We may get it wrong, of course, or only appreciate the point of the law a long time after it has come into force. Civil law that appears to be arbitrary will be difficult to apply since there is no sound framework for decision-making among the legal authorities.

Religious law is different, in two respects. One rather significant one is that it is perfect and stems from the creator of its subjects. The other is that the thinking behind it might not be accessible to us, given that we are mortal and

 | HTTPS://DOI.ORG/10.1163/9789004755567-017

limited and God is the opposite. This leads to interesting discussions of religious law where adherents of a faith end up supporting something that seems to be legal but is obviously morally problematic. One might point here to slavery or the rather distinct roles for men and women in Islam. While at one time there was nothing unusual about such institutions, today there is, and yet divine law is supposed to be unchanging and perfect. How could it have been right then and wrong now? Sometimes apologists suggest that while the law is problematic, it is less problematic than the laws which prevailed at the time, and so counts as an advance on the existing ways of doing things. Perhaps God is using the law to point us in the right direction and suggesting future changes that might be beneficial, but that suggests that He could not have legislated perfectly in the first place, and that is not how religious law is normally seen. It is perfect from the start and we need to establish it entirely in line with what the divine author specifies.

Then there are laws for which no rationale is provided. The very first law laid down by God in the Jewish bible is one such law, not to eat from a particular tree. God says the inhabitants of the Garden of Eden should not do it, but not why, something that the snake made good use of in tempting them to break the law. God told them it would not be in their interests to break the law, and indeed that is how it turned out. They are punished for breaking a law they do not understand, a theme which is continued in the Book of Job. Here Job calls on God to explain how the ways in which things work out in the world are just, because they often seem to be arbitrary and capricious. God's reply is that He is very powerful and knows everything, unlike us. This brings us to an important difference between divine and human law, and that is the existence of mystery in the affairs of the world. That is, we may accept that everything that happens is caused by God and is just but not accept that we understand how this is the case. That seems to be where Job is left, and he is happy at least to have got a reply from the deity.[1]

This brings us to two ways of seeing religion. One view is that it is straightforward and perspicuous: we are told to do things that are in our interest, and we have no difficulty in finding out what we should do. Then there is another view in accordance with which we often do not understand why we are asked to act as we are told, and do not expect to get that information in the first place. It might even be suggested that we do not need such information if we have trust in the source of the legislation, ultimately of course the deity. We are after all so different from God that it is quite reasonable to think that we would

1 The Job in the Qur'an, Ayyūb, is of course a very different character; see Oliver Leaman, *Evil and Suffering in Jewish Philosophy* (Cambridge: Cambridge University Press, 1999).

not be able to plumb His thinking in any case. It is worth spending some time looking at the language of the Qur'an on God, since much of it magnifies the huge gap between us and Him, and surely the corollary is that we would not understand what He does, and perhaps could not. So there is no problem in not really understanding some at least of what we are commanded to do and what to resist.

1 The Peripatetic Thinkers

This is an issue on which the *falāsifa* were particularly interested given their adherence to a way of understanding religion that is too difficult for most members of the community to understand. That is, for them you really need to be a philosopher in order to understand religion, and yet of course most people are not philosophers. Are these poor creatures going to have to spend their lives in ignorance and confusion? Certainly not, since they have available to them a variety of religions and even more importantly rituals that they can understand. It makes sense to them since it is expressed in language they can understand, language that is very material in character. Most people are only used to thinking in concrete terms and would not understand what the philosophers thought religion was all about, since the latter relied on more spiritual and abstract versions of that religion. Most people could not work with these ideas and indeed should not since it would threaten their faith to do so and probably also the lives of the philosophers, who would be accused of heresy. This is not to claim that ordinary believers are incapable of understanding what the philosophers can, although this may be the case, but more that their interests do not lie in that direction and so they are provided with a version of the truth that is agreeable to them, and is actually also of course true.

This is not the place to go into the details of such a theoretical position, nor to assess its validity.[2] It sounds cynical and patronising, but we may reflect that there are many areas of life where we give up our thinking skills to those we trust to guide us in areas like health, taxes, and technology. When the plumber comes to fix the bathroom we are not saying that this is something we could not possibly ever understand how to do. When he explains to us what the problem is he or she will express themselves in a way that they think their audience will grasp and will try to leave out the technical issues that go above the heads of their customers. After all, if the latter understood plumbing, they would fix

2 These issues are dealt with in Oliver Leaman, *Islamic Philosophy: An Introduction* (Cambridge: Polity, 2009).

the issue themselves, other things being equal. We could try to understand and do everything ourselves but it would not be an efficient way of operating. Like countries that try to produce everything themselves, it often can be done but involves great effort which could be better employed in concentrating on just a few more specialised activities.

It might be argued that this example does not work for our relationship with God, which after all is not something that relies on skill or training but is based on what the Qur'an calls our *fiṭra*, our natural disposition. Even animals are said to worship God, and so it is regarded as something smooth and easy, not something that requires huge intellectual effort or skill. Islam refers to religion as something easy to follow, and for most followers it surely is just something they do and think about as part of their ordinary lives, without huge mental conflict or ratiocination. After all, and this is something the *falāsifa* emphasise, religion is for everyone while philosophy is only for a limited number of people. It would have been cruel for God to have created everyone differently and then made them suffer due to that difference.

2 The Role of *Taqlīd*

Should we just obey the rules because of *taqlīd*, the blind imitation of others and their practices? Certainly blind imitation is always going to be questionable. It also runs into the danger of making religion stale and boring, something that al-Ghazālī sought to challenge in his *Iḥyāʾ ʿulūm al-dīn*, which literally refers to the breathing of new life into the rules of religion. Any practice can be so automatic that we lose our enthusiasm for what it is for, like a marriage that is so lengthy it becomes stale. The way to stop ritual from becoming stale is to recognise that over time it will have different sorts of meaning for us and we should accept those meanings and work with them. For something to be the framework within which we act it needs to be in the background most of the time, although capable of surviving occasional examination. Ibn Taymiyya also steadfastly opposed *taqlīd* and following the rules of any one *madhhab*, and certainly there is a great deal of flexibility in going back to the interpretation of the law as practised by the *salaf*. For one thing what one thinks that interpretation is can be very much a personal opinion, perhaps explaining why Fazlur Rahman sees Ibn Taymiyya as someone interested in opening the gate to absolute *ijtihād*.[3] The rules of a legal school may be seen as restrictive but, on the other hand, there are rules, and by contrast, the *ittibāʿ al-salaf* might seem

3 Fazlur Rahman, *Islam* (London: Weidenfeld and Nicolson, 1966), 79.

to throw us very much at the mercy of whoever takes on himself or herself the task of explaining what they think the views of the early generations were.

This is the problem that al-Ghazālī identified: religion needs to be revived since over time it can become tedious and over-familiar, so that we just fall into an unthinking role. He wants us to see religion as exciting and intellectually and personally fulfilling, not just some rote exercises in behaviour and tradition. The *Iḥyā'* expands on this at length, and his putting down of tradition is most marked by his casual use of *ḥadīth*, where he often abandons a strong *ḥadīth* for a weaker one, as though the whole science of *ḥadīth* is really irrelevant as far as he is concerned. He is just interested in the effect that religion has on the emotions and thinking processes of the believer, and how he gets there appears to be rather secondary. Sufism has often been controversial because of its emphasis on feeling and lack of emphasis on traditional rules, although al-Ghazālī of course tries to reconcile both in his *Iḥyā'*. One cannot help suspecting that for him it is the emotions that are significant without which religion has no flavour, and he puts his finger on a significant issue. When we do something a lot we tend to stop thinking about it, it becomes automatic and unexamined, and we might worry, then, that although the ritual is correct, the feelings that go with it are not, like a relationship between people which is still perfectly proper but essentially empty.

3 The *Maqāṣid* Strategy

This is where the connection between *maqāṣid* language and how we should think of religious rules comes in. Once we know the point of what we are doing, or are persuaded to think about it, then the rule becomes refreshed. It is not something we just do but has a point and a rationale. But we always knew this anyway, we just did not know what the rationale was. God would not ask us to do things arbitrarily, there must be a point to them, although in some cases it may be that the point is just to dispose us to do what God tells us to do. Any training tends to involve doing things like following instructions we do not understand but just in order to get us to follow instructions. A language is often like that: we follow certain rules, we do not know why they are the rules, but they are and we obey them if we want to speak and write the language. If we are forever going to try to work out why the rules are the rules, as linguists may do, we will find it impedes our casual use of the language. Would God really give us rules to follow that have no point except to train us to obey Him? Well, think of the laws of purity in any religion, and it is not difficult to accept their arbitrary nature. Why should certain foods or drinks which we know are fine to eat and drink be banned, or why should certain animals or even people be regarded as impure and requiring some ceremony afterwards to clean ourselves from contact with them, unless they have some communicable disease of course? It is of course in itself ridiculous, but as a measure to separate one community from another and help to acclimatise people to do what they are told to do even in cases where it seems to have no point it is very effective.

The trouble with the *maqāṣid al-sharīʿa* approach is that despite the sophistication of its adherents such as al-Shāṭibī it is banal and dangerous. It is banal because it ends up with justifying law in terms of some general formula that is so loose it really does not have any purchase on reality. A law is supposed to increase our welfare, we are told, and this is so vague that one might wonder if a kind of rule utilitarianism is being advocated here. How is general welfare defended or increased by family law which is weighted towards men and we know has caused a great deal of human misery over the centuries? This is not a charge directed at any particular religious legislation but Jewish and Islamic law do seem to be partial to one side of the gender divide, and legislation that is skewed to one side of the gender divide often leads to suffering and inequality. Perhaps it would be worse for most of us most of the time if we did not live under a system of such laws, but how would we establish this and what would count as evidence? The danger exists that once we think we can establish why we have a law, we can quite easily work out ways of changing it if we think the rationale makes it desirable. In general, religious law places quite specific limits on how far others may be harmed but it is easy to make exceptions when you can claim that public welfare is at stake, a slippery slope that is familiar to critics of utilitarianism and its project of cashing in moral claims in terms of happiness. What looks like flexibility to one person may look like self-serving casuistry to another, and rightly so.

But we are told that the laws are not arbitrary so how can we disengage them from aims like our welfare? What we should consider is whether how they contribute to our welfare should be available to us. This is a familiar feature of older religions such as Judaism, where it is often freely admitted that some laws and rituals are so old that we do not know why they exist. We can speculate and people do, but none of this speculation solves the issue. There is an interesting juxtaposition of words in the Torah when the Israelites are said to have committed themselves to the law before they heard what it was (*Exodus* 24:7), a very imprudent thing to do, but, on the other hand, if God asks us to do something should we quibble and ask why? Subsequently the Jews did not succeed in upholding their original bold choice, and the Torah itself is full of backsliding, not to mention the Prophets and the Writings. This is something that the Qur'an of course criticises the Jews for in the second sura. Perhaps if we do not really know why we should follow a law we are less likely to follow it. Religions are very keen to simplify law and embody it in a few or even one general principle, with the idea, no doubt, that if believers know what the law is for, they will be more assiduous in performing it. This idea is worth unpacking, since it is a popular trope in religion. In Judaism, for instance, there are many attempts at summarising law and finding a nice neat principle that we can refer to when considering how to behave. There is an entertaining debate about this in which different formulae are in competition with each other, and the winner is a very boring reference to temple sacrifices. What is the relevance of this to a time when there is no temple nor any sacrifices? The answer is taken to be that this ritual involves daily religious commitment, regular orientation towards God, and that is what religion is about. The specific point of the law itself is nothing we can be expected to know about. It was proclaimed so long ago and in such different circumstances. Perhaps there is a reason why *niyya* or intention is not a term found in the Qur'an. *Irāda* or volition is, of course, but the Qur'an had every opportunity to say what the intention of the law is, and declined to do so. Perhaps this is not information we should have, or would understand, or is unnecessary to those who are really *muttaqīn*.

Yet the *maqāṣid* approach remains popular and influential. Its basis rests on the significance of five principles, maintenance of religion, life, intellect, progeny, and property. These have been supported as aims of the law by al-Ghazālī, al-Shāṭibī, al-Ḥakīm al-Tirmidhī, and al-Juwaynī. They represent *maṣlaḥa*, welfare, and our interests, or so we are told, and yet the evidence is not there to support such a view. Why are there restrictions about food which we know is perfectly acceptable to human bodies? Finding a reason for rules of purity is always tough unless we go for the option that the rule is just that we do what God tells us to do. There is no obvious welfare in not touching certain people, nor in wearing particular clothes, or even in praying in a certain way – unless that is one thinks that this is what God wants us to do and so we do it. The welfare here is not that of the eventual reward, although that is a constant Qur'anic theme. The welfare comes from knowing that we have done our best to please someone to whom we are attached, someone we trust and admire. It is like a child setting the table for breakfast the next day because she knows her father would like it to be done. She does not do it to avoid punishment nor to acquire a reward, but just because of her relationship to him. This does lead to her welfare in the sense that she feels she has completed a task worth doing, and that feeling may be stronger than the tedium of the daily task. But it may not. The significant point here is that the welfare is irrelevant to the meaning of the task, and so welfare cannot be the rationale for religious law.

4 Who Is a Muslim?

Here we need to take seriously the idea that being a Muslim involves, among other things, being guided by the Qur'an, and that guidance is directed at the *muttaqīn* (Q. 2:2), those who are already aware of God. They believe in the *ghayb*, the unseen, and that means that they believe that not everything needs to be on the surface or obvious, a point to which we shall return at the end. The world was not created for no reason at all (Q. 3:191) or for divine amusement (Q. 44:38), and we are told that there are many signs in that creation of what is behind it and how well it is done (Q. 42:29, 45:4). There is no reason to think that we can understand what they all are, however. The language of *maqāṣid* goes against this theme in the Qur'an, suggesting that what we have in the Book is an account of the higher objectives of Islam. God taught Adam the names of things (Q. 2:31–33) and forbade him and his wife from eating from a particular tree, something Iblīs (Satan) persuaded him to do. He was given an order, he did not obey it, he was given no reason for the order, and later on he was forgiven since this is a sign to those who disobey that unless they repent there are serious consequences (Q. 2:39). Iblīs had sound arguments for refusing to bow to Adam, arguments God rejects, and he is punished for his disobedience, and refuses to repent. Of course, he has a role to play in the life of humanity from that time on, but it is worth pointing out God refers to the *ghayb* when justifying His decision to elevate Adam over Iblīs. Adam's knowledge is always limited, as is Iblīs's, and piety is to be aware of this and try to act in accordance with divine instructions.

One might mention the danger of the assiduous completion of empty rituals. It is worth resurrecting a question that Aristotle asks in the seventh chapter of the *Nicomachean Ethics* about morality, where he wonders if it is better to do the right thing but struggle against a strong desire not do so, or whether it is better to do the right thing without ever being tempted contrariwise. He suggests that the virtuous person is not subject to being tempted. The equivalent here would be to ask whether it is better to act in accordance with religion while being strongly tempted often to do differently, or to just find it easy to go along with religion and never know what it would be like to even contemplate another course of action, except perhaps as a vague possibility. This thought experiment would need to be an option to distinguish us from angels, for whom going against what is divinely commanded is an impossibility. Or so it is said, but Iblīs of course managed to go against the grain, and perhaps he was created uniquely in order to do so, since he had a divine role to play in fostering our evil side. The Qur'an emphasises how religion fits in with our natural inclinations and Islam in particular is supposed to value balance and ease in living, and so the various duties and tasks we are asked to perform should not normally be experienced as arduous or extreme. If they become too automatic and smooth, though, perhaps we will not really orient ourselves to God, since we are so comfortable with religious practices and are not forced to think much about what they represent. They are just there, like our lives, as Wittgenstein would say.[4] Does this mean they are empty, though? Not at all; like an old friendship, one does not have to constantly revive our passion for a friend as though one were starting on a new relationship. The familiar behaviour of the past continues into the future and establishes a pattern that regularity brings with it.

5 Ritual and Routine: a Jewish Example

Spinoza would be suspicious of the idea that laws in religion are not obviously rational. He wanted to emphasise the rationality of the principles as he saw it that religions are based upon. Attaching ourselves to aspects that are not those principles is to take the wrong view of religions and what they are about. He does have a point here since it is difficult to justify someone adopting a peripheral feature of an activity and confusing it with something essential. On the other hand, the distinction between them is often quite difficult to establish and this is something that the Talmud discusses frequently. Some commentators seek to summarise the Torah in a neat and pithy sentence that expresses its essence. The most famous is Hillel who, when asked to do this, says we should do to others what we would like them to do to us, and then he says that we should study, an addendum that is often conveniently forgotten. But others point to some obscure ritual, and suggest that is the essence of the religion. We may doubt the value of seeking the essence of any religion, of course, but the idea of summarising something is important, since it enables us to think about what we see as the key words or concepts. The danger of such an approach is that it looks like we might think of that summary as representing what the religion is all about, and everything else linked with it is superfluous. Levinas sees ritual as something that makes it possible for us to be religious since it provides a structure for our lives and a discipline in accordance with which we can orient ourselves toward God and the rest of humanity. He is obviously impressed

4 Ludwig Wittgenstein, *Philosophical Investigations*, trans. G.E.M. Anscombe (Oxford: Basil Blackwell, 1958), 559.

with a passage from the aggadic story found in *Ayn Yaakov*,[5] which is a compilation of such stories, that he quotes.[6] It is about a debate among the major characters of the Mishnah as to what is the single most significant passage in the Torah. What is the one verse that seems to express the essence of Jewish life more than any other? This is a popular activity in religion, trying to summarise the religion in terms of some important idea or phrase. A whole variety of stirring and general principles are mentioned, like that of Hillel. Some are important prayers or general moral principles. Shimon Ben Pazi says we have found a more inclusive verse than all of those and it is 'The first lamb you shall sacrifice in the morning and the second lamb you shall sacrifice in the evening' (*Shemot* 29:39; *Bamidbar* 28:4) (referring to the daily *Tamid* (perpetual) offering brought every morning and evening). Rabbi Ploni stood up and said that the halacha (religious law) is in accordance with Ben Pazi. Yet the other general claims seem much more fundamental to what religion is about. It is like in Islam comparing a rule about washing before prayer and the general principle to do with justice and kindness. The latter seem much more fundamental than the former.

What seems rather perplexing is the teaching of Shimon Ben Pazi. How does his statement about the daily offering of a lamb brought morning and evening compare with the seemingly all-encompassing statements of the previous sages? How can a Midrash state that the accepted view is that of Ben Pazi? After all, he talks about daily lambs and the others talk of fundamental principles. The Maharal suggests that the explanation of Ben Pazi is taken to be a greater teaching of the Torah as it emphasises that a person should serve God regularly and carry out the orders that he has received. Ben Pazi believes the only way to transform our lives in a sustainable way is through such continual daily conduct. It has often been argued that Judaism is more about actions than abstract ideas and the daily carrying out of the rituals and practices of the religion mentioned by Ben Pazi is in line with this approach.

The passage about the *olat tamid*, the daily sacrifice, is legal or halakhic in direct and obvious ways, whereas the rather more abstract competing suggestions are not, so we should not be surprised that it wins the competition. Spinoza offers 'To love God above all things and one's neighbor as oneself'.[7]

---

5 See R. Jacob Ibn Habib, 'Introduction to *Ein Yaakov*', Sefaria, www.sefaria.org/Ein_Yaakov_(Glick_Edition)?tab=contents.

6 Emmanuel Levinas, *Difficult Freedom: Essays on Judaism*, trans. Seán Hand (Baltimore: Johns Hopkins University Press, 1997), 19.

7 Spinoza, *Tractatus Theologic-Politicus*, Gebhardt Edition (1925), trans. Samuel Shirley (Leiden: Brill, 1991), 165.

This is even worse in leading us further away from practical activities. Even if we focus on loving our neighbours we are left in perplexity, since what does it mean in terms of what we should do? But the daily ritual is easy to understand and doing something on a regular basis just because God has ordered it is a very tangible indication of our attitude towards Him. Similarly, we could move on from that in ways that Spinoza would dislike, to suggest that the rules of Judaism give their practitioners a way of expressing their love for God and those around them in tangible and comprehensible ways. A ritual is established and followed and it allows believers to link themselves with their creator and each other, which is after all the point of ritual.

6 Rituals and Rationality

The routine can continue to link people quite acceptably even though it is routine, and in the words of Ben Pazi, a relationship based on regularity should be the basis of such a friendship, and not on wondering what the relationship is actually for. That is the trouble with *maqāṣid* language: it is always looking at a rule teleologically, asking what its aims and objectives are, whereas for much of life we want to stay in the moment and make the most of it. Where it is going or why we are there in the first place is not something we need to contemplate much of the time.

Does not this discussion avoid recognising that there are areas of the world where religious law is carried out without question or refinement, countries like Afghanistan or in the past Saudi Arabia, among others? Similarly there are countries where government legislation is carried out without murmur or objection, since once the law has emerged in the accepted way, it is as the Book of Daniel has it, like the laws of the Medes and the Persians, irrevocable (6:12) – until presumably the Medes and the Persians decide to change it, as seems to have occurred in the Book of Esther. They would not even need to say it had changed, but the ways in which the law went on to be interpreted would make clear that the original ways of understanding the law were no longer apposite now. Some people like the idea that justice is short and sharp, strict and direct, but in practice even in states where this is the principle behind much legislation, the facts on the ground are very different. Those states, for example, that support the idea of capital punishment for many offences do not exhibit equal application of those penalties, on the whole. The wealthy and the well-connected often escape such sentences, if they are ever sentenced at all, while the poor and marginal are less fortunate. There is always scope for judges to be swayed in their judgements by arguments at best or other forms of pressure and influence, and for them to take all sorts of factors into account. Those factors will vary with the relevant context, such as scientific knowledge, the political situation, and so on, and it is right that it do so. The hermeneutic authority is devolved to some sort of local body that better encapsulates where the community is and what its views of the law are.

This seems to be a strange form of argument when we consider divine law, since it assumes that God could not get the law quite right from the start and needs others to fill in the blanks. The analogy is, of course, only an analogy but the idea that there is something special about how the law originates does not imply that it is perfectly determinate. It may be perfect but it still needs to be applied and it is here that the problems arise in thinking that all one needs is the law. This is a point often made about ritual too, to counter the idea that rituals just go on and on in an unchanging manner. That idea is very important to many believers but it defies our understanding of religious history. Rituals do change all the time, and it is important that they do, since religions have to be flexible if they are to survive changing circumstances.

There is a famous story of the founder of Hasidism, the Baal Shem Tov, and Wiesel reports it thus:

> Whenever the Jews were threatened with disaster, the Baal Shem Tov would go to a certain place in the forest, light a fire, and say a special prayer. Always a miracle would occur, and the disaster would be averted.
>
> In the later times when disaster threatened, the Maggid of Mezritch, his disciple, would go to the same place in the forest and say, 'Master of the Universe, I do not know how to light the fire, but I can say the prayer.' And again the disaster would be averted.
>
> Still later, his disciple, Moshe Leib of Sasov, would go to the same place in the forest and say, 'Lord of the World, I do not know how to light the fire or say the prayer, but I know the place and that must suffice.' And it always did.
>
> When Israel of Rizhyn needed intervention from heaven, he would say to God, 'I no longer know the place, nor how to light the fire, nor to say the prayer, but I can tell the story and that must suffice.' … And it did.[8]

It is worth pointing out that the issue in this story is not whether to follow a ritual, but how to act when the ritual is no longer available to us. Originally the ritual was known and over time it was gradually forgotten, and it does not seem to make much difference, so why bother with the ritual in the first

8 Elie Wiesel, *The Gates of the Forest*, trans. Frances Frenaye (New York: Holt, Rinehart & Winston, 1966), prologue.

place. This seems to fit into the idea of *maqāṣid al-sharīʿa*, where intention is all-important. The ritual can change, or even be entirely relinquished, and yet its meaning can continue to exist in some other form, an example of how change is possible in religion. The change does not really change anything significant, just the ritual itself, and if that is seen as standing in for something else, then provided that something else continues to flourish, the ritual can be relinquished or changed in some way without any problem. This idea might be extended to cover cases in which the ritual is not forgotten but no longer resonates with its public, and so the time has come to change it. Yet this is very far from the arguments of the Jewish thinkers who emphasised the significance of the strict performance of the rituals of religion. These thinkers were not antinomians. They were convinced of the perfection of their religion and of the rituals within it, whether derived directly from the Torah or from the wider legal background.

7 Two Types of Qur'anic Language and the *Ghayb*

It might be said that God has expressed His views with great clarity in the Qur'an, and so what need is there for any legal discretion in how those views are actually embodied in practice?[9] Well, the Qur'an itself actually distinguished between two types of Qur'anic statements, some of which are entirely clear and some of which are not (Q. 3:7). The language surrounding this distinction is a little strained since the implication is that those who find passages ambiguous are not perhaps looking at them in the right sort of way. There is a suggestion in the second sura that the Jews play around too much with the rules they are supposed to follow (Q. 2:67–71) and this is a result of their not really wishing to follow what God wants them to do. We are familiar with the ways in which people who do not want to follow a rule can try to argue that the rule does not mean what it seems on the surface to mean, although good legislation makes this difficult. Surely divine legislation is good in this sense? Yet even the Qur'an points out that some of its passages require at the very least more thought, since perhaps they are rather complex and we need to work out how to apply them properly. Human life is itself so complex that it is hardly surprising that issues are constantly raised about how to adapt it to religious instructions and advice.

9 Oliver Leaman, 'Modern Developments in Qur'anic Studies', in *The Oxford Handbook of Qur'anic Studies*, ed. Mustafa Shah and Muhammad Abdel Haleem (Oxford: Oxford University Press, 2020), 39–51.

This looks like an invitation just to change the rules when they become inconvenient or apparently out of date. In recent times there have been influential calls to change the rules to do with who counts as an unbeliever (a 2019 *fatwā* backed, we are told, by 20,000 *ʿulamāʾ*) and the role of the Sharīʿa in political life (something called for by Nahdlatul Ulama in Indonesia). It is certainly true that institutions that last a long time constantly change and adapt to different circumstances. Yet this admirable interest in flexibility should perhaps be moderated by a sense of humility. It has been argued here that we do not know why many of the rules we have in religion are as they are, God does not tell us, and so we need to be cautious about changing those rules. The language of the Qurʾan itself, with its emphasis on the vast difference between us and the deity, and on the scope for indeterminacy in assessing meaning, supports such caution. It suggests that the issue is not so much whether there should be scope for change, since of course there should. The issue is more about what mechanisms and institutions should determine the nature of change, and that is something I hope to discuss elsewhere.

In conclusion, it is worth looking at what the Qurʾan says about the hidden, a topic frequently mentioned in the Book. We are told that believers fear God (Q. 3:94, 21:49, 35:18, 36:11, 50:33, 67:12) where the text refers to the hidden (*bi-l-ghayb*). Part of the definition of being pious is accepting the unseen (Q. 2:3). This is hardly surprising, for having faith means believing things you cannot see or prove. It is part of being tested: anyone can accept something they can see and understand, but it is calling on an exercise in faith to commit ourselves to something that is hidden. This does not just apply to things or states like the next world or predictions about the future that are at present unknown to us. It could also be taken to apply to the reasons for the rules; they are known by God but there is no reason to think they need to be known by us. One thinks here of the long dialogue (Q. 18:65–82) between Mūsā and al-Khiḍr in which the latter calls for quiet patience at the events on their journey, and Mūsā constantly demands answers. He gets them in the end but the suggestion is that he should just have trusted in God to do what is right. No doubt the Qurʾan expects the same from the rest of us. So the Qurʾan itself implies that even if religion and its rules are based on reasons, there is no need for us to know what they are.

Bibliography

Auda, Jasser. *Maqasid al-Shariah as Philosophy of Islamic Law: A Systems Approach*. London: International Institute of Islamic Thought, 2008.

Duderija, Adis, ed. *Maqasid al-Shari'a and Contemporary Reformist Muslim Thought: An Examination*. New York: Palgrave Macmillan, 2014.

Ibrahim, Abdul Halim, Noor Naemah Abdul Rahman, Shaikh Mohd Saifuddeen, and Madiha Baharuddin. 'Maqasid al-Shariah Based Islamic Bioethics: A Comprehensive Approach'. *Journal of Bioethical Inquiry* 16, no. 3 (2019): 333–45.

Kamali, Mohammad Hashim. 'History and Jurisprudence of the *Maqāṣid:* A Critical Appraisal'. *American Journal of Islam and Society* 38 (2021): 8–34.

Leaman, Oliver. *Evil and Suffering in Jewish Philosophy*. Cambridge: Cambridge University Press, 1999.

Leaman, Oliver. *Islamic Philosophy: An Introduction*. Cambridge: Polity, 2009.

Leaman, Oliver. 'Modern Developments in Qur'anic Studies'. In *The Oxford Handbook of Qur'anic Studies*, edited by Mustafa Shah and Muhammad Abdel Haleem, 39–51. Oxford: Oxford University Press, 2020.

Levinas, Emmanuel. *Difficult Freedom: Essays on Judaism*. Translated by Seán Hand. Baltimore: Johns Hopkins University Press, 1997.

Opwis, Felicitas. 'Maqāṣid al-Sharī'ah'. In *The Oxford Encyclopedia of the Islamic World: Digital Collection*, edited by John L. Esposito. Oxford: Oxford University Press, 2022. www.oxfordreference.com/display/10.1093/acref/9780197669419.001.0001/acref-9780197669419-e-254?rskey=ml2yzv&result=250.

Opwis, Felicitas. 'Maqāṣid al-Shari'ah'. In *Routledge Handbook of Islamic Law*, edited by Khaled Abou El Fadl, Ahmad Atif Ahmad, and Said Feres Hassan, 195–207. London: Routledge, 2019.

Opwis, Felicitas. *Maṣlaḥa and the Purpose of the Law: Islamic Discourse on Legal Change from the 4th/10th to 8th/14th Century*. Leiden: Brill, 2010.

Peters, Rudolph. '*Idjtihād* and *Taqlīd* in 18th and 19th Century Islam'. *Die Welt des Islams* 20 (1980): 131–45.

Rahman, Fazlur. *Islam*. London: Weidenfeld and Nicolson, 1966.

al-Raysūnī, Aḥmad. *Imam al-Shatibi's Theory of the Higher Objectives and Intents of Islamic Law*. Translated by Nancy Roberts. London and Washington, DC: International Institute of Islamic Thought, 2005.

Spinoza. *Tractatus Theologic-Politicus*. Gebhardt Edition (1925). Translated by Samuel Shirley. Leiden: Brill, 1991.

Wiesel, Elie. *The Gates of the Forest*. Translated by Frances Frenaye. New York: Holt, Rinehart & Winston, 1966.

Wittgenstein, Ludwig. *Philosophical Investigations*. Translated by G.E.M. Anscombe. Oxford: Basil Blackwell, 1958.

CHAPTER 16

Reconstruction of Sharīʿa through Judicial *Ijtihād*

Inheritance Rights of Childless Widows under the Ithnā ʿAshariyya School in Pakistan

Muhammad Zubair Abbasi

> The teaching of the Qur'ān that life is a process of progressive creation necessitates that each generation, guided but unhampered by the work of its predecessors, should be permitted to solve its own problems.[1]

1 Introduction

In December 2021, the federal legislature of the Islamic Republic of Pakistan added a new provision to the statutory law, namely, that a childless widow of a Shīʿa husband will receive a one-fourth share in the property of her deceased husband.[2] This amendment was prompted by the judgement of the Lahore High Court which declared that the Qur'an prescribes a one-fourth share to a childless widow without limiting her share to movable property only.[3] The exclusion of a childless widow from the inheritance right to immovable property is peculiar to the Twelver Shīʿa school (Ithnā ʿAshariyya *fiqh*). The jurists of other schools (four Sunnī and two Shīʿa, Ismāʿīliyya and Zaydiyya) do not exclude a childless widow from inheriting the immovable property of her deceased husband.[4] The courts in the Indian subcontinent have been applying the exclusionary rule since the mid-nineteenth century and it continues to be applied in India and Bangladesh to this day. Therefore, the statutory intervention in Pakistan is significant as it changed an Islamic legal rule that has been in practice for the past several centuries.

1 Muhammad Iqbal, *The Reconstruction of Religious Thought in Islam* (Oxford: Oxford University Press, 1934), 160.

2 The Muslim Family Laws (Amendment) Act 2021, section 2.

3 *Khalida Shamim Akhtar v Ghulam Jaffar* PLD 2016 Lahore 865.

4 Lucy Carroll, 'The Ithna Ashari Law of Intestate Succession: An Introduction to Shia Law Applicable in South Asia', *Modern Asian Studies* 19, no. 1 (1985): 85, 99–100.

 | HTTPS://DOI.ORG/10.1163/9789004755567-018

This chapter examines the jurisprudential discourse on a childless widow's inheritance under the Ithnā ʿAshariyya school by analysing the seminal judgements in which the judges evaluated the sources of the law to formulate and reformulate the relevant legal rules. Two of these judgements were rendered during the colonial period in British India and the other two were delivered by the judges in Pakistan. Based on this analysis, I argue that judges in Pakistan have adopted the methodology of judicial *ijtihād* (independent reasoning) to reform legal rules.[5] Under this methodology, the judges directly rely upon the principal sources of Islamic law (*fiqh*), the Qur'an and Sunna, while also referring to the secondary sources such as *fiqh* books, legal commentaries, and the scholarly opinions of contemporary jurists.[6]

The first part of this chapter briefly highlights the distinctive features of the legal theory of the Ithnā ʿAshariyya school which led to a different interpretation of the relevant verse of the Qur'an regarding the inheritance right of a childless widow. The second part provides a very brief historical context of the hybrid legal system of Pakistan. The third part evaluates the four judgements in which the judges relied upon various legal sources to first formulate and then reformulate the legal rule related to the inheritance right of a childless widow under the Ithnā ʿAshariyya school.

2 Source Material of Sharīʿa and Legal Theories

Qur'anic verses prescribe the share of various legal heirs in detail. The historical context of the revelation of these verses suggests that their main objective was to improve the rights of women who were deprived of inheritance

---

5 Both Sunnī and Shīʿa judges are appointed at the superior courts in Pakistan (High Courts and Supreme Court). The judges of the Federal Shariat Court (FSC) and the Shariat Appellate Bench (SAB) at the Supreme Court include ulema judges. While Shīʿa ulema have been appointed at the Council of Islamic Ideology, which has an advisory function to the legislature, they have not been appointed as the judges of the FSC and SAB. Sarah Holz, *Governance of Islam in Pakistan: An Institutional Study of the Council of Islamic Ideology* (Liverpool: Liverpool University Press, 2022).

6 Some textbooks on Sunnī *uṣūl al-fiqh* (principles of Islamic jurisprudence) describe *ijtihād* as a source of Islamic law along with the Qur'an, Sunna, *ijmāʿ* (scholarly consensus) and *qiyās* (analogical reasoning). See Mohammad Hashim Kamali, *Principles of Islamic Jurisprudence* (Cambridge: Islamic Texts Society, 1991), 366. Other textbooks describe *ijtihād* as a methodology. See Muḥammad Abū Zahrā', *Uṣūl al-fiqh* (Cairo: Dār al-Fikr al-ʿArabī, 1958), 379–80; Abdur Rahim, *The Principles of Muhammadan Jurisprudence: According to the Hanafi, Maliki, Shafiʿi and Hanbali Schools* (London: Luzac & Co., 1911), 168–69.

rights under the pre-Islamic Arabian customary practices.[7] Q. 4:12 sets out the spouse's share:

> In what your wives leave, your share is a half, if they leave no child; but if they leave a child, ye get a fourth; after payment of legacies and debts. In what ye leave, their share is a fourth, if ye leave no child; but if ye leave a child, they get an eighth; after payment of legacies and debts. If the man or woman whose inheritance is in question, has left neither ascendants nor descendants, but has left a brother or a sister, each one of the two gets a sixth; but if more than two, they share in a third; after payment of legacies and debts; so that no loss is caused (to any one). Thus is it ordained by Allah; and Allah is All-knowing, Most Forbearing.[8]

The expressions in the above verse to the extent of numbers (a half, a fourth, and an eighth) are definitive (*qaṭʿī*). But three expressions are probable (*ẓannī*) and open to multiple interpretations: (i) 'if they leave a child', (ii) 'what ye leave', and (iii) 'after payment of legacies and debts'.[9] This chapter focuses on the expression 'what ye leave'.[10] A majority of Muslim jurists belonging to the Sunnī and Shīʿa schools do not make any distinction between movable and immovable property. Jurists of the Ithnā ʿAshariyya school, however, make such distinction regarding the inheritance right of a widow based on the opinion of Imām Jaʿfar al-Ṣādiq, who referred to a statement of the Prophet Muhammad to this effect. The rationale for this rule according to Imām al-Ṣādiq is 'because

7 Shahbaz Ahmad Cheema, *Islamic Law of Inheritance* (Islamabad: Shariah Academy, 2017), 27; Mariam Sheibani, 'Marriage, Divorce, and Inheritance in Classical Islamic Law and Premodern Practice', in *The Oxford Handbook of Islam and Women*, ed. Asma Afsaruddin (Oxford: Oxford University Press, 2023), 168–73.

8 Translation from Abdullah Yusuf Ali, *The Holy Qur'an* (Kuala Lumpur: Islamic Book Trust, 2007).

9 Jurists of the Ithnā ʿAshariyya school permit a will in favour of legal heirs, but the Ḥanafī jurists hold that such a will is invalid without the permission of all legal heirs. This means that a Shīʿa husband has the right to make a will in favour of his wife to the extent of one-third of his property that may include both movable and immovable properties.

10 In one judgement, the Supreme Court of Pakistan held that a childless widow, who is not entitled to inherit from her deceased Shīʿa husband's (propositus) immoveable property, includes (i) a widow who never gave birth to a child from the propositus and (ii) a widow who had children with the propositus, but the children did not survive the propositus. *Noor Bibi v Ghulam Qamar* 2016 SCMR 1195.

a woman's relation with a man is temporary and not a blood relation [which is permanent, like his parents and children]'.[11]

Both Sunnī and Shīʿa jurists regard the Qur'an and traditions of the Prophet Muhammad (*sunna*) as the basic sources of rights and obligations (*fiqh*).[12] While the Shīʿa jurists consider the Qur'an and Sunna as the sources of Islamic law, they accept a *ḥadīth* as valid if it is narrated by an Imām descended from the Prophet Muhammad.[13] One distinctive feature of Shīʿa jurisprudence is the fundamental belief that the true successor of the Prophet Muhammad was his cousin and son-in-law, ʿAlī b. Abī Ṭālib. This belief in the religious and political leadership of ʿAlī and his family (*ahl al-bayt*) is the defining feature of three major Shīʿa schools: Twelver (Ithnā ʿAshariyya), Ismāʿīliyya, and Zaydiyya.[14] Generally, Shīʿa jurists regard the Imām to be the final interpreter of the law. Only the Imām and, in his absence, the *mujtahidūn* (jurists) can provide the correct interpretation of the law. In this way, jurists play an important role in the development of legal rules in the Shīʿa schools.[15] Another distinctive feature of Shīʿa jurisprudence is that it includes human reasoning (*ʿaql*) as a valid source of law. Therefore, the sources of legal authority under the Ithnā ʿAshariyya school are expansive and include the texts (Qur'an, Sunna, *ḥadīth/akhbār*, *ijmāʿ*) and rationality.[16]

In the South Asian context, jurists, judges, and legal commentators relied upon a variety of legal sources while formulating the rule on a childless widow's right to inheritance under the Ithnā ʿAshariyya school. To evaluate how the legal rule was formulated and reformulated, I analyse four judgements: two delivered during the colonial period in British India and the other two delivered by the judges in the Islamic Republic of Pakistan. Before embarking on

---

11 Muḥammad b. al-Ḥasan al-Ḥurr, *Masāʾil al-Sharīʿa*, translated as *Wasāʾil al-Shīʿa* by Muḥammad Ḥusayn al-Najafī (Sargodha: Maktabat al-Sibṭayn, 2017), 17:316.

12 There are three major Shīʿa schools: Twelver (Ithnā ʿAshariyya), Ismāʿīliyya, and Zaydiyya. The Twelver school has the majority of worldwide followers, including most of the Shīʿa in Pakistan. Therefore, the courts presume that Shīʿa Muslims follow this school unless proved otherwise. *Ghulam Shabbir v Mst Bakhat Khatoon* 2009 SCMR 644.

13 Liyakat Takim, *Shiʿism Revisited: Ijtihad and Reformation in Contemporary Times* (Oxford: Oxford University Press, 2022), 56–65; Asaf A.A. Fyzee, *Outlines of Muhammadan Law*, 5th ed. (New Delhi: Oxford University Press, 2009 [1949]), 27–28.

14 Hashim Bata, *Exploring the Mind of God: An Introduction to Shiʿite Legal Epistemology* (Leiden: Brill, 2023), 14.

15 Ibid.

16 Robert Gleave, 'Imami Shiʿi Legal Theory: From Its Origins to the Early Twentieth Century', in *The Oxford Handbook of Islamic Law*, ed. Anver M. Emon and Rumee Ahmed (Oxford: Oxford University Press, 2018), 207.

this analysis, it is prudent to first provide a brief historical overview of the legal system in British India.

3 Historical Contexts of the Hybrid Legal System in South Asia

Muslim merchants, Sufi saints, and invaders from Arabia, Central Asia, and Persia introduced Islam in the Indian subcontinent.[17] Muslim Arab merchants arrived in the subcontinent in the early eighth century. During the following centuries, Muslim preachers and invaders from Arabia, Central Asia, and Iran spread Islam through migration and conversion. Both Sunnī and Shīʿa schools flourished though the Sunnī Ḥanafī school gained official patronage through the imperial project of the compilation of *al-Fatāwā al-ʿĀlamgīriyya*, which was completed around 1672, at the behest of the Mughal emperor Aurangzeb Alamgir.[18] In 1757, the British East India Company occupied one of the biggest Indian provinces, Bengal, and continued to expand until 1857, when after the unsuccessful uprising against the company rule, India formally became part of the British Empire. As a result, a hierarchical judicial system was introduced. It was structured in the form of local civil and criminal courts, the appellate provincial high courts, and the highest court of appeal, the Judicial Committee of the Privy Council in London.[19] The Imperial Legislative Council promulgated various substantive and procedural codes such as the Penal Code 1860, the Codes of Civil and Criminal Procedures including the Evidence Act 1872, and the Specific Relief Act 1877, the Contract Act 1872, the Trusts Act 1882, and the Transfer of Property Act 1882.[20] The new legal codes were based on English common law which remained uncodified in England.[21]

17 Jamal Malik, *Islam in South Asia: Revisited* (Leiden: Brill, 2020), 12–16.

18 Muhammad Zubair Abbasi, '*Al-Fatāwā al-ʿĀlamgīriyyah*: Ḥanafī Legal Code of the Mughal Empire', *Islamic Studies* 59, no. 4 (2020): 451. *Al-Fatāwā al-ʿĀlamgīriyya* (known as *al-Fatāwā al-Hindiyya* in the Arab world) was the most comprehensive Ḥanafī work of its time and because of its scholarly significance many leading publishers of *fiqh* books in Cairo and Beirut published it during the late nineteenth and early twentieth century.

19 The British established the Federal Court under the Government of India Act 1935. But the Federal Court was not the highest court of appeal.

20 M.C. Setalvad, *The Common Law in India* (London: Stevens & Sons Limited, 1960), 27–28; Bijay Kisor Acharyya, *Codification in British India* (Calcutta: S.K. Banerji & Sons, 1914).

21 David Skuy, 'Macaulay and the Indian Penal Code of 1862: The Myth of the Inherent Superiority and Modernity of the English Legal System Compared to India's Legal System in the Nineteenth Century', *Modern Asian Studies* 32, no. 3 (1998): 513–57.

The exceptions to English law were the personal laws of various religious communities, which were based on their uncodified religious legal texts that were translated into English and treated as 'codes of law'.[22] The judgements of the provincial high courts, based on the translated religious texts, were binding on lower courts and the judgements of the Judicial Committee of the Privy Council were binding on provincial courts. In this way, adjudication was the second modes of the transformation of parts of the Sharīʿa into state-enforced law.[23] Legal commentators systematically organised the judgements along with the text of the 'codes of law' into various chapters for the use of lawyers and judges. Law students were taught these legal commentaries to become practitioners, judges, and civil servants. Thus, the processes of translation, adjudication, legal commentaries, and education reformulated parts of the Sharīʿa to incorporate it into the structure of the British imperial legal system. These processes continued to operate after independence from colonial rule in Pakistan.

The legal commentaries produced during the colonial period such as Dinshah F. Mulla's *Principles of Mahomedan Law* are still taught at law schools in universities and are updated through latest judgements of the superior courts.[24] Some rules of Muslim Personal Law have been reformed through colonial statutes such as the Muslim Personal Law (Shariat) Application Act 1937 to recognise inheritance rights of Muslim women, and the Dissolution of Muslim Marriages Act 1939 to expand divorce rights of Muslim women. After independence, the most important legislative reform in Pakistan was introduced through the Muslim Family Laws Ordinance 1961 that required registration of marriage and divorce, regulated polygamy, and provided inheritance rights to orphaned grandchildren. Other changes related to Muslim women's unilateral right to no-fault divorce (*khulʿ*) and divorced mothers' right to custody of children have been introduced through judicial *ijtihād*.[25] In one judgement related to the interpretation of Islamic legal rule on a female's right to exercise the

---

22 R.K. Wilson, 'Should the Personal Laws of the Natives of India Be Codified?', *Asiatic Quarterly Review* 6 (1898): 225.

23 Dirk H.A. Kolff, 'The Indian and British Law Machines: Some Remarks on Law and Society in British India', in *European Expansion and Law: The Encounter of European and Indigenous Law in 19th- and 20th-Century Africa and Asia*, ed. Wolfgang J. Mommsen and Jaap A. de Moor (New York: Berg Publishers, 1992), 210–13.

24 Shahbaz Ahmad Cheema, 'Mulla's *Principles of Mahomedan Law* in Pakistani Courts: Undoing/Unraveling the Colonial Enterprise?', *LUMS Law Journal* 4 (2018): 56.

25 Muhammad Zubair Abbasi, 'Judicial *Ijtihād* as a Tool for Legal Reform: Extending Women's Right to Divorce under Islamic law in Pakistan', *Islamic Law and Society* 24, no. 4 (2017): 384–411.

option of puberty to end her marriage, Justice Anwarul Huq held, 'It would not be correct to lay it down as a positive rule of law that the present-day Courts in this country should have no power or authority to interpret the Qur'an in a way different from that adopted by the earlier jurists and Imams.'[26] He argued that the denial of such authority to the courts would be against the 'the true spirit of Islam' and would 'endanger the dynamic and universal character of the religion and laws of Islam'.[27]

4 Construction and Reconstruction of Interpretative Authority within the Modern State

The religion-based personal law played an important role in the administrative structure of British India. While acknowledging and respecting religious diversity in India, it asserted the authority of the state in the administration of justice under a uniform and hierarchical judicial system.[28] The personal laws applied to various religious communities and sub-communities based on their religious beliefs. Individuals could not opt out of a particular personal law applicable to them without converting from their faith.[29]

After taking political control in Bengal in 1765, Nawab Governor General Warren Hastings promised that the personal affairs of Muslims and Hindus would continue to be regulated according to their religious laws. The East India Company primarily continued to operate the existing institutional structure of administration. Hindu and Muslim law officers advised the British judges on local laws and customs. The administrators of the East India Company were dissatisfied with this arrangement and wanted to exert direct sovereign control with minimal local agency. Therefore, a few legal texts such as the *Hidāya*

---

26 In *Khurshid Jan v Fazal Dad* PLD 1964 (West Pakistan) Lahore 558, the majority of the bench held that 'the Courts must be given the right to interpret for themselves the Qur'an and Sunnah; and that they may also differ from the views of earlier juris-consults of Muslim Law on the grounds of Istiḥsān (i.e. equity) or Istiṣlāḥ (i.e. public good) in matters not governed by a Qur'anic or traditional text or an Ijmāʿ or a binding Qiyās'.

27 Ibid.

28 Scott Alan Kugle, 'Framed, Blamed and Renamed: The Recasting of Islamic Jurisprudence in Colonial South Asia', *Modern Asian Studies* 35 (2001): 257; Michael R. Anderson, 'Legal Scholarship and the Politics of Islam in British India', in *Perspectives on Islamic Law, Justice, and Society*, ed. Ravindra S. Khare (Oxford: Rowman & Littlefield, 1999), 65–91; Elisa Giunchi, 'The Reinvention of *Sharīʿa* under the British Raj: In Search of Authenticity and Certainty', *The Journal of Asian Studies* 69, no. 4 (2010): 1119.

29 Farrah Ahmed, *Religious Freedom under the Personal Law System* (Oxford: Oxford University Press, 2015).

and *Sirājiyya* were translated into English in the late eighteenth century.[30] Later, parts of *al-Fatāwā al-ʿĀlamgīriyya* for the Ḥanafī school and the *Sharāʾiʿ al-Islām* for the Ithnā ʿAshariyya school were also translated into English.[31] The British judges relied on these translations to adjudicate, and the advisory posts of local legal experts were abolished in 1864.[32] Through the processes of translation and adjudication, the British were able to cement colonial domination through monopolising interpretative authority over legal texts.[33]

Neil B.E. Baillie's translation of the *Sharāʾiʿ al-Islām* provided the following translation on the share of a widow in inheritance:

> When the wife has had a child by the deceased she inherits out of all that he has left; and if there was no child she takes nothing out of the deceased's land, but her share of the value of the household effects and buildings is to be given her. It has been said, however, that she is to be excluded from nothing except the mansions and dwellings; while Moortuza (may God be pleased with him) had expressed a third opinion to the effect that the land should be valued and her share of the value assigned to her. But the first opinion is that which appears to be best founded on traditional authority.[34]

The author of the *Sharāʾiʿ al-Islām* preferred the view that a childless widow does not inherit land of her deceased husband. But other Shīʿa jurists expressed a wide variety of views as discussed in the judgement of Justice Syed Mahmood.[35] Some of them held the view that even a widow with children did not inherit land.[36] Diametrically opposed to this view was the opinion of a few jurists who held that widows (with or without children) would inherit land.[37]

---

30 Charles Hamilton, *The Hedaya, or Guide: A Commentary on the Mussulman Laws*, vol. 1 (London: T. Bensley, 1791); Sirāj al-Dīn Muḥammad b. Muḥammad Sajāwandī, *Al Sirājiyya: or, the Mahommedan Law of Inheritance with a Commentary by Sir William Jones* (Calcutta: Joseph Cooper, 1792).

31 Neil B.E. Baillie, *A Digest of Moohummudan Law* (London: Smith, Elder & Co, 1865); Neil B.E. Baillie, *A Digest of Moohummudan Law*, pt. 2 (London: Smith, Elder & Co, 1887).

32 Act XI of 1864 (an act to repeal the law relating to the offices of Hindu and Muhammadan Law officers and to the offices of Kazi'-ul-Kuzaat and of Kazi', and to abolish the former offices).

33 Jorg Fisch, 'Law as a Means and an End: Some Remarks on the Function of European and Non-European Law in the Process of European Expansion', in *European Expansion and Law*, 38.

34 Baillie, *Digest of Moohummudan Law*, pt. 2, 295.

35 *Fazal Rab v Khatun Bibi and others* (1892) ILR 25 All 29.

36 Ibid., 42–43.

37 Ibid., 41.

Still, others expressed the view that if there were multiple widows, then the ones with children would inherit land and the childless widows would not.[38] Some other jurists distinguished various types of properties such as immovable (gardens, farms, and dwelling houses) and movable (personal utensils, weapons, and cattle) while allocating a widow (with or without children) different rights either in the substance/corpus of the property or in its price.[39]

The diversity of juristic opinions in the extant legal literature required expertise of scholars to draw enforceable legal rules. By translating a few legal texts, the administrators of the East India Company transferred the individual interpretative authority of jurists to the institutional authority of the judiciary which operated under the common law doctrine of precedent. Therefore, once the Anglo-Indian high courts adopted the preferred view expressed in the translation of the *Sharāʾiʿ al-Islām*, it became a binding rule. This was notwithstanding the fact that Muslim judges such as Syed Mahmood referred to a wide variety of legal sources in their judgements.[40] The binding authority of the judgements was based on the institutional structure of the colonial state rather than its accuracy and conformity with the primary source of Islamic law, the Qurʾan.[41]

The relevant Qurʾanic verse regarding the inheritance right of a widow was so clear that it was hard for judges to ignore it. Therefore, a Muslim judge of the Allahabad High Court, Karamat Hussain, raised the issue of conflict between the relevant Qurʾanic verses and judicial precedents in 1909.[42] In this case, a widow filed a petition to recover her inheritance share in land that was denied to her on the basis that a widow was not entitled to a land inheritance share. Justice Karamat Hussain noted that the inheritance share of a widow

---

38 Ibid., 39.

39 Ibid., 38.

40 Ibid. Justice Syed Mahmood quoted the translation of texts from ten different sources and identified diversity of opinion among Shīʿa jurists. The main issue in this case involved whether the wife of a lunatic husband could be appointed as his guardian, since the Lunacy Act 1858 barred a legal heir from becoming a guardian. Therefore, Justice Mahmood did not have to conclusively decide on the entitlement of a childless widow's right to the landed estate of her deceased husband. Justice Mahmood held that the wife was not eligible to be appointed as a guardian of his estate under the act because she was a legal heir.

41 In *Aga Mohamed Jaffer Bindaneem v Koolsom Bee Bee* [1897] 24 IA 196, the Privy Council observed, 'It would be wrong for the Court on a point [reconciling between the Qurʾan and juristic views] of this kind to attempt to put their own construction on the Koran in opposition to the express ruling of commentators of such great antiquity and high authority.'

42 *Syid Murtaza Husain vs Musammat Alhan Bibi* (1909) 2 Ind Cas 671.

is specified in the Qur'an clearly and observed that 'a so-called rule of the Muhammadan Law which is in direct opposition to a rule of law laid down in the Qur'ān cannot possibly be a rule of the Muhammadan Law'.[43] As a judge, however, he was bound to follow judicial precedents. He acknowledged that other legal commentaries of the Shīʿa school such as *Jawāhir al-kalām* are more authoritative but felt himself to be bound by the precedents which adopted the *Sharāʾiʿ al-Islām* and held:

> I only hold that in cases of a conflict between the Sharaia [*sic*, i.e. *Sharāʾiʿ al-Islām*] and any other work of recognised authority on the Shia Law the Courts in British India in administering the Shia Law must follow the Sharaia and must not discard it in favour of any other works of established merits.[44]

He regarded it as 'a highly dangerous course' to adopt a view that does not follow the judicial authorities which are based on the translation of the *Sharāʾiʿ al-Islām*.[45] Therefore, he held:

> I have not come across any reported case in which the authority of the Sharaia [*Sharāʾiʿ al-Islām*] was superseded by the authority of any other work on the Shia Law. To disturb the authority of such a work after more than a century is against the well established principles underlying the administration of justice.[46]

The above judgement established that the case law replaced juristic opinions as the source of Muslim law within the institutional structure of British India. Unlike in other areas of Muslim law such as family endowments (*awqāf*) wherein legal commentators challenged the authenticity and accuracy of judicial precedents,[47] prominent legal commentators such as Syed Ameer Ali, Faiz B. Tyabji, and Asaf A.A. Fyzee (belonging to the Shīʿa community)

43 Ibid., para [11].

44 Ibid., para [15].

45 Ibid., para [14].

46 Ibid., para [16]. He observed that a later legal commentary on Shīʿa law provides a different view and was more authoritative. 'The Jawahir in fact is the best and the most exhaustive work of the last century on the Shia Law. Whenever any text of the Sharaia is to be interpreted or explained recourse must be had to the Jawahir and other works.'

47 Beverley argues that Muslim legal scholars such as Syed Ameer Ali and Faiz Tyabji challenged the interpretative authority of English judges in their legal commentaries. Eric Lewis Beverley, 'Property, Authority and Personal Law: Waqf in Colonial South Asia', *South Asia Research* 31, no. 2 (2011): 155.

endorsed the rule that a childless widow does not inherit land.[48] They referred to the judgements of the Privy Council and Indian high courts in support of their view.[49]

The common law doctrine of precedent played a central role in the formulation of this rule to ensure legal certainty and uniformity. In many ways, this doctrine was like the Islamic legal doctrine of *taqlīd* (following precedent). The objective of both these doctrines was to ensure legal predictability, certainty, and uniformity while facing the challenge of diversity of juristic opinions. In his study of the history of the Mālikī school, Mohammad Fadel has highlighted the role of concise handbooks (*mukhtaṣar*) in promoting legal certainty by providing one preferred view among multiple juristic opinions.[50] His observation also applies to the Ithnā 'Ashariyya school as the *Sharā'iʿ al-Islām* described multiple juristic opinions and specified one to be the 'best founded on traditional authority'.[51] The judges founded the judicial precedent on this preferred opinion.

Judicial *taqlīd* or precedent continued to be the defining feature of the legal system of Pakistan after independence in August 1947. Under this doctrine, once a legal rule was firmly laid down then judges could not change it even after realising that the rule was based on incorrect interpretation of the legal authorities.[52] Only the legislature could change such a rule after passing a statute. In the late colonial period, the Muslim Personal Law (Shariat) Application Act 1937 was passed to replace the customary law of inheritance with Islamic law. This process continued after the creation of Pakistan and several Shariat Application Acts were passed in 1948, 1951, and 1962 to make Islamic law the

---

48 Syed Ameer Ali traced his ancestry to the Prophet's family and the Tyabji and Fyzee clan belonged to a small branch of an Ismāʿīlī Shīʿa sect known as Sulaymani Bohras. Gregory Kozlowski, *Muslim Endowments and Society in British India* (Cambridge: Cambridge University Press, 1985), 116–17.

49 Syed Ameer Ali, *Mahommedan Law*, 2nd ed. (Calcutta: Thacker, Spink and Co., 1894), 118; Dinshah Fardunji Mulla, *Principles of Mahomedan Law* (New Delhi: LexisNexis, 2012 [1905]), 131; Faiz Badruddin Tyabji, *Principles of Muhammadan Law* (Bombay: D.B. Taraporewala Sons, 1913), 630–32; Asaf A.A. Fyzee, *Outlines of Muhammadan Law*, 4th ed. (New Delhi: Oxford University Press, 2002 [1949]), 466.

50 Mohammad Fadel, 'The Social Logic of *Taqlīd* and the Rise of the *Mukhataṣar*', *Islamic Law and Society* 3, no. 2 (1996): 193–233.

51 Baillie, *Digest of Moohummudan Law*, pt. 2 , 295.

52 Abdur Rahim, a legal commentator and later a judge of the Allahabad High Court, observed: 'If a rule of Mohammedan Law is laid down by a judgment of the Privy Council or has been settled by a uniform course of decisions of the Indian High Courts, it must be accepted even though it may not agree with a proper reading of the original authorities.' Abdur Rahim, 'A Historical Sketch of the Growth of Mohamedan Jurisprudence', *Calcutta Law Journal* 3 (1906): 268–69.

main source of legal rules for inheritance.[53] The most important reformative legislative was enacted in the form of the Muslim Family Laws Ordinance 1961, which laid down various legal rules related to the registration of marriages and divorce, regulation of polygamy, and provided inheritance rights to orphaned grandchildren. This legal reform was supported by the doctrine of *ijtihād* that was relied upon by modernist scholars who argued that the legislature in the Islamic Republic of Pakistan was vested with the right to reform the rules of classical Islamic law.[54]

Around the same time in the late 1950s, the judges of superior courts in Pakistan delivered a few judgements in which they did not follow the precedents laid down during the British colonial period. The judges referred to the primary sources of *fiqh*, the Qur'an and Sunna, to reform the existing legal rules or to formulate new ones that differed from or supplanted the juristic rules found in the textbooks of classical Islamic law (*fiqh*). I describe this methodology of the judges as 'judicial *ijtihād*'.[55] One of the earliest examples of judicial *ijtihād* is the judgement of the Lahore High Court in which Justice Muhammad Shafi held that a mother does not lose her right to the custody of her child even when she remarries a person who does not fall within the prohibited degree of marriage with the child.[56] Another important example of judicial *ijtihād* is the judgement of Justice B.Z. Kaikaus in which he referred to relevant verses of

---

53 Matthew J. Nelson, *In the Shadow of Shariʿah: Islam, Islamic Law, and Democracy in Pakistan* (London: Hurst & Company, 2011), 163.

54 The report of the commission that proposed legislation, which eventually was enacted in the form of the Muslim Family Laws Ordinance 1961, criticised the Anglo-Muhammadan law for its being conservative and rigid. The report also described the doctrine of *taqlīd* as inflexible. The authors of the report argued that 'law is ultimately related to life experiences, which are not a monopoly of theologians'. 'Report of the Commission on Marriage and Family Laws', 20 June 1956, 8.

55 Under the Ḥanafī school, a judge may exercise independent reasoning (*ijtihād*) regarding issues on which no valid authority can be found or on which jurists hold divergent views. If a judge is not capable of exercising independent reasoning, he may rely upon the opinion of a jurisconsult (*muftī*). al-Shaykh Niẓām, *al-Fatāwā al-ʿĀlamgīriyya*, vol. 3 (Calcutta: Nawal Kishawr, 1865), 310–12. The *Hidāya* provided that a *qāḍī* should be capable of performing *ijtihād*. However, it clarified that the approved doctrine is that this requirement is merely preferable but not indispensable. Muḥammad b. ʿAbd al-Wāḥid Ibn al-Humām, *Sharḥ Fatḥ al-qadīr ʿalā al-Hidāya*, ed. ʿAbd al-Razzāq Ghālib Mahdī (Beirut: Dār al-Kutub al-ʿIlmiyya, 2003), 7:238–40.

56 *Rashida Begum v Shahab Din* PLD 1960 Lahore 1142 (Justice Shafi held that there is no provision in the Qur'an that a divorced woman should lose the custody of her child if she marries a man not related to the minor within the prohibited degree of marriage). *Zohra Begum v Sh. Latif Ahmad Munawar* PLD 1965 Lahore 695 (the court held that if there is difference of views among Muslim jurists, the court may form its own opinion on a point of law).

the Qur'an and traditions of the Prophet to hold that a Muslim wife does not require the consent of her husband to exercise her right to no-fault dissolution of marriage (*khulʿ*).[57] Justice Kaikaus held:

> On a question of interpretation we are not bound by the opinions of jurists. If we be [*sic*] clear as to what the meaning of a verse in the Qur'an is, it will be our duty to give effect to that interpretation irrespective of what has been stated by jurists.[58]

The Supreme Court of Pakistan confirmed the rule/principle laid down in the above judgement in 1967.[59] In these judgements, judges held that the Qur'an is the basis of all the fundamental laws of Islam and directly referred to the Qur'anic verses to draw new legal rules. In doing so, the judges overruled the precedents laid down by the Privy Council which refused to directly refer to the Qur'an to draw new legal rules.[60] The exercise of judicial *ijtihād*, however, was limited to the rules of personal law which were non-sectarian or were limited to a Sunnī majority. This made sense as the sectarian nature of personal laws rendered any intervention by state institutions sensitive.[61]

In 1972, the issue of the inheritance right of the childless widow under the Ithnā ʿAshariyya school reached the Supreme Court of Pakistan. The appellant

---

57 *Balqis Fatima v Najam-ul-Ikram* PLD 1959 Lahore 566.

58 Ibid., 584.

59 *Khurshid Bibi v Baboo Muhammad Amin* PLD 1967 SC 97. In *Khurshid Jan v Fazal Dad* PLD 1964 (WP) Lahore 558, the court held that judges have the authority to adopt one of the conflicting views and also a view from some other Sunnī school in order to 'mitigate the hardship or the rigor of a particular school of law ... if the facts of the case so merit'. The court further held 'the Courts must be given the right to interpret for themselves the Qur'an and Sunnah; and that they may also differ from the views of earlier juris-consults of Muslim Law on the grounds of Istiḥsān (i.e. equity) or Istiṣlāḥ (i.e. public good) in matters not governed by a Qur'anic or traditional text or an Ijmāʿ or a binding Qiyās.'

60 In *Baker Ali v Anjuman Ara* (Oudh) [1903] 30 IA 9, the Privy Council held, 'Their Lordships think it would be extremely dangerous to accept as a general principle that new rules of law are to be introduced because they seem to lawyers of the present day to follow logically from ancient texts however authoritative, when the ancient doctors of the law have not themselves drawn those conclusions.'

61 While laying down the processes for the Islamisation of laws, the drafters of the Constitution of the Islamic Republic of Pakistan 1973 provided that the enforceable rules of personal status would be based on the interpretation according to the rules of respective schools of each sect. The Constitution of the Islamic Republic of Pakistan 1973, Article 227. An explanation added to Article 227(1) of the Constitution provides: 'In the application of this clause to the personal law of any Muslim sect, the expression "Qur'ān and Sunnah" shall mean the Qur'ān and Sunnah as interpreted by that sect.'

argued that the exclusion of a childless widow from inheritance right in land was not in conformity with the clear verses of the Qur'an. A bench of three judges headed by Chief Justice Hamoodur Rahman heard the appeal. In his detailed judgement, Chief Justice Rahman meticulously examined the relevant precedents and authoritative textbooks of the jurists of the Ithnā ʿAshariyya school. He referred to the legal commentaries of Syed Ameer Ali, Shama Churun Sircar, Tyabji, Mulla, and Fyzee, judicial precedents, and the translation of the *Sharāʾiʿ al-Islām* to conclude that 'according to the Shia Fiqh [*sic*] the principle appears to be well-settled that a childless widow is deprived of her share of inheritance in the lands of the deceased'.[62]

This rule/principle, however, did not conform with the clear and definitive verse of the Qur'an (4:12). Therefore, Chief Justice Rahman explored the sources on which this rule/principle was based. He observed that the rule/principle was based on a tradition relied upon by the founder of the Shīʿa school, Imām Jaʿfar al-Ṣādiq, who found it written in a book of the Prophet's cousin and son-in-law, ʿAlī. According to that tradition, widows do not have any share in the lands of their deceased husbands. Chief Justice Rahman noted that the Qur'an is the primary source of law along with the traditions of the Prophet.[63] He observed that the difference between the Shīʿa and Sunnī schools was based on different interpretative authority over the Qur'an. In his words:

> The Shias claim that the differences between Shias and Sunnis arise as a result of their different interpretations of some of the Quranic texts. The Sunnis, it is said, accept the interpretations given by the four Imams, namely; Imam Abu Hanifa, Imam Malek, Imam Ahmad and Imam Shafi'e whereas the Shias rely on the Interpretations of the Holy Qur'an given by only the Ahl-e-Bait (Members of the Household of the Holy Prophet) beginning with Hazrat Ali and ending with the last Imam and, as such, they claim that their interpretation is likely to be more correct. No one, they maintain, could have known the Holy Qur'an better than Hazrat Ali himself who in his Book had recorded these interpretations according to the instructions of the Holy Prophet himself.[64]

Chief Justice Rahman could not ignore the contradiction between the settled rule/principle that only deprives a childless widow from inheritance in land and the traditions of the Prophet which do not make any distinction between

62 *Syed Muhammad Munir v Abu Nasar, Member (Judicial) Board of Revenue, Punjab* PLD 1972 Supreme Court 346.

63 Ibid.

64 Ibid.

a childless widow or a widow who has a child. From the analysis of the primary sources of Islamic law, it was clear that despite various judicial authorities, the foundation of the legal principle that deprives a childless widow from inheriting land was controversial. He could have followed the reformative spirit of the judiciary which initiated the practice of judicial *ijtihād* in the late 1950s and continued to follow it. However, given that the issue involved Shīʿa law, Chief Justice Rahman preferred to exercise judicial restraint. In his words:

> In view of this difference in the interpretation of the Qur'anic text itself, we feel that it would not be proper on our part at this stage *to attempt to put our own construction in opposition to the express ruling of commentators of such great antiquity and high authority*. To depart from a rule of succession which the Shia community has universally been following ever since the days of Imam Jafar Sadek, as evidenced by the unanimous opinions of the Shia Jurists on this point, would be wrong. It is not open to us to change a settled rule of succession, having the force of Ijma' behind it at this late stage. If a change is desired to be made this work should be undertaken by the Legislature itself after consulting the Shia Community.[65]

From the emphasised words in this passage, it is clear that Chief Justice Rahman followed the precedents laid down by the Privy Council in *Aga Mohamed Jaffer Bindaneem v Koolsom Bee Bee*[66] and *Baker Ali v Anjuman Ara*.[67] But unlike the judges of the Privy Council, the judges of the Supreme Court of Pakistan observed that this rule could be changed by the legislature 'after consulting the Shia Community'.[68]

When they were consulted, however, Shīʿa jurists did not reach a consensus on this issue and therefore the legislature could not change this rule/principle even though the issue was debated in the parliament. A prominent Shīʿa cleric who was also a member of parliament, Allama Mufti Syed Tyeb Agha Musavi Jazairi, opposed the proposed amendment. He argued that the rule excluding a childless widow from inheriting agricultural lands is based on the opinion of

65 Ibid. (emphasis added).
66 [1897] 24 IA 196.
67 (Oudh) [1903] 30 IA 9.
68 Ibid.; Jeffrey A. Redding, 'Constitutionalizing Islam: Theory and Pakistan', *Virginia Journal of International Law* 44, no. 3 (2004): 759; Matthew J. Nelson, 'Islamic Law in an Islamic State: What Role for Parliament?', in *Constitution Writing, Religion, and Democracy*, ed. Asli Ü. Bâli and Hanna Lerner (Cambridge: Cambridge University Press, 2017), 235–64.

Imām Jaʿfar al-Ṣādiq and on the tradition of the Prophet Muhammad.[69] In the absence of any legal reform by the legislature, the courts continued to follow the rule laid down during the colonial period.

Several decades later, the issue of a childless widow's right to inherit land was raised before the Lahore High Court in 2016. A childless widow, Khalida Shamim Akhtar, claimed her share in the estate of her deceased husband from his brothers. The brothers argued that as a childless widow she was not entitled to a share in the inheritance of her deceased husband under the Ithnā ʿAshariyya school. After the rejection of her claim by the district court, she filed an appeal before the Lahore High Court. Justice Ibad-Ur-Rehman Lodhi was struck by the contradiction of the established rule under the Ithnā ʿAshariyya school with the clear verse of the Qur'an. He observed that the Supreme Court dealt with the issue in 1972 and it recommended reformative legislative which did not materialise ever since. Therefore, he invited Shīʿa jurists to provide legal assistance to the court to resolve this issue. Such assistance was provided by Allama Syed Iftikhar Hussain Naqvi Najafi, who was also a member of the advisory Council of Islamic Ideology, a constitutional body that advises the legislature regarding the conformity of laws with the injunctions of Islam as laid down in the Qur'an and Sunna.[70] Allama Najafi referred to the opinions of Shīʿa jurists such as Ali Sistani, Ali Khamnai, and Imām Khomeini to express the view that a childless widow of a Shīʿa husband is entitled to her Qur'anic one-quarter share in the estate of her deceased husband.[71] Allama Najafi did not mention classical legal authorities such as the *Sharāʾiʿ al-Islām* or *Jawāhir al-aḥkām fī sharḥ Sharāʾiʿ al-Islām*. Rather, he relied upon the legal opinions of leading contemporary Shīʿa jurists based in Iraq and Iran.

Justice Lodhi referred to the expert opinion of Allama Najafi to assail the legal authority of legal commentaries such as Mulla's *Principles of Mahomedan Law*, mentioned above, which stated the legal rule related to a childless widow's inheritance right as laid down in judicial precedents. He referred to the judgement of the Federal Shariat Court in *Muhammad Nasrullah Khan v The Federation of Pakistan*,[72] in which the court identified the Qur'an, Sunna, *ijmāʿ*,

---

69 He referred to the rationale of this rule by stating that the widow does not belong to the family of the deceased husband, and hence is excluded from any inheritance in land to avoid disputes, which are likely to occur if she remarries and thus introduces an outsider in the family. A pamphlet written by Allama Jazairi, *Beevi ki Meeras* [Wife's inheritance], is quoted in *Syed Muhammad Munir v Abu Nasar, Member (Judicial) Board of Revenue* PLD 1972 SC 346.

70 *Khalida Shamim Akhtar v Ghulam Jaffar* PLD 2016 Lahore 865, para [4].

71 Ibid., para [8].

72 Shariat Petition No.06/I of 2013.

and *qiyās* as the sources of the Sharīʿa and held that 'if any Book is proved to be different from Qur'an and Sunnah, that would be invalid'.[73] Therefore, he held that the exclusion of a childless widow of a Shīʿa husband from inhering land of her deceased husband is against the Qur'anic verse 4:12.[74]

Justice Lodhi recommended that the legislature should promulgate a law to protect the rights of childless widows of Shīʿa husbands. After this judgement, a bill was proposed by Allama Najafi in May 2019 to provide a childless widow inheritance right in land under the Ithnā ʿAshariyya school. The Statement of the Objects and Reasons of the Bill referred to the judgement of the Lahore High Court and proposed that the following subsection must be added to section 4 of the MFLO:

> (2) If a Muslim male from Ahl-e-Tashih [the Ithnā ʿAshariyya school] dies issueless, his widow shall receive one-fourth share from the estate of the deceased and if the deceased has left more than one widows, the widows shall receive equal share from the one-fourth share of the estate.[75]

The proposed section removed any distinction between movable and immovable property in the inheritance right of a widow under the Ithnā ʿAshariyya school. This is exactly what Justice Lodhi of the Lahore High Court had required in his judgement. The final enactment, however, was more detailed and it introduced two important changes. Firstly, the one-fourth share of inheritance right of a childless widow to the immovable property was limited to the extent of 'the fixed price or value of the property'.[76] She was not entitled to receive this share in the corpus of the property and would become 'entitled to her due share in the corpus of immovable property' if the other legal heirs of her deceased husband did not give her the due share.[77] This legal provision is similar to the amended law in the Islamic Republic of Iran.[78] Secondly, the new law provided for arbitration through 'the Mujtahid-e-Alam' in case of

---

73 *Khalida Shamim Akhtar*, para [6].

74 Ibid., para [7].

75 Report of the Standing Committee on Law and Justice on the Muslim Family Laws (Amendment) Bill, 2020 (National Assembly Secretariat).

76 The Muslim Family Laws (Amendment) Act 2021, section 2.

77 Ibid.

78 In 2009, the Iranian Parliament amended the relevant articles of the Iranian Civil Code 1928 to grant the widow a right to inheritance to *the value of immovable property* after the Supreme Leader issued a *fatwā* (religious edict). Previously, a widow did not receive any share in land. Nadjma Yassari, 'Intestate Succession in Islamic Countries', in *Comparative Succession Law, Volume II: Intestate Succession*, ed. Kenneth Reid, Marius de Waal, and Reinhard Zimmermann (Oxford: Oxford University Press, 2015), 435. It is worth

any dispute.[79] This shows that in return for their support to the legal reform, Shīʿa scholars received the recognition of the interpretative authority of jurists (*fuqahāʾ*) from the lawmakers.

5 Conclusion

The judicial discourse on a childless widow's inheritance right reflects the processes through which interpretative authority over religious texts was formulated and reformulated. In vesting final authority in the translated text of the *Sharāʾiʿ al-Islām*, British judges of the Indian high courts did not show deference to the religious sentiment of Shīʿa Muslims. Rather, they established institutional authority of the judicial system of the British Empire. The *Sharāʾiʿ al-Islām* had the binding authority because the judicial precedents conferred this authority on it. Therefore, the judges continued to follow judicial precedents based on this text, which was written in the thirteenth century, even after realising that it was supplemented with later works such as the nineteenth-century *Jawāhīr al-aḥkām fī sharḥ Sharāʾiʿ al-Islām*. Judges, legal commentators, jurists, and the Shīʿa community continued to follow judicial precedents for over a century and half despite questioning the authenticity of such precedents. Such was the institutional authority of the precedents that even the parliament in Pakistan could not reform the rules based on these precedents. Legal reform was made possible when the judges performed judicial *ijtihād* by directly referring to the verses of the Qurʾan and sought the support of contemporary Shīʿa jurists. These jurists relied upon the interpretative authority of a transnational network of scholars and conferred legitimacy to the state legislation to extend childless widows' rights to inherit land.

noting that this law does not differentiate between a childless widow and a widow with children.

79 Ibid. '(7) In case of dispute, the parties or any of the parties may have recourse to a court of competent jurisdiction or by approaching the Mujtahid-e-Alam from the panel maintained by the Council of Islamic Ideology. The decision of Mujtahid-e-Alam shall have a status of an award and the same shall be dealt with in accordance with the provisions of the Arbitration Act, 1940 (X of 1940).

Explanation. The expression "Mujtahid-e-Alam (Faqih-e-Azam)" means a juris-consult, religious scholar or doctor of [the] Shia school of thought well versed with Shariah having international repute and of such recognition. The Council of Islamic Ideology shall maintain a panel of Mujtahid-e-Alam having aforesaid qualifications.'

Bibliography

Abbasi, Muhammad Zubair. '*Al-Fatāwā al-ʿĀlamgīriyyah*: Ḥanafī Legal Code of the Mughal Empire'. *Islamic Studies* 59, no. 4 (2020): 451–76.

Abbasi, Muhammad Zubair. 'Judicial *Ijtihād* as a Tool for Legal Reform: Extending Women's Right to Divorce under Islamic law in Pakistan'. *Islamic Law and Society* 24, no. 4 (2017): 384–411.

Abū Zahrāʾ, Muḥammad. *Uṣūl al-fiqh*. Cairo: Dār al-Fikr al-ʿArabī, 1958.

Acharyya, Bijay Kisor. *Codification in British India*. Calcutta: S.K. Banerji & Sons, 1914.

Ahmed, Farrah. *Religious Freedom under the Personal Law System*. Oxford: Oxford University Press, 2015.

Ali, Syed Ameer. *Mahommedan Law*. 2nd ed. Calcutta: Thacker, Spink and Co., 1894.

Anderson, Michael R. 'Legal Scholarship and the Politics of Islam in British India'. In *Perspectives on Islamic Law, Justice, and Society*, edited by Ravindra S. Khare, 65–91. Oxford: Rowman & Littlefield, 1999.

Baillie, Neil B.E. *A Digest of Moohummudan Law*. London: Smith, Elder & Co, 1865.

Baillie, Neil B.E. *A Digest of Moohummudan Law*. Part 2. London: Smith, Elder & Co, 1887.

Bata, Hashim. *Exploring the Mind of God: An Introduction to Shiʿite Legal Epistemology*. Leiden: Brill, 2023.

Beverley, Eric Lewis. 'Property, Authority and Personal Law: Waqf in Colonial South Asia'. *South Asia Research* 31, no. 2 (2011): 155–82.

Carroll, Lucy. 'The Ithna Ashari Law of Intestate Succession: An Introduction to Shia Law Applicable in South Asia'. *Modern Asian Studies* 19, no. 1 (1985): 85–124.

Cheema, Shahbaz Ahmad. *Islamic Law of Inheritance*. Islamabad: Shariah Academy, 2017.

Cheema, Shahbaz Ahmad. 'Mulla's *Principles of Mahomedan Law* in Pakistani Courts: Undoing/Unraveling the Colonial Enterprise?'. *LUMS Law Journal* 4 (2018): 56–80.

Fadel, Mohammad. 'The Social Logic of *Taqlīd* and the Rise of the *Mukhataṣar*'. *Islamic Law and Society* 3, no. 2 (1996): 193–233.

Fisch, Jorg. 'Law as a Means and an End: Some Remarks on the Function of European and Non-European Law in the Process of European Expansion'. In *European Expansion and Law: The Encounter of European and Indigenous Law in 19th- and 20th-Century Africa and Asia*, edited by Wolfgang J. Mommsen and Jaap A. de Moor, 15–38. New York: Berg Publishers, 1992.

Fyzee, Asaf A.A. *Outlines of Muhammadan Law*. 4th ed. New Delhi: Oxford University Press, 2002 [1949].

Giunchi, Elisa. 'The Reinvention of *Sharīʿa* under the British Raj: In Search of Authenticity and Certainty'. *The Journal of Asian Studies* 69, no. 4 (2010): 1119–42.

Gleave, Robert. 'Imami Shiʿi Legal Theory: From Its Origins to the Early Twentieth Century'. In *The Oxford Handbook of Islamic Law*, edited by Anver M. Emon and Rumee Ahmed, 207–30. Oxford: Oxford University Press, 2018.

Hamilton, Charles. *The Hedaya, or Guide: A Commentary on the Mussulman Laws*. Vol. 1. London: T. Bensley, 1791.

Holz, Sarah. *Governance of Islam in Pakistan: An Institutional Study of the Council of Islamic Ideology*. Liverpool: Liverpool University Press, 2022.

al-Ḥurr, Muḥammad b. al-Ḥasan. *Masāʾil al-Sharīʿa*. Translated as *Wasāʾil al-Shīʿa* by Muḥammad Ḥusayn al-Najafī. Sargodha: Maktabat al-Sibṭayn, 2017.

Ibn al-Humām, Muḥammad b. ʿAbd al-Wāḥid. *Sharḥ Fatḥ al-qadīr ʿalā al-Hidāya*. Edited by ʿAbd al-Razzāq Ghālib Mahdī. Beirut: Dār al-Kutub al-ʿIlmiyya, 2003.

Iqbal, Muhammad. *The Reconstruction of Religious Thought in Islam*. Oxford: Oxford University Press, 1934.

Kamali, Mohammad Hashim. *Principles of Islamic Jurisprudence*. Cambridge: Islamic Texts Society, 1991.

Kolff, Dirk H.A. 'The Indian and British Law Machines: Some Remarks on Law and Society in British India'. In *European Expansion and Law: The Encounter of European and Indigenous Law in 19th- and 20th-Century Africa and Asia*, edited by Wolfgang J. Mommsen and Jaap A. de Moor, 201–35. New York: Berg Publishers, 1992.

Kozlowski, Gregory. *Muslim Endowments and Society in British India*. Cambridge: Cambridge University Press, 1985.

Kugle, Scott Alan. 'Framed, Blamed and Renamed: The Recasting of Islamic Jurisprudence in Colonial South Asia'. *Modern Asian Studies* 35 (2001): 257–313.

Malik, Jamal. *Islam in South Asia: Revisited*. Leiden: Brill, 2020.

Mulla, Dinshah Fardunji. *Principles of Mahomedan Law*. New Delhi: LexisNexis, 2012 [1905].

Nelson, Matthew J. *In the Shadow of Shariʿah: Islam, Islamic Law, and Democracy in Pakistan*. London: Hurst & Company, 2011.

Nelson, Matthew J. 'Islamic Law in an Islamic State: What Role for Parliament?'. In *Constitution Writing, Religion, and Democracy*, edited by Asli Ü. Bâli and Hanna Lerner, 235–64. Cambridge: Cambridge University Press, 2017.

Niẓām, al-Shaykh. *al-Fatāwā al-ʿĀlamgīriyya*. Vol. 3. Calcutta: Nawal Kishawr, 1865.

Rahim, Abdur. 'A Historical Sketch of the Growth of Mohamedan Jurisprudence'. *Calcutta Law Journal* 3 (1906): 255–71.

Rahim, Abdur. *The Principles of Muhammadan Jurisprudence: According to the Hanafi, Maliki, Shafiʿi and Hanbali Schools*. London: Luzac & Co., 1911.

Redding, Jeffrey A. 'Constitutionalizing Islam: Theory and Pakistan'. *Virginia Journal of International Law* 44, no. 3 (2004): 759–827.

Sajāwandī, Sirāj al-Dīn Muḥammad b. Muḥammad. *Al Sirājiyya: or, the Mahommedan Law of Inheritance with a Commentary by Sir William Jones*. Calcutta: Joseph Cooper, 1792.

Setalvad, M.C. *The Common Law in India*. London: Stevens & Sons Limited, 1960.

Sheibani, Mariam. 'Marriage, Divorce, and Inheritance in Classical Islamic Law and Premodern Practice'. In *The Oxford Handbook of Islam and Women*, edited by Asma Afsaruddin, 155–80. Oxford: Oxford University Press, 2023.

Skuy, David. 'Macaulay and the Indian Penal Code of 1862: The Myth of the Inherent Superiority and Modernity of the English Legal System Compared to India's Legal System in the Nineteenth Century'. *Modern Asian Studies* 32, no. 3 (1998): 513–57.

Takim, Liyakat. *Shiʿism Revisited: Ijtihad and Reformation in Contemporary Times*. Oxford: Oxford University Press, 2022.

Tyabji, Faiz Badruddin. *Principles of Muhammadan Law*. Bombay: D. B. Taraporewala Sons, 1913.

Wilson, R. K. 'Should the Personal Laws of the Natives of India Be Codified?'. *Asiatic Quarterly Review* 6 (1898): 225–49.

Yassari, Nadjma. 'Intestate Succession in Islamic Countries'. In *Comparative Succession Law, Volume II: Intestate Succession*, edited by Kenneth Reid, Marius de Waal, and Reinhard Zimmermann, 421–41. Oxford: Oxford University Press, 2015.

Yusuf Ali, Abdullah. *The Holy Qur'an*. Kuala Lumpur: Islamic Book Trust, 2007.

CHAPTER 17

'Do Not Prohibit the Good Things That God Has Made Lawful to You' (Q. 5:87): Ethical Vegetarianism in Islam and Beyond

Sarra Tlili

Killing for food is one of the most enduring ethical problems in human history. At least on the surface, depriving one creature of its life to satisfy one's craving for meat or even to sustain one's own life does not seem intuitively consistent with the principle of justice. Despite the legitimacy of this concern and the centrality of the notion of justice to Islamic doctrines, among the world's faith traditions, Islam is probably the most resistant to moral vegetarianism. This does not imply that the tradition has been indifferent to the problem. Indeed, the broader theme of animal suffering and the sub-theme of killing for food have preoccupied Muslim theologians, Qur'anic exegetes, and other thinkers; however, vegetarianism was rarely among their proposed answers.[1]

Against this backdrop, in the last couple of decades a small but growing number of academics and lay advocates have striven to demonstrate the compatibility of moral vegetarianism with Islamic doctrines.[2] Although, in most cases, this group's aim is merely to carve a place for vegetarianism without questioning the basic permissibility of animal products, some have crossed this threshold to argue that a vegetarian lifestyle is more consonant with Islamic teachings. Besides, many animal rights advocates and Islamicists treat Islam's resistance to the vegetarian ideal as a sign of anthropocentrism.[3] One of the aims of this article is to examine and evaluate these views. Although I share with advocates of Islamic vegetarianism their egalitarian aspirations

1 For example, see Margaretha T. Heemskerk, *Suffering in the Muʿtazilite Theology: ʿAbd al-Jabbār's Teaching on Pain and Divine Justice* (Leiden: Brill, 2000), 187–89.

2 For example, see 'Fatwas on Vegetarianism', Animals in Islam, www.animalsinislam.com/halal-living/fatwas/ (a site which compiles fatwas affirming the permissibility of vegetarianism); Remona Aly, 'You Are What You Eid: Ramadan for Vegans', *Guardian*, 30 May 2019, www.theguardian.com/food/2019/may/30/you-are-what-you-eid-ramadan-for-vegans; and 'Aiysha Younas Explores the Links between Veganism and Her Religion', Vegan Society (blog), 19 August 2022, www.vegansociety.com/news/blog/veganism-and-islam.

3 For example, see Richard Foltz, *Animals in Islamic Tradition and Muslim Cultures* (Oxford: Oneworld, 2006), 93.

 | HTTPS://DOI.ORG/10.1163/9789004755567-019

and agree that these aspirations are rooted in the Qur'an, I believe that their treatment of this subject leaves much to be desired.[4] Likewise, the unquestioned conviction that killing for food is a sign of anthropocentrism shows a lack of critical engagement with the principle of vegetarianism.

More importantly, I would like to argue that although it may appear paradoxical, killing for food is consistent with egalitarianism and justice, provided it abides by specific rules. This is not to deny the paradox inherent in this problem. I readily admit that the animal whose life is sacrificed experiences a significant loss; however, animal life costs are not unique to meat-inclusive diets. Vegetarian and vegan diets also involve a cost in *animal* life, though one that tends to be less noticeable or dismissed as undeserving of moral consideration. Moreover, if carried to its logical conclusion, moral vegetarianism is bound to raise severe conceptual and empirical problems, affecting many vulnerable human groups and the animals it seeks to protect. Thus, close analysis – as I hope to demonstrate – reveals that moral vegetarianism is founded on an uncritical appeal to intuition and fails to consider the complex webs of life.

This chapter's first section aims to demonstrate that Islamic scriptural sources authorise responsible killing for food in unambiguous terms and that they disallow any interference with this authorisation. I will describe and analyse pertinent scriptural themes to build this argument. Second, I will cite and discuss the arguments adduced to defend Islamic vegetarianism. In this section, I will mainly be in conversation with Richard Foltz, Kecia Ali, and Zinnira Shaykh, whose works capture the main arguments in favour of this ethic. In the third section, I analyse and evaluate the principle of moral vegetarianism. The aim is to highlight the complexity of the factors underpinning food ethics and to argue that such complexity dictates deeper engagement with the question of killing for food.

1 Scriptural and Legal Foundations

The main reason for Islam's resistance to vegetarianism is rooted in the Qur'an, which not only authorises killing for food but also prohibits any interference with this authorisation. Q. 5:1 states, 'O you who have believed, fulfil your pacts. Lawful to you are grazing cattle (*bahīmat al-anʿām*) except that which is

4 For an egalitarian, non-anthropocentric reading of Qur'anic animal themes, see Sarra Tlili, *Animals in the Qur'an* (New York: Cambridge University Press, 2012); and Sarra Tlili, 'All Animals Are Equal, or Are They? The Ikhwān al-Ṣafā''s Animal Epistle and Its Unhappy End', *Journal of Qur'anic Studies* 16, no. 2 (2014): 42–88.

recited to you, hunting being prohibited when you are in the state of pilgrim sanctity. God decrees what He wants.' Q. 5:4 adds, 'They ask you what is made lawful to them. Say, lawful to you are all good things. As for the hunting animals that you teach in the way that God has taught you, eat of what they catch for you and mention God's name over it. Fear God, for God is swift in reckoning.' Q. 5:96 reiterates the prohibition of hunting for those observing the state of pilgrim sanctity but authorises fishing and food from sea provenance. Including for those observing this state. Thus, while imposing several restrictions, these verses clearly establish the permissibility of killing for food.

None of these injunctions, however, require Muslims to eat animal products. Muslim jurists understand the imperatives 'hunt' and 'eat' in these passages as authorisations rather than as mandates. What lays behind the Islamic resistance to moral vegetarianism is Q. 5:87, which disallows Muslims to treat as impermissible something that God has declared as permissible. It says, 'O you who have believed, do not prohibit the good things that God has made lawful to you and do not transgress. God indeed does not love transgressors.' Together, these verses indicate that a Muslim may follow a vegetarian diet without violating Qur'anic injunctions, provided they do not assume that their abstention from meat is more pleasing to God or more consistent with God's purpose, do not question the legality and ethicality of meat consumption, and do not promote vegetarianism as a more ethical path. In other words, the prohibition pertains only to *moral* vegetarianism. Those who do not consume animal products because of financial or health restrictions, for example, or even simply because of taste preferences, are free to follow a vegetarian diet.

The *ḥadīth* literature expounds further on this point. A narrative in several *ḥadīth* compendiums relates that some of the Prophet's Companions asked his wives about the acts of worship he performed in private; however, when they learned about them, they thought they should do more. This led one of them to vow celibacy, another to abstain from meat, and a third to give up sleep at night to dedicate his time to prayer. When this reached the Prophet, he said, 'What is it with people that they say such-and-such things? I myself spend part of the night in prayer, but I also sleep; I fast on certain days but not on others; and I marry women. Anyone who rejects my way is not one of my followers.'[5] Other versions of this *ḥadīth* do not mention meat but convey the same prohibition of deviating from the Prophet's example or trying to outperform him.

The theme of animal sacrifice further complicates this question. The Qur'an ordains pilgrims who combine the minor and major pilgrimages (*ʿumra* and *ḥajj*, respectively) to offer a sacrificial animal. However, it provides alternatives

5 Muslim b. al-Ḥajjāj, *Ṣaḥīḥ Muslim* (Beirut: Dār al-Kutub al-ʿIlmiyya, 1991), 2:1020.

for those who cannot meet the requirements. Q. 2:196 states, 'Those who enjoy *ʿumra* followed by *ḥajj*, let them offer what is easy to obtain of sacrificial animals (*fa-mā staysara min al-hady*), but for those who do not find the means, let them fast three days during pilgrimage and seven when they return.' *Ḥajj* is a mandatory, once-in-a-lifetime ritual that every adult Muslim who is physically and financially able must perform,[6] whereas *ʿumra* is a supererogatory act of worship. Although Muslims typically join the two rituals, technically, they are not obligated to do so. They may thus perform *ḥajj* alone (*ifrād*), in which case the animal sacrifice is no longer compulsory. However, opting for *ifrād* with the sole or primary purpose of avoiding the sacrifice appears inconsistent with the ritual's intent. As I explain later, the Qur'an presents animal sacrifice as a blessing from God and emphasises its goodness. This suggests that striving to avoid it is not pleasing to God.

Within the *ḥajj* context, the Qur'an also imposes a sacrificial penalty on those who intentionally violate the ban on hunting. It says, 'O you who have believed, do not kill game when you are in pilgrim sanctity; whoever of you kills it intentionally the penalty is an equivalent of sacrificial animals as shall be judged by two men of equity among you, an offering to reach the Kaʿba, or, by way of expiation, the feeding of the indigent or the equivalent of that in fasting, that he may taste the evil consequences of his action' (Q. 5:95). Muslim jurists expand this rule to include other violations of the *ḥajj* ritual, including accidental ones. For example, many consider that someone who forgets to pelt some or all the pebbles (*ramy al-jamarāt*) at the designated time – one of the compulsory rites of *ḥajj*[7] – must offer a sacrifice in expiation (*ʿalayhi dam*).[8] As usual, the Qur'an provides other alternatives, but the aim in this case is to ease the burden of those who cannot meet the sacrifice penalty rather than to offer a preferable option.

Affirming the goodness of animal sacrifice is one of the main themes of Sūrat al-Ḥajj (Q. 22), which traces the ritual back to Abraham and links it to feelings of piety and reverence. In Q. 22:28–29, God addresses Abraham, saying, 'Proclaim pilgrimage among humankind: they shall come to you on foot and every lean steed, coming from every deep and distant place, that they may witness benefits for them and mention the name of God, during appointed days, over the grazing animals that He has provided for them. So, eat of them

6 Aḥmad b. Ḥanbal, *Musnad Aḥmad* (Beirut: al-Risāla, 2001), 4:151.

7 For more on this rite, see Muhammad Ilyas Abdul Ghani, *The History of Makkah Mukarramah* (Medina: King Fahd National Library, 2004), 175–79.

8 Ibn al-Mundhir Abū Bakr al-Nīsābūrī, *al-Ishrāf ʿalā madhāhib al-ʿulamāʾ* (Ras al-Khaimah: Maktabat Makkat al-Thaqāfiyya, 2004), 3:334.

and feed the destitute poor.' One of the aims of the rite is thus to feed the poor, but it also serves as a reminder of God's generosity, which pilgrims should celebrate joyfully and in gratitude. The next verse (Q. 22:30) reiterates the permissibility of cattle and appears to provide another warning – reminiscent of the one in Q. 5:87 – to not tamper with this rite. It says, 'And whoever venerates God's sacred rites (*ḥurumāt Allāh*), that is better for him with his Lord. Cattle are permissible for you except that which has been pointed out [as forbidden]. Therefore, eschew abominations and eschew false speech.' Thus, the verse urges believers to revere God's sacred rites, which in this case consist of animal sacrifice, and reaffirms the permissibility of cattle. To claim otherwise, the verse appears to insist, would amount to false speech.

The sura shortly continues,

> We have assigned the sacrificial camels and cattle (*budn*) for you among God's rituals. There is good for you in them. So, mention God's name over them when they line up, and when they have fallen upon their flanks eat of them and feed the needy and the mendicant. Thus have We made them serviceable to you that you may give thanks. Neither their flesh nor their blood will reach God, but your veneration reaches Him! Thus has He made them serviceable to you so that you reverence God for guiding you. Give glad tidings to the righteous. (Q. 22:36–37)

This passage establishes the goodness of animal sacrifice. It declares that sacrificial animals are among God's rituals and affirms that there is good in them for pilgrims or, more generally, for Muslims (*lakum fīhā khayr*). Among the ritual's many benefits is that it fills the believer's heart with reverence and creates a joyful occasion to feed the needy and enjoy God's blessings. Before this passage (Q. 22:32), the sura stresses that 'He who venerates God's rituals, that is from the reverence of the heart (*min taqwā al-qulūb*).' Given that the sura declares that sacrificial animals are among God's rituals and affirms that the veneration of God's rituals is a sign of piety, it clearly expects believers to honour this ritual.[9]

While the forgoing focuses on offerings in Mecca, some have interpreted Q. 108:2, 'So pray to your Lord and sacrifice', as mandating animal sacrifice on the rest of Muslims on the Sacrifice Day. In the view of Ḥanafī jurists, this is, in fact, the only mandatory form of animal sacrifice incumbent on all

9 For more on this point, especially on the cultic dimension of slaughter, see Muhsin Goudarzi, 'Worship (*Dīn*), Monotheism (*Islām*), and the Qur'ān's Cultic Decalogue', *Journal of the International Qur'anic Studies Association* 8, no. 1 (2023): 56–60.

non-travelling Muslim households who possess the means.[10] Interestingly, the Ḥanafī position frees many pilgrims – in their capacity as travellers – from the obligation to observe the sacrifice (unless, as pointed out earlier, they combine the two forms of pilgrimage or violate certain bans) while imposing the sacrifice on non-pilgrims. Other schools of law adopt various stands. Many Mālikī jurists, including Mālik (d. 179/795) himself, consider the sacrifice mandatory (or nearly mandatory) on non-pilgrims,[11] whereas most others, including the majority of Mālikī jurists and Twelver Shīʿa, view it as an emphatically recommended act (*sunna muʾakkada*), yet not binding. Therefore, in the view of the majority, a Muslim who does not observe the sacrifice incurs no blame, but s/he becomes eligible for ample divine reward for observing it.[12]

While authorising killing for food, the Qurʾan also imposes important restrictions on this sanction. The most detailed verse on the subject states,

> Prohibited to you are carrion and blood, the flesh of swine and that which has been dedicated to other than God, animals that are strangled or beaten to death, those killed by falling or the goring of horns, and animals mangled by beasts of prey except the ones that you slaughter properly while still alive; [prohibited also are] animals that are sacrificed on stone altars and what you allot with divining arrows. (Q. 5:3)

The two factors underlying most of these prohibitions are the party to whom the animal is consecrated and the mode of death or killing. Animals whose flesh is permissible must not be consecrated to deities other than God. The Qurʾan, in fact, repeatedly reminds Muslims to invoke God's name over the animals they kill for food (Q. 5:4, 6:118, 22:3) and to avoid the meat over which God's name has not been pronounced (Q. 6:121). Based on this, both Sunnī and Shīʿī jurists generally consider it mandatory to invoke God's name at the time of killing. However, mere forgetfulness does not affect the legality of the carcass. Shāfiʿīs adopt a laxer position. In their view, a Muslim, by definition, does not consecrate animals to a deity other than God, leading them to deduce that the invocation of God's name is highly recommended, though not mandatory. The

10 Muḥammad b. Aḥmad al-Sarakhsī, *al-Mabsūṭ* (Beirut: Dār al-Maʿrifa, 1989), 12:8.

11 Abū Saʿīd al-Barādhiʿī, *al-Tahdhīb fī ikhtiṣār al-Mudawwana* (Dubai: Dār al-Buḥūth li-l-Dirāsāt al-Islāmiyya, 2002), 2:42. Two statements are attributed to Mālik: one says, 'The sacrifice is incumbent (*wājiba*) on the person who can afford it'; the second, 'I prefer that it be observed (*lā uḥibbu tarkahā*).' The first statement indicates that he views it as compulsory whereas the second indicates that he views it as recommended. Ibid., 37.

12 Abū Ḥasan b. Ḥabīb al-Māwardī, *al-Ḥāwī al-kabīr* (Beirut: Dār al-Kutub al-ʿIlmiyya, 1994), 15:71.

position that all schools share, and which is clearly articulated in the Qur'an, is the prohibition of the flesh of animals consecrated to a deity other than God.[13]

The mode of death or killing is the second important factor. The Qur'an prohibits the consumption of the flesh of land animals that expire naturally (*mayta*, carrion) or from violent death, whether accidental or purposely inflicted. The latter include animals that die or are killed by strangulation (*munkhaniqa*), are beaten to death (*mawqūdha*), are thrown or fall from a height (*mutaraddiya*), are gored (*naṭīḥa*), or are devoured by a beast of prey (*mā akala al-sabuʿ*). However, if the animal is slaughtered correctly (*tadhkiya*, literally purification) before it expires from these injuries, its flesh becomes licit. The Qur'an does not elaborate on the notion of *tadhkiya*, or proper slaughter, but Islamic law provides ample details based on *ḥadīth* instructions. The editors of *The Study Quran* capture the legal stance succinctly in their commentary on Q. 5:3. They write:

> Proper ritual slaughtering in Islamic dietary law requires that the animal's throat be slit, preferably severing the jugular vein, in order to kill it quickly and cause the least suffering, and the blood must be allowed to drain out. One must mention the Name of God over the animal and face it in the direction of the canonical prayer (*qiblah*). Additionally, the animal should be treated with kindness: the killing should not be preceded by a violent struggle, the animal should be well rested, and it should be killed with a sharp knife, so that it causes the least pain. One should also turn one's face away from the animal when slaughtering it and remain aware that it is only by God's permission that one may kill and eat the animal. All of these practices have the effect of removing the slaughterer's sense of absolute power over the animal and of maintaining the comfort and dignity of the animal to the extent possible.[14]

Tony Milligan observes that the act of killing is not just about ending an animal's life but also about stripping away a sense of creaturely dignity.[15] The ritualistic nature of slaughter appears mainly aimed to address this point: it seeks to minimise the animal's pain and to nurture feelings about the sanctity of her life. It also simultaneously addresses feelings of entitlement and guilt. It

13 Kuwait Ministry of Endowments and Islamic Affairs, *al-Mawsūʿa al-fiqhiyya* (Kuwait: The Ministry of Endowments and Islamic Affairs, 1983), 21:189–91.

14 Seyyed Hossein Nasr, ed., *The Study Quran: A New Translation and Commentary* (New York: Harper Collins, 2015), 534.

15 Tony Milligan, *Beyond Animal Rights: Food, Pets and Ethics* (London: Continuum International Publishing, 2010), 41.

is a reminder that life belongs to God and may thus be taken only with God's permission, but once God has granted that permission, one should also accept the gift both in humility and in gratitude.

From these and related teachings in the *ḥadīth*,[16] Muslim jurists derived the legal precept that animals may *only* be killed for food and that such killing is the only pain one is authorised to inflict on them (*lā yajūzu taʿdhībuhā wa-lā dhabḥuhā illā li-maʾkala*).[17] Although some schools of law, especially the Ḥanafī, have expanded this authorisation to include non-dietary benefits as legitimate reasons for taking an animal's life, others, particularly the Shāfiʿī, insist on strict adherence to this principle. Thus, in the Shāfiʿī view, if a sheep swallows a precious stone whose market value exceeds its own, it is blameworthy to kill it with the primary intention of recovering the stone, even if one intends to consume the flesh subsequently. This is because scriptural sources, they argue, authorise killing only for food.[18]

All schools of law also agree on the prohibition or blameworthiness of inflicting physical and psychological pain on animals, naturally, excluding the act of killing for food. The Ḥanafī scholar Abū Bakr al-Zabīdī (d. 800/1397) recommends the clipping of one's fingernails before milking an animal lest they hurt her.[19] The Mālikī scholar al-Ḥaṭṭāb al-Ruʿaynī (d. 954/1547) writes that it is impermissible to separate between a mother ewe and her lamb because this causes her to suffer (*al-tafriqa taʿdhīb lahā*).[20] Al-Ṣāwī al-Mālikī (d. 1241/1825) writes that it is forbidden to catch an edible bird or any other animal to confine him for one's gratification (*yaḥrumu iṣṭiyādu maʾkūlin min ṭayrin wa-ghayrihi bi-niyyati ḥabsihi aw al-furjati ʿalayhi*).[21] Abū Ḥāmid al-Ghazālī (d. 505/1111) states that if one does not own feed for their animals, they are authorised to extort it if the animals' lives are endangered. Relatedly, travellers who are short on water must prioritise animals' need for it over the ablution ritual.[22] The

16 For more on the *ḥadīth*'s position on this topic, see Sarra Tlili, 'Animals Would Follow Shāfiʿism: Legitimate and Illegitimate Violence to Animals in Medieval Islamic Thought', in *Violence in Islamic Thought from the Qurʾān to the Mongols*, ed. Robert Gleave and István Kristó-Nagy (Edinburgh: Edinburgh University Press, 2015), 227–29; and Sarra Tlili, 'Animals', in *Muhammad in History, Thought and Culture: An Encyclopedia of the Prophet of God*, 2 vols., ed. Coeli Fitzpatrick and Adam Hani Walker (Santa Barbara: ABC-CLIO, 2014), 1:25–29.

17 Abū Ḥāmid al-Ghazālī, *al-Wasīṭ fī al-madhhab* (Cairo: Dār al-Salām, 1997), 6:248.

18 For more on this point, see Tlili, 'Animals Would Follow Shāfiʿism'.

19 Abū Bakr al-Zabīdī, *al-Jawhara al-nayyira* (Beirut: Dār al-Kutub al-ʿIlmiyya, 2006), 2:281.

20 al-Ḥaṭṭāb al-Ruʿaynī, *Mawāhib al-jalīl fī sharḥ Mukhtaṣar Khālil* (Nouakchott: Dār al-Riḍwān, 2010), 5:173.

21 Aḥmad al-Ṣāwī, *Ḥāshiyat al-Ṣāwī ʿalā al-Sharḥ al-ṣaghīr* (Cairo: Dār al-Maʿārif, 1986), 2:178.

22 al-Ghazālī, *al-Wasīṭ*, 6:249.

interests of other animals thus take precedence over the strict adherence to rituals and legal regulations and impose various obligations on their owners.[23] For their sake, one may even violate humans' property rights, otherwise treated as sacrosanct in Islamic law.

This level of attention strongly suggests that the position on killing for food is neither arbitrary nor unreflective. Scriptural and legal sources clearly take the well-being of non-human animals seriously. It is hard to accept that a tradition attentive enough to spare a sheep pain as minimal as the one resulting from accidental scratching of her udder by one's unclipped fingernails would take her life and the pain resulting from slaughter lightly. Therefore, before cursorily treating the position on killing for food as a sign of anthropocentrism or trying to explain it away, one should first explore other possible reasons that can plausibly reconcile these apparent contradictions.

2 Islamic Vegetarianism: Valid Concerns, Invalid Answers

Although premodern Islamic tradition took animals' interests seriously at the concrete level, conceptually, it viewed them as inferior creatures. Because of this, many Muslims sought to rationalise the scriptural authorisation to kill for food using anthropocentric justifications, claiming, for example, that God created other animals for humans' use. Defences of Islamic vegetarianism have justifiably contested this perceived hierarchical paradigm. Commenting on Ibn ʿAbd al-Salām's (d. 660/1262) statement to the effect that humans are justified to kill other animals because of their superior status, Richard Foltz notes that many 'contemporary animal rights activists would label such positions as "speciesist"'.[24] Foltz's criticism is not without problems. His attribution of universal validity to animal rights theory betrays a hegemonic undertone; nonetheless, he has a point. Indeed, Ibn ʿAbd al-Salām's view is problematic not only by modern animal rights standards but also seems inconsistent with scriptural tenets. As I argue in much of my work, this hierarchical paradigm is more likely projected on, than stemming from, Islamic scriptural sources.[25]

23 Premodern Islamic sources prevalently treat humans, angels, and jinn as animal species. On this point, see Sarra Tlili, 'The Meaning of the Qur'anic Word "*Dābba*": "Animals" or "Nonhuman Animals"?', *Journal of Qur'anic Studies* 12, no. 1–2 (2010): 167–87.

24 Foltz, *Animals in Islamic Tradition*, 35.

25 For example, see Sarra Tlili, 'Qur'anic Creation: Anthropocentric Readings and Ecocentric Possibilities', in *The Routledge Companion to the Qur'an*, ed. George Archer, Maria M. Dakake, and Daniel A. Madigan (New York: Routledge, 2021), 135–44; and Sarra Tlili, 'I Invoke God, Therefore I Am: Creation's Spirituality and Its Ecologic Impact in Islamic

Kecia Ali draws attention to the interplay between anthropocentrism and androcentrism and argues that both are rooted in the same patriarchal ideology. 'Hierarchical cosmologies', she writes, 'affirm male dominance in family and society and affirm human dominion over animals, legitimating their use, confinement, slaughter, and consumption.'[26] This argument is valid, as demonstrated by both secular and religious scholarship. Ali also rightly points out that 'a parallel between female and animal is implicit in a good deal of Muslim thinking'.[27] This is, for example, clear in the views of Abū al-Aʿlā al-Mawdūdī (d. 1399/1979), she notes, who claims that 'men/human beings have been assigned viceregency over animals and that males have been assigned viceregency over females'.[28] She also points out the inconsistency of these views with Islam's scriptural ethos, at least according to recent readings proposed by Muslim feminists and animal ethicists. From these parallels and as a matter of consistency, Ali urges Muslim feminists to show the same concern for animals as they do for women.

These are valuable insights. Centric ideologies indeed have much in common, and all of them can be dismissive of the interests of the other. Moreover, close analysis shows that one of the aims of the Qur'an's theocentric discourse is to disrupt all forms of creaturely centrism. The Qurʾan insists on all creatures' vulnerability (Q. 4:28, 22:73), accountability,[29] and punishability[30] and consistently reminds us that God extends His mercy and providence to all creation (Q. 7:156, 40:7). Despite the centrality of these themes, the tradition has not only embraced many forms of centrism but has often presented them as stemming from scriptural sources, though often through recourse to flawed interpretative strategies. Challenging these hierarchical paradigms is essential because of its potential social and environmental impacts and because it appears to be more consistent with Islam's scriptural ethos.

Defences of vegetarianism also highlight the excessive cruelty and disastrous environmental impact of intensive animal farming and question Muslims' uncritical participation in this system. Zinnira Shaikh not only provides a

---

Texts', in *A Global History of Literature and the Environment*, ed. John Parham and Louise Westling (New York: Cambridge University Press, 2017), 107–22.

26 Kecia Ali, 'Muslims and Meat-Eating: Vegetarianism, Gender, and Identity', *Journal of Religious Ethics* 43, no. 2 (2015): 269.

27 Ibid., 276.

28 Ibid., 277.

29 On the accountability of non-human animals, see Tlili, *Animals in the Qurʾan*, 202–6 (*taklīf*).

30 See Q. 69:46, 17:75, 33:30, 4:172–73, 21:29. These verses indicate that even the Prophet, his wives, and angels are punishable.

disturbing assessment of the livestock industry, but she also questions the credibility of *ḥalāl* certification given the numerous instances in which cartels and corrupt government agencies tampered with it.[31] This is a valid point not only because of the cases of corruption but also because it is highly questionable that intensive farming can satisfy the tradition's moral requirements. The fact that contemporary Muslim scholars and government agencies have yet to take animals' interests seriously in gauging the permissibility of intensive animal production stands in stark contrast with the stances of the premodern tradition, which often prioritised the interests of other animals and devised legal and social mechanisms to ensure their implementation. Drawing attention to this flagrant disregard is thus one of the many strengths of Shaikh's contribution and, more generally, Islamic animal advocacy.

Live trade is another problem Shaikh highlights. Given that Muslim countries are among the major importers of live animals and that these animals are transported in egregiously harsh conditions, this point deserves serious attention. In her description of one shipment from Australia to a Muslim country, Kristen Stilt writes, 'in one voyage … about 2400 sheep, more than 3% of those onboard, died due to the heat. The sheep, packed in to pens on the multi-story ships, literally cooked to death, covered in waste and desperately gasping for air and water in extreme heat.'[32] It seems impossible to find a way to reconcile such neglect and cruelty with the *ḥadīth*'s numerous injunctions about animals.

Millions of the animals shipped to Muslim-majority countries are acquired for sacrifice. Among these, the animals provided for pilgrims survive the transportation trauma only to be exposed to mass slaughter dictated by current pilgrimage conditions.[33] The Prophet, it should be pointed out, is reported to have said, 'God has decreed goodness (*iḥsān*) in everything. When you kill, kill well, and when you slaughter, slaughter well. Let the one [who slaughters an

31 Zinnira Shaikh, 'Heresy or Moral Imperative? Islamic Perspectives on Veganism', in *Routledge Handbook of Islamic Ritual and Practice*, ed. Oliver Leaman (New York: Routledge, 2022), 437–58.

32 Kristen Stilt, 'Trading in Sacrifice', in *Studies in Global Animal Law*, ed. Anne Peters (Berlin: Springer, 2020), 53.

33 According to some news outlets, Saudi Arabia imported 3 million sheep and camels to cover the demand of the pilgrimage season of 2015: 'Kingdom Imports 3 Million Sheep and Camels for Haj', Eye of Riyadh, 31 July 2015, www.eyeofriyadh.com/news/details/kingdom-imports-3-million-sheep-and-camels-for-haj. S.A. Rahman estimates the number to range between 1 and 3 million per pilgrimage season. S.A. Rahman, 'Middle East', in *Long Distance Transport and Welfare of Farm Animals*, ed. M.C. Appleby, V. Cussen, L. Garcés, L.A. Lambert, and J. Turner (Cambridge, MA: CABI, 2008), 400.

animal] sharpen their blade and comfort the animal.'[34] In the view of traditional Muslim scholars, comforting the animal means that one should avoid sharpening the knife in front of her, killing one animal in the presence of another (*lā yadhbaḥ wāḥida bi-ḥaḍrat ukhrā*),[35] pulling the animal violently (*lā yajurruhā li-l-madhbaḥ bi-ʿunf*),[36] and throwing her to the floor (*lā yaḍrib bi-hā al-arḍ*).[37] The transportation conditions illustrate the stark departure from these injunctions, and given the time and space constraints and the number of sacrificed animals, it seems impossible to satisfy any of the remaining ones. Thus, Shaikh is justified in calling for the need to rethink the sacrifice ritual, especially since the Qur'an itself provides other alternatives, as she pertinently points out.

2.1 Invalid Answers

However, despite their validity, these criticisms only show the incompatibility of industrial animal production with traditional Islamic doctrines and point out inconsistencies in the tradition's conceptualisation of the animal. They do not lead to a case for vegetarianism, much less to one on Islamic scriptural grounds. A thorough case must first address the daunting task of explaining away the scriptural prohibition of questioning the permissibility of what God has declared as permissible, something that has yet to receive adequate attention. It must also take a closer look at the principle of vegetarianism. What would happen to domestic animals if universal vegetarianism came to pass? Is domestication inherently exploitative and, therefore, morally indefensible, as most animal rights theorists maintain? Is it inconsistent with the Qur'an's ethos? If we are to end it, how can we do so without violating the integrity of animals' bodies and affecting their psychological well-being? What would happen to societies whose survival depends on domesticates? Is contextual vegetarianism – the version that takes age, gender, and social variables into consideration – without conceptual problems? At an even more basic level, do vegetarian diets have no blood cost? Is plant agriculture indeed better for the environment? As we delve deeper into these and related questions, we discover that vegetarianism is more elusive than many seem to realise and too

34 Muḥammad b. ʿĪsā al-Tirmidhī, *Sunan al-Tirmidhī* (Cairo: Muṣṭafā al-Bābūm, 1962), 4:23.

35 Muḥyī al-Dīn b. Sharaf al-Nawawī, *al-Minhāj sharḥ Ṣaḥīḥ Muslim b. al-Ḥajjāj* (Beirut: Dār Iḥyā' al-Turāth al-ʿArabī, 1972), 13:106–7.

36 ʿAbd al-Ra'ūf al-Manāwī, *Fayḍ al-Qadīr sharḥ al-Jāmiʿ al-ṣaghīr* (Beirut: Dār al-Maʿrifa, 1972), 1:347.

37 Ibn Abī Zayd al-Qayrawānī, *al-Nawādir wa-l-ziyādāt* (Beirut: Dār al-Gharb al-Islāmī, 1999), 4:359.

fraught with ethical and practical dilemmas to be uncritically proposed as a superior model.

2.2 Explaining Away the Scriptural Prohibition

The primary challenge facing a plausible case for moral vegetarianism on Islamic grounds is addressing the scriptural stance. As I explained in the first section, although the Qur'an only authorises, rather than requires, killing for food, it also prohibits any interference with this authorisation. The *ḥadīth*'s position is consonant with the Qur'anic one. The Prophet himself is reported to have consumed animal products, to have personally killed animals for food, and to have warned against deviating from his example.[38]

Although the defences of Islamic vegetarianism reflect an awareness of this point, they stop short of addressing it. Ali, for example, maintains that foundational texts are susceptible to pro-vegetarian interpretations, stating that 'just as Qur'anic verses on marriage and sexuality have been reinterpreted by Muslim women in egalitarian ways', one can perhaps do the same with animal themes.[39] Beyond this hazy appeal to the principle of egalitarianism, however, she does not explain how a *plausible* reinterpretation could be attained. Furthermore, Ali appears to take it for granted that the vegetarian ethic is more egalitarian than the meat-inclusive one, failing to perceive its socially elitist, anthropocentric, and androcentric undertones, which I discuss further below.

Ali presents the tradition's overall attitude towards food as another potential path towards the vegetarian ethic. In her opinion, the fact that the tradition counsels moderation in food consumption and encourages scrupulousness about foodstuff's origins can at least serve as a starting point for a deeper conversation.[40] However, whether in Islamic sources or secular defences of meat-inclusive diets, moderation is consistently presented as a virtue in its own right, not as a step towards abstention. Both cases treat abstention as a new and potentially harmful imbalance.

Ali also makes the strange claim that the Prophet is reported to have speculated on two occasions about foregoing meat consumption out of concern for animals, citing in support of this view an article that merely discusses Muḥammad's kindness towards a camel and a doe.[41] Indeed, the episodes

---

38 Muḥammad b. Ismāʿīl al-Bukhārī, *Ṣaḥīḥ al-Bukhārī* (Beirut: Dār Ibn Kathīr, 2002), 1414.

39 Ali, 'Muslims and Meat-Eating', 272.

40 Ibid., 272–73.

41 Ibid., 273; Giovanni Canova, 'Il Profeta Muḥammad e gli Animali: La Leggenda del Cammello e della Gazzella', *Oriente Moderno* 89, no. 2 (2009): 257–75.

involving these two animals are mere specimens of the overarching theme of Muḥammad's kindness to animals, which permeates the *ḥadīth* and is the main reason the tradition takes the question of animal welfare so seriously. However, this theme exists alongside the explicit authorisation to kill for food and, more importantly, the proscription to tamper with this authorisation.

Advocates of Islamic vegetarianism are also aware of the importance of the sacrifice ritual and consequently strive to de-emphasise it. Based on the Qur'anic affirmation that it is the believer's righteousness, rather than the animals' meat or blood, that reaches God (Q. 22:37), Shaikh is one of many who argue that taking the animal's life is not an end in itself, but rather that the sacrifice 'is meant to be used as a means to serve a social need'.[42] Other advocates propose that the ritual aims to sacrifice one's ego rather than an animal.[43] Although these can be among the ritual's aims, a close reading shows that these aims are to be attained *through* the sacrifice ritual, not by bypassing it.

As I have already pointed out, the Qur'an presents the sacrifice ritual in a favourable light. It states that sacrificial animals are among God's signs or symbols (*shaʿāʾir Allāh*, Q. 22:36) and that the veneration of God's symbols is 'from the piety of hearts' (Q. 22:32). This strongly suggests that the Qur'an links piety to the fulfilment rather than to the omission of this ritual. Furthermore, the clear reminder of the permissibility of grazing livestock, along with the need to revere God's ordinances and to avoid false statements (Q. 22:30, discussed earlier), appear to be clear deterrents against the reinterpretation of the sacrifice ritual. This further corroborates the view that the Qur'an treats the celebration rather than the avoidance of the ritual as a sign of piety. A further indication is found in Sūrat al-Māʾida. After ordaining believers to 'not prohibit the good things that God has made lawful' (Q. 5:87), the passage continues by saying, '*Eat* of what God has provided for you – lawful and good – and *fear God* (*ittaqū Allāh*) in whom you have believed' (Q. 5:88, emphasis added). Again, the sign of righteousness consists of eating rather than abstaining from or re-evaluating the permissibility of what God has declared lawful.

Be that as it may, the sacrifice theme poses a serious challenge, but it is not the major hurdle facing the case for Islamic vegetarianism. Shaikh and others are right to point out that, generally, there are ways around this ritual, though, by scriptural standards, it is questionable that these ways constitute the superior option. The real hurdle is explaining away the Qur'anic injunction to not interfere with something that God has declared permissible. Shaikh, Ali, and

42 Shaikh, 'Heresy or Moral Imperative?', 446.

43 'The Sacrifice of "Eid al-Adha"', Animals in Islam, www.animalsinislam.com/islam-animal-rights/sacrifice-eid-al-adha/.

Foltz not only fail to address this point, but they also criticise those who take it seriously. This results in several inconsistencies. Shaikh, for example, complains that although some Muslim authorities – such as Mufti Ebrahim Desai – accept veganism as permissible, others continue to hold that it is completely prohibited. Contrary to her claim, Desai's position conforms to the mainstream one. She cites him as saying,

> A Muslim may be a vegetarian. However, he should not regard eating meat as prohibited ... One should not think that it is better to abstain from eating these foods, that doing so will be rewarded, or that being a vegetarian is closer to Allah than not, and so on. It is not permitted to draw closer to Allah in this way. The Prophet, peace and blessings be upon him, who is the best of mankind and the closest to Allah, used to eat meat and honey and drink milk.[44]

Desai here describes the mainstream position that only *moral* vegetarianism is objectionable. He is far from being alone in holding that a Muslim may be a vegetarian. The tradition does not require its members to consume meat against their taste preferences, despite health or financial restrictions, or in the case of the unavailability of meat that conforms to scriptural injunctions.

Advocates of Islamic vegetarianism also make the strange claim that Muslims did not know about or were unconcerned with the idea of vegetarianism. Shaikh, for example, writes that the unfamiliarity of veganism to Muslims made it easy for them to associate the veganism of Abū al-ʿAlāʾ al-Maʿarrī (d. 449/1057) – the medieval Syrian poet and the most famous Muslim 'vegan' – with foreign influence and even heresy.[45] Contrary to this claim, the tradition knew about but deliberately rejected veganism. This was primarily out of religious commitment but also out of critical engagement. The medieval author Abū ʿUthmān al-Jāḥiẓ (d. 255/868) pertinently situates humans' participation in killing for food within the broader phenomenon of predation, an important dimension that defences of Islamic vegetarianism fail to address. He also challenges selective approaches to killing, a hallmark of moral vegetarianism. In response to those who avoid killing the so-called blooded animals to the exclusion of those who have no blood, he asks, 'Is it because blooded animals have an increased sensitivity to pain? How do we know, and what evidence can we

44 Shaikh, 'Heresy or Moral Imperative?', 447.

45 Ibid., 449.

produce to support this claim?'[46] Al-Jāḥiẓ's defence results from deeper critical engagement rather than unfamiliarity or lack of concern for other animals.

Similarly, Ali approvingly cites Foltz, who complains that 'preoccupation with the rights of nonhuman animals' – and vegetarianism more particularly – 'remains firmly outside the mainstream in Muslim societies around the world today'.[47] This view is at best uninformed and at worst a specimen of hegemonic tendencies. Through its uncritical reliance on the 'rights' language and frustration with Muslims' continued resistance to the vegetarian ethic, it assigns the animal rights theory a universal status while showing no interest in engaging with the other's point of view. As I hope to show later, despite their many merits, animal rights theories are not without serious conceptual and empirical flaws and are thus not above critical assessment.

2.3 Flawed Premises and Unsound Strategies

As is the case with secular literature, the defences of Islamic vegetarianism are founded on several flawed premises. Foltz cites the original Islamic Veg site as saying, 'The purpose of this site is to show what many Muslims have long suspected: eating meat, dairy products, and eggs conflicts with Islamic teachings of kindness to animals. Not only that, animal industries are responsible for vast environmental pollution and destruction and also contribute to many deadly human diseases.'[48] Thus, from the compelling proposition that animal industries are objectionable, this statement concludes that consuming *all* animal products conflicts with Islamic teachings despite clear evidence to the contrary. This tactic is the same as the one used by many secular animal rights theorists who, as Vicki Swinbank points out, 'in critiquing and condemning meat eating they invariably cite the cruel and exploitative conditions of factory farming systems … whilst ignoring or denying that a possible viable alternative exists, namely non-intensive, free-range farm animals'.[49]

---

46 Abū ʿUthmān al-Jāḥiẓ, *Kitāb al-Ḥayawān* (Cairo: Muṣṭafā al-Bābī al-Ḥalabī, 1950), 4:427–36. Al-Jāḥiẓ appears here to refer to a group of Christians who allow the consumption of fish during Lent, claiming that fish do not have blood. He finds this argument unconvincing because all animals, he argues, have blood or 'something akin to blood' (*lā budda li-jamīʿ al-ḥayawān min dam aw shay' yushākil al-dam*). Ibid., 434.

47 Ali, 'Muslims and Meat-Eating', 273.

48 Foltz, *Animal in Islamic Tradition*, 114. Foltz refers to an article that can be accessed through this link: www.islamicboard.com/miscellaneous/38819-islam-vegetarianism-read.html.

49 Vicki A. Swinbank, 'The Sexual Politics of Food: A Radical Feminist Analysis of Food Production, Preparation and Consumption' (PhD diss., University of Melbourne, 2008), 187.

Though barely referring to this point, Shaikh still appears to accept that traditional farming could be ethical, yet she claims that in today's world, it has become impossible.[50] This is a myopic claim. Traditional, small-scale animal farming not only continues to be the primary type for many societies around the globe but is growing in popularity even in urban and industrialised centres. Hannah Ritchie writes that 84 per cent of the world's 570 million farms are smallholdings (less than two hectares in size). Although in her assessment, small farms produce only one-third of the world's food (as opposed to the claim that they produce up to 70 or 80 per cent), they still contribute a significant proportion and, more importantly, they are the primary source of sustenance for *most* of the world's population.[51]

In the West, small-scale farming, as Julian Agyeman notes, 'has garnered significant ... participation among certain segments of the population', leading to a 'proliferation of farmers' markets and community-supported agriculture projects and programs (CSAs)'.[52] CSAs have indeed become a distinctive feature of urban centres around the world. In their 2012 article, Deborah Greenwood and Robin Leichenko mention that these farms numbered more than 1,000 in the United States alone,[53] and according to the USDA.gov website, by 2020, the number jumped to more than 7,000. Greenwood and Leichenko also affirm that the system is prominent in Latin America, Asia, Africa, and Europe[54] and that its products include milk, eggs, and meat.[55]

Zooming into small-scale farming, Noha Fikry tells the story of low-income Alexandrian families who use their rooftops to raise small animals. Commenting on this practice, she writes,

> Rooftops are a zone of existence in Egypt, a country of the Global South ranking 54th of 107 countries in the 2020 Global Hunger Index, struggling with malnutrition, food affordability, and food quality, especially among underprivileged groups ... The practice [of rearing rooftop animals] therefore narrates not only

50 Shaikh, 'Heresy or Moral Imperative?', 448.

51 Hannah Ritchie, 'Smallholders Produce One-Third of the World's Food, Less than Half of What Many Headlines Claim', Our World in Data, 6 August 2021, https://ourworldindata.org/smallholder-food-production.

52 Julian Agyeman, *Introducing Just Sustainabilities: Policy, Planning, and Practice* (London: Zed Books, 2013), 60.

53 Deborah Greenwood and Robin Leichenko, 'Community-Supported Agriculture', in *Food and Famine in the 21st Century*, 2 vols., ed. William A. Dando (Santa Barbara: ABC-CLIO, 2012), 1:88.

54 Ibid., 89.

55 Ibid., 87.

> human–animal bonds of nurturance but also an everyday struggle of the majority of working- and lower-middle-class families to make ends meet and keep their bellies full.[56]

Fikry notes how these families refer to the animals they raise as their 'rooftop children', extending to them the same nurturing care that they show to family members, yet without losing sight of the fact that they will one day end up on their plates. Thus, contrary to Shaikh's claim, traditional animal farming is alive and well and fills an important economic niche for most of the world's population. Failure to consider this betrays a lack of interest in the daily struggles of the less affluent, who comprise most of the world's population. The growing interest in small-scale farming among more affluent societies further underscores its importance. Although it is far from becoming dominant, its mere existence and growing popularity show that many still believe in ethical animal farming, which reformative movements can tap into. In fact, even if small-scale farming were to disappear altogether, the mere conceptual possibility of its existence should still be considered.

Following the same strategy of conflating small-scale and intensive farming systems, proponents of Islamic vegetarianism also appeal to health and environmental and social justice as additional motives for adopting a vegetarian diet. The negative impact of the meat industry in recent decades is not a point of controversy. It is firmly established that the dramatic increase in meat consumption has become a significant contributor to the intertwined problem of environmental degradation and social inequity and is the leading cause of many health problems. However, meat per se is not the problem. Although rarely the main staple, meat has been part of humans' diet since the dawn of the species' existence,[57] and with the advent of agriculture, other animal products were added to the menu. This mere fact shows that meat is not inherently harmful. Milligan is right to point out that 'A vegetarianism of any defensible sort may have to accept that meat is not nutritionally compromised, that it does us no physical harm to eat it (in suitable amounts, with suitable preparation and so on) … [The] idea that meat per se is physically harmful is, at the very least, ill-informed.'[58]

56 Noha Fikry, 'Tarbiyya', in *Changing Theory: Concepts from the Global South*, ed. Dilip M. Menon (New York: Routledge, 2022), 52.

57 See, for example, Katharine Milton, 'Hunter–Gatherer Diets: Wild Foods Signal Relief from Diseases of Affluence', in *Human Diet: Its Origin and Evolution*, ed. Peter S. Ungar and Mark F. Teaford (London: Bergin & Garvey, 2002), 120.

58 Milligan, *Beyond Animal Rights*, 49–50.

Likewise, meat-related health issues are the result of overconsumption, on the one hand, and the unhygienic conditions in which factory farm animals are raised, on the other. As Danielle Nierenberg explains, these conditions 'can sicken farm animals and create the perfect environment for the spread of diseases'. Compounded with 'the arsenal of unnatural ingredients' that are fed to factory farm animals, the negative impact of these products on human health is hardly surprising.[59] Similarly, the link between meat production and environmental and social equity issues is characteristic of intensive (not all types of) farming. In other words, the ecological and social problems often attributed to animal production result from the *intensive* and exploitative nature of the profit-centred economy. As I briefly point out towards the end of this chapter, intensive production modes affect plant farming similarly, leading to the same ecological and social problems and affecting both human and non-human animals.

3 Beyond Islamic Vegetarianism

A careful case for Islamic vegetarianism must apply to the vegetarian ethic the same critical rigour it strives to apply to Islamic sources. This ethic is more complex than initial impressions might indicate. First, it covers a broad spectrum, ranging from veganism, which opposes the use of any animal products, to flexitarianism, a primarily plant-based diet that occasionally includes meat. Ethicists also differ on the scope of this ethic. Traditional animal rights theory generally considers veganism a universal moral imperative. In contrast, ecofeminism tends to embrace a more nuanced position, conceding that some social contexts and individual needs may justify killing for food. None of these models is without problems. Diets that eliminate meat but include other animal products have been criticised for their inconsistency, as they depend on a system that requires animals to be killed. As Milligan says, 'Cows have to be pregnant in order to produce milk. If their offspring is a bull calf, it will be killed immediately or else it will be absorbed back into the food chain and killed later.' This leads him to conclude that 'if you consume dairy products, as vegetarians do, then your diet will ... be linked indirectly to slaughter'.[60] Milligan still condones ovo-lacto vegetarianism because, in his view, one does not need to aim for perfection – in the sense of doing it all or leaving it all. The problem,

59 Danielle Nierenberg, *Happier Meals: Rethinking the Global Meat Industry* (Washington, DC: Worldwatch Institute, 2005), 5–6.

60 Milligan, *Beyond Animal Rights*, 54.

however, is that the moral (as opposed, for example, to the health-motivated) ovo-lacto vegetarian's ability to afford the 'superior' moral choice is contingent on the fact that someone else is taking care of the 'dirty job' of animal slaughter. This person maintains the veneer of innocence as if her consumption of eggs and milk does not have a cost in animal life, whereas, in reality, it does.

The vegan model avoids this problem but falls into a host of complications. Among the thorny challenges it creates is what to do with domestic animals. Also, the assumption that all human individuals and communities are equally capable of abstaining from animal products reflects a lack of awareness of many people's lived realities and special needs. Contextual vegetarianism/veganism, which strives to be attuned to various needs and circumstances, is not without conceptual problems. Given the limited scope of this article, I will discuss the issues of domestication and contextual versus universal vegetarianism in more detail and then briefly touch upon a few other problems.

3.1 Domestication

Domestication is a millennia-old institution without which human civilisation would not have emerged. It has also modified domestic animals' bodies and psychological make-up to such an extent that most of them have become dependent on humans for survival. Without human demand for animal products and labour, domestication will no longer be cost-effective, and domestic animals must cease to exist. This is a monumental outcome involving the destiny of billions of animals and entailing monumental ecological and social repercussions.

Defenders of Islamic vegetarianism are surprisingly silent on this point despite its crucial importance, but animal rights theorists – the main advocates of universal veganism – embrace this outcome wholeheartedly. Gary Francione, the leading proponent of this position, describes domestication as institutionalised exploitation and blames it for creating animals who are entirely and perpetually dependent on us through selective breeding and what he characterises as other forms of manipulation. Because of this, he demands that we continue to care for animals now in existence but that we produce no more.[61]

Ironically, in its attempt to dismantle anthropocentric cultures, this position must resort to anthropocentric conceptions and abusive methods. First, Francione takes a narrow view of domestication. He assumes it started as an

61 Gary Francione, *Why Veganism Matters: Critical Perspectives on Animals* (New York: Columbia University Press, 2020).

intentional, goal-oriented process – as if neolithic humans had a long-term vision to eventually subdue other creatures. This is an implausible scenario. More plausibly, Richard Bulliet argues that 'domestication came about as unintended, unremembered, and unduplicable consequence of human activities intended to serve other purposes'.[62] Francione's is also a human-centred conception that strips other creatures of agency. As Marcelo Sánchez-Villagra points out, 'interactions between humans and other animals were voluntary on both sides; therefore, from this perspective, the agent is not as obvious.'[63] Deriving her data from animal sciences, genetics, and archaeology, Melinda Zeder argues that domestication has followed several pathways and that human intervention is only one among several factors that have determined its direction.[64] Sánchez-Villagra writes,

> The tempo and mode of domestication are unique for each species. Straightforward and simple narratives of a place and time of domestication involving human agency and goals with a path toward use and exploitation have been discredited repeatedly by diverse kinds of evidence, with literature going back decades and growing exponentially as ancient DNA and zooarchaeological studies expand.[65]

Thus, historical analysis and research founded on close study of empirical data not only refutes the claim that humans were the only determining factor in domesticating other animals but also exposes the anthropocentric undertone of the rightist position. In their attempt to vilify domestication, rightists create a narrative that aggrandises the role of humans and reduces other animals to passive, compliant creatures.

Second, even if we agree that domestication is inherently exploitative, it is unclear how we can end it without resorting to paternalistic methods. Drawing an analogy between domestication and slavery, animal rightists call for the abolition of this institution. However, they also acknowledge that, unlike human slaves, most domestic animals cannot survive 'emancipation', which leads them to propose that we gradually phase domestics out of existence. The problem with this scenario, as Sue Donaldson and Will Kymlicka point out, is

---

62 Richard Bulliet, *Hunters, Herders, and Hamburgers: The Past and Future of Human-Animal Relationships* (New York: Columbia University Press, 2005), 46.

63 Marcelo Sánchez-Villagra, *The Process of Animal Domestication* (Princeton: Princeton University Press, 2022), 2.

64 Melinda A. Zeder, 'Domestication as a Model System for the Extended Evolutionary Synthesis', *Interface Focus* 7, no. 5 (2017): https://doi.org/10.1098/rsfs.2016.0133.

65 Sánchez-Villagra, *The Process of Animal Domestication*, 35.

that it would require 'a massively increased (and probably impossible) human effort to forcibly sterilize and/or confine all domesticated animals'. In other words, this process requires 'precisely the sort of coercion and confinement that AR [animal rights] theorists say makes domestication unjust'.[66]

The paradoxes inherent in the rightist position are indeed manifold. To protect animals from the physical and psychological pain associated with killing, it must violate animals' bodily integrity in the case of sterilisation or genetic modification and suppress their psychological desire to mate in the case of confinement. It thus involves new forms of physical and mental harm. Donaldson and Kymlicka remind us that 'left to their own devices [domestic animals] would continue to reproduce and undergo the experience of parenting'.[67] However, the rightist position follows a paternalistic path by assuming that domestic animals do not know what is good for them and that we must decide on their behalf. It thus infantilises domestic animals and dismisses their preferences as unworthy of consideration.

The call to end domestication also fails to assess the eventual impact of this move on traditional, less affluent societies. In his well-documented survey of the role of 'livestock' animals in Ottoman Egypt, Alan Mikhail illustrates the centrality of these animals in nineteenth-century Egypt's economy. The heavyweight of building materials precludes the possibility of building ships or carrying out construction jobs without the help of camels. Irrigation and processing of agricultural products would be too strenuous without the help of cattle. Without camels and equines, travel to distant destinations would be too arduous.[68] Although for a large segment of the world population, animal labour has now been taken up by sophisticated machinery, such machinery is not within everyone's means. Many continue to depend on domestic animals to perform many agricultural and other tasks. The end of domestication would result in a dysfunctional state for those who cannot afford modern equipment. More use of this machinery is also bound to increase carbon emissions and lead to a greater reliance on synthetic fertilisers, thus exacerbating ecological problems.[69]

---

66 Sue Donaldson and Will Kymlicka, *Zoopolis: A Political Theory of Animal Rights* (New York: Oxford University Press, 2011), 80–81.

67 Ibid., 273.

68 Alan Mikhail, *Animals in Ottoman Egypt* (New York: Oxford University Press, 2013).

69 Ample research shows that traditional farming systems, relying on domestic animals, are ecologically more sustainable than technological ones. For example, Vassilis D. Litskas says, 'organic materials such as animal waste are promising to ensure food security in combination with low environmental impact.' Vassilis D. Litskas, 'Environmental

Since this chapter concerns Islamic vegetarianism, it is also important to consider the Qur'an's stand on domestication. The notion itself is not Qur'anic, but the phenomenon to which it refers – the fact that humans find a group of animals naturally tame and use them as a source of food, fibre, and labour – is Qur'anic. Indeed, whereas secular theories present domestication either as a human-guided and exploitative project seeking to dominate other creatures or as an interactive process whereby humans and non-humans negotiate forms of cooperation and mutual adaptation, the Qur'an presents the amenability of some animals as God's work. It is because God has made cattle/camels (*anʿām*) amenable for use (the concept of *tadhlīl*) that humans can own, ride, and derive food items from them (Q. 36:71–72).[70]

The Qur'an also presents the possibility of benefiting from other species as an expression of God's kindness and a remedy for humans' weakness. It states:

> And cattle He has created; in them, you find warmth and benefits, and from them, you eat. You see beauty in them when you bring them home and when you take them out to pasture. They carry your burdens to a land that you would otherwise reach with great hardship; Your Lord is indeed Kind, Merciful. And [He has created] horses, mules, and asses that you may ride them and as a source of beauty. (Q. 16:5–8)

Thus, from a Qur'anic standpoint, the possibility of deriving benefits from *anʿām* (cattle/camels) and equines – the group of animals that roughly corresponds to so-called domesticates – is a sign of God's mercy intended to address humans' vulnerable condition. Animal rightists tend to ignore this point. Their discussions emphasise the vulnerability of domestic animals, forgetting that vulnerability is a shared condition affecting all living creatures.

In a comment that captures the central paradox characterising moral vegetarianism, Dominique Lestel writes, 'the ethical vegetarian's position is tenable only if it is radical, but its very radicality is completely unacceptable for the majority of vegetarians. For this position is antianimal.'[71] Treatments of the problem of domestication are one good illustration of this paradox. The moral vegetarian who opposes the consumption of meat but condones the consumption of other animal products ignores that her diet is inextricably linked with

Impact Assessment for Animal Waste, Organic and Synthetic Fertilizers', *Nitrogen* 4, no. 1 (2023): 24.

70 For more on the notion of *tadhlīl*, see Tlili, *Animals in the Qur'an*, 75–91.

71 Dominique Lestel, *Eat This Book: A Carnivore's Manifesto*, trans. Gary Steiner (New York: Columbia University Press, 2016), xix.

animal slaughter; her position is untenable because it is not radical enough. The moral vegetarian who opposes the use of all animal products avoids this problem, but his position is anti-life and anti-animal. At the concrete level, it requires domestic animals to cease to exist, a goal that can only be attained through the suppression of their desires and the violation of their bodily integrity. Moreover, this position carries a demeaning view of domestic animals. It fails to acknowledge their agency and appreciate their resourcefulness in choosing to cooperate across species boundaries. Furthermore, the radical position discriminates against traditional societies, which would suffer much more severe consequences with the abolition of domestication. It is even imperialistic, given that abolition would eventually increase the dependence of traditional societies on industrial ones. The universal vegetarian imperative is thus harmful to both human and non-human animals and results in different types of inequalities and injustices.

3.2 Contextual versus Universal Vegetarianism

The radical nature of the animal rights position has given rise to more nuanced theories. While sharing the conviction that non-human animals are entitled to inviolable rights, political animal theorists, for example, reject the premise that this inviolability translates into a categorical prohibition of using them. As in intra-human relations, creaturely interdependence dictates that we use one another. Such use is not necessarily exploitative or derogatory; in fact, it is more typically beneficial to all parties involved.

Attention to context is particularly salient in ecofeminist theory. Grounding this ethic in the notion of care, ecofeminists avoid animal rights theory's abstract and purely rational language and stress interconnectedness and concrete relationships. This leads them to recognise that the universal vegan imperative disproportionately burdens many communities and individuals, leading many to embrace contextual rather than universal moral vegetarianism. While affirming his commitment to the vegetarian ideal, Deane Curtin also admits that certain geographical locations preclude such commitment. For example, the 'Ihalmiut ... whose frigid domain makes the growing of food impossible, do not have the option of vegetarian cuisine'.[72] Karen Warren elaborates that attention to context means attention to personal relations; gender, ethnicity, and class needs; geographical location; and culture.[73] Ecofeminists

72 Deane Curtin, 'Toward an Ecological Ethic of Care', *Hypatia* 6, no. 1 (1991): 70.

73 Karen Warren, *Ecofeminist Philosophy: A Western Perspective on What It Is and Why It Matters* (New York: Rowman & Littlefield, 2000), 133.

thus recognise that the vegetarian ideal is not always feasible and readily concede that those who cannot live up to it should be excused, but they accept this option only as a concession in the face of certain constraints. Otherwise, they share the rightist position that vegetarianism is morally superior to carnivorism.

On the surface, contextual moral vegetarianism appears to have appealing features. Thanks to its attention to geographical constraints and cultural differences, it avoids the pitfalls of essentialism and cultural imperialism. The fact that it requires vegetarianism only from those who can follow it while excusing nutritionally vulnerable groups appears more consistent with the principles of justice and fairness. However, a closer look at the vulnerability principle makes us rethink this initial evaluation. As Kathryn Paxton George's survey of nutritional literature shows, dietary vulnerability is far more common than some may assume. It comprises infants, children, and adolescents; pregnant, lactating, and pre-and post-menopausal women; and the elderly. The cause of vulnerability in this case is either the accelerated growth rate characteristic of the early stages of life or declining health in older age. Both conditions create more significant needs for certain minerals and vitamins, such as iron, calcium, zinc, and vitamin D, which are more readily obtainable from animal products. One notes that women are nearly constantly among the 'nutritionally vulnerable' because of their more significant role in childbearing and the nature of their reproductive system, whereas adult males living in industrialised countries are the least affected by the vegan or vegetarian lifestyle.

Vulnerable groups can still live healthily as vegetarians or vegans; however, nutritional guides consistently stress that they must monitor their diet carefully. This is precisely where part of the problem lies.[74] As George points out, the need for careful planning 'systematically imposes greater burdens on women, children, and the elderly', showing that the vegetarian moral rule is partial to adult males.[75] More problematically, it gives a normative status to the male adult body while treating women and children as outliers and exceptions who do not fit expected norms.[76] This stance reinforces rather than disrupts patriarchy. Of course, the contextual version readily excuses any individual or

74 See, for example, Roger A. Shewmake, 'Nutrition', in *Health Promotion and Disease Prevention in Clinical Practice*, ed. Steven H. Woolf, Steven Jonas, and Evonne Kaplan-Liss (Philadelphia: Lippincott Williams and Wilkins, 2008), 199.

75 Kathryn Paxton George, 'A Paradox of Ethical Vegetarianism: Unfairness to Women and Children', in *The Animal Ethics Reader*, 2nd ed., ed. Susan J. Armstrong and Richard G. Botzler (New York: Routledge, 2008), 275.

76 Kathryn Paxton George, *Animal, Vegetable, or Woman: A Feminist Critique of Ethical Vegetarianism* (Albany: State University of New York, 2000), 97.

group who cannot meet the vegetarian ideal, but the idea of 'excusing' itself is problematic. As George explains,

> If women, and infants, and children, and the elderly, and those who live almost everywhere else besides Western societies are *routinely* excused for doing what would normally be considered wrong, in practice, this relegates them to a *moral underclass* of beings who, because of their natures or cultures, are not capable of being fully moral. They are *physiologically* barred from 'doing the right thing' because they are not 'being the right thing'.[77]

The same hierarchical stance is evident in the economic and cultural dimensions. A healthy vegetarian diet not only presupposes affluence but also carries the tacit approval of the often-unsustainable economies that generate it. As noted earlier, a healthy vegetarian diet often requires careful monitoring, which presupposes access to medical care. It must also incorporate fortified foods and/or vitamin and mineral supplements. This presupposes a type of health awareness shaped specifically by Western or Westernised educational institutions and a complex industrialised food system capable of researching, manufacturing, preserving, and distributing these products.[78] Given that a healthy vegetarian diet should be diversified to maximise the intake of needed nutrients, the ethic presupposes access to global rather than just local markets. Societies who cannot afford these luxuries are, of course, excused. Still, the moral virtuousness of vegetarianism carries an implicit assumption that they would do better by 'emulating' the industrialised model. As a matter of logic, a system more favourably disposed towards the superior ethic must be superior and worth emulating. This view is problematic not just because it implies that affluence is morally good and lack thereof hinders full morality but also because it pays no heed to the many environmental and social problems associated with this industrialised model. When non-industrialised societies are magnanimously 'excused' for their inability to be vegetarian, they are inadvertently excused for not being wealthy enough and for adhering to more sustainable economies.

3.3 Plant Farming, Predation, and Extensionism

The vegetarian ethic raises many other problems, but I briefly discuss only a few more because of space limitations. The assumption that plant-based diets

77 Ibid., 106 (emphasis in the original).
78 For more on this point, see George, 'A Paradox of Ethical Vegetarianism', 279.

are ethically superior is highly doubtful. Lindsay Garcia's investigation of the farming of bananas, one of the main staples of the vegetarian diet, shows that it is responsible for environmental destruction, inhumane labour conditions, the killing of many animals, and habitat fragmentation.[79] She pertinently invites vegan studies scholars and vegans to 'direct their attention to plant to see the ways in which animals are harmed sometimes halfway around the world for the plants on the table of everyday Americans'.[80] This shows that vegetarian diets have a cost on *animal life* and that many of the problems that are often blamed on killing for food are due to the intensive nature of modern farming.

One must also explore the potential impact of the vegetarian ethic on predators. Although most ethicists 'excuse' these animals because of their inability to adopt a different diet, this is not a unanimous position. Because predation 'causes vast suffering among its innumerable victims [and deprives] those victims of the good experiences they might have had were they not killed', Jeff McMahan argues that we should strive to eradicate it.[81] Most advocates of the vegetarian ethic disagree with this position; however, McMahan's position appears to be the most consistent. If killing for food is morally wrong, then we may be obligated to do something about wild predation. Most ethicists and environmentalists, however, would find such intervention morally unjustifiable and environmentally detrimental.

Vegetarianism becomes even more elusive when one considers the cost in insect and other so-called pest life in plant farming. Western animal advocacy mostly dismisses invertebrates from moral consideration under the pretext that they are insentient and unconscious, but a growing body of research contradicts these assumptions.[82] These unfounded assumptions are in fact troublingly reminiscent of the ones used in previous centuries to exclude all animals from moral consideration. This stance also points to the problem of extensionism in the field of animal ethics in Western academies. So far, the field has been striving to broaden the moral community to include more animals, but it uses humans as the standard against which other species are measured to determine whether they possess relevant capacities. The more

---

79 Lindsay Garcia, '"Cruelty-Free" Cruelty: How Vegan Rhetoric Hides the Truth of Banana Production', in *The Rhetorical Construction of Vegetarianism*, ed. Cristina Hanganu-Bresch (New York: Routledge, 2023), 120.

80 Ibid., 118.

81 Jeff McMahan, 'The Moral Problem of Predation', in *Philosophy Comes to Dinner: Arguments about the Ethics of Eating*, ed. Andrew Chignell, Terence Cuneo, and Matthew C. Halteman (New York: Routledge, 2016), 273.

82 Irina Mikhalevich and Russell Powell, 'Minds without Spines: Evolutionarily Inclusive Animal Ethics', *Animal Sentience* 29, no. 1 (2020): https://doi.org/10.51291/2377-7478.1527.

different a given species is from the human one, the more it is assumed to lack these capacities and the less likely it is to be accorded moral consideration. This approach reeks of anthropocentrism and is inconsistent with what I believe is the Islamic stand on insect ethics.[83]

4 Conclusion

The vegetarian ethic, whether in Islam or beyond, raises legitimate questions and challenges us to think more seriously about animals. The feelings of compassion that motivate the ethic deserve respect and recognition, and the vegetarian movement's effort on behalf of animals is commendable in many ways. Advocates of Islamic vegetarianism should also be acknowledged for their thoughtful critiques and their attempt to reinstate animals on Muslims' moral landscape. These favourable elements notwithstanding, moral vegetarianism is poorly conceptualised. It entails many empirical and conceptual challenges that receive no answers from advocates of Islamic vegetarianism, and what strikes me as unpersuasive answers from the broader field. Advocates of moral vegetarianism generally hold the preconceived view that killing for food is inherently wrong; however, by considering the complications that the ethic entails, it should at least become clear that the controversy is genuine. Advocates of Islamic vegetarianism have the additional responsibility of addressing the Qur'anic prohibition to question the permissibility of something that God has declared as permissible. Vague appeals to the principles of egalitarianism and compassion are not sufficient to build a solid case and would not resonate with most Muslims. In my view, by taking what I see as the Qur'an's stand against moral vegetarianism at face value and situating it within the broader scriptural teachings about animals, Islamic animal advocacy would not only build an intellectually more robust case but also an impactful and far-reaching one.

Bibliography

Abdul Ghani, Muhammad Ilyas. *The History of Makkah Mukarramah*. Medina: King Fahd National Library, 2004.

83 Sarra Tlili, 'An Islamic Case for Insect Ethics', in *Animals and Religion*, ed. Dave Aftandilian, Barbara R. Ambros, and Aaron S. Gross (New York: Routledge, 2024), 112–16.

Agyeman, Julian. *Introducing Just Sustainabilities: Policy, Planning, and Practice*. London: Zed Books, 2013.

Aḥmad b. Ḥanbal. *Musnad Aḥmad*. Beirut: al-Risāla, 2001.

'Aiysha Younas Explores the Links between Veganism and Her Religion'. Vegan Society (blog), 19 August 2022. www.vegansociety.com/news/blog/veganism-and-islam.

Ali, Kecia. 'Muslims and Meat-Eating: Vegetarianism, Gender, and Identity'. *Journal of Religious Ethics* 43, no. 2 (2015): 268–88.

Aly, Remona. 'You Are What You Eid: Ramadan for Vegans'. *Guardian*, 30 May 2019. www.theguardian.com/food/2019/may/30/you-are-what-you-eid-ramadan-for-vegans.

al-Barādhiʿī, Abū Saʿīd. *al-Tahdhīb fī ikhtiṣār al-Mudawwana*. Dubai: Dār al-Buḥūth li-l-Dirāsāt al-Islāmiyya, 2002.

al-Bukhārī, Muḥammad b. Ismāʿīl. *Ṣaḥīḥ al-Bukhārī*. Beirut: Dār Ibn Kathīr, 2002.

Bulliet, Richard. *Hunters, Herders, and Hamburgers: The Past and Future of Human-Animal Relationships*. New York: Columbia University Press, 2005.

Canova, Giovanni. 'Il Profeta Muḥammad e gli Animali: La Leggenda del Cammello e della Gazzella'. *Oriente Moderno* 89, no. 2 (2009): 257–75.

Curtin, Deane. 'Toward an Ecological Ethic of Care'. *Hypatia* 6, no. 1 (1991): 60–74.

Donaldson, Sue, and Will Kymlicka. *Zoopolis: A Political Theory of Animal Rights*. New York: Oxford University Press, 2011.

Fikry, Noha. 'Tarbiyya'. In *Changing Theory: Concepts from the Global South*, edited by Dilip M. Menon, 51–63. New York: Routledge, 2022.

Foltz, Richard. *Animals in Islamic Tradition and Muslim Cultures*. Oxford: Oneworld, 2006.

Francione, Gary. *Why Veganism Matters: Critical Perspectives on Animals*. New York: Columbia University Press, 2020.

Garcia, Lindsay. '"Cruelty-Free" Cruelty: How Vegan Rhetoric Hides the Truth of Banana Production'. In *The Rhetorical Construction of Vegetarianism*, edited by Cristina Hanganu-Bresch, 117–35. New York: Routledge, 2023.

George, Kathryn Paxton. *Animal, Vegetable, or Woman: A Feminist Critique of Ethical Vegetarianism*. Albany: State University of New York, 2000.

George, Kathryn Paxton. 'A Paradox of Ethical Vegetarianism: Unfairness to Women and Children'. In *The Animal Ethics Reader*, 2nd ed., edited by Susan J. Armstrong and Richard G. Botzler, 274–79. New York: Routledge, 2008.

al-Ghazālī, Abū Ḥāmid. *al-Wasīṭ fī al-madhhab*. Cairo: Dār al-Salām, 1997.

Goudarzi, Muhsin. 'Worship (*Dīn*), Monotheism (*Islām*), and the Qur'ān's Cultic Decalogue'. *Journal of the International Qur'anic Studies Association* 8, no. 1 (2023): 56–60.

Greenwood, Deborah, and Robin Leichenko. 'Community-Supported Agriculture'. In *Food and Famine in the 21st Century*, 2 vols., edited by William A. Dando, 1:86–93. Santa Barbara: ABC-CLIO, 2012.

Heemskerk, Margaretha T. *Suffering in the Muʿtazilite Theology: ʿAbd al-Jabbār's Teaching on Pain and Divine Justice*. Leiden: Brill, 2000.

al-Jāḥiẓ, Abū ʿUthmān. *Kitāb al-Ḥayawān*. Cairo: Muṣṭafā al-Bābī al-Ḥalabī, 1950.

'Kingdom Imports 3 Million Sheep and Camels for Haj'. Eye of Riyadh, 31 July 2015. www.eyeofriyadh.com/news/details/kingdom-imports-3-million-sheep-and-camels-for-haj.

Kuwait Ministry of Endowments and Islamic Affairs. *al-Mawsūʿa al-fiqhiyya*. Kuwait: The Ministry of Endowments and Islamic Affairs, 1983.

Lestel, Dominique. *Eat This Book: A Carnivore's Manifesto*. Translated by Gary Steiner. New York: Columbia University Press, 2016.

Litskas, Vassilis D. 'Environmental Impact Assessment for Animal Waste, Organic and Synthetic Fertilizers'. *Nitrogen* 4, no. 1 (2023): 16–25.

al-Manāwī, ʿAbd al-Raʾūf. *Fayḍ al-Qadīr sharḥ al-Jāmiʿ al-ṣaghīr*. Beirut: Dār al-Maʿrifa, 1972.

al-Māwardī, Abū Ḥasan b. Ḥabīb. *al-Ḥāwī al-kabīr*. Beirut: Dār al-Kutub al-ʿIlmiyya, 1994.

McMahan, Jeff. 'The Moral Problem of Predation'. In *Philosophy Comes to Dinner: Arguments about the Ethics of Eating*, edited by Andrew Chignell, Terence Cuneo, and Matthew C. Halteman, 268–94. New York: Routledge, 2016.

Mikhail, Alan. *Animals in Ottoman Egypt*. New York: Oxford University Press, 2013.

Mikhalevich, Irina, and Russell Powell. 'Minds without Spines: Evolutionarily Inclusive Animal Ethics'. *Animal Sentience* 29, no. 1 (2020): https://doi.org/10.51291/2377-7478.1527.

Milligan, Tony. *Beyond Animal Rights: Food, Pets and Ethics*. London: Continuum International Publishing, 2010.

Milton, Katharine. 'Hunter–Gatherer Diets: Wild Foods Signal Relief from Diseases of Affluence'. In *Human Diet: Its Origin and Evolution*, edited by Peter S. Ungar and Mark F. Teaford, 111–22. London: Bergin & Garvey, 2002.

Muslim b. al-Ḥajjāj. *Ṣaḥīḥ Muslim*. Beirut: Dār al-Kutub al-ʿIlmiyya, 1991.

Nasr, Seyyed Hossein, ed. *The Study Quran: A New Translation and Commentary*. New York: Harper Collins, 2015.

al-Nawawī, Muḥyī al-Dīn b. Sharaf. *al-Minhāj sharḥ Ṣaḥīḥ Muslim b. al-Ḥajjāj*. Beirut: Dār Iḥyāʾ al-Turāth al-ʿArabī, 1972.

Nierenberg, Danielle. *Happier Meals: Rethinking the Global Meat Industry*. Washington, DC: Worldwatch Institute, 2005.

al-Nīsābūrī, Ibn al-Mundhir Abū Bakr. *al-Ishrāf ʿalā madhāhib al-ʿulamāʾ*. Ras al-Khaimah: Maktabat Makkat al-Thaqāfiyya, 2004.

al-Qayrawānī, Ibn Abī Zayd. *al-Nawādir wa-l-ziyādāt*. Beirut: Dār al-Gharb al-Islāmī, 1999.

Rahman, S.A. 'Middle East'. In *Long Distance Transport and Welfare of Farm Animals*, edited by M.C. Appleby, V. Cussen, L. Garcés, L.A. Lambert, and J. Turner, 387–411. Cambridge, MA: CABI, 2008.

Ritchie, Hannah. 'Smallholders Produce One-Third of the World's Food, Less than Half of What Many Headlines Claim'. Our World in Data, 6 August 2021. https://ourworldindata.org/smallholder-food-production.

al-Ruʿaynī, al-Ḥaṭṭāb. *Mawāhib al-jalīl fī sharḥ Mukhtaṣar Khālil.* Nouakchott: Dār al-Riḍwān, 2010.

Sánchez-Villagra, Marcelo. *The Process of Animal Domestication*. Princeton: Princeton University Press, 2022.

al-Sarakhsī, Muḥammad b. Aḥmad. *al-Mabsūṭ*. Beirut: Dār al-Maʿrifa, 1989.

al-Ṣāwī, Aḥmad. *Ḥāshiyat al-Ṣāwī ʿalā al-Sharḥ al-ṣaghīr*. Cairo: Dār al-Maʿārif, 1986.

Shaikh, Zinnira. 'Heresy or Moral Imperative? Islamic Perspectives on Veganism'. In *Routledge Handbook of Islamic Ritual and Practice*, edited by Oliver Leaman, 437–58. New York: Routledge, 2022.

Shewmake, Roger A. 'Nutrition'. In *Health Promotion and Disease Prevention in Clinical Practice*, edited by Steven H. Woolf, Steven Jonas, and Evonne Kaplan-Liss, 169–207. Philadelphia: Lippincott Williams and Wilkins, 2008.

Stilt, Kristen. 'Trading in Sacrifice'. In *Studies in Global Animal Law*, edited by Anne Peters, 47–55. Berlin: Springer, 2020.

Swinbank, Vicki A. 'The Sexual Politics of Food: A Radical Feminist Analysis of Food Production, Preparation and Consumption'. PhD diss., University of Melbourne, 2008.

al-Tirmidhī, Muḥammad b. ʿĪsā. *Sunan al-Tirmidhī.* Cairo: Muṣṭafā al-Bābūm, 1962.

Tlili, Sarra. 'All Animals Are Equal, or Are They? The Ikhwān al-Ṣafāʾ's Animal Epistle and Its Unhappy End'. *Journal of Qurʾanic Studies* 16, no. 2 (2014): 42–88.

Tlili, Sarra. 'Animals'. In *Muhammad in History, Thought and Culture: An Encyclopedia of the Prophet of God*, 2 vols., edited by Coeli Fitzpatrick and Adam Hani Walker, 1:25–29. Santa Barbara: ABC-CLIO, 2014.

Tlili, Sarra. *Animals in the Qurʾan*. New York: Cambridge University Press, 2012.

Tlili, Sarra. 'Animals Would Follow Shāfiʿism: Legitimate and Illegitimate Violence to Animals in Medieval Islamic Thought'. In *Violence in Islamic Thought from the Qurʾān to the Mongols*, edited by Robert Gleave and István Kristó-Nagy, 226–44. Edinburgh: Edinburgh University Press, 2015.

Tlili, Sarra. 'I Invoke God, Therefore I Am: Creation's Spirituality and Its Ecologic Impact in Islamic Texts'. In *A Global History of Literature and the Environment*, edited by John Parham and Louise Westling, 107–22. New York: Cambridge University Press, 2017.

Tlili, Sarra. 'An Islamic Case for Insect Ethics'. In *Animals and Religion*, edited by Dave Aftandilian, Barbara R. Ambros, and Aaron S. Gross, 112–16. New York: Routledge, 2024.

Tlili, Sarra. 'The Meaning of the Qur'anic Word "*Dābba*": "Animals" or "Nonhuman Animals"?'. *Journal of Qur'anic Studies* 12, no. 1–2 (2010): 167–87.

Tlili, Sarra. 'Qur'anic Creation: Anthropocentric Readings and Ecocentric Possibilities'. In *The Routledge Companion to the Qur'an*, edited by George Archer, Maria M. Dakake, and Daniel A. Madigan, 135–44. New York: Routledge, 2021.

Warren, Karen. *Ecofeminist Philosophy: A Western Perspective on What It Is and Why It Matters*. New York: Rowman & Littlefield, 2000.

al-Zabīdī, Abū Bakr. *al-Jawhara al-nayyira*. Beirut: Dār al-Kutub al-ʿIlmiyya, 2006.

Zeder, Melinda A. 'Domestication as a Model System for the Extended Evolutionary Synthesis'. *Interface Focus* 7, no. 5 (2017): https://doi.org/10.1098/rsfs.2016.0133.

CHAPTER 18

'Clear' Verses of the Qur'an (*Āyāt Muḥkamāt*) and Environmental Ethics

Etin Anwar

This chapter presents a response to the environmental crises by using 'clear' verses (*āyāt muḥkamāt*) in the Qur'an. Such verses are often cited to determine 'what is clear and certain' in divine law (*sharīʿa*) and its legal objectives (*maqāṣid al-sharīʿa*) to govern Muslim behaviours. These legal objectives, which include the preservation of religion (*ḥifẓ al-dīn*), the preservation of life (*ḥifẓ al-nafs*), the preservation of a sound mind (*ḥifẓ al-ʿaql*), the preservation of progeny (*ḥifẓ al-nasl*), and the preservation of property (*ḥifẓ al-māl*), are principles of legal reasoning widely used among Muslim scholars and environmentalists. Earlier scholars such as Nasr, Foltz, Denny, Baharuddin, Abdul-Matin, and Gade provide foundational knowledge that has been useful in framing human behaviours and their relationship to nature in Islamic traditions and in showing the development of environmental discourses and activism in Muslim contexts.[1] My work adds to the discussion on the relationship between Islam and the environment by elaborating on how the Qur'an sets an ethical norm that undergirds the ideal relationship between God, oneself, other human beings, and nature through 'clear' verses (*āyāt muḥkamāt*). It focuses on the intersection between humans' ability for destruction (*fasād*) on earth (Q. 30:41) and their role as repairers or restorers (*muṣliḥūn*) (Q. 2:11).

My intervention consists in the use of the 'clear' verses to provide a workable framework that addresses humans' inclination to damage and repair the environment. There are two ways to achieve this. First, the discursive narratives of 'clear' verses on the environment need to be situated within humans' complicit behaviour in their own destruction and their potential for repair. Secondly, these verses call for new ways to enact faith in addressing

1 Seyyed Hossein Nasr, *Man and Nature: The Spiritual Crisis of Modern Man* (London: Unwin Paperbacks, 1976); Richard C. Foltz, Frederick M. Denny, and Azizan Baharuddin, eds., *Islam and Ecology: A Bestowed Trust* (Cambridge, MA: Center for the Study of World Religions, Harvard Divinity School, 2003); Ibrahim Abdul-Matin, *Green Deen: What Islam Teaches about Protecting the Planet* (San Francisco: Berrett-Koehler Publishers, 2010); and Anna Gade, *Muslim Environmentalisms: Religious and Social Foundations* (New York: Columbia University Press, 2019).

 | HTTPS://DOI.ORG/10.1163/9789004755567-020

environmental imbalances. As humans have the capacity for environmental destruction as well as for repair to address climate issues, they have opportunities to change their complicit behaviours and to provide solutions to environmental imbalances.

In what follows, I first examine the meaning of what is clear (*muḥkamāt*) drawn from Q. 3:7 and its potential to be read in relation to environmental protection. This verse juxtaposes what is clear (*muḥkamāt*) and what is ambiguous (*mutashābihāt*). At the same time, it shows that verses in the Qur'an have their own historical contexts and meanings. To read Q. 3:7 or any other verse in an environmental lens, the Qur'an must be considered as an ethical perspective. This ethical consideration is necessary to the environmental vision of human stewardship and care towards the environment. In depicting the environmental and ethical values in Q. 3:7, I will refer to what scholars such as Muḥammad Rashīd Riḍā (d. 1935), Muḥammad ʿAbduh (d. 1905), and Ibn ʿĀshūr (d. 1973) offer in explaining the concepts of *muḥkamāt* and *mutashābihāt* and explain how these concepts relate to the environment. I have chosen these modern authors to show a common thread of the intertwining relationship between *muḥkamāt* and *mutashābihāt*. I demonstrate the meaning of clear verses from Ibn ʿĀshūr's discussion of *muḥkamāt* as presented in the second section. I conclude the chapter by discussing the 'glory motif' in clear verses and its ethical implementation in repairing (*iṣlāḥ*) the environment.

1 Framing Environmental Issues with 'Clear' Verses of the Qur'an (*Āyāt Muḥkamāt*)

Attempts to present the Qur'anic view of the contemporary discourses of environmental issues must be exercised with care. This careful consideration is important to note because the discourses on the need for world religions and faith communities to embrace the shared mission of environmental stewardship have emerged primarily in the Western contexts. Interestingly, while this call for stewardship emerged in the Western hemisphere, it is not necessarily shared by everyone. Movements that deny the climate crisis and the prevalence of mass consumption affect how people perceive climate change as a threat. These anti-climate attitudes have shaped discourses and policymaking in addressing climate mitigation and climate advocacy. Such denial is also present in the non-Western context.

Despite these controversies, we have witnessed a growing awareness in the West about the need to view the earth as sacred, to move away from consuming fossil fuels, to transition to green energy, and to value climate mitigation as part of the solutions to climate change. On a global scale, these efforts have brought about a series of conceptual changes on how Islam and Muslims address climate change. Gade shows how the Western framework of the world religions and activism by NGOs like the Alliance of Religion and Conservation (ARC), the Nature Conservancy, and the World Wildlife Federation (WWF) interpret Islam from a Western environmentalist perspective.[2] While this demand on Muslims to offer religious responses, especially when considered in light of Western environmentalism, runs the risk of essentialising Islam, it brings about an Islamic treatment of the environment to the fore. On the one hand, Muslims are conditioned to employ a Western framework on how religious response to the climate crisis should look like and, on the other hand, they draw from Islamic legalist, exegetical, mystical, and psychological traditions to show what Islam has to say about the environment. For this reason, any understanding of the Qur'anic messages on the climate crisis needs to consider the ongoing debates on environmentalism in the Islamic context. I will make the case with Q. 3:7 as the starting point to discuss the clear passages of the Qur'an dealing with environmental issues.

Q. 3:7 plays an important role in debating what is clear (*muḥkam*) in regulating Muslim life, stating:[3]

> It is He who has sent down to you, [O Muhammad], the Book; in it are verses [that are] precise – they are the foundation of the Book – and others unspecific. As for those in whose hearts is deviation [from truth], they will follow that of it which is unspecific, seeking discord and seeking an interpretation [suitable to them]. And no one knows its [true] interpretation except Allah. But those firm in knowledge say, 'We believe in it. All [of it] is from our Lord.' And no one will be reminded except those of understanding.

The immediate urgency in reading this verse is to discover how it receives its importance and whether it has the potential to be read through an environmental lens. Q. 3:7 is one of the most important verses for Muslim scholars debating on how to interpret God's word in the absence of the Prophet Muḥammad.[4] The discursive concepts of *muḥkamāt* (clear) and *mutashābihāt* (ambiguous or similar in meaning) are debated to reach certainty (*yaqīn*) in defining and embodying Islam. The pursuit for certainty is theologically more nuanced when it comes to ambiguous verses. Any Islamic Teachings drawn

---

2 Ibid., 38.

3 See https://corpus.quran.com/wordmorphology.jsp?location=(3:7:8).

4 Leah Kinberg, '*Muḥkamāt* and *Mutashābihāt* (Koran 3/7): Implication of a Koranic Pair of Terms in Medieval Exegesis', *Arabica* 35, no. 2 (1988): 93.

from ambiguous verses require legal and theological analyses before certainty is reached as they use language whose meaning is not transparent. These include verses that convey 'the timing of eschatological events; the meanings of the separate letters at the beginning of some sūrahs; and references to the attributes of God, which some see as anthropomorphic'.[5] While these ideas fall within the category of ambiguous topics, they are used to reiterate certainty (*yaqīn*) in faith.

The intertwining relationship between *muḥkamāt* (clear) and *mutashābihāt* (ambiguous or similar in meaning) shows how faith receives new meaning and utility depending on contexts, pre-texts, and texts. For instance, Haleem connects Q. 3:7 to 2:106[6] and 16:101[7] to demonstrate the changing society with the coming of Islam.[8] He proposes to situate Q. 2:106 with the abrogation of previous revelation and Q. 16:101 with the religious orientation of the Meccans that requires a gradual change as demonstrated in the prohibition of intoxicated drink. He also uses Q. 31:20[9] to show that God's blessing is either present around us (*ẓāhir*) or hidden (*bāṭin*) and to debate whether a hidden (*bāṭin*) interpretation has a Qur'anic foundation. Haleem insists that the Qur'an teaches what is inside us (microcosm) and outside us (macrocosm), but its interpretation needs to accord with what is apparent (*ẓāhir*) in the texts.[10]

It is partially within this context of change and flux in the seventh-century Arabia that calls for ethical treatment of the environment are invoked. The ethical consideration to which humans are called for is to be responsible for the earth and to be grateful to God for what He has provided in the seen and unseen world. In showing God's generosity towards humans, the term '*taskhīr*' is used. This Arabic term, which derives from the root *s-kh-r*, is translated as 'subjection'. Although the Qur'an mentions *sakhkhara* in the context of God's

---

5 Muhammad Abdel Haleem, 'Interpreting the Qur'an: Qur'an 3:7; 2:106; 16:101; 31:20', in *Communicating the Word: Revelation, Translation, and Interpretation in Christianity and Islam*, ed. David Marshall (Washington, DC: Georgetown University Press, 2011), 134.

6 'If We ever abrogate a verse or cause it to be forgotten, We replace it with a better or similar one. Do you not know that Allah is Most Capable of everything?' (Q. 2:106), https://quran.com/2?startingVerse=106.

7 'When We replace a verse with another – and Allah knows best what He reveals – they say, "You Muḥammad are just a fabricator." In fact, most of them do not know' (Q. 16:101), https://quran.com/16?startingVerse=101.

8 Haleem, 'Interpreting the Qur'ān', 136.

9 'Have you not seen that Allah has subjected for you whatever is in the heavens and whatever is on the earth, and has lavished His favours upon you, both seen and unseen? Still there are some who dispute about Allah without knowledge, or guidance, or an enlightening scripture' (Q. 30:21), https://quran.com/31?startingVerse=21.

10 Haleem, 'Interpreting the Qur'ān', 138.

subjection of His creation in heaven and earth and what is provided in the seen and unseen world, such verses prompt a worldview of not abusing the environment. Q. 31:20 states that 'Allah has subjected for you whatever is in the heavens and whatever is on the earth', whether it is seen (*ẓāhir*) or unseen (*bāṭin*).[11] While the act of subjecting nature amounts to the imposition of God's will on earth, the concept of '*taskhīr*' empowers humans to protect nature. The Qur'an indicates that humans' transgression and their denial of God's signs in the seen (*ẓāhir*) and unseen (*bāṭin*) world will be punished in the hereafter (Q. 20:127).[12] Such transgression also reflects humans' ungrateful and unjust behaviours in thanking God's favour of life and the bounties on earth (Q. 14:32–34).[13]

While human history is full of examples of mistreatment of nature, pathways for stewardship and reform are present within Islam. Such efforts call for enacting the book (*al-kitāb*) and wisdom through the Sharīʿa, which offers paths to achieving the Truth (*ḥaqīqa*). Nasr explains that the Sharīʿa for Muslims functions as the basis for religious life as it is 'the circumference of a circle whose radii are the *Ṭuruq* (plural of *Ṭarīqah*) and whose center is the *Ḥaqīqah* or Truth, that is, the Source of both the Law and Way as well as the center for one who begins on the circumference, journeys along one of the radii, and finally reaches the center, which is also his or her own center'.[14] As the Sharīʿa plays a central role in cultivating the self's piety, enacting a harmonious relationship with God, humans, and nature, and addressing environmental imbalances we are facing, it is imperative to rethink ways in which clear verses (*āyāt muḥkamāt*) are debated as they relate to environmental issues.

2 Defining Clear Verses and Their Utility in Framing Environmental Ethics

Efforts to link clear verses (*āyāt muḥkamāt*) with the environment should take into consideration how the relationship between *muḥkam* (clear) and *mutashābih* (ambiguous) is interpreted. Scholars like Riḍā and ʿAbduh explain how the Qur'an could be understood entirely as *muḥkam* and as *mutashābih*.

11 See Q. 31:21, https://quran.com/31?startingVerse=21.
12 See https://corpus.quran.com/wordmorphology.jsp?location=(20:127:4).
13 'And He has granted you all that you asked Him for. If you tried to count Allah's blessings, you would never be able to number them. Indeed humankind is truly unfair, totally ungrateful' (Q. 14:34), https://quran.com/14?startingVerse=34.
14 Seyyed Hossein Nasr, *The Garden of Truth: The Vision and Promise of Sufism, Islam's Mystical Tradition* (New York: HarperOne, 2008), 5.

Q. 11:1[15] supports the claim of the Qur'an as *muḥkam* since it establishes a system or structure of understanding and enacting faith and encourages seeking wisdom beyond the literal texts of Qur'anic verses; and as *mutashābih* in terms of its utility as guidance, its eloquence, and its freedom from contradiction as expressed in Q. 39:23.[16] Ibn ʿĀshūr also echoes a similar view by showing the link between *muḥkamāt* and *mutashābihāt* and explains that the Qur'an as a whole could be seen as *muḥkam* as expressed in Q. 10:1, 11:1, and 31:2, and could be perceived as *mutashābih* as exemplified in Q. 39:23 in terms of its beauty, its eloquence, and its truth.[17] The Qur'an says that it does not have major discrepancies (Q. 4:82), so we can assume that, from its own perspective, there is no contradiction between *muḥkam* and *mutashābih* as different verses or contexts require different expressions. As both *muḥkamāt* and *mutashābihāt* together comprise the Qur'an, they provide a framework to address all areas of life, including environmental issues. In this section, I will draw from contemporary thinkers, such as Riḍā, ʿAbduh, and Ibn ʿĀshūr, to discuss how both *muḥkamāt* and *mutashābihāt* undergird the ethics of care for the environment.

Riḍā, ʿAbduh, and Ibn ʿĀshūr all agree on the basic meaning of *muḥkamāt* and *mutashābihāt*. Riḍā and ʿAbduh explain that the term '*muḥkamāt*' comes from the expression *aḥkama al-shay'*, meaning, 'to make something strong', and points to the general meaning of 'preventing something from happening', whereas the term '*mutashābihāt*' refers to verses that resemble each other or have ambiguous meaning.[18] Ibn ʿĀshūr, however, emphasises a different aspect of the discursive meanings of *muḥkamāt* and *mutashābihāt*.[19] *Muḥkam* is understood in terms of 'precise/clear' meaning because the clarity of argumentation prevents the possibility of causing doubts and *muḥkamāt* (regulative) verses are described as '*umm al-kitāb*' (the mother of the book), referring to the root of the book (*aṣl al-kitāb*) or reference. Unlike *muḥkamāt*, *mutashābihāt* point

15 'Alif-Lām-Ra. This is a Book whose verses are well perfected and then fully explained. It is from the One Who is All-Wise, All-Aware' (Q. 11:1), https://quran.com/11.

16 'It is Allah Who has sent down the best message – a Book of perfect consistency and repeated lessons – which causes the skin and hearts of those who fear their Lord to tremble, then their skin and hearts soften at the mention of the mercy of Allah. That is the guidance of Allah, through which He guides whoever He wills. But whoever Allah leaves to stray will be left with no guide' (Q. 39:23), https://quran.com/39?startingVerse=23. See also Muḥammad Rashīd Riḍā and Muḥammad ʿAbduh, *Tafsīr al-Qur'ān al-Ḥakīm: al-Shahīr bi-Tafsīr al-Manār*, 3rd ed. (Egypt: Dar al-Manār, 1948), 3:163.

17 Muḥammad al-Ṭāhir Ibn ʿĀshūr, *Tafsīr al-Taḥrīr wa-l-Tanwīr* (Tunis: Dār Suḥnūn li-l-Nashr wa-l-Tawzīʿ, 1997), 3:155.

18 Riḍā and ʿAbduh, *Tafsīr*, 3:163.

19 Ibn ʿĀshūr, *Tafsīr*, 3:154–55.

to multivalent meanings, each of which could be the intended meaning. At the same time, the correctness of its meaning could take various forms ranging from resemblances to opposites. Ibn ʿĀshūr gives the example of Q. 43:11, 'and He is the One Who sends down rain from the sky in perfect measure, with which We give life to a lifeless land. And so will you be brought forth from the grave.'[20] Ibn ʿĀshūr considers this verse to carry multiple meanings as it expresses how God resurrects dead humans in the same way He restores vegetation in barren land. This verse is ambiguous because the manner of resurrection is explained in a metaphorical way. It is not clear whether this resurrection is a purely spiritual resurrection of the soul, or whether it also includes the body. The topic of resurrection is of course beyond the scope of this chapter. However, what is clear is that understanding the intertwining relationship between *muḥkamāt* and *mutashābihāt* verses in the Qur'an is necessary in having faith in God with certitude (Q. 69:51). That is to say, death is expected for each human, but whether resurrection is going to happen bodily or spiritually is open to interpretation.

Although *muḥkamāt* and *mutashābihāt* are mutually reinforcing faith in God, Ibn ʿĀshūr's discussion of the concept of *muḥkamāt* offers more nuance about what is clear and what is not. He describes the characteristics of *muḥkamāt* (clear) verses as follows: (1) verses containing principles that encompass perfection in belief (*itqān*); (2) verses containing the legislation of divine law (*al-tashrīʿ*); (3) verses that enjoin respectful etiquettes (*al-ādāb*); and (4) verses that give admonition (*al-mawʿiẓa*).[21] Ibn ʿĀshūr's account of *muḥkamāt* shows that this concept offers a multivalency of meaning and could be used for theological, legal, ethical, and mystical discourses. The various meanings associated with *āyāt muḥkamāt* offer a wide array of avenues for how to orient life towards God and to care for fellow humans and, by extension, nature.

As *āyāt muḥkamāt* serve as a framework for the care for nature, they include addressing the environmental crisis. ʿAlī Jumʿa (the former Grand Mufti of Egypt) argues that caring for nature involves two dimensions: theological and judicial (*fiqhiyya*). The theological dimension explains the relationships between humans, nature, and God; whereas the legal dimension shows how jurisprudential premises formulate Islamic law (*al-aḥkām al-sharʿiyya*) and the systemisation of the relationship between humans and God, other humans, and nature.[22] The judicial dimension of *āyāt muḥkamāt* pertaining to the environment is called *fiqh al-bīʾa* (the jurisprudence of the environment). Jumʿa

20 Ibid., 155 (see translation at https://quran.com/43?startingVerse=11).

21 Ibid.

22 Nūr al-Dīn ʿAlī Jumʿa, *al-Bīʾa wa-l-Ḥifāẓ ʿalayhā min Manẓūr al-Islāmī* (Cairo: Dār al-Wābil al-Ṣayyib, 2020), 11.

uses the term *'al-bī'a'* (the environment) referring to humans and everything around them because there is no logical reason to exclude them from being part of the environment.[23] While he positions human beings as the most important part of the environment, he argues that the well-being of the environment depends on humans. Humans and nature are co-dependent in survival; otherwise, humans' lack of interest in protecting their mental, intellectual, and physical well-being and in projecting their care for themselves in nature will lead to the most calamitous injury to their lives, not to speak of their environment.

Unfortunately, humanity's destruction of the environment is ongoing. We are facing climate change as the potent destructive force that is coming our way. From the Qur'anic standpoint, all calamities in the world are seen as a test as stated in Q. 2:155, 'We will certainly test you with a touch of fear and famine and loss of property, life, and crops. Give good news to those who patiently endure.' As a response, humans ought to repair injury to the best of their ability (Q. 2:286). Ibn ʿĀshūr shows that clear verses (*āyāt muḥkamāt*) offer a reliable framework, guiding Muslims on what to do and what to accomplish. While Ibn ʿĀshūr does not discuss the specific topic of environmental care, he argues that *āyāt muḥkamāt* establish the necessity of responsible stewardship towards nature. I will expand Ibn ʿĀshūr's examples of *āyāt muḥkamāt* and use them as a starting point to explain the dimensions of environmental ethics in what follows.

2.1 *Āyāt Muḥkamāt* for Enacting the Unity of God (*Tawḥīd*)

One of the clear messages of *āyāt muḥkamāt* is the belief in the Oneness of God (*tawḥīd*). The teaching of *tawḥīd* undergirds faith (*īmān*) and submission (*islām*) in Islam. Having faith in Islam requires the recognition of God and the Prophet Muḥammad as His messenger. The metaphysical foundation of the faith in God is found in Q. 96:1–5. These verses were revealed to the Prophet Muḥammad teaching him about the knowledge of God as Creator, His creation, His character, and His position in the world. Q. 112:1–5 also reiterate the attributes associated with God, such as the One, the Self-Sufficient Master, the Origin, and the End. As the belief in the Oneness of God (*tawḥīd*) expects Muslims to perceive what is present around us (*ẓāhir*) and what is hidden (*bāṭin*) as one, it implies that God exists in everything He creates.

Ibn ʿĀshūr uses Q. 42:11 to connect the notion of *tawḥīd* to the nature of God, humans, and the environment:

23 Ibid., 5.

> [He is the] Creator of the heavens and the earth. He has made for you from yourselves, mates, and among the cattle, mates; He multiplies you thereby. There is nothing like unto Him, and He is the Hearing, the Seeing.

Ibn ʿĀshūr uses this verse to emphasise the nature of God as the Creator of the world and that there is nothing like unto Him (*laysa ka-mithlihi shay'*). As humans are God's creatures, they have a likeness (*tashbīh*) to Him. However, since He created them, He is completely transcendent to them (*tanzīh*). By putting humans and nature on the same footing as God's creatures, their connection to the natural world presupposes the human obligation to submit to God. It also presupposes the obligation to take care of each other and nature. Furthermore, since humans share some likeness to God, with the capacity to imitate His characteristics, and since God is the creator and preserver of nature, humans must also endeavour to perform the same virtue. This imitation takes various forms in everyday life through the embodiment of divine characteristics such as compassion, generosity, or forgiveness. The enactment of God's divine attributes brings purposiveness to human life and the natural world. Humans' purpose in the world began with the Pre-eternal Covenant of *Alast* affirming the statement 'Am I not (*alastu*) your Lord [who cherishes and sustains you]?' (Q. 7:172). This 'Covenant of *Alast*' inscribes a permanent imprint of the Oneness of God (*tawḥīd*) in the human heart by endowing each person with a proclivity for knowing God (*fiṭra*) and having equal moral agency.

2.2 *Āyāt Muḥkamāt* for Establishing Equal Moral Agency in Humans

The belief in the Oneness of God (*tawḥīd*) presupposes that humans are moral agents with the responsibility to submit to God and enact His teachings. The equality of humans is embedded in clear verses (*āyāt muḥkamāt*). Human knowledge of such agency and responsibility comes from being God's steward on earth (*khalīfa*) and from accepting the Trust (*amāna*) (Q. 33:72).[24] As humans agree to their role as God's stewards, they assume the responsibility to make the planet a better place than they find it. Such roles are not given in vain, but any acts will be counted.

24 'Indeed, We offered the trust to the heavens and the earth and the mountains, but they all declined to bear it, being fearful of it. But humanity assumed it, for they are truly wrongful to themselves and ignorant of the consequences' (Q. 33:72), https://quran.com/al-ahzab/72.

Humans' knowledge of their accountability reflects the importance of clear verses. For instance, Ibn ʿĀshūr uses Q. 21:23, 'He cannot be questioned about what He does, but they will all be questioned', to demonstrate the connection between human agency to enact faith and the accountability of it in the eyes of God. This verse also reiterates how God reckons what people do and have done in their life, good or bad, which is also reflected in Q. 29:13. God will question humans of what they have done and reward them even if it is an atom's weight (*dharra*) (Q. 4:40). Such good deeds are inclusive of honouring the dignity of humans and taking care of nature.

2.3 *Āyāt Muḥkamāt* for Performing Faith with Ease (*Taysīr*)

While enacting faith to serve God and honour His creation requires adherence to the injunctions of the divine law, it also comes with the device of ease, which facilitates the enactment of faith by easing the rigours of certain obligations. The Qur'an offers this device by explicitly mentioning and repeating it (Q. 54:17). This narrative has implications of how to practise Islam daily and how to enact it in human contexts and their environment. One of the examples that is often used to reiterate Islam's flexible approach to performing faith is fasting in the month of Ramaḍān. Q. 2:185 states:[25]

> The month of Ramaḍān [is that] in which was revealed the Quran, a guidance for the people and clear proofs of guidance and criterion. So whoever sights [the crescent of] the month, let him fast it; and whoever is ill or on a journey – then an equal number of other days. Allah intends for you ease and does not intend for you hardship and [wants] for you to complete the period and to glorify Allah for that [to] which He has guided you; and perhaps you will be grateful.

Ibn ʿĀshūr offers three characteristics of ease in legal discourse. First, it eases the commission of ordinances to accommodate the general circumstance of human beings. Second, it reduces the strictness of legal rules and provisions to alleviate hardship. Third, it emphasises the idea that God is a better lawgiver, not in spite of making exceptions and accommodating the capacities of people to perform the law, but because of it. This endows them with a deeper understanding of the nature of the law (Q. 5:50).[26] The discursive narrative of

25 See Q. 2:185, https://quran.com/2?startingVerse=185.
26 Muhammad al-Tahir Ibn Ashur, *Treatise on* Maqāṣid al-Shariʿah, trans. Mohamed El-Tahir El-Mesawi (London and Washington, DC: The International Institute of Islamic Thought, 2006), 202–3.

ease provides justification for each Muslim to act wisely in relation to God, fellow humans, and nature. It can be inferred from Q. 2:185 that any attempt to address social and environmental challenges must also exhibit the accommodating and flexible aspects of *taysīr*.

To view the principle of ease through the environmental lens, we can look at the Islamic Declaration on Global Climate Change, which was announced on 18 August 2018 during the International Islamic Climate Change Symposium in Turkey.[27] This declaration proposes the need of Muslims to recognise the role of Islam in addressing the environmental challenges brought forth by climate change and its impact on the rising temperature of the earth and the loss of biodiversity. This recognition must come by firstly affirming the role of Muslims as God's creatures who must display compassion and care to the world. At a glance, the Qur'anic verses cited in this declaration may not speak to the current risk of climate change, but they are useful in framing how Muslims may easily translate the moral call to affirm their status as created beings (Q. 1:1, 30:30), to appreciate the inherent value of all created beings (Q. 44:38–39), to recognise their contribution to the destruction of the earth due to relentless economic and political pursuits (Q. 30:41), and to do their part in tackling the existing climate change crisis. The citation of these verses in the Islamic Declaration on Global Climate Change provides us with examples of how clear verses are utilised in addressing environmental issues.

2.4 *Āyāt Muḥkamāt* for Avoiding Corruption on Earth

While the concept of ease (*taysīr*) allows believers to enact faith at any time and situation, the admonition against causing corruption (*fasād*) signals self-control over tendencies to destroy the relationship with God, humans, and nature. For example, Ibn ʿĀshūr lists the statement that God does not like corruption (*wa-Allāh lā yuḥibb al-fasād*) to explain how avoidance of environmental destruction is clearly stated in the Qur'an. Q. 2:205 states, 'and when they leave you, they strive throughout the land to spread mischief in it and destroy crops and cattle. Allah does not like mischief.' This verse, according to Ibn ʿĀshūr, provides a categorical and clear textual proof (*qaṭʿiyyat al-matn*) against the commission of action that leads to natural destruction.[28] This

27 Madeleine Arnaout, 'The Islamic Declaration on Climate Change', Ummah for Earth, 19 February 2022, https://ummah4earth.org/en/story/8808/the-islamic-declaration-on-climate-change/.

28 Ibn Ashur, *Treatise*, 17.

serves as a framework for Muslims to engage in environmental protection and climate mitigation.

The intersection between environmental ethics and clear verses (*āyāt muḥkamāt*) provides a theoretical underpinning for undertaking righteous actions daily that are in line with the ideal of stewardship of nature. Righteous action could stem from an equal partnership among people across religions, cultures, and territorial boundaries (Q. 49:13) and from the enactment of piety among believers (Q. 33:35). In return, all humans are rewarded equally for submitting to God, believing in Him, doing good, being trustworthy, patient, humble, charitable, and chaste, fasting, and remembering Him. Once these pious norms become internalised and embodied into experiential conduct, they will shape the believer's ethical worldview.

The Qur'anic expectation of piety falls into the category of clear verses (*āyāt muḥkamāt*). The pious norms in Q. 33:35, for instance, are clearly stated. This verse guides male and female with moral conduct in relating to oneself, other humans, and nature. A pious person is expected to neither look down on other human beings nor act arrogantly as depicted in Q. 31:18, 'and do not turn your nose up to people, nor walk pridefully upon the earth. Surely Allah does not like whoever is arrogant, boastful.'[29] As ethical conduct intersects with how individuals carry themselves in their environment, such ethics is tied to what humans do before God, namely, glorifying Him along with all creatures in the world and heaven (Q. 17:44).

3 The Glory Motif of Clear Verses and Its Ethical Implementation in the Environment

One of the ethical implications of clear verses (*āyāt muḥkamāt*) deals with humans' relationship with God and nature. This relationship reiterates humans' equal status with nature in the eyes of God. Such status brings about the duty to always glorify God. The Qur'an employs the root word of *s-b-ḥ* and its derived forms to teach humans the importance of glory as one of God's attributes and the expectation set for created beings to glorify Him. Q. 17:44 reaffirms the connection between the created nature of His creatures and the expectation that they glorify their creator.[30] The duty to glorify God frequently appears when discussing the duality of obedience and disobedience. The

29 See Q. 31:18, https://quran.com/31?startingVerse=18.

30 'The seven heavens and the earth and whatever is in them exalt Him. And there is not a thing except that it exalts [Allah] by His praise, but you do not understand their

discourses of obedience to God are taught through texts and the natural world. The Qur'an explains the importance of how humans and nature are expected to obey God through acts of glorification; likewise, the transgression of texts and nature counts as disobedience. In this section, I will explore how the glory motif in clear verses (*āyāt muḥkamāt*) that deal with the natural world necessitates the need for humans to care for nature and to restore any damage (*iṣlāḥ*) done to the environment.

The clear verses (*āyāt muḥkamāt*) call for a total embrace of pious and virtuous conduct and avoidance of disobedience as a token of obedience. Such a call appears to be obvious to people of reason (*ulū al-albāb*). Both Q. 3:7 and 3:190[31] dictate the importance of having a sound intellect when deciphering texts and the natural world. 'Alī Jum'a concurs that the natural world (*al-kawn*) teaches Muslims about obedience to God as the whole universe and its ecosystem (Q. 16:68–69) glorify Him (Q. 24:14) along with humans (Q. 21:79).[32] I use the invocation of glory motif as found in the macrocosm and microcosm to show that clear verses situate humans and nature relative to God. Humans and nature are God's creatures and both belong to Him. Even when humans are granted the world and its contents, they are bound to be responsible for what they receive in their lifetime and will be held to account in the afterlife. For this reason, the glory motif of God in nature invites Muslims to obey God and glorify Him.

The goal of obeying God fosters the need to cultivate virtue and contribute to the flourishing of the community. Ibn 'Āshūr uses the term '*samāḥa*' (magnanimity) to describe individuals endowed with 'moderation, justice, and temperance ... being the middlemost position between the two extremes of excessiveness (*ifrāṭ*) and negligence (*tafrīṭ*), [as] moderateness constitutes the backbone of all virtuous qualities'.[33] Such individuals could make up a moderate community as indicated in Q. 2:143.[34] I maintain that the Qur'anic concept of moderate community (*umma wasaṭiyya*) is inclusive of protecting the

---

[way of] exalting. Indeed, He is ever Forbearing and Forgiving' (Q. 17:44), https://quran.com/17?startingVerse=44.

31 'Indeed, in the creation of the heavens and the earth and the alternation of the day and night there are signs for people of reason' (Q. 3:190), https://quran.com/3?startingVerse=190.

32 Jum'a, *al-Bī'a*, 21–23.

33 Ibn Ashur, *Treatise*, 87.

34 'And so We have made you believers an upright community so that you may be witnesses over humanity and that the Messenger may be a witness over you. We assigned your former direction of prayer only to distinguish those who would remain faithful to the Messenger from those who would lose faith. It was certainly a difficult test except for those rightly guided by Allah. And Allah would never discount your previous

environment. The ethics of moderation as expressed via the environmental lens promotes climate justice as a matter of public good (*maṣāliḥ ʿāmma*). By attributing efforts to climate justice as part of a moderate community, Muslims are required to fulfil their collective duties. Earlier, I cited Q. 2:205 to show the prohibition of spreading human-made destruction and destroying crops and cattle as indicators of environmental protection. Such prohibition coincides with the importance of maintaining balance (*mīzān*) and establishing justice (*qisṭ*) in the environment (Q. 57:25).[35]

The Qur'an ties maintaining balance (*mīzān*) and justice (*qisṭ*) with environmental protection. What constitutes balance and justice in environmental protection includes the injunction to not harm people's goods, to withhold from stealing their property, and to prevent destruction on earth (Q. 11:85). The ethics of avoiding harm to others is a duty for Muslims. Muslims acting in a harmful manner and causing injury to people and their goods are perceived to commit wrongdoing (*ẓulm*). Such wrongdoing transgresses the boundaries set forth by the Qur'anic text and the natural world as God ordains what He creates with exact due measure. The violation of God's order in the natural world disturbs balance (*mīzān*) and justice (*qisṭ*) and causes harm to the environment.

Harmful acts lead to destruction and widespread corruption (*fasād*) on earth. The clear verses define *fasād* as something to avoid. Here, the term '*fasād*' is used to describe the destruction of something that was initially good, such that human beings can no longer benefit from it. Such destruction comes from humans and the natural world.[36] Ibn ʿĀshūr shows that *fasād* on land refers to (1) the lack of benefits derived therefrom, (2) the increase of environmental risks, and (3) the appearance of epidemic outbreak. As for *fasād* in the sea, it refers to the diminishing benefits that can derived from it, whether this is due to the extinction of marine life, such as whales, pearls, and corals, the depletion of water in the river, and the lack of rain, which is needed for humans and the environment.[37] While Ibn ʿĀshūr's discourse of corruption (*fasād*) on earth may not fully address current climate change challenges, he

acts of faith. Surely Allah is Ever Gracious and Most Merciful to humanity' (Q. 2:143), https://quran.com/2?startingVerse=143.

35 'Indeed, We sent Our messengers with clear proofs, and with them We sent down the Scripture and the balance of justice so that people may administer justice. And We sent down iron with its great might, benefits for humanity, and means for Allah to prove who is willing to stand up for Him and His messengers without seeing Him. Surely Allah is All-Powerful, Almighty' (Q. 57:25), https://quran.com/57?startingVerse=25.

36 Ibn ʿĀshūr, *Tafsīr*, 21:109.

37 Ibid.

points to the importance of understanding clear verses as they relate to environmental care and protection.

A similar effort by Jumʿa shows how the discourse of *fasād* is theologically tied to human behaviours, such as disobedience (*maʿṣiya*), wrongdoing (*ẓulm*), and a broken tie with God.[38] He explains that human disobedience manifests in wasteful behaviour (*isrāf*).[39] The Qur'an expresses a broad understanding of wasteful behaviour, from excessive eating (Q. 7:31), hoarding food (Q. 6:141), treating people unjustly (Q. 17:33), and immoderate spending (Q. 25:67).[40] Since the Qur'an outlines how to obey God, the wilful transgression of divine law is tantamount to cutting ties with God and His teaching. It diminishes personal virtue, leads to abandonment of other humans, and ends up destroying nature.

Muslims' abandonment of nature intertwines with destruction that is cemented in what Moore calls the concepts of '"big history" – imperialism, capitalism, industrialization, commercialization, patriarchy, [and] racial formations'.[41] These social processes have dominated the world as they proliferated globally through colonial machinery and postcolonial forces. Most Muslim countries were subjected to colonialism and, through these social processes, they came to embrace the dualistic conception of humanity and nature. The postcolonial project of modernising less developed countries is largely based on the Western model, one that prioritises economic development at the cost of environmental destruction and social conflicts with indigenous peoples. At the same time, Muslim countries also lost sense of their identities, their connection to their people, and their spiritual linkage to nature as their nations attempted to rebuild what their colonisers destroyed for decades and even centuries. The colonial project left the infrastructure and geopolitics of many Muslim countries underdeveloped and unstable. Such countries are far more vulnerable to climate change disasters and in need of climate mitigation as they face multiple crises ranging from abrupt leadership change, corrupt governments, economic development, political instability, and the unrealistic demands of economic prosperity.

The decline or civilisational fall of countries is not new. Q. 30 shows how humans actively contribute to their own destruction. Q. 30:41, in particular, is

38 Jumʿa, *al-Bīʾa*, 72–74.

39 Ibid., 81.

40 See the relevant Qur'anic verses at https://quran.com/.

41 Jason W. Moore, 'Anthropocene or Capitalocene? Nature, History, and the Crisis of Capitalism', in *Anthropocene or Capitalocene? Nature, History, and the Crisis of Capitalism*, ed. Jason W. Moore (Oakland: PM Press, 2016), 4.

important to discuss as it points to the destruction on land, sea, and air.[42] Ibn ʿĀshūr explains that this verse deals with giving lessons (*mawʿiẓa*) for Muslims to believe in the divine message.[43] I use Q. 30:41 to show the relationship between corruption on earth and the glory motif. This verse articulates how negligence of a balanced relationship with God, humans, and nature violates divine order and messages and confirms the prediction that humans often lie about submitting themselves to God as indicated in Q. 6:11.[44] Humans shamelessly destroy what God has put in balance and claim that they are repairers or transformers (*muṣliḥūn*). As a corollary, humanity's footprint of destruction is cemented on land, sea, and air.

A deeper look at current global destruction shows how environmental imbalances seep into all spheres of life. Globally, the need for 'food, fuel, and cost crises exacerbate societal vulnerabilities' and the fight to protect the most vulnerable groups leads to political polarisation.[45] Similarly, the increased risk brought forth by climate change and the failure to address it will cause the world ecosystem to fail, which in turn will have devastating economic, health, social, and political consequences globally.[46] The gradual decline of economic, environmental, political, and social stability leads to social polarisation and the deterioration of welfare, which become emerging drivers of conflicts.

Awareness of the glory motif would be useful for Muslims who wish to address the current climate change. Q. 30:41 clearly calls for returning to God and caring for His creation as something good. The invitation to return to God carries broad ethical implications. Abdul-Matin, an American environmentalist, emphasises the Islamic teaching to care for God's creation as it will bring the relationship between the Divine, humans, and nature closer. He introduces six ethical principles that could invigorate ecological awareness by 'understanding the Oneness of God and His creation (*tawhid*); seeing signs of God everywhere (*ayat*); being a steward of the Earth (*khalifah*); honoring the covenant, or trust, we have with God (*amana*) to be protectors of the planet; moving toward justice (*ʿadl*); and living in balance with nature (*mizan*)'.[47] These

42 'Corruption has spread on land and sea as a result of what people's hands have done, so that Allah may cause them to taste the consequences of some of their deeds and perhaps they might return to the Right Path' (Q. 30:40), https://quran.com/30?startingVerse=40.

43 Ibn ʿĀshūr, *Tafsīr*, 21:109.

44 'Say, "Travel throughout the land and see the fate of the deniers"' (Q. 6:11), https://quran.com/6?startingVerse=11.

45 World Economic Forum, *Global Risks Report 2023* (Geneva: World Economic Forum, 2023), 9.

46 World Economic Forum, *Global Risks Report*, 31.

47 Abdul-Matin, *Green Deen*, 2.

ethical principles teach Muslims to nurture an ecologically oriented self and to project such an interiority by embracing God's creation as signs (*āyāt*) and enacting justice with humans and nature. By envisioning a balanced relationship with God, humans, and nature, we make no hierarchy among creatures.

The utility of the Islamic ethical framework provides theoretical underpinning for how to address negligence (*mafsada*) and cultivate good (*maṣlaḥa*) within oneself. Q. 2:11–12 establishes the dualistic character of humans in perceiving the relationship with nature.[48] These verses call for relinquishing blameworthy character, namely, negligence (*fasād*) and for setting what is right (*ṣalāḥ*) in relation to the environment. Such a call is reiterated in Q. 7:56, asking humans to 'not spread corruption in the land after it has been set in order. And call upon Him with hope and fear. Indeed, Allah's mercy is always close to the good-doers.'[49] Ibn ʿĀshūr explains that setting what is right (*ṣalāḥ*) and removing corruption (*fasād*) are in the mission of the Sharīʿa.[50] The dialectical relationship between good (*maṣlaḥa*) and harm (*mafsada*) serves as a lesson, guidance, or advice (*mawʿiẓa*) of how the righteous (*ṣāliḥūn*) will be rewarded. The Qur'an promises that 'whoever does good, whether male or female, and is a believer, We will surely bless them with a good life, and We will certainly reward them according to the best of their deeds' (Q. 16:97).[51] To reap such reward, both men and women are invited to pursue the making of their virtuous characters and to repair their blameworthy traits.

Repairing blameworthy character traits is multifaceted. Such an effort takes into consideration how clear verses (*āyāt muḥkamāt*) are translated into daily life. While a total embrace of what is good (*maṣlaḥa*) is personal and context specific, its impact pervades in communities and their localities. The utility of clear verses (*āyāt muḥkamāt*) provides an epistemological foundation regarding how doing good (*maṣlaḥa*) contributes to our personal and societal transformation. The Qur'an encourages inward transformation as a starting point towards the acknowledgement of God's glory, the fulfilment of the rights of all human beings, and the performance of personal and public duties for the sake of the broader community. This expectation reaffirms the purpose of a creation that is uniquely endowed with 'the best of stature' (Q. 95:4).[52] At the same

48 'When they are told, "Do not spread corruption in the land," they reply, "We are only peace-makers!" Indeed, it is they who are the corruptors, but they fail to perceive it' (Q. 2:11–12), https://quran.com/2?startingVerse=11.

49 See Q. 7:56, https://quran.com/7?startingVerse=56.

50 Ibn Ashur, *Treatise*, 96.

51 See Q. 16:97, https://quran.com/16?startingVerse=97.

52 See Q. 95:4, https://quran.com/95?startingVerse=4.

time, humans could descend to 'the lowest of the low' for neglecting duties to themselves, God, other humans, and nature (Q. 95:4–5).

4 Conclusion

This chapter attempts to elaborate on how *āyāt muḥkamāt* of the Qur'an (clear verses) provide an epistemic foundation of how environmental ethics could be formulated and systematised. I have shown how clear verses place moral and ethical responsibility on humanity to engage in environmental protection and to address negligence towards the environment. I utilise clear verses to show the role of the Qur'an as an ethical source of pursuing a meaningful life, which is structured around the obligation of fulfilling God's rights and cultivating a healthy relationship with other humans and nature. In this sense, clear verses of the Qur'an refer to what shapes the making of individual virtues, what prevents the development of blameworthy character, and what fosters the flourishing of the community and environment.

While the chapter attempts to explore environmental ethics in regulative verses, my analysis is limited to the meaning of the *muḥkam* (clear) verse in Q. 3:7, and its potential to be read in conjunction with environmental ethics. It emphasises how setting what is right (*ṣalāḥ*) and removing corruption (*fasād*) are ethical and in accordance with God's divine message. As both concepts of good (*ṣalāḥ*) and corruption (*fasād*) are debated in the context of showing God's glory in the universe, honouring Qur'anic values, and having the wisdom of understanding the past destruction, they are useful in framing the current environmental imbalances and the global risks associated with the failure of addressing climate change and its mitigation.

While I have argued to use the clear verses to discuss environmental challenges and ethics in Islam, I am aware that any discussion of the Qur'an as it relates to contemporary issues, like environmentalism and climate change, has its own limitations. I cannot apply key ideas such as 'environment' or 'environmentalism' drawn from the Western epistemology to each verse that is discussed in this chapter. Similarly, the existing discussion of the mentioned verses also proposes a more literal meaning or interpretation. The use of Q. 3:7 above, for instance, is tied to how scholars such as Riḍā, 'Abduh, and Ibn 'Āshūr discuss *muḥkamāt* and *mutashābihāt* and how they understood the concept of abrogation. Looking for connections between clear verses and environmental protection is always challenging especially if scholars do not engage with environmentalism as it is debated in the West. For this reason, additional research on clear verses regarding environmental ethics needs to go beyond Q. 3:7 and move towards the explorations of the relationship between the Qur'an and community advocacy in addressing climate change and its mitigation.

Bibliography

Abdul-Matin, Ibrahim. *Green Deen: What Islam Teaches about Protecting the Planet*. San Francisco: Berrett-Koehler Publishers, 2010.

Arnaout, Madeleine. 'The Islamic Declaration on Climate Change'. Ummah for Earth, 19 February 2022. https://ummah4earth.org/en/story/8808/the-islamic-declaration-on-climate-change/.

Chishti, Saadia Khawar Khan. '*Fiṭra*: An Islamic Model for Humans and the Environment'. In *Islam and Ecology: A Bestowed Trust*, edited by Richard C. Foltz, Frederick M. Denny, and Azizan Baharuddin, 67–82. Cambridge, MA: Center for the Study of World Religions, Harvard Divinity School, 2003.

Clarke, L. 'The Universe Alive: Nature in the *Masnavī* of Jalal al-Din Rumi'. In *Islam and Ecology: A Bestowed Trust*, edited by Richard C. Foltz, Frederick M. Denny, and Azizan Baharuddin, 39–65. Cambridge, MA: Center for the Study of World Religions, Harvard Divinity School, 2003.

Gade, Anna. *Muslim Environmentalisms: Religious and Social Foundations*. New York: Columbia University Press, 2019.

Haleem, Muhammad Abdel. 'Interpreting the Qur'ān: Qur'ān 3:7; 2:106; 16:101; 31:20'. In *Communicating the Word: Revelation, Translation, and Interpretation in Christianity and Islam*, edited by David Marshall, 133–41. Washington, DC: Georgetown University Press, 2011.

Haraway, Donna J. 'Staying with the Trouble: Anthropocene, Capitalocene, Chthulucene'. In *Anthropocene or Capitalocene? Nature, History, and the Crisis of Capitalism*, edited by Jason W. Moore, 34–76. Oakland: PM Press, 2016.

Ibn ʿĀshūr, Muḥammad al-Ṭāhir. *Tafsīr al-Taḥrīr wa-l-Tanwīr*. Tunis: Dār Suḥnūn li-l-Nashr wa-al-Tawzīʿ, 1997.

Ibn Ashur, Muhammad al-Tahir. *Treatise on* Maqāṣid al-Shariʿah. Translated by Mohamed El-Tahir El-Mesawi. London and Washington, DC: The International Institute of Islamic Thought, 2006.

Jumʿa, Nūr al-Dīn ʿAlī. *al-Bīʾa wa-l-Ḥifāẓ ʿalayhā min Manẓūr al-Islāmī*. Cairo: Dār al-Wābil al-Ṣayyib, 2020.

Kinberg, Leah. '*Muḥkamāt* and *Mutashābihāt* (Koran 3/7): Implication of a Koranic Pair of Terms in Medieval Exegesis'. *Arabica* 35, no. 2 (1988): 143–72. https://doi.org/10.1163/157005888x00314.

Klein, Naomi. *This Changes Everything: Capitalism vs. the Climate*. New York: Simon & Schuster, 2014.

McKibben, Bill. *Falter: Has the Human Game Begun to Play Itself Out?* New York: Holt Paperbacks, 2019.

Moore, Jason W. 'Anthropocene or Capitalocene? Nature, History, and the Crisis of Capitalism'. In *Anthropocene or Capitalocene? Nature, History, and the Crisis of Capitalism*, edited by Jason W. Moore, 1–33. Oakland: PM Press, 2016.

Moore, Jason W. 'The Rise of Cheap Nature'. In *Anthropocene or Capitalocene? Nature, History, and the Crisis of Capitalism*, edited by Jason W. Moore, 78–115. Oakland: PM Press, 2016.

Nasr, Seyyed Hossein. *The Garden of Truth: The Vision and Promise of Sufism, Islam's Mystical Tradition*. New York: HarperOne, 2008.

Nasr, Seyyed Hossein. *The Heart of Islam: Enduring Values for Humanity*. New York: HarperOne, 2004.

Nasr, Seyyed Hossein. *Man and Nature: The Spiritual Crisis of Modern Man*. London: Unwin Paperbacks, 1976.

Özdemir, Ibrahim. 'God, Humans, and Nature: Toward an Understanding of Environmental Ethics from a Qur'anic Perspective'. In *Islam and Ecology: A Bestowed Trust*, edited by Richard C. Foltz, Frederick M. Denny, and Azizan Baharuddin, 3–38. Cambridge, MA: Center for the Study of World Religions, Harvard Divinity School, 2003.

Riḍā, Muḥammad Rashīd, and Muḥammad 'Abduh. *Tafsīr al-Qur'ān al-Ḥakīm: al-Shahīr bi-Tafsīr al-Manār*. 3rd ed. Egypt: Dār al-Manār, 1948.

https://ummah4earth.org/en/story/8808/the-islamic-declaration-on-climate-change/ — Assessed on June 4, 2024.

https://quran.com/ — Assessed on June 4, 2024.

Index

 | HTTPS://DOI.ORG/10.1163/9789004755567-021